LEARNERS WITH MILD DISABILITIES

A Characteristics Approach

EILEEN B. RAYMOND

The State University of New York at Potsdam

PEARSON

Boston ∎ New York ∎ San Francisco
Mexico City ∎ Montreal ∎ Toronto ∎ London ∎ Madrid ∎ Munich ∎ Paris
Hong Kong ∎ Singapore ∎ Tokyo ∎ Cape Town ∎ Sydney

Executive Editor: Virginia Lanigan
Editorial Assistant: Robert Champagne
Executive Marketing Manager: Amy Cronin Jordan
Editorial Production Service: Raeia Maes
Manufacturing Buyer: Andrew Turso
Cover Administrator: Joel Gendron
Electronic Composition: Omegatype Typography, Inc.

For related titles and support materials, visit our online catalog at www.ablongman.com

Between the time Website information is gathered and then published, some sites may have closed. Also, the transcription of URLs can result in typographical errors. The publisher would appreciate being notified of any problems with URLs so that they may be corrected in subsequent editions.

Library of Congress Cataloging-in-Publication Data
Raymond, Eileen B.
    Learners with mild disabilities : a characteristics approach / Eileen B. Raymond.—2nd ed.
        p.   cm.
    Includes bibliographical references and index.
    ISBN 0-205-38606-7
    1. Learning disabled children—Education—United States.   2. Children with mental disabilities—Education—United States.   3. Hyperactive children—Education—United States. 4. Problem children—Education—United States.   I. Title.
    LC4705.R39 2004
    371.92'6—dc21   2003043706

Printed in the United States of America

10 9 8 7 6 5 4 3 2 1   08 07 06 05 04 03

Photo credits: Chapter **1,** Brian Smith; **2,** © 1970 United Artist Corporation/The Kobal Collection; **3,** Brian Smith; **4,** Michael Newman/PhotoEdit; **5,** Will Hart/PhotoEdit; **6,** David Young-Wolf/PhotoEdit; **7,** Tony Freeman/PhotoEdit; **8,** Michael Newman/PhotoEdit; **9,** Michael Newman/PhotoEdit; **10,** Michael Newman/PhotoEdit; **11,** Tony Freeman/PhotoEdit; **12,** Will Hart/PhotoEdit; **13,** Catherine Ursillo/Photo Researchers, Inc.

CONTENTS

CHAPTER THREE

Issues in Assessment and Identification   57

CHAPTER FOUR

Issues in Curriculum and Instruction   77

CHAPTER SEVEN

Learners with Learning Disabilities   153

UNIT III   WHAT ARE LEARNERS WITH MILD DISABILITIES LIKE?   237

CHAPTER TEN

Cognitive and Perceptual Characteristics   239

CHAPTER THIRTEEN

Social–Emotional Characteristics   345

BOXES

IN THE CLASSROOM

Throughout history, disability has been conceptualized primarily as deviance, with individuals with disabilities diagnosed, labeled, and treated in accordance with that deviance. Disability services have been justified by determining that the individual met the criteria for one of the established disability categories, that the individual was "eligible" and in need of special treatment. For those disabilities that had medical etiologies and a profound effect on the functional ability of the individual, this approach may have been appropriate.

As society began to demand higher levels of literacy and reasoning, increasing numbers of children began to struggle in school. These learners presented milder and more diverse cognitive and emotional disabilities that compromised their success in school. As local communities began to serve learners with an increasing variety of mild disabilities under the Individuals with Disabilities Education Act (IDEA), it became increasingly apparent that it was difficult to identify many youngsters as belonging to one and only one category. The cost of evaluating youngsters for eligibility escalated over the years, and the utility of the diagnoses themselves was called into question.

Increasingly, schools are investigating alternatives to categorical service delivery models, especially for the large group of learners with milder forms of disability. Special education teachers frequently serve students with a variety of labels, students who share a variety of common needs. In the years to come, special educators must be able to accurately and comprehensively describe students' strengths and needs, not just focus on applying diagnostic criteria and categorizing learners. *Learners with Mild Disabilities* provides the special educator of the future with an understanding of the definitions currently in use and a variety of alternative definitions, as well as a discussion of the limitations of categorical processes. In addition, this book presents the conceptual frameworks needed by educators as they identify and interpret a broad range of student behaviors and problems from a non-categorical perspective.

Learners with Mild Disabilities provides the knowledge base needed to serve all learners, including those from varying cultural and linguistic backgrounds. Given an increasingly diverse school population, educators are expected to provide instruction that is culturally sensitive. *Learners with Mild Disabilities* highlights the need to focus on the child, not on a category and not on a particular language or ethnic group. By becoming sensitive to the characteristics of individual children, educators will be able to identify the needs not only of students with unique cultural and linguistic backgrounds but also those with a variety of disabilities. Educators will be able to use this information to design more effective and relevant instruction for all students.

Learners with Mild Disabilities is designed for use at the undergraduate and graduate levels as the main text in courses addressing mild mental retardation, learning disabilities, attention deficit/hyperactivity disorders, and emotional and behavioral disorders. Such courses are typically the first specialized courses taken as part of a teacher preparation program in special education. This text should be especially useful to students in programs preparing pre-service teachers in the growing area of generic special education.

Organization of the Book

Learners with Mild Disabilities departs from earlier categorical approaches to disability. It is based on an awareness that the notion of discrete disabilities has not been well supported by recent experience and philosophical discussions in special education. It develops an alternative model for the preparation of special educators for careers in the complex world of mild disabilities while still equipping them with the ability to discuss categorical processes intelligently. *Learners with Mild Disabilities* looks first at the high prevalence disabilities from the conventional, categorical perspective, and then it presents the reader with a variety of alternative conceptual frameworks for looking at these learners from the perspective of individual strengths and needs.

- Unit I sets the context for the study of disability. It addresses issues of classification, categorization, and labeling and it provides a historical context for current special education practice. Unit I then addresses current issues relating to assessment and identification, curriculum and instruction, and placement of students with mild disabilities, providing updated information on the IDEA Amendments of 1997. Extended case studies are used to help the reader apply the concepts developed in the text to real-life identification, instructional planning, and placement dilemmas.
- Unit II describes learners with mild high-prevalence learning and behavioral conditions, including mental retardation, learning disabilities, emotional or behavioral disorders, and other conditions including attention-deficit/hyperactivity disorders and Asperger Syndrome. It explains the development of the definitions currently found in the IDEA and in many state regulations. Each chapter identifies a variety of concerns about the adequacy of those definitions, as well as the causes, prevalence, and common characteristics of each disability. Readers are given the opportunity to apply the current disability definitions through extended case studies designed to help readers identify critical issues related to these conditions and the usefulness and implications of current definitional processes.
- In Unit III the reader considers the characteristics of learners with mild disabilities with respect to cognitive, linguistic, academic learning, and social-emotional characteristics. *Learners with Mild Disabilities* develops conceptual frameworks related to learner functioning, illustrating the use of these frameworks to analyze a particular child's difficulties and strengths. Moving beyond the categorical perspective, *Learners with Mild Disabilities* focuses on the characteristics of learners that may be related to each learner's particular difficulties. The reader is guided in applying conceptual frameworks for analyzing any learner's skills and deficit areas, regardless of the labeled condition. Extensive use of short vignettes and extended case studies help readers apply the frameworks to individual children as an aid to diagnosis and instructional planning.

Special Features

The second edition of *Learners with Mild Disabilities* retains many of the distinctive features found in the first edition, with content updated as appropriate. The second edition still includes a number of features designed to facilitate the active learning of readers. The juxtaposition of the traditional categorical approaches to mild disability with crosscategorical and noncategorical approaches helps highlight the complexity of determining student needs. It provides the special education professional with the knowledge needed to understand both approaches, and then it challenges the reader to synthesize this information into a more useful approach to identification, planning, and programming. It challenges the simplistic notion that merely determining the correct label or finding the perfect definition is the most important task in designing interventions and supports. Throughout the text, *Learners with Mild Disabilities* does not avoid conflicting philosophical perspectives, but instead it uses such apparent discontinuities to stimulate the reader's analytical skills.

Learners with Mild Disabilities includes a number of case studies drawn from the experiences of real children and teachers that provide practice material that is both realistic and relevant. These cases are longer and more complex than are usually found in books of this type. Because they are composites based on actual experiences, they are realistically messy and unfinished. They present challenges to the analytical skills of the reader, provide the basis for interesting class discussions, and as Piaget theorized, promote the disequilibrium necessary for learning. Discussions based on the questions accompanying each case provide opportunities for significant active learning in cooperative learning groups and whole class instruction.

Learners with Mild Disabilities provides a variety of approaches to thinking about the disabilities. In addition to presenting IDEA disability definitions, Unit II includes alternative definitions of high-prevalence disabilities, including

- The 1992 and 2002 AAMR definition of mental retardation
- The NJCLD, ICLD, and LDA definitions of learning disabilities
- The DSM-IV-TR definition of ADHD
- The definition of emotional or behavioral disorders developed by the Mental Health and Special Education Coalition

Learners with Mild Disabilities uses person-first language throughout the book when referring to individuals with disabilities, modeling for the reader the use of appropriate and accurate language. In addition, the principles and rationale for person-first language are presented in Chapter 1.

Throughout *Learners with Mild Disabilities*, the following structural features used to highlight the chapter topic and assist student learning have been retained:

- *Questions to Guide Your Study* serve as advance organizers.
- *Opening vignettes,* such as "*Meet Clarence,*" set the stage for the content in the chapter.
- *Spotlights in History* present adapted original texts as contextual elements.
- *Vignettes* and examples help illustrate concepts and facilitate understanding.
- *Extended case studies* at the ends of chapters allow readers the opportunity to apply the concepts presented in the chapter.

The book continues to maintain a balance with respect to reference citations. In-text citations provide historical and current references appropriate to the content, with specific emphasis on current references. However, the number of citations has been controlled to avoid interfering with the readability of the text. When a particular concept is found generally within the special education literature, that content has been treated as common knowledge and has been allowed to stand on its own with minimal documentation.

In the second edition, the chapters have been reordered to facilitate use of the book. Chapters dealing with general practices have been grouped together in Unit I, with Unit II focusing on categorical considerations and Unit III presenting the noncategorical characteristics perspective. Chapter 9 has been expanded to include a brief discussion of other conditions such as Autism Spectrum Disorders (Asperger Syndrome) and other low incidence disabilities that may manifest themselves at the milder range of severity. In addition, the content on cognitive and perceptual characteristics has been combined into one chapter and condensed to improve coherence and readability.

Features new to the second edition include the following:

- *Focus on Culture and Diversity* sections have been added to the end of each chapter, highlighting the issues related to diversity presented by the chapter content. Although *Learners with Mild Disabilities* infuses the discussion of linguistic and cultural diversity throughout the text rather than isolating this discussion within a single chapter, the Focus sections in each chapter highlight the understanding that issues of language and culture affect all aspects of a student's life.
- *Resources on the Web* at the end of each chapter provides an annotated listing of web sites to extend the reader's consideration of the chapter content.

Acknowledgments

No effort of this kind would be possible without significant support from a variety of individuals. In particular, I want to express my continuing appreciation for the support of my colleague, John W. Marson. John provided detailed feedback on preliminary drafts of the text and during the field testing of the final drafts at SUNY–Potsdam. Many of the instructional activities in the ancillary materials are derived from our collaborative teaching efforts. I also wish to thank the students in the special education program at SUNY–Potsdam for their feedback on drafts of this work.

The book would not have been possible without the stories that students and fellow teachers have shared with me over the years. The vignettes and case studies are fictional composites, but they are based on the collective experiences of real children and teachers in real school settings. Their basis in reality provides the reader with many useful application experiences, and I express my appreciation to everyone who has shared a story with me.

As with any writing project, editorial assistance is critical. I extend my appreciation to my student assistants, Catherine Boula, Lisa Selby, and Shannon Whitney, who have worked on drafts throughout the process. Their careful reading and feedback have helped ensure an accurate and well written manuscript. I thank the following peer reviewers who read and commented on the manuscript: Linda K. Carey, Northern Arizona University; Moniqueka E. Gold, Austin Peay State University; Bernard J. Graney, Springfield College; and Dianne M. Gut, Ohio University. My appreciation also goes to Virginia Lanigan and Robert Champagne for their assistance in producing this second edition. Their support, encouragement, and feedback have been critical to seeing this project through to completion.

Finally, I want to thank my family and friends for their encouragement and forbearance during this long project. I am especially grateful to Donna for her expert proofreading of the manuscript and for helping me find the time to complete this work.

SETTING THE STAGE

Educators in contemporary society face many challenges. We expect our schools to provide solutions to myriad social problems by preparing the next generation of citizens to assume their adult roles more competently than previous generations have. We ask that our schools educate all children, and we voice the philosophy that all children can learn. We recognize that our classrooms are filled with learners representing significant diversity, including students who differ from one another with respect to gender, race, ethnic background, language, socioeconomic class, religion, sexual orientation, and ability. It is the specific issue of diversity in learning ability that this book addresses.

To develop an understanding of classification, diagnosis, and intervention with children who differ from others in their age group, we need to gain a perspective on the nature of ability and disability as well as on the historical development of our attention to persons with disabilities. A visit to any classroom will confirm that in any group of children, no two are alike. They differ from one another on a wide variety of variables, and this diversity presents challenges to instructional staff seeking to help each child master critical skills and knowledge.

The concept of disability develops from the determination by various persons within society, and finally by the community itself, that the degree to which a particular individual's behavioral characteristics differ from others in the group is unacceptable, that the behavior is deviant to the extent that special attention is warranted (Speece & Harry, 1997). By extension, the individual is then seen as being significantly different so that differential treatment is needed; frequently, this leads to the identification of the individual as having a disability.

Unit I considers the meaning of disability and some of the reasons for focusing on mild disability. It first considers contemporary responses to children with disabilities in the schools, both by the U.S. Congress and by those advocating in the courts for the rights of children to appropriate educational services. It looks back at the way in which individuals with disabilities have been viewed and treated during certain periods of history, with a specific focus on American history. It discusses the process by which some students become classified as learners with disabilities, and it explores the ramifications of such classifications. Finally, it considers the impact on children's lives of being identified as deviant, of being determined to have a disability.

Chapters 3, 4, and 5 will explore some of the implications of IDEA 1997 for assessment and identification, curriculum and instruction, and placement of learners with disabilities. Specifically, the following issues will be considered, questions that must be discussed and answered by special educators in the future, such as:

- How can we best assess student learning, especially when that learning may be hindered or obscured by a mild disability?
- Is categorical identification the most useful process for understanding a learner and for making programming decisions?
- How do students with disabilities relate most appropriately to the general education curriculum?
- Are there instructional practices that are effective for both those students with and those without disabilities? Are there practices that are effective only with students with disabilities?
- What accommodations are appropriate in providing access to the general education curriculum?
- What do we really mean by inclusion? Is it appropriate for all learners?

It is important to note that Unit I will identify a number of issues important to the field of education today. All of them are beyond the scope of this book to address fully. The reader is encouraged to continue to acquire information about issues, practices, and strategies by reading current research in the field.

CHAPTER ONE

PERSPECTIVES ON DISABILITY

QUESTIONS TO GUIDE YOUR STUDY

- Why is it important to study mild disabilities?
- Why might it be useful to study high-prevalence disabilities together?
- What is a disability? What is a handicap?
- What are the advantages of and problems with using generic categories to classify students with disabilities?
- Describe the three levels of prevention and their relationship to categorical services.
- What are the major requirements of the IDEA?
- Can we assure rights without labels?

Meet Clarence

The first day she kept an especially close eye on the boy called Clarence. Clarence was a small, lithe, brown-skinned boy with large eyes and deep dimples. Chris watched his journeys to the pencil sharpener. They were frequent. Clarence took the longest route around the room, walking heel-to-toe and brushing the back of one leg with the shin of the other at every step—a cheerful little dance across the blue carpet, around the perimeter of desks, and along the back wall, passing under the American flag, which didn't quite brush his head. Reaching the pencil sharpener, Clarence would turn his pencil into a stunt plane, which did several loop-the-loops before plunging into the hole. . . . Clarence noticed things. He paid close attention to the intercom. His eyes darted to the door the moment a visitor appeared. But he paid almost no attention to her lessons and his work. It seemed as if every time she glanced up, Clarence wasn't working. . . . The other children were working. . . .

Chris had received the children's cumulative records, or "cumes." . . . Clarence's cume was about as thick as the Boston phone book. . . . One teacher whom Chris trusted had described him as probably the most difficult child in all of last year's fourth grade classes. Chris wished she hadn't heard that, nor the rumors about Clarence. . . . She'd try to ignore what she had heard, and deal with the

(continued)

problems as they came. Clarence's were surfacing quickly. He came to school the second day without having done his homework. He had not done any work so far, except for one math assignment, and for that he'd just written down some numbers at random. . . .

On the third day of school, a Friday, several children including Clarence came in without homework, and Chris told them they were in for recess. . . . Clarence objected to the news about being in for recess. He threw an eraser at one classmate and punched another. . . . She called him to her desk. He came, but he stood sideways to her, chin lifted, face averted. She told him, in a matter-of-fact voice that wasn't very stern, that he could put someone's eye out by throwing things, and that he could not hit anyone. He didn't say a word. He just stared away, chin raised, as if to say, "I'm not listening to you." . . .

He did a little work after lunch, but he came to a full stop when, late in the day, she asked the class to write a paragraph and draw some pictures to describe their visions of the lives of Native Americans. . . . All the other children got to work, quite happily, it seemed. Clarence said he didn't understand the assignment. She explained it again, twice. . . . The other children bent their heads over their papers, working out their impressions about Indians. Chris saw Clarence take out his ruler, and put it on top of his pencil. Grinning, he tapped the ruler with his finger. It spun like a helicopter blade. . . . Chris watched the ruler spin. She understood this as defiance. The lines were being drawn. . . . Clarence is an angry child, she thought. Angry at the whole world. Worst of all was that stony, averted face he wore when she tried to talk to him. How could she ever get close enough to reason with a child who put up a barrier like that? . . . On his first report card he'd flunk everything, and that would tell him the same old news, that he didn't have to do the work because he couldn't.

Have you met Clarence or a student like him? The focus in this book will be on students with milder forms of disability, students perhaps like Clarence. Schools and teachers increasingly find that they are called upon to serve a variety of children with mild disabilities, students with difficulties in learning, thinking, and behavior, students like Clarence.

Historically, special education and services for people with disabilities in general have dealt almost exclusively with more severe levels of disability. As a result, the vocabulary and practices that have emerged over the years have focused on the significant differences that these individuals exhibited when compared to typical individuals (Council for Exceptional Children, 1994b). These children and adults called attention to themselves because of their physical and behavioral differences, and the resulting classification system solidified these differences into categories and labels.

This system, based on difference, overlooked those students who differed less dramatically from the typical child. Children with milder physical, learning, or behavioral problems were either overlooked entirely or were counseled into less demanding academic and vocational pursuits. In a society that needed a large supply of unskilled labor to work in fields and factories, unschooled labor had value, and mild levels of disability did not restrict people from performing productive work. For the first three centuries of American history, mild levels of disability were neither identified nor considered to be problematic.

As our schools and larger society began demanding higher levels of academic functioning and skills in the twentieth century, the classification system was steadily extended upward to include those youngsters with milder problems. Children who fell outside the "typical" mold found themselves identified with classifications indicating their dysfunction. Words like *defective, retarded, impaired, disadvantaged, disturbed, disabled, handicapped,* and *disordered* were attached to more and more children who "just didn't fit in."

With the advent of universal special education services in 1975, students with milder levels of disability, as defined by the schools, began to account for a significant majority of students receiving special services (MacMillan, Keogh, & Jones, 1986). These learners were described by MacMillan et al. as "inefficient school learners," students who were characterized by school achievement and social adjustment so different from their peers that specialized interventions were deemed necessary. MacMillan et al. noted that typically these youngsters were unremarkable in appearance and lacked obvious physical manifestations of disability; in short, they looked much like all the other students. Depending on the accounting method used, students identified as having mild disabilities now account for 70 to 95 percent of all students receiving special education services (Gartner & Lipsky, 1987; Reynolds & Heistad, 1997; Salend, 2001).

Since the middle 1980s, increased awareness and concern about students who fail to successfully complete the minimum educational program has spawned a new category of learners, the *at-risk student,* students perceived as potential school dropouts. In the tradition of social concern that gave us students with *economic and cultural disadvantage* in the 1960s and 1970s, schools have set up new identification procedures and special programs for these students, many of whom test and perform just above the cutoff line for eligibility for special education services. When the learning and behavioral characteristics and needs of these students are enumerated, it is apparent that they often are very similar to students with mild disabilities (Reynolds & Heistad, 1997).

In light of these trends, it seems useful to focus on the needs of all such students, those with mild disabilities as well as those like Clarence who remain unclassified but present significant problems in school, for the following reasons:

- The majority of students being served by special education are in the mild range of disability.

- Since the classification system used to categorize learners with mild disabilities evolved upward from the terminology developed to connote more severe disabilities, and since this classification system often does not adequately describe these learners and their capabilities, study of this population by itself may be more useful (MacMillan, Siperstein, & Gresham, 1996).
- Students with mild disabilities are often similar to other students who have problems learning, so understanding the life experiences of those with milder levels of disability may help us serve similar but not yet classified students.

Studying High-Prevalence Disabilities

The focus of study in this book will be on the high-prevalence disabilities included in the Individuals with Disabilities Education Act (IDEA) (e.g., learning disabilities, mild mental retardation, and emotional or behavioral disorders), as well as other disorders such as attention-deficit/hyperactivity disorder (ADHD) and Asperger Syndrome. It is important to note that although ADHD is not identified for services under the IDEA, children with ADHD are frequently served in special education programs based on the presence of another disability. (See Chapter 9 for more discussion of this seeming paradox.) Together these four conditions account for 70 to 90 percent of all children served under the provisions of IDEA, depending on the degree of overlap among and between these categories and the category of speech and language impairments (see Table 1.1). Students with learning disabilities alone account for about 50 percent of all students in special education, with mental retardation and emotional disorders accounting for about another 10 percent each.

The definitions for these four areas of disability are not now and never have been clearly definitive enough to establish the sharp boundaries among and between the categories. Learners in all four groups may exhibit learning and academic difficulty, problems with cognitive processing of information including attention deficits, problems in social-emotional adjustment, and language-related deficits. The overlap in characteristics among and between these categories has led many school systems to serve these learners together in noncategorical or cross-categorical programs, with instructional strategies selected to meet a particular learner's needs.

A study by Cranston-Gingras and Mauser (1992) indicated that, while eighteen states (35 percent) still certified teachers categorically, fourteen states (27 percent) had begun to issue noncategorical certifications for special education teachers, and nineteen states (37 percent) used a combination of categorical and noncategorical certificates. In a number of the latter cases, all or some portion of new certifications were being issued in noncategorical form as the state began the transition to noncategorical service models for milder levels of disability; in other cases, only certificates for teaching students with certain disabilities or with more severe disabilities were issued as categorical (e.g., severe disability and visual or hearing impairment). Reynolds and Heistad (1997) reported that almost one-fourth of all special education teachers at work in 1992–93 were working in cross-categorical programs. As Hobbs (1975a) predicted, we seem to have learned from our experience serving youngsters with mild disabilities that knowledge of the classification alone rarely, if ever, provides enough information to plan programs effectively. Given this aware-

TABLE 1.1   Percentage of Students Served by Category

Disability	Number of Students Served under IDEA by Disability (1999–2000)	Percent of Students Served in Special Education (1999–2000)
Specific Learning Disabilities	2,871,966	50.5
Speech and Language Impairment	1,089,964	19.2
Mental Retardation	614,433	10.8
Emotional Disturbance	470,111	8.2
Multiple Disabilities	112,993	2.0
Hearing Impairments	71,671	1.3
Orthopedic Impairments	71,422	1.3
Other Health Impairments	254,110	4.5
Visual Impairments	26,590	0.5
Deaf-Blindness	1,845	0.1
Autism	65,424	1.2
Traumatic Brain Injury	13,874	0.2
Developmental Delay	19,304	0.2
All Conditions	5,683,707	100.0

Notes: Figures for students with ADHD are not currently reported separately since it is not an identified IDEA disability; students with this condition may receive services under the categories of specific learning disability, emotional disturbance, or increasingly under the category "other health impairment."

Some students with a learning disability or mental retardation may be counted in the category of speech and language impairment and vice versa.

A significant, although unspecified, percentage of students served under the category of mental retardation are hypothesized to fall in the milder range of that disability.

Developmental Delay was added as a category in 1997 and likely includes additional children ages 0–9 with learning disabilities, mental retardation, and emotional disorders.

From: U.S. Department of Education (2001).

ness, it is reasonable to consider the usefulness of looking at the specific characteristics of individual learners as an alternative to categorical services and as a means of achieving more effective program development.

Mild Does *Not* Mean "Not Serious"

When the degree of disability is described as mild, moderate, or severe, those levels indicate the extent to which the person differs from others. The more similar the students are to typical students, the fewer the modifications needed to accommodate them in the standard curriculum (Hoover, 1987). This suggests that the fewer accommodations needed by the student, the milder the disability. The word *mild* is commonly interpreted as meaning "not a lot." By extension, it can be interpreted as meaning "not serious." A mild cold means you have the sniffles, but basically you are expected to go about your day as usual; it's "not serious." A student with a mild disability is frequently perceived to require few or minor accommodations to facilitate access to the general education program.

However, before we conclude that a mild disability is less serious than a more severe one, we must consider the effect of being "almost like everyone else" on a person's life. When students look and act similarly to their age peers, parents and teachers tend to have similar academic and behavioral expectations of them. For the most part, milder disabilities tend to be invisible. The student bears none of the physical stigmata that elicit understanding, assistance, or sympathy. Physically these students appear as if they should be able to learn and behave like the typical student. They can approximate age-appropriate behaviors, but their disability may cause them to be enough "off the pace" to compromise their success. When their disability even slightly impairs this ability to function, it can lead to failure in ordinary activities and have disastrous effects on their self-esteem and sense of competence. Let's consider some examples:

Meet John and Jim

John is a student with a severe behavioral disorder. His aggressive behaviors are so severe that he has been placed in a restrictive residential program. There he is served in a structured behavior program and receives counseling and social skills training. No one expects him to function in a regular classroom. In fact, no one will have him in a regular classroom.

Jim, on the other hand, has a mild behavioral disorder. He has problems with impulse control. Most of the time, he functions like the others in his sixth grade class. When frustrated, however, he is apt to lash out without thinking about the consequences. His teacher tends to respond to him as if his behaviors are volitional and so responds to these outbursts with punishment. Since Jim looks like the other students, his teacher feels justified in treating him like the others and doesn't believe he needs help with his impulse control disorder. Jim has come to internalize this "bad boy" image.

Meet Jane and Jamie

Jane's birth was a difficult one, resulting in a period of anoxia that left her with cerebral palsy and severe mental retardation. As a sixteen-year-old, she must have all her personal needs met by others. Her special program is designed to increase muscle control and teach her basic daily living skills like self-feeding. Rightly or wrongly, expectations for Jane are low because of her severe disabilities.

Jamie, on the other hand, looks like any other sixteen-year-old girl. Her mild level of retardation has made learning academic tasks difficult. She can read at about the fourth-grade level and is served in a vocational education program. Because she looks like everyone else and can carry out basic tasks, her parents, teachers, and peers expect her to be able to exercise the social judgment required of a teenager. They were all astonished when she allowed a group of boys to have sex with her, resulting in her becoming pregnant.

When we think of mild disabilities, we must consider the problems of these students as serious and worthy of our understanding and assistance. We must understand that constantly being almost able to compete credibly in common activities is very difficult to accept.

We must acknowledge the significant effect on a student's self-esteem of not being able to do what everyone else finds easy and of not knowing why. We must seek to understand the effect on a student's ability to function when it is not easily apparent what can be done to change the situation. This awareness results in an appreciation of the reason so many students with mild disabilities develop learned helplessness or other inappropriate social behaviors (e.g., noncompliance) when faced day in and day out with expectations that they can't meet and aren't helped to meet. Being "just a little different" can indeed be very serious.

The Power of Language

Human beings are distinguished from other animals by our use of a complex symbol system (i.e., language) to communicate with one another. Through language, we exchange information, and we communicate our ideas, emotions, feelings, and even our prejudices. Language has often been used to categorize and stigmatize groups of people. For example, the use of terms like "retarded" to refer to an entire group of people makes it easier to lose sight of their unique characteristics and to think of them in a devalued way. Because words can mean different things in different contexts, we need to be aware of the effect our words can have.

This book pays special attention to the effect of the words we use to describe these learners, especially the difference between a disability and a handicap. A *disability* is a condition that a person possesses; it is, however, only one characteristic of that individual. A disability is identified when an expected, specific human ability is curtailed or absent. Quite simply, it is the lack of an ability, and it is a describable, measurable condition. By itself, it implies absolutely nothing about the ability of the individual to carry out desired life functions.

A *handicap,* on the other hand, results from the interaction of that condition with the environment. A handicap results when the environment cannot or will not be modified to permit the individual to carry out functions. It is this problematic interaction that results in interference with the individual's ability to carry out a desired function (American Psychological Association, 2001; Illinois Department of Rehabilitation Services, 1994).

To give an example of the difference in these two terms, consider Ellen, who has myopia that results in a measurable lack of distance vision. In fact, her unaided visual acuity is over 20–200 in both eyes. We would be accurate in saying that she has a visual disability since she lacks the visual ability we expect people to have. However, since her vision is amenable to correction and she has been provided with glasses, she is not handicapped in tasks such as acquiring information from text or in mobility (e.g., driving a car). If she broke her glasses or if her vision was uncorrectable with glasses, she would be handicapped in acquiring information from text or in mobility—unless she or her friends were able to find another way for her to carry out those functions. Environmental accommodations that would eliminate the handicap might include listening to books on tape or riding to school with a sighted driver. When we think about Ellen, it is quite apparent that the lack of an ability (i.e., having a disability) does not necessarily mean the lack of a function and a resulting handicap.

A related term, *handicapism,* refers to the beliefs and practices that promote differential, unjust, or unequal treatment of a person based solely on an apparent or presumed disability. It involves taking actions on behalf of an individual based on the assumption that presence of a disability necessarily implies a handicap. Handicapist attitudes or actions include viewing persons with disabilities as victims, as afflicted with their disabilities; pitying persons with disabilities; seeing only the disability, not the person; avoiding people with disabilities; seeing people with disabilities as automatically valiant and brave; and speaking about individuals with disabilities in their presence rather than speaking to them.

As we work with learners with disabilities of various kinds, we should use language carefully, communicate accurately, and avoid reinforcing the stereotypes of helplessness. Some suggestions for more appropriate use of language include:

- Avoid using shorthand terms like "the handicapped" or "the disabled" to refer to a group of people with disabilities; these terms imply that all individuals with that characteristic are alike, that all members of the group are identical in their abilities and needs, an assumption that is not valid.
- Avoid using the word "handicapped" as a generic term to refer to people with disabilities; this word implies that a person with a disability is handicapped in functioning, an assumption that is also not necessarily warranted.
- Put the person first in sentence construction; this emphasizes the positive individuality of the person. For example, when we say, "The student with a learning disability . . ." rather than "The learning disabled student . . . ," it implies that the disability is but one facet of that student.
- Use active rather than passive language to diminish the implications of helplessness and victimization. For example, say that "She uses a wheelchair for mobility" rather than "She is confined to a wheelchair." In addition, do not use such terms as "victim" and "affliction" to refer to the person or to the disability.
- Avoid the use of "state of being" verbs in sentence construction. Say "He has a learning disability," rather than "He is learning disabled." The first sentence indicates that the person possesses a particular characteristic (among many), while the second implies a status. If this seems like a minor point, consider whether it would make a difference if you were to say "He is cancerous" instead of the more usual wording, "He has cancer."

Even the name of the legislation that governs our work with children reflects the increasing awareness of the potential of language to stereotype. P.L. 94–142 was originally titled the Education for All Handicapped Children Act. In 1990, the reauthorization of those provisions included a name change. We now put the person first, and the law is called the Individuals with Disabilities Education Act.

Labeling and Classifying

Bogdan and Taylor (1976, 1994) have provided a first-hand view of the life and thoughts of a person with a disability. Ed Murphy is an adult who was classified as a person with mental retardation when he was a child, and who subsequently spent a number of years in a state residential school for individuals with mental retardation and other severe disabilities. Listen to Ed's comments on labels:

> A lot of people are like I was. The problem is getting labeled as something. After that you're not really a person. It's like a sty in your eye—it's noticeable. Like that teacher and the way

she looked at me. In the fifth grade—in the fifth grade, my classmates thought I was different and my teacher knew I was different. One day she looked at me and she was on the phone to the office. Her conversation was like this, "When are you going to transfer him?" This was the phone in the room. I was there; she looked at me and knew I was knowledgeable about what she was saying. Her negative picture of me stood out like a sore thumb. That's the problem with people like me—the schools and the teachers find out we have problems, they notice them, and then we are abandoned. That one teacher was very annoyed that I was in her class. She had to put up with me. I was putting her classwork behind. If I were to do it over again, I think I would try harder to make it in school.

Ed Murphy believed that the classification, or label, he received and the special treatment that followed were caused by the fact that he and his problems in school stood out, that had he tried harder to be like everyone else, he could have avoided being singled out and pushed out of school.

The classification issue is far from simple. Labels affect those who receive the labels, those who give the labels, those who use the labels, and those who live with those who are labeled. The classification system is designed as a vehicle for communication about the child's disability, although it frequently implies some degree of stigma (Hobbs, 1975a). It affects all future interactions with the person. Blackman (1989) discussed children in special education classes as having "been assigned a disability" and referred to them as children with "negative school labels" (p. 459).

The line between typical and exceptional is far from being an absolute. As we will discover in Chapter 2 when we consider the history of disability, the values and needs of a society or culture determine what constitutes deviance, who is determined to be an outsider, and what response is called for to deal with deviance. The creation of categories of difference serves to define the boundaries between what is acceptable and typical in that society and what is not (Hobbs, 1975a). Classification identifies those individuals who are viewed as stigmatized or threatening, and it allows the culture to establish a barrier between those individuals and the "normal" members of the group. The barrier between groups can be physical, as is represented by an institution wall, or it can be psychological, as when we subtly reduce our expectations of an individual.

To Classify or Not to Classify

A number of justifications have been advanced to support the utility of disability classifications as well as arguments against the use of such categorical labels. Reasons often given for classifying students with disability labels include:

- Classification by disability is currently required to qualify a child for services. If we don't place the youngster in a disability category, the child cannot receive special education services under IDEA.

[1]Excerpted by permission of the publisher from Bogdan, R. & Taylor, S. J. *The Social Meaning of Mental Retardation: Two Life Stories.* (New York: Teachers College Press. © 1994 by Teachers College, Columbia University. All rights reserved.) pp. 33–34.

- Funding schemes generally require reports of children served by category to allow for the flow-through of funding. The categories justify the funding. Through classification, we are able to control allocation of resources and govern access to them.
- A classification attached to a particular individual may indicate why the individual has been experiencing difficulties in learning and other areas of functioning; it may hold the prospect that specialized help may remediate the problem.
- Some classifications have educational or medical relevance for treatment.
- It is frequently asserted that categories are needed for educational research, since the classifications are used to define groups for study. Categories are thought to provide a way of describing the characteristics of a group of subjects; without clearly defined categories for groups of individuals, it is more difficult to combine the research done by different investigators to discover useful patterns.
- Classification helps establish justification for specialized professional service providers to interact with that group of individuals; those being served are thought to require special services that can be provided only by professionals with special credentials.
- A more subtle use of classification was identified by Hobbs (1975a) when he asserted that labeling allows society to maintain stability by identifying and subsequently isolating the deviant members.

On the other hand, many problems and unintended outcomes have been attributed to the use of classifications or categories, including the following:

- Categories tend to rigidify thinking about the prospects for a given individual. They affect teacher and parental expectations of the student, usually in a negative way. Once it is known that a student has a disability, the classification explains the lack of progress; efforts to help the child learn may be affected in the belief that the child is achieving as well as can be expected and that additional efforts at remediation may not be useful.
- Classifications are often stigmatic. Negative associations with a particular category are extended to the individual, even when those characteristics are not displayed by that person.
- The individual can "become" the classification, either living up or down to the stereotypes carried by that word.
- Classifications related to etiology or medical treatment are frequently of little value for school program planning decisions, as Stevens and Birch argued in 1957 in their discussion of the terms used to refer to individuals with learning disabilities.
- Psychometric thresholds on tests used to make classification decisions falsely imply sharp demarcations among disabilities and between disability and ability.
- Disability classifications do not convey the specific information needed for designing programmatic interventions, although it is frequently assumed that they do. When a child is identified as a student with a learning disability, it may be assumed by parents and teachers that the child displays letter and number reversals and sees words backwards. This assumption leads to particular ideas about appropriate interventions, which may have little relevance to the child's actual problems. When a child is identified as a student

in need of special education services, we still know very little about the specific manifestations of that disability until someone describes that student's specific characteristics.

- Funding incentives based on differential funding for certain disabilities or levels of severity may lead to inappropriate or erroneous classifications. If classifying a child gets funding and services, a child whose diagnosis is questionable may be classified anyway, because it is a way to get services. If more funding accrues to particular placement options, children may be placed in settings that are not consistent with their needs. The IDEA Amendments of 1997 recognized this possibility when it required funding practices to result in neutral effects on placement (Council for Exceptional Children, 1998a; National Association of State Directors of Special Education, 1997).
- Categories tend to reinforce the notion that the reasons for school failure lie primarily within the student, relieving schools and teachers from responsibility, and downplaying the importance of teacher-student interaction in achieving success in school learning.
- Categories tend to serve as explanations for problem behaviors rather than as descriptors of that behavior.

It may be useful here to differentiate between classification and diagnosis. *Classification* is the systematic grouping of individual subjects into groups based on shared characteristics or traits. The classification does not mean that all members of the group are identical, just that they share some characteristics or traits. Classification refers to the formal and systematic conceptual schemes for describing individuals and their problems (Hobbs, 1975a).

Diagnosis, on the other hand, refers to the process of identifying or determining the nature of a specific individual's disease, condition, or manner of functioning. It is the analytical and descriptive process undertaken to determine etiology, current manifestation of the condition, treatment requirements, and prognosis of the child's condition (Hobbs, 1975a; see Box 1.1). Going far beyond the simple act of classification, diagnosis actually determines the factors that are unique to that individual and that are useful or essential in planning an intervention program.

To use an example from medicine, the classification process for determining if a person belongs to the group called "diabetic" is a blood sugar test. That test, among others, establishes that the person belongs to the general group of people with diabetes. This classification helps the doctor decide about additional diagnostic tests. However, each person with diabetes is unique. Factors such as age, gender, body weight, physical activity level, degree of disability, and emotional adjustment are all investigated and considered as the doctor plans a treatment plan that may include insulin supplementation, diet, physical activities, and other therapies. It is the diagnostic process that guides treatment planning, not the classification of diabetes.

The tendency with disabilities is to stop with classification. Persons working with individuals with mental retardation or any other disability often act as if all their clients have identical needs and expectations. Nothing could be farther from the truth. The needs of each child in a special education program are as unique as the needs of a child with diabetes. We wouldn't dream of giving all individuals with diabetes the same dosage of insulin. In a similar way, we must base programming for children with disabilities on their unique needs, not on their classification.

SPOTLIGHT IN HISTORY: Nicholas Hobbs and the Project on Classification of Exceptional Children

The Project on Classification of Exceptional Children was undertaken in the early 1970s at the direction of Eliot Richardson, U.S. Secretary of Health, Education, and Welfare. He justified the study on the basis of the serious consequences of inappropriate classification of children as delinquent, retarded, disordered, or disturbed. Noting that there were problems with the diagnostic procedures used to classify children, he charged the project team with reviewing the practices and consequences of labeling and developing recommendations for improving professional assessment practices.

The combined efforts of ten federal agencies of the Department of Health, Education, and Welfare resulted in the publication of three volumes: *The Futures of Children* (Hobbs, 1975a) summarized the findings of the interagency task force and formulated a number of policy recommendations. The accompanying source books, *Issues in the Classification of Children,* Volumes 1 and 2 (Hobbs, 1975b, 1975c) contained articles by a number of the participants in the study. Together these books comprised a comprehensive summary of the thinking of the time about classification and problems associated with the classification process.

Hobbs's (1975a) classic discussion of these problems at the beginning of the P.L. 94–142 era made a strong argument for a process that would be based on a description of each individual child's abilities and deficits, revised frequently. He called for a state and federal funding system that would be based on the needs of students rather than on classifications.

Concluding his discussion of the categorizing process, Hobbs stated:

> Classification, then, is not a simple, scientific, and value free procedure with predictably benign consequences. Rather, it arises from and tends to perpetuate the value of the cultural majority, often to the detriment of individual children or

classes of children. The majority has made the rules, determined what is good, normal, or acceptable, and what is deviant, exceptional, or unacceptable. Classification seeks to identify children who do not fit the norms, who are not progressing normally, and who pose a threat to the equilibrium of the system, so that they may be changed or isolated. Seen in this light, classification becomes a mechanism for social control. It institutionalizes the values of the cultural majority, governs the allocation of resources and access to opportunity, protects the majority from undue anxiety, and maintains the status quo of the community and its institutions. Clearly many of the negative consequences and abuses . . . can be understood and remedied only within this broader cultural context. (pp. 40–41)

> Each child is unique, the center of a unique life space. To design a plan to help him grow and learn requires much specific information about him and his immediate world. The best way we have discovered to get the information needed for good program planning is to construct a profile of assets and liabilities of the child in a particular setting and at a particular time. The profile should describe physical attributes, including salient features of a medical, psychological, and educational evaluation. It should specify what the child can do and what he cannot do, what he can be taught to do, and what is expected of him. It should include the people who are important in his life: parents, brothers and sisters, teachers, a social worker perhaps, or a physician, other children, other significant adults, and also the people who make the profile and plan and carry out a program to help him. Settings are important too: the neighborhood, community center, church, the child's school, sometimes an institution. In effect, a profile of assets and liabilities describes the transactions between the child and people significant in his life, always in particular settings and at particular times. . . . The profile should be the basis for specification of treatment objectives and of time limits for accomplishing goals. (pp. 104–105)

Hobbs criticized simplistic labeling systems for their lack of information capacity and value. For example:

> Jane shows up on summary school records and state reports as "mentally retarded, educable." What is not recorded is that Jane cannot read, that she is attractive and pleasant, that she needs dental care, and that she is very good with children and has held a child care job with a family for five years. There is no record of services needed. (pp. 106–107)

He asserted that even this simple sketch conveyed far more useful information than the bureaucratic category of "mentally retarded, educable." He held that the accounting systems then employed by the federal government and most states were responsible for "encouraging the neglect of individual differences among children and obscuring their individual service requirements" (p. 108). He concluded:

> When a skilled teacher or therapist or child-care worker undertakes to help an individual child, categories and labels (in their familiar and gross form) recede from the picture. They poorly fit the complex reality of the living child; they provide meager guidance for what to do for him; they are an inherent encumbrance in the educational or treatment process. A stigmatizing label may have to be dealt with as one of the child's problems, but it is essentially useless in the design of a program for him. (p. 113)

Another problem with tying programming decisions solely to a classification relates to the observation that children's learning and behavioral needs lie on a continuum, not in dichotomous or discrete groups. Many schools operate under the assumption that students who do not have a classification are all typical learners, and that it is reasonable to expect them all to learn and behave in the same environment. We know that this is not true, but since we do not utilize diagnostic procedures regularly with all children, classified or not, many children struggle in classrooms with instructional programs that do not meet their unique needs. The recent move to classify some students as at-risk testifies to this fact. The creation of this new category is consistent with the assumption that we do not need to provide differentiated programming unless a child is first classified as different. Educators need to examine the logic behind this phenomenon and consider the feasibility of designing diagnosis-based planning rather than using only classification-driven programming.

Current Thinking on Labeling

In response to national concern about educational reform and standards in the 1980s, the Council for Exceptional Children (CEC) developed a policy on labeling and categorizing children that addresses many of these concerns (Appendix A). This policy emphasizes the importance of planning an educational program that is appropriate for a child, based upon the child's individual learning needs and strengths rather than on a label or other external factors. Furthermore, this policy highlights the valuable skills that special educators bring to education reform, namely the knowledge and expertise that enables teachers to provide appropriate, individualized instruction to a variety of learners. The policy sought to underscore the fact that all learners can benefit from an education system that focuses on the educational needs and capabilities of students rather than on a label or category.

A policy recommendation developed to respond to concerns about labels and educational placement was issued in 1987 by the National Association of School Psychologists, the National Coalition of Advocates for Students, and the National Association of Social Workers. This position paper, "Rights without Labels," suggested an alternative to categorical systems that safeguards the rights of currently classified students while expanding the process of diagnosis as the primary programming procedure (Appendix A). This model creates the possibility of moving toward a unitary system of service delivery. The framers of this policy recognized that while IDEA mandates educational services for students with disabilities, it does not necessarily require a separate special education system. The "Rights without Labels" philosophy has yet to achieve widespread national acceptance. This is due in part to the fear among parents that the services they worked so hard to acquire for their children would be wiped out if classifications and the means for determining eligibility were to be eliminated.

Prevention of Disabilities

One of the most convincing arguments for classification is that the knowledge of a cause may lead to effective prevention in the future and to more effective services for a specific youngster. As we discuss various disabilities and possible causes, it is useful to consider any implications that certain conditions may be preventable or that the severity of their effect may be alleviated. With increasing knowledge about mild disabilities and their causes, we have developed some ways to prevent those conditions or to at least reduce their effect on an individual's life.

Rowitz (1986) and Scott and Carren (1987) described a three-tier model of prevention efforts, including primary, secondary, and tertiary prevention levels. This model may be useful in developing action plans designed to ameliorate the effects of a variety of conditions and disorders (see Table 1.2). AAMR (2002) describes this framework as a form of therapeutic support.

Conditions that are amenable to primary prevention are those that have a known causal agent and those whose causes can be eliminated so that the condition never occurs. Examples of such conditions are disabilities resulting from maternal rubella infection or maternal alcohol consumption. Effective immunization programs that reach all women before childbearing years will eliminate rubella as a cause of retardation and other defects in infants. In other cases, education campaigns that inform prospective mothers about the dangers of alcohol consumption and counseling abstinence during pregnancy can reduce the use of alcohol in expectant mothers and therefore reduce the incidence of fetal alcohol syndrome and other birth defects in newborns.

Secondary prevention efforts require (1) knowledge of the causal agent, (2) an efficient means of screening for the condition in potentially affected individuals in the early stages, and (3) effective treatment for the condition. Phenylketonuria (PKU) is an example of such a condition. The cause of PKU is a known genetic defect that can be identified in the newborn by a simple and effective blood test. Dietary treatment is virtually 100 percent effective

TABLE 1.2   Levels of Prevention and Their Goals[1]

Level of Prevention	Goal of Prevention Efforts
Primary Prevention	To change the conditions that are associated with the disability so that it does not occur in the first place
Secondary Prevention	To identify the disability as early as possible, and change the environment so that the person is affected as little as possible and the duration of the disorder is shortened
Tertiary Prevention	To provide support in educational and social environments over the life span to maximize the level of functioning and prevent the condition from deteriorating any more rapidly than necessary

[1]Based on AAMR, 2002; Rowitz, 1986; Scott & Carren, 1987.

in eliminating the mental retardation associated with this condition, permitting normal development. In the case of lead poisoning, it is known that high levels of lead in the blood may result in mental retardation, learning disabilities, or ADHD. High-risk populations, such as preschool children who live in high-lead environments, can be routinely screened for lead. Once lead poisoning is detected, medical interventions can lower the level of lead in the blood, and environmental actions can eliminate the source of the lead, preventing recontamination and future intellectual damage.

Tertiary efforts are appropriate when there is not a known cause or a procedure to remove the cause or cure the condition. In such cases, we must manage the environment to maximize the development of the child in spite of the condition. Youngsters with Down syndrome are an example of individuals who respond well to tertiary efforts. While we know the condition is related to chromosomal abnormalities, we do not usually know why it happens, nor can we alter the chromosomal makeup of the affected individual once it occurs. Education efforts across the life span, beginning with infant stimulation and early intervention in preschool, reduces the effect of the condition and allows the child to develop to the maximum extent possible.

This framework can be applied to any disability or condition. In the discussions of mental retardation, learning disabilities, attention deficit hyperactivity disorder, and emotional or behavioral disorders, it is useful to consider the extent to which primary, secondary, and tertiary prevention efforts that will eliminate or lessen the effect of those conditions can be identified. To the extent that knowledge of a cause allows effective prevention efforts to be mounted, then the categorization is a useful venture (AAMR, 2002).

Overview of the Principles of the IDEA

As we begin our study of learners with mild disabilities, it may be useful to outline the major provisions of the Individuals with Disabilities Education Act. In 1975, Congress passed the Education for All Handicapped Children Act (P.L. 94–142), renamed the Individuals with

Disabilities Education Act (IDEA) in 1990. This landmark legislation followed decades of advocacy on behalf of children with disabilities and court rulings that repeatedly held that all children have the right to a public education. The passage of this legislation made identification and services for students with mild disabilities the responsibility of schools, districts, and states. In the years since, there have been modifications and additions to the law, including the reauthorization of the IDEA in 1997, which continue to provide the foundation for services to children regardless of the severity of their disabilities. A more complete discussion of the implications of IDEA 1997 appears in Chapters 3, 4, and 5 of this book, but a brief overview of the major components of the law will help set the context for our discussion of these children.

Prior to the passage and implementation of IDEA, fewer than half of children with disabilities were being served in school programs, and the appropriateness of those programs was debatable (Turnbull & Turnbull, 1998). Since the implementation deadline for P.L. 94–142 in 1978, school districts have been held accountable for assuring that all children are provided with a *free and appropriate public education (FAPE)*. This provision established the principle of *zero reject* in public education. No longer could a child be barred from school and educational services because a disability was too severe, because the school didn't have a class or teacher able to handle students with a particular disability, or because the child had not accomplished certain developmental milestones, such as toilet training. All children in the designated age range for school attendance in a district were entitled to an education funded by public monies. It became the responsibility of the district and state to determine how to provide that education and how to pay for it. In addition to the guarantee of a free and appropriate public education, IDEA established five additional principles to help achieve the aims of Congress:

- Nondiscriminatory evaluation
- Individualized education programs (IEPs)
- Least restrictive environment (LRE)
- Parental participation
- Procedural due process

Nondiscriminatory evaluation procedures were mandated for determining eligibility and placement in specialized educational programs. This means that assessment must include a variety of valid and reliable measures of the child's abilities, that instruments used must be culturally fair and age appropriate, and that testing must be in the child's primary language. All evaluations must be performed by appropriately trained personnel, and the parents or guardians must give consent for and be informed of the results of the evaluation.

When the evaluation process confirms the presence of a disability requiring special education services, IDEA requires that an individualized education program (IEP) be developed, and that an individualized transition program (ITP) should be in place by the time the child is fourteen. Individualized family service programs (IFSP) are required for services to children from birth to age five. The creation of the IEP addresses the requirement that the education provided be appropriate to the student's needs. Teachers, parents, and support personnel, as well as the student if appropriate, collaborate to translate the assessment results into a plan of goals and objectives that will guide the student's educational program for the next year. These "I-Plans" (Turnbull & Turnbull, 1998) identify the skills and behaviors the student has developed, the skills and behaviors that are reasonable goals for the next year, and the resources, supports, and personnel needed to help attain those goals. They indicate the measures that will be used to evaluate the student's progress and the date of the next annual review and planning meeting.

Once an I-Plan has been developed, the team must determine the setting most likely to provide the opportunity to achieve those outcomes. The IDEA requires that school placements be in the least restrictive environment (LRE) possible—the setting that most appropriately meets the child's identified educational needs, that will confer educational benefit on the child, and that will maximize contact with children without disabilities. This means that the multidisciplinary team must consider all possible options and then determine which placements would provide the necessary supports for the youngster to function and develop. LRE has also come to require that once the need for certain levels of support has been confirmed, the team should consider the possibility that those supports could be provided in a less restrictive setting and in a setting that provides for more contact and time in normalized environments with peers who do not have disabilities. The team must indicate the amount of time the learner will be involved in general education settings and the supports that will be needed from special education and related service providers to allow the student access to the general education curriculum.

A model for thinking about placement decisions is the continuum of services, ranging from the general education classroom to residential placements (Deno, 1970; Reynolds, 1989; Ysseldyke, Algozzine, & Thurlow, 2000). The planning team should move a student in the direction of increasingly restrictive settings only as far as necessary. The team should then develop a program of support and instruction that will enable the student to develop the skills and behaviors needed to move as quickly as possible back into settings that are less restrictive and that provide a more normalized school experience. States and districts vary considerably in the implementation of the continuum. However, national data indicates that close to half of all students with disabilities are educated in the general education classroom for 80 percent or more of the day, another 28 percent are out of the general education class for 21–60 percent of the day, and only 20 percent are removed from general education for more than 80 percent of the time. Only 4 percent are served in segregated facilities or residential placements (U.S. Department of Education, 2001). The national trend over the 1984–2000 period has been increasingly to serve students with disabilities in the general education classroom and in regular school buildings (see Table 1.3).

In addition to location, placement patterns vary with respect to the ages and disabilities of the students. In general, younger students are more likely to be served in integrated placements while older students (especially those in the eighteen to twenty-one age group) are increasingly found to be served in specialized, separate settings (Table 1.4). One explanation for this phenomenon may be that students remaining in school until age twenty-one are more likely to have more severe disabilities, which may warrant more specialized placements. Another explanation is that older students began their school careers when more restrictive service models were commonplace, and their schools and parents continue to see those as the best model for those students. When we look at the placement distribution by disability,

TABLE 1.3   Percentage of Students with Disabilities (Ages 6-21) Educated in General Education Classrooms More Than 80 percent of the Day and Percentage Educated in Regular School Buildings: 1984–1998

	1984	1986	1988	1990	1992	1994	1996	1998
General Education Class More Than 80% of Day	24.6	26.4	30.5	32.8	39.8	44.5	45.8	47.4
Educated in Regular School Buildings	93.0	93.9	93.8	94.4	94.9	95.7	95.7	95.9

From U.S. Department of Education, 2001, p. III-2.

TABLE 1.4   Percentage of Use of Placement Options Utilized by Age (1998–1999)

Placement	Ages 6–11	Ages 12–17	Ages 18–21
Consultant/Inclusion	57.21	38.42	31.14
Resource Room	23.63	33.85	27.66
Special Class	16.95	22.53	28.89
Special School	1.76	3.50	8.95
Residential	.23	1.01	2.10
Home/Hospital	.22	.67	1.26

From U.S. Department of Education, 2001, Tables AB 3, 4, and 5.

students with milder disabilities are generally served in integrated or part-time special education settings, while those with more severe levels of disability are served in special classes, schools, or residential settings.

Throughout the evaluation, planning, and placement process, IDEA holds that parents must be central to all decisions. The procedures mandated by IDEA and reaffirmed in the 1997 IDEA reauthorization assured that parental participation would be an expected event, recognizing the importance of different perspectives in understanding the needs of a particular student. Parents are viewed as an important source of information about the strengths and needs of the child and as an essential partner in the delivery of services.

Finally, the IDEA contains language that ensures that schools and parents must work together to provide an appropriate education for every child. The due process requirements ensure that districts will develop procedures to involve all parties in decision making and planning, including requirements for notice and timely completion of various tasks. These provisions also govern responsibilities of schools in the event of a parental appeal of a decision made by the multidisciplinary team. The presence of due process procedures encourages schools and parents to collaborate with one another and to develop an appropriate education plan for every child.

Amendments to P.L. 94–142

In 1986, Congress passed legislation amending P.L. 94–142, extending special education services downward to include preschool children aged three to five and to provide incentive grants for serving infants and toddlers (birth to age 2). The law also required that individualized family service plans (IFSP) be developed to make appropriate educational and support services available for these young children and their families. Interagency cooperation was also mandated to provide appropriate services to children with disabilities.

In 1990, Congress passed P.L. 101–476, which changed the name of the nation's special education law to the Individuals with Disabilities Education Act, or IDEA. This change reflected the philosophy of considering the person first before the disability. These amendments also recognized the importance of support during the transition to adult life by requiring the development of individualized transition plans (ITP) for all youngsters no later than age fourteen.

In 1997, Congress once again amended this landmark legislation with the IDEA Amendments of 1997 (P.L. 105–17), improving and strengthening its provisions. The implications of those provisions will be discussed in Chapters 3, 4, and 5. With these amendments, Congress reaffirmed the commitment of the federal government to the education of persons with disabilities to age twenty-one. The laws and its amendments mandate services that appropriately meet the needs of children and youth from ages three to twenty-one, and they support the philosophy that schools, families, and students must work together to ensure that all children and youth receive needed educational services in the least restrictive environment.

Focus on Culture and Diversity

This chapter highlights a critical issue when considering human diversity and cultural differences—the degree to which we as human beings perceive each other as different, name those differences, and then isolate ourselves from those who are perceived to be different. Our use of language to categorize people, whether by race, ethnicity, language, gender, sexual orientation, socioeconomic class, or ability, carries with it the power to stigmatize and segregate. Our recent history with identifying children as being at risk shows us that when we confront a problem, we tend to attempt to solve it by creating a group to epitomize the problem and then develop interventions to "fix" that group, that is, to remove or diminish their differences, with limited effectiveness.

Our challenge as educators in the twenty-first century is to assure that programs like IDEA, which were put in place to help solve problems for groups of learners, do not have the unintended outcome of further marginalizing them. We have seen the problems that were created when we provided segregated services for those with disabilities, and we are moving toward more inclusive practices. However, as long as children are viewed as special education students rather than as students with special learning needs, we have not solved the problem. As subsequent chapters will discuss, the history and current practice of special education have tended to see cultural differences and diversity as part of the problem, resulting in actions that further divide human beings.

Resources on the Web

IDEAS That Work

www.ideapractices.org

>Provides information and updates on IDEA, links to federal publications, and other resources for teachers and parents; operated by the Council for Exceptional Children and the U.S. Office of Special Education and Rehabilitative Services.

National Information Center for Children and Youth with Disabilities

www.nichcy.org

>A national, IDEA-funded information and referral center; provides information on disabilities for families and professionals.

National Association of Protection and Advocacy Systems

www.protectionandadvocacy.com

>A nationwide, federally mandated system of offices; provides information on the rights of people with disabilities and lists of state advocacy offices.

Person-First Language

www.kidstogether.org/pep-1st.htm

>Provides information and examples of person-first language.

Words with Dignity

www.paraquad.org/wwd.htm

>Provides examples of person-first language, as well as posters highlighting the abilities of persons with disabilities rather than their disabilities.

Summary

A significant majority of students served in special education programs today have mental retardation, learning disabilities, attention-deficit/hyperactivity disorders, or emotional or behavioral disorders. Study of these high-prevalence conditions reveals that difficulties with cognition, learning, language, and behavior are of concern for each disability. An integrated perspective on the four conditions allows teachers and others to have a more accurate and comprehensive understanding of the students they serve.

The majority of learners with disabilities have milder forms of disability. Nevertheless, mild disabilities still cause significant problems for students. Often the disabilities go undetected, leaving the students to struggle on their own. In addition, the students are often blamed for their lack of achievement or their problem behavior. Study of various aspects of mild levels of disability will help teachers and others recognize the effect of mild disabilities on their students and will equip them to serve those needs more effectively. These awarenesses and skills can frequently also be helpful in working with learners whose problems are not severe enough for the student to be classified as a student with a disability.

The language we use to describe students with disabilities conveys much about our view of them. Consistent use of person-first language requires us to consider the child a person and not a disability. It is also important to understand the difference between a disability and a handicap. Disabilities are conditions in which a typical human ability is curtailed. Handicaps are restrictions on functioning that result from the interaction of the environment and the person with a disability. Handicaps occur when the environment cannot or will not be modified to allow the person to perform needed or desired functions.

Classifying and labeling raise complex philosophical and political issues with positive and negative implications. People working in the field of special education continue to struggle with the effects and the utility of classifications. Central to this discussion is the fact that implementation of the IDEA currently requires that students be classified in order to receive services.

One reason for using classification systems is to guide prevention efforts. In some cases, knowledge of a cause allows primary prevention interventions to keep the disability from occurring in the first place. Early detection of a condition allows effective secondary interventions to ameliorate the effect on the individual and prevent subsequent restrictions on functioning. Tertiary prevention efforts continue throughout life to maximize functioning despite the continued disability.

The IDEA contains procedural requirements (nondiscriminatory evaluation, LRE placement, IEP development, due process, and parental participation) that reduce the negative implications of labeling, but questions and concerns remain. Proposals such as the "Rights without Labels" movement help us consider other ways to implement our mandate to provide free, appropriate public education to all children.

ED MURPHY: A Case Study

For the most part, the historical record of special education has been told through the words of those providing services. Recently, as we have sought to expand beyond our own limited experience of what it is like to be deemed different, we have begun to seek out the perspectives of those judged to be exceptional themselves (Safford & Safford, 1996). Through autobiography and ethnographic interviewing, and following in the tradition established by Edgerton (1967), Bogdan and Taylor (1976, 1994) sought to see the world from the perspective of those thought of as "other," specifically, through the eyes of two individuals labeled as having mental retardation. They sought to understand the interactions of these individuals in their cultural milieu, and to reveal the degree to which those interactions defined those individuals, both in the eyes of others and in their own eyes. As the life stories of these two individuals unfolded, it became clear to Bogdan and Taylor (1994) that the participants viewed the programs designed to help them somewhat differently from the way those providing the services saw them. They also became aware that it was the perceptions of the participant that really determined the outcomes.

(continued)

When Bogdan and Taylor first met Ed Murphy, he was working at a sheltered workshop. As they got to know Ed better, they sensed the richness of the story he had to share. Over several years, they recorded numerous extended interviews with Ed, which they reproduced in their book, *The Social Meaning of Mental Retardation*. It is from this book that the information in this case study is drawn.

Ed was born in 1948 with a variety of developmental disabilities. His mother was told he would probably not live and certainly never walk. She refused to give up on him, and in 1954 he began school. At age eleven, he was finally removed from regular class and placed in special education. His parents died when he was fifteen, and after a brief period living with neighbors and in foster care, Ed was placed in a state residential training school for individuals with mental disabilities. He remained at "Empire State School" for almost five years. After an additional four years of "family care," he moved to a boarding house, and shortly thereafter, at age twenty-five, he began to work in a nursing home.

As one reads Ed's story, the power of his story and his perceptiveness shine through. Ed credits his language ability to being a good listener and to hours spent listening to television. The editing of the interviews may be responsible for some of the strength of the narrative, but Bogdan and Taylor assert that they have faithfully represented the man in his own words.

Despite the level of his functioning, the psychologists assigned Ed the label of mental retardation. The diagnosis was justifiable given the standards of the time, since Ed's intelligence test scores ranged only from the high 40s to the low 60s over the years. To put perspective on these scores, here are Ed's own words about what the label "retarded" has meant in his life:

There is discrimination against the retarded. There are people out of ignorance who have hurt retarded children. It really doesn't help a person's character the way the system treats you. One thing that's hard is once you're in it, you can't convince them how smart you are. And you're so weak you can't convince them how smart you are. And you're so weak, you can't really fight back. Some of the help you get isn't help. Like the way they talk to you, "I'll help little Eddie . . . you're so nice." Not that I'm saying that they intentionally treat you that way.

I'm talking like an expert. I had to live it. Shit, I'm not really different. I only had different experiences in my life than you. When you are talking about state schools you need experts. Experts are people who have lived it. I'm not taking anything away from scholars who have sat for years in offices and know the problem. But I know the problem too. (pp. 29–30)

I don't know how old I was when I started talking. It takes time to learn little things when you're handicapped. It's not easy to learn to tie your shoe. Not to know these little things when you're young and everyone else knows them is hell. (p. 31)

My family had problems and it was all over the block that I was this kind or that kind of kid. In school, growing up, it was the same kind of thing. It's very annoying because it follows you around. My mind was slow. I can't deny that. A lot went on when we were kids. My mom and dad weren't really ready for us. They got in over their heads. The family was bogged down. (p. 32)

In elementary school my mind used to drift a lot. Concentrating was almost impossible. I was so much into my own thoughts—my daydreams—I wasn't really in class. I would make up stories in my head. I would think of the cowboy movies. The rest of the kids would be in class and I would be on a battlefield somewhere. The nuns would yell at me to snap out of it, but they were nice. That was my major problem all through school, that I daydreamed. I think a lot of people do that. It wasn't related to retardation. I think a lot of kids do that and are diagnosed as retarded but it's nothing to do with retardation at all. It really has to do with how people deal with people around them and their situation. I don't think I was bored. I think all the kids were competing to be honor students but I wasn't interested in that. I was in my own world—I was happy. I wouldn't recommend it to someone, but daydreaming can be a good thing. I kind of stood in the background—I kind of knew I was different—I knew that I had a problem, but when you're young you don't think of it as a problem. (p. 33)

The way the other kids treated you was a kind of invisible meanness. The meanness you have to look carefully to see. I would get pretty upset when I was teased, but then I learned I had to keep control of myself. It's a lot harder to do that when you're weak. The teasing was one thing, but here was this meanness that you couldn't see that kept after you. (p. 36)

Looking back on it now, when I was in special classes—it really wasn't fair a lot of things that happened. One thing that I remember is that we didn't have a representative on the school senate. We should have been able to vote. We weren't represented. If we had representatives we could have had the advantages the others had. There was a time that everyone voted.

The big thing to get to understand is what the hell is going on around you. They kept us away from the others. The important thing when talking about teaching the retarded child is that we have to teach him to do it for himself. That is real hard. (p. 37)

If you're going to do something with a person's life you don't have to pay all that money to be testing them. I had no place to go. I mean here I am, pretty intelligent, and here are six psychologists testing me and sending me to the state school. How would you feel if you were examined by all those people and then wound up where I did? A psychologist is supposed to help you. The way they talked to me, they must have thought I was pretty intelligent. One of them said, "You look like a smart young man," and then I turned up there. I don't think the tests made any difference—they had their minds made up anyway. . . .

When the psychiatrist interviewed me he had my records in front of him—so he already knew I was mentally retarded. It's the same with everyone. If you are considered mentally retarded there is no way you can win. There is no way they give you a favorable report. They put horses out of misery quicker than they do people. It's a real blow to you being sent to the state school. (p. 40)

Your first day at the institution is an unusual day. It's not like any other day in your whole life. The thing that's so different is, you are different. You're different, the people you are going to be with are different. Going there makes you feel different. I couldn't describe it, but I do think that. I think I almost knew what I was in store for, but on the other hand, I had no idea. I did know about Empire before I went, but I didn't know what it was. When I got to Empire the word

"retarded" was something I had to deal with. I had my own way of thinking about myself—I had my own little world. Looking at it from that point of view, I don't know if I looked at myself from the point of view of me being retarded. I knew I had problems when I went to Empire, but I wasn't sure how I thought about it. (p. 42)

I almost didn't make it. . . . I don't like the word "vegetable"—but in my own case I could see that if I had been placed on that low-grade ward I might have slipped to that. I began feeling myself slip—they could have made me a vegetable. If I would have let that place get to me and depress me I would still have been there today. Actually it was one man that saved me. They had me scheduled to go to P-8—a back ward—when just one man looked at me. I was a wreck. I had a beard and baggy state clothes on. I had just arrived at the place. I was trying to understand what was happening. I was confused. What I looked like was P-8 material. There was this supervisor, a woman. She came on the ward and looked right at me and said: "I have him scheduled for P-8." An older attendant was there. He looked over at me and said, "He's too bright for that ward. I think we will keep him." To look at me then I didn't look too good. She made a remark under her breath that I looked pretty retarded to her. She saw me looking at her—I looked her square in the eye. She had on a white dress and a cap with three stripes—I can see them now. She saw me and said, "Just don't stand there, get to work." (pp. 43–44)

It's funny. You hear so many people talking about IQ. The first time I heard the expression was when I was at Empire State School. I didn't know what it was or anything but some people were talking and they brought the subject up. It was on the ward and I went and asked one of the staff what mine was. They told me 49. Forty-nine isn't 50 but I was pretty happy about it. I mean I figured that I wasn't a low grade. I really didn't know what it meant but it sounded pretty high. Hell I was born in 1948 and 49 didn't seem too bad. Forty-nine didn't sound hopeless. I didn't know anything about the highs or lows but I knew I was better than most of them. (p. 55)

The narrative continues with Ed's account of his transition to adulthood, including living arrangements and jobs. In closing the narrative, Bogdan

(continued)

and Taylor (1994) recorded Ed's reflections on the issue of disability and handicap at that point in his adult life:

> I never thought of myself as a retarded individual, but who would want to? I never really had that ugly feeling down deep. You're not knowledgeable about what they are saying behind your back. You get a feeling from people around you—they try to hide it, but their intentions don't work. They say they will do this and that—like they will look out for you. They try to protect you, but you feel sort of guilty. You get the feeling that they love you but that they are looking down at you. You always have a sense of a barrier between you and the ones that love you. By their own admission of protecting you, you have an umbrella over you that tells you that you and they have an understanding that there's something wrong—that there is a barrier.
>
> As I got older, I slowly began to find myself becoming mentally awake. I found myself concentrating—like on television. A lot of people wonder why I have good grammar—it was because of television. I was like a tape recorder—what I heard, I memorized. Even when I was ten or twelve I would listen to Huntley and Brinkley. They were my favorites. As the years went by, I understood what they were talking about.
>
> People were amazed at what I knew. People would begin to ask me what I thought about this and that. Like my aunt would always ask me about the news—what my opinions were. I began to know that I was a little brighter than they thought I was. It became a hobby. I didn't know what it meant, that I had a grasp on a lot of important things—the race riots, Martin Luther King in jail—what was really happening was that I was beginning to find something else instead of just being bored. It was entertaining. I didn't know that meant anything then. I mean I didn't know that I would be sitting here telling you all this.
>
> When you are growing up, you don't think of yourself as a person but as a boy. As you get older it works itself out—who you are deep down, who you ought to be. You have an image of yourself deep down. You try to sort it out. What is happening to it? You know what you are deep inside but those around you give you a negative picture of yourself. It's that umbrella over you.
>
> The fact that you have a handicap follows you around. People don't like the word. We persecute people. The child goes through everything, and all of a sudden—you're marked with a big "R." By the time you reach the situation you're going to grow into, there isn't too much difference with what people are going to say about you.
>
> People tell you you are handicapped in different ways. You're in a restaurant and you may see people watching you eat and people make excuses for you. They go over and talk to them. They say, "The kid is retarded." Make an excuse for him. I've seen that. I've heard them say it, but you love them so you put up with it. For some reason you put up with it.
>
> It makes me sad to see someone who is forty years old taking a child's lunch box to work. It almost makes me want to cry. It's not easy, because parents don't want to let go.
>
> Right now schools discriminate against the retarded. You can mix handicapped with regular kids, but they won't do it. Parents of normal kids don't want the retarded kids in their school. I think if they got the kids in there when they were younger, then they would grow up being used to each other. The rest of the world can think of you as retarded, but you don't have to think of yourself as retarded. (pp. 86–87)

Ed Murphy reveals himself to be a knowledgeable informant about the nature of the social context from which the construct of mental retardation is drawn. His story helps us see the contradictions involved in dividing people into two groups: the "normal" group and those with retardation. He helps us see that in many important ways, the notion of disability or handicap is derived from how we see ourselves and others.

DISCUSSION

If the only information available to you was that Ed Murphy has the label of mild-to-moderate mental retardation based on measured IQ scores in the range of 40 to 60, what would you actually know about Ed Murphy? Make a list.

Next, make a list of what you know about Ed Murphy from these excerpts from his life narrative as recorded by Bogdan and Taylor.

Now, compare the two lists, and discuss the implications of this information and analysis with respect to the process of diagnosis and classification.

CHAPTER TWO

HISTORICAL PERSPECTIVES AND CONTEXTS

QUESTIONS TO GUIDE YOUR STUDY

- What can we learn from the history of special education?
- Give several examples of the way attitudes and values of a society or a time determine how people with disabilities are viewed and treated.
- What rights for people with disabilities have been secured through the courts?
- What trends do we see in the history of services for students with disabilities?

Meet Victor

A wild boy—a savage found running in the woods and foraging in the fields in the south of France in 1797, who was captured and then escaped—this child focused the attention of the professional community and the world on the nature of difference and disability. In many ways, the story of the "Wild Boy" changed how we think about people with disabilities. The boy was finally apprehended and taken to Paris, where he was placed at the Institute for Deaf-Mutes because of his apparent sensory and language deficits. Jean-Marc-Gaspard Itard, a French physician, met the Wild Boy of Aveyron there at the end of 1800, and against the advice of his mentors, he took on the challenge of educating the "savage." Itard set five goals for his training of the child:

> 1st aim. To interest him in social life by rendering it more pleasant for him than the one he was

then leading, and above all more like the one he had just left.

> 2nd aim. To awaken his nervous sensibility by the most energetic stimulation, and occasionally by intense emotion.

> 3rd aim. To extend the range of his ideas by giving him new needs and by increasing his social contacts.

> 4th aim. To lead him to the use of speech by inducing the exercise of imitation, through the imperious law of exercise.

> 5th aim. To make him exercise the simplest mental operations upon the objects of his physical needs over a period of time afterwards inducing the application of these mental processes to the objects of instruction. (p. 10–11)

Some time later, Itard writes of the naming of the boy:

(continued)

One day when he was in the kitchen occupied with cooking potatoes, two people had a sharp dispute behind him, without his appearing to pay the least attention. A third arrived unexpectedly, who, joining in the discussion, commenced all his replies with these words, "Oh, that is different!" I noticed that every time that this person let his favorite "Oh!" escape, the Savage of Aveyron quickly turned his head. That evening when he went to bed, I made some experiments upon this sound and obtained almost the same results. I went over all the other simple sounds known as vowels, but without any success. This preference for "O" obliged me to give him a name which terminated with this vowel. I chose Victor. This name remains his, and when it is called, he rarely fails to turn his head or run up. (p. 29)

Itard's work with Victor is the first detailed account of a therapeutic and instructional program designed to alleviate the effects of a disability. It is the story of a real child with a disability, a real child with a name . . . Victor!

Quotations from *Wild Boy of Aveyron by Itard* by (trans.) Humphrey/Humphrey, © 1962. Reprinted by permission of Prentice-Hall, Inc., Upper Saddle River, NJ.

The Historical Context of Disability

The degree to which persons with disabilities are included in social environments is always set in the context of a particular society and time. Economic and social conditions have always defined and driven decisions about the role education plays in a society and about society's response to disabilities and deviance of any kind (Bogdan & Taylor, 1994; Safford & Safford, 1996; Smith, J. D., 1998). Changes in social climate have led to changes in the perception of individuals with disabilities. Historical events are a product of the existing social forces, which are mediated by the personal values and beliefs of the participants. At times, it seems that the response of a society to those who differ may even serve as an indicator of that society's social progress. Throughout history, we see documented trends (although not without some backward steps) toward a greater appreciation of the basic humanity possessed by all members of the society, moving from initially rejecting and neglecting, to tolerating and protecting, and finally to accepting and appreciating those with differences.

The issues surrounding our response to disability and difference have changed over the years. Today we debate issues related to the naming of differences in our discussions about labeling and noncategorical approaches. We discuss the degree to which special education may have been used as a tool to keep individuals with disabilities "in their place," as we discuss alternatives in assessment and placement. We make plans and develop programs to address the needs of the individual throughout the life span and in various contexts, making use of such programs as early intervention, family support mechanisms, transition and vocational services, accessibility programs, and adult services. We now recognize the need to develop the professional skills of teachers and other support personnel, roles not even imagined in previous ages.

To help us understand how we have come to this point, it is useful to review examples of pivotal events in prior eras and ages. Our review will be somewhat cursory as it is impossible to include all of the important events and movements throughout human history in a single chapter. For more detailed treatment of these topics, the reader is referred to the work of Safford and Safford, 1996; and Winzer, 1993; as well as to the special issue of *Remedial and Special Education* (Smith, J. D., 1998). This historical overview will allow us to create a context within which to begin to appreciate our progress as well as to identify continuing challenges as we seek to create a social environment in which all can contribute.

Early History

In the classical civilizations of Greece and Rome, noticeable levels of disability were generally viewed as a threat to the economic and cultural vitality of the society. Individuals who did not appear to be capable of full participation in life were seen as the embodiment of evil or as a public threat. Those viewed as "weak" or "stupid" were generally believed to have an evil nature.

In ancient Greece and Rome, it was generally held that the strength of the state was its citizenry. This led to the fairly common practice of eliminating those children who did not appear to have the potential to contribute to building the civilization (Safford & Safford, 1996). Aristotle (300 B.C.E.) recommended infanticide in such cases (Winzer, 1998). Plato (400 B.C.E.) suggested that marriage and procreation be restricted to those who had the potential to advance civilization. Hippocrates (400 B.C.E.) discussed the question of which children should be raised. Child abandonment and exposure were widely practiced, usually resulting in the death of the infant; such practices continued as a way of ensuring the development of a capable citizenry until shortly before the beginning of the Common Era. When allowed to live, persons with developmental disabilities sometimes served as jesters and clowns.

In the classical period, when treatment was available, it took the form of medical intervention rather than education (Apter & Conoley, 1984). There was more concern with the causes of the condition than with a cure. Hippocrates proposed that emotional disturbance resulted from natural causes rather than from supernatural powers. He believed that emotional disturbance arose from imbalance in bodily fluids and recommended a regime of rest and supportive companionship (Safford & Safford, 1996). Chinese physicians held that disturbance was a result of imbalance in the yin and yang forces and recommended similar treatment.

Under Hebraic law, the response to persons with disabilities was more likely to take the form of benign protection. Scriptural directives in Exodus, Leviticus, and Deuteronomy admonished the Hebrews not to put barriers in the way of people with disabilities who were, after all, created by God (Safford & Safford, 1996). "A curse upon him who misdirects a blind man" (Deuteronomy 27:18, New English Bible). In response to Moses' protestations that he was slow and hesitant of speech and not up to the task set before him, the Lord said, "Who is it that gives man speech? Who makes him dumb or deaf? Who makes him clear-sighted or blind? Is it not I, the Lord? Go now; I will help your speech and tell you what to say" (Exodus 4:10–13). Later, the Hebrews are commanded, "You shall not treat the deaf with contempt nor put an obstruction in the way of the blind" (Leviticus 19:14).

During this early period, those with very severe birth defects would not have survived because of the lack of the medical knowledge needed to save them. It is also true that only persons with the most severe levels of disability would have been identified as different. In an era when literacy skills were not common, persons with milder levels of intellectual disability would simply have merged into the population. Not calling attention to themselves, they escaped being singled out for unwanted treatment.

The Middle Ages and the Renaissance

During the early years of the Common Era through the Renaissance and the Reformation (100–1700 C.E.), treatment of persons with disabilities was largely shaped by religious beliefs (Safford & Safford, 1996). The phenomenon of cloistering grew out of the general monastic movements within early Christianity. The monasteries not only protected the religious from the chaotic times, but they were also uniquely suited to provide refuge for persons with such disabilities as blindness or mental retardation (MacMillan, 1982). St. Nicholas cared for persons with mental retardation, and the legends about him led to his being named their patron saint.

This benign outlook was not shared by Calvin and Luther. They believed that people with disabilities did not have souls, and that people with retardation or mental illness were possessed by the devil. Luther and Calvin shared the belief that society had no responsibility for the welfare of such people. The period of the Reformation was generally characterized by the persecution of persons with disabilities and a return to demonology and superstition. Persons with disabilities were viewed as clowns and demons, or occasionally as persons capable of divine revelations (MacMillan, 1982).

Those not fortunate enough to find shelter with the nuns and monks often lived as beggars, court jesters, or fools (MacMillan, 1982). The belief that emotional disorders were the result of demonic possession or other supernatural forces frequently led to severe and abusive treatment of persons with emotional disorders, including torture, exorcism, and witch hunts. Services, if any, were limited to housing and food. As in the classical period, individuals with mild retardation and other less obvious mild disabilities largely escaped notice and were able to blend into the general population.

The Enlightenment

Large institutions called madhouses, lunatic hospitals, bedlams, or asylums were established in Europe and America during the eighteenth and nineteenth centuries. These facilities were created in response to the higher visibility of persons with significant disabilities (e.g., mental retardation, mental illness, blindness, deafness, orthopedic disabilities), as well as to house the poor, the widowed, the orphaned, and those with such infectious diseases as tuberculosis. These institutions were created largely to protect society from all those who were defined as deviant. The inmates were shackled and poorly fed. No therapeutic interventions were available. Punishment was the only "treatment" provided.

The French philosophers of this period ushered in a new era (Winzer, 1998). They gave voice to belief in the natural goodness of human beings, and they asserted that the ideal society would be one in which everyone's rights were protected. They set about changing the way society viewed itself as well the individuals who constitute society. In particular, the philosophies of Rousseau and Locke laid the foundation for equal rights for all people, including children as well as persons with retardation (Safford & Safford, 1996).

John Locke (1632–1704) stated in *An Essay Concerning Human Understanding* (1690) that all of our ideas are derived from our experiences, that we enter the world "tabula rasa," a blank slate upon which experience writes. This theory led to consideration of the possible utility of habilitative and rehabilitative efforts (Winzer, 1998). Jean-Jacques Rousseau (1712–1778) became fascinated with the concept of childhood as a time of innocence, leading to his interest in education as a social tool (Safford & Safford, 1996). Denis Diderot (1713–1784) focused on the possibility of using education to help people with disabilities. He was particularly interested in those whose disability involved the loss of one of the senses, and he proposed using sensory education to allow the individual to learn through the other intact senses. Because of this, Diderot is sometimes considered the father of special education.

These philosophers of the Enlightenment and their contemporaries focused attention for the first time on the effect the environment can have on an individual's development (Safford & Safford, 1996). No longer was it a given that a person's fate was sealed at birth or that any deviance was an act of God or demons and therefore outside the power of human beings to change. The experiences that help human beings develop were seen as critical, and it was asserted that society had the power to enhance those experiences through education and training. By the end of the eighteenth century, special education was an accepted idea, if not a major force, and psychology and psychiatry had emerged as separate disciplines of medicine. Medicine had begun to replace theology as the guide to social policies and treatment of people with disabilities. Social rights and education were a significant part of the public discourse.

Phillipe Pinel (1745–1826), a French physician and one of the first psychiatrists, literally unchained patients at the Bicetre Hospital in France in 1793 and instituted a regimen of more humane therapeutic treatment. Before Pinel assumed the leadership of the hospital, inmates were controlled by use of brute force and inhumane handling. Believing that violence and coercion are not ways to cure mental illness, Pinel prescribed sympathy, respect, and humane treatment. He provided inmates with respites from their restraints and the opportunity for more normal human interaction. He called his approach "moral treatment," and it included the teaching of "good habits." The improvements that were noted in his patients led to the beginning of a revolution in the treatment of persons with mental illness. Pinel also implemented a system of differential diagnosis, recognizing that mental disturbance was not a homogeneous condition. Because of these accomplishments, Pinel is credited with introducing the notion of habilitation and rehabilitation (MacMillan, 1982; Safford & Safford, 1996; Zigler, Hodapp, & Edison, 1990).

Jean-Marc-Gaspard Itard (1774–1838), a student of Pinel's, carried out a series of instructional experiments with Victor, a wild boy found wandering in the forest who is now assumed to have had mental retardation or perhaps an emotional disorder (Lane, 1976; Smith, T. E. C., 1998). Itard published an account of that work, *Wild Boy of Aveyron,* in 1801. His experiments with systematic instruction indicated that persons with conditions such as retardation could be taught, although Itard himself was disappointed that he achieved only limited success in teaching Victor to speak. Itard ultimately became convinced that mental retardation was incurable. Nevertheless, Itard gave a human face to disability when he introduced Victor to the world.

Building on the work of Pinel and Itard, Edouard Sequin (1812–1880) helped to establish schools in France in the 1830s and 1840s for children referred to as "idiots." He was committed to the belief that all children could learn if they were well taught through very specific sensory and sensory motor exercises, and he brought those principles to America in 1848 (MacMillan, 1982; Westling, 1986).

Throughout this period, the focus remained as on individuals with more severe levels of disabilities. With the development of philosophies that supported the educability of human beings, even those with disabilities, and with a growing sense that disabilities might be alterable, the ground was laid for more supportive services for all persons identified as needing assistance to function more fully in society.

Disabilities in the United States: 1800–1900

Public special education in America had its roots in the establishment of universal public education. In 1837, Massachusetts established the first state board of public education and appointed Horace Mann (1796–1859) as the first secretary to the state board of education. Free public schools were established for the express purpose of socializing all children into the common culture. In 1840, Rhode Island passed a *compulsory education law* that ultimately formed the foundation for the claim to education as a right for students with disabilities. In 1852, Massachusetts passed the first compulsory *school attendance* law. Even so, it would not be until 1909 that the first compulsory school laws for children with disabilities would be enacted in America (Winzer, 1993; Yell, Rogers, & Rogers, 1998).

Residential Services

In the late 1700s in America, Benjamin Rush (1745–1813) advocated that corporal punishment and other cruel physical forms of discipline be abandoned in the treatment of children with emotional disorders (Apter & Conoley, 1984; Winzer, 1993). He went on to implement his own version of Pinel's "moral treatment" with his patients at the Pennsylvania Hospital in Philadelphia in 1783 (Winzer, 1993). Rush asserted that mental illness was more generally associated with life events rather than an innate predisposition and that treatment and improvement were possible with humane treatment. These views may have been influenced by his personal experiences with the mental illnesses of his brother and son. Through these efforts, people of the time begin to view mental illness as something to be treated instead of an immutable result of sin (Safford & Safford, 1996; Winzer, 1993).

Institutions were gradually established throughout the 1800s to serve youngsters with disabilities too severe for the public schools to serve, including learners with hearing and/or visual impairments, as well as those with mental retardation (Apter & Conoley, 1984; Winzer, 1993; Zigler, Hodapp & Edison, 1990). Thomas Gallaudet (1788–1851) directed the first residential school for deaf children in Hartford, Connecticut, in 1817. The success of this institution led to subsequent establishment of schools for the deaf in New York, Pennsylvania, and Kentucky, with 55 such schools in operation by 1880 (Winzer, 1993).

The Massachusetts Asylum for the Blind (later to be renamed the Perkins School for the Blind) was opened in 1832 with Samuel Gridley Howe (1801–1876) as superintendent. The school program provided training in the symbol system developed in 1834 by Louis Braille for persons with severe visual impairments to use in reading and writing, making education and literacy for these children a real possibility. By 1900, there were 37 residential schools for the blind in the United States, some serving deaf students as well as those with blindness.

In 1848, H. B. Wilbur (1820–1883) established a private treatment center for 13 individuals with mental retardation in Barre, Massachusetts. Several months later, Samuel Gridley Howe established an experimental program for training individuals with mental retardation in a wing at the Perkins School for the Blind with support from Horace Mann and funding from the Massachusetts legislature (Smith, J. D., 1998; Winzer, 1993). The results from Howe's experimental program led the state of Massachusetts to set up a permanent facility in 1850, the Massachusetts School for Idiotic and Feeble-Minded Children, in Waverly (later to be named the Fernald School).

In 1854, when the New York legislature sought an administrator for a new state school in Albany, New York, for youngsters with retardation, they asked Wilbur to assume that responsibility based on his experience in Barre. Wilbur was assisted in these endeavors by Edouard Sequin (1812–1880) who had arrived in the United States several years earlier, bringing with him the philosophies and training techniques common in Europe at the time, including the principles of "moral treatment." These experimental projects firmly established the residential institution or school as the treatment of choice for youngsters with cognitive or sensory disabilities in America (Zigler, Hodapp & Edison, 1990). By 1890, fourteen states had organized institutions designed to serve children with mental retardation. Most were based on a colony plan and consisted of a custodial department, a training school, an industrial department, and a farm (Winzer, 1993).

Throughout the middle of the nineteenth century, Dorothea Dix (1802–1887) campaigned against the maltreatment of all persons in asylums (Payne & Patton, 1981; Safford & Safford, 1996; Winzer, 1993). In 1843, she spoke before the Massachusetts Legislature, advocating for more humane treatment for persons with mental illness and retardation. Speaking across the country, she was responsible for raising the consciousness of Americans about the treatment of those in institutions, resulting in gradual improvements in treatment and facilities, although her efforts primarily addressed adult services.

The establishment of these institutions was generally justified on the grounds of expedience, charity, and duty. Concern with the needs of these youngsters with severe disabilities, combined with the inability of the newly forming public schools to handle them, and the prevailing emphasis on the medical aspects of disability, led to the establishment of institutions as the predominant provider of special education services beginning in the nineteenth century.

Isolation from community life in mainstream settings characterized these schools. For the most part, they were set apart from major population areas and were based on the premise that country living would be the most healthful environment (Winzer, 1993). Indeed, one could make the case that removing these children and youth from inadequate and unhealthy living conditions in the urban centers of the day may actually have been of some therapeutic value. Organizationally, many of these schools were generally established as separate corporations with self-perpetuating boards of trustees, financed primarily through donations, endowments, and tuition. However, by the mid-1800s, some states had begun to assume some measure of financial responsibility and control (Safford & Safford, 1996; Winzer, 1993). Exhibitions of residents of these institutions at work was a common practice used by their founders to raise the necessary operating funds from state legislatures and private individuals (Trent, J. W., 1998; Winzer, 1993).

At the close of the nineteenth century, the institutional model of service was firmly entrenched as a way to protect and control persons who deviated from normal expectations to the extent that they caused problems in community environments. This period was one of disillusionment in the field of mental retardation when expected cures failed to materialize (Payne & Patton, 1981). The general optimism about the promised effectiveness of rehabilitation prevalent at mid-century had begun to dissipate, leaving institutions to perform a more custodial function. Promoters of institutionalization during this period said that persons functioning as mentally subnormal must be protected and cared for as children, and the "schools" became viewed more as "asylums."

By 1900, a number of issues were being raised. The cost associated with institutionalization was becoming harder to justify when improved functioning failed to result (Safford & Safford, 1998). The physical and social isolation of the facilities themselves heightened the sense of difference, deviance, and dependency of the persons residing in them. There was discussion about the right to an education for all children and whether or not there were indeed limits to that right. Children and youth (like Ed Murphy in Chapter 1) were institutionalized when their deviance or disability led to problems that could not be accommodated in their schools and communities (Bogdan & Taylor, 1994). The issue of the definition of *dis-*

ability was central to many of these discussions. Diagnoses during this period were more reflective of medical and social judgments than they were related to conditions that could be empirically verified.

Public Special Education

These issues led to the establishment of a two-track system of public educational services, one for typical children, the other for children with disabilities. Remnants of this organizational pattern remain with us today. It should be noted that such services were implemented only for those children with more obvious disabilities. Youngsters with milder learning and behavior problems still existed unnoticed in their local communities and schools, joining the work force at early ages.

In particular, children whose disabilities were in the area of behavior usually found themselves outside the school-yard fence (Apter & Conoley, 1984). Educators frequently found it easier to expel them or to leave their fate to the courts. They were seen as outside the capabilities of the public schools to manage. Correctional youth facilities were established using the same punitive methods found in adult prisons. Industrial schools were developed as an alternative, promoted by those who felt that the answer lay in removing the youngsters from problematic homes and families, and then by providing them with training needed to develop skills for useful productive living. Children with deviant behaviors were among the first young people to be provided with separate educational settings (Safford & Safford, 1996). A special education class for "truant, disobedient, and insubordinate" children, the first in the country, was opened in 1871 in New Haven, Connecticut, for the purpose of removing difficult or recalcitrant children from regular school programs so that regular classes could proceed without impediment.

The first psychological clinic serving children with learning and behavior problems was established by Lightner Witmer at the University of Pennsylvania in 1896 (Winzer, 1993). Witmer is credited with using the term *clinical psychology* for the first time. The child guidance movement evolved from these clinics, established to serve children with serious problems (Apter & Conoley, 1984). Over the years, the focus shifted to youngsters who were judged to be predelinquent. The mental hygiene movement promoted the idea that schools were especially stressful environments for children and that early intervention was necessary if there was to be any hope of restoring the child to appropriate behavior. By the end of the nineteenth century, concerns were frequently voiced about children whose behavior was problematic in society. Support was growing for compulsory schooling as a means of socializing problem youth. These developments established a basis for viewing schools as responsible for all children, even those with disabilities (Safford & Safford, 1998).

Disabilities in the United States: The Early Twentieth Century

At the turn of the century, large institutions served persons with severe disabilities, such as severe mental retardation, emotional disorders, and visual and hearing impairments. Those with less severe disabilities stayed at home. Some attended special education classes. Events in Europe laid the foundation for what was to come in the United States.

Eugenics in Europe and the United States

Charles Darwin's *Origin of the Species,* published in 1859, outlined his theory of natural selection and led to the articulation of the principles of social Darwinism. Social Darwinism held that heredity alone was responsible for the nature of an individual, and that defects could be prevented by eliminating "imperfect people." Francis Galton's *Hereditary Genius,* published in 1869, stated that individual traits, notably intelligence, are inherited and are normally distributed in the general population (Safford & Safford, 1996). In 1883, Galton further refined his theory of "eugenics," a word he derived from the Greek words for "good stock." Discussing the interaction of nature and nurture, Galton put the emphasis on the nature (i.e., heredity) side of the question. He maintained that society has the power to alter the inborn qualities of future generations by restricting the reproduction of those with defective physical or mental qualities.

The eugenics movement was given further impetus by Itard, Sequin, and Montessori, whose work showed that education alone could not remove disability. The eugenicists believed that there were five groups of people: those with great talent and genius, the normal class, the dependent class, the delinquent class, and the defective class (Winzer, 1993). They held that the classes of dependents, delinquents, and defectives should be restricted or prevented from reproducing so that the human race could advance.

Attempting to substantiate the eugenic theories of the time, Henry Goddard (1912) traced the genealogy of a girl he called Deborah Kallikak who resided at the Vineland Training School in the early 1900s (see Box 2.1). His work presented the evidence from his genealogical study of the Kallikak family. Goddard was convinced that this work supported the idea that the condition then called "feeble-mindedness" was hereditary, and that persons with disabilities should not be allowed to marry or reproduce. He believed that mental retardation represented a great social threat engulfing the "normal" middle class, and that measures restricting reproduction were necessary to stem the tide of crime, prostitution,

---

BOX **2.1**

SPOTLIGHT IN HISTORY: H. H. Goddard and the Kallikaks

H. H. Goddard's (1912) historic, though seriously flawed (Smith, 1985), study of the Kallikak family sought to answer the question of the inheritability of intelligence. As superintendent of the Training School at Vineland, New Jersey, Goddard supervised the Department of Research, which had been established to determine the mental and physical characteristics of children identified as feeble-minded (as mental retardation was referred to at the time), as well as to determine the cause of such mental retardation.

Goddard began by relating the story of Deborah Kallikak, who arrived at Vineland from the almshouse at the age of eight. He follows her progress over fourteen years, making many behavioral observations, including the following:

> disobedient . . . graceful . . . knows a number of words . . . good in entertainment work . . . plays the cornet . . . played hymns in simple time . . . excellent worker in gardening class . . . helps make beds and waits on table . . . is quick with her work, but very noisy . . . her mind wanders . . . is good in number work . . . her attention is hard to keep . . . knows how to use a sewing machine . . . can write a fairly good story, but spells few words . . . (pp. 2–7)

He concluded with these observations:

> This is the typical illustration of the mentality of a high-grade feeble-minded person, the moron, the delinquent, the kind of girl that fills our reformatories. They are wayward, they get into all sorts of trouble and difficulties, sexually and otherwise, and yet we have been accustomed to account for their defects on the basis of viciousness, environment, or ignorance. It is also the history of the same type of girl in the public school. Rather good looking, bright in appearance, with many attractive ways, the teacher clings to the hope, indeed insists, that such a girl will come out all right. Our work with Deborah convinces us that such hopes are delusions. . . . Today, if this young woman were to leave the Institution, she would at once become a prey to the designs of evil men or evil women and would lead a life that would be vicious, immoral, and criminal, though because of her mentality she herself would not be responsible. The question is, "How do we account for this kind of individual?" The answer is, in a word, "Heredity"—bad stock. We must recognize that the human family shows varying stocks or strains that are as marked and that breed as true as anything in plant or animal life. (pp. 11–12)

Goddard then proceeded to describe the research methods by which this conclusion was reached. Field workers from Vineland collected family tree data on residents over a several year period. "Our field worker occasionally found herself in the midst of a good family of the same name, which apparently was in no way related to the girl whose ancestry we were investigating. . . . These cases led to the conviction that ours must be a degenerate shoot from an older family of better stock" (p. 16). The outcome of the investigation of the Kallikak family led to the compilation of "data" going back seven generations that Goddard believed showed how the defective strain entered this family. He traced the family tree to an illegitimate child born of the "mating" of a Revolutionary soldier named Martin Kallikak with a "nameless feeble-minded girl," a barmaid. Using suspect data (Smith, 1985), Goddard contended that all the 496 descendants of Martin's marriage to a "respectable girl of good family" were "normal people, including doctors, lawyers, landholders, educators. . . . in short respectable citizens" (pp. 29–30). In contrast, Goddard reported that there were 480 descendants of Martin's liaison with the nameless barmaid, of whom 143 were "conclusively" feeble-minded, 43 were normal, and the rest were doubtful. He also counted 36 illegitimate births, 33 sexually immoral persons, 24 alcoholics, 3 epileptics, 3 criminals, 8 who kept "houses of ill fame," and 82 who died in infancy (pp. 18–19).

This study was used as research validation for the eugenics movement, which for many years led to the routine sterilization of persons with mental retardation. According to Goddard's line of reasoning, the only hope for society was to keep such individuals from reproducing and to keep those who were born in a protective ghetto so that they could not fall prey to the ills of the environment. He wrote:

> A scion of this (respectable) family, in an unguarded moment, steps aside from the paths of rectitude and with the help of a feeble-minded girl, starts a line of mental defectives that is truly appalling. . . . Fortunately for the cause of science, the Kallikak family in the persons of Martin Kallikak and his descendants are not open to question. They were feeble-minded and no amount of education or good environment can change a feeble-minded individual into a normal one. (pp. 50–53)

Excerpts from Goddard (1912).

illegitimacy, venereal disease, pauperism, alcoholism, and poor school performance. He saw segregation from normal society and mandatory sterilization as the only answer to these social ills.

Although Goddard's results have subsequently been discredited on the basis of serious methodological flaws in his work (Smith, J. D., 1985), his efforts and ideas led to the enactment of a number of laws that resulted in the forced sterilization of large numbers of persons with mental retardation and other disabilities. Indiana enacted the first sterilization law in the United States in 1907. In 1927 in *Buck* v. *Bell,* the U.S. Supreme Court upheld the constitutionality of mandatory sterilization laws. Thirty states enacted sterilization laws between 1907 and 1958, and over thirty-thousand persons with mental retardation were sterilized (Winzer, 1993). The successful enacting of eugenic measures was due less to the power of the argument than to the social and political context of the times, with immigration, two world wars, and the Great Depression raising concern about the future of our society. By the 1940s, the popularity of these practices was declining, in part because of the horror generated by the reports coming out of Hitler's Germany (see Figure 2.1). The use of sterilization as a social tool was largely abandoned.

The Testing Movement in Europe and the United States

The testing movement was initiated in France in 1905 when Alfred Binet and Theophile Simon developed an instrument to determine mental age (Payne & Patton, 1981). This test was developed at the request of the French Ministry of Public Instruction, which sought a way to identify students who were not likely to succeed in the regular school program (Safford & Safford, 1996). Believing that intelligence was a fixed trait, Binet and Simon developed their test to predict a prospective student's probable success in school and to screen out those students who would not benefit from schooling.

In 1910, Goddard translated the Binet–Simon intelligence scale into English, and in 1916, Lewis Terman revised Binet's test for use with Americans. Terman also coined the term *intelligence quotient* to refer to the ratio of mental age to chronological age. The Army Alpha and Beta Test, the first group intelligence test, was developed in 1917, based on this earlier work with individual testing. The results of the widespread use, or misuse, of this test with military recruits suggested that mental retardation was much more prevalent than once thought, raising alarm about the direction in which society was moving.

Edgar Doll developed the Vineland Social Maturity Scale in 1935 to assess adaptive or functional behavior, developing the norms with institutionalized populations. Terman published the Stanford revision of the Binet-Simon scale in 1937, as the *Stanford–Binet Intelligence Test.* David Wechsler was to later develop the Wechsler Intelligence Scale for Children (WISC) in 1949, a scale specifically designed for use with children. All these tests found an enthusiastic audience in the American public because they appeared to provide definitive and simple answers to the difficult questions, "Can this person learn? If not, why not?" One outcome of easily available norm-referenced tests was that for the first time there was a marker for mild disability. Educators could use test results to rank-order children and define a line between "normal" and "disabled." Youngsters did not have to have an obvious disability in the moderate to severe range to be identified by educators as deviant, and students in the milder

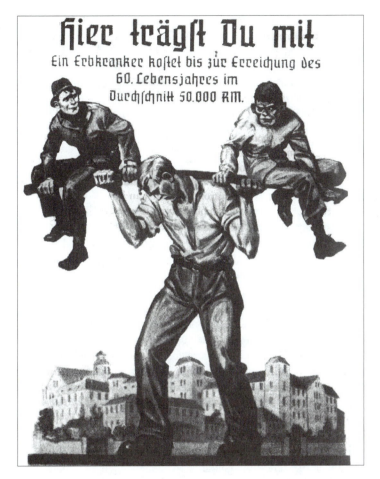

Translation:
"You are bearing this too," informing German workers that a hereditarily ill person would cost them 50,000 RMS to maintain until he or she has reached age 60.

FIGURE 2.1   A World War II German Propaganda Poster

From Burleigh (1994), p. 188.

ranges of disability were identified in ever-increasing numbers. Testing programs and more rigorous school demands made it less possible for students with disabilities to escape notice.

Serving Children Identified as Having Disabilities

At the end of the nineteenth century, Samuel Gridley Howe (1801–1876) and later Alexander Graham Bell (1847–1922) had both voiced concern about the effect of serving children in settings that allowed youngsters to associate only with peers with similar disabilities (Winzer, 1993). They believed that this type of residential segregation tended to reinforce and exaggerate disabilities. Both Bell and Howe advocated for contact with typical peers to the largest extent possible. They further argued against the removal of children from their family homes unless absolutely necessary. At a meeting of the National Education Association in 1898, Bell stated that children with disabilities had the right to an education in the public schools. He proposed setting up special classes in public schools for deaf children with specially trained teachers hired to instruct students. Such an arrangement would allow children with hearing impairments to interact with hearing children during parts of the school day, and he believed that would result in improved learning.

About the same time, others were also beginning to view instruction as an answer to milder levels of disability. In Italy in 1906, Maria Montessori (1912) established an experimental day school for children with mild and moderate levels of mental retardation. Using a curriculum based on practical life activities, sensory training, and formal academic instruction, she was successful in teaching many of them to read, although their disabilities remained (Safford & Safford, 1996; Westling, 1986).

The idea that nurture (i.e., environmental influences) was significant in determining the functional level of human beings was supported by the work of Skeels and Dye in 1939. They published the results of their study of orphaned infants raised by institutionalized women with mental retardation. The children who were nurtured by these women displayed significantly higher levels of later intellectual functioning than the members of the control group who were not talked to and held. This study indicated that environmental factors such as attention and interaction significantly affect intellectual outcomes, suggesting the importance of environmental factors in the development of intelligence. This research began to counterbalance the philosophical effect of the eugenicists.

Compulsory school attendance laws were enacted and enforced during the early twentieth century in response to increasing numbers of children in the community, notably due to the influx of immigrant children and restrictions on child labor (Safford & Safford, 1996; Yell, Rogers, & Rogers, 1998). The public schools were faced with new challenges from children not previously served in formal educational environments. School districts increasingly addressed these challenges by establishing segregated special classes so that students perceived as difficult would not disrupt or interrupt the learning environment in general education classes, nor lower the school's standards for achievement. In many cases, the main purpose of these classes was to manage students who did not conform to the school's behavior standards. Many of these youngsters probably looked much like learners from diverse cultural backgrounds who still find their way into programs for students with mild disabilities.

Public school special education classes became more common in the early twentieth century. Laws mandating education for children with mental retardation were passed in Massachusetts in 1911 and in New York in 1917 (Winzer, 1993). Compulsory attendance laws for children with mental retardation and vision and hearing impairments were also passed in New Jersey. In larger cities, self-contained day classes appeared for students with severe visual and hearing impairments, mental retardation, and emotional disorders. By the 1920s, more than 100 large cities had created a variety of special classes, and the role of special education teacher was established (Winzer, 1993). The increasing emphasis on the validity of education and training for children who differed from their age peers caused many institutions to be renamed "schools," whether their mission had changed or not.

During the first half of the twentieth century, public schools saw their total enrollments grow. The number of special education classes also increased. For example, in 1898, Boston had a single special education class for children with mental retardation; by 1941, there were

141 classes serving students with disabilities in the Boston city schools (Winzer, 1993). Many of the teachers serving these classes had originally been employed in institutional teaching positions. The curricula they implemented in public school special education classrooms frequently included heavy emphasis on crafts and manual training activities, similar to programs they had used in the institutions. In addition, special education curricula frequently contained a strong component of "social training" designed to teach desired school behaviors.

Special Education as a Profession

During the early part of the twentieth century, the field of special education was established within the teaching profession. Although the National Education Association and Alexander Graham Bell had used the term *special education* as early as the 1880s, they failed to establish an organization of special education professionals (Winzer, 1993, 1998). It wasn't until 1922, when Elizabeth Farrell successfully organized a group called the International Council for the Education of Exceptional Children, that the profession of special education came into its own (Safford & Safford, 1998). The group evolved from two college classes taught by Farrell at Teachers College at Columbia University in New York. The group was founded with the express purpose of advocating for the education and treatment of all exceptional children, including the gifted, as well as those with mental retardation, visual impairments, hearing impairments, physical disabilities, and social or behavioral disorders. In 1933, the name of the organization was changed to the Council for Exceptional Children (CEC) to reflect the concern of the organization with all aspects of the lives of exceptional individuals, not just education. The group grew from a membership of fifty that first year to over four thousand in 1944, and sixty-five hundred in 1950 (Winzer, 1993). CEC membership had risen to fifty thousand by the year 2002.

Disabilities in the United States from 1950 to the Present

By midcentury, parents became increasingly active as advocates for their children with disabilities. Disability-specific parent organizations were formed to lobby schools and state and federal governments for the rights of family members with disabilities. Among these were National Society for Crippled Children (1921), the United Cerebral Palsy Association (1949), the Association for Retarded Citizens (1950), and the Association for Children with Learning Disabilities (1964). These groups provided needed support to families dealing with difficult issues, established local schools and services to meet immediate needs, and fought for governmental support for publicly funded programs through the courts and in the halls of legislatures across the country. Their tireless efforts and the power of their message was largely responsible for the progress made in the last half of the twentieth century (Yell, Rogers, & Rogers, 1998).

Another pivotal influence from Europe was provided by the publication of a monograph by Wolfensberger and Kugel in 1969 which described the concept of normalization (Zigler, Hodapp, & Edison, 1990). Based on concepts developed earlier by Bengt Nirje and other Scandinavian writers, *normalization* refers to the practice of "making available to the mentally retarded and other disabled individuals the patterns and conditions of everyday life which are as close as possible to the norms and patterns of mainstream society" (Nirje, 1969, p. 181). Normalization seeks to use culturally normative means to increase the likelihood of achieving ends, or outcome behaviors, that are more culturally normative. As the principle of normalization evolved, the emphasis shifted from the normalization of lifestyles to the normalization of services. This shift suggested that curricular and programming decisions should be based on the degree to which activities are age appropriate and functional. Such practices were believed to reduce the stigmatizing discrepancies between persons with and persons without disabilities. It was expected that self-esteem would be enhanced and that rejection and ostracism would be decreased. Wolf Wolfensberger's (1972) articulation of the principle of normalization profoundly affected the course of legislation and educational practice, and it has continued to influence delivery of services to the present day.

Lloyd Dunn (1968) discussed the services being provided to students with mild retardation in similar terms. He questioned whether segregating these students for special treatment was really necessary, and he called for educators to consider delivering services in general education in a more normalized environment (see Box 2.2 for more information on his concerns).

General Education Initiative and Inclusion

Another influential movement in the latter part of the twentieth century has been the general education initiative, or *inclusion* (formerly referred to as the regular education initiative). Fueled by Madeleine Will's (1986) paper on shared responsibility (see Chapter 5), there has been significant progress toward including children with disabilities in general education

---

BOX **2.2**

SPOTLIGHT IN HISTORY: Lloyd Dunn

In 1968, Lloyd Dunn published an article in *Exceptional Children* that was destined to become a classic in the fields of mental retardation and special education as a whole. In it, he asked the question, "Special education for the mentally retarded: Is much of it justified?" He stated that while he had previously supported and promoted special education classes for children with mild learning problems, he had come to question their effectiveness with that population:

A better education than special class placement is needed for the socioculturally deprived chil-

dren with mild learning problems who have been labeled educable mentally retarded. Over the years, the status of these pupils who come from poverty, broken and inadequate homes and low status ethnic groups has been a checkered one. In the early days, these children were simply excluded from school. Then . . . with the advent of compulsory attendance laws, the schools and these children "were forced into a reluctant mutual recognition of each other." This resulted in the establishment of self-contained special schools and classes as a method of transferring these "misfits" out of the regular grades. This practice continues to this day, and unless counterforces are set in motion now, it will probably become more prevalent in the immediate future. . . . The number of special day classes for the retarded has been increasing by leaps and bounds. . . . This expensive proliferation of self-contained special schools and classes raises serious educational and civil rights issues which must be squarely faced. It is my thesis that we must stop labeling these deprived children as mentally retarded. Furthermore we must stop segregating them by placing them into our allegedly special programs. . . .

Regular teachers and administrators have sincerely felt they were doing these pupils a favor by removing them from the pressures of an unrealistic and inappropriate program of studies. Special educators have also fully believed that the children involved would make greater progress in special schools and classes. However, the overwhelming evidence is that our present and past practices have their major justification in removing pressures on regular teachers and pupils, at the expense of the socioculturally deprived slow learning pupils themselves. . . . Homogeneous groupings tend to work to the disadvantage of the slow learners and underprivileged. Apparently such pupils learn much from being in the same class with children from white middle class homes. (pp. 5–6)

Dunn also raised the question of the efficacy of self-contained classes for children with mild disabilities. He cited several studies that indicated that children with mild mental retardation and emotional disorders did as well or better in regular classes than in special classes. He made the following proposal:

Existing diagnostic procedures should be replaced by expecting special educators, in large measure, to be responsible for their own diagnostic teaching and their clinical teaching. In this regard, it is suggested that we do away with many existing disability labels and the present practice of grouping children homogeneously by these labels into special classes. Instead, we should try keeping slow learning children more in the mainstream of education, with special educators serving as diagnostic, clinical, remedial, resource room, itinerant and/or team teachers, consultants, and developers of instructional materials and prescriptions for effective teaching. (p. 11)

Dunn called for a moratorium on the expansion of special classes. He envisioned a specialized cadre of special educators who would develop curricula and who would take referrals for diagnostic evaluations, resulting in the development of educational prescriptions. He saw these specialized educators being available to help any child who was experiencing difficulty, not only those who had received a disability label. He closed with the following charge:

The conscience of special educators needs to rub up against morality. In large measure, we have been at the mercy of the general education establishment in that we accept problem pupils who have been transferred out of the regular grades. In this way, we contribute to the delinquency of the general educations since we remove pupils that are problems for them and thus reduce their need to deal with individual differences. The entente of mutual delusion between general and special education that special class placement will be advantageous to slow learning children of poor parents can no longer be tolerated. We must face the reality—we are asked to take children others cannot teach, and a large percentage of these are from ethnically and/or economically disadvantaged backgrounds. Thus much of special education will continue to be a sham of dreams unless we immerse ourselves into the real environments of our children . . . and insist on a comprehensive ecological push—with a quality educational program as part of it. (p. 20)

While Dunn's language is somewhat dated by current sensitivities, his message sounds hauntingly familiar. Many of the arguments he raised in 1968 are still being raised today. The IDEA sought to respond to these issues, but it remains the task of all educators to find ways to effectively help all children learn.

environments for some or all of the school day, and toward delivering their needed accommodations within the general education program (U.S. Department of Education, 2001). The
principle of inclusion takes the principle of least restrictive environment one step further. It
states that the general education classroom is an appropriate learning environment for all (or
most) children, and that special education services can often be delivered more efficiently and
effectively in that environment. Such a model of service is designed to avoid the fragmentation of services that Will observed in noninclusive special education and compensatory programs. While the debate about the effectiveness and appropriateness of inclusion for students
with disabilities is far from over, it has significantly affected special education in recent years
and will likely continue to do so. (See Chapter 5 for more discussion of this topic.)

Legislative and Governmental Initiatives

Changes were also occurring within the political and governmental sphere. The Department
of Special Education was established within the U.S. Office of Education in 1931. The
National Mental Health Act was passed by Congress in 1946. By 1952, forty-six of the forty-
eight states had passed legislation providing educational services for children with mental
retardation, but these laws still did not require educating *all* children with retardation or other
disabilities.

   The Elementary and Secondary Education Act of 1965 (ESEA) provided federal funding for the improvement of public schools, including support for remedial and compensatory
education under Title I (Yell, Rogers & Rogers, 1998). The ESEA provided the framework
for federal mandates and support of educational programs in local public schools. When the
ESEA was amended in 1966 to include support for children in state-supported schools for
students with disabilities, its effect on special education services went far beyond the funds
it provided.

   In 1972, the Pennsylvania Association for Retarded Citizens (PARC) successfully
sued the state of Pennsylvania on behalf of the right of children with retardation to a normalized free and appropriate public education. In the *Pennsylvania Association for Retarded
Citizens (PARC)* v. *Pennsylvania* consent decree, the parties agreed that it was the right of all
children in the state, even those with mental retardation, to receive a free and appropriate
publicly funded education. The provisions of the consent decree formed the basis for the provisions of the federal Education of All Handicapped Children Act in 1975 (Yell, Rogers, &
Rogers, 1998).

   In 1973, the passage of Section 504 of the Amendments to the Vocational Rehabilitation
Act guaranteed equal access for persons with disabilities to all programs and services supported by federal funds. It also prohibited discrimination based solely on disability. It required
that reasonable accommodations be made to permit access to programs by people with disabilities. This vital civil rights law remains a basic protection for children and adults with
disabilities today (Yell, Rogers, & Rogers, 1998). In 1974, the Developmental Disabilities
Assistance and Bill of Rights Act was passed, defining developmental disabilities and safe-
guarding the rights of those with developmental disabilities. The Americans with Disabilities
Act (ADA) of 1990 later extended these civil rights protections to all persons with disabilities,
asserting their right to access to all public services, not merely those receiving federal support.

The Education for All Handicapped Children Act, passed in 1975, required a free and appropriate public education (FAPE) for every school-aged child with a disability in the United States. It established the principle of least restrictive environment (LRE), based on the principle of normalization as articulated by Wolfensburger (1972), requiring that learners be served in those environments in which they can succeed and that are most typical of those in which typical peers are educated. Additionally, the law required local districts to assertively attempt to identify all children in their region who might need special education services. "Child Find" efforts in local communities are designed to identify preschool children and others who may not have come to the attention of the schools but could benefit from special educational services to develop maximally.

With the passage and implementation of the Education for All Handicapped Children Act came renewed discussion about classifying and labeling children with disabilities. Hobbs addressed these issues in 1975 with the publication of *The Futures of Children* and *Issues in the Classification of Children* (see Chapter 1). Because the act tied federal support of special education services to the numbers of children identified with disabilities, there was concern about the effect of labeling on increasing numbers of children. As Hobbs (1975a) stated, "by *classifying* we mean the act of assigning a child or a condition to a general category or to a particular position in a classification system. . . . By *labeling* we mean to imply more than the assignment of a child to a category. We intend to include the notion of public communication of the way a child is categorized" (p. 43).

When the U.S. Office of Education achieved separate cabinet status as the Department of Education in 1983, the Office of Special Education and Rehabilitative Services was maintained and expanded. In 1986, Madeleine Will, Assistant Secretary for Special Education, published a position paper, entitled "Educating Children with Learning Problems: A Shared Responsibility," calling for reform in the way special education and compensatory education services were being provided and asserting that the system had been shown to be a failure. She called for efforts to design more effective systems in which everyone shares the responsibility for the outcome (see Chapter 5).

The Education for All Handicapped Children Amendments of 1986 extended the provisions to children from ages three to five and supported initiatives for children from birth to age two. In 1990, the Individuals with Disabilities Education Act (IDEA) reauthorized these provisions, adding a requirement for transition planning during the adolescent years to aid in the transition to post-school environments. IDEA 1997 has added an emphasis on participation in the general education curriculum and on accountability for outcomes on the part of teachers and schools (see Chapters 3, 4, and 5 for more discussion of the requirements and implications of IDEA 1997).

History of Rights Won in United States Courts

Throughout the last half of the twentieth century, the courts have repeatedly been asked to rule on issues involving the civil rights of persons with disabilities, especially the right to equal treatment under the law. In some cases, those rulings led to subsequent legislation to implement the rights won through litigation. For example, the consent decree in *Pennsylvania*

Association for Retarded Citizens (PARC) v. *Pennsylvania* which secured the right to education for students in Pennsylvania in 1972 provided the foundation for the passage of the Education for All Handicapped Children Act in 1975 (Yell, Rogers, & Rogers, 1998). In other cases, the courts ruled on the failure of schools to implement the provisions of the law; for example, the *Honig* v. *Doe* decision in 1988 reaffirmed the rights of students with behavioral disabilities to an appropriate public education.

The modern civil rights era began when the U.S. Supreme Court ruled in 1954 that racially separate education was inherently unequal and, by implication, inferior. In *Brown* v. *Board of Education,* the Supreme Court established that education was the right of every child, stating that the rights of children who were denied equal educational opportunity by virtue of exclusion or segregation were being violated. Access to a free and appropriate public education for children with disabilities became the focus of subsequent cases, building on the foundation established by *Brown* v. *Board of Education* (Yell, Rogers, & Rogers, 1998). The 1972 consent decree in *PARC* v. *Pennsylvania* established the right to public education for all children with mental retardation in Pennsylvania. The court ruled that since the state had undertaken to provide public education, it must make education available to all citizens on an equal basis.

In *Mills* v. *District of Columbia Board of Education* (1972), the court heard a case on behalf of seven children who had been excluded from school because of their disabilities. The school district asserted that it could not afford the cost of the services required by these children. In the ruling, the court reaffirmed the right to education for all children with disabilities and stated that they could not be expelled without a hearing. Furthermore, the court stated that the burden of funding shortages could not weigh more heavily on students with disabilities than it does on those served in regular education. This case provided the foundation for the due process components of IDEA (Yell, Rogers, & Rogers, 1998).

In the 1960s and 1970s, several cases dealt with inappropriate and discriminatory testing and placement procedures. In 1967, the federal courts were asked to review the practice by District of Columbia public schools of assigning elementary children to ability tracks based on standardized tests. In the *Hobson* v. *Hansen* ruling, the judge abolished the tracking system in use in the District of Columbia, saying that it denied equal educational opportunity and therefore was a violation of the Constitution. He specifically noted that the practice resulted in students' being assigned to special education classes not because they had an innate inability to learn, but more often because of their racial and socioeconomic status.

In *Diana* v. *State Board of Education* (1970), the court held that the rights of Mexican American students had been violated when they were placed in classes for students with mild retardation based on intelligence tests that were culturally biased and not given in the students' primary language. This case established testing guidelines for evaluating children in their primary language and for determining the appropriateness of special education services.

In 1972, 1979, and 1984, the courts ruled in *Larry P.* v. *Riles* that the San Francisco school district had violated the rights of African American students by using culturally biased intelligence tests for placement (MacMillan & Forness, 1998). The court substantiated this claim with data showing that disproportionate numbers of minority children were being served in special education classes in San Francisco schools. This ruling strictly limited the use of individual intelligence tests as the sole placement indicator. In a later case, the Illinois courts ruled in *PASE* v. *Hannon* (1980) that individual intelligence tests do not unduly discriminate against children from African American backgrounds and allowed their use as long as other measures were also employed in making special education placement decisions. Other cases that have upheld the basic rights of children with disabilities to equal educational opportunity are found in Table 2.1.

TABLE 2.1 Additional Court Cases Supporting Equal Opportunity to Education

1972 *Wyatt v. Stickney (AL)*

Institutionalized persons have a right to treatment, including education, based on their fourteenth- and eighth-amendment rights.

1979 *New Mexico Association for Retarded Citizens v. New Mexico*

New Mexico violated Section 504 by failing to include all school-age children in an appropriate educational program; this led to New Mexico's agreeing to adhere to P.L. 94-142.

1982 *Board of Education v. Rowley*

Districts are responsible for procedural due process under the Education for All Handicapped Children Act, but mandatory services are limited to those required to provide educational benefit to the child.

1988 *Honig v. Doe*

Suspension or expulsion represents a change of placement for students with disabilities. If the behavior that resulted in the removal from school is deemed to be a result of the disability, the multidisciplinary team must determine a more appropriate service plan.

1989 *Daniel R. R. v. State Board of Education*

The two requirements for determining if a placement is in the least restrictive environment are: (1) determine if services can be provided in a general education classroom with supplemental aids and (2) determine if the child has been mainstreamed to the maximum extent possible.

1989 *Timothy W. v. Rochester (NH) School District*

Every child, regardless of the severity of the disability and the amount of expected benefit, is entitled to a free and appropriate education.

1993 *Oberti v. Board of Education*

Placement in a general education setting must be offered prior to consideration of a segregated setting; a student cannot be excluded just because modifications are required.

1999 *Cedar Rapids Community School v. Garrett F.*

Students requiring intensive and continuing (nonphysician) health services to enable them to attend school must have those services provided as related services, regardless of their cost.

Trends in History

The history of special education, according to Reynolds (1989), has been characterized by a degree of progressive inclusion. He noted that while there are still many children with disabilities in the world who receive no education at all, children with disabilities in the United States have progressively received more education, and they have received it closer to home and more often in the company of their typical peers. He identified four progressive, albeit gradual and as yet incomplete, trends in the history of special education, including the following:

- Moving from distal to proximal arrangements
- Shifting from separation to integration
- Changing the purpose of evaluation from using tests to make decisions about selection and rejection, to using evaluation to make placement decisions
- Shifting from the use of program options that might be characterized as "two-box arrangements" (e.g., special education vs. general education) to service delivery in a single "one-box" system, including an integrated continuum of services for all students

The transition from distal to proximal services is exemplified most clearly by the earlier placement in large, isolated residential institutions followed by the more common practice in recent years of placing children in the neighborhood schools they would be attending even if they had no disabilities. This move has helped to normalize the life experiences of children with disabilities by keeping them in their neighborhoods and communities so that they can engage in all their expected family and friendship relationships.

In previous centuries and generations, children with disabilities were separated from their typical peers either by death or by placement in institutions. Even when kept at home, they were closeted, hidden from view. They had no contact with mainstream society, and they had little or no access to peer role models displaying typical behaviors. Increasingly, such children are now integrated within their neighborhoods and schools. The principle of least restrictive environment increases the probability that they will spend at least part of their day in integrated mainstream settings, and they may even receive all of their support services in such settings. Regulations governing access to public services, such as those included in the Americans with Disabilities Act, help assure that persons with disabilities have the opportunity to participate in community life in a fully integrated manner.

Early public special education efforts operated on a selective basis. Children with disabilities were tested and then may have been denied access to general education programs based on their level of impairment. Likewise, children were selected into special programs based on a variety of evaluation criteria. Programs with an educational mission selected only those who they thought could benefit from those programs. Adapting programs to meet individual needs was not a common occurrence. Children whose disabilities were too severe could be denied access even to special education. With the implementation of IDEA, these practices have changed. Assessment is now used to determine the most appropriate placement and program for the child, not to exclude students from participation. Placement teams interpret the available information, determine the likelihood of success in a particular setting, and determine what supports will help the student be successful in those settings.

Reynold's fourth trend is the most incomplete. Traditionally, we have had a two-box system, general education for most children and special education for those who don't fit the general education program. Over the years, the special education box has changed configuration from a large isolated institution, to a special school, to a special class, to a resource room, but it has still been clear that the student with a disability was the responsibility of the special education program and staff. The general education initiative (GEI), or inclusion, encourages special and general educators to look at their roles differently, to see themselves as professionals within a unitary system with a continuum of services available to all children who need them. Educators are also being asked to consider the possibility that the presence of a disability is related more to the context than to some innate characteristic of the individual, and that disability may not be a chronic state.

Focus on Culture and Diversity

Throughout history, services for people with disabilities have been determined by the culture and beliefs of the times. In western cultures, deviance was first feared, then pitied, then avoided. As racial groups in the United States began to assert their claim to full civil rights, they laid the foundation for the disability rights movement. Gains made by African Americans in *Brown* v. *Board of Education* provided the basis for legal action to obtain access to quality public schooling for children with disabilities.

Unfortunately, children from racially diverse cultures did not always benefit from this increased access. Assessed with discriminatory instruments, African American children and those with limited English proficiency found themselves classified as students with disabilities when their difficulty in public schools was actually related to cultural differences. A series of court cases, including *Diana* v. *State Board of Education* and *Larry P.* v. *Riles,* provided mandates for nondiscriminatory evaluation, including testing in the child's primary language. The courts also required multiple sources of data to support classification decisions. The Education for All Handicapped Children Act codified these rulings into educational law. However, at the turn of the twenty-first century, we still see evidence of disproportionality in classification, suggesting that we do not yet have a culturally fair process.

Resources on the Web

Disability Social History Project

www.disabilityhistory.org

Describes accomplishments of various individuals with disabilities throughout history, some of whom also contributed to the development of special education.

Disability Rights Movement: Virtual Exhibition at the Smithsonian Institution

www.americanhistory.si.edu/disabilityrights/welcome.html

Provides an interactive virtual tour of the Smithsonian's disability history exhibit.

Disability Rights Education and Defense Fund (DREDF)

www.dredf.org

> A national law and policy site that provides information on civil rights issues related to disabilities; founded in 1979 by people with disabilities and parents of children with disabilities.

Wrightslaw: The Special Ed Advocate

www.wrightslaw.com

> Provides resources related to special education law and advocacy and provides a free on-line newsletter.

Summary

In our review of the historical contexts of special education, we have seen societal responses change from rejection, to protection, to isolation, to integration. In each case, the response of society to those with disabilities has been determined by the demands and values of the times. In early civilizations, disabilities represented the unknown. People did not have the knowledge or the ability to understand and treat individuals with disabilities. They knew only that these individuals were a burden, and the response was to reject individuals who differed significantly from the norm. Individuals with milder disabilities did not call attention to themselves and were not generally identified at all.

With the advent of Christianity, explanations for disabilities were based primarily on theology. Disabilities were either assigned by God or were the result of demonic possession. The mandate by Jesus to care for the poor provided the impetus to protect those with disabilities and those who were unable to care for themselves. Alternatively, the call to drive out sin and the Devil sometimes resulted in continued persecution and rejection of those with disabilities. In either case, the response came from the context of the times.

The Enlightenment brought more explanations about the nature of disability and more skill in treating various conditions. With increased knowledge about the nature of disabilities, professionals became more willing to try to help, but the general public was still uneasy. The result was the location of services for people with disabilities in isolated institutions for education and custodial care.

During the twentieth century in America we have moved steadily toward more integration and education in normal environments. Our ethical sense and technical abilities have brought about significant changes in the treatment of people with disabilities. We have found ways to provide effective education in normalized environments, and we have committed ourselves through our federal and state governments to doing so. We have seen treatment of those with disabilities make the transition from distal, segregated services for those who qualified, to more proximal, integrated services for all based on their needs. We are moving toward the day when a unitary society will include all its citizens and will meet the needs of each individual as fully as possible.

PATTY: A Case Study

Patrice (called Patty by her family) was born in 1980 with Down syndrome. Her parents were unprepared for the news that their first-born child was "Mongoloid," as the doctor put it. Fortunately, a nurse in the obstetrical wing put them in touch with the local Down syndrome support group as a source of current information about the condition and current strategies for helping youngsters develop as fully as possible. Before Patty's mother left the hospital, a mother with a child with Down syndrome had visited her. The other mother told her that it was possible to raise Patty at home, that institutionalization was no longer the routine response when children like Patty were born. She told Patty's parents that they were lucky; their suburban community provided early intervention services for infants with Down syndrome. She gave Patty's parents the number for the local health department and urged them to call as soon as they got home.

An intervention specialist was assigned to Patty and her family. Physical activities were devised to assist Patty's motor development. Her parents were encouraged to talk to her and to touch her as much as possible, maximizing the stimuli that would help Patty grow and develop both cognitively and physically.

Although it was soon apparent that there was some retardation, Patty's family responded by refusing to accept less than she was capable of doing. They were very supportive. She was included in all family activities, and they treated her as they would any child. By the age of three, she had made significant progress, although there was a noticeable delay in her speech acquisition.

Patty's school district had recently instituted an early intervention preschool program that provided Patty with a half day of specialized programming at age three. She did well in the class, and in most skills she was clearly at the head of the class. District testing of her intellectual functioning potential led to the classification "borderline retardation."

Patty's parents began to be concerned that the special education preschool might not be challenging enough to develop all of her skills, particularly in the areas of language and social skills. They began talking with her early intervention teacher about adjustments to her program when Patty was ready to enter kindergarten. Her parents believed that more contact with peers without disabilities would provide Patty with more challenging learning opportunities and skilled role models. They also felt that she could now profit from a longer school day.

At the IEP review meeting that year, the district reluctantly agreed to allow Patty to participate in a regular kindergarten class for half of the day and to continue with the special education class for the other half of the day. The district said, however, that they were not sure that Patty would benefit from the activities in the kindergarten class since the program was not designed for nor did it include any children with disabilities. It was further mentioned that the teacher of that class was new and had no experience working with "a child like Patty."

Patty's parents suggested that the problems could be addressed as the team worked out modifications to the kindergarten program required to allow Patty to benefit from placement in the regular kindergarten class. It was then that the school stated that modifications to the regular classroom program were not possible, and that the IEP process was designed to address only the areas taught by special education staff in special education settings. They asserted that the IEP provisions do not apply to general education activities, based on the principle of mainstreaming, which allows participation only in those general education activities that are unaffected by the disability.

Even with this setback, Patty's parents decided to try the kindergarten plan, since it would at least give her exposure to other children with a variety of abilities. The next problem involved lunch. Because Patty would be spending the entire day at school, she would need to eat lunch in the cafeteria, a new and potentially confusing experience. Neither her special education nor her kindergarten

(continued)

classmates would be eating lunch, and this school was not Patty's home school, where she might have known other children from the neighborhood. For these reasons, her parents requested that the school arrange for a "lunch buddy." The school voiced the same objection as before—lunch was for students who could handle it, and no modifications would be made. If Patty couldn't handle it, then she shouldn't be there. The result of the meeting was that Patty would attend the morning kindergarten class with no modifications, eat lunch alone, and then go to the early childhood special education class in the afternoon.

Patty's parents knew how helpful it had been to them to learn more about children with Down syndrome, and they decided that it might help if the kindergarten teacher had some information about Down syndrome. Patty's mother contacted the teacher, gave her a book, and told her about an upcoming conference about educational issues with students with Down syndrome. She also suggested that the kindergarten teacher might confer with the special education teacher so that the programs could be better coordinated. The kindergarten teacher did not do any of these things.

Problems began almost from the first day of the school year. The special education class went as expected, but Patty's parents were told repeatedly that she did not belong in the kindergarten class. The teacher said that Patty was unable or unwilling to participate in the usual class activities. Her language was unintelligible, and she frequently resorted to nonverbal ways of communicating her displeasure with activities in the classroom. She would climb under her desk, cover her ears, or dart out of the room to express noncompliance. She would scribble on her paper while others copied from the board. The teacher reported that her nonparticipation and noncompliance were disruptive to the classroom program.

Patty's mother visited the kindergarten class to observe her behavior. She made several suggestions about changes the teacher might make, but the only one that was adopted was to let Patty use large-handled scissors and large crayons. Following

another observational period, Patty's mother suggested a modification to an activity relating to the concepts of *same* and *different* that would not disrupt the class but would still allow Patty to participate with the other students. The teacher refused, saying that this was too much to ask and that mainstreaming was appropriate only if Patty was capable of doing the activities without modifications.

By October, the situation had reached a critical level. The school had Patty's parents come in for a conference. When they arrived, they found that the conference was actually an IEP meeting, convened to consider changes to Patty's placement and IEP. The school was adamant that Patty be removed from the kindergarten class, lunch, and recess, and that she could come to school only for the early intervention special education class. Patty's parents repeated their contention that without contact with typical peers, Patty would be unlikely to make significant progress in her language and social skills. The school's compromise was that she could come to lunch three days a week, but only if her mother was with her, and that she could attend recess, but that it would come out of her special education class time.

For Patty's parents, this was not an acceptable compromise. How could Patty learn to socialize with other children at lunch when her mother was always there? How much socialization would occur on the playground when she knew none of the other children? Would cutting two and a half hours a week from her special education program for recess be in her best interest? The parents requested a due process hearing.

The hearing officer's opinion stated that the kindergarten class was not appropriate for Patty and was in fact harming her. He stated that Patty was functioning at such a low level that she could not master the curriculum. He further stated that according to school personnel, Patty was requiring 100 percent of the teacher's and aide's time, and that this was unfair to the other students. He concluded by telling the parents that they were entirely unrealistic in their hopes for their daughter and that insisting on this course of action would harm Patty.

This case is loosely based on the events leading up to *Daniel R.R.* v. *State Board of Education*, 1989.

DISCUSSION

In light of the history of special education, discuss the different scenarios that might have resulted if Patty had been born in a different time period:

- Classical period
- Early Christian era
- Enlightenment
- The 1800s in the United States
- The 1900s in the United States, prior to passage of the Education for All Handicapped Children Act in 1975
- Today

Discuss the implications for Patty and her family.

CHAPTER THREE

ISSUES IN ASSESSMENT AND IDENTIFICATION

QUESTIONS TO GUIDE YOUR STUDY

- What requirements relating to assessment and identification were added to the IDEA in the 1997 amendments?
- What are four purposes of assessment?
- What is the difference between norm-referenced assessment and criterion-referenced assessment?
- What are the advantages of using alternative assessment techniques such as performance assessment and portfolios?
- What is the purpose of grading? How might that purpose best be achieved?
- In what three ways may students with disabilities meet the requirements of state and district assessment programs?
- What is meant by the phrase the *social construction of disability*?
- What is meant by noncategorical alternative to identification? What are the implications of a noncategorical process for identifying and serving youngsters with learning and behavioral differences?

Meet Jeffrey

Jeffrey is an active youngster in Mrs. Greene's third grade classroom. He has struggled academically since the beginning of the year, but even more troubling to Mrs. Greene is his behavior. He seems to always be doing something other than what he is assigned to do. She says that if he would mind his own business as much as he minds everyone else's, he'd be fine. She is concerned that he is not learning and that his behavior is beginning to affect the learning of others.

She finally decides to pick up a special education referral form from the office. Filling it out, she describes the central problem this way:

Jeffrey's academic performance is significantly lower than other students in the class, with specific problems in reading. He is struggling with the second grade reader. His lack of attention leads to his not doing assignments or doing them incorrectly. He shouts out in class, disturbs others, and engages in a variety of other off-task behaviors.

(continued)

Following screening by the special education teacher, it was determined that Jeffrey should receive a full evaluation to determine if a disability exists. After securing his mother's permission, the school psychologist administered a series of tests including the WISC-III, the K-TEA achievement battery, and the Formal Reading Inventory. She also had Mrs. Greene complete the Connors Teacher Rating Scale, as well as the Walker Problem Behavior Identification Checklist. Finally, the special education teacher conducted a direct observation of Jeffrey in Mrs. Greene's class, coding instances of inappropriate behavior during three one-hour periods.

The multidisciplinary team determined from the testing that Jeffrey had a delay in acquiring basic academic skills, particularly in reading, but that the problem was not severe enough to classify him as having a learning disability. The behaviors, although certainly bothersome, did not appear to be significantly different from those of other children, and since his academic performance was not significantly affected, he did not meet the criteria for placement as a child with a behavioral disorder.

Mrs. Greene was puzzled. Jeffrey and she needed extra help, but it appeared that they would not be able to get it through the special education process. What was she to do?

IDEA 1997: Assessment and Evaluation Requirements

It is appropriate to begin this consideration of assessment and identification of learners with mild disabilities with a discussion of the assessment requirements codified in the federal special education law. Since 1975 when P.L. 94–142, the Education for All Handicapped Children Act, was passed, the law has been amended several times. In the IDEA amendments of 1997, Congress reviewed the basic IDEA requirements, seeking to evaluate, clarify, and modify them with the aim of improving the quality of programming for children and youth with disabilities. Congress focused attention on outcomes for student learning, increasing the accountability of states and districts for performance outcomes toward high standards for all students, including those with disabilities.

Some of the changes and clarifications in IDEA 1997 related to assessment and identification (Council for Exceptional Children, 1998a, 1998b; National Association of State Directors of Special Education, 1997; Yell & Shriner, 1997) are as follows:

- Schools are required to use a variety of assessment tools and information sources to gather data on student progress. IEP teams must consider all existing data, including data supplied by parents, in making determinations of disability and in designing educational plans.
- Technically sound assessment instruments must be used when evaluating students' abilities in such areas as cognitive functioning, behavior, physical abilities, and developmental progress. Such tests must be normed on a population appropriate for the purpose and must not discriminate against students on the basis of such variables as race, culture, language, or disability.
- Assessments must be provided in the child's native language (e.g., Spanish, Russian) or mode of communication (e.g., sign language, motoric responses).
- Schools are specifically directed to gather and use information about students' progress in the general education curriculum for all students considered for or served in special education programs. Teams must identify strengths as well as deficits. The effect of the disability on the student's involvement and progress in the general education curriculum must be evaluated and addressed by the IEP team.
- Children may not be found eligible for special education services if they have not had the opportunity to learn, or if their learning difficulties are related primarily to limited proficiency in the English language. This provision requires that IEP teams carefully consider all the factors that might be impeding a youngster's ability to learn before classifying a child. Congress' intent was to halt special education placement of students with cultural and linguistic differences unless they also had a disability.
- Reevaluations must occur at least every three years. However, it is no longer necessary to repeat all previous testing or to gather additional data unless parents or teachers feel it is necessary. Reevaluation now becomes a process of reviewing existing information, gathering additional information only if necessary, and determining whether a disability still exists.
- The development of annual goals and short-term objectives or benchmarks for a student's IEP must be based on an evaluation of the child's progress in relation to the general education curriculum.
- The parents of each child in special education should be provided with a progress report related to the IEP goals and objectives as frequently as parents of students in general education classes are provided with progress reports.
- Congress dictated that all children will participate in all mandated state and district assessments (with or without modifications), unless it can be shown that no portion of the general education curriculum is applicable to a specific student. The IEP team determines whether the child needs modifications to the testing procedures or an alternative assessment. Those few students for whom any participation in the general education curriculum is inappropriate, due to the severity of their disability, must be

provided with an alternative standardized assessment process. In all cases, account-ability for student outcomes is now the goal of the law. States are expected to report summary and disaggregated data on the performance of students with disabilities just as they do for students in general education.

Purposes of Assessment of Students with Special Educational Needs

When assessing students, we are most interested in acquiring information that we can use to describe their current functional capability in a variety of areas and that can be used over time to monitor their progress. We use such information for several purposes:

- Classification: the process of using assessment results to determine if a learner has a disability
- Diagnosis: the use of assessment results to provide more specific information about the effect of a child's disability for the purpose of designing appropriate individual-ized interventions
- Formative evaluation of progress: the process of using assessment data to document student growth or progress as the basis for determining the effectiveness of a stu-dent's program and for making changes if improvement is not indicated (Fuchs & Fuchs, 1986)
- Summative evaluation of progress: the process of using assessment data to make decisions about the learner, such as determining if a learner has demonstrated suffi-cient mastery of skills to move to another level or grade

Types of Assessment Instruments and Techniques

To most effectively achieve the purposes listed above, educators must employ a variety of instruments and procedures. In fact, the IDEA requires that multiple sources of information be used for all special education determinations. A full discussion of these practices is beyond the scope of this text; the reader is encouraged to consult current texts and journals on assessment for a more detailed description (e.g., McLoughlin & Lewis, 1994; Overton, 1996; Taylor, 1997; Venn, 1994).

Norm-Referenced Assessment

Some purposes of assessment require instruments that allow the evaluator to compare the per-formance of a child to typical children of that age or grade. Norm-referenced tests permit such comparisons. A new or revised test is given to a significant number of comparable individuals (the normative sample), and the results of that administration are used to derive scores that describe typical performance. The test is then given to other students, and the scores of those students are compared to the derived scores. From this comparison, a determination can be made about the degree to which any student performed less well than, the same as, or better than others of the same age or grade. Examples of norm-referenced tests include:

- Intelligence/aptitude tests (e.g., WISC-III, Stanford-Binet IV, K-ABC)
- Achievement test batteries (e.g., K-TEA, PIAT, WIAT)
- Diagnostic achievement tests (e.g., Test of Written Language, Key Math)
- Adaptive behavior scales (e.g., Vineland Adaptive Behavior Scales, AAMR Adaptive Behavior Scale)
- Behavior rating scales (e.g., Behavior Rating Profile, Walker Problem Behavior Identification Checklist)

Norm-referenced tests are useful for these purposes only if the technical qualities of the instrument are adequate. IDEA 1997 reiterates the requirement that tests used to determine the presence of a disability must be normed on populations similar to the individuals being tested if the conclusions drawn from those comparisons are to be valid. This suggests that the normative sample should be inclusive of racial and language groups in the general population, and that individuals with disabilities should be explicitly included in the normative sample if we are to assume that the test is valid for testing youngsters with disabilities. If the test is being given to a child who uses a language other than English, the test must have been normed in the translated version as well as in the English version. Tests must be *reliable* (yield similar scores on repeated administrations) as well as *valid* (measure what they purport to measure).

Norm-referenced instruments are useful when comparable measures of performance or aptitude are required, such as for identification and classification or for general placement in graded curricula. However, such tests are not able to provide the specific information needed for program planning. They are based on the notion that there is a general body of knowledge and skills that all children, wherever they live, will have learned by a certain age, but it cannot be assumed that the test content matches and measures accurately the learning in any particular classroom or school curriculum. Additionally, anyone who conducts assessments should be familiar with and observe the standards for fair and responsible testing and interpretation as outlined by the American Psychological Association (1985), and by the Joint Committee on Testing Practices in Education (1988).

Criterion-Referenced and Curriculum-Based Assessment

Criterion-referenced or curriculum-based assessment is an alternative to norm-referenced tests that is frequently more useful in diagnosis and program planning. Rather than comparing one individual to another as normed tests do, criterion-referenced tests determine whether the learner has achieved mastery of particular skills or learnings.

Criterion-referenced assessment is particularly useful when combined with task analysis, the process of identifying the subskills required to ultimately achieve a terminal objective. By identifying subskills essential to the desired outcome competency, the evaluator can devise a series of measures that determine if the student has achieved the prerequisite and component skills identified in the task analysis (see Table 3.1). Criterion-referenced tests are most often created by teachers or teams of teachers to assess curricular outcomes in a specific district, school, or class, although they can include more formal, published tests, such as the Brigance

TABLE 3.1   Task Analysis

Terminal Objective

Given a picture prompt, the student will write a paragraph composed of at least five complete sentences and having a clear topic, supporting details, and a concluding sentence.

Task Analysis

Identify parts of a complete sentence (subject and predicate).

Determine if a sentence is a complete thought.

Write a complete sentence that has a subject and a predicate.

List details relating to a given topic or prompt.

Write a topic sentence.

Write detail sentences.

Write a concluding sentence.

Organize sentences into a coherent paragraph.

Inventories (Brigance, 1981; 1991; 1999), the chapter and periodic tests that accompany most reading and mathematics basal series, and certain state assessment systems, such as South Carolina's Basic Skills Assessment Program.

Whether criterion-referenced tests are teacher-made or are published in a standardized format, the purposes are the same: to determine if the student can perform a specific set of skills, to document the amount of progress toward a longer-term goal, and to determine if the student is ready to progress to the next stage of learning. The effectiveness of these instruments in providing useful information will depend on how closely they match or are aligned with the instructional activities engaged in by students.

Performance Assessment

Concern over the validity of information derived from the traditional processes of norm-referenced and criterion-referenced testing has led teachers, schools, and states to look for other more authentic and valid indicators of student achievement. The new generation of state assessments (e.g., the New York English/Language Arts and Mathematics Tests) includes items and tasks that require students to demonstrate the ability to apply knowledge and skills while completing complex and extended tasks, rather than to merely choose answers on multiple-choice examinations. Students are asked to work with others and to develop free-response answers.

Performance tasks generally require the learner to use more complex thinking and reasoning, and to construct rather than merely select the answer. They also involve direct observation of the student completing tasks similar to those found in the real world. Through such observation and analysis, teachers seek to determine the nature and quality of the thinking processes engaged in by the student (Coutinho & Malouf, 1993; Schnitzer, 1993). These assessments emphasize meaning, and they involve performance of tasks perceived to have value in themselves. They are believed to have more validity, especially when dealing with learners from diverse cultural and linguistic backgrounds as well as with students with various disabilities that may prevent them from performing accurately on more typical standardized assessments (Dean, Salend, & Taylor, 1993).

Portfolio Assessment

Another form of assessment that combines performance assessment with evaluation of permanent products is portfolio assessment. A portfolio is a collection of student work over a period of time, intended to show the full range of student endeavor and accomplishment. Such collections have been used for many years in performance areas such as art and music, but they are just finding their place in the battery of general assessment techniques (Salend, 1998). In addition to deciding which work they will include in their portfolios, students are usually also asked to select what they believe to be their "best piece" and to explain why.

As Mills (1996) relates in his description of the implementation of a statewide system of portfolio assessment in Vermont, guidelines can be established that permit the use of portfolios in place of current standardized tests for accountability purposes. It is necessary to develop scoring rubrics to evaluate the evidence contained in each portfolio and to use this information to understand more clearly what students have learned to do and how it compares with what students are expected to have learned. Trained evaluators then use the rubrics to review portfolios and determine whether the evidence supports the claim that students have learned and that districts and teachers have been successful in helping them learn.

Functional Behavioral Assessment

Functional behavioral assessment is the process of gathering information about a student's problem behaviors that seeks to determine the purpose of the behavior in addition to its antecedents and consequences. IDEA 1997 instituted this new requirement for all students who exhibit problem behaviors, regardless of their defined disability (McConnell, Hilvitz, & Cox, 1998). By identifying the purpose of the behavior as well as describing the context in which the behaviors occur, teams are able to design more effective behavioral interventions, ones that include positive behavioral supports (Sugai, Horner, & Sprague, 1999). Key to this process is developing a hypothesis about the function of the behavior, determining what need the behavior may be fulfilling for the student. Common purposes are to seek attention, to escape difficult or painful situations, or to gain control in one's environment. Effective positive behavioral support plans use the results from the functional behavioral assessment to identify alternative and acceptable ways for the student to meet his or her needs.

Reporting on Student Progress: Grading

The report card is a long-standing tradition in American schools. Every six to nine weeks, children across the country take home a card or a piece of paper on which a teacher has recorded symbols that indicate the level of achievement attained by the student during that grading period. The ritual of showing the card to parents or guardians, or of trying to find a way not to, is a common experience of childhood.

Common, that is, except for students with disabilities: these students have not always participated fully in this rite of childhood. Being excluded from general education classroom settings has sometimes meant that the student is not graded as others are and that parents do not receive regular progress reports on their child. Sometimes a brief narrative note or an alternative grading system is used, but often the annual IEP review replaces more frequent periodic reporting. The typical listing of academic subjects and letters or numbers is frequently viewed by special educators as irrelevant for students with disabilities. But with IDEA 1997, the law now requires that parents of children with disabilities receive information on their children's progress as often as other parents do. Schools and teachers are faced with the challenge of constructing a reporting system that communicates useful information.

The purpose of grading, and report card grading in particular, is the central issue. Grades are meant to be communication vehicles. As noted by Carpenter (1985), if the message intended by the recorder of the grade is not interpreted correctly by the receiver of the report, then the purpose has not been met. Any system of grading must be clear and precise if it is to be useful.

In a national survey, Bursuck et al. (1996) assessed common practices with respect to grading students with disabilities by general education teachers who serve some students with disabilities. In general, these researchers found that teachers favored pass-fail grades for students with disabilities, although letter and numerical grades were the system of choice for other students. Written comments and checklists were viewed as helpful for both types of students. The survey asked questions about the acceptability of adaptations to the grading system. The majority of teachers (73.4 percent) responded that adapting grades only for students with disabilities would not be fair. Interestingly, about half of the teachers who had concerns about modified grading said that adaptations would be fair if all students could receive adapted grades as needed. Examples of adaptations include basing grades on improvement or IEP objectives, giving separate grades for effort, and adjusting grades and the weighting of grades according to ability. Bursuck et al. point out, however, that inflating grades based on effort may inadvertently keep some students from receiving needed help since the students may appear to be making adequate progress. Carpenter (1985) suggested that using a multiple symbol grading system with separate symbols to convey different messages was one solution to this dilemma. Good practice suggests that each symbol should convey only one piece of information (see Table 3.2).

Finally, the survey indicated that half the general educators assume full responsibility for grading, while 40 percent of them share the grading tasks with their special education counterparts. Shared grading responsibility would appear to support the necessary communication between general and special educators. It would also help ensure that teachers were using the symbolic system in a uniform way, thus enhancing communication with parents.

State and District Assessment and IDEA 1997

As noted in the discussion of IDEA 1997, assessment continues to play a major role in serving youngsters with disabilities. We must use a variety of technically sound procedures to

TABLE 3.2   **Examples of Options for Reporting on Student Progress**

Letter or Numeric Averages	Symbols are used to summarize student performance on tests and other indicators
Pass/Fail (or No Grade) System	P/F grading denotes mastery of objectives; "no grade" option indicates work still in progress
Grading Using Multiple Symbols	Separate symbol systems indicate ability, achievement, and effort
Grade-level Symbols	Achievement symbol is paired with symbol indicating the grade level at which the student is working
Weighted Grading Systems	Learning activities are given varying weights in computing final grade; can be varied to meet student learning styles
Personalized Grading Plans	Student, teacher, and parent design an individual grading system that reflects communication needs and individual differences (Munk & Bursuck, 2001)
Improvement Grades	Grades are based on changes in performance from period to period
No Progress Grades	Option for performance not indicating mastery (Glasser, 1990)
Competency Checklists	Objectives are rated as "completed," "in progress," or "not attempted"
Narrative Reporting	Teachers provide narrative comments on student learning activities and progress; may supplement letter/numeric grades or serve as the sole reporting system
Portfolio Grading	Grades based on evaluation of portfolio; based on rubric
Contract Grading	Grading based on teacher/student contract identifying standards and requirements for specific grades
IEP Reporting	Assigns grades based on accomplishment of IEP objectives; report status toward mastery of objectives
Combination Systems	System using a variety of the above practices to better communicate to parents and others

Based on Carpenter, 1985; Glasser, 1990; Munk & Bursuck, 2001; Salend, 2001; Salend & Garrick Duhaney, 2002.

assess students' abilities and disabilities prior to identification and placement, and to monitor student progress toward their IEP goals and objectives after placement (Fuchs & Fuchs, 1986). Teachers must now report frequently to parents on that progress, and the reports must be meaningful to the parents and, in the case of parents from diverse linguistic backgrounds, in language they can understand. This makes periodic and routine assessment even more of a necessity.

The 1997 amendments to the IDEA posed one additional new requirement for students with disabilities and their teachers. With the effective date of the law in June 1997, states had to ensure that all children with disabilities were included in state and district assessment programs, with modifications as necessary. By July 1998, states were also required to establish performance goals and indicators for learners with disabilities. The performance of students with disabilities on those assessments must be reported regularly to the U.S. Secretary of Education and to the public as an indicator of the effectiveness of special education programs and the state's progress toward meeting the goals set for youngsters with disabilities.

These requirements have met with some concern. For many years, it has been conventional wisdom that such tests are inappropriate measures of the achievement of students with disabilities. IEP teams have routinely excused students with disabilities from state and district exams, substituting the individual assessments associated with their annual reviews (Council for Exceptional Children, 1998b). In IDEA 1997, however, Congress established three acceptable means for special education programs to demonstrate progress toward meeting state, district, school, and individual goals for students with disabilities:

- Students can participate in the regular state and district assessments without any modifications or accommodations.
- Students can participate in the regular assessments with accommodations as necessary to ensure that the results are valid indicators of student achievement. Accommodations relate to the way in which the test is administered, not to the content of the test. Accommodations can include some or all of the following (Heumann & Warlick, 2000; Yell & Shriner, 1997):

    Flexible settings (e.g., testing in a separate room, in a small group)

    Different timing or pacing (e.g., splitting the test into smaller increments, rearranging the sequence of test sections, allowing extended time to complete sections of the test)

    Alternative presentation format (e.g., having test questions read, paraphrasing or demonstrating directions, using taped questions or a sign language interpreter)

    Alternative response format (e.g., oral responses, use of a computer, use of a scribe for written essays)

- Students for whom the general education curriculum and assessments are deemed to be entirely inappropriate due to the severity of the disability will be required to participate in specially designed alternative assessments, which states must have in place by July 2000.

By including these additional requirements in IDEA 1997, Congress clearly intended that districts and states should be held accountable for the progress or lack of progress of all students, including those with disabilities. According to the U.S. Department of Education (2001), state participation rates for students with disabilities in state-wide assessments in 1999 ranged from 33 to 97 percent with varying levels of performance. It is clear that in the future, students with mild disabilities will be expected to participate more fully both in the general education curriculum and in state and district assessments, and that schools and teachers will be held accountable for their learning.

Best Practices in Assessment of Children and Youth with Disabilities

From this discussion and the assessment literature in general, a number of principles emerge that help define "best practices" in assessment and evaluation of students with mild disabilities and of all students. Frequent and ongoing assessment of student achievement toward established goals is critical to good educational planning and program delivery (Allinder, 1996). The use of formative curriculum-based assessment helps guide those who work with children to determine when learning has occurred and when additional instruction and support is required (Fuchs & Fuchs, 1986).

Use of a variety of tools is necessary, since each type of assessment yields only a portion of the information, and since not all children respond maximally on all kinds of tests. Increasingly, however, undue emphasis on norm-referenced tests will be seen to be counterproductive, since such tests relate to any particular curriculum only in the most general way. Teachers, districts, and states must create valid and effective criterion-referenced performance measures and utilize portfolio and performance assessments to document student achievement. Such measures must relate directly to the curriculum as taught.

Attention must be paid to the validity of all assessment measures with diverse learners. Students from differing cultural and linguistic backgrounds may not be well served by some standard assessment techniques. Learners with various disabilities may not respond well to certain types of assessment even though they have the skills and knowledge being tested. Some types of tests interact poorly with certain types of learners (e.g., timed tests with students with learning disabilities or ADHD; tests in English for students whose primary language is not English). Increasingly, teachers and administrators are finding that extended performance tasks and portfolio assessment enable all kinds of students to more adequately demonstrate what they have really learned.

As students with mild disabilities begin taking mandated state and district tests, with or without modifications, there will be an effect on the curriculum provided to these students. Good practice requires that curriculum, teaching techniques, and assessment be aligned, ensuring that the curriculum established for the children of the district or state is the curriculum that is taught and tested (Hoover, 1987). As will be discussed in Chapter 4, use of individual curricula for students with mild disabilities instead of the general education curriculum has not always served them well.

When IEP teams are designing modifications for state and district tests for particular students, the goal is to identify the accommodations that will allow each student to demonstrate what he/she really knows. It is important for special education teachers to know their students well enough to suggest appropriate accommodations and to be able to explain and sometimes defend the legitimacy of those modifications to others. Tests must measure the learners' skills and content knowledge, not their disabilities.

Issues in Identification

The task of identifying students in need of special education services by use of an appropriate classification system is far from simple. The definitions used to develop operational criteria have been and still are subject to frequent debate and change, as well as to uneven implementation (Cullinan, Epstein, & McLinden, 1986; Mercer, Jordan, Allsopp, & Mercer, 1996; Mercer, King-Sears, & Mercer, 1990; Wright, Pillard, & Cleven, 1990). The instructional groups resulting from this classification process are far from being the homogeneous groups that researchers and educators had envisioned, much as Dunn (1968) asserted many years ago (see Chapter 2).

The needs of the students with mild disabilities are extremely variable. Students vary in cognition, language, academic performance, and social-emotional adjustment. The profiles of two students within the same classification may differ significantly from each other, while two students in different disability categories may present very similar profiles. Identifying a learner with a classification that falsely implies a similarity to others poses serious problems. Reynolds and Heistad (1997) reported on research indicating that there seems to be no educational justification for the categorical divisions among students with mild disabilities. As an alternative, they proposed the use of simple direct assessment of progress as a way of determining which students are in need of more assistance to maintain adequate progress, much as the proponents of "Rights without Labels" advocate (see Chapter 1 and Appendix A). Susan and William Stainback (1987) concurred, asserting that when we actually look at the data about the characteristics of individual children, we find that the information available is much more specific and precise than any categorical label can be, and that categories are virtually useless in educational planning. They maintained that the only purpose of the categorical system was to rule some students eligible for assistance while denying others, a situation that may militate against a coherent plan for meeting the needs of all youngsters.

In a study of instructional practices in self-contained special education classes, Algozzine, Morsink, and Algozzine (1988) reported that special education teachers in general use a variety of pedagogical techniques associated with effective teaching and learning. They did not, however, detect significant differences among teachers with respect to the category of the students. Instruction in classes for students with learning disabilities was similar to instruction in classes for students with emotional disorders and in those for students with mild mental retardation. Categories of learners seem to be educationally irrelevant, and the overlap of characteristics across categories was much more significant than the average differences among groups (Jenkins, Pious, & Peterson, 1988).

Since 1975, many writers have questioned the need for and validity of creating two dichotomous groups of students, one special and one regular or "normal" (Gartner & Lipsky, 1987; Reynolds, 1989; Reynolds & Heistad, 1997; Stainback & Stainback, 1984; Will, 1986). These authors assert that all students are individuals with a variety of characteristics that vary on a continuum. Disability definitions create an arbitrary cutoff point on one or two of those characteristics at the most, and in so doing, they designate some youngsters as deviant and in need of special services, while others like Jeffrey are found to be ineligible.

It was this focus on deficits as the defining characteristic of an individual that concerned Madeleine Will (1986), former U.S. Assistant Secretary for Special Education and Rehabilitative Services. Will questioned a system that restricted special assistance to only those students who demonstrated serious levels of disability, saying that such a system focused only on failure. She noted that the very language used within special education is a "language of sep-aration, of fragmentation, of removal" (p. 412), and she called for all levels of government and both general and special education to create ways to resolve these problems. Jenkins, Pious, and Peterson (1988) noted that programs based on the categorical identification of students with a variety of difficulties in school are often disjointed and fragmented, with duplication and conflicting methods sometimes employed with the same child.

The concern about the validity of defining categories of students is reinforced by ques-tions about the validity and reliability of many of the norm-referenced instruments used in the identification process. The validity of the content in achievement tests is of concern because of the likelihood that either the content itself or the way it is presented and tested does not align with the specific curriculum to which the learner had been exposed. If the tests are not valid or reliable, it is legitimate to ask how cutoff scores can be used meaningfully for classification of some learners as having disabilities.

The identification of a disproportionate number of students from diverse cultural and linguistic backgrounds as needing special education gives further cause for concern (see Table 3.3). When procedures that are purported to be objective and scientific nevertheless result in the identification of students in numbers that are significantly different from the demographics of the general population, the tests may be responding to cultural or linguistic differences, not identifying legitimate differences in learning abilities and needs.

Finally, the effect of differential funding patterns on the rates of identification and de-certification in various states suggests that the procedures used for confirming the existence of a disability do not form an objective science. Some state funding schemes reward districts for more restrictive placements, or they penalize districts for decertifying students who appear to no longer need full services (Council for Exceptional Children 1994b). To under-score this concern, it is important to note that IDEA 1997 specifically addressed this issue when it called for states to revise any funding policies that have resulted in rewarding

TABLE 3.3 Percentage of Students Served by Disability and Race/Ethnicity, 1999–2000 School Year

Disability	American Indian/ Alaska Native	Asian/ Pacific Islander	Black (not Hispanic)	Hispanic	White (not Hispanic)
Learning Disability	1.4	1.6	18.4	16.6	62.1
Mental Retardation	1.1	1.8	34.2	9.1	53.8
Emotional Disturbance	1.1	1.2	27.3	8.9	61.5
All Disabilities	1.3	1.8	20.3	13.7	62.9
Total School Population	1.0	3.8	14.5	16.2	64.5

Data from U.S. Department of Education, 2001, p. II-27.

districts for placing youngsters in placements that are more restrictive than are needed by each student. The law now requires states to ensure that funding policies have a neutral effect on identification and placement decisions.

Categories as Social Constructions

A concern raised by some writers about virtually all of the mild disabilities is whether these disabilities are merely social constructions that are used to exclude and/or excuse difference. What part does the social context play in identifying and describing a disability? Murphy and Hicks-Stewart (1991) discussed learning disabilities and ADHD, in particular, from an environmental interactionist point of view. They noted that the social expectations of society define which behaviors are acceptable and which are deviant. When children, for whatever reason, fail to learn in school and violate the rules of the community, they may be determined to be different, deviant, and in need of special accommodations. Thus, one may make a case for the definition of disability with reference to the degree of adaptability in a social context (Reid & Button, 1995).

This discussion builds on the early description of the "six-hour retarded child" phenomenon (President's Committee on Mental Retardation, 1970), as well as Bogdan and Taylor's (1976, 1994) ethnographic work with persons labeled as having mental retardation, and then continues with similar arguments about learning disabilities (Murphy & Hicks-Stewart, 1991; Reid & Button, 1995; Sleeter, 1986), attention-deficit/hyperactivity disorder (Armstrong, 1995), and emotional or behavioral disorders (McIntyre, 1993; Reid & Button, 1995; Reilly, 1991). Some of the questions include: Are these real differences? Are they merely a variation in human behavior that we find inconvenient? Are we unwilling to accept variation in ability? Do we need to account for diminished performance by using the disability as an excuse? Such questions come from all sides of the political spectrum, addressing the central concept of "goodness of fit" between the individual and the environment.

At the central core of the discussion is concern about the validity of the concept of classification. Questions continue to be raised about the validity of the categories given inconsistent prevalence rates. Interventions relate only weakly to specific classifications and indeed are frequently used across disability categories. Those preparing to enter the field of special education will need to consider these and other questions for which there are no easy answers.

Noncategorical Models of Service: An Alternative?

One solution that is frequently proposed (Reynolds and Heistad, 1997) is being implemented in some states and localities. This proposal suggests that students who are experiencing difficulty in school environments should be identified by their needs, and programming should be designed to build on strengths and ameliorate deficiencies. Proponents of this noncategorical approach see no point in expending time and money to define a category of disability when categories are not viewed as being useful in designing interventions. The CEC policy statement about labeling and categorizing of children (Council for Exceptional Children, 1994b) raised concerns about the labeling process (see Appendix A).

MacMillan, Siperstein, and Gresham (1996) have suggested that the nature of mild retardation, in particular, differs significantly from more severe levels of the disability, and they question the use of the categorical term *mental retardation* with this population at all. MacMillan et al. observed that mild mental retardation is defined chiefly by the interaction between the individual's cognitive inefficiencies and the demands of the environment. These researchers stated that there is rarely an identifiable biomedical cause. They further noted that, in many cases, it is difficult or impossible to make an accurate discrimination between mild mental retardation and learning disabilities. They pointed out that in a number of cases, the categories of learning disabilities, mild mental retardation, and ADHD are used interchangeably, depending on the degree of acceptability to the various members of the multidisciplinary team. MacMillan et al. suggested that individuals who are currently labeled as having mild mental retardation should perhaps receive a completely different designation, one that indicates a generalized inefficiency in learning, such as "educationally handicapped" (as suggested by Reschley, 1988), "students with school learning disorders" (Dunn, 1968) or perhaps "generalized learning disabilities" or handicaps (in contrast to specific learning disabilities). Their point is that contextually situated forms of mild disability are frequently more similar to each other and more variable than more severe disorders, and that attempts to discriminate among them may be futile.

Reynolds and Heistad (1997) took this reasoning one step further. They proposed "to drop the partitioning practices that have become so pervasive in schools" (p. 447), which they claim have immobilized special education in many schools today. These researchers claim that the cost of making determinations about subgroups of students with mild levels of disability is unacceptable. They suggest that the distinctions do not improve instruction and the funds could be more effectively used in direct services. They proposed that schools use direct assessment of progress in school learning as an indication of the need for intervention and as a measure of program efficacy. As Murphy and Hicks-Stewart (1991) concluded, "The questions remain: (1) What are the educational needs of these children? [and] (2) How are these needs to be met in our schools?" (p. 388)

The 1997 amendments to IDEA have begun to address this issue by recognizing that it is not always useful to try to definitively determine the specific category of impairment, particularly in young children. According to the provisions of IDEA 1997, school districts may now exercise the option of serving youngsters between the ages of three and nine in special education under the rubric of developmental delay (Yell & Shriner, 1997). This option allows schools to get about the business of providing early intervention services without the necessity of satisfying specific disability criteria. In young children, the degree of deficit is often not severe enough to meet the formal criteria used to place children in categorical programs, potentially delaying useful formal interventions. Comments recorded in Senate deliberations on the 1997 amendments noted that:

> The use of a specific disability category to determine a child's eligibility for special education and related services frequently has led to the use of the category to drive the development of the child's IEP and placement to a greater extent than the child's needs. In the early years of a child's development, it is often difficult to determine the precise nature of a child's disability. Use of "developmental delay" as part of a unified approach will allow the special education and related services to be directly related to the child's needs and prevent locking a child into a disability category which may be inappropriate or incorrect.[1]

---

[1] From *IDEA 1997: Let's Make It Work,* by The Council for Exceptional Children, 1998, p. 13. Copyright © 1998 by The Council for Exceptional Children. Reprinted with permission.

In light of these comments, it is perhaps ironic to note that many educators and legislators alike seem to still be unable or unwilling to apply this analysis and reasoning more generally across the age span.

Focus on Culture and Diversity

Cultural implications of assessment have concerned educators for many years. Special education classrooms frequently seem to include students of color in disproportionate numbers. In 1970, the President's Committee on Mental Retardation voiced concern about students of color or those with limited English proficiency being classified as having mental retardation, when the real cause of their school problems appeared to be a matter of cultural difference. Tests normed on the general population were found by the courts to be biased when assessing those whose life experiences differed from the normative sample. The courts found these assessment practices to be discriminatory, often resulting in inappropriate placements. Even today (see Table 3.3), the numbers of students of color in various special education categories seem disproportionate to their population numbers.

Educators of the future will need to continue to address this issue. Use of more authentic assessments may provide more accurate and valid indications of students' strengths and needs. Working with families and members of the community may also provide important insights into the behaviors and learning problems faced by children from diverse backgrounds in school, allowing educators to better determine if a pattern of behavior is dysfunctional or merely related to cultural difference (Fox, Vaughn, Wyatte, & Dunlap, 2002).

Resources on the Web

IDEA Practices

www.ideapractices.org

Provides current resources pertaining to the assessment regulations included in IDEA 1997, including IEPs, state and district assessments, and functional behavioral assessments.

National Center on Educational Outcomes

www.coled.umn/edu/NCEO

Resources on assessment of students with disabilities, with particular focus on state and district level assessment programs.

ERIC Clearing House on Assessment and Evaluation

www.ericae.net

Searchable database in the ERIC system, devoted to assessment resources; also has a test locator link.

Fairtest: National Center for Fair and Open Testing

www.fairtest.org

> Site dedicated to advocacy issues and the elimination of bias in testing; supports the use of authentic assessment in lieu of standardized measures.

Center for Effective Collaboration and Practice

www.cecp.air.org

> Focuses on improving assessment and services for students with problem behaviors (e.g., functional behavioral assessments and design of positive behavior support plans).

Summary

The 1997 amendments to the Individuals with Disabilities Education Act have significant implications for the assessment and identification of learners with mild disabilities. The amendments reinforced the requirements that evaluations be composed of multiple measures conducted with technically sound instruments valid for the purposes being used. They state that the learner must be evaluated in the child's primary language, and that children cannot be determined to have a disability if they have not had the opportunity to learn the skills being assessed. The law requires that assessments relate to progress in the general education curriculum, and that students with disabilities must participate in all mandated district and state assessments. IDEA 1997 further requires that parents must be provided with progress reports as often as parents of children in general education classes are.

Assessment may be used for the purpose of classification and diagnosis. It may be used for determining the presence of a disability and for gathering information about strengths and deficits for the purpose of designing interventions. Formative evaluation is used to determine the effectiveness of ongoing interventions, while summative evaluation is used for making decisions about outcomes.

A variety of instruments may be employed to provide needed information for program planning. Norm-referenced instruments give an indication about how well the youngster does when compared to others, while criterion-referenced tests evaluate progress toward mastery of skills or content. Performance assessments ask students to demonstrate their understanding and skill by completing complex, realistic activities. Portfolio assessments examine the permanent products that result from instruction and take note of the evidence of progress in the collected materials. Functional behavioral assessments aid in the development of effective intervention plans.

The IDEA 1997 requirement that all students take the mandated general education assessments means that attention will have to be paid to the curriculum provided to students with disabilities. In addition, students will be able to have modifications in those assessments as prescribed by the multidisciplinary team. For the small number of students with very severe disabilities for whom none of the general education curriculum is appropriate, state-level alternative assessments must be developed.

The complexity of determining the presence of a specific disability indicates that the task of identifying students in need of special education services by use of an appropriate classification system is far from simple. The definitions for the various disabilities are subject to frequent debate and change as well as to uneven implementation. In addition, numerous critics have suggested that there is no educational justification for the identification process and that the costs of such procedures are unacceptable.

One additional issue related to the process used to identify students as having disabilities is the concern that much of what we regard as mild disabilities may actually be socially constructed. The degree of fit between the individual and the environment is largely responsible for the determination of deviancy and disability. The degree to which disability may be constructed remains to be sorted out.

An answer that has been frequently proposed for the above problems and questions is to use a noncategorical approach to providing services. This approach identifies those students who are not making progress in the general education curriculum and provides assistance to them without identifying a discrete condition. The IDEA 1997 has taken a step in this direction by allowing states to serve children between the ages of three and nine in a general category called "developmental delay."

SHARON: A Case Study

Sharon is a fifteen-year-old repeating freshman in a large urban high school. She is functioning well below grade level in all academic areas. She failed to move on to the sophomore level this year because of excessive absences and poor academic performance last year. She does not work well independently, "hates" school, and rebels against all forms of authority. Sharon responds to adults and peers in a very defensive and defiant manner. She frequently uses abusive language in her interactions with peers and adults. If she misplaces her papers, pencils, or books, she attempts to shift the blame to someone else. She seldom accepts personal responsibility for any of her inappropriate behaviors.

According to her parents, Sharon has been in a perpetual state of motion since she was very young. As a young child, she seldom slept long enough at any one time to give them relief from her active, disturbing behaviors. As she grew older, Sharon continued to respond impulsively to situations regardless of the consequences. Her parents tried all the "parent things"—scolding, spanking, denying privileges, sending her to her room, promising rewards for good behavior—in their attempts to change her behavior. They feel that nothing they have tried has had any effect, and they are "at their wit's end."

Referral for psychological evaluation had been considered often by school personnel, but it wasn't until Sharon was caught using drugs on the school grounds that her case was finally scheduled for formal consideration by the multidisciplinary team. Meanwhile, Sharon's parents had secured the services of a private clinical psychologist who agreed to work with Sharon on a weekly basis. Sharon refused to see the psychologist, however, until she was threatened with expulsion from school following the drug incident.

When educational testing was finally completed, it was reported that Sharon had achieved an intelligence score in the high-average range on the Stanford-Binet-IV (IQ of 124). Sharon's scores on the Peabody Individual Achievement Test revealed that her general performance in reading recognition, reading comprehension, spelling, and general information was similar to that of students at the fifth grade level, significantly below her current ninth grade school placement. The school psychologist noted in the evaluation that these scores might be lower than her true skill levels because of Sharon's resistance to the testing activities.

Informal observations by regular and special education teachers confirm that her low level of academic performance on the standardized tests is apparent in actual classroom settings as well. Her teachers report that Sharon completes work hurriedly, if at all, and that her accuracy in the work she does finish suggests a low level of mastery. In contrast, Sharon is an avid reader at home, withdrawing into herself with novels by Stephen King, Dean Koontz, and Anne Rice.

Sharon has consistently refused to participate in school and classroom activities. She has been cutting classes and skipping school entirely since she entered middle school in sixth grade. Even the promise of a car next summer if she attends school regularly and does well has not altered this behavior pattern. When she is in school, she often refuses to do assignments or participate in class. For example, one day in math class, the teacher passed out a test. Sharon sat there doing nothing. When the teacher asked why she was not working, Sharon said she had no paper. When the teacher gave her a piece of paper, Sharon still refused, saying, "You know I don't do math."

Her classmates also seem to view Sharon in a negative manner. A recent sociogram drawn from the answers to the question, "Who would you like to work with on the science project?" showed that no one selected Sharon to be in their group. The two students Sharon chose to work with, Susan and Cathy, are capable students who seem to be well accepted in their class, but Sharon has had little previous contact with them at school or in the neighborhood. Shortly after the sociogram was administered, Sharon did approach Cathy about working with her on a class assignment. Since then, Mrs. Jones, the classroom teacher, has continued to assign them together on projects with some success. Sharon seemed to respond positively to the opportunity to work with a student perceived as academically and socially successful.

The multidisciplinary team decided that Sharon met the state criteria for classification as a student with a learning disability and that placement in a self-contained classroom program for students with learning disabilities at the high school would be the most appropriate for her. They cited her low level of academic progress in spite of her above-average intellectual ability as the reason for this decision. They believed that remediation in the self-contained classroom would increase Sharon's academic skills so that ultimately she would experience more success in school, with a resulting improvement in her behavior. Her IEP was developed to address reading, math, and writing skills, coupled with a self-monitoring program for on-task behavior and attention. It was decided to delay her change in placement until the new semester in January to ease the transition.

Just before the semester break, Sharon was gone when her father went to wake her for school. Her duffel bag, suitcase, and clothing were missing. Her parents called the police and all of her friends. Everyone was mobilized to find Sharon. Fifteen hours later, she was finally found by her boyfriend in a hangout area in the woods, and she reluctantly returned home. She was hungry, cold, and tired. Sharon's parents feel like they are back to zero.

DISCUSSION

Identify Sharon's strengths and needs. Then sort those characteristics into two groups:

- academic learning characteristics
- social-behavioral characteristics

Given your list, what might be the outcome of identifying Sharon as a student with a learning disability and placing her in a self-contained classroom for students with learning disabilities with the goal of remediating her academic weaknesses?

In considering the implications for placement and programming, as presented in the case study, how useful is it for the teacher to know that Sharon meets the criteria for students with learning disabilities? Is there any evidence that the knowledge of the classification had any effect on the intervention plan developed by the team?

■ ■ ■ ■ ■

CHAPTER FOUR

ISSUES IN CURRICULUM AND INSTRUCTION

QUESTIONS TO GUIDE YOUR STUDY

- What provisions related to individualized education program planning are found in the 1997 IDEA amendments?
- What does the word *curriculum* mean within the context of the 1997 IDEA amendments?
- What must be included in a student's IEP?
- Why is it important to distinguish between the explicit curriculum, the hidden curriculum, and the absent curriculum?
- What is the difference between a modified curriculum and an alternative curriculum?
- What is the difference between curriculum and instruction?
- What does IDEA 1997 mean by "individualized instruction"?
- Identify and describe five instructional practices or strategies that can be implemented with students in general education and special education to support higher achievement.
- Describe four programming models, identifying the purpose of each for serving students with disabilities.
- Identify four dimensions of instructional adaptations that may help a student with a disability benefit from general education instruction.

■ ■ ■ ■ ■

Meet Enrico

Enrico has been identified as a student with a learning disability since third grade. As he prepares to enter ninth grade in the fall, the multidisciplinary team has convened to evaluate his IEP and progress thus far. As with many students with learning disabilities, Enrico's academic performance is most seriously affected by his lack of reading skills. He has been taught with alternative reading curricula and instructional materials since his initial special education placement. Every year he makes modest progress, but when September rolls around, he seems to have lost most of the skill he gained and must essentially begin anew. Depending on the measure used, his skills in reading are equivalent to an average third grader's. He reads in a halting, word-by-word manner, and it appears that he is just saying the

words, with little indication that he expects to derive meaning from them. His special education teacher continues to work with him on basic decoding skills, using the *Recipe for Reading* curriculum, an alternative reading curriculum based on instruction in synthetic phonics. In the general education classroom, Enrico is frequently observed to be off-task during reading activities, although he shows adequate attention and participation in class discussions.

The team is concerned about Enrico's lack of progress, and they suspect that it indicates that the alternative curricula and instructional approaches used in the past have not served Enrico well. As they look ahead to his high school years and to the post-school transition, they begin to consider other options. Mr. Thompson, the special education teacher, reminds the team that IDEA 1997 states that they must consider the general education curriculum first in developing the IEP, and that Enrico will be required to participate in the statewide assessments next year. He noted that alternative cur-

ricula are appropriate only when no portion of the general curriculum is applicable to the student. Enrico's class participation in nonreading activities indicates that he can benefit from the general education curriculum.

The team reviews the data and makes the following decisions: Enrico should be able to benefit from the general education curriculum with the supports of taped textbooks in the content areas and participation in Mr. Thompson's Learning to Learn elective class, which will teach him reading strategies designed to enhance his ability to profit from grade-level materials. The general education teachers should receive support from the consultant teacher in making any necessary modifications to the activities and demands of the classroom. It is decided that these supports will help ameliorate Enrico's needs while recognizing and developing his strengths in learning, and that this program of goals and services will better prepare him for the statewide assessments and his future.

IDEA 1997: Curriculum and Instruction Requirements

The IDEA has always required the development of an individualized education program (IEP) for each student found to be in need of special education services. The IEP has generally been regarded by parents and teachers as "the curriculum" for each student with a disability (Sands,

Adams, & Stout, 1995). Prior to 1997, IEPs typically focused only on special education services and objectives, with little or no consideration of the general education curriculum. Special education teachers were often told that only those services specifically related to special education needed to be described in the IEP. It has been noted by some writers that this exclusive focus on special education services in curriculum planning frequently resulted in fragmented programs, with little or no consideration of the interactions between special and general education (Will, 1986; Yell & Shriner, 1997).

In IDEA 1997, the IEP continued to be a central component of the law, but Congress included some significant changes. The 1997 amendments reemphasize that the IEP is to be developed around the strengths and needs of the child, with parents and school personnel actively participating in the planning. For the first time, the law also stipulates that the IEP is to focus on the student's participation in the general education curriculum, that it is to be developed with the assistance of the general educator, and that it must be linked to the state's learning standards.

Procedures used to develop the IEP vary widely from state to state and from district to district. The composition of the team, the procedures used to draft the goals and objectives, the way goals and objectives are written, and the nature and extent of expected parental participation are all variables that have created very different outcomes, depending on where the child lives. For example, all of the following parental roles have been observed in schools by the author of this book:

- Nominal invitations are extended to parents to participate, but with no encouragement or accommodation in scheduling to facilitate attendance, frequently resulting in no parent in attendance.
- Parents are encouraged to attend, and then presented with a document previously prepared by the special education teacher (perhaps with the assistance of a computerized database of objectives), with the school personnel and parent expected simply to ratify the document.
- The IEP is drafted by the parent and special education teacher in an informal meeting, and then presented to the entire team for ratification.
- The IEP is drafted by a team composed of a variety of special education and administrative personnel as well as a parent advocate—a parent selected to serve on all teams to represent parents' interests, regardless of whether the child's own parent can attend.
- The IEP is written from scratch by the team at the meeting, perhaps with the assistance of a computerized database of goals and objectives.

The 1997 IDEA amendments sought to clarify and strengthen existing IEP provisions to increase the likelihood that the resulting plan would be designed around the needs of the child, developed collaboratively by those closest to the child, and referenced to the child's progress in the general education curriculum. Major provisions of the IDEA 1997 amendments include the following (Council for Exceptional Children, 1998a, 1998b; Yell & Shriner, 1997):

- The following people are required to be part of the IEP development team: the child's parent, a general education teacher, a special education teacher, and a representative of the local educational agency (LEA). At least one member of the team must be knowledgeable about the instructional implications of evaluation data, although a school psychologist is no longer required to be present. IDEA 1997 also supports the participation of the student with the disability, whenever appropriate.

■ The IEP team must consider the child's strengths, not just the deficits, and must also address the parents' information and concerns about their child's functioning. Special concerns must be explicitly addressed, including the communication needs of students who are learning English as a second language and of children with hearing impairments, needs for assistive technology, needs for Braille instruction for students with severe visual impairments, and behavioral concerns that impede learning, regardless of the disability category.

■ The content of the IEP must include the following:

Present levels of performance, with particular emphasis on how the child's disability is affecting progress in the general education curriculum

Measurable annual goals and short-term objectives or benchmarks, with particular attention to the child's needs in relation to the general education curriculum

Criteria for determining progress, and the means for evaluating attainment of goals and objectives

Related services required to meet annual goals, including assistive technology

An explanation of the child's inclusion in or restriction from participation in the general education curriculum

Modifications required for the child to participate effectively in general education assessments

Projected dates for implementation and duration of services

Beginning at least by age fourteen, a plan addressing the transition needs for the postschool environment

A central theme in the 1997 IDEA amendments is the repeated reference to the general education curriculum as the starting point for all instructional planning considerations. In the past, reference to the general education curriculum has always implied consideration of the appropriateness of activities in a general education *classroom*. In 1997 IDEA, Congress removed the emphasis on location when considering the meaning of least restrictive environment. The concept of curriculum is no longer associated with a discrete physical location, but rather with the educational program itself, wherever and however it is delivered (Council for Exceptional Children, 1998b).

In the future, this emphasis on the general education curriculum as the foundation for all student programs will create some significant challenges for special educators. According to a study by Sands, Adams, and Stout (1995), over half the 592 teachers they surveyed believed that each student receiving special education services must have an individual curriculum. They believed that the IEP goals served as the basis for each child's curriculum. In contrast, only 15 percent of the teachers believed that the general education curriculum served as the primary curriculum for their students. When questioned about the sources used to determine curricula for students with disabilities, the respondents most frequently noted (1) the special educator's professional judgment, (2) the student's IEP, (3) student and teacher needs as determined on a daily basis, and finally (4) the general education curriculum. The authors of the study indicated that this individualized and somewhat subjective nature of curricular planning raised serious questions about program and educator accountability. It may indeed be that IDEA 1997 requirements with regard to curriculum and assessment of outcomes were necessitated by these same accountability concerns.

Curriculum and Students with Disabilities

Whenever educators discuss curriculum, it quickly becomes clear that they assume that everyone means the same thing by the word. It soon becomes equally clear that there are a variety of meanings represented in any such discussion (Richardson & Anders, 1998). To compound the problem in special education, the *curriculum* and *individualized education program* are frequently used interchangeably (Dever & Knapczyk, 1997; Sands, Adams, & Stout, 1995).

Although there is general agreement that *curriculum* in some way relates to the activities and experiences students encounter under the direction of a school (Hoover, 1987), some of the other more frequently provided definitions include the following:

- Reference to the basal series in use in a given class, grade, or school
- The scope and sequence charts related to a particular field of study (e.g., reading, mathematics)
- A listing of the goals and related objectives that define the content of instruction, as determined by a teacher, school, district, or state
- State or district syllabi or curriculum guides
- State and national standards
- A course of study (e.g., toward a degree)
- Everything that goes on in a school

These variations in meaning create obvious problems whenever educators discuss the general education curriculum as it relates to learners with mild disabilities.

In addition to the problem of achieving consensus on a basic definition, educators must address the multidimensional nature of implemented curricula, as described by Hoover (1987), Richardson and Anders (1998), and others. Curricula may be viewed from at least three perspectives:

- The explicit curriculum, or the curriculum as written and tested
- The hidden curriculum, or the curriculum as taught
- The absent curriculum, or the curriculum that is not taught

The *explicit curriculum* is defined as the formal, written curriculum that teachers and schools are expected to follow. It is the public curriculum that schools say they are providing to students. Increasingly, it pertains to the state's learning standards, those learning goals that have been identified as critical for all students to achieve. It also relates to the curriculum as tested on district and statewide assessment programs. Complications arise when the explicit curriculum as written and the curriculum as tested are not congruent.

The *hidden curriculum* is the actual curriculum as implemented in any classroom. It results from the interaction of the explicit curriculum with organizational decisions made by teachers (e.g., grouping practices, time allocation) and with the teachers' selection of peda-gogical approaches to teaching content. The hidden curriculum also relates to the implicit values of teachers and students that guide those decisions and the degree to which certain behaviors and values are rewarded and supported (Myles & Simpson, 2001; Richardson & Anders, 1998). The manner in which varying cultures, languages, genders, lifestyles, and so on are handled within any classroom culture is a significant component of the hidden cur-riculum. Thus, the hidden curriculum results in a number of important learnings, most of which are not explicitly intentional. The hidden curriculum varies from class to class and school to school despite a seemingly uniform explicit or public curriculum.

The *absent curriculum* includes those topics or learnings that are left out of what is taught. Content may be left out of the explicit curriculum by the curriculum developers (e.g., certain topics in sex education). Alternatively, specific content may be left out by individual teachers as they implement the hidden curriculum due to time constraints, personal prefer-ences, or assumptions about what students already know and can do.

One issue related to the absent curriculum that is of considerable importance to stu-dents learning English as a second language is the omission of English language survival skills in most general education programs. This occurs because of the widespread assump-tion that all students understand English sufficiently to profit from instruction. Comprehen-sion is assumed, unless a student's performance indicates that there is a problem.

As policymakers, parents, and others seek to reform school practices to allow more successful inclusion of students with disabilities, attention to the hidden and absent curricula as well as to the explicit, public curriculum is crucial to the outcomes for those students. Such efforts frequently fail because they consider only the explicit curriculum. The class-room procedures and expectations that are central to the hidden curriculum must be made explicit to teachers, students, parents, and the support staff so that these important learnings can be made more intentional. In addition, identifying elements of the absent curriculum may be crucial to the success of certain learners in the general education curriculum. The identification and teaching of content and skills that are omitted or assumed can be used to improve the match between the student and the curriculum. This is particularly true when such knowledge is used to supplement the implemented curriculum with crucial cognitive strategies or prerequisite skills that a student with a disability may lack.

Instructional materials, including textbooks and basal series, are frequently the most obvious indication of the explicit curriculum in place in classrooms and schools. When gen-eral education classroom teachers report that the curriculum used for their students with dis-abilities is the same or mostly the same as that provided to other students, they generally mean that the students use the same texts. On the other hand, special education resource teachers (see In the Classroom 4.1) are more likely to say that their students use a curriculum that is different from the one provided in general education classes, meaning that they use materials that are different from the ones other teachers use (Deno, Maruyama, Espin, & Cohen, 1990; Simmons, Kameenui, & Chard, 1998). Often the process of making modifications for students with special learning needs focuses primarily on adapting or supplementing the textbooks used by other children.

IN THE CLASSROOM **4.1**

Curriculum in Special Education Classes

As the Johnson Central School District prepared for the visit of state special education auditors, Ms. Perkins, the Director of Special Education, spoke with the district's special education staff to ensure that everyone was ready for the visit. When Ms. Perkins met with Mr. Clark, a resource teacher at Johnson Elementary, she asked him what curriculum he used with his students. He confidently replied that he used an alternative curriculum, comfortable that

this was the desired answer. Ms. Perkins responded quickly, "No, you use the general education curriculum. Your students are learning the same things all students do, you just give them different ways to learn them." Mr. Clark was puzzled; after all, didn't the law require "specially designed instruction" be provided to students with disabilities? How could the general education curriculum be appropriate for his students?

Alternatives to the General Education Curriculum

As noted, IDEA 1997 established the general education curriculum as the foundation for the education of all children in a district or state. The *general education curriculum* may be defined as the set of curricular expectations for students to achieve at each grade and level. It consists of the set of skills and knowledge that a graduate of the system will be expected to know and be able to demonstrate as an adult. In some states and localities, these expectations are clearly defined and written down; they are specific, measurable, and tested. In other schools, the curriculum is a vague sense of what a child should learn, sketched in broad generalities and determined by textbook selection. However it is presented, the general education curriculum delineates the competencies expected of adults in that community. For this reason, it is appropriate to view the general education curriculum as the primary guide for the design and delivery of all educational services.

In IDEA 1997, Congress placed special emphasis on the general education curriculum and the assessments designed to measure progress in that curriculum. The language used in the 1997 IDEA amendments and the commentary recorded during deliberations (Council for Exceptional Children, 1998a), suggest that Congress meant the term to refer to the K–12 continuum of skills and knowledge available to all students. It is also apparent that Congress regards curriculum as independent of place or pedagogy, that they are referring to the body of skills and knowledge deemed as critical for all students to acquire, including those with disabilities. From this perspective, it appears that Congress was referring to the explicit curriculum of a district or state when it used the term *general education curriculum.*

The tendency to equate this curriculum with services provided in the general education classroom is problematic. Since general classroom services are not yet uniformly supportive of students with disabilities, equating those services with the concept of curriculum may lead special educators and parents to oppose the whole notion of the general education curriculum as appropriate for most students. In this discussion, it is important to keep in mind that curriculum is a *thing,* not a *place* and not a *how.*

For many students with mild disabilities, the general education classroom may be an appropriate and normalized place to participate in the general education curriculum, with or without supports. However, the skills and knowledge that comprise the general education curriculum can be delivered anywhere by any teacher. It is crucial that even special educators who deliver part or all of their students' programs in separate environments be aware that the content of that instruction should relate to the general education curriculum to the greatest extent possible if their students are to be prepared to function fully as adults. Since IDEA 1997 now requires that all students be assessed by general education assessment programs, it is also essential for the content of their instruction to relate to that curriculum if those measures are to be valid indicators of ability and competence. It is important that all curricular decisions be referenced to the state's learning standards.

Modified Curricula

In some cases, modifications may be necessary for the general education curriculum to be useful for a particular student with a disability. In such instances, a modified curriculum may be appropriate. A modified curriculum is one in which modifications or substitutions are made in *content.* A modified curriculum is appropriate whenever an element of the general curriculum is determined not to be appropriate for a particular student. For example, for a student with a severe visual impairment, we might substitute instruction in reading Braille for instruction in print decoding. When we use the term *modified curriculum,* it is important to realize that we do not mean accommodations to the general education teaching methods. Curriculum relates to the content of instruction. Students who require accommodations to profit from instruction in the general education curriculum are still being provided with the opportunity to participate in the general education curriculum. They are not receiving a modified curriculum.

Another framework for considering the content of the curriculum is the planning pyramid (Deshler, Ellis, & Lenz, 1996; Schumm, Vaughn, & Leavell, 1994). This model (see Figure 4.1) suggests that teachers ask three questions:

- What should all students learn?
- What should most students learn?
- What content might some students benefit from learning?

In conducting this type of analysis, educators identify those learnings most critical to successful adult living as well as those that might be of more supplemental importance. When efficiency in learning is impaired by a disability, it may be more important to focus on helping students learn those critical concepts and skills that build a strong foundation for later learning. This framework keeps open the possibility that learners will acquire more than minimum skills, but it ensures that at least the foundation will be attained.

A final concern about curriculum and appropriate modification relates to students who are learning English as a second language. As noted in Chapter 12, ability to understand instruction is a critical determiner of the amount of time needed to learn. Educators must consider the effectiveness of the learner in comprehending and expressing curricular content

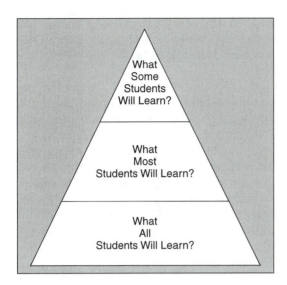

FIGURE 4.1   Planning Pyramid

From *Teaching Adolescents with Learning Disabilities* (2nd ed.), p. 429, by D. D. Deshler, E. S. Ellis, and B. K. Lenz, 1996, Denver: Love. Copyright © 1996 by Love Publishing Company. Adapted and reprinted with permission.

and develop instructional supports for those students as needed. Such supports and modified curricula may include intensive English as a second language (ESL) instruction or alternative means for the students to be provided with the content, such as bilingual education programs. Teachers cannot assume that students understand what is being said just because they appear to be listening. Frequently, students with difficulty comprehending spoken English will pay very close attention, but will still miss significant concepts. Regular assessment of student understanding is critical, especially when competency in the language used for instruction is a noted need for a particular learner.

Alternative Curricula

Alternative curricula and assessments are appropriate only for that small percentage of students with disabilities for whom no portion of the general education curriculum is applicable, those with the most severe levels of disability. Such students frequently are provided with a curriculum including self-care and daily living skills not generally considered part of the K–12 curriculum. Reading, writing, mathematics, science, and social studies are not generally relevant for such students, and therefore an alternative or substitute curriculum is called for. For all other students, some level of competence in the general education curriculum should be a viable goal. The issue for general and special educators alike is how to provide access to that general curriculum.

Instruction and Individualized Education Programming

The previous discussion suggests a contradictory set of requirements, both of which are contained within IDEA. On the one hand, the law requires that each student with a disability be provided with an individualized education program (IEP). On the other hand, Congress has dictated that the curriculum provided to students with disabilities should be the general education curriculum, with accommodations as needed. How can IEP teams and teachers accommodate these seemingly opposing requirements?

The answer lies in differentiating between curriculum, or the content of education, and instruction, or the methods used to develop content and skill competence. One legitimate goal of education, as indicated by Dever and Knapczyk (1997), may be defined as achieving independence in functioning; the role of teachers then becomes assisting young people in the process of growing up to be productive, contributing, and independent members of society. This curricular goal is clearly applicable to all children and youth, whether they have disabilities or not. Even the hierarchical listing of subskills needed to attain independence would be applicable to all. The fact that some learners will not make as much progress toward that goal over a year or a school career is irrelevant; the goal remains the same (Dever, 1990).

If we consider the difference between this curricular goal and the instructional methods and practices used to achieve the goal, the resolution of the apparent contradiction becomes clearer. As teachers and schools work to develop independence in learners, they will employ a variety of activities, and they will pace those challenges in accordance with learner responses. It then becomes obvious that it is the instructional practices that are to be individualized, not necessarily the curriculum.

In discussing some of the issues involved in individualizing instruction, Lloyd (1984) concluded by observing that there are some methods of instruction that have been empirically demonstrated to be effective with a variety of learners, including those with and without disabilities and those who have cultural and linguistic differences. Lloyd agrees that educators should base their instruction on the specific learning characteristics of students, rather than on disability categories. "We cannot know that special education is better for students [with disabilities] and regular education is better for normal learners. . . . It may be that special education would benefit [students without disabilities] just as much as it does special education students" (p. 13). Lloyd suggested that all teachers should individualize instruction on the basis of the skills students have yet to learn and by using a variety of instructional methods that seem to match their individual learning patterns and needs. He and others have implied that this would constitute effective instruction for all students, that "whatever is special about special education has relevance for all effective teachers" (Aber, Bachman, Campbell, & O'Malley, 1994, p. 50).

From this reasoning then, the resolution of our apparent contradiction becomes clearer. Learning problems appear to result most directly from the failure of teachers, despite the environment of instruction, to modify instruction to better match learner characteristics. Instruction in general education (and frequently in special education as well) suffers from too little variation and adaptation for all learners.

Instructional Strategies to Enhance Curriculum Access

As we consider ways to provide more effective access to the general education curriculum for students with disabilities, it is useful to look at educational practices that have been shown to be effective with students in both general and special education settings. Increasingly, researchers are finding that practices that work with one type of student are also effective with others (Cannon, Idol, & West, 1992). This finding supports the premise that the integrated delivery of the general education curriculum is feasible and may be far more effective and efficient than maintaining separate programs. Bickel and Bickel (1986) stated that:

> There is a growing knowledge base about how to effectively organize schools and instruction that is relevant to both special and regular educators and that there is a growing rationale for special and regular educational programming to become more integrated at the school level, at least in terms of [students with mild disabilities]. Special and regular educators have much to learn from each other. (p. 497)[1]

In a review of instructional practices found to be useful with learners at risk of or who are experiencing failure, Simmons & Kameenui (1996) identified six critical instructional factors: (1) focusing on the big ideas; (2) making learning strategies explicit; (3) providing scaffolding to support learners; (4) assisting with integrating knowledge; (5) making connections to background knowledge; and (6) providing structured review opportunities. These principles are relevant in supporting the learning of any student in need of assistance, and they can guide the individualization of any instructional activity.

Research reports concerning the effectiveness of particular instructional practices, strategies, or materials with students with disabilities have frequently produced contradictory results (Marston, Deno, Kim, Diment, & Rogers, 1995). This suggests that practitioners should consider the following factors when reviewing research reports and findings:

- Most research studies report group outcomes. In special education, we are charged with providing individually designed instruction. Attention to individual results and to the variation within the groups often suggests that some approaches work better with certain learners.
- Basic principles of effective instruction frequently form the foundation of any instructional intervention. The positive results of a study may in fact be due to the presence of these critical teaching behaviors or the degree to which the study participants used such principles, rather than to the technique itself.

While it is beyond the scope of this text to discuss specific pedagogical techniques in detail, it may be useful to identify a few of the practices that have been identified in the literature as being related to effective instruction in both general education and special education.

Direct Instruction

Direct instruction, or explicit teaching, is a set of teaching behaviors that have been repeatedly validated through research for over two decades, as described in a variety of synthesis reports (Bickel & Bickel, 1986; Brophy & Good, 1986; Larrivee, 1986; Rosenshine, 1986;

[1] From "Effective Schools, Classrooms, and Instruction: Implications for Special Education," by W. E. Bickel and D. D. Bickel, *Exceptional Children, 52*(6), 1986, p. 497. Copyright 1986 by The Council for Exceptional Children. Reprinted with permission.

Rosenshine & Stevens, 1986). Referred to variously as *direct instruction, explicit teaching,* or *effective teaching principles,* these behaviors include six instructional functions: (1) reviewing and reteaching as necessary; (2) explicit presentation of new content by the teacher; (3) guided initial practice; (4) feedback and correction; (5) independent practice; and (6) weekly and monthly reviews to support maintenance (Rosenshine, 1986). In general, research on direct instruction indicates that the teacher should play an active and direct role in the instructional process, provide relevant practice, and verify that learning has occurred before moving on (Algozzine, Ysseldyke, & Campbell, 1994; Englert, 1984; Levin & Long, 1981; Lloyd, 1984). Although these practices are particularly useful in teaching lower-level skills and in teaching any skill to youngsters who find learning difficult, direct instruction has been found to be useful in both general education and special education and for a wide variety of levels of learning tasks.

Related to research on direct instruction is the body of work that looks at how time is used in classrooms (Bickel & Bickel, 1986; Brophy & Good, 1986; Carroll, 1963; Denham & Lieberman, 1980). Academic learning time is defined as the time a student spends actively involved in a learning task and with a high rate of success (Bickel & Bickel, 1986). Academic responding time is defined as the amount of time students actually spend in responding to academic tasks and challenges, as opposed to waiting or engaging in task management activities (Morsink, Soar, Soar, & Thomas, 1986). Unfortunately, classroom research and informal classroom observations, in both general and special education settings, indicate that a significant amount of students' time does not meet the criteria of either academic learning or academic responding time.

Peer Tutoring

Reviews of effective practices in inclusive classrooms serving heterogeneous groups of students have indicated that peer tutoring is associated with significant gains in learning by students with disabilities on learning tasks involving factual information such as math facts and spelling words (Cook, Scruggs, Mastropieri, & Casto, 1985–86; Fisher, Schumaker, & Deshler, 1995; Villa & Thousand, 1988). In peer tutoring arrangements, one student is trained to provide skill practice and feedback to another. Peer tutoring is frequently an effective way to increase the amount of individualized instructional attention. Improvement in student learning is attributed to the increased opportunity for academic responding time coupled with immediate feedback. Peer support networks and "peer buddies" have also been associated with more effective social integration of students with disabilities. The purpose of these structured peer relationships is primarily nonacademic, and they provide an opportunity to support the development of social skills and social relationships among students with and without disabilities (Villa & Thousand, 1988).

Cooperative Learning

Cooperative learning refers to a family of instructional practices characterized by the use of teams to support academic learning (Johnson et al., 1984; Johnson & Johnson, 1996). In cooperative learning, positive interdependence is fostered while individual accountability is retained. Instructional objectives are selected to include both academic content learning and group work skills. Attention is given to actively teaching and coaching the group work skills so necessary for effective everyday adult functioning. The efficacy research on cooperative learning among learners in general is substantial and robust (Johnson et al., 1984). Positive changes have been observed in study after study, including increased academic learning for most students regardless of ability, increased skill in higher order problem solving, and positive social skill development (Johnson et al., 1984). Pomplun (1997) found that, in general, students with disabilities were able to participate and to learn effectively in such groups, with the exception of students with behavioral disorders or mental retardation. Outcomes with these students suggested that some students with disabilities might need more specific assistance in developing appropriate and useful group work skills prior to involvement in cooperative learning environments.

Cooperative learning is well-suited for supporting learning in inclusive and heterogeneous classrooms (Fisher, Schumaker, & Deshler, 1995; Pomplun, 1997; Villa & Thousand, 1988). One of the strongest and most versatile models, developed by David and Roger Johnson, makes use of heterogeneous teams. As students interact on the team over time, they support each other as their complementary skills allow; and through peer tutoring and mutual support, they work to achieve higher levels of learning for all students in the group (Johnson et al., 1984). Cooperative learning is frequently cited as a way for classroom teachers to provide more relevant practice and feedback, to accommodate individual differences, and to obtain enhanced learning for all.

Cognitive Strategies

Cognitive strategies are techniques that assist a student in learning how to learn, including self-instruction, self-questioning, self-monitoring, self-evaluation, and self-reinforcement. They help students become self-regulated learners, allowing them to direct and evaluate their own learning. Cognitive strategy instruction is particularly useful with middle school and secondary students as they attempt to deal with more complex, independent learning tasks. Cognitive strategies are developed incidentally by capable learners, but research indicates that they are often missing from the repertoire of a student experiencing academic difficulty.

One example of cognitive strategies instruction, the strategies intervention model developed at the University of Kansas, includes a collection of learning strategies that can help students acquire information, store and retrieve facts and skills, and express knowledge in a variety of ways (Deshler, Ellis, & Lenz, 1996; Fisher, Schumaker, & Deshler, 1995). Other examples of approaches that address cognitive strategy development include cognitive behavior modification techniques such as self-instruction and self-monitoring (Hallahan, Kauffman, & Lloyd, 1999; Meichenbaum, 1977), mnemonic strategies such as keyword techniques (Mastropieri & Scruggs, 1991), and content enhancement strategies such as graphic organizers and guided notes (Lenz, Bulgren, & Hudson, 1990).

Positive Behavioral Supports

IDEA 1997 requires that IEP teams design behavioral intervention plans that include positive behavior supports for any student with a disability who is experiencing problems with behavior (McConnell, Hilvitz, & Cox, 1998). Positive behavioral supports include changes to antecedents and consequences of the problem behavior so that the triggers are diminished.

They also include curricular strategies and instructional supports that may increase the student's ability to resolve problems and interact socially in an acceptable manner, while limiting the need for and occurrence of the problem behavior. Critical to the success of the plan is the identification of alternative ways for the student to meet the personal needs that seem to be related to the problem behavior (Sugai, Horner, & Sprague, 1999).The strength of positive behavioral supports as a pro-active school or class-wide intervention lies in the potential for preventing problem behaviors from occurring by creating supportive environments that are designed to allow all students to meet important needs with socially acceptable and personally satisfying behaviors (Sugai & Horner, 2002).

Programming Models: Enhancements to General Education Pedagogies

A programming model is the organizational scheme by which instructional practices are organized, and the model chosen will relate to the ultimate goal for which the services are being instituted. As such, programming models have implications for both curriculum and instruction. These models do not dictate a particular physical location for service; rather they imply the school's or district's philosophy about the goals such services should be working to achieve (Robinson, Patton, Polloway, & Sargent, 1989). At least four models exist currently in the United States as organizational templates for special education services:

- Remediation in basic academic skills
- Tutorial services to assist students in the provided curriculum
- Cognitive strategies or study skills instruction
- Life skills or functional curricular approaches, including vocational and work-study programs

Following is a brief examination of the rationale for each of these models and the grade levels and levels of disability most often associated with each one.

Remediation in Basic Academic Skills

Programs using a remediation model operate under the philosophy that ameliorating basic academic skill deficits, particularly in reading, writing, spelling, and mathematics, is essential to later functioning. Instruction is provided at the learner's estimated functioning level. This means that a twelve-year-old whose instructional level for reading is at a second-grade level would work on skills needed at that level, using second-grade-level materials, and would gradually move into more advanced materials as competencies increase.

Remedial programs are most common at the elementary level, although they are also sometimes found in middle and high schools. Remediation is most useful in the early school years, when students have not yet fallen too far behind their peers and the gap to be remediated is not too large. They are deficit-driven, focusing on what a student cannot yet do. Remediation models frequently present problems with generalization of the remediated skills to other settings. Typically, the usefulness of this approach diminishes as the gap between classroom demands and student achievement increases. The stigma associated with a high school student's still doing "baby work" generally leads educators of adolescents to adopt one of the other models.

Tutorial Services

In this model, special education is viewed as a support to instruction in other content areas. The staff provides short-term assistance in the content areas in which the learner is having difficulty, using techniques such as content enhancement. The role of the special educator in a tutorial model is to keep the student functioning in the general education classroom. For example, a student might come to the resource room one day and receive help completing a science assignment, while another day, the special education teacher might provide drill on social studies content for a test the following period. Tutorial programs are typically instituted as students begin serious content-area study in the intermediate and middle school years, and are frequently perceived as being necessary for the students to "get by." Students tend to respond well to this model because of the help they receive in doing assignments, and general education teachers appreciate having someone to refer students to, thereby relieving them of having to provide the tutorial assistance themselves.

In other applications of this model, paraprofessionals are frequently involved in providing tutorial support in all grades, especially for students in inclusive settings. In some cases, a one-on-one instructional aide is assigned to a student and provides whatever support is needed to maintain the student in the general education classroom setting. A study by Giangreco, Edelman, Luiselli, and MacFarland (1997) investigated these relationships, finding that support by paraprofessionals must be used very carefully. Some of the negative outcomes associated with tutorial and behavioral support provided by one-on-one paraprofessionals included disruptions of social interactions of the student with a disability with class peers, a tendency for the student to develop significant dependence on adults, and an observation that the tutorial assistance and teaching by the paraprofessional does not always constitute the most competent instruction.

Cognitive Strategies or Skills Instruction

This approach, developed by Meichenbaum (1977) and Alley and Deshler (1979), is based on studies of the characteristics of students with disabilities and the match with school demands. These approaches work from the perspective that it is more efficient and effective to teach the student the thinking and organizational strategies used by capable learners than to teach content that quickly becomes obsolete. This philosophy is similar to the maxim that says, "Give a man a fish and he eats for today; teach him to fish and he eats for a lifetime."

This model has gained increasing support since the late 1980s. It is especially useful with middle and high school students as they struggle to function as independent learners in new settings. The cognitive strategy class may be offered as a curricular elective for any student experiencing difficulty with the secondary curriculum, or the instruction may form the basis of the student's support in the special education resource room. While instruction in cognitive strategies has been repeatedly shown to have long-term benefits, students who are accustomed to receiving tutorial services in the resource room may be resistant to using that support time to work for a distant goal. In addition, students whose reading and writing levels are too low may be unable to derive as much benefit from such instruction.

Life Skills or Functional Curricular Approaches

The goal of this model is to teach the student the most critical skills for functioning in the post-school world. The life skills curriculum includes survival reading skills, consumer mathematics, and other daily living skills. These programs may also address basic job skills and provide introductory work experiences. It is critical that the skills included in such a program have community validity and that they be taught in a way that facilitates generalization to home and community. The life skills teacher functions much like a coach, developing skills needed for independent living and economic self-sufficiency.

The life skills and functional curriculum approach is most often used with older students and with students who have more severe levels of disability, for whom some or all of the general education curriculum seems inappropriate or irrelevant. It is important that such models not be used prematurely or exclusively, closing off other future paths. In accordance with IDEA 1997, this model may be used with fewer students in the future. The case can be made, however, that a life skills focus allows relevant instruction to proceed in the goals and objectives of the general education curriculum, particularly for older students. The same reading, mathematics, and problem-solving skills are taught, but they are taught within a contextual setting that allows the student to apply them immediately. Students with and without disabilities, in other curricular models (e.g., diploma programs), may also benefit from such instruction and should not be excluded from participation in life skills programs.

Instructional Accommodations and Curricular Access

Studies indicate that teachers are generally aware of the limitations of commercially available instructional materials in supporting good instruction. Some teachers profess knowledge of a number of ways to modify instruction to better meet student needs, while others view their preparation as inadequate to meet the needs of students with disabilities (Welch, 1997). The research also indicates that in practice, actual modifications are minimal or nonexistent, and that modifications that are made often do not appear to involve changes sufficient to enable all students to learn (Baker & Zigmond, 1990; Simmons, Kameenui, & Chard, 1998; Vaughn, Moody, & Schumm, 1998). The research indicates that most instruction in general education classrooms is reasonably uniform, undifferentiated, and unresponsive to individual student needs (Baker & Zigmond, 1990).

In the context of such observations, it is easy to see why parents and special educators are wary about returning students with disabilities to general education classrooms. Their concern about the appropriateness of the general education curriculum is understandable when that curriculum is equated with teaching every student from the same basal textbook in the same way. Parents and special educators alike have difficulty imagining how sufficient accommodations can be made to the general education classroom instruction to the degree necessary to promote the learning of all children.

It is important to note, however, that these problems are not restricted to instruction in general education environments; similar findings have also come out of research on practices within special education. Studies on the use of instructional time and adaptations to curriculum to accommodate student needs within special education classes indicate a serious lack of time spent on direct instruction and relatively little individualization (Morsink, Soar, Soar, & Thomas, 1986; Steinberg & Knitzer, 1992; Vaughn, Moody, & Schumm, 1998). When individualization occurs, it most frequently is equated with individually assigned seatwork packets, but with little direct instruction, differentiated or otherwise (Haynes & Jenkins, 1986). Clearly the answer to instructional effectiveness is not related to small class size or to categorical or separate models of service. Answers must come from the body of research on effective teaching in general (Cannon, Idol, & West, 1992; Simmons & Kameenui, 1996).

As special educators and general education teachers seek to provide access to the general education curriculum for students with disabilities on a more equal footing, decisions will be needed about appropriate instructional accommodations with respect to content, instructional strategies, behavioral expectations, and instructional settings or contexts. In some cases, the degree of dissimilarity to classroom peers may even dictate an alternative location for the delivery of the general education curriculum.

One of the most obvious ways to increase access to the general education curriculum is to provide accommodations that will allow students to interact with the academic content unimpeded by their specific area of disability. Appropriate accommodations are designed to allow the student to focus on the essential nature of the learning task without being impeded by deficits in skills that are only indirectly related to the learning. Welch (1997) developed a decision-making structure, MATS, that focuses on the three parts of the instructional process: input, practice, and output. Instructional modifications can include adaptations to the ways in which students receive information; assistance with practice needed for storing and retrieving information, and tailoring the demands for expression of knowledge and skill to elicit what the student actually knows and can do. Within each of the three phases of instruction, adaptations can be designed relating to the four domains of instruction: materials (texts, audiovisual materials), activities (student behaviors during input and practice), teacher behaviors (modeling, strategy instruction, effective teaching practices), and student-grouping (cooperative learning, peer tutoring). MATS provides a structured process for teachers to use in identifying accommodations to resolve access problems for particular students (Welch, 1997).

Teachers frequently assert that making such accommodations is not fair to the other students. For example, in a vignette described by Buzzell and Piazza (1994), a general education history teacher responds to the request from the special educator for modifications for a student with a disability: "Don't expect those things to happen in my class. She seems like a nice kid, but she's going to sink or swim like the rest of them. It's not fair that her program gets modified like that and the other kids' programs don't. What am I supposed to tell them? Is Jodi that special?" (p. 212). An answer provided by Richard Lavoie (1989) is that it is fair because Jodi needs the accommodations, and the others don't. As long as teachers would make the same accommodations for any student who needed them, then it is fair. In fact, it would not be fair to withhold needed accommodations from a student like Jodi who needed them.

Universal Design for Learning

One answer to concerns about accessing the general education curriculum lies in the principles of universal design for learning (U.S. Office of Special Education Programs, 1999). Universal design is based on the philosophy that there are many ways to learn and to demonstrate the results of learning and that it is not reasonable to expect everyone to learn given a narrow range of options. Instruction that provides multiple means of engaging in learning tasks will be responsive to the needs of more learners. Instruction can be made available in a variety of modes of learning, and all students can be given access to productivity tools such as calculators and computers. Universally designed activities accommodate differing rates of completion. They also involve students and teachers working collaboratively. The teacher communicates high expectations for achievement and designs classroom supports to make that possible for diverse learners. While universal design does not eliminate the need for accommodations for some learners, it does reduce that need and opens up possibilities for learners who might have been overlooked or marginalized in classrooms with a more narrow perspective. For more information, readers may want to check the following web site: http://www.cast.org.

Focus on Culture and Diversity

It is not uncommon today for diverse students and their families to report feeling uncomfortable in classrooms because of a lack of fit with the curriculum or the pedagogical approaches in use. This discomfort may be related to the individual's race, ethnicity, language, religion, socioeconomic class, disability, gender, or sexual orientation. Among the principles of Universal Design for Learning is the assertion that instruction should be designed to be welcoming and inclusive of all students. Teachers who strive to create classroom climates that convey their comfort with diversity in the classroom convey to their students a deep respect for diverse talents. This principle is critical to assuring that all learners feel safe enough in the classroom to devote their energies to learning.

While the principles of Universal Design for Learning are certainly pertinent to curriculum and instruction for learners who differ with respect to ability, they also mean that the curriculum and instruction should be as inclusive as possible so that all students find relevance in it. It focuses on building a community of learners. It suggests that students of diverse backgrounds and learning preferences should find support for how they learn best, not as an add-on or special intervention, but as an everyday occurrence. While individual accommodations will still remain necessary from time to time, adherence to universal design will sharply reduce that need and include more students as a matter of course (U.S. Office of Special Education Programs, 1999).

Resources on the Web

Office of Special Education Programs (OSEP)
www.ed.gov/offices/OSERS/OSEP/IEP_Guide

Provides an excellent guide for parents and teachers about IEP regulations.

Center for Research on Learning

www.ku-crl.org

>   Contains information about learning strategies and the Strategies Intervention Model.

Cooperative Learning—Response to Diversity

www.cde.ca.gov/iasa/cooplrng2.html

>   Provides links to resources supporting cooperative learning in heterogeneous environments (California Department of Education).

OSEP Technical Assistance Center

www.pbis.org

>   Provides resources to assist in developing positive behavior support plans for students exhibiting problem behaviors.

National Center on Accessing the General Curriculum

www.cast.org/ncac

>   Provides information on Universal Design for Learning; makes the general education curriculum more accessible to students with broad ranges of abilities.

Alliance for Technology Access

www.ataccess.org

>   Provides resources related to assistive technology as well as Universal Design for Learning; includes resources for families as well.

ABLEDATA

www.abledata.com

>   Provides information on assistive technology devices useful for designing accommodation plans for students with disabilities.

Summary

IDEA 1997 brings clarification and some changes to the way special educators plan for instruction. The law stipulates that the IEP is to be organized around the needs of the child as they relate to the general education curriculum. The team must consider the strengths a student possesses, not only the deficits. Parents must be involved more fully in the process.

In the past, special educators have often viewed the child's IEP as the child's curriculum. Today, it is important to understand that Congress intends *curriculum* to refer to the general education curriculum for all students. It is important to understand the content of the explicit or public curriculum. It is also essential for the IEP team to consider the hidden curriculum, or the curriculum as taught. Finally, there are planning implications associated with the absent curriculum, those skills that are not taught, but that students with disabilities and others may need in order to benefit from instruction.

The *general education curriculum* refers to the content of instruction, not the location. Some students will be provided with access to that curriculum in the general education classroom with or without adaptations, while others will have it provided in other settings. For a small number of students, a modified curriculum may be designed, adapting specific content of the general curriculum that is not applicable to the student. For an even smaller number of learners with very severe disabilities, an alternative curriculum will be necessary.

While the curriculum is expected to be the same for all students, instruction may not be. It is in the design of instructional presentations and activities that teachers are asked to accommodate individual student needs. It is apparent from the body of educational research that there are many strategies that are helpful for students with varying needs. Some of these strategies include direct instruction (or effective teaching), peer tutoring, cooperative learning, and cognitive strategy instruction. In the future, it will be even more important to identify additional instructional practices useful in supporting the learning of heterogeneous groups of learners.

Programming models for students with disabilities are distinguished from one another by their purpose. Remediation is designed to make up deficits in basic literacy and mathematics skills. Tutoring models support learners in meeting the requirements of ongoing content instruction. Cognitive strategies instruction teaches students how to learn and how to profit from instruction across subject areas. Functional or life skills models focus on the application of basic skills to everyday living and working in preparation for independent functioning after graduation.

Instructional accommodations are frequently necessary if all students are to benefit from the general education curriculum. Research indicates that classrooms frequently offer few modifications and undifferentiated instruction. Appropriate accommodations allow the student to benefit from the central nature of the learning, unimpeded by the effect of the disability. Adaptations may be needed in content, in the instructional setting, in the behaviors needed to perform tasks, and in the demands for cognitive strategies. A variety of models are available for designing appropriate modifications, including Universal Design for Learning. Collaboration between general and special education teachers will ensure that the instruction is provided in a way that is both useful and appropriate.

ANGIE: A Case Study

Angie, a fourth grader in Ms. Allison's class, receives special education services in Ms. Peter's resource room. Angie began school in kindergarten in a suburban school. She made normal progress in the kindergarten curriculum, which was based on language development, content knowledge enrichment, and academic social skills. Her problems began in first grade with the early reading curriculum. She just didn't seem to be able to associate letters with sounds, and throughout the year she fell farther and farther behind. Her first grade teacher told her mother that Angie was careless and unmotivated. Her teacher said that Angie's problems in the reading curriculum

were undoubtedly due to these motivational factors, since Angie was obviously capable of learning. Frequently, Angie had to stay in for recess and revise reading worksheets that she had done incorrectly.

She was retained in first grade after her teacher suggested that another year might allow Angie to catch up developmentally with the others in her class. Angie's primary problem areas in reading and spelling continued the following year; it was as if she decided, "If you think I'm dumb, I'll just show you how dumb I am." She sat back and basically did as little as she could get away with. Despite her lack of effort, she made enough progress to move to second grade the next year. As the second grade curriculum broadened into more complex math skills and the beginning study of science and social studies, Angie began to blossom—as long as she didn't have to read. Her teachers still believed that motivation was her problem. Since she did well in the subjects she "liked," it must be that she wasn't working hard enough in reading and spelling.

The next summer, the family moved to Littletown, where Angie entered third grade. Her new teachers noted that she had very specific problems in reading, making slow progress in the basal reading curriculum. Her most significant difficulties in reading seemed to be related to difficulty with phonetics. Somewhere along the way, she became convinced that the goal in reading is to precisely and accurately sound out all the words. Angie tried hard to please her teachers and to prove to them that she wasn't lazy. This belief and her motivation to achieve resulted in her reading in a very labored way, a behavior that appeared to compromise her comprehension. Phonics deficits also showed up in her difficulty with spelling.

In fourth grade, Angie's classroom teacher suggested that Angie be referred for possible special education needs. Her full scale IQ score on the WISC-III was 119, and she achieved the following standard scores on the PIAT-R:

Subtest Scores	Standard Score
Reading Recognition	85
Reading Comprehension	95
Total Reading	86
General Information	129
Mathematics	120
Spelling	90

Based on this testing, it was determined that she met the district criteria as a student with a learning disability, and she began to receive special education services in spelling and reading. Angie worked hard in the resource room, but the teacher could tell that she was bored by the repetition and by the low cognitive level of the material she was given to read. Progress was very slow.

In the general education classroom, Angie continued to excel in her math and science work. Her teacher, Ms. Allison, noted that Angie really loved science. She loved doing experiments. She loved to use scientific words, the bigger the better, and she was excited about learning about computers. Her scores on a math achievement test indicated that she was significantly above her peers in math. On the most recent statewide achievement testing, she scored in the eighty-fifth percentile in math and science, receiving an award for this achievement. Her speaking vocabulary and expressive language skills were both highly developed.

Ms. Allison was glad that Angie was successful in these areas, and now that her reading and spelling were being taken care of by the special educator, those problems were of little concern to her in the general education program. Angie's reading and spelling difficulties faded from concern. Angie learned how to effectively compensate for her learning disability. Throughout all this, her mother was a significant support, telling her that she could do anything, that she knew that Angie would figure out her own way to get tasks done.

Ms. Peters, the resource room teacher, described Angie as a shy child who tended to become scared at times. Angie was not very secure with herself, and her self esteem was not as high as it could be. Despite her demonstrated areas of high achievement, the difficulties in reading and spelling led others, and sometimes Angie herself, to believe that she wasn't very smart. Ms. Peters was puzzled by this. She knew that the resource program was not challenging enough for Angie, and that because of her problems in reading, Angie was also not exposed to some of the more challenging opportunities in the general education curriculum.

Ms. Peters decided to investigate the possibility of Angie's participating in the district's honors program in fifth grade, while still receiving her learning disability services. The teacher in the honors program said she had heard of students who were both bright and had learning disabilities, but she had never seen one. She wasn't even sure she believed they existed. She also said that the criteria for the honors program were "very strict," so the idea was never pursued. Ms. Peters now wishes that she had pushed it. Angie shows such good thinking and her oral skills reflect a much higher level of functioning than indicated by her spelling and reading scores. Despite all the assistance Angie has received, it seems to Ms. Peters that something is still missing.

DISCUSSION

From the perspective of the general education curriculum, analyze the information provided about Angie. Have her teachers provided her with access to that curriculum? How?

To what extent does it appear that the basic skills remediation Angie has received in the resource room has been effective? Can you identify other approaches or instructional strategies that might increase her participation in the general education curriculum? What effect might these strategies have on her overall performance?

Consider the implications for instruction and curriculum of having significant intellectual strengths in addition to having a specific learning disability. How would Universal Design for Learning benefit a student like Angie?

CHAPTER FIVE

ISSUES IN PLACEMENT

QUESTIONS TO GUIDE YOUR STUDY

- What two factors does the IDEA identify as critical with respect to determining placement options for students with mild disabilities?
- What is the appropriate sequence of tasks in making programming and placement decisions for learners with disabilities?
- What does least restrictive environment (LRE) mean?
- Describe the continuum of services model and explain how it may be used to guide the placement process.
- What is inclusion?
- How does the philosophy of inclusion relate to the requirements of IDEA?

Meet Tamika

Tamika was first classified as a student with a learning disability when she was almost eight years old; she had repeated kindergarten and was in second grade. She had an IQ score of 97, but her reading was below the pre-primer level, as were her math and spelling skills. She was placed in a self-contained class for students with learning disabilities at Smithboro Elementary School, where she remained for the next two years.

At that time, Tamika and her family moved to another state, where she continued to receive special education services, but this time, she was provided with a couple of hours of resource room services each day, spending the rest of her day in a mainstream fourth- and fifth-grade classroom. Two years later, after a short stay in Illinois, the family moved back to Smithboro Elementary, and Tamika reenrolled as a sixth grader.

When she was evaluated on her return to Smithboro Elementary, Tamika's reading had remained at the pre-primer level, although her math had improved to skills at the second grade level. She

(continued)

was once again placed in a self-contained classroom, where she continues to struggle. Her teacher wonders how the moves have affected Tamika, and she is puzzled by the different placement decisions arrived at in the different states when Tamika's performance and needs apparently remained unchanged.

IDEA 1997: Location of Services

P.L. 94–142 was passed in 1975 to provide procedures for addressing three main questions: (1) Which students require assistance in order to benefit from their educational programs? (2) What educational objectives or learnings are appropriate for each student at a particular point in time? and (3) Where and by whom can those learnings best be achieved? In practice, the sequence in which these three questions have been answered has not always supported the best practice in serving youngsters with disabilities. The most commonly observed scenario at IEP planning meetings is shown in the vignette about Stephen (In the Classroom 5.1).

In the Classroom 5.1 illustrates several of the major concerns addressed by Congress as they passed the 1997 amendments to the IDEA. First, the team and the process focused only on identifying Stephen's areas of deficit. Although it is likely that Stephen possessed some areas of strength, the whole process was focused on determining what his problems were, whether their severity was enough to warrant special education, and where his special education needs could best be served. With the IDEA 1997 amendments, Congress explicitly states that the whole child must be considered, strengths as well as deficits, and not just with respect to academic performance.

Secondly, the process in In the Classroom 5.1 moved directly from identification to placement, matching Stephen's deficits with the variety of service models available. The team determined that the restrictive environment of the self-contained special class was most compatible with the disability category assigned to Stephen. In fact, if this district is like many, the mere fact that Stephen was identified as having an emotional disturbance probably assured that the only placement given serious consideration was the special classroom. In IDEA 1997, Congress stressed that the focus of discussion must return to the needs of the

IN THE CLASSROOM **5.1**

Placement and Planning Process in Action

Stephen's behavior had become more disruptive over the year. By February, Ms. Scott had submitted a referral for special education evaluation. Following the evaluation process, the team met and learned that Stephen exhibited aggressive behaviors toward peers significantly more often than others in his seventh grade classes did. His educational progress had been virtually nonexistent for about two years as indicated by state and individual assessments. Consequently, the team found that he met the criteria for identification as a child with an emotional disturbance.

Based on that determination, they reviewed the available placement options and determined that the self-contained classroom was the least restrictive placement that could address his demonstrated problem behaviors. Finally, they addressed what Stephen should be expected to achieve during the next year, and they drafted an IEP with appropriate goals and objectives. These goals and objectives were consistent with the programs already in place in Mr. Reynold's special education classroom, and Stephen was reassigned to that class beginning the following week.

child, particularly to those needs as they relate to the general education curriculum. Placements and plans must be based on students' needs, not on their disability category. As we will discuss in Units II and III, youngsters with the same disability label can vary significantly from one another in their needs. Plans based exclusively on a classification rarely adequately address the individual needs of children.

Thirdly, Stephen's IEP in In the Classroom 5.1 was developed after the placement had been determined. This common sequence of decisions increases the likelihood that the content of the IEP will relate more to the curriculum already in place in that particular special education classroom than it does to the student's needs and strengths. This is in conflict with the central premise of the IDEA and the 1997 amendments (see Chapter 4). The only valid educational reference points for educational planning, according to IDEA 1997, is the general education curriculum and the child's needs. The fact that this book has discussed educational planning and curricular issues prior to discussing placement, and as is demonstrated in Brandy's story in In the Classroom 5.2, highlights the process intended by Congress to ensure that services are delivered in the least restrictive environment.

Implementation of IDEA 1997 therefore supports and affirms the following sequence for program planning for youngsters with disabilities, as illustrated in In the Classroom 5.2:

- First, the team makes a careful assessment of the learner's strengths and needs with respect to participation in the general education curriculum, resulting in a full and detailed description of the student.
- Second, the interaction of those strengths and needs is evaluated with respect to the general education curriculum, and then goals and objectives are developed that will enable the student to progress in that curriculum.
- Finally, decisions are made about where the services should be provided and who should provide them, based on the premise that services should be provided in the

IN THE CLASSROOM **5.2**

Example of an Appropriate Placement Discussion

Brandy is in fourth grade and has been identified with a specific learning disability for two years. She is participating in the general education curriculum in all subject areas, but up to this time, she has been receiving her reading and spelling instruction in the resource room. At the IEP meeting, her fourth grade teacher and the resource room teacher described Brandy's year. She has made some progress in reading, having just completed the 2–2 level of the basal series used in the school. Her difficulties in spelling persist. Brandy's teachers observed that while she listens with good comprehension and has reasonable comprehension in silent reading, her oral reading and spelling have remained problematic. They concurred that Brandy's strengths in conceptual understanding and visual forms of language have enabled her to function fairly well this year in the fourth grade content. Her needs in the curriculum are related to her need to acquire independent study skills in content-area reading and to be able to write independently with accurate spelling.

The team decided that the rich context of the fourth grade content was an asset to Brandy, and that her objectives should focus on effectively using context clues for silent reading comprehension. In addition, since spelling is a tool skill that she was having trouble developing, it was decided that an objective related to efficient use of word processing would be appropriate at this point. After considering a few more areas of curricular concern, the team turned to the placement issue.

Although this instruction could certainly continue to be provided in the resource room, it was determined that the goals could be met equally as well within the general education class, and Brandy would not be missing ongoing instruction while traveling to and from the resource room. It was determined that next year Brandy would be best served by receiving indirect and direct services from the consultant teacher in the fifth grade classroom, with instruction and support for developing study skills and word processing expertise.

environment that provides the most access to the general education curriculum and to settings in which other children are served. Placement in a general education classroom, with supports as needed, should always be considered first.

Concept of the Least Restrictive Environment (LRE)

The concept of placement in the least restrictive environment (LRE) was originally defined in 1975 as part of P.L. 94–142, and the general principle remains in place in federal statute and state regulations guiding special education practice today, having been reauthorized by Congress in the IDEA 1997. In this landmark legislation, Congress mandated free and appropriate public education for all children and required that states and localities ensure that

to the maximum extent appropriate, children with disabilities, including those in public/ private institutions or other care facilities, should be educated with children who are not disabled, and that special classes, separate schooling, or other removal of children with disabilities from the regular educational environment occurs only when the nature and severity of the disability is such that education in regular classes with supplementary aids and services cannot be achieved satisfactorily. (U.S. Office of Education, 1977b, p. 42497)

IDEA implementation regulations also require states and districts to insure the availability of "a continuum of alternative placements to meet the needs of children with disabilities for special education and related services" (U.S. Office of Education, 1977b, p. 42497). A full continuum of services should include supplementary aids to support general education classroom placements, such as the services of consultant teachers, resource rooms, and itinerant instruction, as well as services in special classes and special schools, homebound and hospital instruction, and residential placement. The "overriding rule . . . is that placement decisions must be made on an individual basis" (U.S. Office of Education, 1977b, p. 42497).

One of the first consequences of the implementation of P.L. 94–142 was the review of all placements of learners in residential and day facilities that were distant from their home communities. New services were established in local districts, and many children were "brought home." One of the most frequently used placements at that time was the self-contained classroom, and many of these students were returned to self-contained classes or special schools nearer their homes. Lloyd Dunn (1968) questioned this reliance on special classes for students with mild retardation (see Chapter 2). He suggested that the needs of students with milder levels of impairment might be served more effectively by keeping them in general education classrooms and by using diagnostic, clinical, remedial, resource, itinerant, and consultant teachers to supplement and support the instruction they received there. He believed that such support personnel, functioning within the general education environment, would help develop programs of remediation that more closely matched the individual needs of the learner. Seven years later, in 1975, Congress agreed, and local school districts have been working on achieving those ends ever since.

Data submitted by school districts and states indicated that from 1984 through 1999, patterns of services for students with disabilities changed significantly. Over that period, use of general education class placements (defined by the federal government as being served out of the general education classroom for less than 21 percent of the school day) increased from 24.6 percent to 47.4 percent. During the same time, there was a corresponding decrease in use of more restrictive settings (U.S. Department of Education, 2001). Other patterns were found in the IDEA data. When placement options for 1998–1999 were analyzed by age, 57 percent of all elementary children with disabilities were served in general education settings, but only 38.4 percent of students in the adolescent years, with a corresponding increase in more restrictive placements. Placement rates varied widely by disability as well, as presented in Table 5.1, with students with mental retardation and emotional disturbance more likely to be served in restrictive settings. Finally, when the placement data is analyzed by race, it becomes apparent that students from racial groups other than white are more likely to be served in more restrictive settings (see Table 5.2).

In most school districts, a variety of placement options are available for consideration by IEP teams. Once a team has determined the strengths and needs of the student and has considered how those characteristics might interact with the general education curriculum, they are ready to determine how to best support the student's learning. "Benefit from their educational program" is the standard established for appropriate services by the Supreme Court in *Board of Education* v. *Rowley* (Turnbull & Turnbull, 1998). For many students with disabilities, it will be determined that supports provided within the general education classroom will

TABLE 5.1   Placement Rates by Disability, Students Aged 6–21 (1998–1999)

Disability	General Education Class	Resource Room	Separate Class	Separate School	Residential Facility	Home/ Hospital
Learning Disabilities	45.11%	38.43%	15.49%	0.64%	0.15%	0.17%
Mental Retardation	13.76%	29.25%	51.07%	5.04%	0.49%	0.39%
Emotional Disturbance	25.52%	23.04%	33.18%	13.30%	3.59%	1.36%
All Disabilities	47.43%	28.44%	20.07%	2.91%	0.68%	0.47%

General Education: Less than 21% of day outside general education classroom

Resource Room: 21–60% of day outside general education classroom

Separate Class: Services out of general education classroom more than 60% of the day

From U.S. Department of Education, 2001, p. A81–89.

TABLE 5.2   Placement Rates by Race, Students Aged 6–21 (1998–1999)

	General Education Class	Resource Room	Separate Class	Separate School	Residential Facility	Home/ Hospital
American Indian	48.2%	34.4%	14.6%	1.5%	0.9%	0.4%
Asian/Pacific Islander	47.0%	26.6%	22.2%	3.1%	0.6%	0.5%
Black	34.8%	28.2%	31.5%	4.2%	0.9%	0.5%
Hispanic	41.2%	29.1%	26.1%	2.6%	0.5%	0.6%
White	52.3%	28.4%	15.3%	2.7%	0.6%	0.5%
Total Population	47.4%	28.4%	20.1%	2.91%	0.7%	0.5%

General Education: Less than 21% of day outside general education classroom

Resource Room: 21–60% of day outside general education classroom

Separate Class: Services out of general education classroom more than 60% of the day

From U.S. Department of Education, 2001, p. III-4.

allow them to benefit from their educational programs. For some, it will be necessary to provide instruction related to some components of the general education curriculum in a resource room or special class setting. For only a small number of students with the most severe disabilities will it be determined that, even with supports, no part of the general education program is appropriate or possible, and placement in the more restrictive settings (special class, special school, or residential settings) will be necessary.

Implementation of the continuum of services is guided by the principles illustrated in Figure 5.1 (Deno, 1970; Reynolds, 1989; Ysseldyke, Algozzine, & Thurlow, 2000). The relative widths of the elements of the diagram are intended to suggest that many more students will be appropriately served at the higher, less restrictive levels than will need to be placed in the lower, more restrictive settings. The IEP team is required to consider the educational

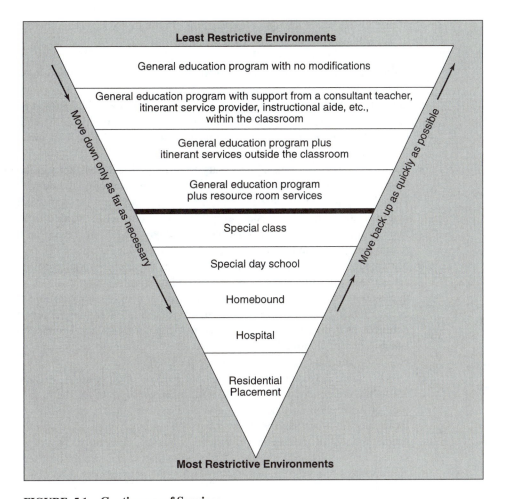

FIGURE 5.1   Continuum of Services
Based on Deno (1970); Reynolds (1989); Yssledyke, Algozzine, & Thurlow (2000).

needs of the child and the instructional goals and objectives they have identified, and then to move only as far down the continuum as necessary to find an appropriate placement. Once the student has been placed, it is the responsibility of all the student's teachers to provide services and supports that will make movement back to a less restrictive environment possible in the future.

Models of Service Commonly Used for Students with Mild Disabilities

Decades of serving learners in a manner consistent with the guidance provided by IDEA, court interpretations, and IDEA 1997 suggests that most learners with mild disabilities can be appropriately served at the upper levels of the continuum of services. The characteristics of these placement options are as follows:

- For some students, the evaluation process will identify accommodations that can be employed within the general education class and that will allow the student to progress in that curriculum without direct service by special education personnel. In such cases, the special education staff will generally provide consultation services (indirect services) to the general education teacher, who will in turn deliver the instructional program to the student.

- For other students, it will be necessary to provide direct assistance in the classroom by a special educator, related services provider, or instructional aide for parts of the school program. Such assistance might involve coteaching and monitoring by the general education–special education team to develop skills needed in that environment. Sometimes an instructional aide assists youngsters in staying on task or with reading support (Giangreco, Edelman, Luiselli, & MacFarland, 1997).

- Some students with very specific educational needs may require out-of-classroom services several times a week by an itinerant provider. Examples of such specialized needs are speech and language services, vision or hearing supports, and physical and occupational therapy, or other related services. Such activities target specific skill deficiencies in areas needed for success in the general education curriculum. Specific training in articulation, for example, can allow a student to participate in the general education language arts program with typical peers.

- Other learners have specific developmental needs (e.g., reading, written language), and while the general education curriculum is appropriate for them, the pacing and type of instruction may not be. In these cases, the general education curriculum in those specific areas may be delivered in the resource room, although the youngster spends the rest of the day in the general education classroom. This type of pull-out service can be disruptive to the child's adjustment, and should be used only when appropriate instruction cannot be achieved in the general education class.

For the vast majority of learners with mild disabilities in learning and behavior, one of these options should be appropriate in meeting their needs in the general education curriculum and allowing them to receive educational benefit from their school programs. In all cases, however, the decision is based on the needs of the individual student, not on the categories and not on the fact that a district has or does not have particular services available.

On occasion, the nature and severity of a specific problem might suggest short-term placement in a more restrictive setting, with the goal of providing intensive intervention and returning the child to a less restrictive environment as soon as possible. Following are two examples of such situations:

- Jim, a student with an emotional-behavioral disorder, exhibits a period of severe problem behavior, making continued placement in the general education class inappropriate for himself or others for the time being. The team may recommend a temporary placement in a special class, day school, or even in a residential setting where Jim can get intensive short-term counseling and behavioral interventions to prepare him to return to his home school and class.

■ Jane, a student with mild mental retardation, recently fell on the ice, resulting in a severe fracture. She is required to stay in bed for two months while it mends. Her physical needs dictate that homebound instruction is appropriate so that her progress in the general education curriculum is not disrupted.

Inclusion: A Continuing Issue in Special Education

Inclusion has been one of the most hotly debated topics in special education since the early 1980s. Articles appear regularly in special education journals, some advocating full inclusion of all students with disabilities, others urging the preservation of separate and specialized educational services. Books such as *Controversial Issues Confronting Special Education: Divergent Perspectives* (W. Stainback & S. Stainback, 1996) and *Critical Issues in Special Education* (Ysseldyke, Algozzine, & Thurlow, 2000) include significant and prominent discussion of the various perspectives on inclusion.

One reason for the continuing debate is the fact that inclusion is defined differently by various people (see Table 5.3). One group of proponents views *inclusion* and *mainstreaming*

TABLE 5.3 Mainstreaming, Least Restrictive Environment, and Inclusion

Mainstreaming

The temporal, physical, instructional, and/or social integration of children with disabilities with typical peers; in general, children with disabilities are "mainstreamed" into environments where their disabilities presents few impediments and where the need for accommodations is minimal; special education services are still generally provided outside the "mainstream" environment

Least Restrictive Environment

The term used in the IDEA to refer to the principle that children with disabilities should be educated with their typical peers as often as possible, and that removal to more specialized (restrictive) settings should occur only when it is not possible, even with the provision of supplementary aids and supports, to serve students with disabilities in general education settings; refers to the principle that services should be delivered in settings as similar as possible to the general education classroom

Inclusion

The practice of providing students with disabilities all of their educational services within the general education program; support services required by any student are integrated into the general education program

Partial Inclusion

A variant on the inclusion model in which most of a student's program is delivered in general education settings with supports, but in which students may also be pulled out of the classroom for specialized services as dictated by their individual needs

as synonymous terms. *Mainstreaming* actually refers to the philosophy that children with disabilities should be educated with children without disabilities to the maximum extent possible and is related to the principle of normalization (see Chapter 2). It generally refers to the placement of children in activities unaffected by their disabilities. It implies nothing beyond physical proximity, although the possibility and utility of modifying the classroom program to accommodate mainstreamed children is frequently discussed. Although the term does not appear in the IDEA, many educators and parents still believe that the law requires mainstreaming.

Inclusion refers to some degree of actual integration of the two systems, from collaboration and partial integration to a fully unified system. The term initially arose from the debate about the efficacy and morality of a dual system of education (Gartner & Lipsky, 1987; Lipsky & Gartner, 1987; Reynolds, 1989; W. Stainback & S. Stainback, 1984; S. Stainback & W. Stainback, 1988; Wang, Reynolds, & Walberg, 1986; Will, 1986). Drawing from the reasoning of the courts in *Brown* v. *Board of Education* (1954) that separate is inherently unequal, these writers questioned the morality of a dual system composed of special education and general education (Biklen, 1985; Zigler, Hodapp, & Edison, 1990). Some suggested that special education in segregated settings is indefensible and inherently discriminatory, even if it were shown to be effective, just as the Supreme Court had found "separate but equal" education for black and white students to be inherently unequal (S. Stainback & W. Stainback, 1988). In addition, special education has not yet demonstrated that it is able to achieve the kind of improvements that disability advocates had projected from an individualized, universally available, separate educational process. Inclusion proponents attributed part of the efficacy problem to the continued separation from real environments and curricula, creating low expectations for students. As Lipsky and Gartner wrote in 1987:

> In education, not only have students with handicapping conditions been ignored in the recent flood of national reports, but the belief persists that they are incapable of learning and behaving appropriately. This leads state education departments, school systems, and the courts to excuse them across the board from the academic, social, and behavioral expectations and standards held for other students. (p. 70)

Lipsky and Gartner went on to call for "changing the mainstream, and making general education flexible, supple, and responsive—educating the full range of students" (p. 72).

Madeleine Will (1986), addressed these issues in "Educating Children with Learning Problems: A Shared Responsibility." Will began with the assertion that the special education system continues to support the premise that children with disabilities cannot be effectively served in general education settings, even with modifications and supports. She believed that reliance on a variety of separate or pull-out programs has led to further separation. Will stated that this system creates the sense that poor school performance is a reliable indicator of disabilities, and she faulted this system, which she said was set up to assist students who had already failed badly, rather than to prevent failure in the first place. Noting that the American educational system was failing more students than ever before, Will urged that attention be directed to developing ways to use our existing resources more efficiently, supporting all children who were having difficulty learning. In closing, Will advocated creating a system in which special education and general education worked in partnership "to cooperatively assess the educational needs of students with learning problems and to cooperatively develop effective educational strategies for meeting those needs. . . . It does mean the nurturing of a shared commitment to the future of all children with special learning needs" (p. 415).

Such calls for the general education program to stretch and take in students with disabilities led to two perspectives relative to inclusion. One group sees nothing short of the elimination of the special education system, with all its categories and special settings, as the way to solve the problem. They envision the return of all children to the general education classroom, regardless of the severity of the disability. They look forward to a day when all education would be "special," when the individual characteristics and needs of all children are addressed as a matter of course, and when all children would be included.

The other group of inclusion proponents takes a more cautious approach, that is more closely allied with the concept of least restrictive environment established in the IDEA and that is consistent with Will's call for shared responsibility. These educators believe that full-time or part-time placement in the general education setting is possible for more children than are now being served there, although some students will still need services that can only be provided in special classrooms and schools. They call for IEP teams to consider more carefully the possibility that the supports currently provided in resource and special classes might be made available in the general education classroom. They believe that in so doing, schools will find that more students are capable of participating full-time in the general education environment while still receiving educational benefit. This perspective is best exemplified by the policy statement on inclusive schools and community settings adopted by the Council for Exceptional Children (1994a; see Appendix A). CEC called inclusion a "meaningful goal," stating that educators could make the general education classroom a viable alternative for more children if general education settings were strengthened with additional supports and resources.

Learning from the Research on Inclusion

One of the most frequently uttered statements with regard to the efficacy of inclusion and other placement models, such as resource rooms, is that there is no good evidence of the effectiveness of various placements—that the limited research which does exist is inconclusive. Support for or opposition to inclusion tends to be founded more on philosophical than empirical grounds. As noted by Vaughn and Schumm (1995), most professional and advocacy organizations have issued position statements on the question. These statements range from unqualified support for full inclusion by the Association for Persons with Severe Handicaps (TASH), to statements supporting inclusion as one element within a full continuum of services (CEC, 1994a) to position statements from organizations supporting continued separate specialized services such as the Council for Learning Disabilities and Learning Disabilities Association.

Despite these expressions of support for one model or another, the existing research base remains plagued by small samples and experimental designs that lack the power to detect differences, much less establish causal links. Researchers frequently have to work with intact groups, comparing children with disabilities served in general education classrooms with those served in resource rooms, as in a study reported by Schulte, Osborne, and McKinney (1990). This team attempted to randomly assign students to one of four conditions: indirect services (consultation), direct services plus consultation, resource room for one period, and resource room for two periods. When pretest data was taken, however, the researchers found that despite their efforts at random assignment, the group receiving two periods of resource room had lower intelligence and achievement scores going into the study. One can conjecture about the reasons for this, but the fact remains that we expect and the law requires that the setting selected for a child will match the child's needs. Comparing the progress of children in inclusion models with the progress made by their counterparts in resource settings frequently produces unconvincing results simply because the groups were not initially comparable.

Research into the efficacy of placement options generally evaluates the outcomes observed in students placed in different environments. A study by Deno, Maruyama, Espin, and Cohen (1990) comparing outcomes associated with resource placements to integrated models failed to support either setting as clearly more beneficial for students with mild disabilities. A study of reading achievement of students after placement in an inclusive setting by Shinn, Powell-Smith, Good, and Baker (1997) indicated that the gains students made were comparable to their general education counterparts, and that the benefit increased the longer the study went on. A qualitative study by Guterman (1995) looked at the opinions of secondary students served part-time in resource classes and part-time in general education classes. In this study, "place" was the only variable considered. The students complained about special education classes that failed to challenge them and about general education classes that were unresponsive to their needs. The results of studies such as these do not allow us to conclude that either special education or inclusion is preferable. The lack of conclusive evidence does suggest that it may be more important to determine what is actually happening in the "place" than to debate what place should be utilized (Coleman, Pullis, & Minnett, 1987).

Krauss (1990) pointed out that the setting frequently becomes part of the service, and that services and settings together become the treatment variable that must be tailored to meet a child's needs. One way of investigating these phenomena is to use the transactional perspective (Ysseldyke, Algozzine, & Thurlow, 2000). This approach holds that all the variables affect the others—that the child's characteristics interact with the setting and the setting affects the child's characteristics. The central questions that must be asked as we evaluate the appropriateness of any setting variable include: What is happening to individual children? Are their individual needs being met? Is the setting supportive of the instructional and social variables needed to support each child's growth and development?

Vaughn and Schumm (1995) reported on one of the few long-term and large-scale studies of the implementation of inclusion of students with learning disabilities. Working with three schools in the context of restructuring efforts, they followed the four-year evolution of three distinct approaches to including youngsters with disabilities in the more normalized environment of the general education classroom. From this research, they identified a number of characteristics of "responsible inclusion," defined as "the development of a school-based education model that is student centered and that bases educational placement and service provisions on each student's needs" (p. 265). They asserted that the goal of responsible inclusion is that each child should be served in the general education setting unless the child's academic and social needs cannot be met there. A full continuum should continue to exist, with inclusion being the component that is considered first by the IEP team

TABLE 5.4   Characteristics of Responsible and Irresponsible Inclusion

Responsible Inclusion	Irresponsible Inclusion
Consider the *student* first: students' needs guide all placement decisions	Consider the *place* first: location is of primary importance
Teachers choose to participate in inclusive models	Teachers are mandated to participate
Adequate resources are provided	Need for resources is not considered; inclusion may be seen as a way to save money
Models are developed by school-based teams to fit the school culture	Model is dictated from district or state level; one size fits all
The full continuum is maintained	Full inclusion is the only model offered
Service delivery is subject to ongoing formative evaluation	No formative evaluation is implemented; model failures are blamed on personnel
Ongoing professional development is provided	Professional development needs are not considered
Philosophy of inclusion is developed by school personnel, and the philosophy guides service delivery	No philosophical base is in place
Curricula and instruction to meet student needs are developed and revised	Specialized curricular needs are not considered

From "Responsible Inclusion for Students with Learning Disabilities" by S. Vaughn and J. S. Schumm, 1995, *Journal of Learning Disabilities, 28* (5), 264–270, 290. Copyright 1995 by PRO-ED, Inc. Adapted and reprinted by permission.

for goodness of fit with the student's needs. Table 5.4 summarizes the characteristics of responsible inclusion models as identified by Vaughn and Schumm.

Implementation of inclusion of students with emotional and behavioral disorders presents additional challenges, as described by Cheney and Muscott (1996). These challenges, which result in such students being more likely than students with other disabilities to be educated in separate classes or schools (U.S. Department of Education, 1994, p. 110), include the following (see Table 5.1):

- The behaviors of these students are extremely variable and often disturbing, requiring additional supports.
- Many general educators seem unwilling to consider that they may have some responsibility for students with challenging behaviors, preferring to defer to special educators for service.
- Classroom teachers generally are underprepared to deal with such behaviors and feel less competent with such students.
- Lack of differentiated curricula and modifications in general education compromises the success of these students in general education settings.

- Students with emotional or behavioral disabilities frequently require other services within and beyond the school day, and general education teachers are not accustomed to working within a coordinated system of services.
- Reintegration of students who have spent time in more intensive and restrictive models is frequently resisted by general education teachers.

Cheney and Muscott (1996) suggested that the same principles of responsible inclusion identified by Vaughn and Schumm (1995) also apply to serving students with emotional or behavioral disorders. They suggested that support to families is particularly critical to the effectiveness of any service model with this group of learners. Finally, they observed that the extreme variation in severity represented by these students makes it critical for the full continuum of services to be maintained, although it is also important to build the capacity of general education settings to serve these youngsters. Clearly, the extent to which schools and teachers are prepared to facilitate inclusion significantly affects the effectiveness of inclusion of students with disabilities.

Much of the debate on inclusion is derived from the experiences of parents, students, and teachers before the implementation of P.L. 94–142 when students with milder forms of disability sat unidentified and unserved in general education classrooms. Concern about inclusion stems from the fear that returning such students from their resource and special class placements to the general education classroom will mean a return to no services at all. This fear is bolstered by the occasional reports that inclusion is being implemented by districts as a way of containing special education costs, with no supports to teachers or students in general education classes.

It is critical to remember that the placement or setting is merely a contextual variable in which the more important social and instructional events occur. The importance of the setting is in its interaction with instructional and social activity. In retracing the history of the development of services for people with mental retardation, Zigler, Hodapp, and Edison (1990) observed that focusing exclusively on the place in which services are delivered is misguided. These researchers observed that it is a mistake to view classrooms only as places, as "social addresses," rather than as locations within which social interactions of importance occur. They pointed out that there is, as of yet, no clear, unambiguous answer to the question of which setting is best. They urged returning attention to the needs of the individual, rather than continuing the philosophical debate about whether special classrooms or general education classrooms are more appropriate settings.

Focus on Culture and Diversity

Issues of culture and diversity have historically played a central role in discussions about where children should receive their educational services. Segregated schools were the norm in the United States until the 1954 *Brown* v. *Board of Education* decision declared that separate is inherently unequal. Placements within special education have followed this pattern as well. Early special education services were in very segregated and isolated facilities. As sensitivities changed, placements became less restrictive, with almost half of all students with disabilities today served in general education for more than 80 percent of their days.

However, not all students with disabilities have benefited from this trend. The rates of inclusion in general education are significantly lower for students with disabilities who are identified as African American or Hispanic (U.S. Department of Education, 2001). They also have higher rates of placement in separate classes for more than 80 percent of the day. These disproportionate placement rates are of concern since one explanation is that the system is affected by institutional racism that is endemic to our evaluation instruments and our referral and decision-making processes (Salend, Garrick Duhaney, & Montgomery, 2002). It has been hypothesized that lack of cultural awareness may lead some educators to see normative cultural behaviors as problematic and in need of special education. Disproportionately low numbers of educators of color compound the problem. Future special education professionals must attend to this phenomenon to assure that all students receive needed services and that special education is not used to exclude students who are characterized as being culturally diverse.

Resources on the Web

IDEAS That Work

www.ideapractices.org

> Provides comprehensive information on IDEA, updates on IDEA regulations related to placement of students with disabilities.

U.S. Office of Special Education and Rehabilitative Services (OSERS)

www.ed.gov/offices/OSERS/IDEA/index.html

> The federal office charged with overseeing special education services; provides direct access to all governmental resources concerning LRE and the IDEA.

National Association of Protection and Advocacy Systems

www.protectionandadvocacy.com

> Provides information on the rights of students with disabilities, including the right to be served in the Least Restrictive Environment.

OSEP Technical Assistance Center

www.pbis.org

> Provides resources to assist in developing positive behavior support plans to facilitate the inclusion of students with disabilities in the Least Restrictive Environment.

Summary

The placement provisions of IDEA 1997 direct educational practice for students with disabilities back to the original intent of the law. By stating that the only valid considerations in planning are the general education curriculum and the interaction of the child's characteristics with that environment, IDEA 1997 refocused attention on meeting the needs of individual children. Thus, determining the placement where services will be provided is the third step in the process, coming after the student's strengths and needs have been identified and the curriculum objectives have been determined.

Least Restrictive Environment (LRE) refers to the provision in the IDEA that students shall not be removed any farther from the general education classroom than is necessary to meet their needs. Furthermore, the law requires that a full continuum of services be available, including the general education classroom, the general education classroom with support, itinerant services, resource room services, special classes, special school, homebound, hospital, and residential placements.

Since the 1980s, philosophical, political, and pedagogical debates have continued over the concept of inclusion. Central to the debate is the fact that there is no common definition of this term. Concern over the lack of efficacy of special education services and the observed fragmentation of services has led some to call for the creation of a unified system, one that meets every child's learning needs without classification and segregation. Research into effective inclusion practices has indicated that programs that are developed by local school staff to meet local needs, that are well supported with resources, and that include a commitment to significant staff development tend to be more effective. One thing is clear: Place alone does not ensure a quality program or good outcomes. The setting, or placement, is merely the context in which services are provided. The critical variable is how the settings and services interact to address a student's needs and to increase positive outcomes.

BENNY: A Case Study

Benny was the youngest child in a family of ten, growing up in a small rural community in western Pennsylvania. His parents were hard-working subsistence farmers who grew most of their own food, with neither employed outside the home. Benny's brothers and sisters had all been in special education during their school years, with the older ones working at minimum-wage jobs. There was a very strong work ethic in this family. There might not have been a lot of money, but they all took pride in working for what they had.

Benny began kindergarten at Mooretown Elementary School. From the beginning, Benny always seemed to be in some kind of trouble. He was very active and lacked appropriate social skills. He didn't seem to know how to act in such a large group of children. He got into trouble for not staying in his seat; even in the kindergarten classroom, a very active place with lots of moving around, he was constantly in need of redirection to stay on task. He was academically behind his peers from the start, lacking

many of the readiness skills needed for academic work, with particular problems in language.

Considering his home environment, Benny's problems were not hard to understand. With only three bedrooms, the house was quite small for such a large family. The television was always on, adding background noise to all the other activity. There was no place for everyone to sit down and eat at one time. The table in the kitchen is always covered with dishes, food, prescriptions, and more. Doing something with the whole family all at the same time was not a part of Benny's experience.

Because of Benny's problems in school, the kindergarten teacher soon referred him for special education evaluation. The testing revealed an IQ score of 72 and confirmed significant deficiencies in academic readiness skills and language development. Some members of the multidisciplinary team thought that he might be most appropriately labeled as a student with mild mental retardation, but they finally decided on the category of speech and language impairment because of his language delays. Benny continued to be served in the kindergarten classroom, where he received in-class services from Ms. Collins, the speech therapist, and from Mr. Brown, the consultant teacher.

Benny was singled out in class because of his appearance. He wore a lot of hand-me-downs, usually ill-fitting, and generally dirty. The other children kept their distance because of his odor. Mr. Brown decided that something needed to be done, so each day when Benny arrived at school, Mr. Brown saw that he got some breakfast and looked him over to see if he was ready for school. Mr. Brown took him to the shower two or three times a week. The first time he took Benny to shower, it became apparent that Benny didn't know how to operate the shower controls; soon, shampoo and water was everywhere. Mr. Brown tried to teach him how to bathe, all the time thinking, "There's no way I could have envisioned this scene in college." By 9:00, Benny would be back in the classroom, presentable enough so that the other kids would work with him.

Benny had a number of other inappropriate behaviors that also caused the other children to avoid working with him. Swearing was a normal form of communication in his home. In conversations at school, it would just come out. He also had a tendency to hug and kiss people as a way of expressing his appreciation for assistance. The other children seemed uneasy around Benny.

At the end of the kindergarten year, Benny's family began working with a caseworker from social services. She told Benny's mother that he really needed to be in a self-contained classroom. Since Mooretown Elementary did not have such a class, this meant that Benny would have to go to another school, leaving his home town. Mr. Brown disagreed; he didn't think sending him out of town to another school was the best thing for Benny. He believed strongly that Benny needed, more than anything, to socialize with a variety of children, and not to spend all of his time only with other students with disabilities. Mr. Brown felt that Benny would learn more and develop more appropriate social skills staying at Mooretown, going to school with the children who would be his playmates after school. Benny's mother was confused by the debate, and she asked Mr. Brown what to do. He explained the options, and also told her that Benny could get the

special help he needed at Mooretown. In the annual review at the end of the year, the multidisciplinary team, including Benny's mother, decided that he should stay at Mooretown for now.

The next fall, Benny was placed in a regular first grade class, where he received special education services for about half the day. His special education services included the services of an aide who worked with him part-time in the first grade classroom, and reading instruction in a small group taught by Mr. Brown.

Math was a strong point for Benny, and he was proud of that. He knew the value of money and was good at addition. One day, when Benny was adding 5 and 6, Mr. Brown asked why he was blinking his eyes. He said, "Well, that's [blink right eye] eleven, and this [blink left eye] is twelve." That was his way of doing it!

However, throughout first grade, Benny continued to have significant problems in reading. He was willing to try almost anything at least once, but he really disliked reading. He didn't know the alphabet, and he had never had the experience of being read to at home. Coming into a school culture that expects children to have had experience with books, to enjoy books, and to be receptive to learning to read, Benny was at a disadvantage because he never had this exposure to books at home.

Though books were foreign to him, Benny did know a lot about trees and animals. Mr. Brown learned that at age six, Benny could already identify about twenty different kinds of trees. He knew how to look for signs of animals, and he could identify their tracks. His family hunted, and he was often out in the woods with his father, cutting wood. Benny was always wondering about things, asking questions, like "What's this?" and "How does this work?" He had a lot of knowledge; it just wasn't *school* knowledge.

Benny was basically a happy child. He had his bicycle and a fishing pole, and to him, that was everything. But school was not a positive experience for him. It seemed to him that every time he was doing something, somebody told him not to do it. He complained to Mr. Brown, "I can't do anything. Everyone is telling me not to do this or that, or do it this way. Why can't I just do it the way I want to do it?"

One day the next summer, Mr. Brown stopped by Benny's house, just to check on him. Benny was

(continued)

muddy from play, wearing just a pair of cut-offs and no shoes. Mr. Brown, Benny, and Benny's mother stood outside talking for a long time. Over the next three hours, other family members joined in, standing around the truck, talking about everything under the sun.

Mr. Brown realized that he had learned a lot from this conversation. Even though Benny's parents might not show up for parent conferences, or send back the folder that went home each Friday, it didn't mean they didn't care about their son. Their way was just different from the school's way. They loved him, and he loved them. Mr. Brown saw that it was difficult for this family to interact with a system that saw them as failures. Benny's mother had quit school in eighth grade and had also spent some time at the state hospital for depression. She believed that her husband saved her from the hospital. However, she told Mr. Brown that Benny's father could also be a "mean, mean man." There was a lot of child abuse in the home. One time his father threatened to put Benny's head in the wood stove, and it took some of Benny's older brothers to keep their father from doing it. Mr. Brown learned that Benny had a temper, too. Once, when he was only six years old, he took a gun and fired it at his father, missing him. Despite these events, Benny talked about his father as the most important man in the world.

The next year in second grade, Benny's academic deficits finally justified his identification as a child with a learning disability. Mr. Brown continued to struggle with the question of labeling, with needing to identify this child as a student with a specific condition. He wondered if Benny had a disability or if the family's cultural differences brought Benny, his brothers, sisters, and cousins into special education. He thought that Benny probably did have some sort of disability; he certainly had a speech problem, and his language and reading skills remained very poor. His behavior also really caused him problems in school. Mr. Brown said, "I try not to get stuck on the label. I told the team that it really doesn't matter what the label is as long as Benny gets the services he needs."

Benny always seemed to make his presence known. Most people saw this as bad, but Mr. Brown viewed it as positive. In class, at an assembly, or at a Christmas concert, wherever Benny was, he always made people notice him. He was always smiling a mischievous kind of grin. To Mr. Brown, these antics seemed like Benny's way of getting people to notice him, of making his mark on the world.

This need to impress people eventually brought about a near-fatal accident when Benny was eight. Benny had ridden downtown on his bike where he met up with some classmates who were playing near the railroad track. The train whistle blew in the distance, and the boys started talking about "making the train stop." In his need to be noticed, to be somebody, Benny was the last to leave the track. When Mr. Brown heard about the incident, he was greatly concerned.

DISCUSSION

Review the information about Benny in the above case study. Identify as many strengths and deficits as you can, information that the team might use to develop an IEP for Benny.

From this analysis, do you believe that any portion of the general education curriculum is appropriate for Benny? If so, identify five objectives that would assist Benny in profiting from that curriculum.

Review the IEP team's placement discussion in light of your analysis. What do you think is the appropriate level of service for Benny? What supports will he need to profit from the general education program? Be prepared to defend your answer.

WHO ARE THE LEARNERS WITH MILD DISABILITIES?

Who are the learners with mild disabilities? How do we identify a child with a disability? In considering these questions, we embark on the most basic of human cognitive activities. Human beings seek to give meaning to people, things, and events by grouping them with like entities. The field of special education has likewise endeavored to create order within the universe of human ability and difference. As individuals were identified who differed from their peers, their central characteristics were enumerated. Those with sufficient similarities were grouped into categories, giving rise to the disability categories we use today.

The challenge then became to develop definitions or rules to determine if a particular person belonged to that group or not. "Definitions cannot be right or wrong, or true or false, but only useful or not useful. A useful definition . . . would aid in the classification system that has two major goals: (1) to benefit those classified by being helpful to their clinicians and service providers, and (2) to bring much-needed order to the field, while directing workers to important issues in need of further study" (Zigler & Hodapp, 1986, p. 63).

The reader is encouraged to consider whether efforts to date have been useful in achieving those two goals. What benefits do learners derive from being classified within our current systems? Do our current systems bring order to the field and facilitate the delivery of services? Are there issues we should continue to address as we seek to support the learning and living of all children and youth?

CHAPTER SIX

LEARNERS WITH MENTAL RETARDATION

QUESTIONS TO GUIDE YOUR STUDY

- What does the history of mental retardation teach us?
- How do we define mental retardation?
- How does the 2002 AAMR definition differ from previous definitions?
- What are the current issues in defining mental retardation?
- How do we designate the levels of severity of mental retardation?
- What are students with mental retardation like?
- How prevalent is the condition we call mental retardation?
- What causes mental retardation?

Meet Caroline

Caroline entered a small rural public school in 1980 as a kindergartner. She was a pleasant child, anxious to please. Her parents were very supportive of their children and the school, always coming in for conferences and asking how they could help. Her teachers in kindergarten and first grade observed that it seemed to take her longer than others in the class to learn concepts, but she worked hard. They appreciated the efforts she made and felt that she would eventually catch on.

In second grade, it was observed that Caroline was continuing to have more difficulty learning, par-

ticularly learning more abstract concepts. Although she got along well in the social environment of the classroom and she was working hard to keep up with the lower math and reading groups in the class, her teacher referred her for evaluation as a child with a possible disability in need of special education services.

The psychological evaluation determined that Caroline had an IQ of 67, and that although her functional and social behaviors and skill were adequate for second grade, it was determined that she qualified for services as a child with mild mental

(continued)

retardation. Her IEP was developed to provide resource room support as needed, particularly in reading and mathematics.

Initially, Caroline came to the resource room an hour a day for extra help, but the resource room teacher quickly determined that the time she was out of the primary classroom setting seemed to be interfering with her skill development. Because of her strong work habits, Caroline seemed to benefit more from staying in the classroom than from the special education services. The resource room teacher continued to monitor her progress, providing indirect services through Caroline's classroom teachers.

Over the next three years, the resource teacher monitored Caroline's progress. Caroline continued to make adequate progress in the basic academic skills, and her good social and work adjustment continued. In fifth grade, however, Caroline began to struggle in the reading program. The vocabulary and stories became more abstract and were not related to her daily life experience. Her effort and coping skills were no longer adequate to maintain progress, and she began to fail. Resource room services were re-

instituted, with additional instruction in vocabulary development and comprehension skills. This extra support enabled Caroline to hold her own through sixth grade.

As the time neared for her to move to the secondary level, the resource room teacher met with Caroline's parents to plan her IEP for seventh grade. They discussed her progress, and then talked about her ultimate goals once her school years were completed, since the IDEA requires transition plans (ITPs) for all students in special education. They discussed her strong social and work skills and her difficulties with abstract levels of learning. Although her grades did not preclude remaining in the typical academic track in junior high, the team decided that it would be better to develop a program for Caroline that began to involve her in the school's prevocational program, while concentrating her academic program on functional reading, writing, and mathematics skills.

Today, Caroline is an independent young adult. She works as a cashier in the local grocery store. She has a social life outside of work, and she manages her own financial affairs.

Historical Foundations of Mental Retardation

Caroline's story is reflective of the time in which she lives and indicative of the way mild mental retardation is conceptualized today. Her story would likely have been quite different had she lived in other times—or in the future. The way people with retardation have been treated, and whether persons with mild retardation would have been identified at all, has been determined more by the attitudes and values of the times in which they happened to be born than by any objective criteria (Payne & Patton, 1981).

As was discussed in Chapter 2, the variable treatment of persons with disabilities such as mental retardation prior to 1700 reflected a general lack of understanding, characterized by confusion and lack of knowledge. Such individuals were treated as buffoons, clowns, and jesters, as demons, or as beings capable of divine revelations. Only those with the most severe levels of disabilities were even noticed in this largely preliterate society.

With the Renaissance and its focus on humanism, society awakened to the idea that all people had rights. This awareness led to the development of a climate that supported efforts to assist those with deficits in intellectual functioning. The 1800s saw the development of optimism about our ability to improve the functioning of those with mental retardation. This early work in the area of mental retardation was conducted almost exclusively by physicians. They focused on individuals with moderate and severe levels of impairment as well as those with accompanying physical disabilities. The work of Down and Sequin in the mid-1800s resulted in the differentiation of types of mental retardation and the awareness that insanity and retardation were indeed different conditions. Through the work of Itard, Sequin, Dix, Howe, Wilbur, and others, a variety of largely residential treatment programs were established, all with great optimism that a cure for mental retardation could be found in these educational efforts.

When these efforts failed to provide the envisioned cures, a period of disillusionment followed in the late 1800s. More institutions were opened, but their function become largely custodial as training programs were phased out. People with moderate and severe retardation were destined to spend their lives in isolated institutions. Those with mild retardation like Caroline continued to blend into a society that valued manual and unskilled labor more than reading and writing.

The public perception was that the residents of these institutions were dangerous and fearsome. Calls for segregation of this population from the larger society were heard throughout the country. With the advent of the testing and eugenics movements, society had the tools to identify, isolate, and eliminate this perceived social menace. New immigrants were believed to be a source of mental deficiency as well, resulting in discrimination and harassment of new arrivals to America. Despite this climate of fear, a few public school day classes were established for children with retardation.

From 1930 to 1950, quiet work was underway. A major breakthrough in biomedical research investigating causes of mental retardation occurred in 1934 when Folling discovered an explanation for the condition called phenylketonuria (PKU). This discovery provided impetus for research designed to identify other genetically determined forms of retardation and possible early interventions. Skeels and Dye (1939) published a study that indicated that the environment also appeared to affect mental development. The testing movement produced new assessment instruments, laying the groundwork for more specific identification and diagnostic procedures for use with children and adolescents with suspected mental retardation. The 1950s saw a reawakening of advocacy on behalf of persons with retardation. The foundation of the National Association for Retarded Children (ARC) created a climate for public advocacy and action.

The "nature versus nurture" debate continued. In response to the eugenicists of the early part of the century, Masland, Sarason, and Gladwin published *Mental Subnormality* in 1958, stressing the connection between social and cultural variables and mental retardation, and highlighting the nurture component of the debate. Jane Mercer's (1973) work on the sociological definition of retardation further underscored the importance of an accurate assessment of a person's ability to function in social contexts before making a diagnosis of mental retardation. At the same time, the nature side of the argument was reasserted when Arthur Jensen (1969) wrote a controversial article arguing that genetic factors are more important in determining intelligence than are environmental factors.

John Kennedy established the President's Panel on Mental Retardation in 1961 to provide a forum for discussion of issues in this field, sparked by his own experience with and concern for his sister who had mental retardation. Edgerton's *Cloak of Competence* (1967) helped persons with mild retardation tell their own stories for the first time, just as Bogdan and Taylor (1976, 1994) were to do later with Ed Murphy (see Chapter 1). Edgerton's work supported the concept of mild retardation as a social construction and underscored the extent to which retardation is defined by the social context of the individual. He helped expose the extent to which the stigma associated with the label of retardation leads individuals to pull a "cloak of competence" around them, to deny their disability, and, more importantly, to pursue the benefits of life in society as others do. Lloyd Dunn published his classic article in 1968, questioning the efficacy of existing segregated services for students with mild mental retardation (see Box 2.2).

Throughout the 1990s, professionals still debated the nature of retardation and the best way to identify those in need of services. The efficacy of many programs was being questioned. The degree to which individuals were able to integrate into the adult world of work concerned many. Lack of appropriate community services threatened the movements toward deinstitutionalization and normalization. The general political climate and economic realities also threatened progress. At the close of the twentieth century, special education professionals and advocates were called on to find ways to ensure that students with retardation continue to advance in the future as they have in the past.

Development of the Definition of Mental Retardation in the United States

In 1919, the American Association on Mental Deficiency (AAMD, now called the AAMR) established the Committee on Classification and Uniform Statistics and charged it with the responsibility of developing a system of classification to aid in providing differentiated treatment programs for individuals with deficits in intellectual functioning. Diagnostic manuals produced over the next four decades provided doctors and other professionals with a common nomenclature to discuss the variety of conditions and syndromes presented by their patients and clients. In 1957, the Committee on Nomenclature recommended that a new comprehensive manual on terminology and classification in the field of mental retardation be developed (American Association on Mental Retardation, 1992; Grossman, 1983).

In 1959, the fifth edition of the manual published by AAMD (Heber, 1959) provided uniformity in terminology for the first time. It also proposed a dual classification system, describing both medical and behavioral aspects of mental retardation. The behavioral section addressed measured intellectual levels and adaptive behavior levels. The manual changed the IQ criterion for classification from less than about two standard deviations below the mean (IQ lower than about 70) to less than one standard deviation below the mean (IQ lower than about 85). This edition added the adaptive behavior criterion to the diagnostic process. Those proposing the higher classification standard felt that by applying the adaptive behavior deficit criterion along with the higher IQ criterion, the possibility of overidentification would be avoided. However, there was considerable concern in the field about identifying such a large segment of the population (potentially about 16 percent) as possibly having mental retardation.

The debate continued until 1973, when the IQ criterion was restored to the traditional pre-1959 level of lower than two standard deviations below the mean (IQ of about 70) for the test used (Grossman, 1973). These changes in criteria between 1959 and 1973 illustrate the arbitrariness of such determinations (Hobbs, 1975a; Zigler & Hodapp, 1986). As illustrated in Figure 6.1, in 1959, with the stroke of a pen, an additional 14 percent of the population could potentially be labeled as having mental retardation. In 1973, the definition in effect removed the potential label of mental retardation from that same 14 percent of the population (Bogdan & Taylor, 1994).

The 1973 manual also went farther in defining deficits in adaptive behavior, providing illustrations of various levels of deficit as guidelines. However, there were problems obtaining standardized measures of adaptive behavior. The AAMD Behavior Scale and other scales

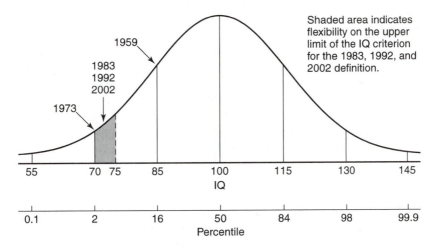

FIGURE 6.1 Effect of Changes in IQ Criterion in the AAMD/AAMR Definitions

for assessing adaptive behavior existed, but their norms were based largely on studies with institutionalized individuals. The 1983 AAMD manual (Grossman, 1983) clarified the use of IQ testing for classification by emphasizing that the IQ score criterion was a guideline only. Diagnosticians were reminded that they should take into account the standard error of measurement on any test used for classification purposes, and that they were expected to use clinical judgment in interpreting all data. In particular, diagnosticians were counseled to consider adaptive behavior in conjunction with the IQ score before making classification decisions.

IDEA Definition of Mental Retardation

The definition of mental retardation currently included in the IDEA is the same definition presented in the 1983 manual published by the American Association on Mental Deficiency (AAMD/AAMR), which reads as follows:

> Mental retardation refers to significantly subaverage general intellectual functioning existing concurrently with deficits in adaptive behavior and manifested during the developmental period.
>
> U.S. Office of Education, 1977b, p. 42478; Grossman, 1983, p. 1.

The AAMD diagnostic manual (Grossman, 1983) further defined the terms used in this definition:

- *General intellectual functioning:* defined operationally as the results obtained from an individually administered intelligence test with appropriate psychometric properties (e.g., Stanford-Binet and the Wechsler family of tests, WPPSI, WISC-III, WAIS).
- *Significantly subaverage:* defined as an IQ score of about 70 or below (or two standard deviations below the mean for the test used). The manual goes on to emphasize that the score of 70 is intended as a *guideline* only, and that it could be extended upward to 75 depending on the reliability of the test used and other relevant factors. The IQ guideline of 70 is derived from the normal curve (see Figure 6.2), which implies that individuals with scores of two or more standard deviations from the mean should probably be considered as part of another population, in this case the population of persons with mental retardation. For example, when using scores on an IQ test where the mean is 100 and the standard deviation is 15, an individual with an IQ score of less than 70 is viewed as having a level of intellectual functioning that differs significantly from the typical person. The various diagnostic manuals and editions repeatedly caution, however, that clinical judgment must always be used in interpreting the meaning and validity of any intelligence measure.
- *Deficits in adaptive behavior:* defined as displaying significant limitations in the ability to effectively meet age-appropriate cultural standards in learning, personal independence, and social responsibility. Adaptive behavior includes all those things people do to take care of themselves and interact with others in daily life. Although these skills are often evaluated informally by making a comparison of the everyday

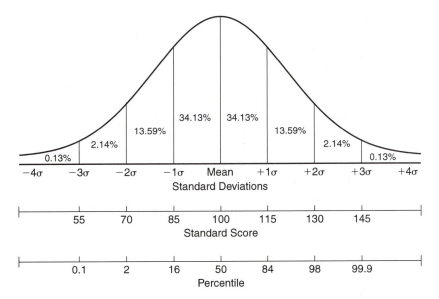

FIGURE 6.2   Normal Distribution of the Population

functioning of the person in comparison to peers, formal evaluations for mental retardation will typically include the use of one or more standardized measures of adaptive behavior. Some of the more commonly used adaptive behavior scales are listed in Table 6.1. School psychologists favor the use of the Vineland Adaptive Behavior Scales over other instruments (Wodrich & Barry, 1991).

- *Developmental period:* defined as the period of time between conception and age eighteen. Deficits in functioning caused by physical trauma or nervous system deterioration after the developmental period are more appropriately classified under the DSM-IV category "Organic Mental Disorders." With persons who develop impairments in mental functioning after development has been completed, one must consider the extent to which previous learning and life experiences affect the nature of rehabilitation services needed; for this reason, it seems inappropriate to classify

**TABLE 6.1   Adaptive Behavior Measures
in Common Use**

AAMR Adaptive Behavior Scales (ABS) (1993)
Adaptive Behavior Assessment System (2000)
Adaptive Behavior Inventory for Children (ABIC) (1977)
Comprehensive Test of Adaptive Behavior—Revised (1999)
Scales of Independent Behavior—Revised (1991)
Vineland Adaptive Behavior Scales (1984)

From Wodrich & Barry, 1991; American Association on Mental Retardation, 2002.

these individuals with the same diagnostic label used for those whose impairment disrupted their experiences during childhood and before learning could occur.

To apply the above definition to the classification process, one needs an IQ score and a standardized evaluation of the individual's adaptive behavior or functioning. Using these two criteria (see Table 6.2), one then determines if this individual meets both of the requirements for classification as a child with mental retardation.

It is important to note, however, that although the 1983 AAMD definition is most often cited in professional literature as the basis for determining whether an individual has mental retardation, a study of state criteria for classification found that only 60 percent of the states used all three criteria, and 10 percent did not mention adaptive behavior in their regulations at all (Utley, Lowitzer, & Baumeister, 1987). A later study of school psychologists' practices (Wodrich & Barry, 1991) revealed other sources of variation in the application of the AAMD/IDEA criteria. Specifically, the researchers found that school psychologists sometimes apply alternative norms when assessing students from different cultural or economic backgrounds, while others vary in their interpretation of the terms *guideline* and *cutoff* in interpreting both IQ and adaptive behavior scores. Some treated the standard score of 70 as the decision maker, while others used professional judgment in the use of that figure.

Although the majority of school psychologists surveyed (Wodrich & Barry, 1991) preferred to use the Wechsler Scales and the Vineland Adaptive Behavior Scales for assessing intelligence and adaptive behavior, others used instruments with different psychometric properties. This is significant when one considers that a given student's score may vary by five or more points from one instrument to another. If a psychologist uses 70 as a cutoff score, then the choice of instruments and the norms applied may have significant effects on the classification of specific students. (See Box 6.1 for a discussion of other classification issues.)

Alternatives to the Current IDEA Definition

1992 AAMR Definition

In 1992, the American Association on Mental Retardation (AAMR) released its ninth classification manual, which defined mental retardation as "substantial limitations in present func-

TABLE 6.2   Classification Criteria for Determining the Existence of Mental Retardation

	Measured Intellectual Functioning	
	IQ below about 70	**IQ above about 70**
Deficit in Adaptive Behavior	Has mental retardation	Does not have mental retardation
No Deficit in Adaptive Behavior	Does not have mental retardation	Does not have mental retardation

From *Classification in mental retardation: 1983 revision* (p. 12) by H. J. Grossman (Ed.), 1983, Washington, DC: American Association on Mental Deficiency. Copyright 1983 by American Association on Mental Retardation. Adapted and reprinted with permission.

BOX **6.1**

SPOTLIGHT IN HISTORY: The Six-Hour Retarded Child

To more fully understand the effect and importance of the adaptive behavior criteria as a necessary precondition for classification of an individual as having mental retardation, we can look to the report issued by the President's Committee on Mental Retardation (1970), entitled *The Six-Hour Retarded Child.* Responding to the concern that children from varying economic and cultural backgrounds were being placed in classes for children with mental retardation in disproportionately large numbers, the conference participants looked closely at the practices that might be related to this phenomenon. One participant said:

> We now have what may be called a 6-hour retarded child—retarded from 9 to 3, five days a week, solely on the basis of an IQ score, without regard to his adaptive behavior, which may be exceptionally adaptive to the situation and community in which he lives. (PCMR, 1970, frontispiece)

The report quoted Wilson Riles, then Associate Superintendent of the California State Department of Education, as asking:

> The rate of placement of Spanish surname children in special education is about three times higher than for Anglo children; the Negro rate is close to four times the Anglo rate. . . . The question must be raised: to what extent are children classified as mentally retarded when the true nature of their learning disabilities stems from environmental factors? (p. 2)

This report underscores the need to include an evaluation of adaptive behavior in a variety of environments to better understand the child's strengths as well as weaknesses. The participants called for an assessment of children's behavior in their homes and neighborhoods. The report further asserted that when the results of the behavioral assessment were not consistent with the obtained IQ score, the child should not be labeled as having mental retardation, but should still receive educational services tailored to the child's strengths and deficits. The committee members believed that this understanding was critical to designing a helpful learning environment for a particular child. In particular, the participants called for a reexamination of the present system of intelligence testing and classification. James Allen, then U.S. Commissioner of Education, asked:

> Is it possible that the term mental retardation is no longer of any value to an educator? Do we need to find a new concept of education for children with special needs—one that does not carry with it the surplus meaning which is threatening to parents and detrimental to children? (p. 15)

Leo Cain of the President's Commission observed that "when we attach a number to a child, we conveniently put him in a slot where we say a program has been devised to fit that particular number" (p. 15). Panel members also questioned the basic assumption that programs adequately match labels and test score criteria, and cast doubts on the utility of the classification process itself.

From President's Committee on Mental Retardation, 1970.

tioning" (AA/MR, 1992, p. 1). This definition also required deficits in at least two of the ten adaptive skill areas. The definition itself and the diagnostic process used to implement it represented a significant departure from previous manuals. Some writers in the field have even suggested that this definition with its focus on present functioning might represent a paradigm shift in the conceptualization of mental retardation (Smith, J. D., 1994). The definition shifted the focus from looking at mental retardation as a personal trait to conceptualizing it as an expression of the interaction of the abilities of the individual and the environment in which that person must function.

The implication of the 1992 definition was that the degree of retardation is not a fixed trait, but in fact may change over time and between environments. Most significantly, it implied that the effective level of retardation may be significantly affected by the level of supports commonly available in the environment. If the individual needs only those supports that are commonly available to all individuals, then no special supports are needed and the diagnosis of retardation would be deemed inappropriate.

The 1992 definition and diagnostic protocols were not without their critics. These concerns as summarized by MacMillan, Gresham, & Siperstein (1993, 1995) included: (1) concern that the 70–75 IQ guideline might lead to increased inappropriate classifications; (2) the difficulty of measuring the ten subdomains of adaptive behavior, given the lack of validated instruments; and (3) the difficulty of reliably determining the intensities of the levels of support needed by an individual. The 1992 definition has to date been adopted by only four states as their definition and criteria for determining if a student has mental retardation (Denning, Chamberlain, & Polloway, 2000).

2002 AAMR Definition

In 2002, the American Association on Mental Retardation (AAMR) released its tenth definition and classification manual, which revised its definition again in response to the concerns raised with the 1992 version. AAMR (2002) now defines mental retardation in this way:

> Mental retardation is a disability characterized by significant limitations both in intellectual functioning and in adaptive behavior as expressed in conceptual, social, and practical adaptive skills. The disability originates before age 18.
>
> From *Mental Retardation: Definition, Classification, and Systems of Support* (p. 1) by American Association on Mental Retardation, 2002, Washington DC: American Association on Mental Retardation. Copyright 2002 by American Association on Mental Retardation. Reprinted with permission.

In applying the 2002 AAMR criteria to the diagnostic process, the manual identifies the following five assumptions underlying the use of this definition for classification purposes. While the text of the definition alone may appear to have abandoned much of what made the 1992 definition unique, a careful consideration of the underlying assumptions suggests otherwise:

1. Limitation in present functioning must be considered within the context of community environments typical of the individual's peers and culture.
2. Valid assessment considers cultural and linguistic diversity as well as differences in communication, sensory, motor, and behavioral factors.
3. Within an individual, limitations often coexist with strengths.

4. An important purpose of describing limitations is to develop a profile of needed supports.

5. With appropriate personalized supports over a sustained period, the life functioning of the person with mental retardation generally will improve.

From *Mental Retardation: Definition, Classification, and Systems of Support* (p. 1) by American Association on Mental Retardation, 2002, Washington, DC: American Association on Mental Retardation. Copyright 2002 by American Association on Mental Retardation. Reprinted with permission.

The 2002 AAMR definition underscores how important it is to look at how the individual functions currently and to evaluate functioning in the environments typical for that person before making a determination of limitations in intellectual functioning. AAMR (2002) also emphasizes the importance of being sensitive to the effects of cultural differences when assessing function. Finally, it points out the need to consider individual strengths as well as needs in identifying the appropriate supports (see Figure 6.3).

This approach seems to address many of the concerns of the President's Committee on Mental Retardation (1970) as described in Box 6.1. It is also responsive to the concerns today about disproprotionate identification of students from culturally diverse backgrounds as students with mental retardation (Patton, 1998; Salend, Garrick Duhaney, & Montgomery, 2002).

Developmental Disabilities and Delay

The term mental retardation has often been criticized because of the stigma generally attached to it. Alternative terms sometimes suggested to indicate problems during normal

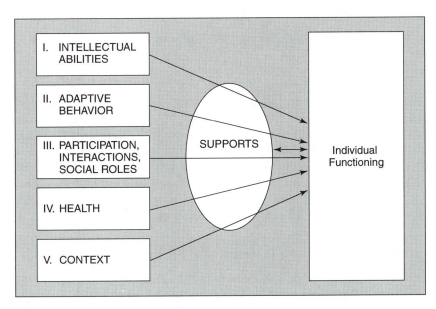

FIGURE 6.3
Theoretical Model of Mental Retardation

From *Mental Retardation: Definition, Classification, and Systems of Support* (p. 10) by American Association on Mental Retardation, 2002, Washington, DC: American Association on Mental Retardation. Copyright 2002 by American Association on Mental Retardation. Reprinted with permission.

development include developmental disabilities or developmental delay. Use of these terms has received mixed reception.

For some, the terms are preferred because of their lack of specificity. Developmental delay is often the term of choice for many early intervention programs where it is not always possible or desirable to apply the classification schemes used with school-age children because of limited language abilities and unstable traits in pre-schoolers. IDEA 1997 allows the use of the term *developmental delay* for children through age nine at the discretion of the state or district whenever a child is experiencing delays significant enough to require intervention in one or more of the following areas: physical development, cognitive development, communication development, social or emotional development, or adaptive development.

The term *developmental disability* has a more specific legal definition, however, and those who seek to use it as a more generic-sounding alternative to mental retardation need to be aware of this. The *Developmental Disabilities Assistance and Bill of Rights Act of 2000* (originally passed in 1974, reauthorized in 2000 as P.L. 106-402), defines a developmental disability by generalized impairment in functioning:

The term *developmental disability* means a severe chronic disability of an individual 5 years of age or older that: (a) is attributable to a mental or physical impairment or combination of mental and physical impairments; (b) is manifested before the individual attains age twenty-two; (c) is likely to continue indefinitely; (d) results in substantial functional limitations in *three* or more of the following areas of major life activity: (i) self-care, (ii) receptive and expressive language, (iii) learning, (iv) mobility, (v) self-direction, (vi) capacity for independent living, and (vii) economic self-sufficiency; and (e) reflects the individual's need for a combination and sequence of special, interdisciplinary, or generic services, individualized supports, or other forms of assistance that are of lifelong or extended duration and are individually planned and coordinated.

(*Developmental Disabilities Assistance and Bill of Rights Act of 2000,* P.L. 106-402, 114 Stat. 1678 § 102(8)(A), 2000)

From this definition, it is apparent that the legal definition of this term implies severe and multiple disabilities of a long-term nature. It applies only when there are very significant deficits in functioning. Estimates indicate that about half of individuals currently identified as having mental retardation would not meet the more stringent criteria of the Development Disabilities Act (AAMR, 2002). Although it does apply to some individuals with mental retardation, and while it appears to represent a less stigmatizing label, it would be inappropriate to apply it generically to all persons with retardation, and it would exclude a number of those currently receiving services for mild mental retardation.

An Alternative Definition with an Instructional Perspective

While the historic and currently used definitions of mental retardation may define the limits of the group of persons with mental retardation for administrative purposes, they provide weak guidance to those involved in providing instruction to students with retardation. Dever (1990) developed an instructional paradigm that teachers and caregivers may find more useful. This instructional definition was not intended to replace more typical classification/administrative definitions but rather to complement them. Dever's purpose was to provide a more useful delineation of the degree of deficit in intellectual functioning of individuals who have been identified as persons with mental retardation. He sought to develop a definition that would be useful in describing the nature of the retardation with respect to instructional goals. He proposed that the following definition be used as a supplement to the formal classification process:

> Mental retardation refers to the need for specific training of skills that most people acquire incidentally and that enable individuals to live in the community without supervision.
>
> Dever, 1990, p. 149.[1]

Dever further clarified the meaning of *independence* as follows:

> Independence is exhibiting behavior patterns appropriate to the behavior settings normally frequented by others of the individual's age and social status in such a manner that the individual is not seen as requiring assistance because of his/her behavior. (p. 151)

In discussing the implications of looking at retardation from an instructional perspective, Dever identified the following assumptions:

- Persons with mental retardation can learn.
- The need for instruction is the central issue in mental retardation.
- The degree of retardation is related to the amount and intensity of instruction needed to achieve the goal of independent community living. The more intense the need for instruction, the more severe the level of retardation.
- If the goal of independent community living has been reached with an individual, the classification of mental retardation is no longer applicable since the need for instruction defines the presence of the condition of mental retardation.
- Some persons with mental retardation will not attain the goal of independence despite instruction; therefore they will continue to be described as a person with retardation.
- The aim of instruction (independent adult living) is the same for all persons; what differs is the fact that individuals will differ in their ability to attain that goal. (pp. 149–151)

---

[1]For this and the following quotations: From "Defining Mental Retardation from an Instructional Perspective" by R. B. Dever, 1990, *Mental Retardation, 28*(3), pp. 145–151. Copyright © 1990 by American Association on Mental Retardation. Adapted and reprinted with permission.

Levels of Severity

The AAMD (Grossman, 1983) definition now in use in IDEA suggests the following process for designating the level of retardation:

- Recognize that there is a delay in developmental milestones.
- Determine that a deficit in adaptive behavior exists.
- Determine the extent of measured general intellectual functioning.
- Determine that both of the criteria for diagnosis of mental retardation exist.
- Use the measure of intellectual functioning to determine the level of retardation, taking into account the adaptive behavior ratings and the standard error of measurement of the tests (see Table 6.3).

The use of a range of numbers as the upper and lower limits implies that clinical judgment based on an evaluation of the individual's actual ability to function is necessary to establish the level of impairment (Grossman, 1983).

Educational Terminology

Schools began universally serving students with mental retardation with the advent of the Education for All Handicapped Act of 1975. Prior to that time, many schools routinely excluded those students who were not deemed "educable." That conceptual framework led to the establishment of a separate level designation system to apply to placement in school programs. The levels were based on the estimate of ultimate school outcomes, and they roughly corresponded to the IQ levels established by AAMD/AAMR Table 6.4).

Students placed in educable classes were assumed to have the ability to become literate at a basic level and to acquire the basic vocational skills necessary for independent adult living. Students placed in trainable classes were expected to develop self-care and daily living skills but not to develop reading and mathematics skills beyond a simple survival level; they were expected to be capable of working only in sheltered environments. Students functioning at the severe/profound level were expected to need custodial care throughout their lives, and their educational program, if any, was designed to develop basic communication and mobility skills, as well as simple self-care skills such as eating and using the toilet.

TABLE 6.3   Levels of Mental Retardation

Level of Retardation	IQ Ranges
Mild	50–55 to approximately 70
Moderate	35–40 to 50–55
Severe	20–25 to 35–40
Profound	Below 20–25

Based on American Association on Mental Retardation (2002); American Psychiatric Association (2000); Grossman (1983).

TABLE 6.4   Terms Used Historically in School Programs for Children with Mental Retardation

Educational Term	Comparable AAMD/AAMR Term
EMH/EMR Educable Class	Mild Retardation
TMH/TMR Trainable Class	Moderate Retardation
PMH/PMR Severe/Profound Class	Severe and Profound Mental Retardation

The use of this terminology has been phased out in recent years. It has been replaced in most programs either by the designations of mild, moderate, and severe disability or by other designators indicating the intensity of supports or the type of curriculum needed by the students in the program. Use of the terms "educable" and "trainable" is generally viewed as offensive and professionally inappropriate today.

2002 AAMR Intensities of Support

In 1992, AAMR abandoned the use of global terms to designate the level of retardation. Acknowledging that each individual possesses strengths and weaknesses among and within the various adaptive skill areas, AAMR proposed a procedure for using those strengths and weaknesses to determine the intensity of support an individual may require to function (Table 6.5). As noted previously, the AAMR 1992/2002 definition assumes that if appropriate levels of support, including instruction, are provided, the person will be assisted in carrying out life functions, and over time these supports should enable the person to function with fewer supports. Therefore, the level of severity is seen neither as global nor chronic but only as a guide to appropriate services. This perspective is similar to and consistent with the instructional paradigm proposed by Dever (1990).

Although it may seem possible or appropriate to equate the older terminology of "mild, moderate, severe, and profound" with these levels of support, it is important to remember that, unlike the earlier global level indicators, this process expects that each adaptive skill area will be evaluated separately (Smith, 1994). It is highly likely that individual students may require differing intensities of support in various skill areas. To provide more or less support than needed in a particular skill area is to compromise the individual's progress toward more effective functioning over time.

Prevalence of Mental Retardation

The determination of the prevalence of mental retardation, or the number of cases at a given point in time, is directly related to the way mental retardation is defined. Most researchers and epidemiologists estimate the prevalence of mental retardation as ranging between 1 percent and 3 percent with 2 to 3 percent being the most frequently cited figure (Drew, Logan, & Hardman, 1988; Zigler & Hodapp, 1986). When one considers that the definition of mental retardation is tied most closely to an IQ score, which itself is based on the normal curve,

TABLE 6.5   AAMR 2002 Intensities of Support

Intermittent

Supports on an "as needed basis," characterized by episodic nature (person not always needing the support(s), or short-term nature (supports needed during life span transitions, e.g., job loss or an acute medical crisis). Intermittent supports may be high or low intensity when provided.

Limited

An intensity of supports characterized by consistency over time, time-limited but not of an intermittent nature, may require fewer staff members and less cost than more intense levels of support (e.g., time-limited employment training or transitional supports during the school to adult period).

Extensive

Supports characterized by regular involvement (e.g., daily) in at least some environments (e.g., school, work, or home) and not time-limited nature (e.g., long-term support and long-term home living support).

Pervasive

Supports characterized by their constancy, high intensity, provision across environments; [and] potential life-sustaining nature. Pervasive supports typically involve more staff members and intrusiveness than do extensive or time-limited supports.

From *Mental Retardation: Definition, Classification, and Systems of Support, Tenth Edition* (p. 152) by American Association on Mental Retardation, 2002, Washington, DC: American Association on Mental Retardation. Copyright 2002 by American Association on Mental Retardation. Reprinted with permission.

it would be expected that slightly over 2 percent of the population would fall below two standard deviations (see Figure 6.2).

In actuality, the figure is somewhat greater than 2 percent, because of cases of mental retardation resulting from organic influences rather than from a normally distributed human trait. Causes shown to result in impairment of mental functioning, such as infection, injury, and toxins, affect the individual only in a negative direction, thus increasing the prevalence at the negative end of the normal curve, boosting the overall number of persons functioning in the range associated with mental retardation (Dingman & Targan, 1960; Zigler & Hodapp, 1986).

Individuals with milder levels of retardation are generally reported to account for about 85 percent of the population of persons with mental retardation. Moderate levels of retardation affect about 10 percent, while those with severe and profound levels account for an additional 5 percent (American Psychiatric Assoc., 2000; Drew et al., 1988). The precise numbers vary from place to place because of the effect of adaptive behavior assessments as well as environmental effects on intellectual functioning. An individual with less ability may be able to function in an environment that places few demands, but noticeably unable to function in a more stressful and demanding environment. Since it is the inability to function independently that most often causes a person to be assessed for possible retardation, prevalence levels would be expected to be somewhat higher in more difficult or demanding environments.

It has been documented that the highest number of new cases are identified during the school years as contrasted with the preschool or post-school years. Specifically, the clinical diagnosis of mild mental retardation appears to be age dependent, with most cases being diagnosed once school activities make new demands on children that may be difficult for them to meet. Severe retardation is noticed much earlier because of the more noticeable gap between the individual's functioning and typical developmental expectations, while milder levels may not be identified until elementary school. Identification of new cases of severe/profound retardation is generally higher in the preschool years.

Finally, since the inception of P.L. 94-142 in 1975, the prevalence of mental retardation among school populations has steadily declined, while the number of students with learning disabilities has increased significantly (MacMillan, Siperstein, & Gresham, 1996; Smith, 1997). From 1976–77 to 1993–94, the number of students with mental retardation dropped 38 percent, while the number of those with learning disabilities increased 207 percent (see Table 6.6). The suspicion that these numbers may not reflect the true prevalence of these conditions suggests that the identification process itself is still flawed.

Typical Characteristics of Persons with Mental Retardation

As noted earlier, the process of classification (i.e., labeling a person as being part of the population of people with mental retardation) implies nothing specifically about the individual's ability to function, nor about what the individual needs from the environment. Without carefully evaluating the individual's strengths and weaknesses in each functional domain and then determining the needed level of support, we can assume virtually nothing. There are an infinite number of possibilities in the degree to which an individual exhibits

TABLE 6.6   Change in Numbers and Percentages of Students with Mental Retardation and Learning Disabilities, 1976–1977 to 1999–2000

	Mental Retardation		Learning Disabilities	
	Number of Students	Percentage of Special Education Students	Number of Students	Percentage of Special Education Students
1976–1977	818,718	25	782,095	24
1990–1991	551,457	13	2,144,017	49
1993–1994	510,107	11	2,402,201	52
1999–2000	614,433	11	2,871,966	51
Change from 1976–1977 to 1999–2000	–204,285 (–25%)		+2,089,871 (+267%)	

Based on data from U.S. Department of Education (1995: pp. 12, 13, A18, A20) (2002: p. II-23).

deficits in intellectual functioning and adaptive behavior. Some individuals have additional physical disabilities or disordered psychological states that further restrict their ability to function independently and that affect their need for habilitative and supportive services. Thus, the one sure statement about persons with mental retardation is that they are a very heterogeneous population. The nature of an individual's characteristics is determined largely by the interactions among three factors: the general level of intellectual functioning, the age of the person, and the favorableness or adaptive fit of the environment.

Learning characteristics are the most obvious concern with persons in this population. A continuing debate addresses the question of whether persons with mental retardation learn the same way as others although more slowly, or whether there is a qualitative difference in their learning patterns that requires unique teaching methods. Since learning is inferred from behavior, individuals who fail to meet age-expected norms of behavior and language are viewed either as not learning or as learning poorly. As a group, learning is slower and less efficient among students with mental retardation than among a group of typical learners.

The efficiency of learning is affected by the degree to which the individual learns incidentally from environmental input. Students with mental retardation tend to respond better to direct, consistent instruction, and learn poorly or inaccurately from unstructured environmental stimuli and incidental learning experiences. Problems occur at various stages in information processing. Attention to relevant details may be less focused and reliable. Grouping or clustering information to process it mentally tends to be inefficient. Rehearsal strategies for transferring information from short-term to long-term memory are often poorly applied, if at all. Transfer of learning in one setting to other appropriate settings is often incomplete. (See Chapters 10 and 12 for discussion of cognitive and academic functioning.)

Social and emotional characteristics are also affected by deficits in learning, as is academic achievement. The experience of repeated failure creates a cycle of failure, resulting in an expectancy of failure and incompetence. The individual learns to depend on external control rather than developing a sense of personal responsibility and competence. This outer-directedness may leave them vulnerable in certain environments as they move into the teen and adult years, and it can result in learned helplessness. Children and youth with mental retardation have psychological needs that are similar to other youngsters (Maslow, 1954). When we help them meet their needs for physical security, emotional security, and acceptance, they are more likely to develop a strong sense of self, which is a necessary prerequisite to an internal locus of control and learned competence. (See Chapter 12 for additional discussion of these characteristics.)

A number of studies have confirmed that adolescents with mental retardation tend to exhibit social skills deficits, particularly at school, and that they tend to be neglected or rejected in school and to display lower levels of personal efficacy (O'Reilly & Glynn, 1995; Siperstein & Leffert, 1997). These deficits persist into adult life and are believed to be a major factor in problems with post-school adjustment. The development of self-determination is an essential step in achieving successful adult status (Wehmeyer, 1992). All adolescents typically question authority, rely on peers, and move toward more independent decision making. Young people with mental retardation have the same needs, but frequently they are not provided with the experiences needed to exercise the decision-making necessary for self-determination because caretakers and teachers question the ability of young people with mental retardation to act effectively and independently (see Chapter 12).

Physically, this group presents significant variations in characteristics. At the mild end of disability, there may be few or no observable physical differences. Slight motoric immaturity or slowness to develop may be the only sign of developmental problems. As the level of disability increases, especially when there are biological or pathological causal factors present, there may be facial differences (e.g., Down syndrome), sensory disabilities (hearing or vision), or seizures or cerebral palsy resulting from brain injury. If lack of adequate nutrition is implicated as a causal factor, physical stature and robust health is likely to be compromised. Throughout life, individuals with mental retardation may have higher instances of injury due to accidents and increased susceptibility to infections. Health and safety education, in addition to appropriate levels of environmental supports, can help ameliorate these problems.

As individuals with retardation become adults, the focus of concern shifts from learning and school environments to concerns about employment, independent living, and the use of leisure time. Although children with mental retardation have been routinely provided with educational programs since 1978, unemployment, underemployment, dependence on governmental services, use of dependent living arrangements, and inadequate social skills still characterize their adult years (Smith & Puccini, 1995). Individuals with retardation have needs and interests in recreational or leisure activities that are similar to other adolescents and adults. However, studies indicate that they participate in these activities less frequently than their peers without disabilities. Hoge and Datillo (1995) suggest that this may be due to lack of leisure education and to problems in securing access to interesting activities. As these individuals increasingly live typical life spans, communities must provide preparation for adult living during the school years, and we must also address the continuing needs for support into the adult years.

Conditions Associated with Mental Retardation

The issue of causation is a difficult one with regard to mental retardation, as it is with many other disabilities. A meta-analysis of 13 studies revealed that in 30 percent of cases of severe retardation and 50 percent of the cases of mild retardation, the exact cause was unknown (AAMR, 1992). In general, most writers report that only in about 25 percent of the cases does the reduced intellectual functioning appear to be related to a specific biomedical condition. In the remainder of cases, a single cause cannot be positively identified although there are frequent multiple environmental risk factors, including social, behavioral, and educational factors, that appear to be related to the retardation (AAMR, 1992, 2002; Zigler & Hodapp, 1986).

The fact is, however, that even when a specific biomedical condition is identified (e.g., Down syndrome, Fragile X, or prenatal drug exposure), it is also true that there are generally a variety of additional risk factors that interact in complex ways to produce a particular level of functioning (AAMR, 1992, 2002). The presence of any particular condition generally associated with mental retardation does not indicate that any particular level of retardation is inevitable. The presence, degree, and nature of retardation are determined by the interaction of a host of biomedical, social, educational, and behavioral factors. In addition, any particular condition may result in a wide variety of functioning levels, including having no impairment at all (AAMR, 1992, 2002). Finally, simply knowing a cause rarely provides definitive guidance in planning differential treatments.

Despite these problems, it is helpful for special education professionals to be knowledgeable about the terms describing various conditions so that they may be discussed appropriately with parents, other teachers, and medical personnel and so that interactions among risk factors may be considered in designing primary and secondary prevention efforts or tertiary interventions once the presence of mental retardation has been confirmed. In the following discussion of conditions associated with mental retardation, the reader is encouraged to consider the prevention implications of the various risk factors. It is useful to consider the extent to which we can identify primary, secondary, and tertiary prevention efforts that will eliminate or lessen the impact of those conditions. (See the prevention framework in Table 1.2).

The AAMR 2002 classification manual presents a multifactorial framework for considering a variety of risk factors associated with mental retardation, including biomedical, social, behavioral, and educational. AAMR (2002) further suggests that clinicians must consider the timing of the onset of the condition (prenatal, perinatal, and postnatal), along with presence of other factors prior to and concurrent with the condition manifesting itself.

Biomedical/Physiological Causes

As noted above, conditions associated with a biomedical or physiological cause are present in only about 25 percent of cases of retardation. In these cases, the pathology is present and identifiable. The retardation is more likely to be severe, although we are increasingly finding that the level of severity can be reduced by appropriate programming and levels of support, particularly during the early years. For example, current experience with individuals with Down syndrome has shown us that previous expectations of severe retardation in these individuals were not justified. With effective early intervention, many individuals with Down syndrome are able to function independently with need for only limited or even intermittent supports in many life skill areas.

Genetic and Chromosomal Abnormalities.   Disorders resulting from genetic and chromosomal abnormalities comprise one group of biological causes. *Phenylketonuria (PKU)* is a genetic condition in which the child inherits a defective gene responsible for the production of the enzyme that helps break down the amino acid phenylalanine in the body. Left untreated, the lack of this enzyme allows phenylalanine to build up in body tissues and causes progressive brain damage and retardation. Fortunately, this condition is now easily and routinely tested for at birth, and children so affected can be placed on a restrictive diet throughout the growing years, virtually eliminating the retardation. Other genetically determined conditions that include the potential for mental retardation include Tay-Sachs disease, galactosemia, neurofibromatosis, and hypothyroidism.

Retardation related to chromosomal anomalies occurs when there is damage to an entire chromosome and therefore disruption of a number of genes. There may be missing or extra chromosomes, or damaged or broken ones. These anomalies are thought to be caused by genetic mutations, radiation, drugs, toxins, viruses, and other environmental factors that can affect the gametes or the embryo during the early cell divisions.

Down syndrome is the most widely known of these chromosomal conditions. Described by Langdon Down in 1854, it was originally associated with moderate to severe retardation as well as a host of physical abnormalities. This led to institutionalization and early death of many affected persons. It is more common in children born to older mothers, but it can occur in any birth. Prominent characteristics of individuals with Down syndrome are upward slanting of the eyes, epicanthic folds, flat broad face, furrowed protruding tongue, and short broad hands, as well as physical defects in the cervical area, the heart, and the digestive tract. As with all syndromes, few individuals have all of the noted characteristics, but a diagnosis of the syndrome requires that the person has enough of the indicators to justify applying the diagnosis.

Current experiences with children with Down syndrome have drastically altered the expectations for these youngsters. Although the chromosomal abnormality cannot be corrected, persons with Down syndrome can reasonably expect to live a normal adult life span with aggressive medical intervention to correct heart and digestive problems. The level of retardation has also been ameliorated for many individuals by effective infant stimulation and early intervention programs. Increasingly, these children are functioning in the milder ranges of retardation or sometimes in the normal range.

The elimination of routine institutionalization of these children has allowed them to benefit from the rich environment of supports available in a home and community situation. The classic research done by Skeels and Dye (1939) provided evidence that the ultimate level of functioning of children such as those with Down syndrome can be altered by tertiary efforts to effect changes in the environment, although there were some concerns raised about the quality of the study itself (Zigler & Hodapp, 1986). In their study, Skeels and Dye selected thirteen two-year-olds who apparently had mental retardation and were living in an orphanage. They placed them in an institution for adult women with retardation. The women nurtured the children, playing with them, talking to them, and "training" them. When these thirteen children grew up, they were all able to live in the community and raise families of their own. Four even went to college. A control group of twelve children who remained in the orphanage until placement had much lower adult IQ scores, and four remained in institutions as adults.

Fragile X syndrome (Santos, 1992) is a more recently identified chromosomal disorder, coming to light in the 1980s. It has been described as the most common inherited cause of mental retardation. Associated with a fragile site on the X chromosome, it is related to mental retardation as well as other learning and behavioral problems, including learning disabilities and disorders of attention, speech, and behavior. Physical attributes include an elongated face, large ears, and hyperextensible finger joints. These physical attributes become more prominent after puberty. Because of its association with the X chromosome, fragile X syndrome is far more prevalent in boys than girls, and the effect on girls is less pronounced. As with Down syndrome, the condition cannot be corrected, but with supportive environments, functioning levels can be improved, sometimes dramatically.

Birth Defects Involving the Neural Tube.

Neural tube defects can affect an infant's mental functioning as well. *Anencephaly* results when the neural tube does not close early in prenatal development, and the brain does not form. These youngsters generally die shortly after birth. *Spina bifida* is another form of a neural tube defect where a portion of the neural tube (in the cervical area or spinal column) does not close, usually resulting in paralysis below the lesion. Unless hydrocephalus is also present, children with spina bifida have physical disabilities but generally display normal intelligence. *Hydrocephalus* occurs when cerebral fluid is not drained normally from the brain. The resulting buildup of fluid pressure results in brain damage and mental retardation. Surgery to install a shunt can usually relieve this problem before significant levels of brain damage occur. With appropriate medical treatment, children born with neural tube defects today rarely have any retardation caused by the birth defect, exemplifying the effectiveness of secondary prevention efforts. Research also indicates that the primary preventive strategy of adding folic acid to the diet of the prospective mother prior to pregnancy appears to be associated with a decreased risk of neural tube disorders.

Infections.   Infectious diseases account for another group of causes of mental retardation, during both the prenatal and postnatal periods. Prenatal infection occurs when the mother becomes infected during pregnancy. Although the placenta protects the fetus from many harmful agents, certain viruses, bacteria, and parasites can pass through the placenta and infect the developing fetus. The damage can be very severe, especially if it occurs during the first trimester of pregnancy. *Rubella,* or German measles, is the best-known of these viruses. Maternal rubella can lead to mental retardation, deafness, blindness, cerebral palsy, and heart defects in the fetus. Primary prevention efforts including routine immunization of children should render this an obsolete cause of mental retardation, but the full benefit of this preventive action will not be realized until all women of childbearing age are immunized in childhood, or before becoming pregnant. *Postnatal cerebral infections,* or encephalitis, subsequent to such childhood illnesses as measles, mumps, rubella, meningitis, and influenza can result in damage to the brain and reduced levels of intellectual functioning. Secondary prevention efforts involving effective and immediate treatment of childhood illnesses can prevent or lessen some of these possible complications. Other maternal infections that are implicated in mental retardation include cytomegalovirus (CMV), toxoplasmosis, congenital syphilis, and HIV infections.

Toxins.   The ingestion of toxic substances, such as drugs and other chemicals, by the mother can also adversely affect the fetus. The well-known devastating effects of the prescription drug thalidomide in the 1960s highlighted the importance for expectant mothers of avoiding toxins of all kinds. This has led to the current practice of carefully monitoring all drugs used by pregnant women, prescribing only those that are necessary to preserve the life of the mother.

There are also a number of common substances that have been shown to have a toxic effect on the fetus. Alcohol, even in moderation, is implicated in what is now called fetal alcohol syndrome (FAS) or the milder form, fetal alcohol effects (FAE). Children born to mothers who consume alcohol during pregnancy can be born with mental retardation, drooping eyelids, and other facial abnormalities, heart defects, reduced physical size throughout life, and other evidence of central nervous system dysfunction.

Smoking by the expectant mother may contribute to low-birthweight babies and the potential for some degree of mental retardation. Other drugs (e.g., crack, cocaine, and heroin) complicate the pregnancy and may leave the newborn addicted. Damage during gestation can result from the mother's drug use. Going through the withdrawal process as a newborn can also result in brain damage and retardation.

Lead poisoning affects the mental growth of the fetus as well as the young child. Common sources of environmental lead are dust from lead-based paint, lead given off by brake linings, and lead in water systems. Young children should be regularly monitored for blood lead levels if there is any reason to suspect that environmental lead is a problem. If caught early, the effects can frequently be reversed; in the more severe stages of toxicity, severe retardation and even death can result.

Brain Injuries.   Injury to the brain, either at birth or in childhood, can result in mental retardation. Trauma to the fetus during birth can occur when the baby's position makes normal vaginal delivery difficult or when labor is prolonged or precipitous. All of these instances put undue stress on the fragile skull structures that protect the brain. Increasing numbers of Cesarean deliveries testify to the widespread belief that birth trauma can permanently damage the child's mental functioning and should be avoided. Fetal monitoring combined with surgical deliveries are frequently credited with reducing or preventing this type of brain damage.

Hypoxia, or lack of oxygen to the brain due to respiration failure, is also implicated in brain injury. Compression of the umbilical cord during delivery is a common cause of hypoxia in the perinatal period. Any time that breathing or respiration is stopped, brain injury is a possibility, and impairment in mental functioning can result. Primary prevention involves good prenatal care and fetal monitoring during labor and delivery.

Childhood traumatic brain injury accounts for additional cases of mental retardation. Injuries to children riding in cars account for a significant portion of these cases. New regulations regarding child safety restraints and the use of seat belts should reduce this cause. Retardation following injuries due to child abuse and neglect also represent preventable cases of mental retardation.

Prematurity.   Infants who are born prematurely or who have low birthweights are at risk for various birth defects and mental retardation. Preterm infants are often born with underdeveloped nervous systems and may not be able to make up that development after birth. Infants who are full term but whose birthweights are low may also show lack of sufficient neurological development. Low birthweight can be attributed to fetal malnutrition, smoking, alcohol or drug use, or other causes. Teenage mothers have a higher rate of premature and low-birthweight babies who are thus at higher risk for developmental delays and disabilities (see the case study about Jennie at the end of Chapter 6). In many cases, good prenatal care can avert these causes of mental retardation.

Environmental Causes

In about 75 percent of all cases of mental retardation, including a majority of those with milder levels of disability, there is no evidence of specific organic disease or pathology. Such cases are presumed to be related to a complex interaction among various adverse environmental influences during the prenatal, preschool, and school years (Zigler & Hodapp, 1986). AAMR (2002) cites a number of social, behavioral, and educational factors that appear to interact and lead to increased risk of mental retardation. Social factors include domestic violence, maternal malnutrition, lack of access to prenatal care, family poverty, and lack of adequate stimulation. Behavioral risk factors include parental alcohol or drug use, parental abandonment, abuse and neglect, inadequate safety measures, and difficult child behaviors. Educational risk factors include parental cognitive functioning deficits, inadequate early intervention, and lack of family supports.

It is generally acknowledged that both innate ability *and* a stimulating environment conducive to learning are necessary prerequisites to intellectual development. Adverse environmental conditions associated with retardation are often related to poverty, and they include inadequate nutrition during the prenatal period or during the periods of rapid development of early childhood, lack of regular health care and immunizations in infancy and childhood, and infections related to poor sanitation. Children growing up in environments that provide insufficient intellectual and language stimulation in the preschool years often appear to have retardation once they begin school. Since lack of age-appropriate language is often seen as an indication of reduced mental ability, a diagnosis of mental retardation is frequently the outcome. As James Allen observed:

> Although many children from the slums score low on intelligence tests and their academic achievement is comparably low, we doubt that it is all due to low intellectual ability. Despite the uncertainties of how and why learning does or does not take place, one thing is clear: No child can be expected to learn satisfactorily in a hostile environment. We are gravely concerned with the thought of children growing up in an environment ridden with health hazards, where rodents carry disease from house to house, where infectious diseases are unchecked, where malnutrition is a way of life. We should be equally concerned with impoverished and dangerous educational environments, where discouragement is a way of life and the infectious diseases of apathy and disinterest interfere with normal educational growth and development. (President's Committee on Mental Retardation, 1970, p. 3)

Compounding the problem is the presence of cultural differences between the family environment and the school environment. If these two cultures differ significantly in their expectations, the child enters school without the adaptive behaviors teachers expect, and the child is at a disadvantage in the school environment (see Box 6.2 and the case study about Benny in Chapter 5.) Since deficits in age-appropriate adaptive behaviors are also an indicator of mental retardation, the child is treated as retarded and may in fact become retarded unless educators are sensitive to the child's skills within the child's own cultural milieu. As Gordon noted, "Educability has been defined less by actual potentials of persons and more by the levels of society's demand for people of certain levels of function" (President's Committee on Mental Retardation, 1970, p. 2).

This discussion leads naturally to the perennial conundrum: Are mental ability and intellectual functioning determined by and related more to nature or nurture? Is the individual's mental ability determined by genetic (and therefore presumably immutable) factors, or is it determined by the environment (and therefore presumably alterable)? The work of eugenicists and Goddard's flawed study of the Kallikaks asserted that deficiencies in mental functioning were largely inherited and that the answer to mental retardation was to prevent those judged to have mental deficiencies from reproducing. In a review of the research on the relative effect of genetics and environment on intellectual functioning, Blanton (1975) concluded that support for the theory of genetic control of traits like intelligence is weak at best.

BOX **6.2**

SPOTLIGHT IN HISTORY: Rena Gazaway in the Appalachian Mountains

Rena Gazaway spent two years in the 1960s living with the inhabitants of an isolated Appalachian hollow she calls "Duddie's Branch." During her stay, she recorded her observations from the perspective of an anthropologist, and her work reveals the extent to which her stay there challenged her beliefs about intelligence as a fixed trait reflected in adaptive functioning. Her observations, documented in *The Longest Mile,* underscored the importance and validity of multiple perspectives on the functioning of individuals within and outside their culture in determining intellectual capability:

> Isolation is not selective; it attacks the young as well as the old. For the first six or more years of life the child is utterly dependent on those who care for him. During that time he acquires deeply rooted social habits in terms of communication, self-awareness and other characteristics that are passed on to him through the social order and biological nature of his being. Since each Brancher interacts only with others of the same kind, the child is doomed to become a carbon copy of the products of his community. He is accustomed to the intensely personal interactions of his immediate family and associates and is incapable of analyzing and developing his attributes. He speaks and walks later than other children, has far less curiosity and imagination, and learns more slowly. The only thing he grasps is the routine of crisis. The result of these experiences tends to glue him to his tradition and to his family. He is passive and shy, and regards the outside world and school as sinister places. Estranged from the outer community, he is committed to a lifetime of nothingness in a mile-long hollow of emptiness. (Gazaway, 1969, p. 70)

Gazaway commented on the lack of response to such special events as the circus or opportunities to visit museums or hear a symphony in the city. As she tried to share her experiences in the world outside the hollow with the Brancher children, she observed:

> The willingness to share my knowledge has little meaning, it serves no worth-while purpose. Sharing sometimes hinders my relationship with those so removed from the world about them. They are unable to understand and I am unable to impart meaning to strange experiences. . . . (p. 71)
>
> Not many of the young people aspire to any kind of achievement that would permit them to become part of the outer society. They cannot read, they cannot write, they cannot draw. In fact they are unfamiliar with most educational materials because they receive little in the way of education. The state law requires school attendance through sixteen years of age, but there is scarcely any enforcement in the rural areas. . . . Parents, too, are responsible for creating an air of indifference among the children. They have not had the advantage of an education and they question its value. The youngsters are not encouraged to make a serious effort because their mothers and fathers cannot appreciate the applicability of what is taught. (p. 72)

She concluded that the isolation of the Brancher's life assured that few would escape this cycle. She observed that "Isolation is to tread backward in time" (p. 73). But as she continued her stay in the hollow, her perceptions changed drastically. She continued with this story:

> Isolation is also selflessness, and ingenuity, and devotion. I was heading out of the hollow at 2:00 a.m. when suddenly I lost control of the jeep station wagon; it somehow turned over in a space scarcely wide enough to admit an automobile. I was stunned. When I regained consciousness I was aware that my hollow friends had come to my assistance.
>
> . . . The Branch was so narrow that the jeep doors could not be opened. Sie lost no time in figuring how to get the back door open and came "sneakin'" through to help me. Water was running six inches deep, and I was cold and wet and sore.
>
> "If'n you's not bad hurt, you's bound t' live," he comforted. "Hit's better fur you's if'n

(continued)

BOX   **6.2**   **Continued**

you's kin worm out. If 'n I's t' pull on you's, I might break off'n somethin' if 'n hit 'ud be jist hangin' by skin." I worked my way out, but could not stand. My skinny, undernourished friends were undaunted. "Sittin's hard anywhar in this branch, but we's plannin' sittin' you's outts warter."

With all the skill of a trained first aid crew, they placed me on a board and moved it "jist fur 'nuf so's you's feets hain't warshin' in 'em warters." The women hovered about and covered me with their threadbare coats that provided little warmth. They made me lean against their scrawny, shivering frames. "You's gonna be feelin' bones, but they's not 's hard 's rocks a-pushin' through you's meat.". . . .

The next project was to get me dry. "Hit 'udn't be fittin' t' take off'n you's wet clothes exposed t' seein' men," Jemima whispered, so the women kept changing the various articles of clothing with which they had covered me.

"We's plannin' t' soak you's duds mostly dry by seepin' 'em out int' our'n."

It worked. (pp. 73–74)

Gazaway continued her account, describing the ingenuity by which the Branchers extricated her jeep from the Branch and finally got her to the hospital. After evaluation by the doctor, her friends carried her back to Duddie's Branch to recuperate. Solicitous attention continued throughout her convalescence. Healing potions were offered, as well as precious gifts of coal.

She concluded her account with this observation and a renewed awareness:

These are the isolated, the "undesirables," the primitives. These are the ones who are destined to live a life of poverty. These are the ones who are excluded from the good things of life, but who do not complain. These are the ones who cannot speak a language that we can understand because it is an idiom that originates from the heart and not the mind. These are my friends. (p. 77)

Quotations from *The Longest Mile* by Rena Gazaway. Copyright © 1969 by Rena Gazaway. Used by permission of Doubleday, a division of Bantam Doubleday Dell Publishing Group, Inc.

Angoff (1988) casts a different light on this question. He suggested that heritability may not be the most useful issue to address, but rather that the central issue is changeability. When we consider the fact that the effects of conditions that are clearly genetically based (e.g., PKU) can be changed dramatically through medical intervention, we must draw the conclusion that heritable does not necessarily mean immutable. Conversely, when we consider how resistant to change certain environmentally induced conditions or habits can be (e.g., smoking, drug use, or nail biting), it becomes obvious that there is little useful connection between heritability indices and the degree to which a behavior is alterable.

It may be more useful to consider the interactive effects of nature and nurture, or heredity and environment. Each person comes into the world with a set of genetic instructions. How those instructions will affect development depends in most cases on the extent to which the environment supports the development of those characteristics. Genetically directed traits have a *reaction range,* a potential range of expression. The manifestation of any hereditary trait will depend primarily on the presence or absence of favorable environmental conditions (Zigler & Hodapp, 1986). A favorable environment will cause the individual to manifest the trait at the upper limit of the range, while a deficient environment will result in the trait being restricted to the lower limits of the range (see Figure 6.4).

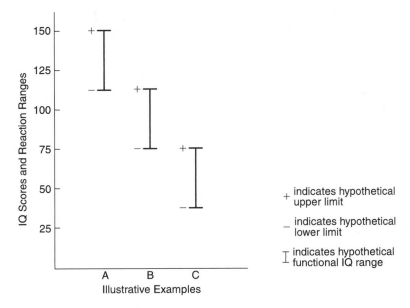

FIGURE 6.4   Illustration of the Concept of Reaction Range

Since we can never be sure what those limits may be for any individual or trait, the most ethical course of action is to maximize the environment for every child. This suggests that as a society, as parents, and as teachers, we should provide good nutrition, health care, and educational opportunities for all children so that they will reach their fullest stature and enjoy vigorous good health. This means that we should seek to provide rich and intellectually stimulating environments for all children so that they will be enabled to function at the upper limits of their range of mental aptitude, whatever that may be.

Focus on Culture and Diversity

The issue of disproportionate representation of students from diverse cultural backgrounds in classes for students with mental retardation has been on the table since before 1970. The President's Committee on Mental Retardation (1970) questioned the adequacy of standard assessment practices in determining if students from diverse cultural or linguistic backgrounds had mental retardation. Two early court decisions, *Larry P.* v. *Riles* (1972, 1979, 1984) and *Diana* v. *State Board of Education* (1970), held that assessment practices using tests that were not culturally fair or that were not presented in the student's primary language could not accurately determine if the child had mental retardation. The central concern related to the validity of instruments commonly used to determine intelligence and the apparent bias of those tests; since their use resulted in a significant overrepresentation of students of color in special education classes, it was suggested that the tests were not adequately assessing the abilities of children from culturally and linguistically diverse backgrounds.

The U.S. Department of Education (2001) confirms that the problem has not lessened in recent years. In 1999–2000, African-American students were much more likely to be identified with mental retardation than would be predicted by their prevalence in the school population, while students from Hispanic or Asian/Pacific Islander backgrounds were less likely to be so identified. In addition, African-American and Hispanic students were more likely to be placed in more restrictive settings once identified. This data suggests that we do not yet have a culturally sensitive assessment and placement process and that students with mental retardation are continuing to be disproportionally represented by race in special education (Salend, Garrick Duhaney, & Montgomery, 2002).

Resources on the Web

American Association on Mental Retardation (AAMR)

www.aamr.org

Provides resources for professionals serving individuals with mental retardation; includes a useful publications link.

The Arc

www.TheArc.org

Provides resources for families, as well as program resources for local chapters of The Arc (formerly the Association for Retarded Citizens), one of the earliest parent advocacy groups.

National Down Syndrome Society

www.ndss.org

Provides a comprehensive information source on Down syndrome, with special attention to parent needs.

Division for Developmental Disabilities (DDD)

www.dddcec.org

Provides a professional site for educators who work with students with mental retardation and other developmental disabilities; a subdivision of CEC.

Summary

Mental retardation, particularly at the severe levels, has been a subject for societal study, concern, and action for a long time. More recently, mild retardation has been defined and addressed by services and supports in the school and community. In current theory and practice, persons with retardation are viewed as individuals with a variety of strengths and needs, and they are served in more normalized and inclusive settings.

Mental retardation has been conceptualized over the past 50 years as a condition defined by significantly subaverage intellectual functioning that exists concurrently with deficits in global adaptive behavior and that manifests itself during childhood and adolescence. The 1992/2002 AAMR diagnostic process suggests that our primary concern should be to determine the current ability of the individual to function in various settings. The diagnostic process assesses adaptive behavior strengths and needs implying that mental retardation is not necessarily a pervasive disorder affecting all facets of the individual's life equally. It also suggests that the levels of support required to enable the person to function (including instruction, training, and coaching) should be factors in the diagnostic determination. Appropriate levels of support might indeed result in improved functioning and possible declassification of the individual in other times and settings.

The terms used to refer to the severity of mental retardation have included at least three levels of mental retardation. Currently, the terms used to denote the levels of severity are mild, moderate, and severe/profound. Current conversations concerning the 1992/2002 AAMR definition suggest that this practice might be inaccurate and not useful for program planning, focusing instead on the domain-specific intensity of needed supports as an indicator. Individuals with mental retardation are a heterogeneous group of people. There are an infinite number of possibilities in the degree to which an individual may manifest deficits in intellectual functioning and in any of the adaptive behavior skill domains. The diagnosis of mental retardation suggests that we may encounter concerns in learning and cognitive functioning, as well as in social-emotional behaviors and physical ability. While the expectation of generalized reduced functioning is present, we must keep in mind that the individual profile of abilities and needs is what should guide program planning.

Mental retardation is believed to affect from 2 to 3 percent of the population, with most of the cases falling in the mild range. About 25 percent of the diagnoses relate to known or suspected biomedical causes, while the majority of cases are generally attributed to the impact of environment and culture on development. There is continuing discussion and debate about the relative impact of nature and nurture on the development of human abilities in general; the "reaction range" model is a useful way to conceptualize the interaction of genetic and environmental factors.

JENNIE: A Case Study

Jennie is an eight-year-old girl who lives in a mid-sized, midwestern city. She is the eldest of four children. She has twin brothers a year younger than she and a baby brother two years old. Jennie lives at home with her mother and siblings. The father has been an infrequent part of their lives due to repeated convictions for drug offenses. The family lives in public housing.

Jennie's mother has had the support of a "Mentor Mom" since before Jennie was born. The Mentor Mom program was established to assist young, inexperienced mothers who otherwise would have few supports in caring for their babies. The Mentor Mom's role is similar to the roles that were played by grandmothers, mothers, and aunts in times when extended families were able to help new

(continued)

parents learn to care for their own children. The Mentor Mom has helped Jennie's mother with child-rearing information and problem-solving support over the years. Jennie frequently spends time with the Mentor Mom at her home in the country. Jennie's mother has been participating in adult basic education programs and counseling for several years, and she wants to make life for her children better than hers has been. Frequently she depends on the Mentor Mom when the demands of living with four young children overwhelm her.

Jennie was born prematurely after a difficult pregnancy. At age six, Jennie was tested by her school system for possible identification as a child in need of special education services. This evaluation was prompted by her lower level of performance and her history of prematurity, neurological problems, and environmental disadvantage. The following psychological report is from Jennie's school file, and was prepared two years ago as part of Jennie's original referral to special education.

Report of Psychological Evaluation

Jennie   Age: 6 years   Grade: 5–K (Kindergarten)

Tests Administered:
  Stanford-Binet Intelligence Scale
      IQ   68   CA   5–11
                       MA   4–6

  Test of Visual-Motor Integration (VMI):
      Standard Score   74
      Percentile Rank   4th
      Age Equivalent   4–3

  Draw-a-Person Test: Estimated Mental Age: 4–5

  Vineland Adaptive Behavior Scale (Classroom edition):

Domain	Standard Score	Percentile	Adaptive Level
Communication Domain	70	2	Mod. Low
Daily Living Skills Domain	80	9	Mod. Low
Socialization Domain	67	1	Low
Motor Skills Domain	60	0.4	Low
Adaptive Behavior Composite	67	1	Low

  Brigance K&1 Screening Test
  Teacher behavioral checklist (district devised instrument)
  Observation of performance of assorted educational tasks

Referral and Background Information: Jennie was referred for evaluation because of behavioral and academic concerns. She has a history of premature birth (two months premature) with a seizure disorder developing at eight months of age. She is currently on Tegretol three times a day for control of the seizures. As a three- and four-year-old, Jennie attended a preschool program for children with developmental delays. Upon completion of the preschool program, a multidisciplinary team determined that she was not eligible for special education and should enter the 4-K Kindergarten in her home school district. She is presently enrolled in the 5-K Kindergarten program.

She is described as engaging in a lot of self-stimulating behaviors such as rocking and making noises, and is said to interact minimally with the other children. Language skills are significantly delayed in both receptive and expressive areas, according to the speech and language evaluation. She does not speak much in class or attend well to group instruction. She is seated preferentially in the classroom to reduce distractibility, and she is involved in a special reading program which places children in ability-appropriate reading groups.

Observations and Behavior: Jennie is a small, dark-haired child who accompanied the examiner readily to the testing room. She was cooperative and appeared to try to do her best throughout the evaluation, which lasted the better part of an hour. Speech was, at times, difficult to understand due to faulty articulation of some sounds. Jennie could give her name, address, and age, but did not know her birthday or telephone number. Some mild tremulousness of the arm was noted when she was engaged in graphic tasks. She was able to hop on both feet and to hop on her left foot quite well. She could not walk heel-to-toe and had trouble balancing on her left foot with her eyes closed. The examiner had difficulty understanding the proper names when she asked Jennie about family members.

Discussion of Test Results: Jennie was found to be functioning within the range of intelligence on the Stanford-Binet-LM that is consistent with the diagnosis of mild mental retardation. She was able to match pictures of animals and shapes, to discriminate pictorial likenesses and differences, and to identify pictures in terms of their functions as well as picture vocabulary. She was able to handle analogous reasoning items at the four-year level, but could not pass the comprehension questions at that level. She simply repeated the questions rather than responding with an answer. At the five-year level she was able to identify pictures in terms of similarities and differences, and to copy a square. Jennie's drawing of a man, copying of the VMI shapes, and Mental Age on the Stanford-Binet were all around the four-to-four-and-a-half-year level. This indicates an average of a two year delay in the areas of functioning assessed by these tests.

Skill-wise, Jennie was able to count orally to twelve, but could not correctly count objects beyond five. While she could count orally, she did not recognize any numerals except one and two. She could match the correct quantity of crayons to the numbers two and one, but to no others. She did not recognize or name any letters of the alphabet, but she was able to sing the alphabet song with only one error in the middle. She cannot print her name at all, but did print a series of letters which looked like J, N, and E when asked to write her name. Jennie was able to identify ten basic colors correctly.

Behaviorally, Jennie's teacher noted on the checklist that there are problems with constant fidgeting, humming, making odd noises, being inattentive, being easily distracted, and crying often and easily. To a lesser degree there are problems with being restless, overactive, excitable, impulsive, overly sensitive, disturbing other children, and having quick and drastic mood changes. The teacher further described Jennie as pretty much tending to isolate herself from other children, appearing to be easily led, lacking leadership, and interfering with the other children's activities. Her attitude toward authority was described as submissive and on the shy side. The teacher indicated that Jennie has very poor socialization skills, that she doesn't assert herself, and that when she does try to interact it tends to be inappropriate.

Summary and Recommendations: This cooperative, friendly, and likable little girl of five-and-a-half has a long history of developmental delays, evidently related to prematurity. She also is reported to have a seizure disorder for which she takes medication. Jennie was found to be functioning within the range of intelligence associated with mild retardation, with developmental levels generally around the four-and-a-half-year level in terms of her cognitive ability and her physical skill development. She appears to be a child with global retardation who is probably rather overwhelmed by the demands of

(continued)

the regular kindergarten classroom where she very likely does not understand much of what transpires. Her inattentive and distracting behaviors in this setting are possibly a reaction to her inability to compete and perform at a level that is comparable to the other children in the class. Her teacher comments that Jennie's socialization skills are similar to those of younger children.

It appears that Jennie needs a small, structured classroom situation where she can receive individualized work at her instructional level. She could benefit from a program with a heavy emphasis on the development of socialization and communication skills. She appears to meet the criteria for an individualized education program (IEP), as a child with mild mental retardation.

The following report was written a year ago, when Jennie was seven, by the staff at the neonatal neurological clinic that has been following her since birth, due to her history of prematurity and her subsequent seizure disorder. It provides some additional information about her history and neurological status at age seven.

College of Medicine • University Hospital
Rehabilitation Center for Children and Adults

PATIENT NAME: Jennie   **AGE: 7 years old**

Jennie is currently a seven-year old female who was born at thirty-three weeks gestation weighing five pounds. She has a history of seizures and frequent otitis media. Jennie was seen in the University Clinic for a speech and language consultation. She was accompanied by her mother. Jennie presently receives speech and language therapy twice weekly at school. One session is in a group setting, while the other session is on an individual basis. Jennie's mother reported that the goals of therapy include improved syntax and sound production. Jennie's mother is pleased with her present speech services.

During today's visit, Jennie was observed for speech and language development. She is a very pleasant young lady who easily engages in conversation. She was able to follow all simple one- and two-step directions. She exhibited some difficulty with regular verb production but this was on an inconsistent basis. Phonological errors were present but they were within expectations for her age. Although syntax errors were evident in her conversational speech, her ability to convey her meaning appears to be appropriate for her overall developmental levels. It is recommended that Jennie continue to receive speech and language therapy in addition to her school program. Her present program is addressing all appropriate speech/language developmental goals. However, it is suggested that Jennie's speech and language development continue to be screened during clinic visits.

Finally, when Jennie turned eight, the following observational report was prepared by an independent educational evaluator to assist Jennie's mother and the Mentor Mom with their planning meetings at Jennie's school. They were both concerned about Jennie's lack of progress in her current school program. Both Jennie's mom and the Mentor Mom voiced the concern that Jennie seemed to be making little progress despite all the years she has been in school. They were looking for information to support their request for a full triennial evaluation, including a repeat of the ability and achievement measures done two years earlier.

Observational Report

Name: JENNIE   **Age: 8 years**

At the request of Jennie's mother, an observation was conducted in Jennie's classroom to determine if her current placement in a primary class for youngsters with mild mental retardation appeared appropriate for her. In addition, a number of informal diagnostic procedures were undertaken.

It was apparent from watching Jennie's performance in her classroom that she has great difficulty with tasks like naming and writing letters and numbers, especially when these tasks are presented without context. In contrast, in preparation for a parent program the following week, she recited a long poem from memory and without prompts. She appears to function as well as or better than most of her classmates. Jennie's class behavior was attentive and conforming. In discussing the class curriculum with the teacher, it appears that the majority of the time is spent on counting, reading color words, and naming and writing letters. The teacher mentioned that the whole language approach had been suggested, but that she didn't think that method was appropriate for students at this functional level. She bases her program on acquisition of basic skills such as counting and naming and writing letters. Until the students have mastered those skills, the teacher feels it is inappropriate to move on.

In subsequent diagnostic teaching observations outside of school, Jennie was presented with a whole word approach to decoding words, using picture cues and repeated self-drill. She quickly learned a half-dozen words she had selected from a book. She seemed to benefit from the meaningfulness of the words and the picture cues. She was taught to drill herself on these selected words using the single-concept picture cards she and the evaluator had created; she also learned to congratulate (reinforce) herself when she was correct. The process appears to have promise for getting her started on reading.

A second activity was making pies for a picnic. As the pie was being made, she and the observer wrote down the steps of the recipe. After each step, the combined recipe was read and reread. With the repetition and meaningful activity, she was able to read the entire recipe at the end of the project.

One incident regarding reading is worth noting. Jennie was holding a book that had been read to her previously. She said she would read it to the observer. She then commenced to "pretend read" the book as many young children do. The difference was that she carefully hid the pages from the observer so that it would not be apparent that she was not actually reading the page. It appears that this child has already decided that she is supposed to be able to read, knows she cannot, and is desperately trying to hide that fact. This behavioral pattern is particularly troubling, since it suggests that she will be increasingly resistant to real attempts to teach her to read.

Behaviorally, Jennie has developed a talent at getting what she wants and avoiding what she doesn't want to do. She bargains with those around her: "Let me do/have this, then I'll do that." The problem is that she frequently resists the less desired activity after having received her reward, refusing to comply. It is essential that any behavior modification program established for Jennie place the reward after the compliance action has occurred.

From all of these observations, it appears that Jennie is a child with a variety of strengths and weaknesses. It appears that she is a child who would benefit from more holistic, experiential forms of teaching. It is recommended that:

- Initial reading instruction should focus on whole words and real language. Appropriate methods might include language experience activities, repeated rereading of trade books with the teacher or her parent (perhaps using Reading Recovery, the Fernald multisensory method for learning whole words, or IBM's Writing to Read program). For now, focusing on individual letters and sounds should probably be abandoned.

(continued)

- Story reading to and with Jennie should be engaged in to reduce her anxiety about not reading.
- Use of a computer and primary word processing software may help with the fine motor problems that have thus far impeded her writing.
- Consistent use of manipulatives in math instruction, using a curriculum such as *Math Their Way,* is essential if numbers are to begin to have meaning for Jennie.
- Her delays in oral language are obvious. Good models and structured language training should be continued.
- Strict adherence to the Premack principle in behavior management is essential. Low interest activities should be paired with high interest activities (rewards). Rewards should be contingent on her completing the required behavior before the reward is received.

DISCUSSION

Using the above information collected over a two-year period, determine whether Jennie's classification as a child with mental retardation is appropriate. First, analyze the data using the current IDEA criteria developed by the AAMR in 1983, and then reanalyze the case using the 1992/2002 approach.

Where you lack information for a full determination, draw tentative conclusions, and make a list of the additional information you would need to complete the evaluation.

CHAPTER SEVEN

LEARNERS WITH LEARNING DISABILITIES

QUESTIONS TO GUIDE YOUR STUDY

- How did the concept of learning disabilities develop?
- How do we define and identify learning disabilities today?
- How is the concept of discrepancy applied to the identification process?
- What issues have been and still are being debated with respect to the concept of learning disabilities?
- What causes learning disabilities?
- How common are learning disabilities; what explanations can you give for the increases in the numbers of students with learning disabilities since 1975?
- What are the characteristics of students with learning disabilities?

Meet Peter

Peter looks like a typical teenager. He has a growing CD collection, he loves his computer video games, and the condition of his room is a source of constant "conversation" with his mother. At age fifteen, he pours over the driver's license manual, looking forward to the day when that magic card will free him from the constraints of parental transportation and curfews.

But Peter differs from his peers in some significant ways. Although he is alert, appears to be knowledgeable about many things, and is apparently no different from others in his school who are planning on college in a few years, he struggles with basic reading and writing and may not be able to pass the state-mandated competency tests required for high school graduation. What makes this so hard on Peter, his family, and teachers is that Peter "looks smart." In fact, he has a measured IQ of 113, well into the average to above-average range. Yet school has always been hard for him.

What makes Peter different is that he was identified as a student with a learning disability in second grade. Peter failed to learn to read from the basal program used by his school, and his handwriting and spelling were very poor. At first, his teachers and parents felt he just wasn't trying, and

(continued)

he was alternatively cajoled and punished in an attempt to get him to exert the effort needed to "live up to his potential." His second grade teacher, trying to find a way to help Peter become a successful learner, sought the help of the school's resource teacher.

After a period of prereferral intervention, it was determined that more information was needed. The evaluation by the school psychologist provided the answer; despite normal sensory and intellectual abilities, Peter's achievement lagged significantly behind his potential. Since no other reason could be found for this lag, it was determined that Peter had a learning disability.

Throughout the next few years, a number of interventions were tried. He learned well when information was provided orally in class discussions. He was able to demonstrate his knowledge in oral recitation and various projects that did not require reading and writing. The skills of reading and writing, however, remained problematic. In middle school, compensatory modifications were initiated. He was provided with books on tape. Tests were given in the resource room, with oral responses permitted. These modifications allowed him to keep learning, but they failed to address his reading and writing deficiencies.

Now Peter is in high school. His inability to read at a functional level has impeded his progress. He is unable to demonstrate his knowledge and understanding through written work and tests. He is having more difficulty with the academic-track coursework, and his teachers wonder if he wouldn't be better served by a general vocational program.

His new special education teacher noted that he seemed to lack the cognitive strategies needed for learning, and in an attempt to help him keep his graduation and college options open, the teacher has begun a program of learning strategy instruction. Peter's general intellectual ability suggests that with help and accommodations for his disability, he should be able to complete college.

For now, Peter reads the driver's manual and looks forward to driving!

Historical Development of the Learning Disabilities Concept

Students like Peter have puzzled teachers for years. These students look "smart" but fail to learn. They are students whom we now identify as having a learning disability. But it hasn't always been so. The field of learning disabilities is fairly young. While it is apparent that there have always been individuals who would now be identified as having a learning disability, the term itself has been in use only since 1963, when it was adopted by the parents who formed the Association for Children with Learning Disabilities (ACLD/LDA). Prior to that time, work with such individuals was carried out largely by physicians, neurologists, and psychologists.

Medical Phase

Work by Franz Gall, Paul Broca, and others in the 1800s investigated the hypothesis that certain functions were governed by specific parts of the brain (Mercer, 1987). In their studies of adults with brain injury, they determined that injuries to specific areas of the brain appeared to be related to specific disorders in functioning, with particular emphasis on language usage. Early twentieth-century neuropsychologists continued this line of research. Hinshelwood (1917) described a condition called "congenital word blindness," documenting his work with a boy who appeared to be intellectually capable but who nevertheless could not read. In 1939, Kurt Goldstein published his work based on a study of the characteristics of soldiers who had suffered brain injury as a result of head wounds in World War I. All of these efforts documented the relationship between specific injuries and specific functional impairments.

Work on brain differences continued through the 1930s. Samuel Orton (1937), a neurologist, concluded from his research that language abilities were controlled by one side of the brain, and that children with language disabilities were those who had not achieved hemispheric dominance. Using multisensory techniques and synthetic phonetics, Anna Gillingham and Bessie Stillman developed remedial approaches based on Orton's work. About the same time, Grace Fernald utilized whole word techniques to develop her own multisensory approach (VAKT) for teaching students with problems in reading and writing.

The medical period in the history of learning disabilities in the United States continued into the 1930s and 1940s with the work of Heinz Werner and Alfred Strauss and their students, Laura Lehtinen, Newell Kephart, and William Cruickshank. Werner and Strauss noticed that, although all of the residents where they worked were diagnosed as having mental retardation, there seemed to be two distinct groups among the patients based on clusters of behavior. They attributed *endogenous* mental retardation to familial or inherited (i.e., congenital) characteristics and they believed that *exogenous* mental retardation was the result of an injury to the brain at or after birth. The characteristics of persons with exogenous mental retardation came to be referred to as *Strauss Syndrome* and included distractibility, hyperactivity, and perceptual motor problems (Stevens & Birch, 1957). These individuals often displayed erratic and inappropriate behavior, disproportionate motor activity, poor behavior organization, faulty perception, and awkward motor performance (Mercer, 1987).

From this, Strauss and his colleagues developed the concept of individual differences and the need for prescriptive teaching (Strauss & Lehtinen, 1947; Strauss & Kephart, 1955). Lehtinen's work concentrated on manipulating and controlling the environment in which these students learned and on identifying ways to teach these students voluntary control skills. Kephart's work focused on perceptual motor development. During the 1950s, there was considerable interest in identifying specific areas of deficit and then designing specific interventions to train these processes. Cruickshank continued this work with children who had cerebral palsy but normal intelligence. He later published his strategies for educating these children in a highly structured environment to help them focus their attention devoid of extraneous stimulation (Cruickshank, Bentzen, Ratzeburgh, & Tannhauser, 1961).

By the end of the 1950s, the foundation for the yet to be named field of learning disabilities had been established. Attention had been directed to the unique learning difficulties exhibited by students with a history of brain injury, as well as by those with similar behaviors but no history of brain injury. However, the term *brain injured* suggested a medical diagnosis and treatment, and educators remained largely uninvolved in either the identification or treatment of individuals with these disorders.

Learning Disability Phase

During the 1960s, general dissatisfaction grew with the concept of brain injury as an explanation for the problems experienced by children with seemingly normal abilities but who were not learning well in school. The term had a very negative and pessimistic tone because it implied severe disability. The term implied a permanency of the condition that reduced hope of normal functioning in the future, and it provided no guidance for educators.

Seeking names for this condition that have more educational relevance, special educators, parents, and others began using such terms as educational handicaps, language disorders, perceptual handicaps, clumsy child syndrome, and hyperkinetic syndrome. Without a clear description or understanding of the condition, parents sought help from other parents in dealing with schools and their own frustrations, forming a variety of organizations such as the New York Association for Brain-Injured Children and the Fund for Perceptually Handicapped Children.

At a meeting of these parents in Chicago in 1963, Sam Kirk noted that the terms brain injured and neurological impairment implied that the problem was a medical one. He suggested that the use of a term more related to teaching and learning would be more useful in the goal of acquiring educational services for these children.

> Recently I have used the term "learning disabilities" to describe a group of children who have disorders in the development of language, speech, reading and associated communication skills needed for social interaction. In this group I do not include those who have sensory handicaps such as blindness or deafness because we have methods of managing and training the deaf and the blind. I also exclude children who have generalized mental retardation. (Kirk, 1963, p. 3; Kirk & McCarthy, 1975, p. 9)

During the 1960s and 1970s, there was increased governmental activity on behalf of these children. Task Force I, chaired by S. D. Clements, was established by the Department of Health, Education, and Welfare to study this disability. Using the term *minimal brain dysfunction* to refer to these children, they identified ten characteristics typically observed in these learners:

- Hyperactivity
- Perceptual-motor impairments
- Emotional liability (i.e., instability)
- General coordination deficits
- Disorders of attention (e.g., short attention span, distractibility, perseveration)
- Impulsivity
- Disorders of memory or thinking
- Difficulty in academic skills (e.g., reading, arithmetic, writing, spelling)
- Disorders of speech and hearing
- Equivocal (or "soft") neurological signs and electroencephalographic irregularities (Clements, 1966, p. 13)

Although the term minimal brain dysfunction minimized the implication of the severity of the organic damage and mental disability, it still had many of the same limitations of the earlier work in brain injury. Thus the term *learning disability* became the term of choice for identifying these puzzling students. The Association for Children with Learning Disabilities/Learning Disabilities Association of America (ACLD/LDA) was formed in 1963 and has continued to work on behalf of the rights of individuals with learning disabilities.

Researchers continued to investigate learning disabilities and developed educational interventions for these students. Newell Kephart (1960) published *The Slow Learner in the Classroom,* which advocated perceptual-motor training as a remedial technique. Sam Kirk and colleagues published the *Illinois Test of Psycholinguistic Abilities (ITPA)* in 1961, which was designed to assess the specific processes of sensory and psycholinguistic processing, (Kirk & Kirk, 1971; Kirk, McCarthy, & Kirk, 1968). Marianne Frostig developed the *Developmental Test of Visual Perception* and training materials for remediation of visual perception disabilities in 1964. However, none of these approaches demonstrated a significant degree of sustained effectiveness, and they are no longer used in programs for children with learning disabilities.

In 1968, the National Advisory Committee on Handicapped Children (NACHC, 1968), chaired by Kirk, was formed by the U.S. Office of Education with the charge to develop a definition of learning disabilities. The Specific Learning Disabilities Act was passed in 1969 and included the definition of learning disabilities that is still used in federal programs today, and with the passage of the Education for All Handicapped Children Act in 1975, the disorder called specific learning disability was firmly established as a defined area of disability.

IDEA Phase

Schools now faced the challenge of identifying and serving these children. The *Federal Register* published regulations issued by the U.S. Office of Education (1976), stating that the presence of a learning disability was to be established by the use of a discrepancy formula to identify a severe discrepancy between expected achievement and ability, and that the impairment did not result from other disabilities.

After a year of comment on the 1976 Federal definition, the overwhelmingly negative reactions caused the government to withdraw the discrepancy formula and to return to the original conceptual definition. The 1977 regulations required that the individual display achievement significantly less than would be expected for the learner's age and ability (U.S. Office of Education, 1977a, p. 65083). Definitional issues have continued to occasion much debate with periodic offerings of new, "improved" versions, including the NJCLD, ACLD, and ICLD definitions that we will discuss later in this chapter (Hammill, 1990). None of the proposed definitions is without critics, and the search for the perfect definition continues.

From 1975 to the present, as increasing numbers of children have been identified as having learning disabilities, the challenge to schools has been to find ways to effectively educate these students. It was initially reasoned that since learning disabilities were related to problems in psychological processing, appropriate remediation of those process deficits should enable these children to subsequently profit from regular instructional methods. However, it soon became apparent that (1) the deficits themselves did not seem to respond to these programs, and (2) academic deficits remained even when the programs seemed to be ameliorating the process deficits (Kavale & Mattson, 1983; Lloyd, 1984). By the end of the 1970s, educators became more critical of and questioned the efficacy of psycholinguistic and perceptual motor models of teaching. In 1978, the U.S. Office of Education established five Learning Disabilities Research Institutes at universities across the country to study particular issues relating to learning disabilities.

Attention then turned to the use of direct instruction and behavioral reinforcement strategies, working directly on the academic deficits rather than the implied processing problems (Treiber & Lahey, 1983). Although these methods were more useful in increasing student achievement, they failed to engage the student actively in his or her own learning. Instruction was often segmented, and students seemed to lack the skills needed to integrate the learning and to generalize it across settings.

By the 1990s, research in the field began to focus on cognitive approaches. Researchers at the University of Virginia and the University of Kansas developed methods and curricula that help students learn how to learn. They addressed the skills of self-questioning, self-instruction, self-monitoring, self-evaluation, and self-reinforcement. The growing research base suggested that these approaches, if well implemented, help students with learning disabilities develop the skills needed to actively pursue their own learning. It has also been suggested that students may benefit even more when cognitive approaches are combined with skill instruction using behavioral approaches. However, no magic cure has been found that will unlock the puzzle for this heterogeneous group of students. Many questions regarding definition, assessment, and remediation remain to be answered.

The 1980s and 1990s also saw increased concern with adolescents and adults with learning disabilities. As individuals who were identified as having learning disabilities during childhood matured into adolescents and then adults, it was found that the disability remained, although the manifestation might have changed. Gordon Alley and Donald Deshler published *Teaching the Learning Disabled Adolescent: Strategies and Methods* in 1979 (revised by Deshler, Ellis, and Lenz in 1996), which laid the groundwork for subsequent efforts with adolescent learners and cognitive interventions in general and a recognition that learning disabilities persisted over the life span.

Current IDEA Definition

The definition currently used in the IDEA to define this population of learners reads as follows:

"Specific learning disability" means a disorder in one or more of the basic psychological processes involved in understanding or in using language, spoken or written, which may manifest itself in an imperfect ability to listen, think, speak, read, write, spell, or do mathematical calculations. The term includes such conditions as perceptual handicaps, brain injury, minimal brain dysfunction, dyslexia, and developmental aphasia. The term does not include children who have learning problems that are primarily the result of visual, hearing, or motor handicaps, of mental retardation, or emotional disturbance, or of environmental, cultural, or economic disadvantage.

U.S. Office of Education, 1977b, p. 42478.

This definition includes five major components:

- "Disorder in psychological processes" relates to the presumed source of the student's learning difficulty, based on the theory that the individual does not process information as efficiently or effectively as others do. Throughout the history of the field, various researchers have taken this to refer to perceptual or perceptual-motor processing, psycholinguistic processing, or cognitive functioning. New diagnostic tools such as magnetic resonance imaging (MRI) have provided evidence that the brains of individuals with learning disabilities differ from typical learners (Shaywitz, B. A., et al., 1997). However, the "disorder in psychological processes" criterion has yet to be defined in a way that leads to valid, reliable, and practical assessment devices. The presence of disorders in processing can generally only be inferred from observation of academic and learning behaviors. At the most, this criterion supplies a conceptual explanation of the learning disability rather than a diagnostic indicator.
- The language component points to the centrality of disorders in understanding or using language. These disorders may be manifested by deficits in the receptive language areas of listening and reading as well as in the expressive language functions of speaking and writing. This component also relates to difficulties in language processing, which includes cognitive language processes (i.e., inner language) in addition to the expressive and receptive functions.
- The ability-achievement discrepancy, or "the imperfect ability to" clause, is generally regarded as one of the major operational diagnostic indicators. Very simply, a student who presents indications of having the ability to perform a particular skill or function at an acceptable level, but who fails to achieve at that level, is viewed as meeting this diagnostic criterion. The discrepancy may be in any single area or it may be in a combination of academic and functional areas. As stated in the proposed rules for the IDEA implementation:

    A team may determine that a child has a specific learning disability if the child does not achieve commensurate with his or her ability levels in one or more of the areas listed [below] if provided with learning experiences appropriate for the child's age and ability levels; and the team finds that a child has a severe discrepancy between achievement and intellectual ability in one or more of the following areas: oral expression, listening comprehension, written expression, basic reading skill, reading comprehension, mathematics calculation, [and] mathematics reasoning. (U.S. Department of Education, 1997a, p. 55106)

  In addition, the finding of a discrepancy must meet a criterion of severity. The standard for determining that a severe discrepancy exists varies from district to district and state to state. A study of state-mandated criteria by Frankenberger and Fronzaglio (1991) found that only 76 percent of the states dictated a specific method for determining discrepancy, and that those states used a variety of methods (e.g., standard score comparisons, expectancy formulas, deviation from grade level, or regression analysis). Mercer, Jordan, Allsopp, & Mercer (1996) and Ross (1995) noted continued variation in the procedures used and the compliance with those procedures.
- The inclusion clause was added to bridge the gap between the present definition and prior eras when multiple terms were used to refer to the group of individuals we now

have agreed to say have "learning disabilities." It does not imply that an individual must have one of the listed diagnoses to qualify as having a learning disability, but merely that individuals who were or might have been identified as having one of the listed conditions may now be referred to as having a learning disability. The one term listed in the definition that has remained in widespread usage is *dyslexia*. In accordance with this component of the definition, students with severe reading disorders, or dyslexia, would be considered to have specific learning disabilities.

■ The exclusion clause was derived from the original conceptual definitions of learning disability in the early 1960s. The term *learning disability* developed because there were children who could not read although they could see, could not speak well although they could hear language, could not learn but did not have mental retardation or emotional disabilities, and did not do well in school although they had access to normal opportunities to learn in the school, home, and community. If any of these other conditions were present, it was reasoned that there were existing categories by which to identify them and classes and methods for serving their needs. Children assigned to this new category were defined primarily by what they were not: They were not learning, and they did not have visual, hearing, or motor disabilities, mental retardation, emotional disturbance, or environmental, cultural, or economic disadvantage that restricted their learning (Lavoie, 1989). IDEA 1997 reinforced this principle when it stated that children who have not had the opportunity to learn may not be identified as having a learning disability (Council for Exceptional Children, 1998a). Thus, the exclusion clause becomes the second operational indicator of the presence of a learning disability.

Assessment and Identification Issues

IDEA requires that students suspected of having any disability receive a nondiscriminatory evaluation using a variety of reliable and valid information sources. Over the years, many instruments have been developed to identify learning disabilities. Many, such as the ITPA and other tests of perceptual functioning, have not been proven to be reliable or valid for the purpose (Algozzine & Ysseldyke, 1988; Council for Learning Disabilities, 1987b; Kavale & Mattson, 1983) and are no longer in general use. The information sources used most often to determine the presence of a learning disability are:

■ Measures of ability (e.g., an individually administered test of intellectual functioning, such as the WISC-III, Stanford-Binet, or K-ABC intelligence tests)
■ Measures of academic achievement, including individual achievement tests
■ Other indicators of academic achievement or underachievement, such as report cards, group achievement tests, teacher anecdotal records, and other reports
■ Screening tests for vision and hearing
■ Social and school history information gained from interviews with parents
■ A variety of other sources, such as classroom observations and results from prereferral interventions

Once gathered, this information is evaluated to determine if the criteria in the definition and state regulations are met. The first task is to document the presence of an area or areas of serious underachievement. Determination of the extent of the underachievement is typically accomplished by comparing the student's achievement and ability measures, using one of several methods for determining if the child is significantly underachieving, given the child's ability or grade. A learning disability may be identified in a single academic skill, such as mathematics, spelling, or written expression, or in several or all academic areas. Underachievement alone is not generally sufficient for classification in most states.

The exclusion criterion is met if the vision and hearing screenings indicate intact sensory abilities and if the measure of intellectual functioning fails to substantiate mental retardation as the cause of underachievement. Social and school history data as well as teacher rating scales and anecdotal reports may be used to rule out the presence of a primary emotional disorder that would account for the learning problem. Classroom observations and prereferral interventions can help rule out environmental causes for the learning problem.

Multiple Perspectives on Severe Discrepancy

In 1965, Barbara Bateman introduced the concept of discrepancy into the conceptual definition of learning disability. Since then, the concept of a severe discrepancy between ability and achievement has remained central to most procedures for identifying learning disabilities, although it is not without controversy (Aaron, 1997). Throughout the history of learning disabilities and the IDEA, many procedures have been proposed and used for determining when a student's learning was different enough from typical learning patterns to warrant the student's being classified as having a learning disability. Three approaches have been widely utilized in the elusive attempt to determine definitively which students do and do not have a learning disability: (1) ability-achievement discrepancy, (2) low achievement for grade, and (3) scatter or variation among various abilities possessed by a given individual. Ability-achievement discrepancy and scatter among abilities represent intra-individual discrepancy determinations, while low-achievement criteria look at differences among individuals with respect to population norms.

Debate about the validity and reliability of any of these methods, and even about the tests on which they are based, has continued over the years. Most studies have found that various formulas overidentify or underidentify individuals with learning disabilities, leading to the conclusion that the use of these procedures creates a false sense of objectivity (Aaron, 1997; Algozzine & Ysseldyke, 1988; McLeskey, Waldron, & Wornhoff, 1990). The Council for Learning Disabilities (1987a) issued a position paper opposing the use of discrepancy formulas. They recommended that when discrepancy formulas are required by law or regulation, they should be used with great caution.

A variety of procedures are used by school districts and states to determine the presence of a severe discrepancy and to identify students with learning disabilities. This makes it possible for a student to be eligible for services as a student with a learning disability in one district or state and not be eligible in another, depending on the criteria used. The following list is representative of the wide variance in procedures used to identify discrepancies in students with potential learning disabilities (Mercer, King-Sears, & Mercer, 1990; Ysseldyke, Algozzine, & Epps, 1983):

Ability-Achievement Discrepancy Criteria (Intra-individual Determination)

- Having a specific difference (e.g., ten, twenty, thirty, or more points) between an IQ score derived from an individual intelligence test (e.g., WISC-III) and a standardized individual achievement measure (e.g., Woodcock-Johnson, WIAT, PIAT)
- Use of a regression formula to transform the standard scores on an achievement test to make them more comparable to the scores obtained on the intelligence test
- Having scores on individual achievement measures that are significantly below a "severe discrepancy level" (SDL), such as the 1976 federal formula: $SDL = CA[(IQ/300) + 0.17] - 2.5$

Use of Scatter Comparisons (Intra-individual Determination)

- A specific difference between the verbal and performance scales on the WISC-III (e.g., nine, twelve, or fifteen points)
- A specific difference (e.g., ten or more points) between the highest and lowest subtest scores on the WISC-III
- A comparison among factors (i.e., groups of subtests) on the WISC-III

Low Achievement Criteria (Inter-individual Determination)

- Achievement scores (in standard score units) below a set criterial point (e.g., 70, 77, 85) on a standardized individual achievement measure (e.g., Woodcock-Johnson, WIAT, PIAT)
- Achievement scores (in percentiles) below a set criterial point (e.g., fifteenth, tenth, fifth percentile) on a standardized individual achievement measure (e.g., Woodcock-Johnson, WIAT, PIAT)
- Deviation from grade level criteria or achievement in an academic area that falls below expected grade level (this criterion is often combined with a requirement of intelligence in the average or above average range)—e.g., performance in an academic area that is
    1.0 year below grade level in the primary grades
    1.5 years below grade level in the intermediate grades
    2.0 years below grade level in junior high school
    2.5 years below grade level in senior high school

Alternative Definitions of Learning Disabilities

Definitions are used to explain the nature of a thing and to establish the boundaries between that entity and others that are not related to the term being defined. There have been numerous attempts over the last thirty years to more clearly and accurately define the condition we now call learning disabilities.

Association for Children with Learning Disabilities (ACLD/LDA) Definition (1986)

ACLD sought to achieve a number of goals in developing its 1986 definition. They wanted to underscore their understanding that this condition was not generalized but rather might be characterized by many possible and specific manifestations. They believed that this condition affects the individual throughout life, not just in childhood. They believed it to be of neurological origin, although they acknowledged that no diagnostic tools existed to confirm this belief. ACLD stated that the effect of the disability varies from person to person and that the disability may affect receptive and expressive language as well as conceptual and thinking processes, integrative skills, and motoric abilities. The condition may also affect educational performance, vocational attainment, social skills, and daily living skills.

> Specific Learning Disabilities is a chronic condition of presumed neurological origin which selectively interferes with the development, integration, and/or demonstration of verbal or non-verbal abilities. Specific Learning Disabilities exists as a distinct handicapping condition and varies in its manifestations and in degree of severity. Throughout life, the condition can affect self esteem, education, vocation, socialization, and/or daily living activities.
>
> Association of Children with Learning Disabilities, 1986, p. 15.

National Joint Committee on Learning Disabilities Definition (1988)

Representatives of eight organizations whose work is related to the field of learning disabilities came together in the early 1980s to discuss improvements to the federal definition. The organizations were the American Speech-Language-Hearing Association, the Council for Learning Disabilities, the Division for Learning Disabilities, the Division for Children with Communication Disorders, the International Reading Association, the Learning Disabilities Association of America, the National Association of School Psychologists, and the Orton Dyslexia Society. Although they were in general agreement with the federal definition, these groups believed it could be made clearer and more specific. The issues addressed in their 1988 revision included describing learning disabilities as a life span issue; eliminating psychological processing as a conceptual element; differentiating among learning disabilities, learning problems, and problems in social behavior; and clarifying the exclusion clause to acknowledge the possible coexistence of learning disabilities with other disabilities.

> Learning disabilities is a general term that refers to a heterogeneous group of disorders manifested by significant difficulties in the acquisition and use of listening, speaking, reading, writing, reasoning, or mathematical abilities. These disorders are intrinsic to the individual, presumed to be due to central nervous system dysfunction, and may occur across the life span. Problems in self-regulatory behaviors, social perception, and social interaction may exist with learning disabilities but do not by themselves constitute a learning disability. Although learning disabilities may exist concomitantly with other handicapping conditions (for example, sensory impairment, mental retardation, serious emotional disturbance) or with extrinsic influences (such as cultural differences, insufficient or inappropriate instruction), they are not the result of those conditions or influences.
>
> NJCLD, as cited in Hammill, 1990, p. 77.

The NJCLD definition has been approved by the majority of the member organizations as the official NJCLD definition, and therefore it represents some degree of consensus among professionals in the field. It has many supporters (Hammill, 1990), but it has not been adopted by the federal government as the conceptual definition of learning disabilities.

Interagency Committee on Learning Disabilities (ICLD) Definition (1987)

In a parallel effort to the NJCLD process, representatives from twelve federal agencies of the U.S. Department of Education and the U.S. Department of Health and Human Services were appointed to an Interagency Committee on Learning Disabilities (ICLD) and were charged with creating a more accurate and useful federal definition. In 1987, the ICLD reported the following definition to Congress:

> Learning disabilities is a generic term that refers to a heterogeneous group of disorders manifested by significant difficulties in the acquisition and use of listening, speaking, reading, writing, reasoning, or mathematical abilities, or of social skills. These disorders are intrinsic to the individual and are presumed to be due to central nervous system dysfunction. Even though a learning disability may occur concomitantly with other handicapping conditions (e.g., sensory impairment, mental retardation, social and emotional disturbance), with socioenvironmental influences (e.g., cultural differences, insufficient or inappropriate instruction, psychogenic factors), and especially attention deficit disorder, all of which may cause learning problems, a learning disability is not the direct result of those conditions or influences.
>
> Interagency Committee on Learning Disabilities, 1987, p. 222.

This definition paralleled the NJCLD definition in many ways. The major difference lay in its addition of social skills deficits as a subtype of learning disability rather than as a condition that was secondary to a primary area of learning disability. Most of the formal comments on this definition have centered on this aspect. It was stated that, while social skills deficits may be a secondary manifestation, to assert that a child might have social skills deficits as the only disability area made clear diagnosis difficult.

Issues Raised by the Alternative Definitions

Throughout its history, the concept of learning disabilities has been difficult to define. Philosophical differences around the concept have continued to occupy the efforts of professionals in the field (Kavale & Forness, 1985). Hammill (1990) conducted an analysis of the major components of the many attempts at definition, and he concluded that, despite the controversy, there is evidence of common themes throughout most of the definitions. He concluded that there is a sense of what constitutes a learning disability conceptually even if practitioners are not always in agreement about how to operationalize those concepts. Specifically, Hammill noted the presence of the following themes in most of the definitions created since 1968:

- Central nervous system dysfunction as the *presumed* cause of the disorder, whether it can be confirmed or not
- Underachievement as a primary diagnostic indicator
- The effect of the learning disability throughout the life span
- The presence and centrality of problems with language, academic learning, thinking, and reasoning
- The possibility of the coexistence of a learning disability with other conditions
- A sense of the heterogeneity of the condition and its many manifestations

The implication of this discussion of alternative definitions is that clinical judgment and good diagnostic data are essential to the determination of the nature and extent of the disabilities a child has in learning. It is unlikely that any two students with learning disabilities will ever present the same diagnostic profile. What is needed is documentation of the nature and effect of the learning disability, followed by the development of an appropriate, adaptive educational plan to facilitate each student's learning.

Conditions Associated with Learning Disabilities

Learning disabilities are generally attributed to presumed causal factors in the environment (extrinsic to the individual) or within the person (intrinsic). As difficult as it has been to agree on what constitutes a learning disability and who has one, it has proven even more difficult to identify causal factors.

Intrinsic factors that have been implicated as causes in learning disabilities are

- Genetic differences, since there appears to be some tendency for family members to show these problems across generations
- Brain injury (prenatal, perinatal, or postnatal), leading to disruption of a specific brain function
- Biochemical imbalances, which are hypothesized to affect brain function
- Unspecified brain differences

Studies have used modern diagnostic procedures such as MRI studies or PET scans to determine where particular functions are housed in the brain. These studies and earlier autopsy studies suggest that human beings differ in brain structure, and that those differences appear to correlate with characteristics in mental and motor functioning (Shaywitz, B. A., et al., 1997). It is unclear to what extent these differences account for "imperfect abilities" and underachievement. Even if they do account for the problems displayed by individual learners, the value of such information for remediation is restricted to diagnosis, since we do not yet have the capability to make significant repairs or alterations to the brain and nervous system structures.

Extrinsic factors have also been studied. Environmental toxins such as lead have been shown to affect children's ability to learn. If caught early enough, the damage seems to be reversible; if left untreated, it leads to permanently diminished learning ability. Food and environmental allergens have also been suspected, although research has not supported this line of thought (Kavale & Forness, 1983). Other environmental problems, such as child abuse and neglect and lack of early stimulation, as well as inadequate or inappropriate instruction, have also been targeted as some of the reasons some children fail to learn despite apparently normal learning capability.

The fact is that in most cases we cannot infer a specific cause for the learning disability from the child's performance or history. Even in the occasional case when we are able to infer a cause, it rarely dictates specific remedial or preventative actions. The causes of this puzzling disability remain an enigma. The primary difficulty with not being able to reliably pinpoint causes is that efforts at primary and secondary prevention are hindered or made impossible. Educators are left to maximize tertiary prevention efforts to improve the functioning of the learner despite the disorder (Rowitz, 1986; see Chapter 1).

Prevalence of Learning Disabilities

The prevalence of learning disabilities as reported by districts, states, and the federal government is related to two factors: (1) the actual number of individuals with learning disabilities, and (2) the methods used to operationalize the definition and to classify learners. Although logically it seems that there should be a discrete number that would answer the first question, in actuality the differences among definitions and diagnostic criteria mean that the reported percentages of children identified as having a learning disability vary widely, ranging from a low of 1 percent to a high of 30 percent. The more stringent the criteria used by a state or district, the lower the rate of identified children.

In studies of the implementation of uniform state guidelines for use in classifying children as having a learning disability, McLeskey and Waldron (1991) and Ross (1995) found that implementation of such guidelines reduced the number of students classified in the state. However, adherence to the guidelines was not 100 percent. They attributed this phenomenon to the tendency of IEP teams to rely most heavily on professional and clinical judgment and to the observation that the information provided by the referring teacher in many cases became the determining factor in classification decisions. It appeared that it was difficult for a multidisciplinary team to ignore the conviction of a concerned teacher that a particular child has a learning disability, even when the outcome of a particular method of classification fails to support the hypothesis.

The uncertainty about the prevalence of learning disabilities has a historical aspect as well. Prior to the Specific Learning Disabilities Act in 1969 and the passage of The Education for All Handicapped Children Act in 1975, this disability was not officially defined, and students with learning disabilities were uncounted and generally unserved. In 1975, it was estimated that perhaps 1–3 percent of children would fall into this new category. Prior to 1975, most of these children were sitting in regular classes, often failing, and generally regarded as "slow learners" or unmotivated students. Some students with learning disabilities were receiving special education services, having been inaccurately classified as learners having mental retardation or with primary emotional or behavioral disorders.

Since 1975, the number of students identified as having learning disabilities has steadily increased. During the first seven years, the increases were dramatic. Since then, the growth in numbers has slowed, but is still increasing slightly. Throughout the 1990s, about 5 percent of all students and approximately 50 percent of students in special education were identified as having a learning disability (see Figure 7.1).

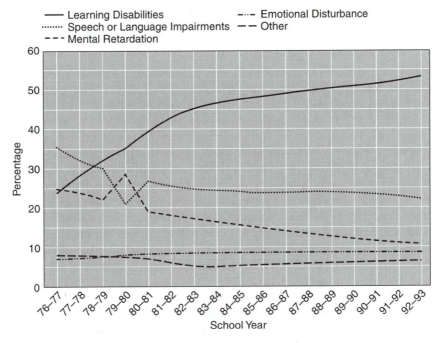

FIGURE 7.1 **Percentage of Students with Learning Disabilities, as Compared to Other Disabilities, 1976–77 through 1992–93**

From U.S. Department of Education, 1994, p. 11.

Several reasons for these trends have been suggested:

- Awareness of the existence of the concept of learning disabilities since 1975 has led teachers, parents, and students to consider it as a possible cause of a student's failure to learn.
- Improved screening procedures have identified students who would have previously gone undetected and unclassified as having learning disabilities.
- Learning disabilities as a classification does not seem to have the stigma often associated with mental retardation and emotional or behavioral disorders. Given an ambiguous case, the classification of learning disability may be chosen by the multidisciplinary team rather than selection of a more stigmatic label.
- As cuts have been made in remedial programs for students in general education classes, teachers and parents who were searching for remedial help for struggling students have pressured schools to utilize the learning disability rubric to get needed help for a student.
- Court cases have repeatedly called into question the use of certain standardized instruments such as intelligence and language tests in making placement determinations for minority students. Coupled with the stigma of mental retardation, schools have tended to use the category of mental retardation very conservatively and only when the testing is unequivocal. It is likely that a percentage of referred students with

borderline testing results have been labeled as having a learning disability instead of being classified as having mild mental retardation, reducing charges of cultural bias.

Because learning disabilities primarily affect academic progress, few children are classified as having a learning disability before school age. As shown in Table 7.1, the numbers rise steadily during elementary school, with the most students being referred between the first and third grades and the majority of cases identified by the end of elementary school (McLeskey, 1992). By sixth grade, students have been in school long enough to establish the pattern of failure in academic learning required by most placement criteria. By junior high school, the number of students being identified for the first time for service in special education begins to fall off, as students who have not previously been identified move into less academically demanding school programs or drop out of school altogether.

Often, by the time these students reach adulthood, they fade into the mainstream population once again, choosing occupations that do not place undue demands on their areas of deficit. Recent studies do confirm, however, that adults with learning disabilities continue to have problems in employment and daily life (Morrison & Cosden, 1997). They tend to be underemployed or unemployed more often than their counterparts. They also have more social problems, possibly related to difficulty using language effectively in social situations. The effect of the learning disability may be more subtle, but it remains. Vocational rehabilitation counselors and college academic support offices report increasing numbers of clients who were identified in childhood as having a learning disability and who are now seeking training and accommodations supports in postsecondary education and employment.

Types of Learning Disabilities

Learning disabilities are characterized by their heterogeneity more than by any other factor. The difficulties these students experience take many forms, and no two students are alike. Perhaps the easiest way to conceptualize the different types of problems students may exhibit is to use the framework suggested by Kirk and Chalfant (1984; Lerner, 1993). Learning disabilities may be divided into two categories: (1) developmental learning disabilities, or disabilities in functions that are usually considered prerequisites to successful academic

TABLE 7.1   **Grade Level at Referral for Students with Learning Disabilities**

Age Level	Percentage	Cumulative Percentage
Primary (K–3)	58.5	58.5
Grades 4–6	23.2	81.6
Grades 7–9	15.4	97.0
Grades 10–12	2.9	100.0

Based on data from McLeskey, 1992.

learning, and (2) academic learning disabilities, or problems in the more traditional areas of school learning (e.g., reading, written language, spelling, mathematics).

Developmental learning disabilities involve skills that develop early in a child's life and are central to later academic success. These include attention, perception, and memory, as well as thinking (or cognitive skills) and oral language (Kirk, 1987). A diagnostic indicator of a potential developmental learning disability is a discrepancy or delay in the acquisition of typical language, attention, and motor skills when compared to other children in the neighborhood or preschool class.

Attention refers to two skills: selective attention, or the skill of selecting and focusing on relevant stimuli, and sustained attention, or the skill of maintaining that attention over time. The child who has underdeveloped attention skills will have a difficult time learning effectively and efficiently. (See Chapter 10 for further discussion of attention characteristics.)

Skill in making perceptual judgments is also essential for learning and cognitive processing. Perception involves the interpretation of sensory stimuli and the labeling of those stimuli with meaningful names. Until a stimulus has been named, the student cannot manipulate it cognitively and cannot connect it to other information stored in memory. Visual and auditory perceptual skills are areas of concern for some students with learning disabilities, and they are essential to later development of reading and written language skills. (See Chapter 10 for more information on perception.)

Thinking or cognitive disorders affect the child's ability to solve problems, to develop conceptual knowledge, and to store and retrieve information in long-term memory. Memory skills include both visual and auditory memory and are likewise central to later reading, language, and mathematics performance. Memory disorders can affect short- and/or long-term memory and may be attributed to problems in storing information and/or retrieving information on demand. (Characteristics related to memory will be discussed in more detail in Chapter 10.)

Oral language skills include young children's abilities to listen effectively and to express themselves orally. Difficulties in the use of expressive and/or receptive language skills are often the most obvious indication of a learning disability in a young child. Unlike articulation problems, deficits in oral language affect the ability of the child to learn and interact with others. Oral language problems frequently are followed by later problems in reading and/or writing. (See Chapter 11.)

Academic learning disabilities manifest themselves in school-age youngsters who have normal learning capacity but who fail to develop age-appropriate skills in reading, written expression, spelling, handwriting, and mathematics. Assessment of academic disabilities frequently reveals the presence of previously undetected developmental learning disabilities. In effect, the learning disability was always there; it just went unnoticed because preschool youngsters vary so greatly in their attention, perceptual skills, use of memory, and language abilities.

When developmental learning disabilities are found to have developed into an academic disability, the program of remediation must consider both areas. According to Treiber and Lahey (1983), when developmental learning disabilities are identified in a school-age child, it is more efficient and effective to work on remediating those perceptual, memory, language, or attention disabilities within the context of the academic skill areas.

Characteristics of Students with Learning Disabilities

From our brief discussion of the two types of learning disabilities, it should be apparent that this is a very heterogeneous group of disorders with the common theme that the disability affects the student's ability to learn in some way. It has been said that there are so many possible combinations of the many difficulties that may be associated with a learning disability, that a teacher is unlikely to ever encounter two students with learning disabilities who have identical needs. This is a critical concept in considering the characteristics students with learning disabilities may present in the classroom. Knowledge that the child has been classified as having a learning disability tells us very little about what that child can do and what supports are needed for learning. The teacher's task is to become familiar with the possible problem areas and to work with each student to discover individual needs. Unit III, Chapters 10 through 13, considers more fully the major areas that may be affected by a learning disability.

Difficulties with language are quite common among these students. Some experience difficulty following what others say to them and comprehending what they hear. Others develop expressive oral language very slowly, with a vocabulary much smaller than others their age. Some use very simple or basic syntactic structures and short sentences that are inadequate to express what they need to say. Others are awkward in their use of social language skills.

Some have trouble learning the auditory-visual associations needed for success in beginning reading, or have difficulty decoding words and blending the sounds. Some can read anything you put in front of them aloud, but have great difficulty comprehending what they read. Some lack the metacognitive skills needed to monitor their own comprehension, and others find content textbooks incomprehensible both in level of reading and in format.

Some find that correct spelling appears to be forever outside their grasp. Others have handwriting that even they can't read. Some write in sentences that are shorter and more simple than those of their peers. Writing may be so inaccurate in syntax and spelling that it is incomprehensible. Other students lack the organization skills and formatting capabilities to create effective paragraphs and compositions, leading to the use of the term *dysgraphia* to describe their condition.

It is frequently believed that mathematics is not a problem for students with learning disabilities, and occasionally teachers believe that a student with a learning disability can be identified because of problems in reading as contrasted with good skills in mathematics. The fact is that mathematics does pose problems for a number of these students, leading to the use of the term *dyscalculia* to refer to this condition. Some struggle unsuccessfully for twelve years to memorize basic number facts. Others have difficulty organizing the numbers on the paper so that they can complete the required calculations. Some have difficulty learning and executing the calculation algorithms, particularly when there are many steps, such as in subtraction with regrouping or long division. Others find that their problems in reading interfere with solving story problems, although often the real problem is that they lack the ability to manipulate the numbers in their short-term memory and to see the relationships among them.

Beyond these language and other academic difficulties, students can have even more basic problems in cognition. Some students may have difficulty focusing their attention, while others have trouble sustaining that attention. Students may lack the strategies needed to effectively store information in their long-term memory and then to retrieve it. Some lack the cognitive skills of clustering and organizing that make it possible to actively work with a number of concepts at a time. Others lack the self-instructional and self-monitoring skills necessary for effective class participation. Some students find taking tests a daunting experience, often because of their anxieties in approaching such tasks and because they do not have strategies for addressing the challenge effectively.

Finally, many of these students display deficits in social skills. They may have a limited repertoire of social responses, leading them to use the ones they have frequently and inappropriately. This often results in other students seeing them as "weird." These students may have learned the necessary social skills but may not be able to use them appropriately. Some may lack the social perception necessary to interpret social cues in the environment and therefore fail to use an adaptive social response when needed. They may be physically awkward and therefore are not desired as playmates.

Students with learning disabilities are an extremely heterogeneous population. Few students with learning disabilities will have all of these problems, and many will have areas of significant strength. They share the name of the disability, and that is frequently all that they have in common. As we approach our work with a particular child, we must remember to let the child show us what we need to do. Programming must be based on individual student needs, regardless of the disability category.

Focus on Culture and Diversity

Concern about disproportionality in disability identification has most often focused on mental retardation or emotional behavioral disorders. Hypothesizing that there might also be a possibility of disparate learning disability identification among students from varying racial groups, Coutinho, Oswald, and Best (2002) analyzed learning disability rates by race, gender, and community variables. They noted several patterns: male students were more likely to be identified as having learning disabilities than female students; American Indian students had a significantly higher identification rate, while Asian/Pacific Islander students had a much lower rate when compared to White students; and finally, districts with higher rates of poverty and larger non-White populations had higher rates of learning disabilities identification.

Coutinho, Oswald, and Best (2002) raised several issues that should be addressed at the district level: (1) poverty as a risk factor seems to make diverse students differentially susceptible to being identified as having a disability; (2) rates may be affected by bias inherent in teacher evaluation of behavior, with differences in learning and behavior seen as a disability rather than a cultural difference; and (3) it appears that districts may not be appropriately utilizing the economic disadvantage exclusion clause, perhaps because teachers believe that special education is the only available way to get help for a struggling student. However, these authors recommend that districts look at the special education outcome data rather than merely focusing on identification rates, since the problem may indeed be the quality of services. If students from non-White groups do more poorly once placed in special education than White students, then it may said that these students are not receiving a free and appropriate education. However if the outcomes are positive, then the placements may also be deemed to be appropriate. Disproportionality may indeed not be the most important issue; the quality of services may be more critical. This complex question will require careful consideration if we are to arrive at the most appropriate solutions.

Resources on the Web

LDONLINE (WETA, Washington DC)

www.ldonline.org

> Resources concerning learning disabilities for teachers, parents, and students with learning disabilities.

Learning Disabilities Association of America (LDA)

www.ldanatl.org

> LDA, the learning disabilities advocacy group for persons, provides publications, fact sheets, position statements on issues, and general information links.

Division for Learning Disabilities (DLD)

www.teachingld.org

> Professional site for educators who work with students with learning disabilities; DLD is a subdivision of CEC.

National Association for the Education of African-American Children with Learning Disabilities

www.aacld.org

> Contains resources for parents and educators for developing quality interventions for African American students with learning disabilities.

Summary

The concept of learning disability was initially derived from research conducted from the late 1800s through the first half of the 1900s on the relationship between brain injury and impairment of mental functioning. Once the relationship was confirmed, parents and teachers seized on the term *learning disabilities* to denote those disorders that impaired learning despite apparently normal intellectual abilities. The disability was presumed to be caused by differences or disabilities in cognitive and psychological processing, particularly involving the use of language.

Defining learning disabilities has been a constant challenge for workers in this field. The key components found in the current federal definition are central to most of the definitions. They include: presumption of central nervous system dysfunction with disorders in psychological processing being a central defining characteristic; disorders in the understanding and use of language in all its forms; a discrepancy between the individual's ability and achievement; and the exclusion of other factors or disabilities as the primary cause of the learning problem. The determination of ability-achievement discrepancy remains the central defining characteristic, although states and districts vary in how they operationalize the concept of discrepancy. The lack of a uniformly applied procedure tends to create confusion in the minds of teachers, parents, and researchers.

Speculation and theories abound about the causes of learning disabilities. Possible intrinsic causes include: brain differences of a genetic nature, biochemical imbalances, brain injury, and other unspecified brain differences. Extrinsic causes that have been advanced include environmental toxins such as lead, food allergies, child abuse and neglect, and even inadequate instruction. The fact is that we rarely can know the precise cause, and in any event, knowledge of the cause is unlikely to affect the remediation and support required by the child in the present setting.

Learning disabilities are among the most common disabilities, accounting for about 5 percent of all school children and half of all students who receive special education services. Since the passage of IDEA in 1975, the number of students with learning disabilities has more than doubled.

Students with learning disabilities are a very heterogeneous group. Any area of functioning may be affected. Learning disabilities may be in developmental learning abilities, such as disorders of attention, memory, cognitive processing, language, and/or perceptual motor skills. Academic learning disabilities account for other manifestations of the disorder, with students having disabilities in reading, mathematics, writing, and/or spelling. In addition, the level of severity varies widely from mild to severe. In truth, any student may possess any combination of these disabilities at any level of severity, resulting in the likelihood that no two students will have the same areas affected.

BOBBY: A Case Study

Bobby is almost eight years old. He lives with his mother, father, and older sister just outside of town on a small farm. Bobby's father has a professional career, and his mother works in the home. Bobby has always been an alert and inquisitive child, but his lack of typical speech development was noticeable by the time he was three. At the suggestion of his pediatrician, Bobby was evaluated at a local speech clinic. It was determined that his expressive language lagged considerably behind his receptive abilities. He was placed in a special nursery school program for children with speech delays, and he also received individual speech therapy for two years.

At age five, Bobby participated in the regular half-day kindergarten program at his neighborhood school and continued to receive speech services from the school speech/language therapist. At the end of the year, the family moved to their present home in Moore Central School District, where Bobby entered first grade. Based on the records Bobby's mother brought with them, the school's multidisciplinary team determined that Bobby would be best served in a regular first grade class with one period of resource help a day and two sessions of speech therapy a week. He made significant progress throughout that year, although his skills in expressive language and handwriting were still noticeably below those of his classmates. By contrast, his receptive language (listening) and mathematics skills were very advanced in comparison to his peers.

(continued)

By the middle of second grade, his classroom teacher felt that since he was making average progress in all areas, he no longer seemed to need special education services. She attributed his continuing problems to carelessness and rushing through his work. She stated that if he would slow down and work more carefully, he would be successful in school. A reevaluation of his placement was requested, resulting in the following report from the multidisciplinary team, which included the results of individual testing conducted by the school district psychologist:

Multidisciplinary Team (MDT) Evaluation Report

Name: Bobby

Age: 7 years, 4 months
Grade: middle of second grade

Background: Bobby moved to the Moore School District last year when he began first grade. An evaluation was done at that time at the request of Bobby's mother, who felt that he was having difficulty mastering certain areas in language arts. He had a history of delay in acquiring expressive oral language and had received intensive language services throughout his preschool years. Although the evaluation conducted last year suggested that Bobby had ability falling somewhere in the average-to-bright normal range, it was recommended that he be served in the learning disability program based on the information provided by his previous school placement. Bobby has been receiving assistance in the resource program for children with learning disabilities since he entered first grade in this district. Additionally, he has received assistance from the speech and language therapist for language and articulation.

Test Results: Throughout the testing session, Bobby paid close attention to the examiner at all times. He seemed extremely well motivated and anxious to please the examiner, and was fairly relaxed and comfortable in the presence of an adult.

WISC-III: Verbal   120   Full Scale   124
          Performance   123

Wide Range Achievement Test:

	Grade Equivalent	Standard Score	Percentile
Reading	3.2	115	84
Arithmetic	3.3	118	88

Peabody Individual Achievement Test:

	Grade Equivalent	Standard Score	Percentile
Reading Comprehension	3.5	112	78

The PIAT comprehension measure is generally commensurate with the decoding measures obtained from the WRAT, and both results are commensurate with the ability scores from the WISC-III, which suggests ability in the average to high-average range.

Interpretation of Assessment Results: At this point, Bobby still seems to have articulation difficulties. No other language problems have made themselves known this year to the regular classroom teacher, special education teacher, or the speech and language therapist. All of Bobby's teachers seem to indicate that his primary problem seems to be related to his being somewhat careless. Bobby tends to complete assignments in as rapid a manner as possible. He fails to check his work, and consequently he tends to make mistakes.

Current evaluations seem to indicate that Bobby has ability within the high-average range. All of the verbal areas on the ability measure corroborate this. In fact, there was virtually no scatter at all within the verbal areas of the ability protocol. On the performance subtest, Bobby showed ability that ranged from the average range to the high-average range. Bobby's highest ability was found in matching designs with blocks. His lowest measured abilities were found in copying symbols for speed and accuracy and in noticing missing details. No measures on the ability tests suggest any sort of difficulty processing information.

All of Bobby's achievement measures (reading and math) suggest that he is able to perform adequately within a regular classroom setting. At this time, he is sometimes able to perform addition and subtraction problems when regrouping is required. Bobby can read one- and two-syllable words. He seems to be able to comprehend at a level commensurate with his ability to decode. In summary, Bobby is functioning at a level that is superior to a number of children in the classroom. His primary difficulties appear related to his haphazard work habits and his inconsistency in checking his work.

Recommendations: The Moore Elementary School multidisciplinary team has determined that these scores indicate that Bobby no longer meets the criteria for identification as a child with a learning disability. The team feels that Bobby does not demonstrate a significant enough discrepancy to warrant this type of special education identification. At this time, it is felt that his primary disability is related to speech and articulation, and it is recommended that his services with the speech/language therapist continue.

During the summer after receiving this report, Bobby's parents sought an independent evaluation from a psychologist at the nearby state college. They were concerned because his performance, although minimally acceptable, did not appear to be consistent with his ability. They were concerned that his expressive language performance would hold him back, particularly as written language demands increased in the upper grades. The independent evaluator produced the following report:

Psychological Assessment
(Performed by an Independent Psychologist)

Name: Bobby   **Grade:** Second (end)   **Age:** 7 years, 11 months

Bobby was referred for psychological assessment by his parents, who were interested in obtaining an independent assessment of Bobby's cognitive development to assist them in educational planning with his school.

Testing Results:
Test of Language Development (TOLD):
  Language Quotient: 105

Subtests	Language Age	Standard Score
Picture Vocabulary	8–11	13
Oral Vocabulary	>8–3	14
Grammatic Understanding	7–9	10
Sentence Imitation	8–1	9
Grammatic Completion	7–9	9

(continued)

Wechsler Intelligence Scale for Children-III (WISC-III):

Verbal IQ:	133	Full Scale IQ:	130
Performance Scale IQ:	121		

Verbal Subtests:

Information	13	Picture Completion	12
Similarities	16	Picture Arrangement	15
Arithmetic	14	Block Design	15
Vocabulary	16	Object Assembly	13
Comprehension	17	Coding	10
Digit Span	9		

Peabody Picture Vocabulary Test-(PPVT):

Standard Score: 104	Percentile: 60	Stanine: 6

Wide Range Achievement Test (WRAT):

Subtest	Grade Equivalent	Standard Score	Percentile
Reading	3.3	107	68
Spelling	3.1	104	61
Arithmetic	3.3	108	70

Goodenough-Harris Draw-A-Person Test (DAP):

Standard Score: 108	Percentile: 71

Bender Visual Motor Gestalt Test (BVMG):

Perceptual Age:	7.0–7.5
Grade Placement:	Beginning Second

Discussion of Test Results:

Intellectual Functioning: Bobby's performance on the WISC-III suggests that he is presently functioning within the very superior range of intelligence. Although the present testing occurred approximately seven months after his most recent evaluation by the school (also employing the WISC-III), his performance suggests that his potential ability level may be even higher than presently estimated. Both the discrepancy between verbal and performance scales (twelve points) and scatter among his subtest scores (eight points) appear to be excessive.

Achievement: Bobby's present achievement, as measured by the WRAT, suggests that he is performing academically at approximately the beginning third grade level in the three areas measured by the test. While his performance appears to be within the average range for his age and grade placement, there appears to be a substantial discrepancy between his present intellectual functioning level and his achievement levels (a discrepancy between his IQ of 130 and verbal IQ of 133, and his standard scores in reading, 107; spelling, 104; and arithmetic, 108.) If, as the assessment of his performance on the WISC-III suggests, his potential intellectual functioning level is somewhat higher than presently obtained, then the discrepancies between achievement and ability would be even greater than estimated here.

Perceptual Motor Skills: Bobby's performance on the BVMG suggests the possibility of a slight perceptual motor deficiency. His reproductions of the Bender forms reflected rotations, distortions, and perseveration. One wonders to what extent this deficiency in perceptual motor skills contributed to his relatively poorer (but still average) performance on the DAP test and Coding Subtest of the WISC-III.

Language: Bobby's performance on the TOLD suggests average language development. All subtest scores fall within the average range except Oral Vocabulary, which fell within the above-average range. He did somewhat better on the subtests involving semantics than on the ones involving syntax. The results of the PPVT substantially agree with the results of the TOLD and reinforce the finding of average language development.

Discussion: Based on the present assessment of Bobby's intellectual functioning, he appears to be a child with very superior intelligence who probably should be viewed as potentially intellectually gifted. Based on available school records, Bobby's present school performance and his performance on the tests used in this assessment, Bobby appears to be a child who possesses the ability, academic skills, and study habits needed to perform satisfactorily in the general education program.

During the present testing, Bobby was a pleasant, cooperative child who appeared eager to please. He seemed to enjoy the tasks assigned to him. His work habits appeared adequate, although he did at times respond too quickly. He was able to maintain effort when confronted with difficult tasks. While it was difficult at times to understand him due to his articulation errors, he appeared to comprehend instructions without any difficulty. It was noted, however, that he was timid and lacked spontaneity in his responses. An informal assessment of dominance found a consistent preference for his right side, although he reported that he usually throws a ball with his left hand. Visual pursuit skills were fair. No evidence of either a hearing or visual problem was found, although he does wear glasses. Bobby manifested some signs of fatigue during the three-hour session, but fatigue did not appear to be a factor in his performance.

An analysis of Bobby's performance on the WISC-III suggests that while he is above average in most factors measured, he experiences difficulty (relatively speaking) with tasks involving concentration and manual dexterity. While no learning channel was found that appeared to be substantially more likely to be successfully used for instruction than another, some evidence was found to suggest that he is somewhat more successful processing auditory information.

In summary, Bobby appears to be a child who is of very superior mental ability. While he is presently functioning within expectations for his age and grade placement, a substantial discrepancy exists between his obtained ability level and achievement level. Should his potential ability be somewhat higher than measured, then the discrepancy between ability and achievement would be even greater. Consequently, a case probably can be made that Bobby is a child who meets the criteria used to identify a child with a learning disability, although it probably should be viewed as mild.

Recommendations

1. Bobby's full placement in general education should be continued, but he should be carefully monitored to determine if special education services will again be necessary to ensure an adequate and appropriate education.
2. Bobby will continue to require the services of the speech/language therapist.
3. Based on the discrepancy between ability and achievement, Bobby should be viewed as an underachiever in need of remedial services to reduce that discrepancy. In particular, his written language skills should be carefully monitored to ensure that past delays in expressive language do not recur.
4. Since Bobby appears to meet the ability criteria for classification as an intellectually gifted child, his progress should be carefully monitored for possible referral to that program.

DISCUSSION

Using the information from these two separate evaluations, determine whether you think the classification of Bobby as a child with a learning disability is applicable.

Specifically, consider the reasons the two psychologists came to somewhat different conclusions and how those conclusions might be related to the method used to determine the discrepancy.

If you identify additional information that would be helpful in making a full determination, create a list of the additional information you would need to complete the identification process.

■ ■ ■ ■ ■

CHAPTER EIGHT

LEARNERS WITH EMOTIONAL OR BEHAVIORAL DISORDERS

QUESTIONS TO GUIDE YOUR STUDY

- Why are there so many different terms to refer to this group of learners?
- What is the history of our concern for children with emotional or behavioral disorders?
- How are emotional or behavioral disorders defined?
- What issues are being debated with regard to this definition?
- How can we most validly and reliably determine if a child has an emotional or behavioral disorder?
- How common are emotional or behavioral disorders?
- How can we conceptualize the levels of severity of this disability?
- What causes emotional or behavioral disorders?
- Identify two major types of emotional or behavioral disorders.

■ ■ ■ ■ ■

Meet Nicki

When Nicki entered first grade, her teachers saw a quiet, somewhat reserved child. Her appearance, clothing, and hygiene were typical for this rural community. It wasn't long, however, before her teacher, Mrs. Smith, became concerned. Nicki seemed tense and jumpy, avoiding the physical touches so casually given in a primary classroom. She also was very possessive of school materials and toys, frequently laying claim to as many as possible and refusing to allow others to play with them. She struggled to acquire initial reading and mathematics skills. Mrs. Smith submitted a special education referral in March.

The evaluation for special education eligibility confirmed the following: Nicki was exhibiting long-standing and significant problems in building and maintaining satisfactory interpersonal relationships, and she was having difficulty learning despite a measured IQ of 94; the social work evaluation of the home environment revealed an authoritarian parenting style in the father, with suspected physical and emotional abuse. The multidisciplinary team (MDT) agreed that Nicki met the criteria for identification as a child with an emotional disturbance and developed an IEP for services in the resource room.

(continued)

For the next three years, Nicki went to the resource room an hour a day, receiving help with her academic skills. However, her behavior in the general education classroom continued to worsen. She was increasingly aggressive toward other students and had difficulty staying on task and completing independent work. At the end of fourth grade, the MDT determined that services in the self-contained classroom for students with emotional disturbance would be beneficial, including group and individual counseling as well as a consistently administered behavior modification program.

Nicki remained in that class for the next two years, and her behaviors appeared to become more controlled. Her teacher felt that Nicki was responding well to the menu of rewards and punishments, and that she was learning to avoid unacceptable behaviors to earn her rewards, although she still seemed to struggle to hold back hostile feelings. In seventh grade, Nicki moved to the junior high school's self-contained classroom, where her problems escalated. In February, the teacher denied Nicki the right to go to recess after lunch because of rule infractions in the morning. Nicki responded by hitting the teacher, resulting in Nicki's immediate removal from school programs. The MDT immediately reconvened, determined that she was a danger to others, and recommended her transfer to the residential treatment program at the state hospital, where she stayed for the next nine months. In the safe environment of the hospital, Nicki blossomed, handling seventh-grade mathematics work and making gains in reading as well. The activity program at the hospital provided her with social activities, the first time she had access to such activities outside of school. Her therapist helped her explore issues relating to her family and others. She was making progress in developing her sense of self. She thrived. Unfortunately, work with the family was minimal, since the father refused to participate.

In November, Nicki returned home to a special education classroom with a new teacher. Unfortunately, nothing had changed at home, and the school program continued to focus on academics and work habits. Work begun at the state hospital on Nicki's emotional issues was abandoned. Two months later, Nicki exploded over a minor disagreement, hitting the teacher again. This time, the school authorities pressed criminal charges, and Nicki was assigned to the custody of the juvenile court system as a youth with social maladjustment.

Terms to Refer to This Group of Learners

Unlike mental retardation and learning disabilities, there is still no universally agreed-upon term to refer to learners like Nicki. The federal designation for such students is *emotional disturbance,* as defined in IDEA 1997. However, terms used in school programs vary from district to district and state to state.

Writers and professionals in the field over the years have used various combinations of words. James Kauffman (2001) illustrated the problem by presenting two lists of terms. He observed that writers and workers in this field seem to combine one or two terms from column A with a term from column B to create a variety of descriptive names for these learners:

Column A	Column B
Emotional	Disturbance
Behavioral	Disorder
Social	Maladjustment
Personal	Handicap
	Conflicts
	Impairment

As Kauffman noted, this process leads to a large number of possible combinations and terms, each used to define the same group of learners, each with subtly different implications, including terms such as a child with:

Emotional disturbance	*Behavioral impairment*
Behavioral disorder	*Social and emotional impairment*
Behavioral disturbance	*Social and emotional disorder*
Emotional disorder	*Social and emotional disturbance*
Emotional handicap	*Personal and social maladjustment*

Generally, professionals select particular terms for very specific philosophical reasons. However, this lack of agreement on a name reflects the significant level of debate on major conceptual issues within this field. How can we begin to address the issue of which children might need services for this disability when the disability itself is conceptualized and even named differently by various authorities in the field?

This book will be using the term *students with emotional or behavioral disorders.* The term has been selected because it focuses on the learner first and is most reflective of the dual nature of the disability: the internal or intrapersonal nature (emotions) and the external or interpersonal nature (behavior). Following the lead of IDEA 1997, the book will not use the adverb *seriously* to modify this term, especially since our focus is on milder levels of impairment within a continuum of severity. In light of stories like Nicki's, it is important to view the entire continuum of behaviors and emotions so that intervention can be developed and implemented before problems have become unresolvable (Bower; 1960; Rutherford & Nelson, 1995).

The designation of a student as having an emotional or behavioral disorder implies a lack of fit between the child, the family, and the larger environment. Our focus in this chapter will be on those students who respond to their environment in ways that are socially unacceptable or personally unsatisfying (Kauffman, 1977). The degree of dysfunction or lack of fit may be interpreted as an indication of the extent to which the individual deals with personal, interpersonal, or larger environmental issues and contexts in a maladaptive manner.

Historical Foundations

The existence of individuals with mental illnesses, those thought to be "mad," has been documented throughout history. However, attention to the phenomenon of emotional and behavioral disorders in children was delayed until the twentieth century. (See Safford and Safford, 1996, for a more complete treatment of the history of services to children with emotional or behavioral disorders.) Psychological clinics for children began to appear at the turn of the century, and the term *emotional disturbance* came into use around 1910. Two prevalent theories sought to explain mental illness. The organic approach held that disturbances were due to specific brain disorders and physical disease. The functionalist approach focused on a study of behavior as a key to the cause of the mental illness, fueling the mental hygiene movement and providing the impetus for new services for children with emotional or behavioral disorders.

The first psychiatric hospital for children in the United States was founded in Rhode Island in 1931. In 1935, Lauretta Bender and her colleagues established a school for children with psychoses at Bellevue Psychiatric Hospital in New York City. Bruno Bettleheim established the Orthogenic School at the University of Chicago in 1944, providing a model of a therapeutic milieu for children with emotional disorders. Fritz Redl and David Wineman opened Pioneer House, an early group home for youngsters with emotional disorders, in 1946 in Chicago. It was there that they developed the crisis intervention technique called the "life-space interview" (Wood & Long, 1991).

In 1961, Nicholas Hobbs and his colleagues established several Project Re-ED programs. Project Re-ED was a comprehensive ecological intervention for children with emotional or behavioral disorders that used short-term residential programming for the child within the community and focused on teaching behavioral skills needed in the present as well as in the future (Knoblock, 1983; Long & Morse, 1996). This residential program was combined with and followed up by interventions with the child's family, school, and community.

In 1960, Eli Bower published his classic work on the identification of children with emotional handicaps, a definition that was later to be incorporated into the federal definition of serious emotional disturbance (see Box 8.1). In 1963, P.L. 88–164 provided federal funding to prepare teachers to work with children with emotional disorders.

B O X   **8.1**

SPOTLIGHT IN HISTORY: Eli Bower and the Classification of Children with Emotional Disorders

Eli Bower's (1960) classic work on the definition of emotional handicaps was the foundation of the federal IDEA definition. Defining students with emotional disorders as those who exhibit one or more problem behaviors to a marked degree and over a prolonged period of time, Bower listed five problem behavior patterns:

(1) An inability to learn which cannot be explained by intellectual, sensory, or health factors.
(2) An inability to build or maintain satisfactory interpersonal relationships with peers and teachers.

(3) Inappropriate types of behavior or feelings under normal circumstances.
(4) A general, pervasive mood of unhappiness or depression.
(5) A tendency to develop physical symptoms and fears associated with personal or school problems. (Bower, 1960, pp. 8–10)

However, unlike the later federal definition, Bower did not include the requirement that school performance be affected in order for a child to be identified as having an emotional or behavioral disorder.

While Bower's work formed the foundation for the IDEA definition, he took issue with the federal definition's focus on only those students with "serious" emotional disturbance (Bower, 1982). He noted that failure to treat problems early, before they had become so severe, would compromise the efficacy of those treatment programs and undoubtedly increase service costs. In his version of the definition, he addressed the varying levels of severity or effect as a guide to design of services. This acknowledgment by Bower that emotional or behavioral disorders vary along the full continuum of severity further differentiates his work from the later federal definition:

> Emotional handicaps may be displayed in transient, temporary, pervasive, or intensive types of behavior. To complete the definition, it would be necessary to establish a continuum in which the handicap could be perceived and perhaps estimated, especially as it relates to possible action by the school. One could begin the continuum with (1) children who experience and demonstrate the normal problems of everyday living, growing, exploration, and reality testing. There are some, however, who can be observed as (2) children who develop a greater number and degree of symptoms of emotional problems as a result of normal crises or stressful experiences such as the death of father, birth of sibling, divorce of parents, brain or body injury, school entrance, junior high entrance, puberty, etc. Some children move beyond this level of adjustment and may be described as: (3) chil-

dren in whom moderate symptoms of emotional adjustment persist to some extent beyond normal expectations but who are able to manage an adequate school adjustment. The next group would include (4) children with fixed or recurring symptoms of emotional maladjustment who can, with help, profit from school attendance and maintain some positive relationships in the school setting. Beyond this are: (5) children with fixed and recurring symptoms of emotional difficulties who are best educated in a residential school setting or temporarily in a home setting. (Bower, 1960, pp. 13–14)

Another significant difference between the two definitions, noted by Bower himself in 1982, is the IDEA exclusion of youths who are socially maladjusted. He stated that meeting the criteria of his definition and the definition found in IDEA was tantamount to a definition of social maladjustment:

> To differentiate between behaviors that are antisocial or active and the so-called neurotic or personality disabilities of a more passive kind as if they were indeed separate entities is unfortunate and misleading. Moreover, to use a definition that operationally and conceptually defines emotional disturbance by their social maladjustments, then disqualifies them on the same basis, fits Tweedledee's logic, "If it was so, it might be; and if it were so, it would be; but as it isn't, it ain't." (Bower, 1982, p. 58)

Nicholas Long, William Morse, and Ruth Newman published *Conflict in the Classroom* in 1965, which led to the establishment of the psychoeducational approach as the major program approach for educating children with emotional or behavioral disorders in schools. Other programming initiatives included pioneering work by Haring, Hewett, and Wood. In 1962, Norris G. Haring described a program for use with children with emotional or behavioral disorders based on highly structured environments and operant conditioning (Haring & Phillips, 1962). His procedures focused on observable behaviors, the use of operant conditioning to achieve change, and the use of data for making instructional decisions. Frank Hewett (1968) published *The Emotionally Disturbed Child in the Classroom* which described the approach he called the "engineered classroom." This approach further systematized the data collection process for assessing behavior, and it established a hierarchical program of activities, using token economies for reinforcement. Later, in 1975, Mary M. Wood and her colleagues developed an intervention program called "developmental therapy," which provided specific activities designed to remediate delays in the development of age-appropriate social and emotional behaviors.

With the passage of P.L. 94–142 in 1975, children with emotional or behavioral disorders were formally brought into the sphere of public school responsibility under the category of "seriously emotionally disturbed." The presence of these children in schools has not been without controversy, and they are more frequently served in self-contained classes, special schools, or residential facilities rather than in general education classrooms. Their troubling behaviors are often described as disruptive to the general classroom environment, and referrals frequently lead to removal to other settings.

An ongoing issue deals with the right of schools to exclude youngsters whose severe behavior disrupts ongoing classroom activities. In *Honig* v. *Doe* (1988), the courts ruled that exclusion from school based on problem behavior judged to be related to the student's disability must be considered as a change of placement, and any such removals must be approved by the multidisciplinary planning team within the context of that youngster's overall treatment plan. IDEA 1997 further clarified the issues of placement and the right of children with problem behaviors to a free, appropriate public education, as we will discuss further in Chapter 13 (Council for Exceptional Children, 1998a, 1998c; Yell & Shriner, 1997).

Current IDEA Definition

IDEA 1997 defines emotional disturbance as follows:

(i) The term means a condition exhibiting one or more of the following characteristics over a long period of time and to a marked degree, which adversely affects a child's educational performance:
  (A) An inability to learn which cannot be explained by intellectual, sensory, or health factors;
  (B) An inability to build or maintain satisfactory interpersonal relationships with peers and teachers;
  (C) Inappropriate types of behavior or feelings under normal circumstances;
  (D) A general, pervasive mood of unhappiness or depression;
  (E) A tendency to develop physical symptoms and fears associated with personal or school problems.
(ii) The term includes schizophrenia. The term does not apply to children who are socially maladjusted, unless it is determined that they have an emotional disturbance.

U.S. Department of Education, 1997a, p. 55069.

Notes:

IDEA 1997 removed the modifier "seriously" to avoid the pejorative implications of the classification, but Congress intended no substantive or legal significance in making this change (Yell & Shriner, 1997).

This definition has been amended several times, alternately including and then deleting autism as a category. In 1990, IDEA finally established autism as a discrete category of service, and therefore it has been deleted as a condition included in the group of students with emotional disturbance.

As commonly interpreted, this definition requires evidence that

- One or more of the identified problem behaviors is present
- The behaviors of concern differ significantly or "to a marked degree" from the behaviors of typical students
- The problem behaviors have been present "over a long period of time" (typically interpreted as six months or more)
- Educational performance has been affected
- The cause of the behavioral problem is not social maladjustment.

While "educational performance" is not defined in the law as a guide to classification decisions, many districts and states interpret this requirement to mean that the student must be having academic problems as manifested by underachievement and failing grades. The exclusion of students with social maladjustment has also been an issue of constant debate, which will be discussed later in this chapter.

The implementation of this categorical definition has been variable at best over the years. States have provided varying levels of guidance to local school districts through statewide special education regulations. Implementation at the local level introduces even more variance. Studies have indicated that the implementation of the definition has resulted in varying prevalence rates from state to state, and that only a third of that variance can be explained by reference to definitional variables (Cullinan, Epstein, & McLinden, 1986; Epstein, Cullinan, & Sabatino, 1977; Tallmadge, Gamel, Munsen, & Hanley, 1985; Wright, Pillard, & Cleven, 1990). A survey of state education departments revealed that states use some combination of the following eleven criteria to identify students with emotional or behavioral disorders (Cullinan et al., 1986; Epstein et al., 1977):

- Presence of disorders of emotion or behavior
- Problems maintaining satisfactory social relationships
- Presence of achievement or learning problems
- Deviation from normative emotions or behaviors; failing to perform to age-appropriate expectations
- Problems that are long-standing and chronic
- Symptoms that are extremely serious or intense
- Attribution of the problem to a specific etiology
- Problems that have a favorable prognosis if special services are made available
- Exclusions from classification (e.g., mental retardation, sensory impairments)
- Need for special education services
- Child meets criteria through the certification process used to determine eligibility.

Disorders of emotions and behavior, interpersonal problems, learning difficulties, and deviation from normative behaviors were the elements included most frequently in state criteria, but the implementation of even these selected criteria varied widely. Subsequent studies have found similar results.

IDEA child count data for 1999–2000 showed that the percentage of the school-age population classified as students with emotional disturbance ranged from a low of 0.08 percent in Arkansas and Mississippi to a high of 1.55 percent in Vermont (U.S. Department of Education, 2001). Within states, districts exhibit the same variability; for example, in 1994, a third of the districts in Texas and Kentucky did not have any students identified with this disability (U.S. Department of Education, 1994). According to statistical analysis of prevalence rates in comparison to definitional elements, about two-thirds of the variance remains unaccounted for (Wright et al., 1990). These observations suggest that there are problems with the definition itself and perhaps with the concept of categorical service delivery models in general.

Social Maladjustment: Definition and Exclusion

The current definition of emotional disturbance (U.S. Department of Education, 1997a) contains an exclusion clause that states that youth with social maladjustment do not qualify for services within this category unless they are also determined to have emotional disturbance. There has been much debate on this issue over the years (Council for Children with Behavioral Disorders, 1990). It has been noted by many that this exclusion is contradictory, since the IDEA definition of emotional disturbance identifies as eligible those students who exhibit "an inability to build or maintain satisfactory interpersonal relationships with peers and teachers, or inappropriate types of behavior or feelings under normal circumstances," characteristics that are included in most conceptualizations of social maladjustment (Bower, 1982). Over half of the states have responded to this inconsistency by not using the exclusion clause in their states' regulations (Council for Children with Behavioral Disorders, 1990).

In the 1990s, however, some school districts and states began using the clause to exclude young people with conduct disorders from receiving special education services, taking the position that social maladjustment is equivalent to having a conduct disorder (Cheney & Sampson, 1990). From the legislative record, however, it appears that the original intent of Congress was to use the exclusion to relieve school systems from the responsibility of serving adjudicated youth, since habilitative and rehabilitative services for these young people were being provided by other governmental agencies (Cline, 1990; Council for Children with Behavioral Disorders, 1990). The debate continues, and students with disruptive behaviors continue to be excluded because they are difficult to serve and are often very disruptive to school environments.

Central to this debate is the lack of consensus on a definition of social maladjustment. The presence of significant antisocial behaviors has been used to define *conduct disorders* (American Psychiatric Association, 2000). Many educators consider such antisocial behaviors equivalent to social maladjustment, resulting in the exclusion from special education of many youngsters with conduct disorder diagnoses (Walker, Colvin, & Ramsey, 1995). Others take the position that students with social maladjustment are those with externalizing behaviors as opposed to the internalizing behaviors evidenced by youngsters with personality and anxiety disorders. Students who have social maladjustment are also sometimes viewed as delinquent or predelinquent. They are frequently characterized as having lower moral reasoning than peers, resulting in antisocial behavior and differences in attitudinal or affective responses to their offenses (Clarizio, 1992). Those taking this perspective assert that students with conduct disorders or social maladjustment are different from students with emotional disturbance and should not be eligible for special education, but instead should receive their interventions under other programs.

An alternative perspective is that *social maladjustment* describes those individuals who choose to engage in antisocial behaviors—those who could conform to societal expectations, but will not do so (Apter & Conoley, 1984). The central issue in this definition is volition. This perspective holds that students who are socially maladjusted are those who choose to engage in antisocial actions; students who have emotional disturbance are believed to have no control or choice in their behaviors.

Center (1989) characterized social maladjustment as an etiologic issue, a problem with the socialization of the young person. He differentiated among the various sources and types of socialization problems. Children who have experienced deficient or inadequate socialization experiences in their homes or communities may as a result exhibit undersocialized aggressive behaviors. These children have not had the opportunity to develop appropriate social responses and behaviors, and therefore they act in ways that hurt others and cause disruption at home and in school. Other children encounter deviant or inappropriate socialization experiences in their homes or environment and learn socialized aggressive behaviors. The antisocial behaviors exhibited by these youngsters are accepted and even expected by the subcultural group with which they affiliate. In many ways, these behaviors can be viewed as an adaptation to a problematic environment, an adaptation necessary for the young person to survive.

Center's (1989) distinction may be useful in understanding the nature of the problems presented to us by these troubled and troubling students, but it still leaves the eligibility question unanswered. The understanding that particular antisocial behaviors might be attributed to different developmental processes may suggest different programs of rehabilitation; nevertheless, it seems reasonable to assume that both groups of young people will need assistance in developing other more adaptive behaviors and emotional responses, regardless of whether the source was deficient socialization or deviant socialization by their parents, schools, or communities.

In 1990, the Council for Children with Behavioral Disorders (CCBD) identified a number of problems related to the issue of social maladjustment that need to be addressed by educators and policymakers in the future:

- Consensus on a definition of the term *social maladjustment* must be achieved.
- If it seems useful to differentiate among subgroups of students with problem behaviors, valid and reliable assessment instruments and procedures must be developed. The results of such assessments must be used for making placement and planning decisions, not for excluding students from receiving needed services and treatment.
- Decisions about which children are eligible for services must be separated from financial and management concerns. IDEA was passed to ensure that all children are accorded the right to a free, appropriate public education. The task facing educators is to determine how to do that, not how to be relieved from the responsibility of doing it.

An Alternative Definition of Emotional or Behavioral Disorders

In light of the problems cited by the CCBD, and based on the general comments and debate about the current federal definition, it may be useful to consider an alternative definition. The

**TABLE 8.1   Organizations Endorsing the Mental Health and Special
Education Coalition Definition of Emotional or Behavioral Disorders**

- American Association for Counseling and Development
- American Orthopsychiatric Association
- Council for Children with Behavioral Disorders
- Council for Exceptional Children
- Federation of Families for Children's Mental Health
- Mental Health Law Project
- National Association of Private Schools for Exceptional Children
- National Association of Protection and Advocacy Systems
- National Association of School Psychologists
- National Association of Social Workers
- National Mental Health Association

Mental Health and Special Education Coalition, 1991.

Mental Health and Special Education Coalition, composed of national organizations (see Table 8.1) in the fields of special education, mental health and related services, and parent and advocacy groups, was formed to study the existing federal definition and to consider alternative definitions. The coalition identified the following specific problems with the current IDEA definition (Mental Health and Special Education Coalition, 1991):

- This was the only disability in IDEA that had the modifier "seriously" attached to the name. In all other cases, we identify and serve youngsters with disabilities ranging from mild to severe if their conditions restrict their ability to receive an appropriate education. By limiting services to those who are "seriously" emotionally disturbed, we risk losing the opportunity to provide interventions in the early stages, when efforts can be most effective. [Note: Although IDEA 1997 has dropped the word "seriously" from the terminology, it has been asserted that this change had no substantive implications (U.S. Department of Education, 1997a; Yell & Shriner, 1997). The fact that the incidence of emotional disturbance has not changed since 1977 supports this assertion.]
- The term "adversely affects school performance" has been generally interpreted by schools and states to imply that a child must be having academic problems as evidenced by underachievement and indicated by poor grades and low test scores. This narrow definition restricts services for some students who are having serious social and behavioral school adjustment problems, since students who are "getting by" academically may not qualify for services even if they display serious problems in social-emotional areas.
- The five criteria or characteristics do not match terminology used by mental health professionals, making crossdisciplinary conversations more difficult.
- The exclusion of students with social maladjustment is problematic for several reasons:
  1. Social maladjustment is not defined.
  2. Social maladjustment is commonly equated with conduct disorders, and conduct disorders are described by two of the criteria: (a) inability to build or maintain sat-

isfactory interpersonal relationships; and (b) inappropriate types of behavior or feelings under normal circumstances. This definition can lead to a child's being identified in one sentence and disqualified in the next (Bower, 1982).

3. Childhood clinical depression frequently coexists with conduct disorders, thus making a child eligible and ineligible at the same time.

- Throughout the history of this definition, the number of identified students has consistently fallen short of the numbers estimated by researchers in this field (Forness & Knitzer, 1992). In addition, the numbers served vary widely from state to state (Tallmadge et al., 1985). This observation suggests that a problem exists with the definition, since one indicator of an effective definition is the degree to which it yields comparable prevalence rates across comparable settings. The variability in prevalence from state to state also suggests that students' right to access to services depends more on where they live than on the nature of their disability.

Members of the Mental Health and Special Education Coalition worked for several years to resolve these issues, resulting in the development of a substitute definition. The coalition definition has been proposed as a substitute for the current definition in IDEA. The U.S. Office of Special Education and Rehabilitative Services (1993) published the proposed definition in the *Federal Register* in 1993, inviting comment. To date, the definition has been considered but has not been adopted as part of IDEA. However, an examination of the definition and the rationale behind its components can help educators better understand the nature of this disability and perhaps help us develop more effective assessment and identification practices. The text of the proposed definition (as revised during the comment period) reads as follows:

Emotional disturbance refers to a condition in which behavioral or emotional responses of an individual in school are so different from his/her generally accepted age-appropriate, ethnic or cultural norms that they adversely affect educational performance in such areas as self-care, social relationships, personal adjustment, academic progress, classroom behavior, or work adjustment.

Emotional disturbance is more than a transient, expected response to stresses in the child's or youth's environment, and would persist even with individualized interventions, such as feedback to the individual, consultation with parents and families, and or modifications of the educational environment.

The eligibility decision must be based on multiple sources of data concerning the individual's behavioral or emotional functioning. Emotional disturbance must be exhibited in at least two different settings, at least one of which is school-related.

Emotional disturbance can co-exist with other handicapping conditions as defined elsewhere in this law (i.e., IDEA).

The category may include children or youth with schizophrenia, affective disorders, anxiety disorders, or with other sustained disorders of conduct or adjustment.

Guetzloe, 1998, p. 1.

In this definition, the coalition intended to resolve the most troubling issues found in the current federal IDEA definition. Specifically, the group made the following points: Use of the words "so different" implies a contrast to typical behaviors without the negative connotation of the word "deviance." In referencing this "difference" to "age-appropriate, ethnic, and cultural norms," the coalition hoped to establish local normative behaviors as the standard of comparison to lessen the stigmatizing and pathologizing of a child who is just responding as others in his environment do and as he has learned to do.

The definition broadens the interpretation of educational performance to include all areas of functioning in a school context. This helps ensure that services will be available to youngsters who are able to maintain passing grades despite significant emotional and behavioral disorders. It recognizes the holistic nature of the school experience and views as important the child's social, vocational, and personal adjustment, as well as academic achievement.

The phrase "more than a transient, expected response to stresses in the child's or youth's environment" is included to indicate that special education services should be reserved for students who require long-term services and whose problems are unlikely to be resolved by standard school counseling services and other typically available interventions. As described in Bower's description of the levels of severity of emotional disorders, the coalition recognized that special education services were most appropriate for youngsters identified by Bower (1960) as being in levels 3, 4, or 5 (see Box 8.1).

In requiring that the behaviors be "exhibited in at least two different settings," the coalition sought to prevent the identification of a child based on the idiosyncratic referral of a single person. If the problem behavior is apparent only in one setting, it is more reasonable to study that setting for the answer, rather than to place the child in special education. The requirement that the problem behavior be unresponsive to interventions applied in general education was included to underscore the importance of providing effective instructional environments in general education for all children. Only when the best that general education can offer in terms of interventions is insufficient is it appropriate to look to special education for assistance.

The statement that emotional or behavioral disorders may exist along with such conditions as learning disabilities, mental retardation, speech impairments, substance abuse, and recognized psychiatric diagnoses was included to ensure that all children, regardless of their classification, would have access to services designed to help them develop behaviors that are personally satisfying and socially acceptable. IDEA 1997 recognized this principle as well when it noted that individualized education programs should include individualized behavior intervention plans for all students whose behavior is problematic, regardless of the student's classification.

Although the coalition definition is not currently in force in the IDEA or in state regulations, it is nevertheless useful for teachers and other professionals who work with these students to consider the points made in the proposed definition. Special education services will likely be more effective with such students if we collect the information from the sources as specified in the coalition definition. Specifically, the routine practice of evaluating students' behaviors from a contextual basis, from a perspective that recognizes the ecological nature of emotional and behavioral disorders, and of determining cultural and age normative behaviors will provide useful data to guide intervention planning. Using the results of intervention attempts as diagnostic information is also considered best practice. Elimination of the modifier "seriously" and recognition of the possible coexistence of this disorder with other disabilities will allow schools to serve such youngsters earlier and more fully.

Assessment and Identification Issues

A major reason for the debate about definition in this field is that an emotional or behavioral disorder does not exist outside a social context (McIntyre, 1993, 1996). Emotional or behavioral disorders exist only to the extent that behavior or emotions are unacceptable or unsatisfying in a particular contextual environment. Any identification of an emotional or behavioral disorder can be made only by comparing the individual's characteristics with existing cultural rules or norms. A behavior will possess different meanings and perform different functions depending on the context. What is disturbed behavior at one developmental stage or in one context might be considered quite typical and even expected in another. For example, hitting and knocking peers down is generally inappropriate, unless the young person is on a football team. Only to the extent that a behavior is seen as significantly different from that of typical peers and as a threat to the stability, safety, or values of the individual, society, or community is the behavior (and by extension, the person) appropriately considered to be disordered.

Unlike sensory, physical, or intellectual deficits—which are viewed for the most part as varying along a single dimension, and for which there are established instruments to measure the degree of functioning and, by extension, the level of deficit—the presence of an emotional or behavioral disorder can be inferred only by comparing the behavior of the individual to that of others in the social context. It is also important to distinguish between difference and pathology. While marked differences in behavior may signal a disorder or pathology, the same behaviors may be present in students who are behaving in a manner consistent with cultural norms. It is critical to ask if there are alternative explanations for the behavior.

By implication, then, any assessment of the nature or degree of disordered behavior will be subjective (McIntyre, 1996). Educators can improve the objectivity of the process by rigorously defining and describing the applicable cultural norms, rules, and expectations, and by developing instruments that describe the person exhibiting the problem behaviors as objectively as possible. By comparing the normative behaviors to the observed behaviors, we can determine the extent of the discrepancy and increase the likelihood of developing a helpful intervention program. Since one of the conceptual biases used against these students is that their behavioral excesses are volitional (Peacock Hill Working Group, 1991), we must also attempt to determine the degree to which the student is making a choice to engage in those behaviors and the extent to which the student could adopt other behaviors if desired. If it appears that the learner is choosing the problem behavior, it behooves the teacher to ask why. What need does the behavior fill for the child?

Such a process might begin by using an adaptation of Frank Wood's (1982) model of behavioral assessment, wherein he suggested that problem behaviors be considered from five perspectives:

- The *disturber* element: Who is the focus of the problem? What do we know about the child? What is the child's gender, age, race, economic background, sexual orientation?

Are there age, cultural, or ethnic norms that help explain (not excuse) the behavior? Are there other disabilities present? What is the home environment like?

- The *problem behavior* element: How do we describe the behavior? How often does it occur? What are the antecedent and consequent events around the behavior?
- The *setting* element: Where does the behavior occur? What are the characteristics of that setting? Where does the behavior not occur? What are the characteristics of those settings?
- The *disturbed* element: Who regards this behavior as a problem? Who is bothered by the behavior? What are the characteristics of the person(s) who regard the behavior as a problem?
- The *functional* element: What goal or need does the behavior appear to help the individual meet; are there alternatives available to allow the child to meet that need?

From this starting point and from the general principles of nondiscriminatory evaluation, it should become apparent that the only defensible process for identifying students with emotional or behavioral disorders is a multiphasic one. The process would include the appropriate use of standardized tests, such as intelligence and personality measures. Appropriate use of such instruments means that the evaluator recognizes that the information value of these instruments becomes apparent only as we collect information from a variety of other sources, including observations. Batteries of psychoeducational instruments alone are rarely of much help in identifying the core issues in a problem behavior or in planning interventions.

Behavior rating scales, such as the Walker Problem Behavior Checklist (Walker, 1983), the Child Behavior Checklist (Achenbach, 1991), the Revised Behavior Problem Checklist (Quay & Peterson, 1987), and the Behavior Rating Profile-2 (Brown & Hammill, 1990), provide information about the *informants' perceptions* of the extent of the problem behaviors. When a scale is completed by several different individuals who know the child, one can begin to have more confidence in the results. A rating scale completed only by the referring person may reflect only the idiosyncratic views of that individual.

Interviewing can also be a valuable source of information. Information can be gathered from parents, teachers, peers, siblings, and even from the child. Using open-ended questions and seeking clarification of the information obtained can result in information that is rich in diagnostic value and that can lead to more effective interventions. Each interview provides significant information in itself, but when the information from all of these sources is "triangulated," a more accurate understanding of the problem emerges (Spradley, 1979).

Finally, direct observation in a variety of settings and by multiple observers is essential. The observer will need to collect information on the frequency, duration, intensity, and topology of the behavior. The observer will compare the nature of the problem behavior with the normative behaviors of peers in the setting. Identifying antecedents and consequences of the behavior helps add meaning to the description of disturbing behaviors and also guides intervention planning. Observing in more than one setting helps sort out the contextual factors that may be involved. Accurate recording of observed behaviors will be essential in describing the problem behavior and in evaluating the effect of a particular intervention after implementation.

Prevalence of Emotional or Behavioral Disorders

Estimates of the number of youngsters affected by emotional and behavioral disorders range widely. Figures ranging from less than 0.5 percent to 20 to 30 percent have appeared throughout the literature and in various government reports, with most estimates ranging from 3 to 6 percent (Forness & Knitzer, 1992; Kauffman, 2001; U.S. Department of Education, 1997b). A three-year longitudinal study by Rubin and Balow (1978) indicated that in any given year 20 to 30 percent of all the children in the study were identified as having a behavior problem, and that over the three-year period, 50 percent of the children had been identified by at least one teacher as having a behavior problem. A more significant finding was that 7.4 percent of the children were rated as having a problem with behavior by *every* teacher over a three-year period. This figure agrees closely with one federal estimate that 7 to 8 percent of all school-age children may have emotional or behavioral disorders severe enough to require treatment, and that one-third to one-half of those would be expected to also display academic difficulties (Forness & Knitzer, 1992; U.S. Department of Education, 1994). These are the students who are believed to be in need of assistance in developing more personally satisfying and socially acceptable behaviors and who may benefit from special education intervention.

According to state reports to the Congress on the implementation of the IDEA, however, fewer than 1 percent of all children are currently served in programs for students with emotional or behavioral disorders (U.S. Department of Education, 2001). Considering that the most conservative professional and governmental estimates cite a prevalence rate of 2 percent (Kauffman, 2001; U.S. Department of Education, 2001), the fact that we are currently serving significantly less than 1 percent of all children in special education raises serious questions.

Another concern with respect to identification rates was identified by the U.S. Department of Education (1994, 2001). They noted that rates of identification vary significantly across racial, cultural, gender, and socioeconomic groups. Disproportionately high numbers of students from low socioeconomic backgrounds are being identified. Disproportionately low numbers of female students become classified as having primary emotional disturbances. Rates vary across racial categories as well (see Table 8.2). The Council for Children

TABLE 8.2   Percentages of Students with Emotional Disturbance by Race

Racial Group	Percentage in the Total School Population	Percentage Served in SED Programs
African American	14.5	27.3
Caucasian	64.5	61.5
Hispanic	16.5	8.9
Asian/Pacific Islander	3.0	1.2
Native American	1.0	1.1

Based on data from U.S. Department of Education, 2001.

with Behavioral Disorders (in preparation) convened a task force to address these trends and to prepare a position paper concerning responses to the disproportionate representation and inappropriate treatment of learners from diverse cultural and linguistic backgrounds in programs for students with emotional or behavioral disorders.

Prevalence by age groups also suggests some interesting comparisons (see Table 8.3). Adolescents account for 60 percent of all students with emotional behavioral disorders, while accounting for less than half of all students with disabilities. One hypothesis that might account for this finding is that students with milder forms of emotional or behavioral disorders are tolerated within general education when they are younger, but by the time they reach the turbulent adolescent years, the problems have become serious enough to demand attention and services.

With all this said, just what is a reasonable estimate of the numbers of children and youth who may need various levels of support for emotional or behavioral disorders? The most reasonable estimates suggest that 3 to 6 percent of the school population may require intensive interventions in a given year, while the federal estimates are widely regarded as entirely too conservative (Forness & Knitzer, 1992). Using the IDEA projections as the expectation, schools would identify only those with the most severe disorders, students who are clearly a danger to themselves and others. This would leave unserved and unnoticed many other students who are not *yet* that severe and who might actually be more amenable to interventions. We would be failing to identify those very students who might be more likely to benefit from interventions and improve their ability to function in personally satisfying and socially acceptable ways, enough so that they no longer require services.

Special educators need to ask why we are so significantly underserving the estimated number of children in need of assistance. There are a number of reasons advanced for this phenomenon:

- As one listens to teachers and administrators discuss these students, particularly those with conduct disorders, it quickly becomes apparent that this group elicits few sympathetic responses. The learner is often described as willfully disobedient or aggressive, as an undisciplined child. It is implied or stated that the children could behave if they wanted to, that they choose not to behave or have never been taught to behave in

TABLE 8.3   Distribution of Students with Emotional Disturbance Compared to All Disabilities by Age Groups

Age Group (in Years)	Percentage of All SED Students	Percentage of All Students with Disabilities
6–11	34	49
12–17	60	46
18–21	6	5

Based on data from U.S. Department of Education, 2001.

accordance with school standards. Frequently, the response is that schools and parents could solve this problem by simply disciplining these youngsters more firmly.

■ The diagnosis of emotional or behavioral disorders is not one that parents are particularly relieved to hear. Because the stigma associated with the condition is applied not only to the student but also to the parents, the parents are more likely to deny that this could be the problem. Society tends to assume that if a child has an emotional or behavioral disorder, it is either because the parents failed to provide appropriate discipline and socialization, or that they abused or neglected the child. Parents will frequently argue for any other possible category in order to avoid this implied stigma and blame.

■ Students who experience withdrawal or depression symptoms are frequently simply overlooked, particularly if they manage to achieve passing grades. Teachers may see these students as a little different, but since they cause no disruptions to ongoing classroom programming, they are often allowed to just sit.

■ Following the *Honig* v. *Doe* ruling in 1988, some school officials have become reluctant to have a child with acting-out problem behaviors identified as having an emotional or behavioral disorder. They believe that the special education label will prevent school staff from using standard discipline practices (including suspension, expulsion, and corporal punishment) to respond to problem behaviors. The conventional, although erroneous, wisdom is that school personnel can't discipline a special education student for behavior that disrupts school activity and safety, that these students can do anything they want, and that no one can do anything to stop them. The fact is, of course, that these children can be and are subjected to various consequences for their actions. The requirement of *Honig* v. *Doe* is that those consequences and changes in placement must be guided by the multidisciplinary team, which must consider what part the child's disability plays in the problem and what actions are most likely to be therapeutic as well as corrective. In any event, children who threaten the health and safety of themselves or others can always be removed, at least temporarily. (See Chapter 13 for a more detailed description of the IDEA 1997 provisions regarding discipline issues.)

■ Services for these learners are typically fairly labor-intensive, requiring significant individual and small group service models. For some students with severe levels of disability, short-term, intensive residential placements may be required. These services are costly, and once a child is labeled, the IDEA mandates that each learner must receive a free and appropriate public education that addresses the disability. Some districts and states have sought to implement restrictive identification procedures, such as excluding students with conduct disorders from classification, with the apparent aim of restricting the numbers of these students and therefore curtailing the costs and challenges associated with serving them.

■ Teaching students with emotional or behavioral disorders requires a significant level of skill and training. In addition, the stress associated with serving these children leads to a significant incidence of "burnout" among professionals working with them. The shortage of specialized personnel can effectively become a cap on identification, since once a student is identified as having an emotional or behavioral disorder, services must be provided, and no exceptions are granted even if a district lacks sufficient qualified staff.

Because the identification of an emotional or behavioral disorder is so context-driven and because the determination of who does or does not belong in this group is relatively subjective, almost any estimate of prevalence could be justified. It has been observed that the classification of behavioral disorders is a social or ecological construct, based mainly on what we as members of the community view as tolerable or desirable (Apter, 1982; Kauffman, 2001; Knoblock, 1983). Since a diagnosis of an emotional or behavioral disorder, like the label of mental retardation, carries a heavy stigma, it seems incumbent on professionals involved in the assessment process to carefully consider the criteria used to define a child as different or deviant with respect to emotions or behavior. The potential for stigma suggests that we need to be sure that the benefit to the learner from being classified as having an emotional or behavioral disorder outweighs the societal burden imposed by use of this category.

Levels of Severity

As previously discussed, IDEA has generally identified in this category only those students who have more serious levels of emotional disturbance. However, students logically fall on a continuum of severity with respect to their emotional or behavioral disorders. As Bower (1960) delineated in his classic definitional work, these disorders may manifest themselves as transient or temporary problems with limited impact or as more pervasive disordered behavior requiring more intensive interventions. He further defined five levels according to the need for intensity of services (see Box 8.1), beginning with problems that require only temporary support and structure within general education and the home to resolve them. As the level of severity increases, problem behaviors may require interventions by special education and support personnel for extended periods of time to maintain the student in school programs. Bower's most severe level of disability is characterized by the need for residential or homebound services, where the disorders are so serious that school programs are not possible until some progress on the behavior is achieved. As we saw in Nicki's story, the level of disability can change over time, depending on the efficacy of the interventions provided.

Emotional or behavioral disorders certainly vary from mild to severe. DSM-IV-TR (American Psychiatric Association, 2000) generally uses the framework that individuals with mild disorders display the minimal number of criteria, while severe disorders are manifested by many behaviors in excess of the minimum. Clarizio and Klein (1995) surveyed school psychologists in an attempt to determine which factors held the most weight in determining a disorder to be more severe. They determined that four factors strongly affected the determination of severity: impairment of functioning, physical danger, frequency, and chronicity. Four other factors were determined to have a moderate effect: degree of suffering, number of settings, bizarreness, and the form of the problems.

Gresham (1991) proposed using resistance to intervention as a means of determining the severity of the disorder. He suggested that students with emotional or behavioral disorders may be described as those whose problem behaviors are resistant to change even when given well-designed school-based interventions. Factors that affect resistance to intervention include severity and chronicity of behavior, and generalizability of behavioral change.

Severity of behavior includes such factors as the topology, intensity, and frequency of the behavior. The more extreme the behavior, the more resistant it is likely to be to interventions. In these cases, if the strength of the initial interventions proves insufficient to significantly alter the behavior, then the individual is appropriately identified as having an emotional or behavioral disorder (Nevin, 1988).

Chronicity of behavior is a key criteria in IDEA and in DSM-IV-TR diagnoses. Gresham concurs with the coalition that use of the chronicity criteria is appropriate only when it is applied to long-standing problem behaviors that persist in the face of intervention efforts. If no attempts have been made to alter the behavior, it might be concluded that the lack of intervention that is the real problem.

More severe behaviors may also be characterized by a failure to achieve generalization of behavioral change. Some behaviors may respond to intervention in highly structured training settings, only to return to previous levels in nonintervention settings. Such behaviors should be viewed as resistant and will require longer periods of intervention, including careful and explicit generalization training and fading. Students with less severe behavioral problems will more easily maintain and generalize the changes following intervention efforts.

Conditions Associated with Emotional or Behavioral Disorders

As with all of the conditions we have discussed to this point, the question that is often asked and that is very hard to answer is, "What caused this problem?" With emotional or behavioral disorders, this question implies the additional questions, "Who is to blame? Whose fault is it?" As discussed previously, unlike other disabilities, an emotional or behavioral disorder elicits little sympathy or empathy. Indeed, the person with this disability is frequently seen to be at fault. The tendency is to "blame the victim." The reasoning employed is that such children choose to act inappropriately and *could* behave appropriately if they wanted to, or they are weak and unwilling to help themselves and could "cheer up" or get better if they just tried. If we don't blame the child, we blame the parents. Suspected inadequate or abusive home environments and perceived deficiencies in parental discipline are easy targets.

Additionally, when discussing causes of emotional or behavioral disorders, as of other disabilities, the implication is that knowing the cause will lead to a cure, and that it is not possible to identify an appropriate treatment in the absence of knowledge of the cause. As discussed in the chapters on mental retardation, learning disabilities, and ADHD, knowledge of the cause of the disorder rarely points to a unique remedial action, and the most effective interventions are based on the observed characteristics regardless of a known or presumed cause.

What must also be understood is that even when home or personal factors may have contributed to the problem, the individual or the parents are often doing the best they can in the context. As we look for factors associated with the emotional or behavioral disorder, our goal should be to use that information to plan interventions, not to excuse school personnel from acting to assist the child. In addition to providing interventions for the youngster, it is generally advisable to use this information to provide interventions within the family context as well in order to achieve long-lasting improvement for the child. Educators can also use this information to develop primary and secondary prevention programs (see Chapter 1) in schools so that fewer children in the future may develop these problems in the first place.

Biological Factors

Biological factors are rarely the sole cause of an emotional or behavioral disorder. It is generally only in the interaction with the environment that biological causes result in specific disorders of emotions or behavior. When such causes can be identified, they tend to be related to more severe disorders, some of which can now be partially treated by use of psychoactive drugs. Research on biological causes has been far from conclusive. Brain damage is often believed to be related to subsequent emotional or behavioral disorders, but it is rarely possible to validate this belief. Only the most serious of brain injuries can be definitively shown to affect emotional development, as is found in youngsters who have experienced certain traumatic brain injuries (Mira & Tyler, 1991).

Some serious disorders, such as schizophrenia and clinical depression, appear to have a genetic explanation. Genetic connections are generally viewed as a *predisposition,* which may develop into the disorder in a complex interaction with a particular social environment, rather than as a simple Mendelian trait (Plomin, 1995). Fragile X syndrome has been linked with behavioral disorders as well as with mental retardation (Santos, 1992). Still other conditions, such as clinical depression and attention-deficit/hyperactivity disorder, now appear to be related to biochemical abnormalities in the brain. In some cases, using psychoactive drugs can help restore near-normal brain functioning. When medication is used along with psychotherapy, the individual can learn to cope with the disorder and achieve a level of functioning that is more normalized (Forness & Kavale, 1988).

Another more indirect biological factor is derived from the research of Thomas and Chess (1977, 1984), who found that children appear to be born with a predisposition toward a particular temperament or behavioral style. Temperament or behavioral style is described as the "how" of behavior rather than the "what" or "why." How an individual responds to environmental stimuli will have a significant effect on that person's life experience. Thomas and Chess identified several patterns of initial reactivity or primary reaction patterns. This inborn temperament of the child interacts with the characteristics of adult caregivers, affecting these crucial early relationships. The temperament that a child is born with may affect the quality of nurturing interactions the child receives from parents and teachers and subsequently with behavioral adaptation (Martin, 1992). (See Chapter 13 for a more detailed discussion of the role of temperament in social adjustment.)

Children's physical illnesses and disabilities also place stress on caregivers and affect both the quality of caregiving and the children's perceptions of themselves as competent people (Gallagher, Beckman, & Cross, 1983). Children can exhibit emotional responses (e.g., depression, anxiety) related to necessary medical treatments. Additionally, some children appear to be biologically predisposed to be vulnerable, resistant, or resilient in the face of deviancy-promoting environments. All these factors, apparently related to biological features, can affect the way a child experiences the environment, leading to differential effects on the emotional or behavioral status of the child.

Family Factors

A number of family factors may also affect the emotional or behavioral development of the child. Among these are family stress, parenting styles, parental psychopathology, and addiction in a family member. Families today experience significant stresses related to maintaining the family unit (Gallagher, Beckman, & Cross, 1983). Factors often implicated in family and parental dysfunction include poverty, unemployment, marital problems (including separation and divorce), domestic violence, and illness or disability of a family member. As our society has become more complex, the isolation of families has also increased, compounding potential effects of family dysfunction when dealing with stressful situations.

While these factors do not in themselves cause children to develop emotional or behavioral disorders, the presence of multiple risk factors and the absence of supportive networks for parents and children significantly increase the risk that children will develop emotional or behavioral disorders (Keogh & Weisner, 1993; Morrison & Cosden, 1997). The issue of risk is complex. Children within a single family will react quite differently to the same environment and stresses; one may develop a behavioral disorder, while another appears resistant or resilient and makes a good adjustment to life. (See Chapter 13 for further discussion of risk and resilience.)

The style of parenting may affect the school and community adjustment of the child. Overprotective parenting may be related to anxiety in the child, causing withdrawal from normal situations which the child perceives as dangerous. Parents who place undue emphasis on the importance of achieving high standards may increase the potential for depression. Abusive discipline has obvious implications for the child's emotional health, although the result is not always predictable. Some children become very conforming, others become overly attached and cling to the abusive parent, while still others act out with abusive behavior toward other people or animals. Another potential problem occurs when the parenting style, be it authoritarian, permissive, or democratic, conflicts with the discipline style in the school. This may result in confusion for the child and may lead to behavioral adjustment problems at home, in school, or both.

Parental mental health and adjustment problems have the potential to disrupt the parent-child relationship. Parents who have emotional disorders themselves, including such conditions as schizophrenia, depression, or addiction, have fewer resources to allocate to and use in the parenting role. If other healthy caregivers are available to the child, the effect of pathology in one family member may be reduced.

The presence of alcoholism or other drug dependency problems in the family setting also affects many children and families today. Every classroom contains some children whose family nurturing is being distorted by the substance abuse of a family member. Children growing up with an alcohol- or drug-dependent person grow up in a home with different rules (Black, 1981). These children learn three basic family rules:

- Don't talk about what goes on at home, and don't talk about what you're feeling.
- Don't trust others to meet your needs. Adults are unpredictable and unreliable; if you don't trust or hope, you can't be hurt.
- Don't feel, particularly your pain and hurt. Convince yourself that it isn't so bad, that it doesn't matter that significant adults are not reliably available for you.

Children growing up in such homes may develop particular coping behaviors and assume specific family roles in order to deal with an unpredictable home environment that revolves around the needs of the alcoholic or drug dependent family member (Wegsheider,

1981). The "super child" or "family hero" does everything and does it well; the message this child seeks to send is that the family can't be so bad if this child is so "good." The clown or "mascot" diverts attention from family distress with antics. The "lost child" withdraws into a private world. The family's "scapegoat" exhibits various acting-out behaviors at school or in the community, diverting attention from other family members. The "placator" takes responsibility for making everyone happy, taking care of other members of the family, and attempting to please significant others. Obviously, some of these roles cause more problems in school situations than others, but all are destructive to children's ability to fulfill their own unique potential, and they all may result in a variety of emotional or behavioral problems that may become severe enough to require intervention.

Environmental, Social, and School Factors

Although there are many environmental factors that can affect a child's ability to develop personally satisfying and socially acceptable responses to life events, school factors are the ones that teachers and administrators have the most control over. Next to the family, the school is the most important socializing force in a young person's life. Causal factors directly related to schools include school failure, developmentally inappropriate expectations and discipline, and incongruity between school and home cultures.

School failure is highly correlated with school adjustment problems and difficulties later. It is not always clear whether academic problems lead to behavioral problems or vice versa. What does appear to be clear is that once the cycle is established, it will continue unless effective academic and behavioral interventions are implemented. Failure in school can lead the child to develop a diminished sense of self-esteem. Peer rejection of students who do not meet social and behavioral norms in the community or school accentuates the problem. Students who experience frequent failure tend to adopt a self-defeating cycle of responses, including setting lower goals and putting forth less effort, leading to more failure (see Chapter 12). Such youngsters see their efforts as less and less efficacious, and come to see their lives as controlled by external forces rather than by their own efforts. When their self-esteem as a learner is under attack, they may respond by giving up, saying "I don't care; it's not important." Alternatively, the student may fight back, saying in effect, "I won't, and you can't make me." When students see themselves as incapable of succeeding in the tasks valued by teachers, they may attempt to find other activities in which they can be competent or "the best." This may include being the class bully or clown. The student may become noncompliant or disinterested in school tasks that present difficulties. Any of these behaviors, extended over time, may result in a referral for special education evaluation.

Schools and teachers increase the likelihood of problems when they hold inappropriate expectations for the student's age, ability, and culture. The likelihood of school failure, with its associated problems, is increased in an environment characterized by the quest for uniformity at the expense of individuality. Children need the opportunity to learn and explore in ways that fit their abilities, temperaments, and interests. They also need to learn in environments that validate their particular cultural realities (including differences of race, religion, language, gender, sexual orientation, economic background, and physical and mental abilities). When the options for learning are narrowly restricted, many students will find no place they fit in that environment, and they may then respond in problematic ways to become self-determined individuals. (See Chapter 12 for more discussion of self-determination.)

Curricula and instruction that are perceived as irrelevant or nonfunctional by students can also be a causal factor in the development of problem behaviors. When the activities of the classroom are seen as uninteresting or not worth their participation, children find other ways to occupy their time. They also learn to discount the guidance offered by their teachers and other school staff. Credibility with students is compromised when curricular offerings are viewed as frivolous and a waste of time. Students are unlikely to take seriously information about drug usage when the rest of the curriculum is seen as a waste of time.

Classroom management and school behavior codes can be another source of confusing information for students. When management of behavior and classroom life is inconsistent, students are likely to discount rules of community life in general. They come to see all rules as arbitrary or capricious. Use of destructive reinforcement contingencies to achieve behavioral control, such as candy rewards and excuse from homework for good behavior and the use of corporal punishment for bad behavior, provide little support for the intrinsic motivation to learn that most youngsters have when they begin school. When adults in the school environment provide inadequate or undesirable models of school conduct, it is not difficult to see why students' actions and attitudes may fall short of desired behaviors.

One of the most common factors affecting the emotional health and behavior of a child is the conflict between and among the norms of the family, the school, and the culture (McIntyre, 1993). Cultural biases may affect evaluation for behavior disorders when the teacher's norms are at variance with the community and family culture. Children who find that their own culture is devalued in the school environment—and who are not helped to learn to navigate the differences in cultures between home and school—frequently fail to develop the ability to adapt in different settings, and the cycle of disorder begins.

A final environmental factor that must be addressed by our society as a whole relates to the effect of mass media on children today. Frequent episodes of violence and inappropriate expressions of sexuality provide destructive models of behavior for young people. They establish new norms of behavior and tend to cheapen regard for the feelings of others and even for human life. Families, schools, and communities must address this issue in a concerted way, expanding the dialogue on what it means to be human.

Types of Emotional or Behavioral Disorders

There are many behaviors and attitudes that young people can engage in that might cause their teachers and parents to become concerned. Psychiatrists use the DSM-IV-TR criteria (American Psychiatric Association, 2000) to arrive at a diagnosis related to the presenting symptoms. While it may be useful for teachers to recognize these psychiatric diagnostic terms, educators do not have the authority to determine that such conditions exist, nor do these categories generally have significant relevance for educational placement and planning. The usefulness of the DSM-IV-TR descriptions for educational personnel is further limited because the manifestations of a number of disorders (e.g., depression) may be different in young people than they are in adults.

Another scheme for conceptualizing the subtypes of emotional or behavioral disorders is provided by Quay and Werry (1986), who divided emotional or behavioral disorders into five groups: undersocialized aggressive conduct disorders, socialized aggressive conduct disorders, anxiety-withdrawal-dysphoria disorders, attention-deficit/hyperactivity disorders, and psychotic and pervasive developmental disorders. See Chapter 13 and references such as Kauffman (2001) and Quay and Werry (1986) for more detailed discussions of these maladaptive behavior disorders.

One of the simplest, most commonly used, and most educationally relevant classification schemes categorizes these behaviors and the conditions themselves into *externalizing* and *internalizing* behaviors (Walker & Severson, 1992; see Table 8.4). Conduct disorders are comprised of externalizing aggressive behaviors of the overt and covert varieties. Anxiety-withdrawal-dysphoria disorders include primarily internalizing behaviors. Behaviors categorized as ADHD or immaturity disorders include both externalizing and internalizing behaviors.

There are two benefits of grouping problem behaviors into externalizing and internalizing behaviors. Such categorization helps us focus on the dual nature of behaviors and may help ensure that children with internalizing disorders do not get overlooked in the screening and referral process. In addition, useful interventions and placement options tend to be different for externalizing and internalizing behaviors.

TABLE 8.4   Examples of Externalizing and Internalizing Behaviors

Examples of Externalizing Behaviors	
Overt, Undersocialized	*Covert, Socialized*
Fighting	Lying
Being disobedient	Stealing
Being destructive	Being uncooperative
Dominating others	Staying out late
Being disruptive	Being truant
"Blowing up" easily	Setting fires
Hitting	Associating with "bad companions"
Temper tantrums	Using alcohol or drugs
Refusing to follow directions	Engaging in gang activity
Being boisterous, noisy	Passive noncompliance
Bullying	Cheating
Swearing	

Examples of Internalizing Behaviors	
Anxious	Fearful
Shy	Timid
Tense	Bashful
Depressed or sad	Hypersensitive, easily hurt
Feelings of inferiority	Self-conscious
Lacks self-confidence	Easily confused
Cries easily	Aloof
Worries excessively	Prefers to be alone

Problem behaviors frequently emerge as stable patterns as early as the preschool and primary levels. Early screening to detect them results in the opportunity for intervention in the earliest stages of the disorder, when treatment is likely to be most successful (Rutherford & Nelson, 1995). The Systematic Screening for Behavior Disorders (SSBD) process assists teachers in screening all children for early indications of the presence of potentially disabling behavior patterns (Walker et al., 1988; Walker & Severson, 1992). The SSBD specifically asks teachers to focus on all of the students in their classes and to determine which students are the most externalizing in their behaviors, as well as which exhibit the highest degree of internalizing behaviors. Using this information, detailed follow-up evaluations can be performed to determine the nature and degree of severity of identified behavioral problems and the need for intervention in either general or special education.

Students who are primarily internalizing in their behaviors generally require different placements and interventions from those who present more externalizing behaviors. Children who are grouped within a single self-contained classroom simply because they are all determined to be eligible for services as students with emotional or behavioral disorders are unlikely to have their needs met very well. Students with anxiety-withdrawal-dysphoria disorders often retreat farther into their shells and become more unhappy when grouped with students who are acting-out and who exhibit externalizing behaviors. The behavioral approaches commonly used with students with conduct disorders are repressive to the child with anxiety symptoms. For these and other reasons, it is more useful to think of students who have emotional or behavioral disorders not as a single group but rather as individual students with very specific personal characteristics.

Since problem behaviors and delays in developing appropriate behavior are not the exclusive property of students with emotional or behavioral disorders, Chapter 13 will discuss developmental delays and maladaptive behaviors among all learners with mild disabilities.

Focus on Culture and Diversity

There are long-standing concerns about the disproportionate classification of students of color as having emotional disturbance. African American and Native American students are overrepresented and Hispanic and Asian students are underrepresented. A study of classification rates by Coutinho, Oswald, and Forness (2002) found that the disparity in rates was related to the characteristics of the student (e.g., race and gender) as well as to the characteristics of the community (e.g., poverty). The authors noted that students of color are "disproportionally exposed to potentially toxic environmental influences" (p. 121) and called for local districts to study all the possible contributing factors before deciding on an intervention.

However, educators must consider the degree to which culturally relevant behaviors explain behavioral differences, and whether those behaviors indicate the need for intervention. The reference to cultural norms was added to the Mental Health and Special Education Coalition definition to address the possibility that learners were being identified as having an emotional disturbance because their behavior and interaction patterns differed from those of their teachers, when those behaviors may, in fact, be normative for their cultural group. McIntyre (1993) believed that the issue is not that clear-cut, voicing the fear that, under the Coalition definition, legitimate emotional or behavioral needs of diverse youngsters (e.g., students of diverse races, economic levels, sexual orientations) may be discounted solely because of their cultural status. It certainly is true that students from such groups should not routinely be placed in programs for students with emotional or behavioral disorders simply because their behaviors differ from those typically expected by teachers. It is also true that young people in such groups may have legitimate needs in developing more personally satisfying and socially acceptable behavioral responses to their environment. To include or to exclude students from services because of their cultural background is to treat them unfairly. Assessment protocols should consider the degree to which each student's cultural status is affecting emotional or behavioral responses. That information can then be used to help create a package of services to address those needs appropriately from within that cultural context (Cartledge, 1999).

Resources on the Web

National Mental Health Association (NMHA)

www.nmha.org

> Provides information and fact sheets on topics related to mental health issues, including depression and suicide, and information on local chapters.

National Association for the Mentally Ill (NAMI)

www.nami.org

> Includes research and other resources, a helpline, books, and topical information on issues related to mental illness.

Council for Children with Behavioral Disorders (CCBD)

www.ccbd.net

> A professional site for educators who work with students with emotional and behavioral disorders; CCBD is a subdivision of CEC.

Summary

Many different terms have been used to describe learners with problems with their behaviors and emotions over the years. The term *emotional or behavioral disorders* reflects the dual nature of this condition and also reflects concern with students across the continuum of severity. This book focuses on all students who exhibit behaviors that are personally unsatisfying and/or socially unacceptable to the extent that their growth and development is affected.

Historically, little attention has been given to these children. The advent of the mental hygiene movement early in this century signaled the awareness that children develop in their emotions and behaviors and that adults can assist in that development. Public school special education classes and programs have evolved slowly and have generally been spurred on by concerns about the effect that "out-of-control" children might have on general education classroom activities.

The IDEA states that students are eligible for services for emotional or behavioral disorders when they exhibit relatively severe problem behaviors for a significant period of time and when those behaviors affect school performance. Students who are determined only to have social maladjustment are excluded from eligibility. Many components of the IDEA definition have raised concern, including the issue of severity levels to be served, the definition of educational performance, the exclusion of social maladjustment, and the overrepresentation of students from ethnic and cultural minority backgrounds.

Assessment and identification of students must be multiphasic, including multiple sources of data. A reliable and valid assessment process will include direct observation in multiple settings, information from a variety of informants (parents, teachers, and the child), and scores from standardized rating scales and other psychometric assessment instruments.

It has been estimated that as many as 7 or 8 percent of all schoolchildren may have emotional or behavioral disorders significant enough to require some kind of intervention. Currently, fewer than 1 percent are served nationwide in programs for students with emotional or behavioral disorders. The reasons for this discrepancy have been widely debated. One reason may be the inadequacy of the current definition. The Mental Health and Special Education Coalition definition was developed in response to these concerns.

Factors associated with emotional or behavioral disorders are not easy or even always possible to identify. When evident, the cause is rarely helpful in designing the intervention. Three groups of factors may be involved: (1) biological, including brain injury and genetic predisposition; (2) family factors, recognizing the family's role as the first socialization agent in the child's life; and (3) school and other environmental factors.

Emotional or behavioral disorders can be separated into two groups: those represented by externalizing behaviors and those characterized as internalizing. Conduct disorders, anxiety-withdrawal-dysphoria, and ADHD are specific conditions regularly encountered in school programs. Specific interventions should be developed in response to the nature of the individual child's condition.

CARTER: A Case Study

Carter was initially referred for possible special education services in first grade, where he was being served in a compensatory classroom at Browning Elementary School. The compensatory class served students who did not reach the criterion score for first grade placement on the district readiness test. This classroom had only fifteen students served by a teacher and a full-time aide.

He was referred by his mother, who had many concerns about her son. She noted that his progress seemed slow, that he not only had problems with academics but had a lot of trouble paying attention, was impulsive, and had poor motor control. Carter's teacher concurred with the mother's concerns. Carter was having very little success in the classroom and was constantly in motion. This had become a problem even in a developmentally appropriate alternative first grade program. He was easily distracted and had trouble delaying gratification. He was impatient and gave up easily. He was easily discouraged, and he complained that he did not have any friends. His teacher reported that Carter voiced fears that were unusual for this age group.

(continued)

Carter was the younger of two children. He had been a large baby (ten pounds at birth), and the pregnancy was complicated by high blood pressure and toxemia. However, no adverse effects were noted after the birth. His mother described Carter as a clumsy child, with repeated falls and bumps. Normal developmental milestones were somewhat delayed. He did not crawl until he was eight months old nor walk until he was two. Speech development was interrupted by a loss of hearing at eighteen months due to ear infections. The speech and language evaluation done at the time of referral confirmed difficulty with some sound frequencies, and it showed poor speech and communication skills. He was also taking Ritalin twice a day, prescribed by his pediatrician for attention and hyperactivity problems (ADHD). Even so, Carter's mother described him as a creative, sensitive, and generally happy child.

At age six and a half, Carter was given a standard battery of tests by the school psychologist. The psychologist noted that Carter was able to concentrate more easily on tasks that involved manipulation of objects, but that he was very distracted in auditory tasks. He needed encouragement and reinforcement to sustain effort during the testing. The results indicated the following:

WISC-III

Verbal IQ	102
Performance IQ	109
Full Scale IQ	105

Subtests:

Information	10
Similarities	12
Arithmetic	10
Vocabulary	12
Comprehension	8
Digit Span	9
Picture Completion	12
Picture Arrangement	10
Block Design	13
Object Assembly	10
Coding	12

Carter also achieved a standard score of 105 (63rd percentile) on the Peabody Picture Vocabulary Test, a measure of receptive language ability, which indicated age-appropriate receptive language skills consistent with the WISC-III results.

Carter was given two measures of academic achievement. The Diagnostic Achievement Battery resulted in the following standard scores:

Reading	109
Math	94

The Wide Range Achievement Test (WRAT-3) yielded the following standard scores and grade equivalents:

Math	103	Grade 1-end
Word Identification	113	Grade 1-middle
Spelling	108	Grade 1-middle

From the evaluation, the multidisciplinary team concluded that Carter was a student of average intelligence who showed no significant strengths and weaknesses. Based on state and federal guidelines, he did not at that time qualify for special education.

He went on to second grade, continuing on the Ritalin for his medically diagnosed ADHD. His classroom teacher was very sensitive to Carter's needs and monitored the effects of his medication carefully. Carter continued to show signs of problematic socialization behaviors. He would pick on other children, and he had significant trouble getting along with others.

In third grade, he moved to another school, where he still received all of his education in the regular classroom program. He returned to Browning Elementary School in fourth grade, where he seemed to be in constant trouble. He was still on Ritalin, receiving the highest dose possible. His mother had sought help and advice from other doctors and agencies, and she was in the process of getting him evaluated by a major regional child evaluation clinic. Carter's behavior at home continued to cause serious problems. He exhibited a lot of unwarranted fears and was obsessed by violence. He could not seem to complete any tasks given to him. For the first time, his math skills fell below grade level. In January of that year, the school support team placed him in the resource room under the new eligibility of "other health impaired" because of his ADHD. He was also receiving counseling at the community mental health clinic.

His problems with attention were causing him difficulties, specifically during transitions, such as from lunch to recess and from recess back to class. Right before lunch, when his morning medication would wear off and before the noon dose would take effect, he was unable to concentrate and do work and was consistently disruptive in the regular classroom. It was suggested that his resource room services could include having lunch with the resource teacher and spending recess in the resource room. This was done for about four months, during which careful anecdotal records were kept on his behavior to determine what would be the best placement for Carter. His mother requested that he be reevaluated. He was also scheduled for a brain scan and other diagnostic testing outside of school.

During this period, he was being weaned off the Ritalin because he had to be completely off it for the planned brain scan to be accurate. As he came off the Ritalin, his attention quickly diminished. By the time he was completely off the drug, he could not sustain attention for more than one or two minutes at a time, even on things that he enjoyed, such as computer games. He was unable to do any academic work at that time.

Problem behaviors toward his classmates, teachers, and other people were still very evident. They didn't change whether he was on the Ritalin or not. His reevaluation by the school psychologist included additional tests to try to uncover Carter's real problem. The reevaluation and the behavioral records helped clarify the nature and extent of his problems. His new fear of crowds caused him to resist going to the lunchroom and to prefer solitude. He made up stories and talked extensively about violence. He would jump from one thing to another in conversation, not seeming to know whether he was telling true or made-up stories. He seemed not to be able to tell what was real from what was not real. By April of that year, the full team met with the mother to determine how to best meet Carter's needs. He had not made any progress during this school year, and the entire experience had been very frustrating for him, his mother, and his teachers.

Everyone at the meeting was aware that Carter had an attention-deficit/hyperactivity disorder. When the team met, the school psychologist reported that the results of the evaluation indicated that Carter's school problems stemmed primarily from his emotional problems, not from the ADHD. The ADHD was a contributing factor, but the primary disability appeared to be the emotional or behavioral disorder. Even when he was on Ritalin, the abnormal behavior continued. The mother and the classroom teacher concurred in this. They saw a special class placement as being the least restrictive environment for Carter at this time, one that would allow him to resume academic learning and to work on his emotional issues and problem behaviors. However, the teacher of the class for students with emotional or behavioral disorders dissented, saying that the ADHD was the root problem.

The committee took all the evidence and decided that the emotional problems were the central issue. Those concerns were always there, on or off Ritalin; therefore, they felt that his emotional problems were the primary cause of his lack of academic success. Carter had never had a successful year since he started school, and because of his past history, it was the committee's sincere hope that intensive work in the self-contained classroom environment would help him finally begin to make progress.

DISCUSSION

Using the above information and the federal definition of emotional disturbance, determine whether the classification of Carter as a child with an emotional or behavioral disorder is appropriate.

How might the diagnosis of ADHD complement or contradict Carter's classification as a child with an emotional or behavioral disorder?

Specifically, consider possible reasons the team and the teacher of the self-contained class might have come to somewhat different conclusions.

If you identify additional information that would be helpful in making a full determination, make a list of the additional information you think would be necessary to complete the evaluation.

CHAPTER NINE

LEARNERS WITH OTHER DISORDERS AND CONDITIONS

QUESTIONS TO GUIDE YOUR STUDY

- What is an attention-deficit/hyperactivity disorder (ADHD)?
- How do we identify students with ADHD? What are students with ADHD like?
- How are learning disabilities, emotional-behavioral disorders, and ADHD related?
- How can students with ADHD be served in the public schools if ADHD isn't listed as a disability in IDEA?
- What conditions are part of the autism spectrum disorders? Which ones might be considered among the mild disabilities?
- What are learners with traumatic brain injury like?
- What conditions comprise communication disorders?
- How do physical and sensory disabilities affect student learning?

Meet Nancy

Nancy makes an impression, and she always has. As an infant, she was fussy and cried a lot. Despite all attempts to soothe her, it appeared impossible to make her comfortable or happy. Her mother wondered if she would ever sleep through the night. As she grew and as her physical abilities increased, life in the house was devoted to keeping her safe, twenty-four hours a day. She learned how to climb the bars and get out of her crib by her first birthday. Child safety latches and gates proved inadequate to the task of keeping Nancy and harm apart. When she was three, her parents were awakened one morning at 4:30 A.M. to the screams of the family cat. They followed the sound, arriving in the bathroom just in time to save the cat from being flushed down the toilet by Nancy. Her pediatrician felt that Nancy was just an active, inquisitive preschooler, and that judgment would come with maturity. Time was the remedy.

At five, Nancy was enrolled in kindergarten. The teacher quickly realized that Nancy was different. Her level of attention was much shorter than the

(continued)

other children, and her levels of impulsivity and activity were much higher. She was not benefiting from the kindergarten program, and the decision was made to move her to the prekindergarten class, assuming that with time, she would develop the attention abilities required to be successful in school, that she was just developmentally immature. Life was no better in the prekindergarten class. She talked incessantly, grabbed what she wanted, and was in constant motion. Nancy wasn't learning, and neither was anyone else.

Finally, when Nancy was in second grade, the school and her parents concluded that a psychological evaluation was in order to determine an explanation for Nancy's problems. The results indicated normal ability and, surprisingly, normal development of cognitive concepts and language. What stood out was her constant movement and her dangerous and disruptive impulsivity, as well as her academic problems in the classroom. Her performance levels in reading, writing, and math lagged well behind her peers. A medical examination was suggested, and the diagnosis made: attention-deficit/hyperactivity disorder, combined type. Based on the above information and the discrepancy between her achievement and ability, as

well as the absence of other disabling conditions, the school's multidisciplinary team determined that she qualified for services as a student with a learning disability.

Today, Nancy is a reasonably successful fourth grader. She still stands out, and she probably always will. A combination of behavioral interventions and psychostimulant medication has brought her behavior under control, although she still has a shorter attention span, is somewhat fidgety, and displays more impulsivity and activity than other fourth graders. She has learned to self-monitor her attention as a result of cognitive behavior modification interventions implemented by the consultant teacher. Counseling sessions with the guidance counselor have helped her accept responsibility for her actions and not to blame her actions on the ADHD or the medication. Nevertheless, her homeroom teacher has a hard time accepting that her behaviors are the result of a disability. Mr. Smith finds it hard to accept that a student who is obviously as capable as Nancy and who *sometimes* pays attention and can control her behavior reasonably well has a "real" learning disability. He suspects that the "attention disorder" is an excuse for letting Nancy do what she pleases.

Children and Youth with Attention Disorders

During the 1980s and 1990s, increasing numbers of children just like Nancy have been identified by physicians, psychiatrists, psychologists, and sometimes schools as having *attention-deficit/hyperactivity disorder (ADHD)*. Schools are increasingly being challenged by parents to provide modified programming and accommodations for these students. School administrators and teachers like Mr. Smith frequently question these diagnoses, voicing concern that the disability rubric is being abused. There is the suspicion that the label is being used to relieve children of responsibility for their own behavior. Articles on one side of the debate or the other appear regularly in the popular press as well the professional literature. The one thing that seems certain about ADHD is that nothing is certain. (Because *attention-deficit/hyperactivity disorder* is the term currently in medical use to refer to this group of learners, in the interest of brevity this book will use the abbreviation *ADHD* to refer to these students.)

Historical Development of the Concept of ADHD

Like learning disabilities, attention-deficit/hyperactivity disorders are a fairly recent phenomenon of study, and the history of ADHD tells of struggles to describe and even name the condition (Epstein, Shaywitz, Shaywitz, & Woolston, 1991; Shaywitz & Shaywitz, 1988). In 1902, a physician by the name of G. F. Still reported his observations of children with "morbid defects in moral control" in terms that parallel current descriptions of children with ADHD. Other researchers and physicians of that period, such as Goldstein and Bender, related these problem behaviors to brain injury or infections of the central nervous system. Werner, Strauss, and Lehtinen similarly described clients with apparent disorders of attention and hyperactivity, which they too associated with a history of brain injury (Stevens & Birch, 1957; Strauss & Lehtinen, 1947). Clements and the members of Task Force I (described in Chapter 4) developed a definition of children with "minimal brain dysfunction" that included children with "various combinations of impairment in . . . control of attention, impulse, and motor control" (Clements, 1966, p. 9).

In 1968, the American Psychiatric Association (APA) added a category to the *Diagnostic and Statistical Manual: DSM-II* and named it *hyperkinetic disorder of childhood,* with diagnostic criteria including overactivity, distractibility, short attention span, and restlessness (APA, 1968). By 1980, the APA had changed the focus to include issues of attention rather than just overactivity (APA, 1980). With its DSM-III definition and diagnostic criteria of *attention deficit disorder,* the APA highlighted the importance of attention in the learning process and daily functioning. In 1987, the APA revised the criteria once again in the DSM-III-R, listing fourteen symptoms and requiring that eight of them be present for a diagnosis of *attention-deficit/hyperactivity disorder* (APA, 1987). In 1994, the criteria for *attention-deficit/hyperactivity disorder* were revised once again in the DSM-IV (APA, 1994) and DSM-IV-TR (APA, 2000), continuing the focus on the dual nature of the condition—inattention and hyperactivity. The DSM-IV also identified three subtypes: hyperactive-impulsive type, inattentive type, and combined type.

From this brief history, it becomes apparent that the conditions of learning disabilities and ADHD have been integrally intertwined throughout their histories. Their histories are identical in the earliest years, and they continued to proceed on parallel tracks in the 1980s and 1990s. Through all the changes in names and revised criteria, the fact remains that these children have a condition that impairs their ability to function optimally in school. Children and Adults with Attention Deficit Disorders (CH.A.D.D.), a parent and support group for individuals with this condition, continues to advocate for effective identification procedures and more treatment options. Currently, medication and behavioral approaches are the primary services available to these students. Increasingly, cognitive behavior modification, self-instructional strategies, and counseling are being used as well.

When Congress reauthorized P.L. 94–142, the Education for All Handicapped Children Act, in the form of the IDEA in 1990, it declined to add ADHD to the list of specific diagnostic categories recognized as special education categories. Instead, Congress directed the U.S. Department of Education to conduct a study of the condition and the extent to which these students were being denied needed services. In 1991, the U.S. Department of Education issued a clarification memorandum, confirming that children with ADHD may be eligible for services under the IDEA when the ADHD impairs their educational performance and prevents them from learning (Davila, Williams, & MacDonald, 1991). The memorandum further asserted that it was not necessary to list ADHD as a separate diagnostic category since these students generally present learning and/or behavioral problems to the extent that they are eligible for services under one of the existing categories, specifically the categories of learning disabilities, emotional disturbance, or other health impairments.

The clarification memorandum stated that youngsters with ADHD may be qualified for services under the IDEA as "other health impaired" if the ADHD constitutes a "chronic or acute health problem that results in limited alertness, which adversely affects educational performance" (Davila et al., 1991). The U.S. Department of Education memorandum also noted that children with attention-deficit/hyperactivity disorders are deemed to be "qualified handicapped persons" under the provisions of Section 504 of the Rehabilitation Act of 1973 if the condition limits their ability to learn or benefit from their educational program, much as the needs of individuals with other physical, sensory, or mental disabilities are addressed. The review process also concluded that many students with ADHD diagnoses were already being served within the guidelines for learning disabilities or emotional or behavioral disorders if a multidisciplinary team determined that their characteristics matched the criteria for those disorders.

The debate continues, however, with many points of view on the relationship of learning disabilities, emotional-behavioral disorders, and ADHD. A study of the comorbidity of ADHD with learning disabilities or behavioral disorders indicated that students who met the criteria for both ADHD and one of the other disability categories generally had more severe levels of disability (Bussing, Zima, Belin, & Forness, 1998). Silver (1990) asserted that attention-deficit/hyperactivity disorders are not learning disabilities, although they are often associated with learning disabilities. One proposed response to this debate is to use functional assessment practices and to serve youngsters in noncategorical treatment programs (Egnor, 1996).

Current Definition in the DSM-IV-TR

The American Psychiatric Association's *Diagnostic and Statistical Manual of Mental Disorders, Fourth Edition—Text Revision* (2000) outlined the diagnostic criteria for ADHD (see Table 9.1). The DSM-IV-TR notes that a criterion is met only if a behavior is observed to

TABLE 9.1   DSM-IV Diagnostic Criteria for Attention-Deficit/Hyperactivity Disorder

A. Either (1) and/or (2):

(1) Six or more of the following symptoms of **inattention** have persisted for at least 6 months to a degree that is maladaptive and inconsistent with developmental level:

Inattention

(a) often fails to give close attention to details or makes careless mistakes in schoolwork, work, or other activities

(b) often has difficulty sustaining attention in tasks or play activities

(c) often does not seem to listen when spoken to directly

(d) often does not follow through on instructions and fails to finish schoolwork, chores, or duties in the workplace (not due to oppositional behavior or failure to understand instructions)

(e) often has difficulty organizing tasks and activities

(f) often avoids, dislikes, or is reluctant to engage in tasks that require sustained mental effort (such as schoolwork or homework)

(g) often loses things necessary for tasks and activities (e.g., toys, school assignments, pencils, books, or tools)

(h) is often easily distracted by extraneous stimuli

(i) is often forgetful in daily activities

(2) six (or more) of the following symptoms of **hyperactivity-impulsivity** have persisted for at least 6 months to a degree that is maladaptive and inconsistent with developmental level:

Hyperactivity

(a) often fidgets with hands or feet or squirms in seat

(b) often leaves seat in classroom or in other situations in which remaining seated is expected

(c) often runs about or climbs excessively in situations in which it is inappropriate (in adolescents or adults, may be limited to subjective feelings of restlessness)

(d) often has difficulty playing or engaging in leisure activities quietly

(e) is often "on the go" or often acts as if "driven by a motor"

(f) often talks excessively

Impulsivity

(g) often blurts out answers before questions have been completed

(h) often has difficulty waiting turn

(i) often interrupts or intrudes on other (e.g., butts into conversations or games)

B. Some hyperactive-impulsive or inattentive symptoms that caused impairment were present before age 7

C. Some impairment from the symptoms is present in two or more settings (e.g., at school [or work] and at home)

D. There must be clear evidence of clinically significant impairment in social, academic, or occupational functioning

E. The symptoms do not occur exclusively during the course of a pervasive developmental disorder, schizophrenia, or other psychotic disorder and are not accounted for by another mental disorder (e.g., mood disorder, anxiety disorder, dissociative disorder, or a personality disorder)

occur considerably more frequently and severely than the behaviors observed in peers at the same developmental level. It is also a requirement that some of the symptoms should have been evident before the age of seven, although the diagnosis can occur later. Impaired function should be in evidence in at least two settings, and the problem behaviors must be judged to be interfering with expected functioning in social, academic, or vocational areas. Although this definition represented an improvement over prior conceptual definitions, which consisted of a vague sense of overactivity, the DSM-IV-TR criteria still lack clear operational procedures for determining if a criterion is met. There is room for considerable subjectivity in the evaluation and diagnosis of ADHD. The DSM-IV-TR acknowledges that there are currently no standardized tests to establish a definitive diagnosis of this condition.

In order to establish a diagnosis of ADHD, the problem behaviors must be present in multiple contexts, such as home, school, work, and social situations; they must also have persisted for at least six months. Behaviors may worsen in situations that require sustained attention and mental effort or that are not intrinsically interesting. Symptoms generally decrease or disappear entirely in very controlled situations, such as when working one on one, or when the activity is particularly interesting, such as playing video games. The DSM-IV-TR cautions that it may be difficult to distinguish between the behaviors of a child with ADHD and the age-appropriate behaviors of normally active children.

Types of Attention-Deficit/Hyperactivity Disorder

The DSM-IV-TR (2000) identified three primary subtypes of ADHD: (1) predominantly inattentive, (2) predominantly hyperactive/impulsive, and (3) combined type. Most individuals are found to have the combined type of ADHD. Those who have one of the other types may develop the combined type later, and vice versa. The three types are described as follows:

- *Predominantly inattentive type (ADHD-I):* six or more indicators of inattention are present, but fewer than six indicators of hyperactivity/impulsivity can be documented
- *Predominantly hyperactive/impulsive type (ADHD-HI):* six or more indicators of hyperactivity/impulsivity are present, but fewer than six indicators of inattention can be documented
- *Combined type (ADHD-C):* both inattention and hyperactivity/impulsivity are present equally, with six or more indicators in each group.

In a field test of the DSM-IV criteria conducted by Lahey et al. (1994), incidence data by subtype were acquired, as presented in Table 9.2, indicating that more than half of the children meeting the criteria for an ADHD diagnosis are judged to have the combined subtype, while 27 percent of the referred were found not to have ADHD at all.

Levels of Severity

As with other disorders, ADHD may be mild, moderate, or severe in its effect on the ability of the individual to function appropriately. DSM-IV-TR (2000) provides the following guidelines for differentiating among the levels of severity:

- *Mild:* few if any symptoms in excess of those required to make the diagnosis; minimal or no impairment in school or social functioning

TABLE 9.2   **Percentage of Students with ADHD in Each Subtype**

	ADHD Subtypes			
	Inattentive (N = 74)	*Hyperactive/ Impulsive (N = 50)*	*Combined (N = 152)*	*No ADHD (N = 104)*
Percent of Children in Each Category (N = 380)	20%	13%	40%	27%
Percent of Children with ADHD in Each Subtype (N = 276)	27%	18%	55%	——

Based on data from Lahey, 1994.

- *Moderate:* symptoms or functional impairment intermediate between "mild" and "severe"
- *Severe:* many symptoms in excess of those required to make the diagnosis; significant and pervasive impairment in functioning at home and in school with peers.

Identification of Learners with ADHD

The diagnostic process used to confirm the presence of ADHD is a complex one, generally involving (1) a medical examination to explore the biological and physiological aspects, (2) a psychoeducational evaluation to determine how the presenting symptoms may be interfering with the child's ability to learn and function, and (3) an ecological assessment to determine the nature of the interactions between the child and the demands and characteristics of the environment.

An appropriate assessment process would include the following:

- *Medical examination, including direct measures of activity level and attending behaviors:* A general physical examination is recommended to determine the medical basis for the condition and to rule out treatable causes. Since ADHD is a condition derived from the medical model and is presumed to have a neurobiological basis, it might also seem reasonable to include a complete neurological examination in the assessment process. The fact is, however, that routine neurological examinations usually indicate normal functioning. The source of the disorder is rather subtle in its manifestation, and the absence or presence of neurological findings does not constitute a diagnosis in itself. It should be noted that although this medical evaluation is recommended, schools frequently base their determination of the need for services on other assessment information derived from psychologists' and teachers' reports.
- *Psychoeducational examination, including measures of intellectual functioning and achievement:* This evaluation will help substantiate any negative effect the condition is having on school performance, and it may also confirm the existence of another

disability, such as a learning disability, emotional or behavioral disorder, or mental retardation.

■ *Ecological assessment, including use of rating scales, interviews, and direct observations:* The ecological assessment should be especially sensitive to cultural or linguistic factors that may be implicated in the behaviors that led to the referral.

Rating scales are one of the principal instruments used to identify children and youth with problems related to inattention, impulsivity, and hyperactivity. These scales are generally based on the DSM-IV-TR criteria, which are broken down into more specific descriptors. By their nature, rating scales are inferential and subjective, and the results are influenced as much by the characteristics of the person completing them as they are by the characteristics of the child being evaluated. Good practice requires rating scales to be completed by as many people as possible who know the child. While rating scales describe the child's behaviors in comparison to a normative sample, they also give some sense of the variability of the behaviors across settings. Some of the more commonly used scales include the Yale Children's Inventory, Child Behavior Checklist, the Connors Parent and Teacher Rating Scales, and the Revised Behavior Problem Checklist.

Other information sources that are useful in assessing the ecological context of the condition include

■ Structured interviews with teachers, parents, peers, and the students themselves
■ Direct observation of behaviors in a variety of naturalistic settings, and comparison of these observed behaviors with those of typical peers.

One of the central components of the ADHD construct is that the condition is relatively pervasive. The individual's ability to attend is seen to be impaired at home as well as at school and at play as well as at work, although the extent of the impairment may vary between settings. This means that while the symptoms may increase or decrease in particular environments, they never completely vanish. If the symptoms were found to be present only in one setting (e.g., in the classroom with a particular teacher), one would not identify the child as having ADHD but would instead look for environmental conditions in that setting that could be altered to improve the ability to function.

Prevalence of Attention-Deficit/Hyperactivity Disorder

ADHD has been referred to as a low-visibility, high-prevalence disorder. It is a low-visibility condition because in many cases the youngsters look and act like their typical peers, unless their hyperactivity is at the severe end of the continuum. It is a high-prevalence syndrome because it is estimated that the incidence of ADHD in children is between 3 and 7 percent (APA, 2000; Davila et al., 1991; Lerner, Lowenthal, & Lerner, 1995). Varying prevalence rates are obtained in different geographic areas, but it is assumed that the variations are due more to different ways of conceptualizing and diagnosing the condition than they are to a true variability (Shaywitz & Shaywitz, 1988). Although students with the inattentive type of ADHD are at significant risk for school failure without intervention, they are less likely to be referred for services than their hyperactive/impulsive peers (Epstein et al., 1991).

The disorder is much more prevalent among males than females, with ratios in the general population ranging from 2:1 to 8:1 in various studies (Shaywitz & Shaywitz, 1988). The range of symptoms displayed by boys and girls is similar, but girls have a tendency to display more cognitive, language, and social deficits, while the boys exhibit more problems with aggression and impulse control (Lerner & Lerner, 1991). The lower numbers of girls identified may be attributed to the observation that boys tend to display more characteristics associated with hyperactivity while girls appear to manifest symptoms of inattention more frequently; this difference can cause boys to be identified more often because the behaviors are more obvious and troubling.

ADHD affects individuals differentially at the various age levels, with the symptoms changing as the individual moves through preschool, elementary school, adolescence, and adulthood. It is often difficult to diagnose ADHD in children younger than four or five years of age because the behavior of young children is much more variable than that of older children, and the symptoms of hyperactivity and impulsivity are typical characteristics of young children. Very young children often display inattention as well, largely because they have not had the reason or opportunity to develop sustained attending behaviors.

Most cases of ADHD are diagnosed in elementary school, when the symptoms begin to significantly interfere with school adjustment. As children move toward adolescence, the symptoms may change again, becoming less conspicuous. Excessive motor activity may be replaced by less conspicuous fidgeting or an inner restlessness. Impulsiveness may lead the young person to break family rules and to display a tendency to avoid sedentary tasks (e.g., at school). It is not clear if or how prevalence figures change in adolescence and adulthood since statistics for those populations are more difficult to acquire and the symptoms are less obvious.

A question that is frequently debated is whether the definition of ADHD should include an exclusionary clause similar to that found in the current federal definition of learning disabilities. Those who favor this approach feel that it would be useful in research and treatment to be able to identify a more homogeneous group of learners whose sole problem area relates to attention and hyperactivity. Other researchers advocate dually identifying learners with ADHD in addition to learning disabilities, emotional disorders, or mental retardation (Shaywitz & Shaywitz, 1988).

Some students with ADHD receive services under the classification of learning disabilities since their primary presenting symptom relates to their inability to learn and perform in school at a level consistent with their ability. In some cases, it appears possible that the ADHD is secondary to the learning disability, developing in reaction to failure in school. An issue in discussing the prevalence of ADHD is the extent to which learning disabilities and ADHD coexist in a single student. The answer to this question is hard to determine due to the varying methods used to diagnose both conditions. It is estimated that up to 40 percent of children with ADHD have difficulties learning commensurate with their measured intellectual ability, while 10 to 20 percent of children with learning disabilities will also manifest symptoms of ADHD (Lerner & Lerner, 1991; Lerner et al., 1995; Shaywitz & Shaywitz, 1988, 1991). In their report to Congress, the Interagency Committee on Learning Disabilities advocated drawing a clearer delineation among learning disabilities, conduct disorders, and attention deficit disorders and exploring the interrelatedness of these conditions (Shaywitz & Shaywitz, 1988, 1991).

The situation is similar when we look at the coexistence of ADHD with emotional or behavioral disturbances. The most frequent problem behavior associated with ADHD is anti-social, aggressive behavior or conduct disorders. Between 30 and 90 percent of children with ADHD are judged to have serious problem behaviors (Frick & Lahey, 1991; Teeter, 1991). These conduct problems are often judged to be related to inattentiveness, overactivity, and im-pulsivity. Students with the inattentive type of ADHD are more likely to display symptoms of disordered affect, such as anxiety and depression (Lahey & Carlson, 1991). Shaywitz and Shaywitz (1988) suggest that the conditions of ADHD and various emotional disorders are so intertwined that it may be impossible to identify a youngster as belonging solely to one classification or the other. To complicate matters further, it has been observed by members of multidisciplinary placement teams that even though identification of the learner as having an emotional disturbance will qualify the student for needed behavioral services, parents often resist this label and refuse the services, due to the significant stigma the label repre-sents. The term *ADHD* or *learning disability* is viewed as a more acceptable category. The perceptions of the varying stigma associated with various categories further complicate the classification process.

Conditions Associated with Attention-Deficit/Hyperactivity Disorder

ADHD is generally regarded to be a chronic neurobiological condition that can interfere with many life functions, disrupting the individual's life at home, school, work, and play. Current thinking holds that both biological and psychosocial factors play a role in the gene-sis of ADHD. One theory holds that the child's biological makeup forms the biological basis for the condition, but that the specific manifestation and expression of the disorder are related to the environmental context (Shaywitz & Shaywitz, 1988). In a review of the litera-ture that included twenty-five studies of ADHD, Goodman and Poillion (1992) identified thirty-eight separate causal factors in five broad categories:

- Organic causes (including genetic conditions)
- Birth complications
- Intellectual/developmental causes
- Psychological issues
- Environmental factors

There is growing scientific evidence (Lerner et al., 1995; Roccio, Hynd, Cohen, & Gonzalez, 1993) that such organic causes as chemical imbalances or deficiencies may account for the difficulties in maintaining attention and controlling physical activity. Specif-ically, it is hypothesized that the attention problems may be caused by a reduced ability of the brain to produce the required neurotransmitters. The lack of neurotransmitters results in a reduction in stimulation from the brain to the central nervous system, thus disrupting the nor-mal process of activity and inhibition. These findings may help explain why psychostimulants work to reduce the symptoms of ADHD. Other researchers hypothesize that neuroanatomical or neurophysiological differences resulting from differences in brain structure may play a role

(Roccio et al., 1993). Still other research studies have implicated thyroid abnormalities, differences in brain structure or function, and problems with glucose metabolism as causal factors (Lerner et al., 1995).

There is also evidence that genetic factors may be involved in some cases, with several members of the same family (e.g., grandparent, parent, child, siblings) exhibiting the symptoms of ADHD. Learners with such conditions as fragile X and neurofibromatosis may display an increased level of attentional and hyperactivity problems. Inheritance patterns of ADHD and Tourette syndrome suggest interrelated patterns of heritability for these two conditions. Children with phenylketonuria (PKU) also seem to have a higher than expected incidence of ADHD, indicating a potential relationship with that genetic condition.

Brain damage was implicated early in the history of the syndrome. According to the DSM-IV, ADHD is sometimes associated with a history of child abuse, lead poisoning, encephalitis and other infections, prenatal drug and alcohol exposure, low birthweight, and birth complications (APA, 1994). Children with seizure disorders are more likely to also display ADHD, although it is not clear if the cause is the seizure disorder itself or the antiseizure medications. All of these factors constitute insults to the brain and central nervous system and thus may be implicated as causes of inattention, impulsivity, and hyperactivity.

Psychological causes (Goodman & Poillion, 1992) are noted by smaller numbers of researchers. Such causes include problematic psychosocial relationships, anxiety, conduct disorders, frustration, and personal space needs. In such cases, it is possible that these conditions are characterized by behaviors similar to ADHD rather than being the cause of the ADHD, since a causal connection has not been determined.

Finally, the environment has recently been considered as a contributing factor in ADHD. The "goodness of fit" between children and the settings in which they learn, live, and play may be critical in whether a child is judged to be inattentive or hyperactive. The ability of the cultural contexts to tolerate the levels of inattention and hyperactivity of normally active children will be central to determining if that child is viewed as deviant. Additionally, the degree to which the environment provides the opportunity and need to develop the ability to focus attention and control activity may be a factor. One hypothesis suggests that hyperactivity may be the child's response to an environment that lacks sufficient stimulation.

Characteristics of Individuals with ADHD

In addition to the DSM-IV-TR diagnostic criteria listed previously, the following characteristics are frequently observed in individuals with this disorder:

- Low frustration tolerance
- Resentment toward family members
- Mood lability (instability)
- Poor self-esteem
- Lack of effort, "laziness"
- Perceived lack of self-responsibility
- Excessive, insistent demands that requests be met

- Temper outbursts
- Stubbornness
- Rejection by peers
- Oppositional behavior
- Antagonism and aggression
- Bossiness.

Individuals with ADHD frequently perform more poorly in school than their typical peers, drop out of school more often, and have less vocational success as adults. Intellectual functioning and development may be adversely affected. The disorder may coexist with a number of other conditions, such as mood disorders, learning disabilities, anxiety disorders, communication disorders, behavioral disorders, and Tourette syndrome.

Poor Delay of Response.   A recently advanced theory about the source of the symptoms of ADHD suggests that the condition may actually arise from poor delay of response (Barkley, 1993). Barkley described these children as having a deficiency in tolerance for delay within tasks and a reduced ability to delay responses. The ability to reflect before acting allows the individual to make informed choices about proceeding with a course of action and to refrain from carrying out impulsive actions that will not lead to desirable outcomes.

Barkley hypothesized that ADHD is better characterized as disinhibition (a deficit in delay of response) rather than a primary deficit in attention. Barkley relates the inability to delay responses to interruption of basic thought processes, including: (1) separating a message into several components (e.g., affect and content), (2) holding a stimulus long enough to perform complex mental operations with it, (3) reflecting on the meaning of a stimulus, with the mediation of inner language, and (4) reconstituting the message into a new thought or concept. Barkley suggested that basic thinking processes may in fact be intact in students with ADHD, but that it is the poor delay of response that does not allow time for thinking to occur before acting. Studies on the effect of stimulant medication suggest this may indeed be true. If this hypothesis is supported by subsequent research, we may more accurately characterize individuals with ADHD as those who act before having time to think, rather than as those who do not think or who lack the ability to attend and think before acting.

Characteristics at Different Ages.   A developmental perspective is essential in determining the presence of ADHD in an individual. As mentioned earlier, it has been determined that the symptoms vary according to developmental age and that the effects of these symptoms on behavior vary as well (Teeter, 1991). While the age at onset and diagnosis may be as early as three, the child who is later identified with ADHD is often retrospectively reported to have cried excessively and to have been difficult to soothe in infancy. Excessive sensitivity to stimuli is noted. Temperamental differences may adversely affect the mother-child bonding process (Lerner et al., 1995; Teeter, 1991).

Preschool children diagnosed with ADHD are frequently described, as Nancy was, as "always on the go," with excessive motor activity as a primary characteristic. Aggressive acts are also frequent, perhaps explained by the lack of inhibitions that characterizes these children. Their natural childlike inquisitiveness can take destructive turns, since they act before thinking about the possibility of damaging property or harming people. They also test their parents regularly by exhibiting more noncompliance than their typical peers (Lerner et al., 1995; Teeter, 1991).

By elementary school age, the motor activity moderates in some children into fidgeting and restlessness. Problems with organization and task completion are frequently mentioned in referrals. Inability to concentrate will eventually affect school performance negatively. The children display a low tolerance for frustration. They respond impulsively, often failing to follow directions because they get started on a task before all the directions have been given. They may take undue risks and engage in dangerous acts, either because of impulsivity or as a means to generate more positive image with their peer group. They may be reported to be disruptive in class and to display oppositional and noncompliant behaviors. They frequently exhibit social difficulties, having difficulty maintaining friendships because of their troubling behaviors (Lerner et al., 1995; Teeter, 1991).

In adolescence, the motoric excesses all but disappear in most individuals, although the young person may talk about being "jumpy" inside. The years of inattention take their toll, and the teenager frequently has growing academic skill deficits. Problems with following rules and achieving self-control are frequently noted by teachers and parents. In fact, at this age, the secondary symptoms of aggression, low self-esteem, problems with peer relation-ships, and problems in learning become the predominant concerns. Concurrent diagnoses with behavioral disorders such as oppositional defiant disorder or other conduct disorders become more common. There is an increased risk of developing depression and problems with substance abuse and antisocial behaviors (Lerner et al., 1995; Teeter, 1991).

In adults, ADHD is usually a hidden disorder, and the manifestation of the disorder is a result of cumulative effects over the years. The adult may exhibit problems maintaining rela-tionships, staying organized, or keeping a job. Substance abuse and problems with impulse control can result in abuse of their spouses or children, similar to the temper tantrums they may have engaged in as young children. Depression and low self-esteem are frequently observed in adults with ADHD who have experienced significant failure in their develop-mental years (Lerner et al., 1995; Teeter, 1991). In some cases, the ability to function in the workplace may improve over previous school performance, due in part to the reduction in motoric activity, but also related to the ability of adults to choose work environments that accommodate their ability to function.

In reviewing the significant body of research on the developmental manifestations of ADHD, Teeter (1991) illustrates the continuing effects of ADHD on affected individuals throughout the life span. It is also obvious that the effect of ADHD over time leads to increas-ing problems with learning, conduct, emotional development, and health. Poor self-esteem, lack of success in learning, and impaired social relationships affect overall development and the ability to function. Treatment plans need to focus on the concerns that are central to the developmental level of the child. Although the manifestation of the ADHD may change over time, the effect on related functioning may well persist throughout the life span. Educators and parents should address these concerns as aggressively as they do increasing attention, time on task, and hyperactivity.

Should ADHD Be a Separate Category in the IDEA?

As indicated previously, ADHD is not currently specified as a separate eligibility category in the federal special education statute, the IDEA. Although Congress failed to add it to the IDEA in 1990, and the U.S. Department of Education has determined that children with ADHD can receive services under existing categories, the debate continues. Special educators need to be knowledgeable participants in these ongoing discussions. To set the context for this debate, it may be useful to summarize the arguments advanced on both sides of the issue.

Children and Adults with Attention Deficit Disorders (CH.A.D.D.), with the support of some professionals in the field, has been among the most vocal proponents of establishing a separate category. Composed primarily of parents, and serving as a support and advocacy group for individuals with ADHD, CH.A.D.D. holds the position that students with ADHD are being denied services due to the lack of a diagnostic category. The arguments advanced by CH.A.D.D. continue in the tradition of parent advocacy established by The Arc, the LDA, and similar groups in the 1950s and 1960s. CH.A.D.D. uses this history as a precedent to underscore the direct connection between formal designation as a separate condition and the provision of services and accommodations in the public schools. CH.A.D.D. contends that without the designation of ADHD as a disability category, the civil rights protections available to individuals with other disabilities are frequently denied to them and their children. Furthermore, they assert that individuals with ADHD require specialized and distinctive treatment plans and services. They advance the position that grouping these children with students with other conditions such as learning disabilities, behavioral disorders, and other health impairments results in their receiving inappropriate services (Lerner et al., 1995).

On the other side of the debate, the position against establishing a separate category in the IDEA was articulated by the U.S. Department of Education in its 1991 clarification memorandum (Davila et al., 1991), as well as by many professional groups. One such group, the Division for Learning Disabilities (1991) of the Council for Exceptional Children, holds that while ADHD is a valid medical diagnosis, appropriate services are already available under current programming options. This position focuses on the premise that special education services should always be designed to meet the individual needs of the child in question, and that the label is merely a vehicle for determining that a child is eligible for such an individualized education program. Others who oppose CH.A.D.D.'s position argue that services already exist in the schools to assist children in learning and in managing their behavior, and that to establish a separate category would unduly complicate teacher certification and school staffing. Many special education professionals agree that specialized methods that apply only to ADHD students do not exist, and that separate programs for learners with ADHD would be redundant (Division for Learning Disabilities, 1991).

ADHD and Other Health Impairments.   One possible course of action identified by the U.S. Department of Education is to classify a student with ADHD as a student with "other health impairment." Currently, the vehicle for identifying a learner as having ADHD is a medical diagnosis as established by the American Psychiatric Association (2000). Thus the condition legitimately may be considered a medical condition. According to the provisions of the IDEA, a health condition constitutes a disability under this law when it results in limited alertness, adversely affecting educational performance. Since deficits in attention can be assumed to affect the alertness needed for learning, the U.S. Department of Education (Davila et al., 1991) has determined that students with ADHD may be judged eligible under this category if their educational performance is affected. They also make the case that if this physical or mental condition results in substantial limitations in a major life function such as learning, the child would also be eligible for appropriate specialized services under Section 504 of the Rehabilitation Act of 1973. IDEA data from 1990–1991 to 1999–2000 suggest that use of the category Other Health Impairments is becoming the option of choice for classifying students with ADHD. Over the decade, while the numbers of all students with disabilities increased 30.3 percent, the numbers of students classified as having other health impairments increased 351 percent! Twelve states reported that their increases in OHI identification were directly attributable to the inclusion of students with ADHD in this category (U.S. Department of Education, 2001).

ADHD and Learning Disabilities. When achievement deficits inconsistent with ability are the primary presenting symptoms, use of the learning disability category appears to be appropriate. This determination is further supported by the fact that attention is considered to be a psychological process, and that learning disabilities are conceptualized as disorders in basic psychological processes; therefore, a disorder in attention that leads to a severe discrepancy between ability and achievement would appear to be justification for determining that a student has a learning disability (see Chapter 7). Silver (1990) voiced an alternate opinion, saying that ADHD is not and should not be considered a learning disability, but he acknowledged that it frequently coexists with a learning disability, and that children with ADHD who also have a learning disability would appropriately receive services for both conditions in programs designed for students with learning disabilities.

ADHD and Emotional or Behavioral Disorders. Finally, it may be determined that the student with ADHD also meets the criteria for services as a student with a serious emotional disturbance (see Chapter 8). If the primary presenting symptoms relate to aggression, non-compliance, oppositional disorders, depression, and other problem behaviors, and if these symptoms and conditions are affecting educational performance, the multidisciplinary team may determine that the instructional and management needs of the student justify classification as a student with an emotional or behavioral disorder. As noted previously, this category is often resisted by parents who fear the stigma associated with the label. They make the argument that the behavioral problems are secondary to the primary condition of ADHD, and that if their child is treated for the ADHD, the behavioral problems will be resolved. As with learning disabilities, it is often difficult to separate the label from the needed services.

ADHD as a Social Construction. These positions have in common the fact that they accept that ADHD is a disabling condition, even though they differ on where and under what rubric services should be provided. Attention-deficit/hyperactivity disorder as a condition, however, is not without its critics. Another position on services for learners with ADHD holds that neither the category nor the services are needed or justified. The rapid increases in numbers of children identified as having ADHD has raised suspicions that this diagnosis is more of a social invention than a true disability (Armstrong, 1995). It is believed by many, including some teachers and parents, that the label is used to explain an undisciplined child. In their review of the literature on ADHD, Goodman and Poillion (1992) identified sixty-nine characteristics of students with ADHD and at least thirty-eight possible causes, leading them to question the utility and future of the category. They noted that there is little agreement on the critical defining issues concerning ADHD, and that the validity and reliability of the construct appear to be questionable.

Those who hold these views make the following points:

- Children learn to control their attention and their behavior when they are expected to do so. Delays in developing these skills may be attributed to lack of the expectation of appropriate behavior by parents and teachers.
- Over the last three decades, schools have consistently expected children to handle more advanced material and to develop academic skills at ever earlier years. It is not uncommon now for three- and four-year-old children to be expected to sit still and complete reading and writing worksheets, and for children to enter first grade knowing how to read. This raises questions about the developmental match between school expectations and these young students. When children are viewed as hyperactive and inattentive in developmentally inappropriate environments (Elkind, 1981), is the problem with the child or is it with the setting?
- Children growing up today are presented with a barrage of stimuli from the earliest years. Television programs like *Sesame Street* teach them letters and numbers, but at a frenetic pace. Some advance the argument that young children have come to expect the world to provide the same fast-paced environment for learning and leisure. When the schools don't provide that level of stimulation, the children lose interest and stop paying attention. If attention and reflection are not nurtured in the child's everyday environment, where are the children to learn it?

These questions and arguments address the issue of the social construction of attention-deficit/hyperactivity disorder. As with all issues of disability, professional educators must always evaluate the rationale used to identify a student as deviant and in need of special education services. Teeter (1991) suggests that the label of ADHD should be reserved for those learners who are most severely affected, and that children with fewer symptoms should be supported within the general education program. If a child is identified as having severe ADHD, the child's individualized education program should be developed to meet specific behavioral and learning needs. Teeter further suggests that a "Rights without Labels" framework (see Chapter 1 and Appendix A) might provide a more useful rubric for service. She suggests that interventions should be available to support all learners who have mild problems with inattention, impulsivity, and hyperactivity. As the general education classroom becomes more responsive to the needs of diverse learners, these authors suggest that it will become more effective for all students. Specifically, the focus on building general education programs that create successful learners should help avert the secondary problems of low self-esteem, aggression, and depression. In light of the concerns about the possible misuse of the diagnosis of ADHD, this recommendation would appear to be a useful first step.

Autism Spectrum Disorders

Another group of disorders that has received increased attention since 1990 are the *autism spectrum disorders*. These disorders include those that affect an individual's social development and the ability to communicate, usually resulting in more severe disability. Some conditions also involve repetitive motor movements. These disorders are of a neurobiological base and result in the student being impaired in the ability to communicate, understand language, play, develop social skills, and relate to others. They are generally considered to be among the pervasive developmental disorders. The Individuals with Disabilities Education Act (1997) defines *autism* as follows:

> a developmental disability significantly affecting verbal and non-verbal communication and social interaction, usually evident before age 3, that adversely affects a child's educational performance. Other characteristics often associated with autism are engagement in repetitive activities, resistance to environmental change or change in daily routines, and unusual sensory experiences. The term does not apply if a child's educational performance is adversely affected because the child has a serious emotional disturbance. (U.S. Department of Education, 1999, p. 12421)

Autism spectrum disorders are considered low-incidence conditions, with only about 1.2 percent of students receiving special education services classified in this category. However, the incidence of students classified in this category nearly doubled in the three years from 1996–97 to 1999–2000, rising from 34,101 to 65,424 (U.S. Department of Education, 1998, 2001). Although autism is generally considered a more severe disorder, there are an increasing number of these students identified as having high-functioning autism (HFA) or Asperger Syndrome (Shore, 2001; Wing, 1981). While prevalence figures are variable, it appears clear that the prevalence of Asperger Syndrome is considerably higher than autism itself (Safran, 2001; Shore, 2001). U.S. Department of Education (2001) data indicate that one-third of these students with autism receive a significant portion of their educational services within the general education, since their relatively high levels of academic functioning allows them to access the general education curriculum with supports.

Asperger Syndrome has received considerable attention in recent years as more of these youngsters have been formally identified. They differ from students with other autism spectrum disorders in that their impairment is almost exclusively within the social interaction area. Students with Asperger Syndrome do not display the cognitive and language deficits more common to autistic disorder. Instead, they are identified, according to the DSM-IV-TR criteria, by a severe and sustained qualitative impairment related to social interactions, accompanied by evidence of restricted and repetitive patterns of behaviors, activities, and interests (American Psychiatric Association, 2000).

Students with Asperger Syndrome frequently develop an all-consuming interest in particular topics about which they acquire as much information as possible, and which they often pursue with great intensity. They frequently become impatient with others who do not share their preoccupation. Another commonly observed characteristic is their ineptness in social skills (Williams, 2001). Their odd behaviors often cause them to be singled out and teased by peers in general education classes. They are naive about social conventions, and they are relatively unable to cope with changes so common in daily social interactions, particularly in the adolescent years. These students also frequently have difficulty conceptualizing and appreciating the thoughts and feelings of others (Barnhill, 2001; Safran, 2001). They often exhibit deficits in social perception and social perspective taking (see Chapter 13).

Although students with Asperger Syndrome generally have average to above average intellectual ability, they can experience difficulties in academic learning due to their tendency to be literal thinkers. This causes problems when school demands include higher level thinking skills and comprehension of complex materials (Williams, 2001). Students with Asperger Syndrome are also frequently characterized by their poor attention. In particular, they have difficulty focusing on the most relevant stimuli. These characteristics, combined with their obsessive interests in particular topics and their well-developed language skills, often lead teachers to assume that they could be more successful in school learning if they applied themselves. To successfully assist the student with Asperger Syndrome in the general education classroom, the teacher must understand how these annoying behaviors relate to the condition, and then work with the parents, student, and special educator to design supportive interventions (Barnhill, 2001). Social skills interventions are valuable, especially when combined with structured teaching strategies (Safran, 2001).

Traumatic Brain Injury

In 1990, Congress added the category of *traumatic brain injury* to the categories covered by IDEA. These students have an acquired brain injury due to external force (e.g., a car accident, fall, gunshot wound, child abuse). The results of these injuries can be many and variable, including physical impairments, sensory impairment, emotional disturbance, disruption of cognition, and language problems. This small and varied group of students includes about 0.2 percent of all students in special education today (U.S. Department of Education, 2001). The injury may be temporary or relatively permanent, mild or severe.

Unlike students with developmental disabilities like mental retardation, students with traumatic brain injury typically retain some of the skills they had learned previously. The interventions with these students therefore involve rehabilitative services. The special and general educators need to work closely together to design the most appropriate program of rehabilitation, maximizing the remaining abilities, and working to regain those that were damaged. School professionals must also be prepared for the manifestations of the injury to vary from day to day and for progress to be intermittent and variable.

Communication Disorders

Communication disorders include disorders in speech as well as language. Speech disorders include those affecting articulation, fluency, and voice quality. They affect the mechanical production of oral language. Language disorders involve an impairment in the understanding or use of the language system, including the spoken or written code, vocabulary, and syntax. Children with speech and language impairments account for about 20 percent of all students receiving special education services. The vast majority of these are youngsters in grades K–3, with most of them placed in general education classrooms and receiving articulation therapy.

Physical and Health Disabilities

Students with physical or health impairments are a small but very diverse group of students with disabilities. This group consists of students with orthopedic conditions, including impairments in movement due to injury or disease of the bones, muscles, or neurological system. It also includes students with a variety of health conditions (e.g., asthma, diabetes, cancer, heart conditions, AIDS, epilepsy) which reduce the students' alertness for learning and therefore affect their educational performance.

One large group of students with physical disabilities are those with *cerebral palsy*. Most have cerebral palsy that is related to an injury during the birth process, typically involving a lack of oxygen to the brain. Others were affected by injury or infection in the early developmental period. The effect of this condition on the child's functioning can range from mild to severe, with most students able to participate in general education with accommodations if there is no additional disability (e.g., mental retardation or sensory impairment). Other conditions affecting a student's physical abilities include spina bifida, muscular dystrophy, arthritis, paralysis, and amputations,

In most cases, related service providers, including physical and occupational therapists, adaptive physical educators, and school nurses, provide the support needed for many of these students to be served in the general education program. The most important understanding for teachers is that this group of students is very heterogeneous and that the ability to learn is often largely unaffected by their conditions. When a student with a physical or health disability is placed in a general education classroom, it is essential that the teacher consult with the parents and the related service providers to learn about that student's specific areas of impairment and the actions required to make the general education program accessible to the maximum extent possible.

Sensory Disabilities

Sensory disabilities involve impairment in one of the primary sensory systems used for learning. Students with visual impairments account for 0.5 percent of all students in special education, while those with hearing impairments account for 1.3 percent (U.S. Department of Education, 2001). In each case, the hearing or visual impairment is significant enough, even with correction, that the student's educational performance is affected.

Students with hearing impairments are classified as *hard of hearing,* or having a mild-moderate hearing loss, if they have enough residual hearing so that processing linguistic information is possible with amplification and other accommodations, but which reduce the effectiveness of educational progress. They can be classified as *deaf* if the hearing loss is so severe that even with amplification, the individual cannot process linguistic information through the ears alone. Most students with hearing impairments have impairment in the mild-moderate range, with only a small number having severe and profound hearing losses requiring more extensive accommodations.

Students with visual impairments are classified as having a moderate visual impairment if they can process print information with the help of visual devices, such as magnifiers. Students with a severe visual impairment can use their vision only with difficulty, while a student with a profound visual impairment cannot use vision for educational purposes and must rely upon adaptive devices such as auditory media and Braille. Most students with visual impairments fall in the moderate range with only a very small percentage having severe and profound levels of visual loss requiring more extensive accommodations for learning.

According to U.S. Department of Education (2001) data, about half of all students with visual impairments are served in general education for more than 80 percent of the day. About 40 percent of students with hearing disorders are served in general education for more than 80 percent of the day.

Focus on Culture and Diversity

The conditions included in this chapter present a number of issues related to culture and diversity, with specific emphasis on issues of gender, race/ethnicity, and socioeconomic status. Issues of gender seem, appropriately or not, to reflect the effect of societal expectations (based on the dominant culture) of normative behavior for boys and girls. Patterns of disproportionality related to race are also well documented over a period of years (U.S. Department of Education, 2001), and poverty has been repeatedly shown to be related as a risk factor to a variety of disabilities.

Males are significantly overrepresented among students with ADHD, particularly among those with the hyperactive or combined types (Shaywitz & Shaywitz, 1988). It has been hypothesized that females may be underidentified since they seem to be more likely to exhibit the ADHD-Inattentive type, leading them to be overlooked for services. This disproportionality by gender suggests that ADHD classifications may be affected by a disparity between the normative behavior expected by female, middle-class teachers and the activity levels exhibited by boys. Similar concerns have been raised with respect to ADHD identification among culturally different groups. Multidisciplinary teams should consider the possibility that the activity levels observed in students from diverse cultural groups may in fact be normative for that cultural group or the community.

It is interesting, however, that the conditions that comprise the autism spectrum disorders seem to be evenly distributed across all racial, ethnic, and social groups (Gargiulo, 2003). However, for reasons yet unknown, there is a higher incidence among boys (Kirk, Gallagher, & Anastasiow, 2003).

Health and physical disabilities tend to occur at higher rates among students from economically challenged backgrounds, including migrant farm workers. This is generally attributed to lack of prenatal care, poor nutrition of mothers and children, lack of access to health care, and exposure to toxic substances (e.g., lead, agricultural chemicals). Infection rates for diseases such as HIV are also on the rise, particularly among racial minority populations. This has been attributed to lack of accurate information about prevention and insufficient medical resources.

The incidence of sensory impairments varies among various racial groups as well. Asian/Pacific Islanders and Native Americans display an increased incidence of hearing impairments and deaf–blindness, while African-American students exhibit more visual disabilities (U.S. Department of Education, 2001). Of particular concern are those students with sensory impairments who also use a language other than English at home. Services to these children must recognize the multiple effects of disability, cultural difference, and sometimes poverty as well.

One cultural issue that is specific to the population of people with hearing impairments is the concept of Deaf culture, with cultural members united by their physical characteristics, language, and needs. Arguments abound on both sides, reflecting the importance of language in defining personal identity and cultural affiliation.

Resources on the Web

National Attention Deficit Disorder Association (ADDA)

www.add.org

> Provides information on adults and young adults with ADHD, including information for parents.

EDLAW

www.edlaw.net/service/504idea.html

> Provides information on the similarities and differences between Section 504 and IDEA; link to SpeciaLaw, which provides links to a variety of other legal resources.

Autism Society of America (ASA)

www.autism-society.org

> Provides information on autism for professionals and families, including information on the variety of treatment approaches.

Asperger Syndrome Coalition of the U.S.

www.asperger.org

> Provides resources for professionals and families about Asperger Syndrome.

The Brain Injury Association of America

www.biausa.org

> Provides resources and support networks for individuals dealing with traumatic brain injury.

United Cerebral Palsy Association

www.ucpa.org

> Provides a variety of links to national resources about cerebral palsy and other disabilities; promotes full inclusion of individuals with disabilities.

Alexander Graham Bell Association for the Deaf and Hard of Hearing

www.agbell.org

> Provides resources and publications related to hearing impairments across the life span for families and professionals; provides contact information for support groups and advocacy.

National Federation for the Blind

www.nfb.org

> Provides links to research and resources about visual impairments across the life span for individuals, parents, and professionals; links to sources of nonprint media.

Summary

Teachers today encounter a variety of other disorders in programs for students with mild disabilities. Attention-deficit/hyperactivity disorder (or ADHD) is the most prevalent of these disorders affecting school performance. ADHD is currently defined in the DSM-IV-TR as a condition in which individuals exhibit significant differences with regard to attention and/or hyperactivity/impulsivity when compared to typical students. It is estimated that approximately 3 to 7 percent of school-age children may be affected by disorders in the ADHD family. Exact counts are not kept by states and the federal government because the disorder is not specifically listed as a special education category in the IDEA.

ADHD is most appropriately diagnosed through the use of a multiphasic assessment process that includes a medical examination, a psychoeducational assessment, and an ecological assessment including direct observations, family history, and teacher rating scales. Multiple sources of data are required to confirm the presence and severity of the disorder and to differentiate it from other conditions.

Students with ADHD display a wide variety of characteristics. Some are predominantly inattentive, while others are mainly characterized by their hyperactivity and impulsivity. The symptoms also vary by age and cause a variety of secondary problems in school achievement and social relationships.

ADHD is not currently a separate category within IDEA. A 1991 Department of Education study indicated that children with ADHD could be and were being served appropriately in programs for students with other health impairments, learning disabilities, or emotional disturbance, or under Section 504, with specific placements and services dependent on the individual's primary presenting symptoms.

Other conditions affecting educational progress include the autism spectrum disorders. Asperger Syndrome is one of these disorders primarily affecting social relationships. Since students with Asperger Syndrome have average to above average intellectual functioning and use language functionally, they are frequently served in general education programs.

Students with a variety of other low-incidence conditions in the mild-moderate range are also frequently well served in the general education environment with supports. These include those with traumatic brain injury, speech and language disorders, physical and health disabilities, and visual and hearing impairments. With appropriate accommodations based on their strengths and needs, these students can generally make adequate progress in the general education curriculum.

FRANK: A Case Study

Frank is a relatively new student to the Rayberg County School District. He is six years, eleven months old. He was referred for evaluation by his first grade teacher due to her concerns that his high levels of distractibility and activity as well as his short attention span were significantly affecting his daily classroom performance. Frank seems to be a happy, easygoing student who is courteous and intellectually curious. He is proficient in verbal skills and is willing to accept suggestions. However, his short attention span affects his concentration as well as his comprehension of directions and his reading skills. He has frequent reversals of letters and numerals when writing, and he is disorganized in his work habits. He appears easily distracted by his own thoughts. His mother has indicated that Frank has stated that he daydreams, and that the daydreams will not stop. When frustrated and tired, Frank reverts to immature behaviors and baby talk. His mother has indicated that teachers have expressed concerns about Frank's behaviors to her since his entrance into kindergarten.

Frank lives with both natural parents and a younger sister who is five years old and in preschool. His father is an engineer whose job takes him away from home frequently. His mother indicates that she was under significant stress during her pregnancy with Frank because her husband was on military duty at the time. Frank was born following a nine and a half month pregnancy and thirty-five hours of labor. His mother was on oxygen for the last eight hours of labor due to a decrease in Frank's heartbeat with each contraction. The umbilical cord was wrapped around Frank's neck at birth. The first APGAR score taken at birth was abnormally low, although the second, taken at five minutes, indicated normal neonatal health.

Frank reached most developmental milestones within expected time ranges, although he did begin walking early at nine months of age. He continues to have occasional temper tantrums when he cannot complete a task. His mother has indicated that he sometimes hits himself on the front of his head with his fist when he is frustrated. He has exclaimed in frustration, "It won't work." His mother has indicated that Frank has always had difficulty paying attention in school.

Frank's school history is complex. He began kindergarten in Alabama. The family then moved to Kansas last summer, where Frank began first grade. In October of that year, the family moved to Indiana for three months before moving on in February to their present home in Rayberg County, where Frank enrolled in first grade at the local elementary school. Although he has attended several different schools, there have been no excessive absences. Each of his teachers has indicated concern about his attention and learning behaviors.

Frank's previous teachers have felt that his difficulties might be due to a hearing problem. Frank has had extensive ear infections that required tubes in his ears when he was almost three years old. However, his hearing has recently been checked and found to be normal. Frank has passed vision screenings for both near and far vision. He began receiving speech therapy in first grade in Indiana, and he continues with speech services at Rayberg for his articulation difficulties.

Strategies that have been used since Frank's enrollment at Rayberg to strengthen his school performance have included modified instruction, which involved immersing him in a multisensory literature-based reading program. He also receives math instruction through an activity-based manipulative program. Supplementary texts and materials such as tapes, word cards, and dictated stories have been used to strengthen his reading skills. Frank has also been consistently praised for appropriate responses. Regular communication between home and school has also been implemented. These efforts have resulted in sporadic improvements in Frank's academic skills and behavioral responses.

Results of the School-Based Screening Testing (Performed by Resource Teacher)

Peabody Picture Vocabulary Test

Standard Score	115
Percentile	84
Age Score	7–11

(continued)

Woodcock-Johnson Tests of Achievement

	Standard Score	Percentile	Grade Equivalent	Age Equivalent
Letter/Word Identification	97	43	1.2	6–8
Passage Comprehension	98	44	1.3	6–7
Calculation	116	86	1.9	7–5
Applied Problems	113	81	2.0	7–7
Dictation	96	40	1.2	6–7
Writing Samples	100	50	1.3	6–9

Cluster Scores:	Standard Score	Percentile
Broad Reading	97	41
Broad Mathematics	115	84
Broad Written Language	99	47

Results of the Psychoeducational Evaluation

A complete psychological evaluation was performed by the school psychologist. Frank entered the evaluation setting without hesitation and was cooperative throughout the assessment. He was attentive to individual activities and seemed to be putting forth good effort. However, he was very bouncy and physically restless, even in the one-to-one setting. He engaged in nearly constant physical movement, either standing beside his chair, bouncing in his chair, or swinging his feet under the table throughout the assessment. Although Frank was fidgety and restless during the assessment, he generally presented himself as a very pleasant student who wanted to perform well.

The administration of the Wechsler Intelligence Scale for Children-III (WISC-III) yielded the following results:

Verbal Scale IQ	119 (90th percentile)
Performance Scale IQ	112 (79th percentile)
Full Scale IQ	118 (88th percentile)

These results suggest that Frank's overall abilities fall within the above-average range for his age. The psychologist indicated that it is difficult to determine whether these results accurately depict Frank's true capabilities due to his physical restlessness and his distractibility throughout the assessment. She thought that the results may underestimate his true potential to some degree.

He had difficulty with the WISC-III block design subtest, although he worked persistently and responded correctly to many of the complex items. He became excited when working with the WISC-III object assembly subtest and began playing with the pieces. When presented with the automobile item of this subtest, he made racing noises. When praised for good work, he commented that he has "a good brain." He bounced up and down in his chair throughout the coding subtest, although he did appear to be concentrating on the items.

Individual subtest scores on the WISC-III verbal scale reflected strength in Frank's vocabulary skills. His understanding of abstract verbal concepts also seems quite strong. Capabilities within the above-average range are noted in his auditory processing and visual memory related to basic math skills as well as in his knowledge of appropriate responses in social situations. His long-term memory for general information seems to be developing at a rate within the average range.

The WISC-III performance scale reflected strength in Frank's visual analysis and sequencing of social events, which also reflects his understanding of cause-effect relationships and in his perceptual motor skills when working with visually abstract symbols and manipulative materials. His visual attention to detail within the environment, visual organizational skills, and concentration on a short, structured pencil-and-paper activity fell within the average range. Although this administration of the WISC-III revealed no significant delays in Frank's basic learning, the inconsistencies noted among his subtest scores may pose some frustration for him.

The Visual Aural Digit Span Test (VADS) is designed to assess Frank's concentration and immediate recall of auditory and visual cues when he is asked to respond orally and in writing. His responses to the individual subtests are reported in age percentile scores as follows:

Visual Aural Digit Span Test

Subtests	Percentile
Aural-Oral	90
Visual-Oral	75
Aural-Written	75
Visual-Written	75

Composite VADS Scores	*Percentile*
Aural Input	90
Visual Input	75
Oral Expression	90
Written Expression	75
Intrasensory Integration	90
Intersensory Integration	75
Total VADS Score	75–90

Frank's responses on the VADS suggested strengths in immediate memory skills for both auditory and visual cues. His speech articulation difficulties were noted throughout the assessment. As has been indicated previously, he bounced in his chair throughout the administration of the VADS. When working on the written items of the Visual Aural Digit Span Test, he reversed several numerals. He recognized his reversals and asked whether it was all right for the numbers to be backwards. Despite the reversals, his strengths in perceptual motor skills as revealed through both the WISC-III and the Bender Gestalt Test of Visual Perception suggested that this is developmental in nature. It is not unusual for children to reverse letters and numerals until about age eight. The fact that he recognized his reversals is a positive sign. However, the formation and spacing of his numerals as well as his placement of the forms on the page suggested some impulsivity in his responses.

The Bender Gestalt Test of Visual Perception revealed five scorable errors involving shape distortion, integration of designs, and figure rotation, yielding an age range equivalent of 7–6 to 7–11. This resulted in a standard score of 109 (average = 100), reflecting adequate perceptual motor skills when working with pencil-and-paper activities. However, his use of space and placement of the forms on the page suggested some difficulty in organizing visually unstructured activities. His actual responses also reflected some difficulty in fine motor control when working with pencil-and-paper activities, although his perceptual skills seemed to be adequate.

The Woodcock-Johnson Tests of Achievement revealed deficits in Frank's academic skills, which are reflected in his classroom performance. He had difficulty with basic phonetic skills, which affected his identification of less familiar words as well as his understanding of content. The resource room teacher believed that some of his correct answers on the passage comprehension test were achieved by guessing rather than by application of decoding skills. He could not recognize many of the words, and he used pictures as clues to content. He would often shake his head and stand up when working. He constantly looked around the room and reached for materials. His responses to the dictation and writing samples subtests reveal both his weak phonetic skills as well as his weak fine-motor coordination skills, which affects his formation of letters. Frank seemed to have difficulty hearing and reproducing sounds, which also affects his writing performance. Some letter reversals were also noted. He seemed to be learning basic math skills more easily than reading skills. In fact, his understanding of math concepts when writing is not involved has developed to a point generally found at the beginning of the second grade. He was able to add and subtract two-digit numbers without regrouping with no difficulty.

Frank's family drawing included both of his parents, his younger sister, family cat, and himself. He presented each family member as smiling and in no unusual distress. However, there were indications of dependency on adults and poor impulse control in his drawing.

The Attention Deficit Disorder Behavior Rating Scale was completed with information supplied by Frank's mother, revealing highly significant concerns about Frank's short attention span and impulsivity as seen in examples of his difficulty completing assigned activities, weak listening skills, poor concentration on difficult activities, high level of distractibility, a tendency to act before thinking, weak organizational skills, a need for consistent supervision, and a tendency to interrupt or speak out of turn. Concerns were also expressed about his academic skills and low self-confidence. Concerns about his activity level were validated through observation of his difficulty sitting still and his fidgeting during the

(continued)

evaluation period. His high activity level was more evident through his restlessness at his seat than through his need for large motor movement. There were lesser concerns about his anxiety level and resistance to requests from adults. The results of this administration of the ADD Behavior Rating Scale suggested to the team that Frank was experiencing physiologically based issues that are affecting his attention and control of impulses. His anger is expressed when he is frustrated, although he is not a student who gets mad easily or who expresses anger when asked to do something. He does not lose his temper easily. Frank seems to be developing adequate social responsibility and is not generally seen as aggressive with others.

Assessment Summary and Placement Recommendations

The results of this assessment suggest that Frank's overall abilities fall within the above-average range for his age. It is difficult to determine whether the results of the WISC-III accurately depict Frank's true capabilities due to his high level of distractibility and physical restlessness during the assessment, and the results are thought to underestimate his potential to some degree. By having a greater than fifteen-point discrepancy between his abilities and achievement, Frank meets one of the eligibility criteria established by Rayberg School District for specialized instructional services through programs for students with learning disabilities in the areas of reading and written language.

It appears that his academic delays are primarily due to physiological factors involving attention deficit disorder. Although he has attended three schools this year, he has had no excessive absences during the year. Each of his teachers has expressed concern about his activity level, listening skills, and weak reading and written language skills. His behavioral responses during the assessment, his classroom performance, and the Attention Deficit Disorder Behavior Rating Scale suggest that Frank's school-related behaviors may be affected by attention-deficit/hyperactivity disorder.

Frank appears to be a student who will benefit from a more detailed medical evaluation to further evaluate his activity and attention, an evaluation which may lead to a trial of stimulant medication to determine whether it can help control his impulsivity and distractibility. In a recent parent-school conference, his mother expressed her interest in pursuing this option due to the continuing difficulty Frank is experiencing in school. His teachers will be in excellent positions to monitor his performance on a daily basis and offer feedback concerning the effectiveness of the medication. His mother has been offered information concerning ADHD and support resources within the community.

Retention in the first grade is being considered due to Frank's academic skills and younger maturity level. His mother has expressed concern that he may not be successful in second grade, particularly if he continues to have significant difficulties with distractibility and impulsivity. However, a decision on retention will be delayed until closer to the end of this school year when information has been gathered about Frank's responses to instruction in reading and math skills as well as to any medication trial. His progress should be followed carefully as he progresses through school to ensure that the programs and services provided for him are meeting his needs appropriately.

DISCUSSION

Using the above information from Frank's evaluation for special education, determine whether it is most appropriate to classify Frank as a child with attention-deficit/hyperactivity disorder or with a learning disability.

Specifically, consider the reasons for choosing one category over the other.

If you identify additional information that would be helpful in making a full determination, make a list of the additional information you would need to complete the evaluation.

SARA: A Case Study

Sara has just turned fifteen and is graduating from Gordon Junior High this year. After a long history of early neglect and abuse in her biological family, she was placed in a foster home and subsequently in a residential program for two years due to her unmanageable behaviors. Sara was finally diagnosed with Asperger Syndrome, and she has lived with her current foster mother for the past two years. Her placement in this therapeutic foster home provides the support services she needs to make the transition back to a normalized community setting. Sara loves to swing, spending long periods of time in the family's backyard. She was very disappointed to find that her junior high school did not have swings.

Sara becomes almost hypnotic when she eats; she continues to eat as long as there is any food available. Her foster mother wonders if this is due to the early physical neglect. When she is asked to slow down, she will blurt out, "Well, I'm hungry!" It is becoming problematic because Sara is beginning to gain weight as a result of the nonstop eating.

Sara seems to have a very high tolerance for pain. One day she was riding down the driveway in the back of the truck and she fell off. She was on the ground, her tooth chipped and her face bruised. Her foster mother said that she had a "bizarre look in her eyes," but she didn't shed a tear. Her foster mother thinks she doesn't express the pain she feels. Sara seems unresponsive to most physical stimuli. Once again, her foster mother wonders if this is part of her condition or the result of her early abuse.

Sara is very intelligent, and she can't understand why the other students aren't getting what the teacher is teaching. She doesn't understand that what is obvious to her might not be obvious to someone else. She sees the world only from her own perspective; she assumes that everyone sees things the way she does. Sara's foster mother is especially concerned about her egocentrism and sees it getting in the way of her making friends at school.

Sara participates fully in her general education classes with the help of Carol, her one-on-one aide, and she makes good grades. Her measured intelligence is in the average range, and she demonstrates grade-level achievement on tests and her report cards. Carol has noticed, however, that Sara needs explicit directions for each task. For example, when the teacher says, "Take out your notebooks," the other children take them out and open them, while Sara just takes hers out.

Sara has a Big Sister named Nancy who is a professor at a nearby community college. Sara and her Big Sister share a love for libraries and books. Sara has written three different books. It often seems that she would prefer to be alone and to read and write her books.

Sara seems to be a very concrete thinker. One day Sara and her Big Sister were talking about sex. Sara told Nancy that she's never getting pregnant, that "I'm going to wait until I'm 21, and then I'll get married to someone I'm really in love with, and then maybe I'll have sex." But then, she added that she guessed she would get pregnant. When asked why she thought that, Sara said, "Well, I saw this sign at school that said that girls who play sports don't get pregnant . . . and I don't play sports." Sara also doesn't understand figurative phrases like "You're on thin ice!"

Sara doesn't seem to realize that sometimes people need to do things they'd rather not, but that doing them is part of the social contract. One day, her aide asked her if she would throw something in the trash can, and Sara said "No!" Another day, Sara hurt her foster sister's feelings by "helping" her by criticizing her singing. Sara's aide takes note of these situations and reports them to Sara's speech therapist. The speech therapist works on these social conversation skills that most young people pick up by observing others. Then Sara's aide, Carol, spends 10 hours a week working with her in a community setting, reinforcing the social interaction skills that her speech therapist has been working on. Her foster mother tries to reinforce them too, but she sometimes tires of being a "24-7" teacher when she would rather just be Sara's mother.

Her foster mother is concerned that at the age of 15 Sara doesn't seem to have a sense of personal boundaries. One day they had a visitor with a beard, something new for Sara. She reached up and pulled his beard and started laughing even when he reacted

(continued)

with pain. At camp last summer she met a boy. She was "all over him, hugging and kissing, like a much younger child." She was happy to have a friend, but she didn't realize what behaviors would be considered appropriate social interaction.

Recently, her foster mother has seen her become very "boy crazy." Sara has become very interested in a boy at school named Bob, but he hardly seems to notice that Sara is there. Sara hates to be ignored and she can't understand why Bob ignores her. She responds by inappropriately putting her hands on him, often with an altercation ensuing. She doesn't appreciate the subtleties of adolescent interactions and responds much like a third-grader who chases another child around the playground to make him be her friend. The problem is that as a young adolescent such behaviors are likely to be seen as sexually inappropriate and definitely odd.

Sara has some long-standing problems with appropriate personal hygiene. She doesn't seem to notice the need to change her clothes or take a shower, even when her clothes are dirty and her body odor has become offensive. She does not appreciate that the changes in her adolescent body require more attention to hygiene if she is to be welcome in social environments. This really bothers her foster mother who can't understand why Sara would be so oblivious to the appearance she presents. She has noted, however, that recently Sara seems to be developing an interest in hygiene.

Another issue that has surfaced is the constant presence of Carol, Sara's aide, in school and in the community. Carol has been consciously attempting to step back a bit and let Sara try to handle her own social interactions. However, she remains vigilant and intervenes as needed. For example, at the graduation practice, Sara was sitting with some other girls, trying to interact with them. Carol became aware that the girls were trying to embarrass Sara by calling Bob over, although Sara was oblivious to their motives. Carol stepped in to stop the teasing. Carol continues to be concerned that Sara doesn't seem to know when others are laughing at her. Sara's foster mother knows that Sara will continue to need her aide's help when she moves to the high school next year, but she hopes that the social coaching Sara receives from Carol and the speech therapist will begin to make her capable of handling the social side of adolescence with fewer interventions from Carol. There seems to be a real deficit in her level of socializing, a deficit that her foster mother fears will continue to cause Sara problems.

Sara's lack of social awareness and skill continues to concern everyone. At the graduation this week, it was painfully obvious that Sara was not at the social level of the other girls. She wants people to like her, but she stands out in her immaturity. When someone does something she doesn't like, she is likely to respond by pushing or biting, because the person "wouldn't leave me alone." These behaviors cause others to avoid her. Recently she was at a parade downtown and tried to greet some girls from school. The girls whispered to each other and walked away. Her foster mother wonders how to explain what happened to Sara. She realizes that these might be girls Sara had yelled at inappropriately just the day before.

How can Sara be helped to develop the social competence to match her academic abilities?

DISCUSSION

From the information provided in your text, identify the descriptive elements that suggest that the diagnosis of Asperger Syndrome is appropriate for Sara.

From the case study information, make a list of Sara's strengths and needs.

WHAT ARE LEARNERS WITH MILD DISABILITIES LIKE?

What does it really mean when we say that Jennie has mild mental retardation, Bobby has a learning disability, Frank has ADHD, and Carter has an emotional or behavioral disorder? Are there other more useful perspectives from which to view mild disability? P.L. 94–142, the Education for All Handicapped Children Act of 1975, had not even been fully implemented when Hallahan and Kauffman (1977) gave voice to the growing concern about the utility of categorical approaches to instructional planning. They contended that the traditional definitions of learning disabilities, mental retardation, and emotional disorders were vague and subject to a variety of interpretations and that these categories provided little useful information for instructional programming. They noted research evidence of overlapping characteristics among the disability groupings (see Figure III.1). Although social adjustment, intelligence, and underachievement are each primarily associated with a specific disability, research has failed to support their exclusive use as a defining categorical trait for any one category.

In light of these concerns, Hallahan and Kauffman (1977) and others over the years have recommended that special education services might be more effectively delivered if intervention planning was based on the student's specific behavioral and academic characteristics and needs rather than on their category. Epstein and Cullinan (1983) voiced the opinion that while categories provided some relevant information, it was nevertheless important to determine the differences and similarities between learners and to base programming

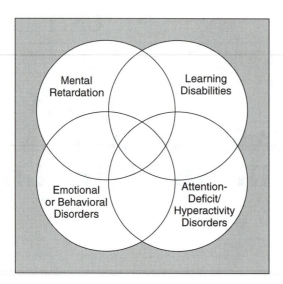

FIGURE III.1   Representation of the Manifestation of Various Mild Disabilities

decisions on those relevant differences. This implies that educators should work on identifying specific functional deficits and strengths, regardless of the categories used for administrative purposes. Indeed, IDEA 1997 requires this.

Unit III will consider the characteristics of all these learners from the perspectives of their cognitive processing, perceptual abilities, use of language, needs and functioning in academic settings, and social-emotional development. A variety of alternative frameworks for looking at the instructional and social needs of children and youth will be developed in Unit III. These frameworks are a useful supplement to the traditional categorical systems for describing children. It is, after all, the specific characteristics of students like Jennie, Bobby, Frank, and Carter that matter most as teachers and parents work with those who are experiencing difficulty developing the skills needed for successful living.

CHAPTER TEN

COGNITIVE AND PERCEPTUAL CHARACTERISTICS

QUESTIONS TO GUIDE YOUR STUDY

- What are the basic assumptions of cognitive theory, and how do they apply to our study of the learning of students with mild disabilities?
- What can we learn from the work of the constructivists (Piaget and Vygotsky) to help us understand the cognitive functioning of learners with mild disabilities?
- What are the characteristics of field dependent and field independent learners?
- What are the characteristics of impulsive and reflective learners?
- What functions do the three structural components of the cognitive model play?
- What functions do the strategic control components perform in carrying out cognitive functions?
- How do selective and sustained attention differ from one another? How do they relate to cognitive functioning in general?
- What is perception? How does perception relate to overall cognitive functioning?
- What is visual, auditory, and haptic perception? What are the subskills associated with each type of perception?
- Should a teacher or psychologist attempt to assess a student's perceptual and perceptual motor functioning? Why? Why not? How?
- What role do the executive control functions play in cognitive functioning?

Meet Robert

Robert is a student in the fourth grade at Smith Elementary School. He is served in the school's resource program for students with learning disabilities. Robert's history is unremarkable. He was adopted shortly after birth and lives with his adoptive family and four sisters. His mother does not work outside the home and has tried to help Robert with his academic work all through elementary school. Robert is described as a sweet and quiet child. He enjoys sports and is physically active.

According to Mrs. Peters, his resource teacher, Robert has the most difficulty with the cognitive processing required for reading, writing, and math activities. He cannot transfer easily from one function to another. For example, he has a problem with listening and then speaking. If Mrs. Peters asks him a

(continued)

question, he needs extended time to process the answer. Sometimes he is not sure enough of himself to even chance an answer. For example, one day Mrs. Peters had worked a math problem with regrouping on the board, and she asked Robert why she put a number in a particular place. It took Robert an extended period of time to process the answer. Mrs. Peters understood Robert's difficulty in processing, so she gave him as much time as necessary. The length of time it takes Robert to accomplish academic tasks has caused him to fall behind in reading,

spelling, and math. He is working with reading and spelling materials at the middle–first grade level. His math tends to be a little higher; he can add and subtract with basic regrouping. He can do basic multiplication tables up to the sevens and eights, but he has trouble with the processing required to use those facts in problem-solving or computation. Robert knows that he has a problem. He recently told Mrs. Peters and his fourth grade classroom teacher that he wants to know why he can't read like the other kids.

Cognitive Theory and Approaches to Mild Disabilities

To understand the difficulties students with mild disabilities have in school learning environments, it is helpful to consider the complex cognitive processes that occur in the minds of students like Robert before, during, and after a specific learning event. This chapter will first look at the way most people incorporate new information into their knowledge bases. Then it will consider how learners with mild disabilities might differ from more typical learners with respect to their cognitive functioning.

Learning theory holds that learning is an active process that results in lasting changes within the learner's knowledge base and leads to stable changes in behavior. Learning may be conceptualized as the process of "coming to understand" (Paris & Winograd, 1990; Stone & Reid, 1994). Children in classrooms may be most appropriately viewed as apprentice learners who are engaged in a variety of interactive and collaborative activities in meaningful social contexts with both teachers and peers (Reid & Stone, 1991). The expert thinker (i.e., teacher or mentor) provides support that allows the novices to develop their own understandings and cognitive structures.

The following assumptions form the basis for this discussion of the cognitive characteristics of children and youth:

- Learners must be active participants in and responsible for their own learning.
- Learning results when a student effectively relates a new learning to previous learning.
- The way individuals organize and integrate information is critical to their success in learning.
- While it is possible and useful to study the individual components of successful learning, any interventions must consider and address the whole learning act.

These basic assumptions apply to all learners, with or without disabilities. However, since recent research into cognitive approaches to instruction has tended to focus specifically on those children who are experiencing difficulty in the learning process, such research findings have direct application to the youngsters we are studying. This research indicates that learners with mild disabilities tend to have more difficulty than typical individuals in cognitively generalizing content and strategies to new situations. They appear to exhibit less ability to appreciate the applications of what they have learned, and therefore their learning appears less effective and useful (McFarland & Weibe, 1987; Reid, Hresko, & Swanson, 1996).

Behavioral theories and frameworks have had a significant impact on educational practice for many years. Behaviorists view learning as occurring when the individual forms an association between a particular environmental stimuli and a pleasant or punishing event (Skinner, 1953, 1974). Stimuli associated with pleasant outcomes result in new learned behaviors; those associated with unpleasant events or that receive no reinforcement are ignored or rejected by the learner. Teachers are seen as those who provide the stimuli to be learned along with the appropriate reinforcers to ensure learning of those behaviors or concepts.

Although behavioral approaches are very common in special education, they have generally failed to develop the students' abilities to learn independently of the teacher. This is because these approaches do not focus on the holistic act of learning, do not involve the youngster actively in that learning, and do not develop the child's ability to cognitively process information independently and create his or her own learning (Alley & Deshler, 1979; Deshler, Ellis, & Lenz, 1996). Two other frameworks may be more helpful in clarifying the cognitive difficulties of students with mild disabilities: the constructivist and information processing frameworks.

Constructivist Perspectives

The constructivists, most notably Jean Piaget and Lev Vygotsky, focused their attention on how children develop or "construct" knowledge from the experiences provided by the environment. Believing that learning is more complicated than a series of simple stimulus–response sequences, Piaget and Vygotsky developed explanations for the complex learning they saw demonstrated every day by active children, children who apparently were busy constructing new knowledge.

Piaget

Based on his fifty years of observational research on the development of cognitive skills in children, Piaget developed the theory that learning occurs in a defined sequence of stages related to maturation of the learner and that learning is self-regulated by learners themselves (Piaget, 1960). Through a combination of maturation and experience, these self-regulated learners construct their understandings of the world, a theory he called *biological constructivism.*

Piaget theorized that learning begins when individuals differentiate between and among various environmental stimuli. This *differentiation* allows learners to recognize specific stimuli as new information. Learning occurs as individuals develop *schema,* or concepts that organize a person's perceptions of the world in some way. The learner develops schema by using the cognitive functions of *organization* and *adaptation.* As new information is received by learners, they are prompted by their own internal self-regulatory processes to fit the information into their existing organizational structures, to relate it to previous learning. Existing schema are modified by adaptation of that organizational structure, that is, by using either *assimilation* (the addition of new and complementary information into an existing schema) or *accommodation* (changing existing schema to accommodate the new and contradictory information and experience).

Piaget believed that each new experience tends to create an unsteady cognitive state, or *disequilibrium,* which the learner seeks to resolve by using the cognitive functions of organization and adaptation, resulting in a new level of *equilibrium* being attained (Figure 10.1). With each new attainment of equilibrium, the learner spirals upward to a new level of cognitive competence.

Piaget noted that the quality of the cognitive processing appeared to change significantly at specific points in development, leading him to divide cognitive development into *cognitive stages* (Table 10.1; In the Classroom 10.1). He observed that once children had achieved specific critical understandings, they were then able to engage in significantly more complex levels of cognitive processing. Piaget attributed learning problems or deficits to a lag in maturation. While learning experiences could be made available to children, Piaget did not believe that learning could be accelerated beyond the limits of maturation.

The processes described by Piaget take on increasing importance in considering the cognitive characteristics of learners with mild disabilities. First, the process of cognitive development is generally slower for learners with mild disabilities, and such individuals may

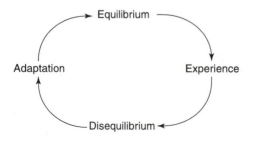

FIGURE 10.1   The Learning Cycle of Equilibrium and Disequilibrium

TABLE 10.1   Piagetian Cognitive Stages

Stage	Age Range (Approximate)	Characteristics
Sensorimotor	Birth to 2	Builds knowledge/concepts through sensory experience and motor activity
Preoperational	Ages 2–7	Begins to think in symbols but is still dependent on direct experience for learning
Concrete Operations	Ages 7–14	Begins to use logic to create new concepts, but only those related to the here and now
Formal Operations	Ages 14 to adult	Develops ability to think abstractly and logically

IN THE CLASSROOM **10.1**

Piaget's Stages of Cognitive Development

Sandy is a student in an early intervention program for children with developmental delays. At age four, Sandy would be expected to be in the preoperational Piagetian stage. Instead she appears to still be in the sensorimotor stage. She is responsive to sensory experiences of all kinds. She bangs objects on the floor and on each other. She likes to be touched and tickled, and she enjoys touching and tickling others. She will place her hand on another person's hand to "ask for help" and then move that person's hand to what she wants done. It is not clear to her teacher if she is building knowledge through her tactile and kinesthetic senses, but it is evident that touch and motor activity are involved in nearly all her daily activities and that they appear to be the primary means by which she incorporates new information into her knowledge base.

Ricky, a first grader with learning disabilities, appears to still be in the preoperational stage. He uses letters, numbers, and some sign language for communication, but he needs direct experience to understand basic concepts. For example, when he was asked, "If we cut the apple in half, how many pieces will there be?" he was unable to answer. He just shrugged his shoulders and said, "I don't know." The look on his face suggested that he didn't even understand the question. Even when the concept was demonstrated for him, he could not answer the question later without seeing the visual model.

Ben, a middle school student with mild mental retardation, seems to be functioning within Piaget's concrete operations stage. He appears to need to connect new information to real-life experiences to give it meaning. During a recent math lesson, he struggled to understand the concept of area until his teacher explained that he might think of area as a floor that needed to be carpeted. With that analogy, Ben was finally able to understand the concept.

reach a plateau before progressing through all the stages. For example, although learners with mental retardation move through the same Piagetian stages as other children, they make slower progress and tend to fixate at lower stages (Drew, Logan, & Hardman, 1988). Progress through the developmental stages may be disrupted or less efficient in learners with ADHD, learning disabilities, or emotional or behavioral disorders as well. In general, they will need more experiences and careful coaching to arrive at the same insights regarding fundamental concepts and processes. Pasnak and others (1995) found that the skills of seriation and classification can be taught, allowing the learner to move to the next stage of cognitive functioning.

The impetus for learning presented by the cognitive disequilibrium may have less significance for a child with a mild disability. This learner may not recognize the disequilibrium created by a particular event and therefore may not process it or learn from it. In some learners, the state of disequilibrium may become so constant that the student sees it as the normal state of affairs, failing to detect the need to develop new cognitive structures to bring his or her experiences and knowledge back into equilibrium. In other cases, it appears that the child indiscriminately uses only the function of assimilation, adding new experiences to his or her knowledge base and failing to notice discrepancies that require that the knowledge base itself be modified to accommodate the new information (see In the Classroom 10.2).

Although Piaget did not believe that cognitive development could be speeded up significantly, evidence has been accumulating in the research that suggests otherwise (McCormick, Campbell, Pasnak, & Perry, 1990; Pasnak et al., 1995; Perry, Pasnak, & Holt, 1992; Reid & Stone, 1991). Studies indicate that well-designed, developmentally appropri-

---

IN THE CLASSROOM **10.2**

Accommodation and Assimilation

Danielle is a middle school student with learning disabilities and secondary emotional problems. Her teacher observed that she is unable to relate one idea to another unless it is essentially a duplication or extension of prior patterns or learning. For instance, she has mastered the process of computation with two addends ("4 + 9" or "22 + 36") but sees computation with three or more addends as an unrelated process ("4 + 9 + 7"). She is unable to modify her schema readily to incorporate new or discrepant information. Danielle is able to learn or process information if it is given in small enough chunks and if teacher assistance is provided to perform the accommodation function.

Eugene, a seventeen-year-old with mental retardation, is still at the concrete operations level of cognitive development. Even more importantly, he experiences difficulty with the cognitive function of accommodation. For example, he can play Rummy with his friends and remembers the rules as he learned them from his brother. He understands that a player needs three of a kind to lay the cards down, and that if you have the fourth card, you can say, "Rummy." However, for Eugene, the idea of laying down three cards in sequence is "cheating." He was taught to play the game in a certain way, and it has been reinforced over time. He is not able to accommodate the new information into his schema or add it to and adjust what he already knows.

ate teaching activities, using significant exposure to manipulatives and hands-on activities and focusing on developing key cognitive concepts, can increase the rate of cognitive development beyond that achieved solely with good academic skill instruction. Furthermore, Reid and Stone noted that the common practice of structuring remedial instruction in very small increments tends to deprive these learners of the opportunity to note and address discrepancies. Breaking down learning into very tiny steps can result in the learner's being unaware of the subtle changes from one concept or skill to the next. This deprives the learner of the experience of resolving disequilibrium needed to develop his or her cognitive functions of accommodation and assimilation.

Vygotsky

Another constructivist approach to learning was developed by Vygotsky (1962, 1978, 1987), who theorized that learning occurs through participation in social or culturally embedded experiences. In contrast to Piaget, Vygotsky does not see the learner as a solitary explorer of the world but rather as one who learns through social interactions in meaningful contexts. His theory of *social constructivism* holds that learning occurs when teachers and others guide the learner in developing new understandings. Vygotsky extended the concept of a social context for learning to include the symbolic social context of shared language systems (Trent, Artiles, & Englert, 1998).

Vygotsky developed the concept of the *zone of proximal development* to indicate that range of learning that students can achieve when they are engaged in meaningful activities with competent others. The zone of proximal development is the distance between what children can do by themselves and the next learning that they can be helped to achieve with competent assistance (Stone & Reid, 1994; Vygotsky, 1987). According to Vygotsky, learning takes place only in the zone of proximal development. It is essential in working with youngsters with disorders in learning and behavior to understand that the success of the learning will be determined first by what the learner already knows, and then by the nature and quality of the support needed for them to learn the "next thing." Vygotsky believed that the zone of proximal development was a better indication of what a person can learn than tests of acquired knowledge.

Vygotsky also used the term *scaffolding instruction* to refer to the role of teachers and others in supporting the learner's development and providing support structures to get to that next stage or level. The "teacher" helps students connect the "known" with the "new." As these interactions proceed, the learner increasingly assumes responsibility for the task and for problem-solving, "appropriating" the goal and plan for achieving the goal from the teacher or guide (Stone & Reid, 1994). Vygotsky further explained that as the learner develops more sophisticated cognitive systems related to fields of learning such as mathematics or language, the system of knowledge itself becomes part of the scaffold or social support for the new learning (McFarland & Weibe, 1987; Reid & Stone, 1991) (see In the Classroom 10.3).

Youngsters with mild disabilities, like Mary and Kathy in In the Classroom 10.3, appear to have smaller zones of proximal development in many areas of academic and social learning. They require more scaffolding by their parents and teachers to achieve firm learning. Teachers can help by orchestrating learning situations in which there is a gap between where the child is and where the adult guide is, and where the expectation is that the child can be reasonably expected to bridge the gap with assistance from the guide (Trent, Artiles, &

IN THE CLASSROOM **10.3**

Scaffolding Within the Zone of Proximal Development

Mary is a middle school student with a learning disability. Her zone of proximal development is smaller than that of her peers in English class. The class moves fairly quickly from chapter to chapter in the novel they are reading. Often Mary has not fully comprehended one chapter when the class moves on to the next. She experiences similar frustrations with the English vocabulary lists. More scaffolding would help Mary achieve firmer learning. She needs more time and instruction, as well as more support than her peers, to master this English content before moving on.

Kathy was diagnosed with mild mental retardation in second grade. She has just begun classes at the high school. Her current math teacher has said that her zone of proximal development is very narrow. Significant scaffolding is required for Kathy to relate new information to previously learned material. Kathy does not assimilate or accommodate new ideas or concepts easily. In math, for example, she does not see the relationship between addition and subtraction, subtraction and division, or division and fractions. She still depends on the scaffolding provided by her teacher's use of manipulatives for basic mathematical operations. She seems to be constantly in a state of disequilibrium, always trying to catch up.

Englert, 1998). This framework is particularly critical in working with learners who have difficulty with social interactions. Expectations of appropriate behavior are reasonable only when the skill is determined to be in the child's repertoire or when it is within the child's zone of proximal development and the environment provides the support or scaffolding needed to learn and use that skill.

Cognitive Styles Research

About the time that the term learning disabilities began to be used to refer to the group of learners with underachievement, researchers began to look more closely at the way in which these learners approached learning tasks. It was reasoned that there might be differences between typical students and those with mild disabilities and that these differences might be useful in designing remedial activities. This research, focusing on the *cognitive styles* of these learners (Blackman & Goldstein, 1982; Claxton & Murrell, 1987), revealed some patterns related to the structure and process of thinking rather than to the content of thought processes. Two concepts have relevance to our work with learners with mild disabilities today: (1) field dependence versus field independence and (2) reflectivity versus impulsivity.

Field Dependence and Field Independence

The degree to which an individual's perceptual and cognitive judgments are influenced by the surrounding environment has been referred to as *field dependence* and *field independence*.

This construct takes note of the extent to which the person interprets perceptual information by independently attending to and considering relevant cues in the environment while discarding irrelevant ones. The degree of field independence is related to the individual's ability to perceive the object or situation without being unduly influenced by or dependent on other information in the surrounding field (Witkin, Moore, Goodenough, & Cox, 1977).

The degree of field independence then is determined by the extent to which individuals resolve conflicting sources of information by reference to a standard derived from within themselves. That standard of comparison is typically thought to be stored in the knowledge base of the individual. Students who function in a field independent manner are more likely to use such inner resources as a mediator for information processing (Reid, Hresko, & Swanson, 1996). Swanson (1991) stated that field independent children are more capable of using inner language to mediate their processing of environmental stimuli. Such learners perform more consistently on school tasks and in learning environments. It has also been determined that the tendency toward field independence tends to grow stronger with age and that learners with learning disabilities and other mild disabilities tend to remain more field dependent for longer periods of time.

Field dependence, on the other hand, is evidenced when the person's perceptions are largely determined by the prevailing external stimuli and information. Such students experience difficulty structuring the stimuli that they take in, and they rely on teacher-generated cues and hints to give meaning to what they see or hear (Reid, Hresko, & Swanson, 1996). Keogh and Donlon (1972) asserted that the tendency for field dependent learners to scan larger portions of the environment for clues may lead to confusion and ambiguity in some learning situations, thereby reducing learning efficiency. Many of the studies on field dependence have found a link between field dependence and academic underachievement (Blackman & Goldstein, 1982).

Later studies (Forns-Santacana, Amador-Campos, & Roig-Lopez, 1993) have concluded that field independence tends to be less well developed in children from lower socioeconomic backgrounds, possibly related to the effect of limited learning experiences on cognitive development. They also reported additional evidence that girls tend to function in a more field dependent manner than do boys.

The concept of field dependence and independence may be applied in social situations as well as cognitive ones (see Chapter 13). Individuals with a field dependent social orientation make extensive use of social referents in determining their feelings, attitudes, and actions. The tendency to view field dependence as undesirable or less adaptive has been questioned by some researchers (Claxton & Murrell, 1987). They note that some cultures (e.g., Mexican-American) place a value on a field dependent cognitive style, suggesting that the use of the term *field sensitive* may be a more appropriate alternative. They recommend that teachers strive to develop a balance of both cognitive styles in their students, asserting that contemporary life requires individuals who can be field independent and field sensitive as the occasion demands. (See In the Classroom 10.4.)

Impulsivity and Reflectivity

This aspect of cognitive style refers to the speed with which the individual reaches decisions and whether the individual thinks about the action before acting. The critical issue is not the

Field Dependence and Field Independence

Mike, a fifth grader with ADHD, has become more field independent since going on medication for his ADHD. Sometimes being field independent works to his disadvantage, however. He now tends to do things entirely on his own. If he does not remember the directions, he makes up his own. If he doesn't know an answer, he skips it. He does not seek the assistance of the teacher when it would be useful to do so. He is proud of being able to control himself now and likes not having to rely on others for support and confirmation. He is happy he can complete his work on his own, whether it is correct or not.

Dennis, a fifth grader with a learning disability, shows signs of both field dependence and independence, depending on the subject or task he is working on. He still exhibits considerable field dependence in writing and spelling. He continually stops to look up the spelling of words when writing a story. When he is told to just write and not worry about the spelling for now, he cannot proceed. He just focuses on the spelling. His teachers have begun having him use a word processor with a spelling checker. When the word processor beeps at an error, he may still ask how to spell it, but he is beginning to try it on his own several times before asking for help. On the other hand, Dennis appears very field independent in math. He considers himself to be a very good math student, and he prides himself on figuring out the answers rather than checking the answers on the cue cards available in his classroom.

actual speed of taking action but rather the presence or absence of an effective and deliberate process prior to acting. Reflective learners evaluate their responses before answering, while impulsive children check their standard of comparison less often and use fewer analytical strategies to evaluate their responses (Swanson, 1991). Impulsivity is characterized by quick decisions and a higher error rate, while reflectivity is described as a more deliberate decision-making process, usually with higher accuracy (see In the Classroom 10.5).

There is some evidence that impulsivity may be associated with underachievement, but the pattern is not consistent (Blackman & Goldstein, 1982). In their summary of research on cognitive styles, Hallahan, Kauffman, and Lloyd (1985, 1999) reported that while children with mild disabilities can be trained to respond in a more reflective manner, just getting impulsive learners to slow down does not generally lead to fewer errors. Also, increased reflectivity in clinical settings does not necessarily generalize to classroom-based tasks. Use of language-mediated cognitive behavior modification techniques has had the most success in developing more adaptive and reflective cognitive styles. Such techniques teach the student to engage in self-instruction while carrying out standard cognitive tasks, thereby promoting reflectivity.

Information-Processing Approaches

Information processing provides another framework for understanding an individual's specific patterns of learning and thinking. This approach to cognitive functioning and learning

IN THE CLASSROOM **10.5**

Impulsivity and Reflectivity

Elaine is ten years old and has a learning disability. She appears somewhat impulsive. She will write down or blurt out the first thing she thinks of, whether it has anything to do with the subject or not. When asked for an explanation of her response, she usually gets defensive and says something like, "It's the best I can do." At times she fails to read the questions or directions before beginning tasks or tests. She does not check over her work unless instructed to do so. She usually finishes an assignment quickly and then immediately wants to hand it in. She states that she doesn't go back to look over her work because "I don't have time." When instructed to do

so, she appears frustrated as she notes her errors and must try again.

John's teacher describes him as surprisingly reflective. He is usually the last student to complete an assignment in his senior high school class for students with mild retardation. In approaching a cognitive task, he consciously and systematically attacks the problem. If he feels rushed for time, he asks the teacher for an extension. Unfortunately for John, his deficits in long-term memory mean that thinking about the task before acting doesn't always result in fewer mistakes.

---

departs from the earlier research about cognitive styles and from the environmental or inter-actionist perspectives of the constructivists and behavioralists. The information-processing framework is based on the premise that cognition is a highly interactive process, and it assumes that individuals interpret all newly received sensory input with respect to what they already know. It is hypothesized that individuals then construct meaning or modify their knowledge bases. The critical factors influencing the success of the learning include the learners' selection of stimuli from all the available environmental stimuli and the processes they use to give meaning to those environmental stimuli.

Information-processing researchers have studied how human beings collect, interpret, store, and modify information received from the environment and retrieved from their own stored information. A variety of functional models and hypotheses have resulted from this study of the complex processes involved in cognition. Within this framework, the process of learning is not viewed as qualitatively different from stage to stage or from age to age. Instead, it is related to each learner's ability to process new information efficiently and effectively. Each cognitive action adds new concepts, skills, and insights to the individual's existing knowledge base, resulting in the learner's being able to use that new knowledge in subsequent learning. The learner associates this new input with previous learning and stores it for use in the future, much as computers do.

Models of cognitive functioning generally are composed of three primary components or functions (Reid, Hresko, & Swanson, 1996; Swanson, 1987; Swanson & Cooney, 1991): (1) structural components, (2) strategic control components, and (3) executive control functions. The structural components of the cognitive model include the sensory register, the immediate memory (composed of short-term and working memories), and the long-term storage or memory. The strategic control components include functions or strategies for completing specific tasks. These strategic components include attention, perception, and the storage and retrieval strategies used to transform information so that it is useful in the next stage of the processing. The executive control functions perform a variety of monitoring activities, evaluating the effectiveness of cognitive processing, directing the flow of information, and allocating resources. The relationship of the structural components, strategic processes, and executive control functions to the processing of environmental stimuli or information is illustrated in Figure 10.2.

Structural Storage Components

Most models of the cognitive processing of information include a multilevel structural storage component, composed of three types of memory (Anderson, 1983; Stone & Reid, 1994):

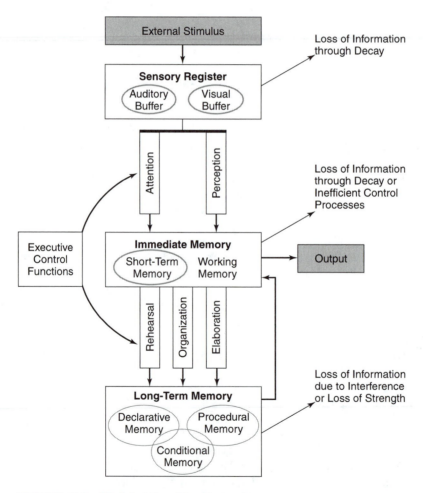

FIGURE 10.2   Model of Cognitive Processing

- The sensory register, or store, which receives and briefly stores sensory stimuli
- The immediate memory, composed of the working and short-term memories, which process information prior to storage or use (output)
- The long-term memory, for indefinite storage.

Sensory Register. The sensory register is the cognitive storage device for all sensory input (Hayes, 1989; Wyer & Srull, 1989). It is capable of receiving significant amounts of sensory information. It stores a relatively complete copy of the physical stimulus—much like photographic film—that is available for further processing (Swanson & Cooney, 1991; Wyer & Srull, 1989). Unless captured by the attention control process, this information decays within three to five seconds. The sensory information is scanned and compared against information in long-term memory, and if no match is found, the thinker determines that the stimulus is not meaningful and the memory of the stimulus is lost through decay.

The sensory register (see Figure 10.2) is composed of separate stores or buffers for the different sensory modalities, including buffers for visual, auditory, tactile, olfactory, and gustatory stimuli. The visual and auditory buffers are most often used in the process of thinking and school learning, and they are the only ones that have been studied extensively. These buffers store pure sensory information without complex meaning. Such information is considered precategorical or unprocessed, with no meaning until it is acted on by attention and perception (Hayes, 1989).

Images stored in the sensory register are operated on by the strategic control process of selective attention, which makes determinations about which stimuli should be captured and used and which should be ignored and allowed to decay. The attention function scans the images, identifying relevant and irrelevant stimuli and filtering out irrelevant environmental stimuli. Problems for some learners may arise at this stage when relevant images are allowed to decay due to inefficient attention processes or when the filtering system allows irrelevant images to remain active in the process, competing with more useful stimuli for processing space (Stone & Reid, 1994). The attention problems of many learners with mild disabilities (see In the Classroom 10.6) mean that information often never makes it past the sensory register and is lost.

Immediate Memory. The structural component devoted to active processing of information is called the *immediate memory,* which is composed of two complementary functions: working memory and short-term memory (see Figure 10.3). *Working memory* has been described as a work table for the temporary storage and manipulation of information derived from incoming stimuli and information retrieved from long-term memory. It is a dynamic and active system where a limited number of pieces of information can be processed rapidly prior to restorage or use (Ashbaker & Swanson, 1996; Swanson, 1994). Working-memory functions require holding on to pieces of information while carrying out cognitive operations.

Immediate memory has another subsection referred to as *short-term memory,* a temporary, passive storage location for information being operated on in the pursuit of a specific cognitive objective. Short-term memory provides a storage buffer for auditory, visual, or other sensory stimuli, holding information for very short periods of time. It also provides a rehearsal stage, serving as a mediator between input, processing, and output (Ashbaker & Swanson, 1996; Reid, Hresko, & Swanson, 1996; Swanson, 1994; Swanson, Cochran, & Ewers, 1990).

IN THE CLASSROOM **10.6**

Sensory Register

Billy, a middle school student with a learning and behavioral disability, exhibits both strengths and deficits in his sensory register. It appears that it is easier for him to pick up and process auditory stimuli than visual stimuli. He is much more comfortable and efficient in listening and talking than he is with reading and writing. When he is trying to read, he has so much difficulty processing the visual symbols that the stimulus is frequently lost before mean-

ing can be attached. Trying to make sense of a group of visual symbols as a complete thought appears impossible. If he is given the same information verbally, he has little difficulty understanding the concepts. Attaching meaning to auditory stimuli is much more automatic, and his efficiency in processing the auditory stimuli allows him to be more successful in attributing meaning to it as a complete thought.

The allocation of space in immediate memory to working and short-term memory is flexible. Some cognitive tasks require more storage, while others demand more active work space to manipulate data. The learner, using the executive control processes, determines the optimal allocation of these limited resources for the immediate task. The limitations of both the working and short-term memories are their storage and processing capacities. Studies indicate that normally about seven independent pieces, or chunks, of information can be held in working memory at one time without the learner's needing to transfer some information into long-term memory or run the risk of losing it (Hayes, 1989). A *chunk* is a collection of stimuli or symbols that is treated as a unit. For example, words are combinations of letters and may be treated as a single chunk; sentences are combinations of words and may be viewed as a chunk. Once the storage limit of the working memory has been exceeded, infor-

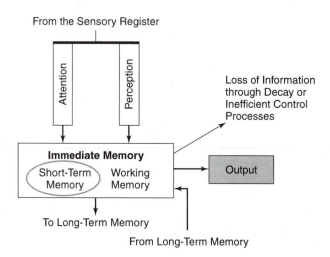

FIGURE 10.3 Components and Operation of Immediate Memory

mation becomes lost. The phenomenon of losing information due to limited storage capacity is called *displacement.*

Immediate memory is limited in its storage capacity. Information stored in the short-term memory buffer will decay on average within twenty to thirty seconds unless it is retained and renewed by strategies such as rehearsal. The time that a specific chunk remains active and available within the short-term memory buffer is variable and is significantly influenced by the actions and strategies of the individual. Repeating the information over and over or actively working with the information can sustain it for longer than this brief time. An alternative is to transfer the information into long-term memory for subsequent use, retaining cues for retrieving it as needed.

The ability of learners to create and use chunks to increase the limited processing capacity of their immediate memory is dependent on the extent of the prior knowledge they can apply to the situation. Sometimes, rearranging the units can reveal even larger chunks (e.g., grouping sets of items into categories to aid in recall). For many learners with mild disabilities, the extent, strength, and accessibility of their knowledge base is frequently inadequate, which compromises their overall cognitive effectiveness. A chunk must be a familiar unit of meaning if the individual is to be able to recognize and handle it as a chunk. When learners are able to recognize a pattern in the information being processed based on their prior knowledge, they can treat that information as a single chunk and therefore can increase the capacity of their immediate memory. Effective use of such "chunking" strategies increases the effectiveness of immediate memory, both in the storage (short-term memory) and the processing (working memory) subcomponents.

Learners with mild disabilites frequently exhibit a variety of difficulties in use of their working and short-term memories (see In the Classroom 10.7). Problems include difficulty in strategically processing information, including less frequent or less skillful use of organizational strategies to chunk information. In general, these learners exhibit less mature memory functioning, more comparable to younger children (Swanson & Cooney, 1991). The memory

---

IN THE CLASSROOM **10.7**

Immediate Memory (Working and Short-Term Memory)

Deficits in his immediate memory have had a critical effect on Chris' academic achievement and functioning in his self-contained classroom for elementary students with emotional disorders. Directions for assignments are a particular problem. His teacher gives him specific directions and routinely asks him to repeat them, checking for understanding. Although he looks at the teacher while she is speaking and gives the appearance of listening, he frequently is unable to repeat what she told him. On other occasions, the teacher gives Chris a specific fact, such as the year he was born, for a form he is filling out; when she immediately asks him to repeat what she said, he is unable to do so. Without the ability to hold information briefly in his immediate memory for use or processing, Chris is unable to perform immediate tasks adequately. He is also unable to add the information effectively to his knowledge base in long-term memory.

strategies and skills of students with specific learning disabilities often do not match estimates of their general intellectual ability. Such students may present a variety of problems in the use of their working and short-term memories, with some learners seeming to have more problems in the storage facilities, while others encounter more difficulty in using executive control strategies to organize their working memories for efficient processing (Swanson, Cochran, & Ewers, 1990). Students with mild disabilities frequently encounter specific problems in reading comprehension because of the inefficient operation of their working memory to handle decoding and perceptual tasks simultaneously (Ashbaker & Swanson, 1996). Students with mental retardation are reported to take longer to achieve automatic and fluent levels of information processing, a factor which compromises the amount of cognitive information they can handle at one time (Merrill, 1990).

Long-Term Memory.   Long-term memory, the main storage facility, appears to have virtually unlimited storage capacity. Once information is stored in long-term memory, it is generally considered to be permanent and accessible for a lifetime. Information may be of a declarative, procedural, or conditional nature and is transferred into long-term memory by the use of strategic control processes (Billingsley & Wildman, 1990; Deshler, Ellis, & Lenz, 1995). Although there is some indication that these three types of information are stored separately, there is also evidence that the three storage units are accessed interactively during cognitive processing (see Figure 10.4).

Declarative knowledge deals with factual information and the acquisition of related concepts. Factual data is encoded for future use and stored in the declarative memory store, which is also called the semantic memory. Prior to storage, information is compared with previously stored information and is either assimilated or accommodated based on that comparison and evaluation. If there is *interference,* or a discrepancy between the new information and the previously stored material, cognitive decisions must be made by the learner about which information to keep or how to modify the knowledge base to accommodate the new data.

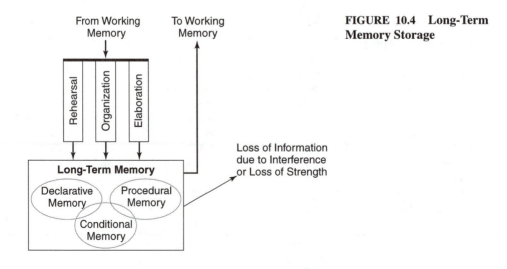

FIGURE 10.4   Long-Term Memory Storage

The structure of information stored in the declarative memory is best described as a hierarchical classification system (McFarland & Weibe, 1987; Reid, Hresko, & Swanson, 1996), with information of a more specific nature stored in relationship to more general or global categories. The learner makes use of various associations or links to store the data as well as utilizing more general organizational structures or frameworks to organize the memory store as a whole. The stronger the relationship between two facts or stimuli, the more easily the learner will be able to retrieve those facts on demand (Hasselbring, Goin, & Bansford, 1988).

Research suggests that the structure of declarative memory in individuals with mild disabilities is similar to that in other persons, but there is some evidence that the extent and accessibility of that information differs somewhat (see In the Classroom 10.8). Hayes and Taplin (1993) reported that while the structure of declarative memory in individuals with mental retardation resembles that of those without such disabilities, children with mental retardation seem most often to develop new concepts based on references to prototypes (that is, by linking the new concept to a generalized and similar concept already stored). Other more-adaptive learners are more able to develop concepts from criterial characteristics extracted from experience with a series of exemplars of such concepts. Hasselbring et al. (1988) observed that when learners with mild disabilities are unsuccessful in retrieving needed information from their declarative memories, they often rely on strategies in their procedural memory to determine the needed facts (see In the Classroom 10.9). While this is sometimes effective in recovering the needed information, this process slows down the cognitive processing and can obstruct higher order thinking.

Procedural knowledge includes information about how to do specific tasks. This knowledge includes basic action-sequences (Derry, 1990), such as how to tie a shoe or how to subtract three-digit numbers with regrouping, as well as the more complex knowledges needed to carry out complex cognitive processing of information. Procedural knowledge is generally composed of a system of condition-action rules, called *productions,* similar to a basic stimulus-response framework. They permit more automatic performance of complex

---

IN THE CLASSROOM **10.8**

Declarative Knowledge

Melissa, a fifth grader with a learning disability, has a difficult time storing and retrieving declarative information in her long-term memory. She is working on learning her multiplication facts by using flash cards with her teacher. She frequently gets "that look" on her face when she appears to know the answer but doesn't answer right away. Her teacher thinks this may be because she has difficulty retrieving the information quickly from long-term memory into her working memory and then forming an adequate response. Melissa's teacher wonders if it is because of inefficient organization of concepts within her declarative memory or if ineffective memory strategies used in the storage process are to blame. Melissa appears primarily to use verbal rehearsal strategies, which may not be the best choice for her since she appears to respond more readily to visual and tactile stimuli.

IN THE CLASSROOM **10.9**

Procedural Knowledge

Donnie, a sixth grader with learning disabilities, continues to experience difficulties in his math class. He started having trouble in math in second grade when the class began to memorize the multiplication tables. He had always been able to complete addition and subtraction computation and problem-solving well. Even though he did not have the facts in memory, he could rapidly count them, and he had a firm grasp on the procedures for doing the calculation. Ever since then, his teachers have been working unsuccessfully on memory of the

multiplication facts. At first he was allowed to use a chart, and he became quite competent in the processes of multiplying and then dividing. Trouble began when his teachers said, "No more chart." Procedural knowledge alone was simply not enough. Donnie's consultant teacher, recognizing his strength in procedural knowledge, has been working with him on the declarative knowledge deficit while seeking to put accommodations in place that will allow him to continue to function in math class with his multiplication chart.

tasks (Derry, 1990; Reid, Hresko & Swanson, 1996), since each step leads automatically to the next once the string has been activated. Such procedural memories make use of data stored in the declarative memory but allow more efficient processing of information within the working memory and in cognitive information processing as a whole, resulting in the capable individual's being able to carry out a variety of such action sequences simultaneously. Youngsters such as Donnie (see In the Classroom 10.9) sometimes find these action sequences easier to learn, perhaps due to the multisensory aspect of most procedural learning. Once learned, procedural sequences may then be used by the learner to compensate for deficits in declarative memory.

The third component of long-term memory is *conditional knowledge,* consisting of the knowledge base that an individual uses to determine when or whether to initiate a particular cognitive process. Conditional knowledge provides the strategy knowledge needed to integrate declarative and procedural knowledge. Conditional knowledge also involves the knowledge of appropriate techniques for monitoring and evaluating cognitive events and as such includes the knowledge of how one's memory and overall cognitive processing operate and have operated in the past. These standards developed from past experiences enable the individual to make use of prior experiences to support their cognitive processing in the present. This is the memory store that is likely to be least well developed in learners with mild disabilities.

Processing within Long-Term Memory.   Long-term memory processing involves the use of three activities (Hayes, 1989):

- Encoding or putting the information into memory
- Organizing that stored information in an accessible manner
- Retrieving or recovering stored information.

Encoding, or preparing the material for transfer into long-term memory, can be accomplished by simple rehearsal. However, in order to effectively fix the information in a form that is strong enough to be easily and reliably accessed later, more complex and elaborative rehearsal techniques are generally required. Such strategies involve making a variety of connections with the new information. The more connections that are made, the more likely that the material will be successfully and effectively encoded for storage and retrieval. Access to stored material and the effectiveness of both storage and retrieval are largely mediated by strategic control functions such as rehearsal strategies (oral, written, or motoric rehearsal), organization strategies (chunking, clustering, mnemonics, and coding), and use of strategies to elaborate on the meaning of the stimuli being processed (use of semantic elaboration or imagery strategies).

Access to stored information can be disrupted by either interference or decay. Interference is usually attributed to conflicts with other learning. When the interference is with a prior experience, it is called *proactive interference.* When the interference is from a later learning, it is called *retroactive interference.* Decay is hypothesized to be related to the insufficient strength of the original learning, resulting in a memory trace that is too weak to facilitate recall (Hayes, 1989). The decay effect can be reduced by practicing overlearning strategies or by reviewing stored information periodically. Learners with mild disabilities experience frequent problems in retrieving stored data due primarily to weak original learning. (See Chapter 12 for a more complete discussion of the stages of learning required for robust learning to occur.) They also may not monitor their memory stores for possible interference with previously stored information, as was discussed in the section on Piaget and the accommodation process.

Strategic Control Components

The processing and transfer of information between the cognitive structural components is accomplished by the use of strategic control processes, including attention, perception, and mnemonic strategies (see Figure 10.2). The application of these strategic control processes is first evidenced when stimuli are being evaluated in the sensory register. At this stage, the information is scanned quickly, attention is focused on distinctive features, and names are generated for specific bits of information. Almost instantaneously, a decision is made about the utility of these stimuli. Unless tagged for further attention, they quickly decay and are lost. Much of what occurs around us fails to pass this initial screening and disappears without notice.

Once information has been given meaning and has passed into working memory, the executive control function evaluates it again and calls up an appropriate mnemonic strategy to transfer it to an appropriate location in long-term memory. Finally, strategic control processes are utilized to combine incoming stimuli with stored information, resulting in a response to the environment. Such responses may be verbal (oral or written) or kinesthetic (including gestural language as well as physical actions).

Attention.　No learning can occur unless the learner is first able to focus on the relevant aspects of the task or concept and to focus on them long enough to process the information, giving it meaning and making it usable. *Attention,* the term typically used to refer to this focusing function, has been conceptualized in a variety of ways over the years. Students with mental retardation, learning disabilities, ADHD, or emotional or behavioral disorders, as well as other low-achieving youngsters, frequently exhibit problems with attention, or one or more of its components, as one of the defining characteristics of their disability (Krupski, 1980, 1986; Richards, Samuels, Turnure, & Ysseldyke, 1990).

Attention is much more than a simple system for taking in information. Information previously stored in the individual's long-term memory is utilized by the attention function to determine what is novel or relevant. Attention is an integral part of the cognitive process, but difficulties in learning are more likely caused by a fundamental limitation in the cognitive functioning as a system than by a deficit in any single function such as attention (Krupski, 1986). For example, the adequacy and availability of prior knowledge are significant determiners of what the learner can and will attend to. Information taken in from the environment through the sensory register is joined with information retrieved from long-term memory; if a match is found, the learner is able to be give meaning to the stimulus within the working memory (Stolzenberg & Cherkes-Julkowski, 1991) (see Figure 10.5). In this way, the attention function interacts with all aspects of the learning and thinking process and may be most appropriately viewed as one of the strategic control functions.

Attention has been described as a multifaceted construct composed of several subfunctions. Although some writers have identified as many as seven attentional subcomponents, most focus on two or three: (1) coming to attention, (2) selective attention, and (3) sustained attention (Conte, 1991; Keogh & Margolis, 1976; Krupski, 1986; Posner & Boies, 1971; Smith, C. R., 1991). All of these components are involved in identifying relevant information and inhibiting the processing of irrelevant information (Klorman, 1991; Krupski, 1986).

Coming to attention.   The initial factor in our ability to attend to relevant stimuli is our alertness, or our receptivity to signals from the environment. Our alertness, or capability of being aroused by external stimuli to "come to attention," varies considerably throughout the day, and alertness varies across individuals. Factors that affect alertness or receptivity to stimuli are

- Our physical state (e.g., tiredness, excitement, physical health, hunger)
- External circumstances (e.g., the weather, the type of activity)
- The presence of advance organizers (information that prompts us to attend)
- The need to allocate attention resources in a setting of conflicting attentional demands (e.g., a crowded room, a busy shopping mall)

All of us exhibit varying levels of alertness over time and situations. Our effectiveness in functioning requires that we moderate our alertness to meet environmental demands. In considering learners with mild disabilities, there is some evidence that their ability to come to attention may be compromised by their conditions. Some children may appear to be under-aroused and to engage in "stimulus seeking" behaviors (Conte, 1991). They appear to be very

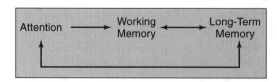

FIGURE 10.5   Interaction of Attention and Memory

IN THE CLASSROOM **10.10**

Alertness or "Coming to Attention"

Dianne is nine years old and has a learning disability. Attention appears to be difficult for her. Her deficits appear to lie primarily in alertness, or coming to attention. Her teacher finds it helpful to give her a little extra time (about thirty seconds) when transitioning from one subject or activity to another. She is then able to effectively come to attention. The teach-er finds that if she asks her to switch her attention focus too quickly, Dianne "gets lost." She is usually focused on the task she has just completed and needs to have some advance warning of what's happening next. When ample time is given to the transition stage, Dianne comes to attention and maintains attention more effectively for longer periods.

distractible and to have problems attending. Other learners seem to be overaroused, resulting in high levels of anxiety and disorganization. The level of alertness becomes problematic when a student exhibits a uniform level of arousal across setting demands (that is, when the student is uniformly underaroused or overaroused), with accompanying lack of ability to adjust attention responses to meet specific daily living demands. Without the ability to come to attention as needed, functioning is certainly impaired (see In the Classroom 10.10).

Selective attention.   Once the individual has become alert to the need to attend to incoming stimuli, the next step in the process is "catching and focusing" the attention (Smith, C. R., 1991). Human beings are bombarded by enormous quantities of stimuli during every conscious moment. It is impossible to attend to and process all of it, and much of the environmental stimuli are not relevant and should not be processed. *Selective attention* refers to the ability to focus on relevant stimuli without being distracted by irrelevant environmental factors (Hallahan & Reeve, 1980). It requires that the individual possess the ability to identify and maintain attention to the target stimulus for several seconds even when distracters are present. It requires that the person engage in decision-making about which stimuli are relevant and should be focused on to the exclusion of other stimuli.

Learners with problems with selective attention often appear to attend to central stimuli and incidental stimuli indiscriminately (see In the Classroom 10.11). Several research reviews indicate that students with mild disabilities frequently have more difficulty with selective attention than other learners or that they may achieve the focus on the central signal more slowly (Conte, 1991; Krupski, 1986; Merrill, 1990). They may also exhibit problems identifying the central stimulus because of problems connecting the stimulus in their sensory register or immediate memory with a concept in their knowledge base, or long-term memory. Hallahan & Reeve (1980) concluded that problems in selective attention are most likely attributable to immature or deficient task-appropriate attending strategies. They noted that repeated studies have failed to demonstrate an increase in attending behaviors when the learner is shielded from distractions. Hallahan and Reeve concluded from this finding that such learners may lack the cognitive skills needed to connect sensory images with concepts and images stored in their long-term memory.

I N   T H E   C L A S S R O O M   **10.11**

Selective Attention

Jerry is a third grader with mild mental retardation. His teacher has ruled out coming to attention as an area of deficit because initially Jerry appears excited to begin work and seems fully focused. He will immediately make comments about the subject being presented. Difficulties begin with his selective attention. He often seems unaware of the main idea and cannot pick out relevant details. His difficulty in selecting the most relevant stimuli is evidenced during classroom discussion. He frequently provides answers that are off the topic, or he displays little if any recollection of material discussed. In a recent discussion of the four food groups, for example, he responded, "I don't remember hearing about all of them."

Tina is a third grader with a learning disability and ADHD. One day, her teacher was reading aloud as the students followed along. Tina appeared to be paying attention for the first few minutes. However, she had a pencil in her hand, which appeared to draw her attention away from the book. When Tina saw or heard the others turn the page, she did so as well. The teacher directed Tina to put the pencil away, and for the remainder of the reading, she appeared to follow along. Her teacher later said that she is unsure whether Tina was unable to sustain her attention on the reading and so turned to focus on the pencil or whether her selective attention left the book and focused on the pencil, shifting her attention away from the more relevant stimulus.

Selective attention does not refer to occurrences when learners appear to choose not to attend to something being presented to them. It also does not refer to a situation when the child attends to some stimuli and not to others. It refers to that adaptive attention function of being able to focus on relevant target stimuli and to ignore other distracting or irrelevant stimuli. It represents a decision-making function, but not in the sense of willfulness or disobedience. It involves catching hold of a stimulus briefly and focusing attention on the stimulus for a few seconds, long enough to utilize other cognitive processes of perception and memory to give it meaning. At that point, the ability to sustain or maintain attention takes over.

Sustained attention.   If continuous attention to the stimulus or task is required once the stimulus has been caught, *sustained attention* takes over. To be effective as learners, students must develop the ability to maintain focus on incoming information over a sufficient period of time for effective cognitive processing to occur. During this time, the learner must also withhold responses to incidental or nonrelevant stimuli. Sustained attention is conceptualized as the ability to exercise vigilance, or the continuous monitoring of stimuli, combined with the evaluative capacity to reject those stimuli that are not relevant to the task at hand.

Individuals should have developed the ability to maintain attention to a task for at least ten minutes to be effective at many school and work activities. Youngsters with learning disabilities, ADHD, or other disabilities seem to be particularly affected by problems with sustained attention and will often be observed making more responses to nontarget stimuli over time (Krupski, 1980, 1986) (see In the Classroom 10.12). Obviously, the ability to attend for significant periods is typically less developed in very young children. Preschool and kinder-

IN THE CLASSROOM **10.12**

Sustained Attention

Martha is in middle school and has been diagnosed as having a mild behavioral disorder. Her main problem is attending to the stimuli presented by her teachers or parents. She cannot always decide what is relevant for her to focus on. Her selective attention has shown signs of improvement since she has learned to check herself on what she should be learning. If she does focus on a relevant stimulus initially, her sustained attention still tends to be a problem; she cannot usually maintain her attention long enough for learning to occur. For example, in English class she verified the story she was to read and began the reading with the others. The teacher checked to see that Martha had begun the task and then went on to another student. Unfortunately, after the first two pages, Martha's sustained attention waned, and when the others had completed the story and were ready to discuss it, she was still on the second page.

garten programs are specifically designed to develop this ability by the early primary grades, since it is so essential to effective learning.

Problems in attention.   Some writers describe attention as a process by which the individual applies concentration and mental powers to an object or task, a process which mediates virtually all other cognitive activities. Others (Merrill, 1990) describe it as the capacity for processing. In this framework, effective allocation of attentional resources is required for success in various cognitive tasks. Problems occur when the learner has difficulty making the associations needed to focus on relevant stimuli and then connecting them to prior learning (Krupski, 1986, 1987).

In an investigation of the attention capabilities of students with learning disabilities and ADHD, Richards et al. (1990) observed that students with ADHD seemed to have more difficulty with sustained attention, while those with learning disabilities were more likely to exhibit problems in selective attention; like Robert at the beginning of this chapter, they seem to need longer response times, indicating a slower speed of cognitive processing in general. These researchers concluded that teachers need to carefully investigate the specific nature of an apparent deficit in attention in order to plan more appropriate interventions. While the source and defining characteristics of the attention problem may differ, the fact remains that deficiencies and inefficiencies in attention create problems in learning and everyday functioning for many learners with mild disabilities. A full diagnostic description of their attention attributes is essential to the development of effective educational plans for these students.

The nature of attention demands.   The ability to sustain attention over time is affected by the voluntary attributes of the attention task. *Involuntary attention,* the most basic and automatic form of attention, is elicited directly by the particular qualities of the stimulus. Such tasks require only passive attending, and they are tasks that the individual cannot avoid attending to.

The attention of infants and young children is largely determined by the characteristics of the stimulus, and they primarily exhibit involuntary attention. Involuntary attention demands are more predictably responded to by older individuals as well. One can hardly ignore or fail to attend to a fire licking at one's heels!

Voluntary attention, on the other hand, requires some degree of personal effort on the part of the attender. The individual must act consciously and actively to focus on and control the processing of stimuli. With maturity, individuals generally develop an increasing ability to employ voluntary attention and to exert more personal and cognitive control over stimuli. With experience and training, children usually learn to use personal effort to command their own attention, making voluntary attention more possible and dependable.

The performance of students with deficits in attention will be compromised most on those tasks that make the greatest cognitive demands and that present voluntary attention demands (Krupski, 1986). In addition, because of the increasing demands attention makes on other cognitive functions, such as storage and retrieval from memory, deficits in voluntary attention are often found to be linked to problems in other areas of cognitive functioning. For this reason, teachers attempting to evaluate the effectiveness of attention in schoolchildren may discover that attention functioning is confounded by problems in memory storage and retrieval and in other strategic and executive control functions (see In the Classroom 10.13).

Factors that affect attention availability.   In evaluating the nature of a child's attention capabilities, it is useful to consider the child within the ecological context, determining how the attention may be affected by environmental factors. Krupski (1981) asserted that the ability to attend or the quality of that attention is affected by the interaction of three variables: the child, the setting, and the task.

When considering characteristics of a child that may be influencing attention capabilities, it is important to consider the nature of disabilities such as mental retardation, learning disabilities, ADHD, or emotional or behavioral disorders, since these conditions frequently reduce the effectiveness of attending behaviors. A history of failure may also affect attention.

IN THE CLASSROOM **10.13**

Voluntary and Involuntary Attention Demands

John is an eight year old with mild mental retardation, and he has just completed first grade. He has demonstrated difficulty maintaining attention in areas that he does not find appealing. On most days, he is fidgety and roams around the classroom. In contrast, John was recently able to listen attentively for over thirty minutes to a presentation on rain forests, and later he could recall the information that had been presented. Relevance in his instruction helps him maintain attention. This example illustrates the differential performance often seen in youngsters when faced with tasks that present involuntary attention demands as compared to those that make voluntary attention demands. Rain forests for John clearly present involuntary attention demands.

Regardless of the presence or absence of a disability, physiological factors such as hunger, fatigue, and pain will adversely affect attention, while good physical health, nutrition, and rest will tend to enhance the ability to attend.

The more structured the demands and the setting, the more difficult it is for any child to respond with appropriate levels of attention. In a highly structured setting such as a classroom, the child's deficits in attention skills are increasingly noticeable and problematic. Such settings permit little leeway in attention responses and penalize the student who is less consistently attentive.

When evaluating the task demands, it is important to determine the extent to which the task requires voluntary attention. Krupski's work (1980, 1981) indicated that the more voluntary the attention demands, the more effort the learner must exert to focus attention. In other words, the more strongly the task draws the attention of the learner, the less the individual has to consciously pay attention and the easier it is to sustain attention.

Sources of deficits in attention.   Some problems in selective or sustained attention may be traced to physiological causes, as was discussed in Chapter 9. In such cases, medication may be prescribed as one component of the total treatment plan. It is important to note, however, that medication alone is unlikely to solve the problem, since attention interacts with all of the components of the cognitive model. Without development of effective strategic processing, performance is unlikely to significantly improve by the use of medication alone (Stolzenberg & Cherkes-Julkowski, 1991).

There is also evidence that some attention problems may be due to a history of failure, which affects the motivation of the learner. Failure frequently reduces motivation and alertness as well as compromises the knowledge base that is integral to completing the attention process. It is also possible that the learner has never learned the subskills necessary to selectively attend and to maintain attention over time. (See Chapter 12 for more discussion of the effect of failure on learning.)

Perception.   Once stimuli are attended to, they must be given meaning. Perception performs this important bridging function in cognitive processing (Faust & Faust, 1980). *Perception* is the strategic control process by which the individual processes stimuli meaningfully. It is the process by which stimuli are named and given meaning, allowing the learner to then work with these mental representations. Once the perception function has effectively assigned a descriptive name to the stimulus, the learner can use that named stimulus to create new cognitive concepts and to relate those concepts to others within the individual's memory structures (see Figure 10.6).

Perceptual skills are often discussed in the research literature in relationship to learning disabilities. However, it is important to keep in mind that perceptual functioning is central to all cognitive activity and that deficiencies in perception can be identified in any learner, regardless of diagnostic category. For example, we focus on perception when we consider the social perceptions of youngsters with emotional or behavioral disorders or when we investigate the visual and auditory perceptual functions of students with deficits in reading, regardless of the disability category (Torgeson, Kistner, & Morgan, 1987; Willows, 1991).

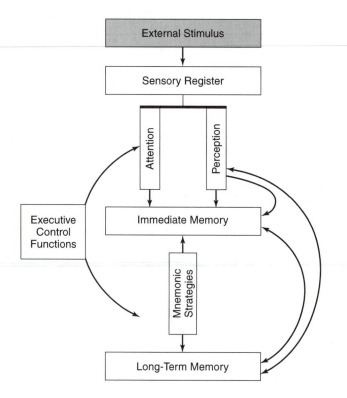

FIGURE 10.6 Role of Perception in the Model of Cognitive Processing

Theoretical frameworks of perception. Using the processes of scanning, selecting, attending to, and categorizing sensory stimuli, perception transforms raw stimuli into meaningful representations. Perception is the capturing of stimuli and the matching of those stimuli with relevant representations in long-term memory, thereby giving the stimuli meaning.

Infants are initially unable to perceive their world as a meaningful place since they have no stored representations to match with new stimuli. Gradually, the young child encounters experiences that resemble a previous group of experiences, and names for those categories of experience are derived. With each concept stored in memory, the process of perception is enhanced. For this reason, perception is most appropriately viewed as an active and constructive process that differs significantly from simple vision or hearing. According to the Gestalt psychologists, perception is an active process involving the organization of incoming stimuli and accomplished by the individual's internal cognitive processes (Dellarosa, 1988).

Torgeson, Kistner, and Morgan (1987) describe perception as coding, as the process of translating sensory input into a representational form that can be manipulated in a person's working memory and stored in long-term memory. This coding may be *denotative,* by which a basic identity is ascribed to the stimulus, or it may be *connotative,* which means that more complex attributes and semantic connections are made with the stimulus. It has been noted that children with a variety of learning problems seem to be deficient in the speed and effectiveness of this coding process (Torgeson, Kistner, and Morgan, 1987; Torgeson & Kail, 1980).

Carroll (1976, 1981; Sternberg, 1988) identified the following components that are related to the process of perception:

- Apprehension: registering the stimulus in the sensory buffers
- Perceptual integration: process used to match the encoded stimulus with a previously stored mental representation
- Encoding: forming a mental representation of the stimulus, including its interpretation in terms of attributes, associations, or meanings
- Comparison: the process of determining if two stimuli are members of the same class of objects

A multiphasic model of perceptual processing may be the most useful construct for special educators working with learners with disabilities. Rather than thinking of perception as a group of independent processing channels (e.g., visual processing, auditory processing), it may be more useful to consider the perceptual functions in relation to the overall cognitive model. Such a model proposed by Melamed and Melamed (1982) includes four components:

- Sensory encoding
- Perceptual integration, including perceptual organization (pattern discrimination and matching); perceptual relating; and spatial patterning
- Storage and retrieval (i.e., memory)
- Cognitive abstraction

Melamed and Melamed proposed that the term *perception* pertains most appropriately to the skills within the perceptual integration component, but they note that it is essential to understand the interactive role of sensory encoding, storage and retrieval from memory, and cognitive abstraction in performing various perceptual tasks (Melamed & Melamed, 1982; Wyer & Srull, 1989). Learning problems attributed to perception may actually be related to or exacerbated by difficulties in other areas of cognitive functioning, such as selective attention (sensory encoding), strategic memory processes, or the inadequacy of the working memory storage area to manipulate information and allow the accurate perceptual matching to occur.

Assessment of perceptual functioning. Although the visual and auditory channels are often discussed and treated as separate entities, teachers have learned that the development of perceptual skills is often enhanced by the interactions among the abilities. For example, visual and motor development frequently interact to aid the development of one another, and auditory perception and visual perception also often support one another. In a similar way, a learner's functioning in the areas of perception can be best assessed through behavioral observations of everyday activities such as:

- Following directions
- Copying letters, including both far- and near-point copying
- Writing; drawing; manipulating various tools and devices
- Listening tasks
- Identifying letters and letter sounds (Ariel, 1992)

Careful investigation of all possible hypotheses for an individual's apparent difficulty with perceptual tasks within an actual academic context allows a teacher to plan appropriate assistive supports (i.e., scaffolds). For an example of such a diagnostic process, see Table 10.2.

Specific perceptual functions and abilities. The general term *perception* refers to the complex processing of visual, auditory, and haptic stimuli. It is important to consider the topic of perception from the perspective of the general cognitive processing model, but it is also useful for teachers to have an understanding of the basic terms used throughout the literature to refer to specific perceptual functions.

Visual perception is the process of ascribing meaning to visual stimuli. Since many school tasks relate to visual stimuli, such as letters, numbers, and words, the ability to process visual stimuli is critical to school success. Visual perception can be broken down into a number of subcompetencies:

- *Visual discrimination* is the ability to identify dominant features in different objects and to use that ability to differentiate among a variety of objects. Features by which

---

TABLE 10.2   Example of Appropriate Assessment of Perceptual Functioning

When asked by her teacher to write her name, Susie falters on the *S,* resulting in distortions of the desired letter shapes, which are frequently reversed. Her teacher wonders why this happens and if Susie may have a "perceptual disability." Having just learned about the cognitive model, and the specific function of perception, her teacher considers a number of possibilities, or hypotheses:

Sensory encoding: Susie does not recognize that letter shapes differ from each other.
   When given a set of letters, can Susie sort the letters into groups?
   When given a set of letters and a card with the letter S *on it, can Susie pick out the* S*'s from the pile?*

Perceptual integration: Susie cannot determine the essential features that determine the letter *S.*
   Can she describe the shape of the letter S*? (e.g., round, two parts of circles)*
   Can she pick out the letter S *from similar letters or numbers (e.g., O, G, C, R, Z, or the number 2)?*
   Can she identify the reversed letter forms, given a stack of letters?

Memorial storage and retrieval: Susie cannot retrieve the name and shape of the letter *S* from memory.
   Is the letter S *stored in her long-term memory?*
   Has she been taught the letter S *as a concept or shape?*
   Does she have a problem retrieving the S *concept from her long-term memory?*
   When shown a set of five letters, can she pick out the letter S*?*

Cognitive abstraction: Susie can only identify as *S* the stimulus letter with which she was taught the letter *S.*
   Can she identify (name) the letter S *when it is presented in a variety of forms and sizes?*

Motoric output/response: Susie has a deficit in the motor control needed to produce the letter.
   Can she copy the letter from a model?
   Does she have similar copying problems (shapes, other letters, numbers)?

objects may differ include shape, color, size, pattern, position, and brightness. The ability to discriminate among stimuli based on their distinctive features is an essential first step in visual perception, and visual discrimination of letters and words is crucial to success in learning to read.

- *Visual figure–ground discrimination* is the ability to distinguish an object from its background. Students who have not developed this ability appear easily distracted by irrelevant stimuli.
- *Object recognition* is the ability to recognize the essential nature of an object. Form constancy refers to the awareness that an object generally retains its identity despite its position. Young children learn early in life to interpret a round shape with a loop on the side as a cup, whether it is right-side up or upside down. This concept is critical to flexible processing of visual stimuli. If the learner is able to identify enough congruency between the stimuli and the stored generalized concept, the image is able to be named for further processing.
- The term *spatial relations* refers to the ability to determine the position of physical objects in space in relation to oneself and other objects. In certain reading and mathematics tasks, form alone is not enough. One cannot attribute meaning to some stimuli without taking into account their relative position in space. In reading, it is important for the student to develop an awareness that spatial position is related to the identity of some stimuli (e.g., letters like *b, d, p,* and *q*). This understanding is often not well established in primary age youngsters who have previously learned that object identity is a constant, regardless of spatial orientation (Lavoie, 1989).
- The term *visual memory* refers to the ability to recall the dominant features of a stimulus no longer present or to recall the sequence of items presented visually. In school, this skill is especially useful in spelling. However, the concept of visual memory has a more generalized function. In order to ascribe a meaning to a specific visual stimulus, the learner needs to call up a visual memory with a tag or label. The ability to name a visual stimulus and complete the perceptual process depends on that ability.
- *Visual closure* is the ability to identify figures that are presented in incomplete form or that have unclear elements. Visual closure is related to visual memory because the remainder of the word or sentence is filled in by the mind's reconstruction of a likely match. Visual closure allows capable readers to read a word or sentence without actually processing all of the elements. Without the skill of visual closure, the speed of perceptual processing of written material is restricted because each element must be individually processed (see In the Classroom 10.14).

Auditory perception refers to the ability to interpret auditory stimuli and to attach meaning to what is heard. Since most auditory perceptual skills develop early in childhood, less attention is given to the development of these skills in the elementary classroom. However, early reading depends on the student's ability to make very fine auditory judgments, and difficulties in this area must be identified and remediated. Some of the auditory perception subskills include the following:

- *Auditory discrimination* is the ability to recognize differences between sounds. Initially, the child must make discriminations between distinctly different sounds, but reading and spelling instruction soon require students to be able to make perceptual judgments

IN THE CLASSROOM **10.14**

Visual Perceptual Skills

Nan is a fourth grader diagnosed with ADHD. She appears to be somewhat delayed in the development of visual perceptual skills. Her spelling and reading are affected by problems with visual memory. She has problems revisualizing common words such as *said, went,* and *was,* words she should have mastered by now. She demonstrates adequate visual discrimination and figure-ground discrimination since she can distinguish the dominant features of different stimuli and distinguish them from the background. Nan appears to have problems with spatial relations, however, which presents itself in her writing, where she frequently reverses the letters *b, p, d,* and *q.*

Joey is a nine-year-old with a learning disability. Recently, when he played Concentration with his tutor, he displayed strong visual memory for pictures. He can also distinguish among items by shape and color, and he can recall the sequence of three objects or pictures. His primary visual perceptual deficit is in the area of spatial relations. In writing, he has difficulty determining where to position his letters. His letters are frequently above and below the line, and spacing between letters and words is erratic. These problems persist even when his tutor provides a model to copy.

Cassie is a twelve-year-old girl with mild mental retardation related to Down syndrome. Her teacher has noted that Cassie experiences recurring problems differentiating between letters that present finer discrimination challenges (e.g., *K* and *R*). Mrs. Green attributes this to problems with visual discrimination. To help Cassie, Mrs. Green taught her some verbalizations to highlight the differences between the visual letter forms, building on her stronger auditory association skills, with positive results.

between very similar sounds. Phonological awareness is an important aspect of auditory discrimination. As children develop the ability to discriminate between the sounds they hear, they also begin to understand the basic structure of language and develop an awareness that language can be divided into words, syllables, and sounds.

- *Auditory blending* is the ability to make a complete word by blending the individual phonological elements. Students without the ability to perceive the whole as a combination of the parts will experience difficulty in reading programs based on synthetic phonetic approaches, or blending letter sounds into words.

- *Auditory figure–ground discrimination* is the ability to distinguish a sound from its background. The individual must have the ability to lift the relevant auditory stimulus from its sound background to be successful in school.

- The term *auditory memory* refers to the ability to recognize and recall previously presented auditory stimuli or a sequence of items presented orally. Rote memory of spelling words and other facts (e.g., multiplication tables) makes use of this skill. Even more important, auditory memory provides a matching template against which new stimuli can be evaluated.

- *Auditory closure* is the ability to identify words and other auditory elements that have been presented in incomplete form or that have unclear elements. Effective auditory closure skills permit perceptual information to be processed more efficiently, especially in lectures and discussion, since the listener does not need to process every phonological element for meaning to be derived.

- *Auditory association* is the ability to relate ideas, find relationships, make associations, and categorize information obtained by listening. It is the final stage in auditory perceptual processing and completes the determination of the meaning of a particular stimulus (see In the Classroom 10.15).

Haptic perception refers to the ability to ascribe meaning to tactile and kinesthetic stimuli. The term *tactile* refers to the sense of touch and the term *kinesthetic* relates to the sensations received through body movement. Information received through the fingers and skin as well as from the movement of parts of the body must be interpreted and given meaning just as visual and auditory stimuli are handled.

Perceptual motor integration involves the interaction of perceptual functioning (using any sense) with a specific motor activity. In school, we are most concerned with the abilities to integrate perceived visual stimuli with the movement of body parts. The abilities to copy, draw, and write each involve significant visual motor integration.

Two areas where the processing of sensory stimuli can become problematic include tactile defensiveness and perceptual overload (Lerner, 1993). *Tactile defensiveness* is characterized by extreme sensitivity and discomfort in response to the slightest tactile stimulation,

---

IN THE CLASSROOM **10.15**

Auditory Perceptual Abilities

Jeremy is a ten-year-old with an emotional disorder accompanied by ADHD. He seems to have a problem making auditory associations. This causes him significant problems in his regular education class when the teacher is presenting information orally. He recently experienced problems in a lesson on outlining. He was unable to use the information the teacher was providing to find the relationships in the information he had already assembled and to use that information to compose his outline. Although he understood the words the teacher was saying, he was unable to associate those words with his previous learning to enable him to perform the task.

Christy is a fifth grader with mild mental retardation and continuing speech impairments. While Christy has great difficulty pronouncing words that are similar (e.g., *etch* and *edge*), she has no difficulty hearing the difference between these similar words.

This strength in auditory discrimination leads her speech therapist to believe that she will eventually be able to articulate the words correctly.

Jonathan is a fourteen-year-old student in a resource program for students with learning disabilities. His teacher has noted that auditory processing appears to be a strength for him. He can recall information that has been presented to him orally, using his auditory perceptual abilities. In particular, auditory memory appears to be a strength, since he has little trouble retrieving material that was presented days before. His teacher has hypothesized that because Jonathan doesn't have to spend time deciphering each word as he does in reading, he is able to listen, attach meaning to the words, and then store the information in his long-term memory. For this reason, Jonathan's IEP provides access to books on tape.

impeding the processing of haptic stimuli by the student. *Perceptual overload* refers to the tendency in some individuals for information from one sensory input system to interfere with information coming in from another. For example, children like Maggie in In the Classroom 10.16 can listen or watch but have difficulty doing both simultaneously.

Issues concerning perceptual assessment and training. Early in the current special education era, especially in the field of learning disabilities, it was believed that assessment and training of such basic cognitive functions as perception would allow students with disabilities to eventually function similarly to typical age peers. Consider this seemingly analogous situation: Physical therapy is prescribed for a person who has experienced a physical injury; exercises are prescribed on the assumption that if range of motion and strength are regained, the person will subsequently be able to perform the full range of physical activities impaired by the injury as well as any new physical skills in the future. It is assumed that once basic physical skills are re-established, remedial training in subsequent activities will not be needed.

In much the same way, it was reasoned that if perception is impaired, providing therapy should improve those fundamental abilities, allowing the learner to then use these improved perceptual skills to master other skills involving perception such as reading and writing without the need for continued therapeutic interventions. In the past, special education services, particularly for children with learning disabilities, operated on this deficit-remediation assumption on the belief that student achievement was being blocked or slowed by a primary perceptual deficit. It was reasoned that if that deficit could be identified and removed, typical levels of functioning could be attained in the future (Wodrich & Joy, 1986).

Experience has cast doubt on this assumption. A meta-analysis of the research on perceptual motor training programs (Kavale & Mattson, 1983) revealed a lack of research support for the "processing deficit and remediation" hypothesis. These researchers found that despite extensive testing of process skills and intensive remedial programs, there was little or no improvement in overall achievement. Kavale and Mattson further stated that their meta-analysis suggested that the effort spent on such ineffective programs wasted valuable time and resources and left these learners even further behind.

IN THE CLASSROOM **10.16**

Perceptual Overload

Maggie is a second grader with a learning disability. Her classroom teacher complains that she is always daydreaming and looking out the window. Surprisingly, though, she often seems to know the answer when she is called on. Her resource teacher noticed one day that when Maggie maintained eye contact with her teacher during oral spelling practice, she often made mistakes, but that when she was looking sideways at the wall, she was 100 percent accurate. Puzzled, the resource teacher talked to Maggie about this. Maggie's answer was, "When I look at the teacher, her face gets in the way of the words."

Finally, during the 1980s, researchers and practitioners began to experiment with other answers (Torgeson, 1991). A focus on direct instruction techniques and cognitive strategies replaced the earlier process training approaches as the treatment of choice. In 1987, the Council for Learning Disabilities issued a policy statement opposing the continuation of measurement and training of perceptual and perceptual-motor functions in special education services (Council for Learning Disabilities, 1987b; see Appendix A).

In response to the questions about process assessment and training, researchers and practitioners then looked for alternatives that were consistent with the growing understanding of learning and cognition. Behavioral models of academic remediation (e.g., direct instruction) were proposed (Rosenshine, 1986; Rosenshine & Stevens, 1986; Treiber & Lahey, 1983) and focused on the academic tasks themselves. Using task analysis of academic skills, they suggested that direct instruction be used to remediate identified academic deficits and to teach needed prerequisite academic skills.

By the 1990s, the focus was returning to the cognitive functioning of students with mild disabilities. Researchers and educators began to use instructional strategies that responded to deficits in cognitive processing, including perception, and to do so in a context that enhances academic achievement (Torgeson, 1991). Such techniques include instruction in metacomprehension strategies, phonological awareness, and other learning strategies (Deshler, Ellis, & Lenz, 1996). Time will tell whether or not these approaches are more effective than earlier strategies, but it is clear that educators of the future will need to recognize and understand the complexity of perceptual and cognitive functioning, the context in which cognitive processing occurs, and the interaction of cognitive skills with academic demands in order to plan effective instruction.

Mnemonic or Memory Strategies. The skills used to encode, process, store, and retrieve information are what most people associate with the word *memory*. These skills and processes involve the efficient and effective application of strategic control processes. It is the ability to use these mnemonic, or memory, strategies that is usually implied when we say a learner has a "good memory" or that a student has "memory deficits." Deficiencies in the use of mnemonic strategies usually lead to academic and other cognitive difficulties. Learners with mild disabilities frequently rely on a small repertoire of strategies or on less flexible ones like rehearsal. These deficits in mnemonic strategies compromise their learning and functioning.

Strategies often applied in this function include rehearsal (verbal, written, or motoric), organization (including chunking, clustering, categorization, mnemonics, and coding or paired associates), and elaboration (including imagery and semantic elaboration). *Rehearsal* is the most primitive of the mnemonic strategies and is heavily used in both immediate memory and long-term memory, particularly by less-sophisticated learners. It is hypothesized that a portion of immediate memory is reserved for use as a rehearsal buffer (Merrill, 1990; Swanson & Cooney, 1991; Torgeson, Kistner, & Morgan, 1987; Wyer & Srull, 1989). The common experience of repeating a telephone number over and over until reaching the phone and dialing it illustrates the application of rehearsal in the immediate memory. It seems as if the repetition makes a deeper, more durable memory trace of the concept or stimulus, keeping it accessible for a longer period. Rehearsal can be oral, written, or kinesthetic. In each case, the purpose is to retain the exact copy of the idea or action, much like a photocopying machine.

Rehearsal strategies are useful in preserving a copy of the stimulus, but they are limited in their usefulness in developing more complex cognitive structures or concepts within long-term memory. Used primarily to develop rote memory of specific facts or automatic performance of specific functions, rehearsal is most applicable to lower-level or convergent thinking, facts, concepts, and actions. Use of rehearsal as a memory strategy does not promote the development of the connections between data elements necessary for efficient and complex thinking. One might imagine it as a cognitive equivalent of the kitchen junk drawer. Everything is stored, but there is no rhyme or reason to the storage, and finding a specific element is often difficult and time-consuming. Learners with mild disabilities tend to rely on simple forms of rehearsal to the exclusion of other strategies, and their learning is less efficient and effective because of this.

Strategies that utilize *organization,* on the other hand, make use of purposeful connections between items to facilitate their storage and ultimate retrieval. Specific strategies include

- Chunking, or grouping items that relate to one another in a meaningful way
- Clustering, or arranging items into categories or in relationship to a superordinate category or concept
- Ordering, or arranging items in some logical sequence
- Paired associates, or the connection of the new term with a term already in the learner's repertoire
- Mnemonics, or the use of an idiosyncratic or artificially meaningful method of organizing items to be remembered (e.g., "Every good boy does fine" to remember the letters of the treble staff in music)

Organization strategies are similar to the addition of trays to the kitchen junk drawer for specific categories of items (e.g., a tray for screws, a tray for small tools, a tray for glue and tape). Grouping these kitchen items makes finding them again much easier and more likely. It also makes storage of new items faster and more effective. Strategies such as chunking, clustering, and paired associates serve not only the basic memory storage function, but they also increase the likelihood that the learner will relate the material being learned to other previously acquired material in a meaningful way, fostering the development of more complex concepts within the long-term memory knowledge base. Retrieval is enhanced as well, since the retrieval of one concept or fact tends to open up access to related and connected information. Learners with mild disabilities tend not to utilize this strategy unless provided with explicit instruction in the connection of one concept to another. Their weaker original learning tends to reduce the likelihood that they will build strong categories of knowledge or that they will see the connection of new learning to prior learning.

Elaboration represents the third grouping of memory strategies, utilizing enhanced images to aid storage and retrieval. Semantic elaboration involves verbal enhancement of the concept(s) to be stored and may include establishing a richer context for the item (e.g., relating the concept to a story, metaphor, or analogy). Imagery involves pairing the concept with a visual image to enhance the strength of the memory trace. In both cases, use of verbal or visual images creates a stronger mental image or representation of the concept. Students with mild disabilities are aided in learning when their teachers help them create rich pictures of the material to be learned or when such techniques as semantic webs are used to connect the material in meaningful ways.

When the need for retrieval of stored data arises, these strategies aid the retrieval process in reverse. Using cues (fragments of information), we reconstruct the information after a search of long-term memory. When the fragment or cue connects with a likely item, the individual reconstructs the image and transfers it back to working memory for use. Information cannot be manipulated until it has been retrieved and returned to the working memory area, much as information on a computer's hard drive cannot be used until it has been brought back to the "desktop" (see In the Classroom 10.17).

Executive Control Functions

Throughout the entire cognitive process, the use of *executive control functions,* or *metacognitive regulation,* is the hallmark of the effective learner. Using these executive control functions, learners determine the possibility and need to use one or more strategic control components and then monitor and evaluate the effectiveness of the processing. Drawing on their conditional knowledge and the ability to plan, organize, monitor, and evaluate, learners engage in making a series of decisions, including deciding on the best mnemonic strategy for

---

IN THE CLASSROOM **10.17**

Mnemonic Strategies

Barry appears to have average memory skills in spite of his diagnosis of mental retardation. He seems particularly successful with the use of rehearsal strategies in learning math facts and spelling. When he writes his spelling words a number of times each day, he does well on the weekly tests. Other practice activities, such as looking up the words in the dictionary and filling in the words in sentences, seem much less effective. His teacher is concerned that his exclusive reliance on rehearsal strategies limits his overall cognitive development in areas of learning where rehearsal is not an effective strategy. When rehearsal fails to help him store information in memory, he tends to become more field dependent and increasingly depends on his teacher or others to structure his learning.

Organization seems to be Ben's preferred memory strategy. If he can relate something to what he already knows, he tends to remember it well. Rehearsal and elaboration are strategies he still rarely uses effectively. His dependence on only one method of storage and retrieval hinders his cognitive processing.

Amanda experiences difficulties in her work in sixth grade due to difficulties in the use of mnemonic strategies. Although she makes some use of rehearsal, her use of other strategies, such as elaboration, is largely nonexistent. She does not have the capability to create or enhance the meaning attributable to particular stimuli. In language arts class, she was recently asked to memorize a short poem. Amanda became upset and said she couldn't do it. The problem was that the task was too much for rehearsal alone, and she lacked other strategies to enable her to do it. Her teacher stepped in, and, by use of drawings and gestures to accompany the words, provided the meaningful elaboration for her. With these cues, Amanda quickly caught on and was able to successfully complete the memorization assignment. Based on this success, her resource teacher plans to work with her on developing her strategic use of elaboration in the future.

a given task, checking on the implementation of the strategy, and determining how effective the strategy was. If the strategy is not proving adequate to the task, further decisions are made about alternative strategies.

A model of cognitive functioning, or metacognition, developed by Borkowski and Kurtz (1987) illustrates the complexity of the multiple and reciprocal interactions between and among the strategic processes and the executive function. These researchers identified three kinds of metacognitive knowledge as essential to effective cognitive functioning: (1) knowledge of specific cognitive strategies, (2) understanding of the relative merits of various strategies in relation to others, and (3) appreciation that effort is useful and essential for successful cognitive activity. They also identified an executive component, which provides direction for the effective deployment of various other strategic processes.

Following experience with a few specific cognitive strategies, typical learners usually develop their general strategy knowledge, including the understanding that the use of strategies increases cognitive effectiveness and that effort is required to achieve the full benefit of strategy use. This general strategy knowledge does not develop until some elements of the specific strategy knowledge base are in place. For this reason, learners such as those with mild disabilities who do not develop and use specific cognitive strategies are also hampered in developing a comprehensive strategic approach to cognitive functioning. As learners begin to develop beliefs about their own self-efficacy and the effect of effort, these motivational understandings also become a part of the general strategy knowledge base and increase the likelihood that the individual will deploy strategies when needed in the future. Such attributional and self-efficacy beliefs are essential for the operation of the system and will be discussed further in Chapter 12.

Tying all of these elements together and providing the needed control for their use is the job of the executive control functions. These executive control functions develop only when sufficient specific, relational, and general strategy knowledge has been accumulated. When faced with an unstructured or ambiguous learning task, the learner must independently evaluate the situation and determine a strategy to be deployed. Executive control functions are used to monitor the effectiveness of that strategy use and to refine specific and relational strategy knowledge based on experience; they also aid in the development of self-regulated cognitive behavior in general. Use of such executive control functions as checking, monitoring, and revising strategies enhances the general and specific strategic knowledge base for future use. The executive control functions may be thought of as traffic officers, orchestrating the flow of information and redirecting traffic patterns as needed. They also function as the highway department, which accumulates information on traffic flow and accidents and then uses that information to modify traffic patterns and the highway system.

The metacognitive skills used by learners to determine the effectiveness of their comprehension during cognitive activities are central to efficient cognitive processing. Such skills include self-instruction, self-monitoring, and self-valuation, as well as metacomprehension skills such as self-questioning. Students with mental retardation, learning disabilities, ADHD, or emotional or behavioral disorders frequently fail to develop these specific strategies and executive control functions, or they fail to use them effectively and efficiently (see In the Classroom 10.18). For these reasons, such students are frequently less successful in learning tasks and environments as well as in problem solving (Merrill, 1990; Ryan, Short,

IN THE CLASSROOM **10.18**

Executive Control Functions

Amy's problems in cognitive processing seem to be related to a breakdown in her executive control functions. She appears attentive, but her processing is slow, and she tries to pay attention to everything. She has difficulty sorting out which information is relevant. While she is able to focus on a specific source—for example, the teacher—she cannot easily identify which information from the teacher is most useful or relevant. She tries to process everything the teacher says. Without a useful repertoire of organizational skills to sort the information in her short-term memory, she gets confused. It is not apparent to the speaker that Amy is not following the conversation while it is taking place until she is asked to respond. She can typically answer questions about the first things the speaker said but not the later. As long as information is presented slowly and in small chunks, she seems to be able to work with it rather well.

Ellie seems to have a number of gaps in her executive functioning. While she seems to be paying attention and she appears to recognize which information is relevant to the task, she seems to lack the ability to determine which strategies to use to relate this new information to what she already knows. She does not have effective executive control functioning that will allow her to access her declarative memory efficiently and effectively. When asked what year she was born, she could not answer, and she was unable to apply any retrieval strategies that might help her find the answer. This suggests a deficit in her executive functioning decision processes accompanied by difficulties transferring information from both her procedural and declarative memories to her working memory. Her teachers have been working on short-term memory functions and will begin working on improving organizational and rehearsal strategies to aid storage and retrieval from her long-term memory. Without further training in general strategy selection and metamemory skills, the specific strategy training is unlikely to be very effective or to generalize to other tasks.

& Weed, 1986; Swanson & Cooney, 1991; Torgeson, Kistner, & Morgan, 1987). Instructional assistance to develop such strategies has been shown to be useful in helping these learners develop more efficient and effective cognitive functions (Deshler, Ellis, & Lenz, 1996).

Focus on Culture and Diversity

When considering the cognitive characteristics of students with disabilities from diverse backgrounds, it is difficult to discern the impact of culture and diversity. However, the documented correlation of poverty and disability rates suggests that there is an impact. When one considers how children typically learn, a hypothesis emerges. Since active children use their cognitive functions to assimilate new concepts into their schema, it becomes apparent that availability of experiences affects the rate of learning. Without these experiences, the child has little to work with. Books and other experiences may be less available in homes affected by poverty. In homes and communities where the language is not English, the learner is further restricted in developing the English concepts valued in schools. Finally, early experiences in cultural traditions that differ significantly from the dominant culture of the school may result in learned behavior and content that contradict what is presented in school. For example, the Hispanic and Native-American cultures, which value the field sensitive cognitive style, do not prepare a child well to operate within the field independent style valued in public schools.

This suggests that what is needed is a focus on the opportunity to learn. As IDEA 1997 states, children cannot be identified as having a disability unless they have had the opportunity to learn, to develop their knowledge base, and to develop the strategic control processes necessary for learning. Educators and families must find ways to work together to provide the rich language and learning experiences required for cognitive development and to bridge the worlds of the family, community, and school.

Resources on the Web

National Attention Deficit Disorder Association (ADDA)

www.add.org

Provides information on the nature of attention problems; provides information for parents and for adults with attention deficits.

Center for Research on Learning

www.ku-crl.org

Provides information about learning strategies and the Strategies Intervention Model that supports the development of cognitive strategies in students with disabilities.

Summary

This chapter has considered the concept of cognitive functioning from a variety of perspectives. The constructivists view learning and cognitive functioning from a developmental point of view. According to Piaget, learning results as children encounter discrepant information and use the processes of assimilation and accommodation to incorporate the information into their cognitive schema. Vygotsky viewed cognitive development from a social constructivist framework and recognized the importance of the skilled mentor in learning.

Cognitive style research focuses attention on the way a learner approaches various tasks. Field dependence and field independence refer to the tendency to depend on cues from the environment in making perceptual decisions. Impulsivity and reflectivity refer to the routine use of reflecting before taking action.

Information processing frameworks provide another useful theory of cognitive functioning. The cognitive model consists of structural components, and strategic control components, coordinated by the executive control functions. The structural components include: (1) the sensory register that receives all sensory stimuli; (2) the immediate memory that stores information briefly (short-term memory) for processing (working memory); and (3) the long-term memory where information can be stored for use at any time in the future.

The structural components are connected by the strategic control components. Attention is composed of three subfunctions: (1) coming to attention, (2) selective attention, and (3) sustained attention. Perception attaches a name and meaning to it before transferring it to the working memory. Mnemonic strategies round out the strategic control components. Coordinating all of these processes and events is the job of the executive control functions that direct the selection of appropriate strategies, monitor ongoing cognitive activity, modify processes to meet cognitive needs, and evaluate the effectiveness of the outcomes.

Individual students with mild disabilities may exhibit a variety of problems in cognitive functioning, all of which can lead to problems in school achievement. Irrespective of their diagnostic categories, these students may develop cognitively more slowly than those without disabilities. Educators working with such students will find it useful to fully identify the learner's cognitive strengths and needs so that the most effective remediation and support can be provided.

CHARLENE: A Case Study

Charlene is a junior at the local high school in the small town where she lives. She has developed considerable artistic talent and hopes one day to be a graphic designer. She appears to be a happy, emotionally stable teenager despite her long-standing learning disability, which is accompanied by the inattentive type of ADHD. Charlene's primary areas of difficulty have involved the use of memory, particularly for auditory stimuli. She also experiences problems in use of expressive language, particularly in the areas of grammar and semantics. It is these areas of concern that initially brought her into contact with special education as a young child.

Charlene was served by special education personnel throughout elementary school and had the services of a one-to-one aide for part of that time. Now she is served by the high school's resource program, receiving supplemental assistance only during study halls. Although this assistance is available on her request, she rarely asks for it. At age seventeen, she places a premium on independent functioning.

As her resource teacher, Mr. Stewart, reflected on Charlene's current levels of functioning in preparation for the annual review meeting, he made a number of observations. Although Charlene seems to want to act in an independent manner, she actually appears to depend heavily on her surrounding environment for cues to guide perceptual decision

making. She needs the reinforcement of having assignments, directions, and procedures written on the board. Often she will check and recheck the directions with a peer before proceeding. Without these guides, she loses confidence and spends extra time going back and checking and rechecking.

Charlene appears to think logically when presented with problem-solving situations, but she often requires the use of manipulatives and other concrete representations of the problem as an aid. With the use of manipulatives, she proceeds to draw her own conclusions. Recently, her American history class was discussing everyday life in the eighteenth century. It was not until her teacher brought in some actual examples of tools and clothing used during that time that she was able to understand the difficulty of life in that period.

Mr. Stewart believes that Charlene's problems in memory are related to her disability in attention. She appears to have difficulty focusing on relevant stimuli. She is easily distracted by irrelevant stimuli, such as people in the hall or candy on another student's desk. She seems unable to make the decisions needed to focus on the relevant features of a task or on the teacher's instructions. If, after a number of attempts and cues, she does focus her attention appropriately, she has trouble maintaining her attention for a sufficient period, despite being on medication for a number of years.

(continued)

Mr. Stewart has noted some factors that might be affecting Charlene's attention. First, the ADHD diagnosis suggests that problems with various attention tasks are to be expected. Next, it seems that the form of instruction and the tasks assigned by Charlene's teachers do not present strong attention signals. Charlene says that school is boring and that it is too hard to pay attention, an observation that appears related to the repetitious nature of the tasks and Charlene's perception of their lack of explicit value to her everyday life. This lack of attention is particularly evident in her academic classes, where instruction is primarily in the form of lectures that do not require much active student participation. Activities in the class continue, with or without Charlene's focusing on what the teacher is saying. Finally, throughout much of the day, Charlene is in a setting that is fairly unstructured in its demands on her, and Mr. Stewart notices that Charlene's attention lapses often go unnoticed and are not viewed as a problem.

If Charlene is able to focus her attention and remain focused, she appears to be able to transfer information effectively into her memory structure. In art and technical drawing classes, Charlene sees the information as interesting and valuable, and she uses appropriate means to store it in her long-term memory. Interestingly, however, her past annual reviews have noted problems in memory retrieval. In English and social studies, she appears to have difficulty dealing with the large amount of information she is asked to process at one time. She is unable to quickly make the connections needed to save the information, and it rapidly passes from her mind. She most often resorts to rote rehearsal as a memory strategy, a practice that seems to be inadequate in dealing with the large amounts of complex material in the eleventh grade curriculum. Lack of access to information in memory results in poor test scores and inadequate performance on other assignments.

Noting Charlene's dependence on rehearsal, Mr. Stewart suspects that this restricted repertoire of memory strategies is impeding learning. When Charlene uses rehearsal instead of other more appropriate memory strategies, her concept development is hindered and retrieval is compromised. Although Charlene is aware of other ways of dealing with memory tasks, she either fails to use them or uses them so inefficiently that she does not benefit from them.

Mr. Stewart has tried to help Charlene by prescribing particular study strategies as well as by monitoring her completion of tasks. At times, Mr. Stewart even completes portions of the assignment for Charlene, modeling the processes. He believes that this coaching will eventually help Charlene learn to apply these organizational and elaborative memory strategies herself. Mr. Stewart is surprised that Charlene still seems to distrust her own abilities and that she continues to look to her teachers for cues and information rather than beginning to depend on her own cognitive and organizational resources.

DISCUSSION

Review the above information about Charlene in the context of cognitive functioning. Specifically, what indications do you see about Charlene's functioning with regard to

- Level and process of cognitive development described by Piaget
- The process of cognitive development described by Vygotsky
- Field dependence and independence
- Impulsivity and reflectivity
- Structural cognitive components: sensory register, immediate memory (including working and short-term memories), and long-term memory
- Attention: alertness, selective attention, and sustained attention
- Perceptual abilities
- Memory strategies
- Executive control functions

JEANNE: A Case Study

Jeanne was referred for possible special education services at the end of first grade, and an evaluation was performed at the beginning of second grade, just after her eighth birthday. Jeanne was initially referred because of her poor reading skills and overall academic problems. In class she was easily distracted and had a short attention span. Her teacher described her as a daydreamer. Her performance was inconsistent from day to day and activity to activity, and she often failed to complete assignments. Jeanne was described as shy, affectionate, and sensitive by her teachers. She didn't seem to have much self-confidence. She seemed to see herself as inferior to other students. Math, however, was her strong point.

Her mother reported that Jeanne's was a normal pregnancy, and although she was born at seven months, there were no apparent difficulties resulting from her early arrival. Since birth, however, she has been hospitalized twenty-nine times for respiratory infections and other types of illness. She also had chicken pox and pneumonia, and once she fell and hit her head. After the fall, she was nauseous and said she "saw things." She had allergies, and displayed sensitivities to dust, pollen, milk, flour, and a number of other substances. Her overall health status was only fair. She was a picky eater and also borderline anemic. Her immune system in general did not work very well, and she was susceptible to any infection that came along. For these reasons, she missed a lot of school. She had already been retained once in the first grade because she was sick that year and missed too many days of school to be promoted.

When she was evaluated to determine the need for special education services, she achieved the following scores:

WISC-III

Full Scale IQ	106
Verbal IQ	114
Performance IQ	96

WISC-III Subtests:

Information	11
Similarities	14
Arithmetic	12
Vocabulary	12
Comprehension	13
Digit Span	12
Picture Completion	10
Picture Arrangement	15
Block Design	8
Object Assembly	9
Coding	6

Jeanne's WISC-III scores indicated that she had a significant discrepancy between her verbal and performance IQ scores, favoring her verbal skills. Her language skills were well developed for her age, but there was a lot of variation in the performance area.

Jeanne had a lot of difficulty with paper and pencil tasks, so her visual-motor skills were assessed further. The Bender Visual Motor Gestalt Test (BVMG) and the Goodenough-Harris Drawing Test revealed that her visual motor skills were similar to a child of six and a half, suggesting that she was performing below expectations in this area.

Next, Jeanne was given the Woodcock-Johnson Test of Achievement, which confirmed that her reading and written language were significantly below what would be expected of a child with Jeanne's general ability. Jeanne's skills in math, however, were appropriate for her ability, especially in the area of applications.

Woodcock-Johnson Tests of Achievement

	Standard Score	Percentile
Reading	85	17
Math	117	87
Written Language	89	23

Woodcock-Johnson Subtests

Letter-Word ID	78	7
Passage Completion	95	36
Calculation	101	54
Applied Problems	128	97
Dictation	87	19
Writing Samples	85	16

From this testing, the multidisciplinary team determined that Jeanne qualified for services as a student with learning disabilities. Although she had

(continued)

high-average verbal ability and her understanding and use of oral language were good, she had problems with tasks requiring perceptual-motor organization and coordination, such as copying and writing. The team decided that placement in the resource room for one period a day was the least restrictive environment for her to receive needed services.

Jeanne began coming to the resource room in second grade. Mrs. Brandon, the resource room teacher, worked with Jeanne on her reading and writing. She also focused on increasing Jeanne's self-esteem. Jeanne showed considerable improvement in reading, but writing was still a problem. She didn't like to write; it was hard for her to concentrate on writing tasks.

During that year, her health also improved. With improved attendance, Jeanne made more progress. She continued to come to the resource room for help in reading and writing at the beginning of third grade. After four weeks of third grade, she was doing very well in reading comprehension, and it was decided that she could be successful in the general education classroom. She would come to the resource room only for support services. During the year, she consistently made progress. She kept up with all of her classwork, making average to above-average grades.

Her writing showed some improvement as well. In the resource room, she and Mrs. Brandon worked on formation of her cursive letters and also on looking back at her own written work, doing self-evaluation to be sure that it was correct. Written language seemed to be "bothersome" for her, like it was something she didn't need to do.

Math was a high point, but she still found the process of going back and checking her work to be tedious and difficult. She understood complicated concepts on the first explanation. The only problem was that she continued to seem "defeated," to have a low level of self-esteem. Mrs. Brandon stated that she seemed to have "a chip on her shoulder."

Jeanne's progress was so pronounced in third grade that it was decided that she would be served in the itinerant level the next year—that is, that she would be monitored and assisted only on an as-needed basis.

DISCUSSION

In the context of the discussion of perception, review the information about Jeanne. What indications do you see from the data that Jeanne may have difficulties in perceptual processing? What specific modalities and skills seem to be impaired? Why might those problems interfere with academic learning?

- Can you hypothesize any causes for the problems?
- Why do you think Jeanne's remedial program appears to have been effective?
- Are there areas you feel still need to be addressed? Why?

CHAPTER ELEVEN

LANGUAGE CHARACTERISTICS

QUESTIONS TO GUIDE YOUR STUDY

- What is language?
- Describe the three components and five skills of language.
- What are some of the important skills involved in pragmatics, the functional use of language?
- What are the two processing channels used in communication? How do they operate?
- Describe the two receptive and the two expressive language functions.
- How do the three types of listening differ from one another?
- Why is it important to determine whether reading problems are related to decoding, to comprehension, or to both areas?
- Why is it important to determine whether problems in written expression are related to comprehensibility, to mechanics (grammar), or to both areas?
- What is the distinction between language differences and language disabilities? Of what importance is this distinction to educators, parents, and students?

Meet Tom

Tom was initially placed in special education at age six due to his difficulties in first grade reading and mathematics. Throughout his years in school, Tom has exhibited difficulties in cognitive processing and the use of language. This fall, at age fourteen, he began eighth grade in a class for students with learning disabilities.

Tom tries very hard to listen when spoken to, and he is usually described as being attentive by Ms. Allen, his teacher. He participates well in class discussions and often volunteers to answer questions. When he knows an answer, he responds confidently. When he is unsure of the answer, his response is generally a simple shrug. He seems to have a diffi-cult time expressing his uncertainty and difficulty saying, "I don't know." At times it seems to Ms. Allen that Tom's lack of response may be related to problems with retrieving information stored in his long-term memory.

Most of Tom's written work is understand-able. Although grammatical errors are common in his writing, the meaning of the written message is apparent most of the time. His spelling is generally phonetically correct, although vowel digraphs and other nonphonetic spelling patterns cause him diffi-culty. Tom takes pride in his very neat cursive pen-manship, voluntarily copying over work that he considers messy.

(continued)

While he is able in many cases to comprehend what he hears, his expressive and receptive skills in social environments often prove to be unreliable. As a young adolescent, these deficits in social communication are beginning to set him apart from his peers. Ms. Allen frequently notes his misreading of social cues and occurrences of inappropriate social behaviors in Tom's classroom and social activities. Messages conveyed by his nonverbal communication behaviors (e.g., facial expressions, body language) frequently do not match his verbalizations. He frequently moves in too close to the person with whom he is conversing, making casual conversation uncomfortable.

Tom tends to misinterpret what peers intend to communicate to him and others. Last week, he was observing two other students playing around in the classroom before school, calling each other names in jest. Tom joined in but was very puzzled when the other students reacted negatively. He couldn't understand why they were blaming him for what he saw as the same behavior in which they were engaging. He failed to take into account the effect of the existing relationship between the other two students, which formed a context for the teasing. Such occurrences are increasingly frequent, as Tom's lack of social language skills interferes with his ability to build normal adolescent relationships. He is mystified by his lack of success in this area. Ms. Allen is concerned that if this problem is not addressed, Tom's language difficulties will become compounded by isolation and rejection.

Definition of Language

Language is that peculiarly human behavior that involves the use of vocal sounds and, in many cultures, the corresponding written symbols to comprehend, form, and express thoughts and feelings. The term *language* is generally used to refer to any code employing signs, symbols, or gestures that human beings use to communicate ideas meaningfully (Bloom, 1988; Bloom & Lahey, 1978; Lahey, 1988; Wallace, Cohen, & Polloway, 1987). As Tom's story shows, it is also a social tool that is used to communicate meanings, feelings, and intentions by use of a system of symbols specifically designed to transmit and receive social messages. Language is an integral part of thought; it is not merely synonymous with or limited to oral expression.

Language competencies are critical to success as a learner (Bashir & Scavuzzo, 1992; Gersten, Brengelman, & Jiménez, 1994; Ripich & Spinelli, 1985; Schoenbrodt, Kumin, & Sloan, 1997). Educators and curriculum designers assume that learners will bring basic competencies in the understanding and use of language to learning events. Language is the vehicle by which content knowledge is presented and elaborated on. Success in learning will depend in large part on the student's ability to effectively and efficiently process information in lecture and textual formats. Language is also the means by which the individual becomes part of the social group. A student's ability to share a common language with teachers and other students will contribute to success in the learning environment. Finally, language is a tool for self-expression, a means by which a young person develops a sense of personal identity as an individual in society (Bashir & Scavuzzo, 1992).

The word *language* is used in this book as a collective noun, referring to all languages human beings use to communicate with one another. The reader should not equate "language" with "English." The concepts developed throughout this chapter can generally be applied to the functional capabilities of most language users, including those who communicate in English, in another language, or in a dialect or subcultural variant of English. As noted in the section on language differences later in this chapter, students who are learning English as a second language do present special concerns, and it is necessary to carefully evaluate the language use of such learners to determine whether their language competencies are being affected primarily by a language disability, a difference, or both (Gersten, Brengelman, & Jiménez, 1994).

Language Components and Skills

Language is generally regarded as having three components: form, content, and use (Bloom & Lahey, 1978; Johnson & Croasmun, 1991; Lahey, 1988; Wallace et al., 1987). Form is related to the rules by which a given communication system, or language, is governed; it is the "how" of language. Content refers to the "meaning" component; it is the "what" that we listen to, and read, talk, and write about. Use, the third component, is the reason, purpose, or "why" of language. Lahey (1988) describes the integration of these three components as knowledge of or competence in language. Bloom (1988) suggests that problems in language may be the result of (1) simple delay in development of language competence, (2) disruption in one or more of the three components of language, or (3) the failure to integrate the three components functionally.

Language is also conceptualized as being composed of five separate skills that are associated with the components of form, content, and use. Form includes phonology, morphology, and syntax; content generally relates to semantics; and use refers to pragmatics. Although there is obviously a relationship and interaction among these skills, there is no implied hierarchical nature to this structure. A skillful communicator will generally have equal facility in all five skill areas, although it is possible for a speaker or writer to have a deficit in one skill and still be able to function to some degree in the others. It is also not expected that the skills will be developed sequentially. Instead, in normal language development, growth in all skills generally occurs simultaneously, and all five skills must be integrated to produce functional language. One might also make the case that phonology, morphology, syntax, and semantics must all work together to support pragmatics, or functional language use (see Figure 11.1).

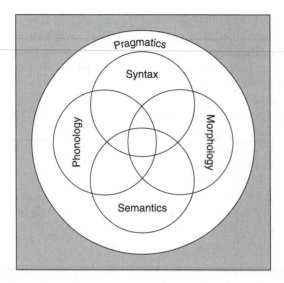

FIGURE 11.1   Functionalist Theory of Language Skills

From: R. E. Owens, Jr., *Language Disorders: A Functional Approach to Assessment and Intervention,* Third Edition, p. 8. Copyright © 1999 by Allyn & Bacon. Adapted and reprinted by permission.

In considering the language abilities of students with mild disabilities, one of the first areas that should be evaluated is their facility with the various language skills and components. Teachers and others should consider how strengths or deficits in any of these language skills may affect the overall functional use of language and, by extension, cognition. The centrality of language to human functioning implies that skill or lack of skill in any of the language components will have a significant effect on the individual's ability to function socially and cognitively. Language is frequently the most observable indicator of the more internal cognitive and perceptual skills discussed in Chapter 10. Deficits in any area of language may also make assessment of cognitive, perceptual, and social skills more difficult.

Phonology

Phonology is the study and use of the individual sound units in a language and the rules by which these units are combined and recombined to create larger language units. Language may be divided into segmental elements (letters, sounds, and syllables) and suprasegmental aspects, which are associated with stress, intonation, and pacing (Johnson & Croasmun, 1991). The smallest unit of sound in a particular language is called a *phoneme*. There are forty phonemes in English, each representing a separate and unique sound used in English speech. The symbols used to represent these sounds are called *phonograms* or *graphemes*. There are twenty-six phonograms or graphemes (letters) in the English language, which are combined and recombined to stand for the various phonemes, which in turn are combined in various ways to create English words.

Every language is composed of unique phonological characteristics, rules and principles the novice communicator must learn. By itself, a phoneme or phonogram has no meaning, but by using a variety of rules particular to the language, an individual can combine those sounds and letters to create words that do convey meaning. For example, in English the letters *p, h, o, n,* and *e* have no meaning in themselves, but we can use the rules governing English words to combine the *p* with the *h* to represent the *f* sound; we can attach the *e* to the end of a word with an *o* in it to represent the *long o* sound; and we can then combine all of these letter and sound units to spell *phone* to refer to the device for talking to distant friends.

Phonological (or phonemic) awareness is defined as the capability of analyzing and manipulating the components of a language without respect to meaning (Jerger, 1996; Torgeson, Morgan, & Rashotte, 1994). Typically, problems in the area of phonology will be evidenced by articulation problems in spoken language, by differences in voice, intonation, and fluency, by decoding deficits in reading, and/or by deficits in handwriting or spelling. The existence and extent of such deficits is most often investigated through careful analysis of spontaneous or prompted samples of language use, spoken or written. Analysis of such samples helps determine the degree to which speech or writing differs significantly from that of peers and the degree to which the communication calls attention to itself instead of to the message.

In addition to the concern about the effect of phonological deficits on oral language, researchers have studied the relationship between difficulty with phonological processing and success in early reading (see In the Classroom 11.1). A number of studies support the hypothesis that paying attention to development of a child's phonemic awareness, letter knowledge, and phonological decoding skills (speech-to-print matching, spelling, and word decoding) within reading-based activities is necessary to support the subsequent development of higher reading skills (Smith, C. R., 1998; Vandervelden & Siegel, 1997).

Morphology

Morphology is the study and use of morphemes, the smallest units of a language that have meaning. Morphemes are those units that cannot be further subdivided while still retaining meaning (Wallace et al., 1987). The morpheme must have a referent for which it clearly stands. In other words, the group of sounds must be recognized as referring to a particular object, action, or idea. For example, *cat* is widely understood to refer to a furry domestic pet that meows, and the pronoun *he* refers to a previously named male person or animal.

IN THE CLASSROOM **11.1**
Phonological Skills

Kathy seems to have problems with phonological processing needed for reading and spelling. She frequently cannot decode words she does not immediately recognize in her reading book, and therefore she cannot attach meaning to either the words or the sentence. When she comes to an unknown word, she appears to examine the letters and to begin to "sound it out," but then she abandons the attempt and guesses. When Kathy spells a word, she spells it as she hears it and says it, so "family" becomes "famly."

Jonathan began receiving speech/language services in kindergarten. Today, at age thirteen, his speech is still marked by misarticulations. He has particular difficulty with the letters *R* and *L,* so a phrase such as "Let me run" comes out as "Wet me wun." This makes him an easy target for classroom teasing, and he is often picked on by other students since his speech sounds "babyish." This juvenile speech is particularly incongruent coming from a boy of his physical size.

Morphemes consist of two types of letter combinations: free morphemes and bound morphemes. Free morphemes are words that can exist by themselves and still convey meaning; the collection of free morphemes constitutes the vocabulary used by an individual. Bound morphemes are units that have meaning but that cannot stand by themselves (e.g., prefixes and suffixes); a bound morpheme must be attached to a free morpheme to function fully. A word may consist of a free morpheme (e.g., "turn") or a combination of free and bound morphemes (e.g., "return" or "returning"). A teacher who investigates a learner's facility with vocabulary and inflected endings as compared with language-competent peers is concerned with this level of language. Students whose vocabulary is limited or inappropriate for the settings in which they must function can be viewed as having problems at the morphological level.

The development of children's vocabulary generally occurs in a reliable sequence (Garcia, 1994). Initially, the young child acquires single nouns and then verbs that have concrete objects or actions as referents. Throughout childhood, the youngster's vocabulary gradually expands to include words referring to more complex and abstract objects and actions. In addition, the limited meanings initially attributed to words within the child's vocabulary develop into richer and more inclusive understandings, including the multiple implications of many common words such as "mother" and "father." Finally, in later childhood and adolescence, most youngsters begin to appreciate the symbolic nature of words, moving more easily past literal interpretations of spoken and written discourse as needed.

For children experiencing difficulty in developing morphological competence, the most common problem is delayed or arrested development of their vocabulary and metalinguistic awareness (Johnson & Croasmun, 1991). Children with impairments in language are more likely to have trouble acquiring new words and maintaining them in their lexicon. Children whose vocabulary is restricted to very concrete words—who are unable to effectively comprehend language unless the explanations are made very concrete—are likely to encounter difficulty in academic classwork as well as in social interactions.

Development of facility with inflections (i.e., bound morphemes) appears to proceed in the same sequence for most children, but children with language impairments tend to develop these skills later and with more difficulty (Johnson & Croasmun, 1991). Such problems will also generally affect the student's syntactic competence as well (see In the Classroom 11.2).

Syntax

Syntax is the study of the rules by which morphemes are organized into phrases or sentences in a particular language (Chomsky, 1957; 1965). The relationships among morphemes are governed by a variety of syntactic rules. This is referred to as the grammar of the language, and it is specific to that particular language. Syntax also allows fuller expression of thoughts and ideas by making references to past and future events possible and by making complex relationships clear. When students use faulty syntax in their expressive functions of speaking or writing, meaning may be quickly obscured. Inability to use syntax as a context clue can impede progress in learning to read. Learners who fail to interpret the meanings imparted by syntactic placement of words in sentences they hear and read will be hindered in their effective use of language. Students who attempt to apply rules of syntax related to other cultural language systems to their study of a new language may also encounter difficulty communicating (see In the Classroom 11.3).

IN THE CLASSROOM **11.2**
Morphological Skills

Susan is a fourth grader with mild mental retardation. Her teacher has observed that Susan uses a very limited vocabulary. She is not exposed to a great deal of language at home, and this lack of vocabulary role models has apparently compounded her problems in school. Susan's vocabulary is functional enough to allow her to express her basic needs, but she seems to have too few words to allow her to explain fully and accurately how she is feeling or what problems she is facing. Most of the time she handles this deficit by keeping quiet.

Ivan's teacher has noted his limited vocabulary. He frequently describes objects in terms of their functions when he is unable to retrieve the words themselves. Yesterday, in a lesson about household objects, Ivan was asked to identify a picture of a light switch. He replied, "The thing that turns the light off." His limited vocabulary is hindering his performance in the general education classroom. Attempts at providing additional supports for learning (i.e., scaffolding) as he deals with the general education curriculum have not been successful in the past because his vocabulary delay is too large. He attends the classroom reading group for exposure to concepts and ideas and for group participation and discussion. His resource teacher has begun preteaching vocabulary in the resource room, a practice that has begun to show some positive effect in his performance in the third grade reading group.

IN THE CLASSROOM **11.3**
Syntactic Skills

Allen is ten years old and is being served in a resource program for students with learning disabilities. His oral language is often characterized by problems with standard English grammar. His oral syntactical errors are indicative of the immature grammar of younger children (e.g., "He don't have brown hair. . . . He runned down the street.") He also frequently makes errors with pronoun usage (e.g., "Me and Willie want to play football."). After talking with Allen's father, his teacher reports that she believes Allen's spoken grammar is a reflection of the language used in his home.

Tara is thirteen years old and placed in a resource program for students with mild disabilities. She exhibits a variety of problems with written language. Frequently, her attempts at written sentences include fragments or run-ons. She can identify nouns and verbs in grammar exercises, but she doesn't self-evaluate her written sentences to ensure that each is a complete and independent thought with a subject and a verb. Although she understands basic grammatical rules, she does not apply them independently. Capitalization and punctuation are erratic, although she can perfectly recite the rules for their use. Her teacher sees Tara as having deficits in language performance but not necessarily in competence (or knowledge) of language.

Semantics

Semantics is the larger meaning component of language. Language is more than a compilation of single words with direct referents. It consists of more complex language patterns such as phrases, sentences, and paragraphs, involving interactions among a number of words in a given context. Semantics refers to the meaning of the entire communication act. It involves the complex use and decoding of vocabulary, including processing with understanding such semantic structures as word categories, word relationships, synonyms, antonyms, figurative language, ambiguities, and absurdities. Often students appear to possess skills in the areas of phonology, morphology, and syntax but seem to have problems in the general comprehension of language. For some, it may be an issue of cognitive skill in processing language, while for others, it may be related to a lack of sufficient language experience to apply to the communication act (see In the Classroom 11.4).

Pragmatics

Pragmatics is the knowledge and ability to use language functionally in social or interactive situations. Pragmatics combines competence (or knowledge) with performance (or use). Many complex knowledges, skills, and abilities are required to become an effective user of language (Owens, 1999; Prutting, 1982; Prutting & Kirchner, 1987). Pragmatics integrates all the other levels of language, but it also involves the knowledge and use of the rules governing the use of language in context.

Language can be correct with respect to form and content and still not be adaptive for the individual, since the appropriateness of the communicative act depends on the context in which those linguistic structures and behaviors are applied. The contexts of language are complex, multidimensional, and ever-changing. Individuals must consider the contexts in which

---

IN THE CLASSROOM **11.4**

Semantic Skills

Marty, a fourth grader with a learning disability, seems to encounter difficulty in reading when he is asked to derive meaning from what he reads. He is so intent on decoding the words that he seems unable to attend to the meaning of the words or the sentences. Frequently, upon completing a sentence, he won't be able to tell his teacher what he has just read. He is even more frustrated by larger units of text such as paragraphs or stories, and he sees no benefit to developing his reading skills. Reading means nothing to him, and he has given up.

Kelly is ten years old and has mental retardation associated with Down syndrome. She has significant problems putting her thoughts and ideas into meaningful sentences, indicating problems with the semantic level of language. Her sentences are quite short, and she rarely develops a thought or a story beyond a single sentence. Subsequent sentences rarely relate in any way to the ones before. She does not understand the jokes told by her general education classmates. The play on words central to many jokes is lost on her.

linguistic interactions are occurring if they are to engage effectively in the functional use of language. They must consider the relevant conceptual and social knowledge, the previous and concurrent linguistic events, and any nonverbal behaviors involved in the interaction (Owens, 1999; Prutting, 1982). Pragmatics builds on the content of the communication, but it goes beyond the simple meanings of the words to consider the manner of communication and the ability of the individual to use social communication rules effectively and appropriately.

While the linguist sees language as a set of words and sentences following particular rules, the functionalist sees language as a vehicle of social competence. It is our knowledge of pragmatics that causes us to vary our speech and writing to fit particular situations. For this reason, the use of appropriate communication is often identified as the most significant indicator of social competence. One's social identity is often negatively affected by a pragmatic speech or language disorder. Students like Tom who fail to pick up social language skills, and who are not taught them by teachers or parents, are frequently excluded from the very social interactions that would help them become more skillful communicators and social beings. Students with disabilities who are placed in more restrictive school environments may lack exposure to and experience with classmates who use language more skillfully. This hinders their development of useful levels of pragmatic language and deprives them of the opportunities to practice pragmatic language skills in natural contexts.

Pragmatics is also the level of language that is least likely to be identified as an area of instruction or to be included as a part of the formal school curriculum or a student's IEP. It is, however, the area most likely to cause continuing problems for learners with mild disabilities, like Tom (Lapadat, 1991; Ripich & Spinelli, 1985). The assessment and intervention of students with mild disabilities should include evaluation of their pragmatic skills. If a learner is found to have deficits in this area, instructional activities should be designed to develop these skills, since they are so essential to functioning in the classroom and in the larger society (see In the Classroom 11.5).

Pragmatic Skills. In order to communicate effectively, people must be able to apply their understandings of the context of language along with their knowledge of a variety of linguistic and pragmatic skills. Linguistic skills include knowledge of phonologic, morphologic, syntactic, and semantic relationships that govern the language in use. Pragmatic skills apply to a variety of aspects of communication, including non-verbal as well as verbal behaviors (see Table 11.1).

Communication participants must be aware of the type of interactions being engaged in and then must be able to tailor their response to that analysis (Prutting & Kirchner, 1987). Some of the basic conversation patterns that a communicator may encounter include

- Directive/compliance: the communication of a personal need or imperative, responded to by an indication of compliance or noncompliance
- Query/response: questioning followed by a response or an indication of uncertainty
- Request/response: direct or implied requests followed by a response
- Comment/acknowledgment: a statement or description followed by a statement indicating that the information has been received and is being considered[1]

[1]Adapted from Prutting & Kirchner, 1987, pp. 118–119. Reprinted by permission of the American Speech-Language-Hearing Association.

IN THE CLASSROOM **11.5**

Pragmatic Skills

Yvonne, a seventh grader with a behavioral disorder, is inconsistent in her ability to communicate with others, a factor that affects her social standing in class. In addition to problems with grammar and semantics, she often interrupts her peers and behaves in inappropriate ways when her ideas are not accepted. She asks questions at inappropriate times and in inappropriate places. During science class last week, she raised her hand and asked what they were having for lunch. She rarely makes eye contact when she engages in a conversation. She glances briefly at the person she is talking to, then looks around the room while continuing to speak.

Terry, a fifth grader with ADHD and learning disabilities, uses correct grammar and has a good vocabulary, but he seems unable to express himself effectively in social situations. He enjoys talking to people and will easily begin a conversation, but unless he is relaxed and rested, his conversation is difficult to follow because he changes topics quickly and fails to use transitional expressions. He does not seem to know how to interpret environmental cues to determine whether it is a good or bad time to make a request or seek attention. When he is under stress, he frequently reverts to threats, crying, withdrawing, or other destructive behaviors.

TABLE 11.1   Pragmatic Skills for Communication

Verbal Aspects	
Skill	*Definition, Example*
Topic selection, introduction, maintenance, and change	Skills used to select topics relevant to the context, make relevant contributions to the topic, make smooth and respectful changes in topic, and end the discussion at an appropriate place
Initiation and response	Initiating and responding appropriately
Repair/revision	The ability to repair a conversation that has broken down and to ask for repair when ambiguity and misunderstandings occur
Pause time	Use of pauses that support the purpose of the conversation and are neither too short nor too long
Interruptions/overlap	Avoiding interruptions or talking at the same time as the communication partner unless necessary; using appropriate interruption behaviors if needed
Feedback to speaker	Listener use of verbal and nonverbal means to provide feedback to the speaker
Contingency	Use of responses that directly relate to partner's previous utterance
Quantity/conciseness	Speaking enough to address topic, but not too much

Nonverbal Aspects

Skill	Definition, Example
Physical proximity and contact	Distance between speakers and amount of physical contact appropriate to relationship and to the purpose of the communication; may be culturally determined
Body posture	Use of body posture that accomplishes purpose of communication (forward lean, etc.)
Foot/leg and hand/arm movements; gestures	Use of movements and gestures to complement verbal communication
Facial expression	Use of facial expressions to complement and encourage verbal communication
Gaze	Maintaining eye contact

Paralinguistic Aspects

Skill	Definition, Example
Intelligibility	Extent to which the utterance can be understood
Vocal intensity	Appropriate selection of vocal volume for the intended purpose
Fluency	Rhythm and flow of the speech
Prosody	Use of varying intonation and emphasis to match message

Adapted from Prutting & Kirchner, 1987, pp. 118–119. Reprinted by permission of the American Speech-Language-Hearing Association.

In each of these communication patterns, it is critical that the initiating act (directive, query, request, or comment) be clearly stated and be appropriate for the context. It is also incumbent on the listener to respond in an appropriate manner (e.g., to indicate whether a directive or request will be complied with and why). Frequently, students with mild disabilities will

- Initiate a conversation in an inappropriate context or manner
- Fail to modify their conversation to fit their relationship with the other person
- Fail to verbally respond to a directive or request in a socially acceptable manner.

Learners with mild disabilities also frequently display response deficits such as not responding at all, being compliant when that is not a useful response, or refusing to comply in a manner that is interpreted by others as being unreasonable or argumentative. Finally, problems can occur when the individual's response repertoire is so limited that there are few adaptive response options available (e.g., the toddler whose only response is a firm "no").

The "Cooperative Principle."   The communicative act is composed of the actions of at least two people reciprocally interacting as both receiver (listener or reader) and sender (speaker or writer). Conversation proceeds most effectively when there is a "cooperative principle" at work (Grice, 1989). This principle holds that the receiver expects the sender to be engaged in conveying a message that is appropriate to the context. Grice observed that conversation is appropriate when it is relevant, true, clear, and only as informative as is required in the situation. The receiver's knowledge of these characteristics and the expectation that they are indeed present provides the motivation to attempt to extract meaning from the message. Individuals whose communications do not follow these rules or who do not expect that the messages others send will adhere to this principle frequently miss the point of the interaction, making their functional use of language unreliable.

Societal Membership. Another concern related to the development of skill in pragmatic language relates to the role language plays in determining the extent to which the individual is accepted as a functioning member of a particular society. Ferguson (1994) asserted that:

> the purpose of all of our [language] interventions . . . is *to enable all students to actively participate in their communities so that others care enough about what happens to them to look for ways to include them as part of that community.* . . . Satisfying, active contributory membership depends upon fostering the kinds of interest, shared meaning, and relationships upon which socially meaningful communication must be based [emphasis in the original].[2]

The question that must be addressed by those who live and work with individuals with mild disabilities is the relationship and interaction between communicative skills and societal membership. As in the proverbial "chicken and egg" debate, it is important to consider the extent to which skill in social communication enhances the person's membership in a social group and the degree to which being considered a member of the group furthers communicative development. As Bruner (1990) wrote:

> When we enter human life, it is as if we walk on a stage into a play whose enactment is already in progress—a play whose somewhat open plot determines what parts we may play and toward what denouements we may be heading. Others on the stage already have a sense of what the play is about, enough to make negotiation with a newcomer possible.[3]

Teachers, parents, and friends all play a role in conferring membership on an individual, in initiating the new arrival into the community, and also in helping the person develop the social language necessary to participate in that community as a full member. An understanding of the individual's pragmatic language strengths and deficits can help parents, teachers, and friends determine effective ways to develop pragmatic competence.

---

[2]From "Is Communication Really the Point? Some Thoughts on Interventions and Membership" by D. L. Ferguson, 1994, *Mental Retardation, 32*(1), p. 10. Copyright © 1994 by American Association on Mental Retardation. Reprinted with permission.

[3]From *Acts of Meaning*, p. 34, by Jerome S. Bruner. Copyright © 1990 by the President and Fellows of Harvard College. Reprinted by permission of Harvard University Press.

Language Channels: Comprehension and Production

Language use is related to the two separate and complementary language channels of comprehension and production (Wallace et al., 1987). The comprehension channel, also referred to as "receptive language," is used to receive language communications from the environment. This channel functions as a decoder of symbolic information and makes use of the functions of listening and reading (see Figure 11.2).

The production channel, or "expressive language," is used to relay information about the individual's thoughts and feelings to others. This channel serves an encoding function, making accessible the content of a person's covert thinking processes (Wallace et al., 1987). The production channel makes use of the functions of speaking and writing and is illustrated in Figure 11.3.

Language Functions

Each of these communication channels is composed of two functions, one related to auditory/verbal processing, the other to visual/written functioning. As illustrated in Table 11.2, comprehension, or receptive functioning, is accomplished by listening and reading. Production, or expressive functioning, involves speaking and writing.

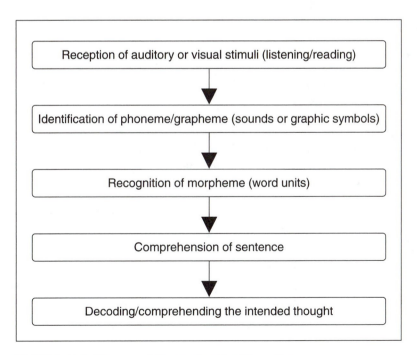

FIGURE 11.2 Process of Comprehension/Reception

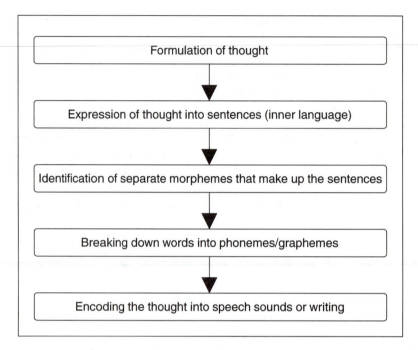

FIGURE 11.3   Process of Production/Expression

Listening

Listening is the receptive language process used to derive meaning from language received auditorily. Listening requires that the individual be able to attend to the message, select the main ideas, and then recall and relate the ideas to one another and to concepts stored in long-term memory. There are three different types of listening, each of which make varying demands on the cognitive functioning of the listener (Mercer, 1987): (1) appreciative listening for entertainment and enjoyment (e.g., listening to a music or a story), (2) attentive listening for the acquisition of information (e.g., listening to a lecture or to directions), and (3) critical or evaluative listening (e.g., listening to a debate or a campaign speech and judging whether the arguments are persuasive).

TABLE 11.2   Language Functions and Processing Channels

	Comprehension/ Reception	Production/ Expression
Auditory/Verbal	Listening	Speaking
Visual/Written	Reading	Writing

Problems that are commonly found among all learners with mild disabilities in the areas of attention and cognitive processing (refer to Chapter 10) frequently also interfere with their ability to perform many listening tasks effectively. Learners may be able to listen appreciatively and still experience difficulty with the more rigorous cognitive processing required for attentive and critical/evaluative listening, the very skills needed for school success (see In the Classroom 11.6).

Speaking

Speaking is the expressive language process used to encode thoughts so that they can be communicated orally to others. Speaking involves accurately making speech sounds (i.e., using correct articulation), speaking fluently, and using a quality of voice (e.g., loudness, pitch, etc.) that contributes to and does not obscure the message. Speaking also involves using adequate vocabulary, syntax, meaning, and social language skills that support the communicative purpose. A study of students with learning disabilities revealed that disabilities in spoken language are common: 23 percent had articulation disorders, 90 percent had language disorders, 1 percent had fluency disorders, and 12 percent had voice disorders (Gibbs & Cooper, 1989). Students with emotional disabilities often display difficulties with pragmatic or social speech, using inappropriate or ineffective means to convey their wants and needs, while children with mental retardation may exhibit speech patterns more common in younger children (see In the Classroom 11.7).

IN THE CLASSROOM **11.6**

Listening

Paul's most developed listening skill is in appreciative listening. He loves to listen to the radio or the television, activities where he does not feel the more intense pressure of attending that he feels in school tasks. He is working with his resource teacher on becoming more capable of attentive listening, however. At the beginning of the lesson, his teacher gives him questions to help him listen for the critical points during the class presentation. This helps him focus on the more relevant pieces of information. Even so, some days it is a real struggle for him to concentrate, and he requires extra coaxing to keep going.

Laurie is a kindergartner in a special class for children with language impairments. Listening, particularly attentive listening, is very difficult for her. She does not process verbal directions well and has to be reminded of where and when she should be somewhere. Each day, Laurie gets off the bus, enters school, and needs to be directed step-by-step through the process of hanging up her coat, storing her lunch, and entering the classroom. At this time, she seems incapable of processing more than one-step listening tasks. Ironically, she seems to be able to listen effectively to more heavily content-laden messages, such as a story or concept presentation. Her teacher is amazed that despite wiggling and failure to make eye contact, she can still answer questions about what was just presented.

IN THE CLASSROOM 11.7

Speaking

Jane is in an early intervention program and is classified as a preschool child with a disability. Her speech is somewhat unintelligible. The staff find they are able to decipher more of her communication when it deals with events in a strong context or with routine matters. When she arrives at school bursting with a new piece of information, the teachers put their heads together to figure out what she might be saying. Her mother and aunt frequently translate; they often know what she wants and needs when her teachers are baffled. Early in the year, staff members were astonished to hear her mother report on the tales Jane told at home about her day at school, since her speech in class sounds only like singsong humming. With the help of her speech teacher, Jane has progressed some during the year. She understands the syntactic meaning of verb tenses and plurals, but she uses these devices infrequently in her own speech. Her teacher is working on sentence repetition to give her practice in speaking in syntactically correct sentences.

Jeremy is eleven years old and in a program for students with emotional disorders. His teacher reports that Jeremy's speech is rapid and soft. He rarely talks in complete sentences, and when he does, he tends to speak in three-word units despite the phrasing needs of the sentence (e.g., "I dressed for—Halloween as a—Terminator"). At times, the teacher says, it seems as if he is saying other things to himself while he is speaking. She says that he frequently adds words or phrases that have nothing to do with what he is trying to tell her. She believes that Jeremy has a lot going on internally. He told her last week that aliens were calling him inside his head. She wonders how he manages to speak at all with such distractions.

Reading

Reading is the receptive language process that utilizes both visual and auditory abilities to derive meaning from the language symbols found in written text. It is an interactive process between the reader and the text for the purpose of deriving meaning. In order to read effectively and efficiently, the reader must be able to (1) decode the graphic symbols to determine their morphemic referents, (2) infer meaning from the combinations of words using syntactic and semantic clues, and (3) perform these decoding and inference functions fluently enough to make this a feasible way to get information. For instructional purposes, these skills are often broken down into two skill components: word recognition and comprehension. However, it is important to consider the whole reading act when evaluating a student's reading skills and problems. Focusing exclusively on techniques to teach phonetic decoding or word recognition may result in students' being able to decode the words accurately while still not achieving the primary purpose of reading, which is to derive meaning from text.

Students with learning disabilities frequently display specific disabilities in reading, and learners with mental retardation may exhibit significant lags in developing reading skills commensurate with their chronological age. In either case, a common remedial approach is to focus on assessing and then developing those beginning reading skills related to decoding and oral reading. The assumption is that these building blocks must be attained before higher level reading skills can be developed, leading to instructional practices that can result in youngsters' approaching middle school age still using first grade materials.

Teachers would be well advised to broaden their assessment of reading behaviors to include comprehension following silent reading as well as oral reading, and listening comprehension as well as reading comprehension. As is shown in In the Classroom 11.8, students are frequently capable of more complex comprehension skills beyond mere sound-symbol associations. An evaluation of the variety of ways in which students might process literary materials may reveal some strengths that can be used to accommodate deficits in word recognition. The key is to determine how students might be helped to see reading as a meaning-based interaction with text. Such a diagnostic profile can then be used to make more appropriate matches between the specific learner and instructional approaches for fostering literacy.

IN THE CLASSROOM **11.8**

Reading

Randy is a third grader with a learning disability whose reading ability is limited to simple words. He is able to read short stories in the pre-primers in his classroom, but he often does not seem to understand what he reads. He basically reads the words, one after the other, in isolation. He is unable to conceive of the meaning conveyed by words as a group. He does have some basic reading vocabulary, and given a strong enough context, he can sometimes figure out an unknown word. He understands initial phonemes and uses this skill to help him read.

Tilly is a ninth grader classified as having a language learning disability. Reading is very difficult for her. She has the ability to decode words, but she appears to derive little meaning from them. She reads aloud with considerable fluency, but when asked fairly straightforward literal comprehension questions after reading aloud, she is unable to provide answers. In particular, she is unable to identify the main idea of a passage with any accuracy.

George, although designated as a fifth grader, continued to experience significant difficulty with simple text reading. His resource teacher, Mr. Cohen, had been working with him with the pre-primer level of an alternative reading series for several months in an attempt to help George master the phonologic code with no significant progress. As the year progressed, George became more frustrated; his efforts were never sufficient. The pre-primer material was uninteresting and presented no cognitive challenge to George, who demonstrated that he possessed the ability to process information as well as his fifth grade peers. Finally, Mr. Cohen decided to make use of this disparity and develop some different approaches. He made audiotapes of books in the content areas of science and social studies available to George, as well as some age-appropriate fiction for more recreational reading. The content of these materials engaged George's mind; he was, for the first time, able to experience the cognitive outcomes of literacy activities. With this stronger meaning base, George began to read along with the tapes, which gradually improved his ability to deal with textual materials. Even more importantly, for the first time he viewed reading and writing as rewarding, engaging activities.

Writing

Writing is the process of encoding thought into graphemic symbols, or phonograms, so that communication can occur across time and space. To be effective, the writer must be able to write in an accurate mechanical form that does not detract from the communication. Written expression is composed of skills in handwriting, spelling, and composition. Handwriting problems are common among students with mild disabilities; their writing may be too slow to be usable or illegible due to difficulty coordinating motoric production with the visual perceptual skills needed for handwriting. Spelling requires the ability to turn phonemes into graphemes, using visual memory and/or auditory discrimination and association, skills that many children with learning disabilities and other mild disabilities find difficult, if not impossible. Written expression involves the use of the preceding skills as well as the ability to organize thoughts and to use vocabulary, syntax, and semantics to say what is desired or needed, and in a form that follows the mechanical conventions of the language.

Many students with mild disabilities seem to view writing activities as particularly threatening, possibly because writing results in a permanent record of their competence in language and content. This fear frequently results in attempts to avoid any participation in writing activities. When they do write, their work often displays problems in the following areas (Kameenui & Simmons, 1990):

- Lack of fluency (using too few words per sentence or too few sentences)
- Limited vocabulary and lack of diversity in the choice and use of words
- Problems with syntactic accuracy, including less complexity in sentence structures
- Problems with the mechanical conventions of English, such as spelling, capitalization, punctuation, handwriting, and appearance
- Less originality in content and organization of the written product than their typical peers

In addition, older students frequently lack the organizational strategies required for the more extensive written assignments given by secondary school teachers (Hallenbeck, 1996).

All these problems interfere with the writer's effectiveness in conveying the intended message to the reader. Problems in written expression can also lead a teacher or parent to significantly underestimate the degree to which the student has successfully mastered academic content and skills. Some of these deficiencies can be remediated or compensated for by the introduction of basic word processing tools to the learner. Word processing programs support the writer's proofreading skills by checking spelling and grammar. The burden of making editing changes is reduced, encouraging writers with disabilities to modify and improve the accuracy of their work. The final typed copy circumvents problems associated with illegible handwriting, producing a more polished paper. In evaluating a student's written expression abilities, a diagnostic trial with word processing software may provide useful information for planning interventions (see In the Classroom 11.9).

As with all language functions, written language includes components related to form, content, and use (function). When evaluating a learner's ability to communicate effectively in written form, it is helpful to be clear about which specific component is being affected by the disability. Issues of form involve the ability to use legible penmanship, to spell with reasonable accuracy, and to use appropriate syntax. Content is concerned with morphology and

IN THE CLASSROOM 11.9

Written Expression

Kim, a student with language learning disabilities, is generally able to complete written assignments in her fifth grade classroom fairly well. She generally writes with good meaning and grammar. Problems occur, however, when she begins to ramble, losing the focus on what she wanted to write about. When she goes off on a tangent, her grammar remains accurate but her ability to convey meaning is lost. Her teacher has provided Kim with some organizational aids such as "webs," "story grammars," and other outlining devices, which seem to be helping. Last week Kim wrote a story that won first prize in a classroom writing contest. Kim was very pleased with her success.

Jim is a middle school student with mild mental retardation. His teachers are very concerned about his writing ability. In preparing Jim for the state test in writing required of all eighth graders, his teacher analyzed a sample of his work to try to determine ways to help him. She noted that all of his errors were in the areas of syntax and spelling. She was able to understand his meaning, but she noted that he writes as little as possible and that his main ideas lack development. She finds that if she asks him questions about his writing to get more detail, she can sometimes get him to expand on his first effort. His problems in grammar and punctuation continue to cause serious problems. His teacher plans to introduce him to basic word processing as the next step.

semantics, which are also affected by organizational strategies. In the category of use, the question is whether the student can use written language to achieve specific purposes, particularly in functional/social written language such as applications and letters.

Giordano (1984) developed a framework for analyzing student writing that may be useful in describing a student's needs more accurately so that an appropriate developmental or remedial program can be designed. He suggested that teachers evaluate each of the errors a child makes by using the dimensions of grammar and comprehensibility. For each error, one needs to ask:

- Is the error grammatically correct?
- Is the meaning comprehensible despite the error?

With the construction of an "error plot" (see Figure 11.4), it is possible to determine the predominant pattern of errors and use that information to plan interventions.

According to Giordano (1984), errors in quadrant I might include problems in handwriting or spelling errors that do not obscure the meaning. Quadrant II errors may indicate a writing disability but also may indicate the effect of earlier instruction that resulted in too much attention to grammar instruction and editing at the expense of meaning. Quadrant III errors usually indicate significant writing disability. Quadrant IV errors may be due to inadequate grammatical instruction or may possibly reflect the influence of a nonstandard dialect or a primary language other than English. (Figure 11.5 presents a sample of writing.)

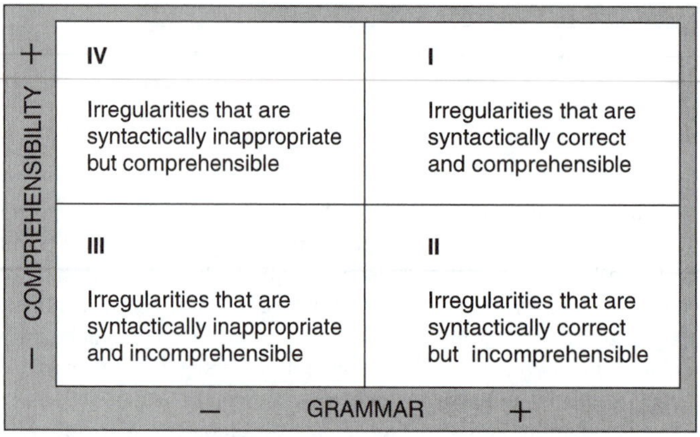

	IV	I
+	Irregularities that are syntactically inappropriate but comprehensible	Irregularities that are syntactically correct and comprehensible
COMPREHENSIBILITY	III	II
−	Irregularities that are syntactically inappropriate and incomprehensible	Irregularities that are syntactically correct but incomprehensible
	− GRAMMAR +	

FIGURE 11.4   Framework for Analysis of Writing Errors

From "Analyzing and Remediating Writing Disabilities" by G. Giordano, 1984, *Journal of Learning Disabilities, 17*, p. 79. Copyright © 1984 by PRO-ED, Inc. Reprinted by permission.

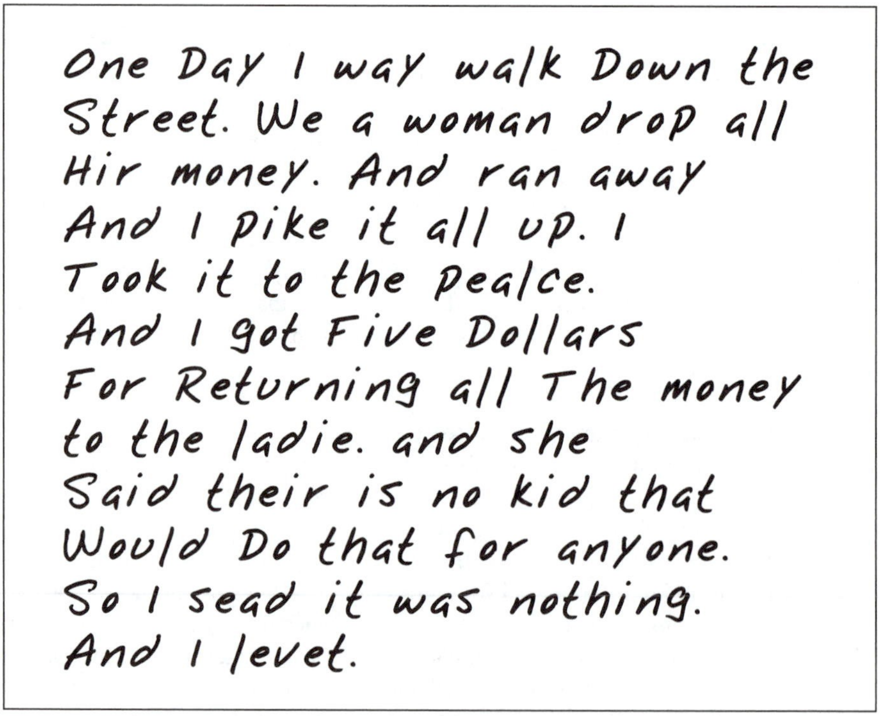

> One Day I way walk Down the
> Street. We a woman drop all
> Hir money. And ran away
> And I pike it all up. I
> Took it to the pealce.
> And I got Five Dollars
> For Returning all The money
> to the ladie. and she
> Said their is no kid that
> Would Do that for anyone.
> So I sead it was nothing.
> And I levet.

FIGURE 11.5   Writing Sample for Analysis: Todd, Age Eleven

Common Language Characteristics of Learners with Mild Disabilities

The language capabilities of learners with mild disabilities are frequently affected in some way by their particular disability. As a group, learners with mild disabilities frequently experience some degree of difficulty in communication, regardless of their diagnostic category (Owens, 1999; Stone & Reid, 1994). These language difficulties further impair their ability to learn and to perform age-appropriate tasks. The significant linguistic demands posed by the instructional practices used by teachers in scaffolding and designing remedial activities may cause even more difficulties for the learner. Multiple and varied words and sentence patterns are often used as a tutor tries to help a student develop a skill or concept, reexplaining the concept multiple times, using different words each time. Such practices increase the processing load the student must handle (Lavoie, 1989). The success of these multiple verbal explanations and interactions depends, however, on the ability of the student to identify the referents of the words used and to interpret the syntactic and semantic structures. These are the very tasks that may prove daunting to learners with language deficits.

Students with mild disabilities may display a variety of characteristics that indicate that the development of language has been impaired in some way (Ripich & Spinelli, 1985). It is important to note, however, that the specific characteristics of an individual learner must be considered when designing effective language learning programs and that, as with Tom, there are potentially an infinite number of combinations of strengths and problems that contribute to the language skill or lack of skill in a specific individual (Calculator, 1985). Individuals may exhibit some of the following problems:

- Difficulty in auditory reception and perception
- Difficulty with verbal expression
- Difficulty with word retrieval in spoken language
- Problems in social conversation
- Incomplete sentences or thoughts
- Difficulty comprehending what has been read
- Difficulty in written expression.

As a group, children with mental retardation tend to develop language more slowly than their typical peers (Pruess, Vadasy, & Fewell, 1987). The delays appear to include delays in understanding as well as in using language, with more delay at the more severe levels of retardation. One hypothesis suggested to explain these delays relates to the inefficiency with which these children make use of incidental learning opportunities critical to early language development. Another explanation relates to insufficient interaction with other children who are more skilled in language use, a situation that may be exacerbated by the use of more segregated educational services and the lack of friends without language disabilities. As the child with mental retardation grows older, a qualitative difference in the speech patterns is frequently evidenced in addition to the rate difference (Owens, 1999). These youngsters are frequently less effective in social communication, a fact that may be attributable to a lack of social language experiences or a lack of skill.

Children with emotional or behavioral disorders are also more likely to display problems in communication than their more socially skilled peers, and those with communication disorders are more likely to display emotional or behavioral disorders (Ruhl, Hughes, & Camarata, 1992). They may possess age-appropriate language skills at the phonemic and morphemic levels but still display difficulties with syntax, semantics, and/or pragmatics. Students exhibiting problems with expressive language encounter more difficulty expressing ideas, feelings, concerns, and needs, and they appear to be at greater risk of developing emotional or behavioral disorders than those with speech disorders involving articulation. The oral language of students with conduct disorders may be laced with profanity and with argumentative and hostile expressions. Their problems frequently include difficulties with inappropriate content and use rather than with the form of language. Students with anxiety, withdrawal, or immaturity disorders may exhibit difficulty with expression of feelings and needs. Youngsters with emotional or behavioral disorders also frequently have difficulty using socially skilled language to express their wants and needs.

Students with learning disabilities, by definition, exhibit problems in the understanding or use of language, spoken or written (see Chapter 7). They frequently display a wide variety of problems with receptive and/or expressive language as well as with the integrative thought functions of inner language. Deficiencies in cognitive processing can result in difficulties with word retrieval in oral language, as well as inefficiency in decoding the messages presented by the speech of others. These students present uneven language abilities in both school and social settings; the exact nature of difficulties depends on the nature and severity of their learning disability (Candler & Hildreth, 1990; Schoenbrodt, Kumin, & Sloan, 1997).

Frequently, youngsters with learning disabilities are also seen as less effective in social communication. Due to their deficits in processing syntactic and semantic cues, these students may miss the subtle meaning of communication acts employing such devices as jokes, idioms, and sarcasm. They may lack the ability to understand and effectively use the rules of social language, such as turn-taking and topic maintenance. In a meta-analysis of studies of the pragmatic abilities of students with learning disabilities, Lapadat (1991) found that students with learning disabilities displayed more consistent and pervasive difficulty in this area than their peers without disabilities. In particular, young people with learning disabilities exhibit more problems in the following:

■ Overuse of nonspecific referents in conversation, leading to ambiguity
■ Word choices that do not enhance understanding
■ Frequent instances of unrelatedness and lack of cohesion in social discourse
■ Lack of skill in the various speech acts
■ Restricted use of the diversity of speech acts
■ Inability to consider their verbal interactions from the partner's perspective.

Furthermore, due to repeated difficulties in social language situations, these learners may gradually develop a communicative role that is predominantly passive and underresponsive.

Although there are few studies of communication skills in youngsters with ADHD, the specific deficits in attention displayed by learners with attention-deficit/hyperactivity disorders may inhibit their ability to concentrate on the relevant features of a conversation and result in their making off-topic contributions that are interpreted by peers as "weird." Their language learning may be delayed by problems in attending to environmental stimuli consistently enough to learn the language rules of their culture. In cases where a learning disability is also determined to be present, language difficulties are likely to be similar to those with learning disabilities alone (Javorsky, 1996).

In looking at the effect of an individual child's disability on use of language, a variety of functional characteristics may be found to be contributing factors. It is unlikely that any two students will have the same problems; even those who have similar deficits in a given area will be found to vary in the severity of those difficulties (Calculator, 1985).

Language Difference or Disability?

A final concern in the area of language development and linguistic characteristics occurs when we ask the question, "Is Juan's difficulty in using and understanding language caused by a deficit in his ability to process linguistic information, or is his use of English affected by his background using a different primary language?" Increasingly, schools in many parts of the country are finding that newly admitted students use languages other than English as their primary means of communication and that their skill in using English for learning is minimal or nonexistent. Teachers are also increasingly recognizing that students who are experiencing difficulty in speaking, reading, listening, and writing are students whose primary language is actually a dialect or cultural variant of *standard English,* that version of English that is used most widely in public oral and written discourse (Garcia, 1994). Since standard English is the language system used in schools as the primary medium of instruction, each of these groups of children is likely to encounter some level of difficulty dealing with the school curriculum and with interacting effectively with other students and staff.

In the past, such children were automatically placed in general education classrooms until their failures caused them to be referred for possible special education classification. Once referred, they would likely have been assessed using standard-English-based instruments. This occurred even though the IDEA and various court decisions have held that students with limited English proficiency must be assessed in their primary language (e.g., *Diana* v. *State Board of Education,* 1970; *Jose P.* v. *Ambach,* 1979); the courts also ruled that evaluations must use instruments that are culturally appropriate and do not result in disproportional placements of children from minority cultural groups in special education (e.g., *Larry P.* v. *Riles,* 1979, 1984). Once placed in special education, such children were frequently not provided with a program that was appropriate to their needs. English-based special education programs frequently did not sufficiently accommodate the special characteristics of students who were learning English as a second language and who had differing cultural and linguistic backgrounds.

Today the scenario might be somewhat different, particularly in larger cities with a significant number of students who are learning English as a second language. In addition to special education services for children found to have disabilities, some schools and districts have established alternative programs to help students with language-different backgrounds learn to function within an English environment as well. The two approaches include (1) bilingual education programs, which provide content instruction in English and in the target language (e.g., Spanish and English instruction for Spanish-speaking youngsters) and (2) English as a Second Language (ESL) programs designed to teach standard

English to students who are learning English as a second language as quickly and appropriately as possible so that students can participate fully in content classes in English. Students who are learning English as a second language entering school may now be automatically assigned to such programs based on the assumption that children with different language backgrounds need only to be taught English and that they are by definition not in need of special education services.

The irony, of course, is that the automatic use of either of these placement procedures (special education, or bilingual education/ESL) is likely to result in programming errors if applied across the board without regard to the educational and developmental needs of each child (Gersten, Brengelman, & Jiménez, 1994; Ortiz, 1997). In some cases, children are hindered in learning and using standard English only because they learned language in a non-English environment or within a different cultural environment. Their skill in understanding and using their primary language or a cultural variant of English is an indicator of an intact ability to learn language. Their needs are predominantly related to the need to learn the new language code we call standard English while maintaining proficiency in their primary language. These children have a *language difference.*

Other learners have language disabilities that are related to a primary disability such as mental retardation, learning disabilities, ADHD, or emotional or behavioral disorders. Their difficulties in developing, understanding, and using language exist in their primary language system as well as in English (Ortiz, 1997). The challenges of functioning in an English-speaking environment may result in a lesser level of competence in English than they currently display in their primary language systems, but there is evidence of impaired language learning in all communication systems. These students have *language disabilities* in addition to language differences.

To illustrate the implications of the interaction of a disability with language learning: Many students with learning disabilities whose primary language is standard English find that, with support, they are able to cope with many of the demands of the high school and postsecondary curricula with the exception of learning a second language. One of the most frequently sought curricular waivers is exemption from second language study. While students with learning disabilities might well be able to function in the United States without mastering Spanish or French, the situation would be quite different if they suddenly found themselves living in a country where Spanish or French is the main vehicle for communication. Learning the second language would then not be optional, it would be a necessity, and it would be very difficult. Their language disability would likely impair their learning of the second language, and they would require specialized teaching methods to be successful.

This is the situation faced today by those students in bilingual or ESL programs who also have disabilities affecting language learning in general. The disability compounds the task of learning the new language. These students frequently have not learned their primary language well enough or have not reached the stage of learning the written form of that language, and these gaps make new language learning more difficult (Poplin & Phillips, 1993). These students are best viewed as having a language disability, not simply because they have lack of skill in using English but because they have some level of difficulty in the use of language in general.

Distinguishing between students who have language disabilities and language differences, or who have a combination of both, is not always an easy task. However, in order to match each student with the most appropriate developmental and support program, it is essential to make the attempt (Gersten, Brengelman, & Jiménez, 1994; Poplin & Phillips, 1993). Evaluation of language learning in children whose primary language is other than English or who use a variant form of English, such as the dialects found in Hawaii, African American communities, and the rural South, should include consideration of the degree to which the student has been successful in that primary language system as an important diagnostic indicator. This assessment requires attention to the phonologic, morphologic, syntactic, semantic, and pragmatic aspects of the first language. One must ask if the student's vocabulary is age-appropriate in size and in complexity; if the child uses the syntactical rules appropriate to that primary language; and if the child uses language functionally, following the culture-specific rules for pragmatic discourse, such as eye contact, turn-taking, and so on. School personnel cannot generally make accurate assessments of a student's level of skill in language learning without seeking the assistance of persons familiar with the language used by the child.

Gazaway's work (1969) with the adults and children living in Duddie's Branch (see Chapter 6) illustrates this principle well. By outsider standards, the language used by the residents of that isolated community appeared deficient. As Gazaway spent more time in the community, she became an insider, able to appreciate the functionality of the language usage. She became able to judge individual's level of competence more realistically, not in comparison to the outside but by the standards of that community. These children would indeed have been at a disadvantage outside of their hollow; they would have required assistance in learning the vocabulary and syntax of standard English. Some of them would have been able to learn that new language system and thus could be viewed as being affected by language differences. Others undoubtedly would have found the task daunting, possibly because they were also eligible for classification as children with mental retardation or learning disabilities. They would be more correctly viewed as having a language disability in addition to their use of a language other than standard English (see In the Classroom 11.10).

Complex issues are involved in assessing and serving the needs of (1) students whose primary language is not English, (2) students who use a dialectical variant of English, and (3) students who have developed oral competencies in their primary languages but have not progressed to learning the written form before beginning the study of a second language. Finding answers for individual learners based on their needs, their stages of development, and the nature of their primary language or dialect is critical for their success. In part, those answers will depend on our ability to separate disability from difference, to treat each appropriately, and to recognize when both conditions coexist within a single learner. Educators interested in continuing their study in this area could begin with the work of Poplin and Phillips (1993), Gersten, Brengelman, & Jiménez (1994), and Garcia (1994) and should keep up with the developing work in this field.

Implications of Language Characteristics for Thinking and Learning

To conclude this discussion of language, the skills by which we communicate with others, it may be useful to return to the discussion of cognition from Chapter 10. In using language symbols, human beings have a powerful tool for communicating the results of their cognitive

IN THE CLASSROOM **11.10**
Language Difference, Language Disability, or Both?

Meet David

David is a third grader in a school that serves elementary students from his Native American reservation. His family uses both English and their native language in the home. When he began his formal education in the prekindergarten class, he was referred for evaluation because of his language difficulties, particularly in the articulation of English sounds, and he began receiving daily speech services.

By second grade, his teacher voiced additional concerns. David was having trouble with memory tasks in mathematics as well as difficulty in the reading curriculum with word recognition and sight word vocabulary. She found that unless concepts were taught and retaught numerous times, he did not retain them. She also stated that David was not one to volunteer information and that unless she prompted more complete expressions, he continued to communicate mainly in single words or phrases. His speech teacher noted some speech improvement but also observed that he continued to lag behind in vocabulary development as well as in attentive listening and in reasoning in a language medium. At the end of the year, the multidisciplinary team determined that David now met the criteria for services under the learning disability classification.

His new teacher in third grade has voiced the opinion that the phonetic approach to reading does not seem to be effective with David and has proposed a trial with a meaning-based whole language approach. Mr. Johnson notes that David loves to draw and wonders if combining his drawings with stories may help him develop a sense of what reading is all about. Ironically, no one seems to have considered the possibility that some of these observed problems might be attributable to the interaction of his native culture and language with the mainstream culture of the school. No one has addressed the differences in these two languages and cultures or discussed the possibility that David might be struggling with reconciling these two linguistic and cultural paradigms.

Meet Tony

Tony was born in the Caribbean and moved to New York City as a toddler. His parents speak only Spanish, and Tony had no English skills when he entered first grade. Throughout elementary school, he learned a little English, and although his oral Spanish is fluent, he has not learned to read in either language above a very basic level. A bout with serious levels of lead poisoning and life with an alcoholic, abusive father led to his deriving little benefit from elementary school. Pushed from grade to grade, he was finally classified as having a learning disability at age thirteen. His adolescence was marked by time spent in a juvenile facility, traumatic times at home, where he and his father became violent with one another, and eventual placement in a state correctional facility for armed robbery at age eighteen. While in prison, Tony has been enrolled in adult basic education classes because of his low level of English literacy.

Tony told his new teacher at the prison that the little English he knows he has learned since coming there. His spoken Spanish is much more fluent, and he uses it whenever he can. However, he was never given the opportunity to learn to read and write in his primary language, so he has to get the help of a friend when he writes letters home to his mother and girlfriend, who speak only Spanish. When he wants to share something with his teacher, he often must use the teaching assistant as a translator.

When Tony tries to communicate in English, his syntax is often more similar to Spanish, with the adjectives following the verbs. His auditory perceptual skills are better in Spanish than in English. He has difficulty processing his teacher's English directions, and again the teaching assistant is pressed into service to translate. His oral and written English competencies are poor, as are his reading and writing in Spanish. He explains that he hears the English, tries to translate it into Spanish, and then responds in the language that seems most accessible at the time.

Mr. Samuels, Tony's teacher, reports that his classroom behavior is very cooperative, and his pragmatic skills seem functional. However, when he is with Spanish-speaking peers during meals and recreation periods, he frequently becomes loud and hostile. He speaks only in Spanish and seems to lose the social behaviors he demonstrates in the controlled classroom setting, reverting to the street culture of his youth. He frequently compounds his problems by challenging security personnel.

When his teacher asks Tony what he wants out of life, he says that he wants to learn to speak, read, and write both English and Spanish and to get his GED. He wants a better life than he had in his home, and he wants to be happy. Mr. Samuels wonders what the likelihood of these things occurring can be, when Tony's problems with language seem to have been overlooked for so long. He is uncertain about the extent to which Tony's problems are a result of language disabilities attributable to his history of lead poisoning and domestic abuse or whether they are due primarily to language differences—or both. Mr. Samuels realizes that Tony has not learned either Spanish or English well enough to use them in the world of adult work, and he wonders if it is too late for Tony to develop these skills.

---

processing of information to others. We can receive interpretable information from our environment, and we have tools for responding to those outside ourselves. Clearly, any condition that disrupts the cognitive processing of information or the use of that information through communicative acts will impede the process of development and learning. Using the frameworks developed in this chapter, educators will find it useful to analyze the language capabilities and disabilities of their students as clues to more fundamental aspects of cognitive functioning and then to use that information to develop effective interventions and learning environments.

Focus on Culture and Diversity

Title VII of the Improving America's Schools Act of 1994 defined students with limited English proficiency (LEP) as those who have "sufficient difficulty speaking, reading, writing, or understanding the English language and whose difficulties may deny [them] the opportunity to learn successfully in classrooms where the language of instruction is English" (U.S. Department of Education, 2001, p. II-31). IDEA 1997 directly addressed this issue when it required that assessments be conducted in the child's primary language and that students should not be identified as having a disability if their difficulties were primarily related to their limited English proficiency. While the goal of this requirement is to help halt inappropriate placements, it does not address the academic and language learning difficulties faced by these students.

According to data cited by the U.S. Department of Education (2001), students with LEP account for about 3.5 million students (7.9 percent) and that close to 6 percent of all students with disabilities are also in need of services for limited English proficiency. Spanish is the primary language for 73 percent, with an additional 10.6 percent speaking a variety of Asian languages (e.g., Vietnamese, Hmong, Cantonese, Cambodian, and Korean). That leaves 16.4 percent speaking one of the hundreds of other possible languages. These students also tend to come from poorer families, and their achievement is on average lower than that of their English-speaking peers. The dropout rate among students with LEP has historically been higher than for speakers of English, indicating that these students are not receiving educational services appropriate to their needs.

Complicating this issue is the fact that students with LEP may differ from native English speakers culturally and socially as well as linguistically and that all three factors can impact the disability assessment process (U.S. Department of Education, 2001). Students with LEP may be referred by teachers who are poorly prepared to provide the needed language instruction and who believe that special educators can provide the support services required for these learners to become successful in school. Compounding the problem is that evaluations using tests normed on White, middle-class, native English speakers, even when they are translated into the child's primary language, are not able to accurately identify the nature of the problems faced by the student with LEP. Educators need to understand that evaluation of students and program planning for students with LEP require cultural and linguistic sensitivity to allow them to distinguish between language disabilities and language differences. Then educators must design appropriate interventions that accommodate all of the learner's needs.

Resources on the Web

American Speech-Language-Hearing Association

www.asha.org

> Resources related to disabilities in communication and hearing; also provides referral information.

National Association for Bilingual Education (NABE)

www.nabe.org

> Discusses a variety of advocacy issues related to bilingual education for learners with limited English proficiency.

Center for Applied Linguistics

www.cal.org

> Provides resources concerning the education of English language learners, including information about both ESL (English as a Second Language) and bilingual education.

ERIC Clearinghouse on Languages and Linguistics

www.cal.org/ericcll

> Provides a searchable database on topics related to language and language learning.

Teachers of English to Speakers of Other Languages (TESOL)

www.tesol.org

> Provides resources for professional TESOL educators.

Summary

Language is that uniquely human behavior involving the use of a symbol system for the communication of ideas and feelings between human beings. The study of language may be subdivided into three components: form (phonology and syntax), meaning (morphology and semantics), and use (pragmatics). Development proceeds simultaneously on all of these skills, and deficits in any area(s) will generally impact overall functioning.

Pragmatics is the area of language that is most likely to be overlooked in assessing language skills, and it is the skill least likely to be included as a part of formal school curricula. Communication achieves its purpose when the message is effectively sent and interpreted. The communicator's ability to use a number of pragmatic skills will determine that effectiveness. The degree to which individuals can use appropriate pragmatic skills will often determine the extent to which they will be included as "members" of a group or society.

Language utilizes two separate but complementary channels. Comprehension (listening and reading) relates to the understanding of communication messages. Production (speaking and writing) refers to the skills needed to send messages to others.

Listening is actually a hierarchy of behaviors. Depending on the purpose for the listening, individuals utilize appreciative listening, attentive listening, and/or critical listening. Reading is the receptive language function that uses visual and auditory abilities to derive meaning from text materials. Readers must be able to decode word units, infer meaning from the sentences, and do so with sufficient fluency.

Speaking is the process used to encode our thoughts into sound units so that we can communicate orally with others. Writing is the vehicle for communicating expressively in a permanent form using written symbols and written syntax. Handwriting and spelling are tool skills used in writing to help reliably transmit the intended message. Composition deals with the meaning component of written expression.

Learners with mild disabilities frequently exhibit difficulties with language, and this difficulty impacts their ability to learn. Intensive use of language as the vehicle for instruction in special education classes may further complicate learning for these students. No two students will present the same profile of abilities and deficits, but it is appropriate to assume that language difficulties may play a role in the youngster's ability to learn effectively.

One further question that must be addressed is the extent to which a learner's problems are due to language differences or language disabilities or some combination of both. Learners affected by language differences are those whose primary language is a language or dialect other than standard English and whose functioning in English is affected by that fact. Learners with language disabilities are those who have a condition that affects their ability to process linguistic information either in one language or in two languages.

CLARK: A Case Study

Clark is fifteen years old and has just completed the ninth grade at his local public high school. Clark lives with his parents and has an older sister. The family lived in Delaware and New York before moving to their current home in Ohio four years ago.

(continued)

Clark has always had good physical health. His only significant health-related problems have been persistent allergies, making him prone to sinus and ear infections. He has never presented any serious behavior problems. He has had some difficulty relating to peers over the years and often tends to be isolated. His oral language is somewhat awkward, and he lacks the skills for natural adolescent banter. At times, he is teased and picked on, but he tends to accept this treatment with resignation. Clark enjoys spending his time reading, working on his computer, and watching TV, all solitary pursuits. He also enjoys basketball but does not get to play much because of a lack of close friendships and a cohesive peer group.

Clark was slow to develop language skills and received speech therapy from age five to twelve. His spoken language remains somewhat deliberate and labored. His handwriting is still poor, often illegible. His written compositions are not structured or organized well. Although Clark has a history of expressive language difficulties, he is currently being served in the gifted program at his school due to his strengths in math and science. In seventh grade, he qualified for participation in the Creative and Talented Youth (CTY) program by scoring 1050 on the SAT examination. This past summer, he participated in the CTY program for three weeks.

Clark gets As and Bs in his classes. He is generally stronger in mathematics-related subjects and struggles in English classes. His written language is plagued by problems with handwriting (nearly illegible); he knows how to use a word processor, but his English teacher is reluctant to let him use it for routine assignments, asserting that he needs to develop his handwriting skills. His spelling, vocabulary, and intellectual functioning are appropriate for his grade, although his handwriting often makes it seem as if he has deficits in these areas. Written syntax is very problematic. His sentences frequently include problems with verb tenses and subject-verb agreement, as well as pronoun referent mismatches and inaccurate use of homophones. His written sentences tend to be short and choppy. His oral speech reflects use of more complex language, and he is able to process very sophisticated language structures in listening and reading.

Clark has problems with the organization of most written assignments, from paragraphs needed for short essay responses on tests to longer compositions and papers. His written work rambles, failing to reflect the complex thinking and reasoning he is clearly capable of. After several attempts with private tutoring in writing failed to improve Clark's writing ability, he and his parents sought an independent educational evaluation. The following testing was conducted to assist in determining Clark's current personal and academic capabilities and needs.

Assessment Results

Intellectual Functioning.   Clark attained the following scores on the Wechsler Intelligence Scale for Children-III (WISC-III):

Full IQ	119	(90 percentile)
Verbal IQ	113	(81 percentile)
Performance IQ	121	(92 percentile)

Although Clark is functioning at the top of the above average range of intelligence, he does show considerable variability among his scores on various mental functions. He is extremely adept at performing rapid hand-eye coordination movements, he displays an excellent capacity for exercising clear and logical judgments, and he has a well-developed fund of general information. His poorest score occurred on a task dependent on auditory learning and spoken response (digit span).

Verbal Subtests		*Performance Subtests*	
Information	13	Picture Completion	12
Similarities	10	Picture Arrangement	11
Arithmetic	11	Block Design	12
Vocabulary	12	Object Assembly	12
Comprehension	15	Coding	18
Digit Span	9		

Academic Achievement.   Achievement testing indicated that Clark is functioning at or above his peers in reading comprehension, spelling, and mathematics. On the Woodcock Reading Test (Passage Comprehension Subtest), Clark displayed accelerated abilities. He comprehends written material well beyond his peers (92 percentile). Consistent with Clark's long-standing difficulties in expressive language, his reading decoding score indicates abilities that lag mildly behind his actual grade placement.

On the Test of Adolescent and Adult Language (TOAL), Clark attained a language quotient of 108, which is in the high average range. However, his scores on the various subtests varied considerably. He attained the following subtest scores (10 is the mean score):

Listening/Vocabulary	10
Listening/Grammar	10
Speaking/Vocabulary	12
Speaking/Grammar	7
Reading/Vocabulary	15
Reading/Grammar	12
Writing/Vocabulary	12
Writing/Grammar	9

All of his scores are average or above with the exception of his performance on tasks dependent on speaking and writing in a grammatically organized fashion. His subtest scores were further analyzed according to the following language skill areas, with a score of 100 considered average:

Listening	100	Spoken Language	98
Speaking	97	Written Language	117
Reading	121	Vocabulary	115
Writing	109	Grammar	100
Receptive Language	112		
Expressive Language	102		

Clark's language-related strengths are apparent when his writing is evaluated for ideas as opposed to technical competence. His strengths are also apparent when he is asked to define vocabulary and answer questions based on listening passages. Relative weaknesses become evident when spoken language and grammar tasks are presented to him.

On the Test of Written Language (TOWL), Clark attained a written language quotient of 101, significantly lower than the estimates of his overall intelligence. On this task, Clark presented an original and creative essay. However, his good descriptive abilities were compromised by frequent grammatical errors, which detracted from idea development and for which he is penalized in classes where written language assignments are required. His handwriting is cramped and at times illegible. The variations among the subtests on the TOWL reflect the difficulties he encounters in integrating the components of effective language skills (average score = 10):

Vocabulary	12	(75 percentile)
Thematic Maturity	12	(75 percentile)
Spelling	11	(63 percentile)
Word Usage	12	(75 percentile)
Style (Punctuation/ Capitalization)	9	(37 percentile)

Personality Functioning

During his conversations with the psychologist, Clark indicated that he frequently feels helpless and overwhelmed and that he has difficulty with activities that require autonomy and independence. He has a strong need for acceptance and support. However, he has learned to expect criticism and rejection and attempts to steel himself against the hurt and frustration associated with rejection. He has developed a "wall of social indifference" to insulate himself from social hurt and pain, but this tactic reinforces his sense of loneliness and isolation. In addition, avoidance and withdrawal interferes with his development of confidence and security and reinforces his self-doubt. His emotional distress may soon deplete his energy and optimism and interfere with his satisfactorily carrying out tasks and responsibilities expected of an adolescent.

During these conversations, Clark was very open. Despite his deficits in expressive language, he gave a forthright description of his concerns, feelings, and reactions. His comments reflected his experience of a good deal of frustration and disillusionment. He appears to be very sensitive and empathetic in his reactions to others. His comment about "secretly imagining stories in my head" reflects his reliance on fantasy in an effort to meet basic needs. Unfortunately, Clark's social avoidance and withdrawal actually limit opportunities for gaining the degree of social attention and fulfillment he craves.

Clark is described as having a quiet, reserved interpersonal relationship style. He appears to particularly enjoy topics that are more theoretical and scientific in nature rather than those having social components. He presents well-developed logic skills. His declaration that "I am best when a new idea interests me" reflects his efforts to invest himself in safer, theoretical, abstract interests rather than

(continued)

in those of a more interpersonal nature. He shows little interest in social gatherings or small talk with others. He tends to invest himself strongly in his interests.

Some of his responses suggested that he has not yet developed appropriate ways of releasing his bad feelings but instead internalizes them. As a result, he may be expending a good deal of emotional energy in containing his feelings, which may also fuel his sense of depression and tension. He did admit to sometimes feeling "melancholy" and that he often "did not know what to do next" and "felt a little too different."

Evaluation Summary

Clark demonstrates above average intellectual ability. He scores beyond his actual grade placement on most academic tasks but has encountered long-standing difficulties in language-related skills, particularly spoken and written expression. Clark is particularly adept in his mathematical skills and has well-developed conceptual and abstraction capabilities. On personality testing, he displays significant feelings of inadequacy and insecurity, relying on avoidance, withdrawal, and fantasy in an attempt to maintain an indifference to the slights and rejections of others. Intellectualization and development of theoretical and individualized interests also serve Clark as a means of protecting himself from uncomfortable feelings. This isolation limits his opportunities for meeting basic needs for attention and acceptance and prompts him to repress his frustrations and impulses.

DISCUSSION

Analyze Clark's abilities and disabilities with respect to language development and use. What information do you have regarding his abilities in the following skills:

- Phonology
- Morphology
- Syntax
- Semantics
- Pragmatics?

What information do you have about his relative abilities in the four language functions of listening, speaking, reading, and language? What are the implications of those differences? How does Clark's language functioning affect other areas of his life?

What concerns and implications for intervention might you derive from this analysis?

■ ■ ■ ■ ■

CHAPTER TWELVE

ACADEMIC LEARNING CHARACTERISTICS

QUESTIONS TO GUIDE YOUR STUDY

- What is learning?
- Identify the goal of each of the five stages of learning.
- How might a student's deficits in cognitive functioning interact with classroom and academic expectations in problematic ways?
- What is the difference between extrinsic and intrinsic motivation?
- Give examples of three sources of intrinsic motivation.
- What is the difference between an internal and an external locus of control?
- How might students' attributions of success or failure affect their performance in the classroom?
- What special concerns are associated with adolescents with mild learning and behavioral disorders in the school environment?
- How does the need to achieve self-determination interact with the way schools provide services to students with disabilities?
- Discuss appropriate uses of the theories of learning styles and multiple intelligences in planning programs for students with mild disabilities.
- What does Carroll's model of school learning suggest to you as a teacher?

■ ■ ■ ■ ■

Meet Barbara

Barbara is an eight-year-old student in Mr. Taylor's special education classroom. She was classified as a student with mild mental retardation about four years ago when her prekindergarten teacher noted language delays, which continue to present serious problems for her today. Barbara has recently begun to experience some success in school. When she accomplishes a desired task, she seems very pleased with herself, and she is likely to continue working hard to refine her skills. Her achievements appear to be motivation enough to keep her trying. She tries very hard to please Mr. Taylor. Unfortunately, her teacher notes that when she fails after attempting a difficult task, she generally pulls back and will not try again. The amount of new information Barbara is able to handle at one time is

(continued)

limited, and her zone of proximal development is narrow. Mr. Taylor finds that it is sometimes difficult to judge how much of a challenge Barbara is ready to attempt.

Barbara learns most effectively when Mr. Taylor makes the learning objective, as well as the activities themselves, very concrete. Barbara requires many attempts and careful monitoring over a period of days and even weeks to reach mastery on basic reading and math tasks. Once she seems to "have it," she needs much more practice to make the skill automatic. She also needs to be prompted to use her new academic and daily living skills in settings other than the classroom where they were taught. It is as if she doesn't recognize that she can apply her new reading skills to books and reading tasks other than the basal reader.

Barbara has recently developed a behavioral pattern that concerns Mr. Taylor. Increasingly, Barbara is unwilling to complete an activity unless Mr. Taylor tells her that the part she has already completed is correct. Yesterday, Mr. Taylor assigned a reading activity that involved reading several short stories and writing a good title for each. After each story, Barbara raised her hand and would not continue until Mr. Taylor had confirmed that her answer was correct. Mr. Taylor has also noticed that Barbara is becoming very dependent on the teaching assistant as well. He is concerned that this dependent behavior will keep Barbara from being successful outside the classroom.

What Is Learning?

Learning is defined as the process by which experience and practice result in a stable change in the learner's behavior that is not explained simply by maturation, growth, or aging. It is the process of going from "not knowing" to "knowing." We can only infer that learning has occurred by observing the performance and behavior of the learner. Because this is only an inference, teachers must use caution when making assumptions about the level of learning resulting from any given experience or practice.

As school administrators and teachers discuss more inclusive models of service for youngsters with mild disabilities, a special consideration is the applicability of social learning theory to academic performance. Social learning theory holds that behaviors are learned by observing the behavior of others and by observing the direct consequences of those behaviors (Bandura, 1986). From that perspective, in making decisions about placements, we must evaluate not only the characteristics of individual student behavior but also the extent to which an environment provides useful models of skillful behavior, and the extent to which the student can make use of those models.

When we discuss learning as a topic, we generally think of school learning. For students with mild disabilities, schools certainly present particular problems. However, it is important to remember that much of what we will discuss in this chapter is also applicable to learning in any setting and context, at home and in the community as well as in school.

Stages of Learning

As noted above, learning is generally viewed as the process of moving from the state of "not knowing" to the state of "knowing" and then to the state of "using." Teachers frequently assume that, once a student demonstrates the ability to perform a skill or demonstrates an understanding, the learning has been completed and teacher and student can move on to the next concept to be mastered. With learners with mild disabilities, this assumption frequently leads to poorly learned content and skills to learning that provides a weak foundation for new learning. It doesn't take many layers of weak learning before the structure collapses and the student is left without the capacity to perform at all.

Weak learning results from the failure to recognize that the learning process must continue past simple acquisition or mastery to proficiency, maintenance, and generalization to become firm. With most students, the process of reinforcing prior learning continues rather easily and incidentally as new skills are presented. With students with mild disabilities, however, attention and conscious effort must be applied to ensure that the student moves satisfactorily through each of the following stages of learning: (1) acquisition, including reversion, (2) proficiency, (3) maintenance, (4) generalization, and (5) adaptation (Mercer, 1987; see Figure 12.1 and In the Classroom 12.1).

Acquisition and Reversion

This stage consists of moving the learner from no skill to basic mastery, or moving from no skill to about 85 percent accuracy. Explicit instruction is most useful at this stage, since it ensures that the student is presented with the most accurate information. During acquisition, learners also benefit from actual experience and active involvement with the content or skill, which helps make the knowledge or skill more relevant. At this stage, making learning meaningful seems to be more helpful than making the task simple.

Incidental learning, while useful to some learners, can result in inaccurate learning for many students with mild disabilities. These students are as likely to learn undesirable, unproductive, or unrelated skills or facts as they are to master the object of instruction. Students

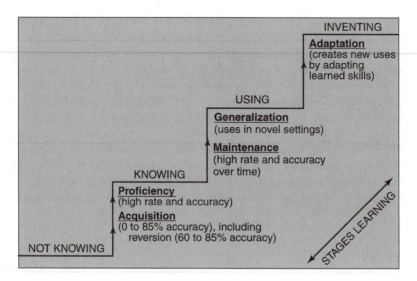

FIGURE 12.1   Stages of Learning

with attention deficits frequently attend to too many stimuli or pick the least helpful one, both of which impede learning at the acquisition stage. At this stage, frequent and specific feedback, including both positive and corrective feedback, is essential so that the student is assured that the learning is accurate.

Throughout the acquisition stage, the goal is accuracy in learning. The performance of students in acquisition is frequently awkward and variable (Graham, 1985). *Reversion* is a critical substage of acquisition in which the learner responds correctly enough of the time (more than 50 percent) to indicate some level of mastery but is nevertheless erratic in accuracy of response. In the reversion substage, the goal is to capitalize on beginning skills and to acquire sufficient practice with immediate feedback to finally achieve the desired accuracy in the learning. Through continued instruction, practice, coaching, and feedback, the student is gradually helped to define the characteristics of accurate learning and to finally be able to perform the skill accurately at least 85 percent of the time. The biggest danger during the period of reversion lies in allowing the student to continue extended practice unmonitored without the frequent and specific feedback needed to refine the skill particularly during the reversion substage. If this occurs, errors and misunderstandings are likely to be practiced and learned, with inaccurate learning the result.

Proficiency and Automaticity

Once a firm understanding or mastery of the skill or concept has been demonstrated, the learner enters the proficiency stage. The goal of this stage is to develop automaticity and fluency with the skill. The advantage of developing proficiency in skills and content is that as performance becomes more automatic, less cognitive capacity is required for execution. As less of the learner's finite cognitive processing capacity in working memory is used for retrieval of facts and execution of basic skills in mathematics and reading, this capacity can be freed up for higher level processing (Hasselbring, Goin, & Bansford, 1988; Samuels, 1987).

To be successful, the learner needs to move past conscious performance of the skill, requiring significant amounts of practice so that the skill becomes automatic. The number of trials needed to achieve fluency varies greatly, depending on the general and specific abilities of the student and the strength of prior learning. Students with mental retardation and other intellectual or learning limitations require many more encounters with a skill or content to make it their own, and they are vulnerable to failure without concentrated practice (Podell, Tournaki-Rein, & Lin, 1992). For example, Hasselbring et al. (1988) reported that students with mild disabilities acquire automaticity in recall of math facts significantly more slowly than their typical peers and are more likely to continue to depend on alternative strategies (e.g., counting on fingers) rather than retrieval from memory to achieve correct answers. This lack of proficiency restricts the student from applying basic skills to more complex learning. Samuels (1987) proposed a similar explanation for the reading problems observed in students with mild disabilities.

Maintenance

During the maintenance stage, the goal is to maintain a high level of performance over time, after the reinforcement associated with instruction ends. Maintenance of skills is necessary if future learning is to build on those skills. This goal requires that students continue meaningful practice in functional contexts with appropriate feedback on their performance. Students with mild disabilities generally require extended practice and review to maintain their skill level. Teachers and parents must keep in mind the fact that if skills are not used and if maintenance opportunities are not provided, the skills will atrophy no matter how firmly it appears they have been learned.

Generalization

The goal of the generalization stage is to extend the use of acquired skills across situations, behaviors, settings, and time. Once learned, a skill should be available to be used in any appropriate setting. It has been stated that generalization is of such importance that if it does not occur, then the learning process has not been successful (Ellis, Lenz, & Sabornie, 1987). The goal of generalization is for the learner to recognize a different stimulus as a prompt to apply a learned skill. For example, if Mary learns to add in math class, she should be able to use those addition skills in home economics, shop, and science without prompting. Learners with mild disabilities often fail to see how a skill learned in one setting might be applied in another. Skills learned in a resource room frequently do not transfer to the general education class unless the teachers work to prompt the use of the skills in the new setting. Without prompts to use the newly acquired skill, students frequently fail to make the connection or to perceive the applicability of the skill to a new situation.

Generalization rarely happens automatically. Initially in this stage, the teacher or parent helps the student see how a skill might apply in a new setting. Ellis et al. (1987) advocate beginning to teach generalization during initial instruction, describing the variety of ways and places a new skill might be used. They also recommend using a continuum of techniques, ranging from teacher-mediated to student-mediated, thereby increasing the likelihood that students will see their own efforts as responsible for their successes and that they will develop internal attributions for those outcomes. (The role of attributions for success and failure are discussed later in this chapter.)

Adaptation

The final stage of learning occurs when the student is able to apply a learned skill in a modified way to a new task without help or prompts. When the stimulus to apply the skill is radically different from the training setting, the learner must modify the manner of performance to meet the new demands (Ellis et al., 1987). The basic skill is the same, but the execution varies. In this stage, the student is firm enough in the learning to see how it can be modified to match the demands of the novel situation. In adaptation, the learner is also able to discern the larger implications of a skill and assumes personal responsibility for carrying the learning farther. As with the generalization stage, coaching and prompting may be needed initially to help students identify the applicability of modifying skills for use in novel situations. Although adaptation is the final stage in learning, not all skills will be learned to the adaptation stage, particularly by students with mild disabilities. Achieving generalization of a skill may be an appropriate end for some learnings and some students.

Cognitive Processing Deficits and Academic Performance

Analyzing the characteristics of learners with mild disabilities in academic learning environments quickly leads back to the model of cognitive functioning. Within the cognitive model (see Chapter 10), the three areas that most affect the success a student experiences in learning are attention, memory, and executive functioning.

Learning cannot occur until a student is able to focus on the relevant details in the environment. Students who encounter difficulty in selective attention functions will almost certainly be viewed as inefficient learners and exhibit attentional problems that interfere with their success in the classroom. Students with learning disabilities along with hyperactivity have significant problems focusing their attention appropriately (Cotugno, 1987). Such students are more narrowly restricted in their scanning of incoming sensory stimuli, and they are more likely to be distracted by extraneous input. They appear to lack the cognitive capacity to sort information for relevancy in an efficient manner. Those learners with the most difficulty focusing on the relevant stimuli will need more teacher coaching to develop efficient selective attention strategies.

A student's efficiency in learning is frequently evaluated by the extent to which the student is able to store information and retrieve facts on demand. Learners with problems in school frequently display problems with memorizing math facts, spelling words, vocabulary definitions, and other content area information (e.g., lists and dates). They also have difficulty demonstrating the basic skills involved in reading and mathematics. On investigation of the strategies these students use to accomplish memorization tasks, we frequently discover that such learners differ in their ability to organize information for recall. Strategies

IN THE CLASSROOM **12.1**

Stages of Learning

John is a third grader with a language learning disability who spends the majority of his day in the general education classroom. He is an enthusiastic learner, willing to try almost anything. He is one of those students who seem to either "get it" quickly or not understand at all. He is frequently the first one to respond to questions and to note similarities in content discussions, but he is also the first one to jump to erroneous conclusions. As soon as a skill is introduced, he is most eager, almost impatient, to use it. Since his tendency is to attempt to quickly apply his knowledge, he often appears to think that he has achieved mastery of a new skill after only one or two examples. It soon becomes obvious that his accuracy and understandings are not as strong as his enthusiasm, indicating that the learning is still at the reversion substage. Without careful monitoring, he is apt to end up practicing skills incorrectly. He responds well to corrective feedback, but he seems to be amazed when it is pointed out to him that he doesn't have it right. His teacher's challenge is to keep John at the acquisition stage of learning longer so that learning is accurate, and then to carefully monitor his practice during proficiency to ensure accurate learning.

Heather is a fourth grader with mild mental retardation. Her teachers have noted that she seems to move through the stages of learning fairly slowly when compared to typical fourth graders. She frequently needs to have material taught in a variety of ways and to have concepts retaught in the resource room. She benefits from extensive feedback during the acquisition process. Achieving proficiency is also difficult, as Heather needs many more opportunities for practice than other students do. Her exclusive reliance on rehearsal as a memory strategy also impedes her learning. Conscious attention to maintenance activities is also necessary. Although Heather had achieved fluency with her multiplication facts, after a period of no specific practice with the facts, she has begun to need the multiplication table again to do calculations.

Frank is in tenth grade, although his mild mental retardation has limited his ability to progress academically. Frank receives significant assistance from his teachers in learning, progressing slowly through the acquisition, proficiency, and maintenance stages in each new skill. He has had some success in developing functional reading and math skills to the fifth- and sixth-grade levels. However, he encounters significant difficulty in generalizing learned skills. Last week, the social studies teacher asked the class to find out how many years ago the Civil War ended. Although Frank can subtract multidigit numbers easily, he was unable to see the applicability of that skill in social studies until his teacher showed him how to figure it out. It is difficult for him to transfer skills across situations, settings, and time. Frank's best friend, Tom, a student with no cognitive disabilities, regularly provides evidence of the ability to use basic math skills independently in a variety of settings (i.e., generalization). He enjoys mental math activities in which he manipulates numbers in creative ways to solve computation problems more efficiently than using pencil and paper. This creative problem solving illustrates that Tom's learning of subtraction is clearly at the adaptation stage, a level his friend Frank is unlikely to achieve.

such as verbal or written rehearsal, coding (associating a new item with a concept already in memory), imagery, and mnemonics are absent, immature, or inefficiently used among younger students and among those with mild disabilities (Leal & Raforth, 1991).

Two helpful strategies that are rarely spontaneously utilized by individuals with mental retardation and learning disabilities for dealing with declarative knowledge are grouping or clustering, and paired associate learning. Both organizational strategies depend on establishing relationships between new stimuli and prior learning, and on the strength of that prior learning. For these reasons, students who do not achieve mastery at the maintenance stage or better in prior learning are unable to use these strategies. Without knowledge of a variety of memory strategies, the students are inefficient or unsuccessful in accomplishing memory tasks. Since so much emphasis is placed on quick recall in school environments, the students are seen as failures or lazy. Teachers can assist students in developing such strategies by clearly explaining how new learnings relate to old learnings, and by modeling ways to store such information in long-term memory.

As was discussed in Chapter 10, declarative memory deals with factual knowledge, and procedural memory stores action sequences and procedures. Teachers may find it useful to treat declarative memory tasks differently from procedural memory tasks and to teach students to deal with them differently (Derry, 1990). Declarative memory depends on establishing strong networks between related bits of content information. This is most effectively done in the early stages of learning, during acquisition. As teachers and students discuss new information, they can develop elaborations on the concepts and the connections, or organization, and make connections between the new data and previously stored information. Students with mild disabilities often fail to see the relevant connections to prior learning without assistance. Taking the time during the earliest learning stages to ensure firm learning will increase the effectiveness of the learner in the later stages of learning.

Procedural memory differs from declarative in that skills (e.g., arithmetic calculation skills) are stored as action sequences that are best learned by repetition (Derry, 1990). Students with mild disabilities tend to appear to respond quickly during initial skill instruction, but then are unable to retrieve the action sequence accurately the next day. Repeated initial demonstration of the skill and extended practice with corrective feedback are needed to develop the necessary level of automaticity in procedural knowledge by students with mild disabilities.

Central to efficient cognitive processing and academic learning is the ability of the individual to make cognitive decisions about the applicability of particular strategies and the effectiveness of learning. These executive control functions (metacognition) include control of attention, metacognitive regulation (self-instruction and self-direction), metacomprehension (self-questioning and monitoring), and reflection (self-evaluation). When a student exhibits deficiencies in executive control functioning or strategic control functions (see In the Classroom 12.2), adults often assume the control and direction of strategy selection, monitoring, and even completing tasks, resulting in learner passivity, outer-directedness, and learned helplessness (Borkowski & Kurtz, 1987). The lack of specific and general strategy knowledge as well as deficits in employing executive control functions or metacognitive regulation can lead to an increasingly negative attitude and avoidance of cognitive tasks. Learners increasingly look to others for cues, are less reliant on their own resources for developing solutions, and may distrust their own abilities. The literature about the utility of metacognitive coaching (Paris & Winograd, 1990) suggests that active interference with this negative spiral by teachers and others is both possible and necessary. By actively working to help students develop metacognitive awareness of their own thinking, teachers can help develop attributions of effort in their students and can enhance their intrinsic motivation for self-determination, leading to increased persistence in the pursuit of that learning. Later in this

IN THE CLASSROOM 12.2

Cognitive Functioning and Academic Performance

Kelly is a sixth grader with learning disabilities and attention deficits. Now that she is changing classes in the middle school, she is expected to organize her time, learning, and herself. Her reduced ability to process information affects her academic performance in several ways. Due to her deficits in selective and sustained attention, her teachers must frequently call her back to attention, with resulting gaps in learning. Rehearsal is the only memory strategy Kelly uses independently, and the demands of the middle school curriculum make this an inefficient mode of learning. Kelly's teachers have begun to assist her in developing other memory strategies. They also provide her with study guides and summaries of reading. Unfortunately, she is not yet developing and using the self-monitoring strategies needed to evaluate her own learning, and she is becoming dependent on the aids her teachers provide.

chapter, the implications of these issues for academic success of learners with mild disabilities are discussed.

The Role of Motivation

Beginning teachers are frequently told that they are responsible not just for teaching their students but for motivating them to learn. Teachers in return frequently attribute a lack of learning to the student's being "unmotivated" or to parents who fail to "motivate" their children. While it is certainly true that motivation affects the learning process and that without motivation, learning is unlikely to occur, the converse is not necessarily true. For example, one cannot reason that if learners are motivated, they will be able to learn anything they are asked to learn. Motivation only encourages students to persist in doing something they are capable of doing. If a learner does not have the aptitude or prerequisite skills to learn or perform a particular skill (e.g., fly out the window or read a story from the basal reader), a teacher could promise that student a million dollars (strong motivation indeed!), and a positive learning outcome would nonetheless be unlikely (Lavoie, 1989). Learners with a variety of mild disabilities present significant motivation concerns in classrooms (Mehring & Colson, 1990; Nichols, McKenzie, & Shufro, 1994; Ryan, Short, & Weed, 1986; Switzky & Schultz, 1988). They tend to develop a failure orientation and perceive that they lack control of their destiny. They also tend to attribute success or failure to forces outside their control, or to see no relationship between task outcomes and their own efforts.

Extrinsic Motivation

Motivation comes from many sources. Extrinsic motivation is provided by sources outside the individual. Examples include rewards that a student earns on execution of the desired behavior and punishments a child seeks to avoid by performing as asked. Extrinsic motivation rarely leads to robust learning. The tendency for the learning to be tied directly to the reward frequently leads the individual to do the minimum to achieve the reward or to avoid punishment (Stipek, 1993). Changes in behavior are likely to disappear once the extrinsic reinforcement is withdrawn unless the change of behavior has created its own intrinsic rewards for the student. In addition, learners may also come to equate the extrinsic reward with the external control of their destiny, reducing their sense of self-determination (Grolnick & Ryan, 1990). This can lead to a cycle in which teachers see students as being unmotivated and students become more dependent on external control of their learning and behavior.

The possibility of earning the extrinsic rewards may actually result in a decrease in natural intrinsic motivation and in the student's interest in the task. When the extrinsic reinforcer is removed, the student may find no reason to continue to perform the task that was previously reinforced (Faust & Faust, 1980; Schultz & Switzky, 1994; Sternberg, 1986; Switzky & Schultz, 1988). Furthermore, it is unlikely that learning based only on extrinsic motivation will have the strength to generalize into other settings. This represents the classic "learn it for the test, then forget it" situation (see In the Classroom 12.3). That said, however, teachers and parents sometimes will find that it is advantageous to enhance a child's weak intrinsic motivation with an extrinsic reinforcer. While they may find it useful to use extrinsic motivators, they must be aware of the dangers of overuse of rewards and punishments, seeking instead to identify and reinforce the learner's intrinsic motivation whenever possible (Kohn, 1993).

IN THE CLASSROOM 12.3
Extrinsic Motivation

Darlene is fourteen years old and is classified as a student with learning disabilities, although her intellectual ability (IQ 75) indicates that she might also be viewed as having borderline mental retardation. Her motivation for learning is affected strongly by her history of failure. When completing classwork, she works hard enough to pass, but not to do well. It appears that she exerts enough effort to avoid the punishment of failing grades, but she shows no evidence of working to achieve the competence represented by good grades. Her history of failure seems to have affected her to the extent that she seems to believe that she cannot obtain a good grade, and she sees no point in exerting the effort to try.

At ten years old, Harry is served in a self-contained classroom for students with emotional disorders. His teachers are concerned with his non-compliance, temper outbursts, and general oppositional behavior. His classroom management system utilizes a point system for earning food rewards, buying items at the school store, and earning privileges. His teachers also utilize response cost procedures and time-out for problem behavior. These extrinsic motivators are only marginally effective with Harry. He wants to receive the rewards and to avoid the punishments, and so will try to adjust his behavior only as much as necessary to achieve those ends. However, it is becoming apparent to the staff that these are not strong motivators, since Harry continues to exhibit the problematic behaviors in spite of the rewards and punishment, and the problem behaviors are persisting outside the school environment.

Intrinsic Motivation

Motivation derived from sources within the individual student, or intrinsic motivation, appears to have the strongest effect on learning. The amount of intrinsic motivation available to achieve a particular level of learning is affected foremost by the individual's sense of competence. Learners are more motivated to learn something that appears to be possible for them to achieve when engaged in meaningful activities with others who already possess the skill or knowledge (i.e., learning that appears to be within their zone of proximal development). They are motivated to learn those things they perceive as possible to learn. On the other hand, uncertainty of prior learning or experience with failure in that learning frequently leads to reduced motivation for new learning attempts.

Additionally, the learner's perception that a particular learning activity has meaning or meets an identified personal need or goal affects the level of motivation to participate in the learning activity. Glasser (1986, 1990) contends that all human behavior is an attempt to satisfy basic human needs: to survive, to belong, to love, to have fun, to gain power, and to be free. He further states that what we choose to do is what we think is the most need-satisfying thing to do at the time. Glasser advocates that teachers ensure that there is potential for students to actually meet their basic needs in school settings, which will lead to students' being motivated to adapt their behavioral responses in ways that make the whole social structure a more productive one for everyone.

Intrinsic motivation to persist in a variety of human efforts, learning or otherwise, follows from at least three basic needs or goals, including the drives for competence, self-determination, and relatedness or affiliation (Adelman & Taylor, 1990; Deci & Chandler, 1986; Stipek, 1993). A student may exhibit one or some combination of these needs, but for any given learning or activity, one of the needs is likely to be the primary motivation (see In the Classroom 12.4).

Some students are motivated to participate in school activities because learning results in an enhanced sense of competence (Deci & Ryan, 1985; Stipek, 1993). *Competence* is derived from activities that extend and enhance the ability to interact effectively with the environment, and master challenges. In addition to the internal sense of accomplishment and personal efficacy, such achievement also often provides recognition from society, thereby blending intrinsic and extrinsic motivations. The competence motivation leads the individual to perform difficult tasks as well as possible in order to achieve a goal. An artist works on a painting, motivated by the need to achieve a masterpiece that will be recognized as significant by peers and the public. The mathematics student works to prove a difficult proposition, motivated by the challenge of the puzzle to be solved. The high school student works to demonstrate competence in chemistry because achieving the grade of A indicates mastery of the subject to herself and others. All of these individuals are motivated by the need to achieve, to demonstrate their competence, to "climb the mountain just because it is there." Competence motivation is often enhanced by recognition and appreciation by significant others, which follows the demonstration of competence.

Individuals are also motivated by the need for *self-determination;* in order to feel self-determining, a sense of perceived control and autonomy is essential (Deci & Ryan, 1985; Stipek, 1993). Individuals may be motivated by their perception of control involved in engaging in an activity that appears to give them power or that demonstrates their power over

Intrinsic Motivation

Peter is twelve years old and is served in a program for students with mental retardation. Everyone who meets him is impressed by his eagerness and positive attitude. They wonder what keeps him resilient in the face of his significant learning challenges. In observing him at work in the classroom, they note that he seems very focused and determined to meet his goals. It appears that he gains a sense of accomplishment and recognition from his achievements. His pride is evident when he completes a project or when he sees his work posted in the hallway. It is apparent that he possesses a strong competence motivation, and that he gives his all to classroom activities to meet that competence need.

Joanne is fifteen, and has ADHD and a behavioral disorder. Her need for relatedness, or affiliation, appears to be the strongest motivation for her actions. Unfortunately, this manifests itself in negative ways. She tends to rush through assignments in Mr. Tallon's resource room, with little effort or concern for quality, so that she can interact with her peers. Yesterday she rushed through a math worksheet, completing only as much as she needed to do

to receive a passing grade. Mr. Tallon convinced her to finish the worksheet, whereupon she rushed off to interact with one of her friends. Since this relatedness motivation is so strong for her, Mr. Tallon has decided to see if he can structure Joanne's learning activities to take advantage of it.

Seth is thirteen years old in a self-contained class for students (mostly boys) with learning disabilities. In this classroom, power struggles are common; and posturing, threatening, and fighting are means of survival. Academic success is not perceived by the students as a way to gain power or control; ironically, it is sometimes even viewed as weakness, indicating that the student has succumbed to the domination of teachers. Arguments among class members involve knowledge of nonacademic subjects such as wrestling, sports, and snowmobiles. Seth's knowledge in these areas accords him a place of importance in the group and possible power and control. His need for self-determination fuels his desire to learn all he can about sports, allowing him to determine the course of events in these classroom discussions.

others or over circumstances. It is this desire to be in control of one's fate that often leads individuals to acquire new competencies, since skills are essential to managing one's environment and to being in control of one's destiny. Learning how to do things for yourself means that you don't have to ask others for help, and therefore you develop increased personal control of your life and become more self-determining. Because you know how to do something better than someone else, you may be hired for a job you're seeking. Having the ability and authority to act competently results in the capability to affect outcomes, to wield power, to determine your own outcomes. We often think of control as a negative, but it is important to remember that depression and helplessness are frequent outcomes of a lack of control or power. Some students are motivated to learn by the need to be self-determining, to have control, so that they won't have to be dependent anymore.

Finally, some students are motivated by the need for *relatedness,* as evidenced by attempts to develop affiliations or friendships to achieve a sense of belonging. The human need for belonging and nurturing is well documented in the early work of Maslow (1954), and of Skeels and Dye (1939). Frequently, students are motivated to stay with the learning process simply because it enables them to interact with others in interesting ways. Learning new skills creates more opportunities for relating to others. This source of motivation is perhaps the most frequently overlooked of all the possible intrinsic motivations for learning. In fact, it is often seen as a detriment to learning. Teachers chastise students who seem more interested in talking about their learning than in completing the work. The research in cooperative learning by Johnson et al. (1984) gives strong evidence of the power of the relatedness motive for learning. When students work cooperatively, they often learn more and better than when they work in individualistic or competitive structures.

As with any human being, any of these sources of intrinsic motivation may exist in learners with mild disabilities. An individual may even exhibit a combination of motivations, depending on environmental and personal factors. In learners with disabilities, competence motivation is likely to be weaker because of the history of failure such students have experienced. The effectiveness of competence in motivating individual actions will depend on the individual's belief that success is possible, a belief that is frequently weak or undermined by prior failures in learners with mild disabilities. The competence or achievement motivation carries with it the possibility of success or of failure (Schrunk, 1992). Teachers and parents must recognize that the lure of achievement or competence as represented by a good report card may be a weak motivator for these students.

Frequently, motivation involving learning as a means of achieving control or personal power and becoming more self-determining, or of interacting with others, will be more influential. As we seek to help students with mild disabilities become more successful in academic settings that have not previously met their needs, we need to help them identify how these school tasks will help them meet their personal needs of becoming more competent, self-determining, or connected to others. Then we have to address the additional motivational issue of competence by ensuring that the assigned task is within their zone of proximal development and that an appropriate level of support is available to help them move to the next level of learning.

Before leaving the discussion of motivation, it is important to discuss some reasons that motivations to meet basic needs might lead to a learner's engaging in destructive behaviors. When considering problem behavior, we must accept the fact that many instances of misbehavior are related to the learners' mistaken belief that, by engaging in the behavior, they will achieve a measure of control, competence, or connectedness. Finally, it is important to note that central to the studies of problem behavior and aggression is the concept of perceived control of one's life (Adelman & Taylor, 1990; Allen & Greenburger, 1980; Grolnick & Ryan, 1990; Schrunk, 1992). Failure experiences can lead to youngsters' developing a low sense of perceived control. Since low levels of perceived control constitute a threat to the individual's self-determination needs, these youngsters frequently turn to other, more destructive means of reestablishing a sense of personal control and self-determination, such as displaying oppositional and aggressive behavior. In such situations, teachers and parents frequently revert to extrinsic rewards to achieve desired behavior. Ironically, such rewards are perceived as external controls and as an additional threat to self-determination, causing the student to react against the reward with diminished effort or increased acting-out behaviors. This suggests a strong connection between developing competence in students and reducing their need to control the environment through aggressive behaviors. Learning and behavior are clearly related in youngsters with mild disabilities.

Locus of Control and Attribution of Success or Failure

Central concepts in the literature concerning low-achieving students in general and those with disabilities in particular are the concepts of locus of control and attribution theory (Borkowski, Weyhing, & Turner, 1986; Rotter, 1966; Schrunk, 1992; Stipek, 1993; Wehmeyer, 1994; Wehmeyer, Agran, & Hughes, 1998). *Locus of control* refers to the degree to which individuals perceive that there is a connection between their actions and the outcomes achieved, and it includes the explanations given by individuals to account for their personal successes or failures. *Attribution theory* focuses on the perception of personal control for outcomes.

External Attributions and Locus of Control

When learners indicate that their success or failure is due to factors outside themselves, such as chance, fate, or the actions of others, we say they are exhibiting an external locus of control or that they display external attributions. Frequently, students with mild learning and behavioral disabilities exhibit characteristics associated with an external locus of control (Wehmeyer, 1994). That is, they tend to attribute their success or failure to the actions of others or to forces outside their control (e.g., luck). They may not see their own efforts as relevant to the outcomes. Research reported by Borkowski, Weyhing, and Turner (1986) indicates that students with mild disabilities are more likely to attribute the outcome of a task to factors not generally within the person's control, such as ability (or lack thereof), luck, a task that is too hard (or too easy), or such factors as the teacher's liking or disliking them (see In the Classroom 12.5). Ironically, if students with mild disabilities do attribute their failures to their efforts, they are still likely to attribute their successes to external factors such as luck or the teacher's being easy on them (Wong, 1991). This pattern underscores the helplessness or lack of efficacy these learners frequently experience. Young children or those who have developmental delays generally display more dependence on an external locus of control. This may be related to the tendency of these same children to display a more field-dependent cognitive style. Students with an external locus of control also tend to adopt failure-avoiding strategies in which they avoid tasks they view as beyond their ability or environments they see as nonproductive (Stipek, 1993).

Internal Attributions and Locus of Control

On the other hand, successful learners are more likely to attribute outcomes to their own efforts (e.g., trying hard or not trying hard enough), a characteristic referred to as an internal attribution or locus of control. Recognition that effort matters is often linked to persistence in the face of difficulty, a factor that is also associated with greater success in learning tasks

IN THE CLASSROOM **12.5**

External Attributions of Success and Failure

Diana, a third grader with ADHD, appears to expect failure and has a tendency to attribute her successes to external factors. When her mother asked her how she did on a recent test on time and money, Diana answered that she had failed. Later, her mother found the test in her backpack, and said, "You didn't fail; you got a 94!" Diana's response was that she did well only because the teacher had them "do time and money so much at school." She did not appear to believe that her efforts played a part in the success. Diana expects failure, and even when she experiences success in her school program, she attributes it to the actions of others.

Mike is eighteen years old and has been served in programs for students with mild mental retardation since first grade. As do many adolescents, he seeks to be in control of his life. Because of his disability, he needs to spend more time on his classwork than the typical student does to be successful. Frequently, however, he spends a minimal amount of time studying. When he experiences failure, he generally blames the instructor for making the test too hard or for not telling him what to study. His tendency to blame everything and everyone else for his situation is evidence of his external locus of control, a fact that undermines the development of self-determination for this young man.

(Licht & Kistner, 1986). Students who come to believe that effort makes a difference will exert more effort, leading them to persist with difficult tasks and subsequently to learn more (Stipek, 1993). An internal locus of control is related to the sense that factors within the individual's control (e.g., personal efforts) are responsible for outcomes. Individuals experience more reinforcement from outcomes they attribute to their own actions.

Effective learning requires increasingly internalizing the locus of control if the learner is to move beyond teachers, parents, school, and home to become an independent learner and problem-solver. Typically, individuals develop a more internal locus of control as they move into adolescence and adulthood, although this is not as generally true of those with disabilities. Students with mild disabilities tend to remain more externally oriented than their typical peers, leading to less adaptive adult outcomes (Wehmeyer, 1994). In light of the discussion of locus of control and motivation, it is also important to note that merely providing instruction in content and cognitive strategies for learning is unlikely to be effective. It is important for teachers to also help youngsters with disabilities see that the effort they put forth in applying such strategies can pay off in improved outcomes, that their efforts result in more success (see In the Classroom 12.6).

Spirals of Failure or Success

The manner in which a learner approaches a task affects the outcome. The expectation of success or failure creates a climate that increases the likelihood of the outcome. Experiences

IN THE CLASSROOM **12.6**

Internal Attributions or Locus of Control

Sue is fourteen years old and currently in eighth grade. Her teacher reports that Sue sees herself as a competent person and that she feels that if she tries, she can affect outcomes positively through her own efforts. If she doesn't do well on a test, she is usually able to identify her actions that may have led to it, such as failing to use a particular study technique. She is in a class with other highly motivated students, and she wants to be accepted by them. She has indicated some ambivalence about her classification as a student with a learning disability. Her teacher has helped her identify her strengths and weaknesses, and together they have worked on strategies she can use to compensate for her deficit areas. Despite her tendency toward an internal locus of control, at times she reverts to behaviors indicative of an external locus of control. For example, last week when she couldn't find an assignment, she quickly assumed the teacher had lost it.

Bill, an eighth grader with a mild behavioral disorder, has just been placed in a full-inclusion program. Academically, he is challenged by the new environment. When he is successful on a project, he takes pride in his effort and accomplishment. When he encounters failure, such as doing an assignment incorrectly or losing his temper, his first impulse is to blame others. Last week, he tore up his science worksheet when the teacher asked him to redo a section. At first he blamed the teacher, saying, "He made me do it." After a short time in the time-out area and a discussion with the crisis counselor, he admitted that he had lost control and that he was responsible for the problem and for getting a new worksheet. This development of more internal attributions for events in his life is evidence of the progress Bill is making with the help of his teachers and counselor.

---

with failure may result in the learner's setting lower goals and exerting less effort, which in turn may bring about subsequent failure, leading to a downward spiral of ever-lower goals and efforts (Licht & Kistner, 1986). Repeated failure erodes the student's motivation to learn, resulting in a lowered sense of personal efficacy, diminished academic self-concept, and external attributions for all outcomes (see In the Classroom 12.7). The student tends to avoid challenges, giving up at the first sign of difficulty and becoming a passive learner in the classroom (Wong, 1991; see Figure 12.2).

A similar but opposite effect tends to follow successful learning experiences. A sense of competence results when a student exerts effort, takes a voluntary action, and is successful. In such cases, students perceive their efforts as efficacious and have a tendency to exert similar efforts on future tasks, increasing the likelihood of further successes. It is important, however, for these successes to truly be achieved by the students as a result of their own efforts. Often, special educators manipulate the learning environment in such a way as to make success inevitable and effortless. In such cases, the student does not attribute the success to effort, but rather to the task's being easy. The student's lack of experience in confronting failure and seeing effort pay off leaves the learner helpless in the face of real challenges (Balk, 1983; Seligman, 1975).

IN THE CLASSROOM **12.7**

Failure and Success Spirals

Megan is 15 years old and has received special education services, under the classification of learning disability, in three states since second grade. After almost ten years of significant failure in school, Megan appears to be firmly planted in a failure spiral. She does not invest full effort in academic tasks, responding "I'm just a 'retard.' I can't do this." When asked a question, she often responds at random with the first word that pops into her head. Her lack of progress appears to have defeated her. Megan recently told her teacher, "There's not enough time left for me to learn. I'll never do it."

Mary, on the other hand, has really benefited from the assistance she has received this fall. Last year was a frustrating one for her, with failing grades in math primarily related to incomplete homework. Her special education teacher this year decided to teach her some organizational and study strategies to help with her content area classes, including math. Mary found that by using the assignment completion strategy for her math assignments, she was able to keep track of her materials better, which encouraged her to actually complete the work. Her teacher reinforced her for handing in her homework, which led Mary to try even harder to be more accurate in the work she hands in and to ask for help when she needs it. This week she received an 87 on her math test, and she attributes the grade to having done her homework every night for the last two weeks. Mary finally appears to be firmly in a success spiral for math.

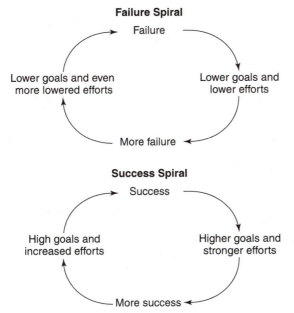

Failure Spiral

Success Spiral

FIGURE 12.2 Failure and Success Spirals

Learned Helplessness

The belief that one's own efforts will not be sufficient to positively affect outcomes, or *learned helplessness,* is another characteristic affecting motivation that is frequently observed among learners with mild disabilities (Stipek, 1993; Wehmeyer, 1992). Defined originally by Seligman (1975), learned helplessness results when individuals repeatedly experience events that can't be controlled by their own actions. No matter what response the learner makes in the school environment, there is no expectation that the response will lead to a positive outcome, or that it will lead to more control and self-determination; rather, it leads to a sense of help-lessness. The students' experience that voluntary efforts seem to be ineffective at achieving the desired results undermines their motivation; they accept failure as inevitable and develop learned helplessness (see In the Classroom 12.8).

Youngsters whose mild disabilities affect their learning and adjustment in school set-tings often receive intensive academic help and guidance, including teachers' monitoring everything they do, and parents' doing their homework or making excuses for their achieve-ment problems. This experience of control by others and their lack of personal control often convinces them that they are unable to act (or learn) on their own, that everything that hap-pens is related to external and uncontrollable forces, and leads to learned helpless behavior. For example, a study of adolescents with mild mental retardation indicated that these stu-dents experienced more learned helplessness than their typical peers. The learned helpless-ness was attributed to the significant levels of school failure experienced by these students, failure that they could not avoid by their own efforts. Learned helplessness appeared to inter-fere with their learning progress and was found to be related to later instances of observed depression (Reynolds & Miller, 1985).

In a similar vein, Brehm and Brehm (1981) found that the loss of freedom and control of one's destiny, particularly when accompanied by the imposition of external restraints or control, generally leads to increased motivation to restore the lost freedom. They called this response "psychological reactance." The more important the freedom, the stronger the moti-

---

IN THE CLASSROOM **12.8**

Learned Helplessness

Ray, a sixth grader with learning disabilities and ADHD, is placed in an inclusion classroom. He tends to rely on external supports such as teacher prompts and assistance even when he is capable of completing a task independently. He quickly gives up on assignments that are only slightly challenging, saying, "I don't know how to do this." His intrinsic motivation for self-determination and control is in conflict with this learned helplessness. Although he is quick to say he can't do something, he is also quick to dismiss assistance offered by his teachers. They recognize these signs of learned helplessness and are developing an intervention program to help Ray de-velop more independence.

vation to regain it. However, they also noted that when individuals become convinced that the freedom is irretrievably lost, they generally abandon the quest, leading to a condition similar to learned helplessness. The degree to which a youngster feels that a task or situation presents impossible demands determines how much motivation will remain. Teachers may want to evaluate the degree to which a youngster views a task as possible as an indication of how much motivation to learn can be mobilized.

Similarly, students with ADHD who take medication for hyperactivity and inattention frequently come to believe they cannot control themselves without it. The next step is for these learners to refuse to accept responsibility for their learning or lack of learning, or for their behavioral control. It appears that children with disabilities can learn helplessness as surely as they learn competence (Balk, 1983).

Adolescents with Disabilities in Behavior and Learning

All adolescent students present special challenges to their parents and educators. Students with mild disabilities are no exception (Kerr, Nelson, & Lambert, 1987). The problems and issues encountered by typical adolescents are compounded for students with disabilities that affect learning and behavior. Challenges associated with identity exploration, self-determination, and biological changes, as well as with the development of the social inter-action and career skills needed for adult life, are faced by all teenagers. These challenges may be exacerbated by specific issues related to the young person's disability, such as

- Poor academic achievement or reaching an academic learning plateau
- Deficits in cognitive processing
- Ineffective study skills and cognitive strategies needed for problem-solving and self-regulated learning
- Social skill deficits and other problem behaviors
- Motivational deficits induced by failure, passive learning styles, and learned help-lessness.

In the 1970s, the Institute for Research on Learning Disabilities at the University of Kansas began investigating the characteristics of adolescents with learning disabilities. As they looked at these young people, they discovered some common patterns of behavior (Alley & Deshler, 1979; Johnston, 1984):

- Growing discrepancy between ability and achievement, including difficulty in reading, spelling, and/or mathematics
- Reduced ability to retain information; disorganized thinking patterns
- Inability to stay on task, although attention appears to improve
- Poor study habits and inconsistent organization of school tasks
- Continued difficulties with fine motor skills (e.g., poor handwriting), although gross motor skills are improved

- More frequent manifestation of emotional symptoms, including a tendency to over-respond to social stresses
- Tendency to be unaware of their effect on others in social situations
- Tendency for learning and behavioral problems to become more covert as increased maturity masks characteristics more common at younger ages.

In addition, these researchers confirmed that the demands of the high school environment are significantly different from the demands encountered in elementary school. Secondary teachers routinely expect that students will be relatively independent in their learning skills. High school teachers tend to concentrate instruction in course content, providing less of the cognitive coaching and skill development activities commonly available in the elementary grades. Secondary teachers expect students to be proficient in independently carrying out the following tasks:

- Acquiring information by studying and note-taking
- Devising ways to remember information
- Demonstrating competence by performance in complex written formats on assignments and tests.

Significant mismatches can occur between the learning profile of a specific student with a disability and the demands of the high school environment, resulting in impaired performance and school failure. One indication of this mismatch is the amount of stress exhibited by these young people and the coping strategies they use to deal with it. In a study of the stresses encountered by young adolescents with learning disabilities, Geisthardt and Munsch (1996) found that these students experienced stressors in similar proportions to other students, although they were much more likely to fail a class and less likely to be chosen for a special school activity. Both of these factors have implications for the adolescent's sense of competence and self-worth. These students were also found to more often respond to academic stresses with cognitive avoidance and denial and were less apt to seek help from a friend when faced with a problem, strategies frequently used when a problem seems out of one's control. These strategies are problematic in the long run, as they indicate the likelihood that the adolescent will move into adulthood without the skills to actively deal with problems and without a support network composed of friends (Wenz-Gross & Siperstein, 1997).

Although these research efforts focused specifically on adolescents with learning disabilities, the patterns and issues have been found to apply generally to students with other mild disabilities as well. Research on students with behavioral disorders indicates that they too face significant academic problems in high school. Their academic difficulty also increases as they move from the elementary to the secondary level; since academic underachievement is a common characteristic of this group, this fact places them at risk from the beginning. Kortering and Blackorby (1992) report that students with behavioral disorders fail to graduate from high school at a rate that is significantly higher (as high as 80 percent) than their typical peers. The students who dropped out were characterized as having frequent school and program placement changes, indicating that their school programs may not have been as appropriate or continuous as one might hope. Foley and Epstein (1992) found that students with organizational deficits in managing time, poor test-taking skills, content reading problems, and an external locus of control—all commonly observed in students with mild disabilities—tended to fare more poorly academically. The picture that emerges of students with behavioral disorders is consistent with the earlier description of those with learning disabilities.

One of the central tasks facing the young person is to develop *self-determination,* the condition of "acting as the primary causal agent in one's life and making choices and decisions regarding one's quality of life free from external influence or interference" (Wehmeyer, Kelchner, & Richards, 1996, p. 632). It involves the experience of acting out of choice rather than responding to coercion or obligation (Deci & Ryan, 1985; Wehmeyer, 1992, 1994; Wehmeyer, Agran, & Hughes, 1998; Wehmeyer, et al., 1996; Wehmeyer & Schwartz, 1997). It develops over the life span, with critical developmental periods in childhood and adolescence. The opportunity to make choices, express preferences, experience personal control over outcomes, take risks, and assume responsibility for personal actions is a highly valued indicator of becoming an adult. The importance of self-determination is reflected in the amendments to the IDEA (1990, 1997) that now require the involvement of adolescents aged fourteen and over in transition planning (Field, Hoffman, & Posch, 1997; Sands & Doll, 1996).

Self-determination is affected by four attributes: autonomy, self-regulation, psychological empowerment, and self realization (Wehmeyer et al., 1996), all of which present particular challenges to adolescents with disabilities. Students with disabilities frequently have had little opportunity to practice autonomous decision-making skills, particularly as the severity of the disability increases. This lack of opportunity to develop the skills required by autonomy promotes passive responses, learned helplessness, and dependency, leading the adolescents and others to believe that they are incapable of making their own decisions. Deficits in metacognition result in less skill in the self-examination and strategic knowledge necessary to solve problems, and in a random or haphazard approach to self-regulation activities. The tendency of youngsters with disabilities to be delayed in self-regulation causes them to interact with significant others in ways that lead others to conclude that they are incapable of making choices and must be protected. Psychological empowerment is derived primarily from a perceived sense of control of one's life. As noted previously, young people with disabilities tend to develop an external locus of control and to attribute their successes and failures to factors beyond their control. Their experience with failure and negative feedback as well as with events that appear unpredictable or uncontrollable affects their persistence and motivation, resulting in a diminished sense of perceived control (Deci & Chandler, 1986). The life experience of adolescents with mild disabilities leads them to focus on what they cannot do, building on their experience of failure (Wehmeyer et al., 1996; see In the Classroom 12.9).

An evaluation of the progress of an adolescent in becoming a self-determined adult is a critical factor in creating an appropriate educational program and in planning for transition. Those students who leave their adolescent years without a strong sense of self-determination are more likely to experience problems in employment and self-sufficiency during their adult years (Wehmeyer & Schwartz, 1997). Teenagers with disabilities must be viewed as active participants in their educational programs. As they play active roles in determining what they need to learn, why they want to learn it, and how they are going to learn it, the likelihood increases that positive outcomes will be achieved and that they will grow in their sense of self-determination (Field, et al., 1997).

Adolescents and Self-Determination

Karen is a tenth grader receiving services for learning disabilities and ADHD. She has developed into a young woman with a strong set of values about what is right and wrong, and she is not easily swayed by others. She says she gets into a lot of fights standing up for her friends or for what she believes. She thinks about possible choices when a problem arises, then "goes with what's right." However, she is influenced by peer pressure in the classroom and frequently will not ask questions for fear of sounding "stupid." Karen says she works hard in school when she has "good days" (Fridays, gym days, soccer days, cheerleading days, days she isn't fighting with anyone). Learning results in an increased sense of competence; when she passes tests she feels good about herself, and she attributes her success to studying and working hard. Failures are often attributed to external forces, such as "the work was too hard," "the teacher didn't read the whole test to me," or "I am stupid." Karen is clearly working on determining her identity; when she is with her friends, she acts in a confident manner, sure of herself; when she encounters difficulty in class, she feels like she is "different."

Learning Styles and Multiple Intelligences

Early in the history of learning disabilities, it was hypothesized that these disabilities were related to deficits in specific processing modalities or channels. It was believed that a prescription of specific procedures to remediate these deficits would allow the child to function normally in the school environment. This hypothesis, called the "aptitude-treatment interaction," is predicated on the premise that a specific treatment matched to a specific ability or deficit will result in skill improvement (Fuchs & Fuchs, 1986; Lloyd, 1984). Subsequent research has failed to support this hypothesis for a variety of reasons: (1) it is not possible to accurately assess many of these aptitudes; (2) it has not been possible to consistently design valid treatments to match specific deficits and abilities; and (3) it has not been possible to measure the interaction, or outcome of intervention, with any degree of confidence (Fuchs & Fuchs, 1986; Kavale, Hirshoren, & Forness, 1998; Snider, 1992). As noted in the discussion of the work of Treiber and Lahey (1983) in Chapter 10, even when children developed their skills in the prescribed remedial activities, they were often not able to transfer those skills to related academic tasks.

That said, it is important to discuss aspects of diversity among students with respect to learning from two additional theoretical perspectives that bear some similarities to the earlier processing deficit theories. The first, learning styles, deals with the context and nature of instruction, suggesting that the instructional environment and teaching methods should be selected to support the learning style of each student. The second perspective, multiple intelligences, focuses on individual students and their innate and varying abilities to solve problems and to create products that are of value in societal interactions.

Learning Styles

While few now support the processing deficit approach to remediation, a similar discussion continues concerning instructional accommodation of different learning styles within instructional settings, both in general education and special education programs. Proponents recommend this approach to instructional programming as an answer to underachievement among students in general, and particularly with students with mild disabilities, despite inconsistent research findings on its general applicability and efficacy (Kavale, Hirshoren, & Forness, 1998).

The basic tenet of learning style theory is that individuals possess certain characteristics that interact with specific learning experiences and environments, resulting in the enhancement of learning or in making learning more difficult. Learning style theory is concerned with how students learn, with the personal abilities they apply to learning tasks, and with the means by which they accommodate and assimilate new information. Specifically, proponents like Rita and Kenneth Dunn believe that it is possible to identify the particular learning style of a student and then to select methods of instruction that match that style, increasing the likelihood that instruction will be successful (Carbo, 1987; Dunn, 1995). Others have suggested that there are three learning styles related to the way individuals prefer to acquire new information: (1) visual learners who are most effective using reading, watching demonstrations, and drawing pictures; (2) auditory learners who learn best through listening, and participating in discussions; and (3) kinesthetic learners who learn most effectively through hands-on experiences with manipulatives and other media (Melton & Pickett, 1997). The work of Rita and Kenneth Dunn has provided the basis for most learning style assessment and procedures (Carbo, 1987; Carbo & Hodges, 1988; Dunn, 1995). They suggest that teachers need to consider the characteristics and preferences of learners as they relate to physical environment, method of instruction, modality preferences, motivation and feedback, and types of working groups when making instructional plans.

Nevertheless, while it is generally recognized that all human beings relate somewhat differently to instruction, and that the act of learning is affected by individual and environmental variables, reversing this reasoning appears to be afflicted with the same problems that characterized earlier process deficit and training theories (Frostig's perceptual-motor training and Kirk's psycholinguistic theories) and aptitude-treatment interaction approaches in general (Kavale, Hirshoren, & Forness, 1998; Snider, 1992). Specifically, the instruments used to assess learning style preferences have been found to have questionable validity and reliability; the teaching methods are only superficially related to any particular style; and the effect of such a match is difficult to measure. While there may be some value in the notion that learners approach learning uniquely, it is not necessarily possible or desirable to individually tailor a child's instructional environment to any specific style. Teachers may be more effective by providing a variety of ways for all of their learners to encounter and practice the skills and content of the curriculum, and then guiding students in identifying for themselves the ones that are most useful for them (see In the Classroom 12.10).

Teachers who plan instruction in accordance with the principles of Universal Design for Learning make classroom activities accessible to most learners, despite disabilities or differences in learning styles.

IN THE CLASSROOM **12.10**

Learning Styles

Aaron and Carolyn are eighth graders with mild disabilities. Aaron's teacher has noted that he does much better in mainstream classes where the teacher uses visual media and demonstrations to explain the content. He has more difficulty in history class where the teacher uses lecture and discussion methods exclusively. This leads his teacher to conclude that Aaron benefits from the use of visual presenta-tion methods and that exclusive use of auditory presentations puts Aaron at a disadvantage for learning. Carolyn, on the other hand, has great difficulty learning from reading but does much better when she can also hear the material. Their teacher concludes that both students will benefit from instruction that includes both visual and auditory input and an opportunity for active involvement in learning.

Multiple Intelligences

Related to this discussion of learning styles is Howard Gardner's theory of multiple intelligences (Gardner, 1983, 1991, 1993, 1995, 1996). In the tradition of cognitive styles research, Gardner has advanced the theory that each individual possesses at least eight distinct ways of thinking and learning, solving problems, and creating valued products: (1) linguistic intelligence, (2) logical-mathematical intelligence, (3) musical intelligence, (4) spatial intelligence, (5) bodily-kinesthetic intelligence, (6) intrapersonal intelligence, (7) interpersonal intelligence, and (8) naturalist intelligence (see Table 12.1). He viewed all of these intelligences as having equal standing. Gardner also hypothesized that each person will exhibit a profile of these intelligences reflecting specific intra-individual strengths. He asserted that these intelligences are not discrete entities but rather function in a variety of overlapping and complementary ways in real life situations. Finally, he proposed that everyone has the potential to develop skills in all eight intelligences (Armstrong, 1994).

Gardner (1983, 1991, 1993, 1995) proposed that the difficulties some individuals experience in our current schooling process may actually be due to the fact that their stronger skills and intelligences lie in areas not generally tapped by common school curricula and practices. It has been asserted by some (e.g., Hearne & Stone, 1995) that schools' preoccupation with linguistic and logical-mathematical abilities may cause other intelligences to be devalued and underdeveloped. The extent to which programming decisions for children are based almost entirely on their deficits in linguistic and logical-mathematical areas may restrict their development in other areas of strength, and the learner may be disadvantaged in the teaching-learning environment because of a lack of fit. (For an example, see the case study of Sammy at the end of Chapter 13.) Ironically, the development of intelligences other than linguistic and logical-mathematical is seen as necessary for success in many post-school environments. Interpersonal and intrapersonal intelligences are particularly needed for students to achieve success in the adult world of work and should be clearly addressed in school programs.

TABLE 12.1   Gardner's Multiple Intelligences

Type of Intelligence	Description of Specific Skill or Ability
Linguistic intelligence	Verbal facility; skill in the use of words
Logical-mathematical intelligence	Symbolic reasoning and skills in dealing with abstract reasoning and problem-solving; recognizing patterns and order
Musical intelligence	Skill in performance and appreciation of musical forms of expression; sensitivity to pitch, rhythm, and tone
Spatial intelligence	Awareness of the structural components of ideas and objects, and the ability to transform structures mentally; ability to work effectively in a three-dimensional world
Bodily-kinesthetic intelligence	Ability to use movement for learning and expression; skillful use of the body and manipulating objects to produce a desired outcome
Intrapersonal intelligence	Ability to understand one's own feelings and emotions as a means of self-development and growth
Interpersonal intelligence	Awareness of others and social interactions; ability to apply social understandings to interactions with others
Naturalist intelligence	Sensitivity to, and ability to differentiate among living things as well as sensitivity to other features of the natural world

Based on Checkley (1997).

Gardner (1996) voiced caution, however, in applying the theory of multiple intelligences in a restrictive and prescriptive manner. He acknowledges that this is an evolving concept, and that practitioners need to work out their own understandings of its implications. Gardner's framework suggests that each person will vary in the means by which learning happens most effectively and by which achievement is demonstrated most clearly. When considering the theory of multiple intelligences, teachers may want to consider ways of creating learning environments that recognize and value all the intelligences rather than focusing exclusively on the linguistic and logical-mathematical forms (Hoerr, 1996).

Universal Design for Learning

Discussion of these theories and perspectives continues. While it is not entirely clear how the frameworks of learning styles and multiple intelligences might affect schooling in general and special education in particular, it appears reasonable to suggest that educators consider all the strengths presented by their students. IDEA 1997 requires educational plans to consider a student's strengths, not merely the deficits. It may well be that developing a student's abilities in other forms of intelligence will assist in the development of the currently valued linguistic and logical-mathematical intelligences. It may be that attention to students' preferred ways of working and learning may help educators design instructional interventions that make use of untapped strengths to support learning, and that by using more diverse teaching methods and activities, more effective learning will occur. As educators develop instructional activities that are consistent with the principles of Universal Design for Learning (see www.cast.org), the likelihood increases that all students will be able to successfully access the learning environment.

Instructional Needs of Learners with Disabilities

As we consider the instructional needs of learners with mild disabilities, we need to consider the variables that affect how well students learn in school and how these variables interact with student characteristics. Carroll (1963) suggested that students will be successful in learning to the extent that they actually spend the amount of time needed to master the task or concept. In his model of school learning, Carroll defined the time spent by the learner as a function of the actual clock time allowed for learning and the persistence or motivation of the learner to stick with the learning tasks. He further defined the time needed by the student as determined by the quality of instruction, the student's aptitude for instruction, and the student's ability to understand instruction.

The rate and efficiency of learning depends on how effectively the time allocated for learning is used (Graham, 1985). If no time is allocated for a learning task, no learning will result. If too little time is spent, then the resultant learning will be incomplete. If the time available is devoted to tasks that are incomprehensible to the learner, or if time is spent repeating errors, learning will not proceed with maximum efficiency. Furthermore, if the learner is required to continue a learning activity past the point of mastery and proficiency, no further learning occurs (see Figure 12.3).

As we consider instructional variables that affect the success and efficiency of learning, it might be useful to discuss each of these elements individually, with particular attention to their relationship to the characteristics of learners with mild disabilities and to the stages of learning discussed earlier.

Time Allowed for Instruction

Learners with mild disabilities are likely to need more actual time to learn. Given actual time constraints, it is important to make careful decisions about the allocation of time in order to insure that the most critical learning has sufficient time allocated to it. Studies of time use in schools indicate that a significant amount of time is used on nonacademic pursuits or in off-task, nonengaged behavior. Time in school is further eroded when students are pulled from their primary classrooms for remedial help, using significant amounts of time traveling the halls (see In the Classroom 12.11). When one measures the actual academic learning time,

Model of School Learning

$$\text{Degree of learning} = \frac{\text{Time actually spent}}{\text{Time needed}}$$

FIGURE 12.3 Carroll's Model of School Learning

IN THE CLASSROOM 12.11

Time to Learn

Gail is in ninth grade and receives resource room services for her learning disability in reading and written expression. Now that she attends the high school, her time in regular classes is not disrupted by these services. In elementary and middle school, she lost instructional time traveling to the resource room and getting back on task on her return to class.

Now, she spends her study hall period in the resource room, where she receives instruction in learning strategies that help her meet the reading and writing demands of her content classes. Her motivation to use this assistance to do well allows her allocated time in the resource room to be fully used in the pursuit of learning.

or the time spent engaged in learning with a high rate of success, it is frequently meager indeed (Denham & Lieberman, 1980).

Persistence or Motivation

As noted earlier in this chapter, students are motivated by different goals and needs. Even more importantly, motivation is affected by the quality of prior learning. Motivation alone cannot cause students to do that which they lack the preparation to do. Difficulty in maintaining attention to academic tasks also affects the student's ability to stay with the task long enough to complete the learning. As teachers, we must assess prior relevant learnings for robustness as we evaluate a specific student's zone of proximal development (see Chapter 10). We can also evaluate teaching and learning activities for the likelihood that participation will help students meet their goals and needs. Finally, we must assess the quality of the attention paid by learners and then modify learning time demands to accommodate and develop their attention spans.

Pupils' Aptitude for Instruction

This variable requires an accurate assessment of the aptitudes and prior learning that students bring to classrooms, and that we use that knowledge to design classroom activities. Obviously, general intellectual functioning is a variable, but we also need to understand how students process cognitive information, the nature of their attention capabilities, their motivation for learning, their specific abilities in using and understanding language, and the quality of prior learning. We also need to consider that the ability of some students to profit from instruction may be reduced by a variety of social or emotional factors.

Ability to Understand Instruction

The factors that affect this variable include competence in the use and comprehension of spoken and written language. Students learning English as a second language will have more difficulty understanding instruction provided in standard English, and they will need to be provided with supports and additional language instruction to become most effective in learning (see Chapter 11). The ability to understand instruction may also be affected by social or emotional demands that command a student's energies needed for learning (see Chapter 13).

Quality of Instruction

Of all the factors in Carroll's model, this is the one most clearly within the teacher's ability to control. Research summarized by Christenson, Ysseldyke, & Thurlow (1989) indicates that a number of critical instructional factors are essential to the learning success of students with mild disabilities (see Table 12.2). One pedagogical concern relates to the nature of the interaction between the student's individual characteristics (such as cognitive reasoning abilities, language competencies, motivation, and emotional and behavioral characteristics) and the method of instruction used by the teacher. In general, research on effective teaching of students with mild disabilities has suggested that direct instruction is preferable to other methods such as inquiry learning (Ellis, 1993). Mastropieri, Scruggs, and Butcher (1997) confirmed this in their study of student performance on an inductive inquiry task in science. In this study, students with learning disabilities and mental retardation were significantly less successful in discovering on their own the rule being demonstrated, and they required much more directive coaching to be successful. This suggests that teachers should use caution in assuming that learning has occurred subsequent to nondirective classroom activity; inquiry learning experiences may need to be followed up with additional direct instruction and practice for these students to fully learn concepts and skills.

Focus on Culture and Diversity

When we consider the academic learning characteristics of students with disabilities, we must eventually consider factors that contribute to making the educational environment feel supportive or hostile to the learner. Unfortunately, today the outcome of hostile school envi-

---

TABLE 12.2   Critical Instructional Variables

- Effective, efficient classroom management
- Positive school climate
- Instruction designed to meet learner needs
- Clear learning goals
- Clarity in lesson presentation
- Support for learners
- Time allocated for academic learning as a priority
- Instruction allowing frequent student responses
- Active monitoring of student understanding and progress
- Frequent performance evaluation

(Based on Christenson, Ysseldyke, & Thurlow, 1989)

ronments is all too evident: bullies and harassment, school violence, and high drop-out rates remind us that a number of students do not find school a place that meets their needs. When students feel excluded, marginalized, or unsafe because of who they are, by virtue of their abilities, race, language, ethnicity, language, religion, gender, physical attributes, family structure, economic status, or sexual orientation, learning is certain to be compromised and may become impossible. Educators must work to see that every child finds school to be a comfortable place to learn.

High school graduation rates are one indicator of the success of an academic program. U.S. Department of Education (2001) data indicates that 57.4 percent of students with disabilities graduated with a standard diploma in 1998–99, but that rates were much lower for students with mental retardation (41.7 percent) and emotional disturbance (41.9 percent). It was also reported that White students with disabilities had a 63.4 percent graduation rate, while only 43.5 percent of African-American students with disabilities graduated. Drop-out rates were highest among Native-American students (44 percent) and African-American students (33.7 percent). It is clear that students with disabilities who are African American and Native American are being left behind. Finally, issues related to family poverty must be considered in any discussion of academic performance. Poverty has repeatedly been shown to be related to academic failure (Coutinho, Oswald, & Best, 2002; Coutinho, Oswald, & Forness, 2002). Unfortunately, students with disabilities whose lives are also affected by poverty and racial or linguistic differences are at significantly more risk of school failure (U.S. Department of Education, 2001). Educators must find out why this is so.

It has been suggested that increasing the number of diverse educators would also help address these problems (Salend, Garrick Duhaney, & Montgomery, 2002). One response to the above findings is for districts to find ways to diversify their staffs, recruiting educators who represent diverse backgrounds and/or who have had successful experiences working with diverse learners.

Resources on the Web

The Arc

www.TheArc.org

Provides a number of resources related to the topic of self-determination.

National Center on Accessing the General Curriculum

www.cast.org/ncac

Explains the principles of Universal Design for Learning, including ways to make the general education curriculum accessible to a broad variety of student abilities.

Teaching Tolerance

www.tolerance.org

Provides a number of teaching resources for educators to use in making the curriculum more supportive of the needs of diverse students.

Gay, Lesbian, and Straight Education Network (GLSEN)

www.glsen.org

Provides information and resources for creating safer school environments for all, with particular emphasis on gay, lesbian, bisexual, and transgender youth.

Summary

Learning is the process of moving from "not knowing" to "knowing and using." Five stages mark the progress of the learner: acquisition, proficiency, maintenance, generalization, and adaptation. Learners with mild disabilities tend to move through the stages more slowly and to need more support or scaffolding to achieve each the goals of the stages.

The ability of learners to process information cognitively is critical to their academic success. Deficits in attention, short- or long-term memory, and executive control functions present special problems as teachers tend to assume the control, direction, and monitoring of learning for the student, often resulting in passive learning styles.

Motivation is critical to all human endeavors, including learning. Extrinsic motivation is supplied by rewards or punishments that reinforce learned behaviors. Intrinsic motivation comes from the individual learner's personal needs and drives, such as the need for competence, self-determination, or relatedness.

Learners also vary in their perceptions of their perceived control of outcomes. Those who view events as determined by luck or the actions of other people are said to have an external locus of control. Those who see outcomes as determined by their own efforts are said to have an internal locus of control, which has been shown to be associated with greater learning effectiveness. Significant experiences of failure frequently lead to a failure spiral, while successes can result in a success spiral. In response to failure, students with disabilities frequently develop learned helplessness, the belief that nothing they do will affect the outcome.

Adolescents with disabilities face unique challenges in school learning. Their areas of deficits frequently prevent them from meeting the expectations of secondary teachers. Self-determination, a crucial learning for all adolescents, is the ability to act as the primary causal agent in one's life, to make choices and decisions independently. The effect of a disability may impede the development of the self-determination so necessary for adult independence.

The theories of learning styles and multiple intelligences suggest that each student approaches the task of learning in potentially unique ways, which suggests the need for tailoring instruction to individual preferences. An alternative approach to meeting individual needs is to plan instruction in accordance with the principles of Universal Design for Learning, which provide multiple ways for learners to access the educational environment.

In concluding our discussion of academic learning characteristics, it is important to note that knowledge of student characteristics can lead us to make more effective decisions about instructional techniques and the type of environments necessary to be most supportive of student achievement. In addition, each student's opportunity to learn will be enhanced by assuring that each student has the time needed to learn effectively and that instructional decisions are made with the primary goal of increasing efficiency of learning.

ALLISON: A Case Study

Allison is an eight-year old girl classified as having mental retardation. She is presently enrolled in Mrs. Riley's self-contained special education classroom. Allison has been progressing nicely in Mrs. Riley's class for the past two months. She has particularly demonstrated growth in mathematics. However, Allison is a timid child who has difficulty functioning in large groups. She becomes easily distracted and anxious when surrounded by more than a few other children. She needs extra support and encouragement to interact with her peers.

Allison's mother, Jane Miller, has been very impressed with her daughter's recent achievement in mathematics. She suggested to Mrs. Riley that Allison be mainstreamed into a general education classroom for math. In response to her suggestion, Mrs. Riley said that although Allison has demonstrated significant improvements in mathematics, she has difficulty functioning in large groups and may need more time to strengthen her self-confidence and social skills. Mrs. Riley thought that Allison would eventually be ready for mainstreaming, but that it was premature to consider it at this stage.

Disappointed by Mrs. Riley's response, Mrs. Miller met with the Director of Special Education and expressed her strong belief that Allison should be mainstreamed for mathematics. She then asked the director to schedule a meeting of the multidisciplinary team to discuss the situation.

The meeting was scheduled within the week, and Mrs. Miller presented her suggestion to the committee. "I am very pleased with Allison's progress in mathematics," she said. "I am also aware that Allison has difficulty socializing; however, I believe that Allison would benefit, both socially and academically, from being mainstreamed in math. She would have the perfect opportunity to strengthen her social skills with a greater number of students, while getting the more sophisticated math instruction she needs."

Mrs. Riley responded, "Mrs. Miller, I am as pleased as you are with Allison's progress in math. I am not concerned with Allison's ability to succeed academically; in fact, Mrs. Armstrong's first grade class is covering the same math concepts that Allison is working on. I have considered Mrs. Armstrong's class as a possibility for Allison to eventually be mainstreamed into. At this point, I strongly recommend that Allison remain in my class where we can work on her self-esteem and improve her social skills. I am afraid that mainstreaming Allison at this point would be too overwhelming. Allison has a tendency to cry when she is surrounded by a group of children, and it is very difficult for her to function appropriately, let alone do her best, in such an environment. Let's wait before we subject Allison to an environment for which she may not be ready."

Mrs. Miller forcefully explained, "If Allison were mainstreamed, it would be a parent's dream come true. It would go a long way to reducing the stigma of Allison's having been labeled mentally retarded. IDEA requires that a child be educated in the least restrictive environment. Let us at least do Allison justice and give her the opportunity to work in a regular classroom with regular kids! We cannot possibly know that Allison would not be able to function in a regular classroom until we give her a chance."

The decision was finalized at the meeting. Allison would be mainstreamed into Mrs. Armstrong's classroom for mathematics beginning the following Monday. It was agreed at the meeting that a student from Mrs. Riley's class would walk Allison to and from Mrs. Armstrong's class until Allison felt comfortable walking by herself.

On Monday, Allison arrived at Mrs. Armstrong's class with her classmate Jenny. Mrs. Armstrong welcomed Allison warmly and introduced her to the class. One of the students in the class said, "Hi! You can sit next to me. My name is Tracey." Allison held tight to Jenny's hand and didn't take another step. Jenny said, "Come on Allison. You're going to sit here," and began walking Allison to the empty seat next to Tracey. Allison sat down apprehensively, and Jenny returned to Mrs. Riley's class.

Five days had passed when the following scene took place. It was a scenario that had become common in Mrs. Armstrong's classroom:

(continued)

Mrs. Armstrong asked, "Tracey, could you please share your crayons with Allison?"

Tracey replied, "I'm not sharing my crayons with her—she never gives them back and she puts them in her mouth!"

Peter added, "Yeah, and she always cries like a big baby when you want your stuff back!"

Allison, with tears in her eyes, pleaded, "Let me go back to Mrs. Riley's class—please, let me go!"

Adapted with permission from "When Mainstreaming Fails" by Karin Otto-Flynn.

DISCUSSION

Discuss Allison's experience with respect to the major topics in this chapter:

- Social learning theory
- Stages of learning
- Cognitive processing and academic performance
- Motivation
- Attributions of success and failure
- Learned helplessness.

Based on this analysis, how might this scenario have had a different outcome? What actions might both teachers have taken to make this a more successful experience?

CHAPTER THIRTEEN

SOCIAL–EMOTIONAL CHARACTERISTICS

QUESTIONS TO GUIDE YOUR STUDY

- List and describe two perspectives from which social-emotional characteristics might be viewed.
- What are the implications of Erikson's psychosocial theory for understanding the emotional development of individuals with disabilities?
- What are some indicators of an individual's level of emotional development?
- How does social perspective taking develop over the life span?
- What are the major components contributing to social competence in learners with disabilities?
- What is the difference between social awareness and social skill?
- Why might social cognitive delay be a common characteristic of learners with mild disabilities?
- What are behavioral flexibility and newness panic? How do they affect a learner's adjustment in the classroom?
- What does IDEA 1997 require of schools in responding to problem behaviors in school?
- When might a behavior be considered maladaptive?
- Describe the difference between the two types of conduct disorders.
- Describe the manifestations and implications of depression in children and adolescents.

Meet Eddie

Eddie is seven years old and a first grader in Mrs. Williams' class. He is one of three children, with a younger sister and an older brother. Mrs. Williams has become increasingly concerned about Eddie's tendency to fly into a rage when he encounters frustration. He responds to frustration with behavior more typical of a much younger child by hitting, kicking, biting, and spitting at other children in the classroom and at home. His mother reports that he is particularly violent with his sister.

Eddie's mother has told the social worker that she is unable to control Eddie at home. She seems to be overwhelmed by the care of three young children. When Eddie loses his temper, her only recourse is to remove the other children from the apartment. She reports that Eddie has been abused by adults in his

(continued)

life—physically by his father, who is no longer in the home, and sexually by an uncle who has been committed to the state hospital.

Eddie was referred to the local mental health agency for an evaluation. The evaluator found that Eddie's intellectual functioning fell within the borderline range of mental retardation with academic measures below grade level but consistent with his IQ of 72. He found evidence of oppositional and controlling tendencies, which supported a diagnosis of oppositional defiant disorder. The school multidisciplinary team recommended placement in a day treatment program for children with emotional disorders. They felt that Eddie should be able to experience success both at home and in his school environment with appropriate therapeutic interventions to address his emotional and behavioral needs, along with small group academic instruction.

Meanwhile, Eddie's teacher, his mother, and the social worker have put in place a behavior modification program involving earning privileges and the use of time-out. They are finding it difficult to carry out the program consistently, however, due to the nature of Eddie's violent outbursts, and the social worker is investigating placement in a therapeutic foster home.

Perspectives on Social–Emotional Characteristics

Behavioral responses are adaptive when they result in socially acceptable and personally satisfying outcomes. On the other hand, social-emotional behaviors are deemed to be problematic when they become socially unacceptable or personally unsatisfying (Kauffman, 1977). Behaviors become problematic in two ways:

- The learner may fail to develop age-appropriate social behaviors or may develop appropriate behaviors more slowly than typical children do, restricting the ability to participate productively in ways that are appropriate for the learner's age or culture. The child may also be blocked in the normal developmental progression, restricting the child's ability to accomplish later social learnings, and leading to accumulating deficits in social behavior.

■ Maladaptive behaviors may be present. The learner may exhibit substitute behaviors that are maladaptive responses to environmental events and personal issues and that take the place of more useful behaviors, compromising the youngster's functioning in critical ways.

The difficulties presented by learners who have problems in identifying, choosing, and using appropriate and adaptive social responses may be considered from two theoretical perspectives that help explain the meaning of the behaviors exhibited by a particular learner:

■ Developmental perspectives, which consider typical social skill progressions observed in learners as they develop age-appropriate levels of social awareness and behavioral responses
■ Ecological perspectives, which describe behavior as a result of the interactions between the characteristics of the individual learner, the nature of the environment, and the behavioral context in which a particular behavior occurs.

At the end of the chapter, we will discuss the most frequent types of maladaptive behaviors presented by some learners with mild disabilities. The concepts developed in this chapter apply to any learner with a disability whose behavior is of concern, including students with mental retardation, learning disabilities, and ADHD, as well as to those with emotional or behavioral disorders.

Developmental Perspectives

Developmentalists such as Piaget, Erikson, and Kohlberg generally hold that behaviors and emotions develop in a predictable manner throughout the life span. Over the years, individuals incorporate learnings from typical life events into their own unique personalities. These theorists suggest that knowledge about normal development in children, adolescents, and adults is useful as a guide when designing instructional interventions for students whose development appears to be following a different path or pace.

Erikson's Theory of Psychosocial Development

Erik Erikson (Erikson, 1963; Papilia & Olds, 1990) formulated his theory of psychosocial development based on his concern about the effect of societal and cultural factors on the development of the ego, or self. He identified eight predictable stages of life, each of which is characterized by a particular life challenge or *crisis*. As individuals work to resolve each of these crises, they develop socially and emotionally. Erikson asserted that the development of a healthy sense of self was dependent on the individual's coming to a successful resolution of each of these eight successive crises (see Table 13.1).

Each stage is characterized by two opposite outcomes. Satisfactory resolution of each stage results in the individual's developing a strong sense of the positive quality, appropriately balanced by the negative. For example, infants who develop a healthy balance in the trust versus mistrust stage come to view the world and people as generally trustworthy, while maintaining enough mistrust to allow them to protect themselves from potential

TABLE 13.1   **Stages of Psychosocial Development**

Stage or Crisis	Virtue/Goal	Time Period
Basic trust vs. mistrust	Hope	Birth to 12–18 months
Autonomy vs. shame	Willpower	12–18 months to 3 years
Initiative vs. guilt	Purpose	3 to 6 years
Industry vs. inferiority	Competence	6 years to puberty
Identity vs. role confusion	Fidelity	Puberty to young adult
Intimacy vs. isolation	Love	Early adult years
Generativity vs. stagnation	Care	Middle adult years
Ego integrity vs. despair	Wisdom	Late adult years

Based on Erikson, 1963.

dangers. Children who fail to resolve this crisis in a positive direction in infancy will continue to view the world as a scary place and are likely to have trouble forming satisfactory interpersonal relationships until they can be helped to develop trusting relationships with significant others.

In the autonomy versus shame stage, the toddler learns to strike an appropriate balance between self-determination and control. The initiative versus guilt stage challenges the child to balance the pursuit of goals with appropriate reservations or caution about carrying them out. The industry versus inferiority stage helps the child develop a sense of competence, value for productive work, and a positive, but realistic self-concept. Adolescents struggle with the identity versus role confusion stage as they determine who they are and to what they will commit their life (e.g., careers, values, loved ones). Through this process, teenagers develop a strong sense of self while keeping themselves open to later growth. The final three stages relate to the challenges faced by adults in developing intimacy, productivity, and wholeness. In each stage, Erikson believed that the individual's experience with significant others will be critical in determining if a healthy sense of self will be the outcome.

As we look at learners with disabilities, we can identify several ways in which normal development may be hindered, affecting the ability of the individual to interact productively with others. Obviously the child whose needs have not been met reliably in infancy is more likely to have problems with trust throughout life. Caregivers during childhood will find it difficult to form relationships with such youngsters. Children like Eddie may exhibit emotional problems in their interactions with others, and it will be important to document and address these trust needs (Arent, 1992).

Toddlers whose world is circumscribed by overprotectiveness or restriction may fail to develop the healthy sense of self-determined behavior necessary for later academic and social learning. Children who are reticent and reserved in attempting new tasks or interacting with new people may have been restricted in setting and achieving goals in their early play experiences. Elementary age youngsters who find school-valued academic tasks difficult due to mental retardation, learning disabilities, or ADHD, or whose special education classification is used by others to excuse their failures, may end up struggling with a sense of inferiority rather than developing a positive sense of self-worth as a learner and worker.

Considering current behaviors of children and youth in light of Erikson's theory may provide some clues to the source of problems and assist in the development of effective interventions (see In the Classroom 13.1). It is also worth considering that the way we serve children in schools may enhance or detract from their psychosocial development. The most obvious implication is that when we classify children, we are confirming their status as problem learners; by pulling them out of the mainstream and placing them in special classes, we may inadvertently communicate to them that they are not capable of the work others can do, and that they are therefore inferior, thus compromising their successful resolution of the childhood crisis of industry versus inferiority. Separate placements may also restrict their interaction with typical peers, resulting in delayed interpersonal development (Bradley & Meredith, 1991).

Emotional Development

Emotions underlie behaviors, and therefore it is important to consider the role emotions may play in an individual's life. In a review of emotional development as it affects students with learning and behavioral disabilities, Dupont (1989) suggested that emotions develop over

---

IN THE CLASSROOM **13.1**

Stages of Psychosocial Development

Susan is eight years old and has mild mental retardation. One day when she approached the door to her resource room, she noticed her teacher talking to another teacher. She looked at the floor and put her fingers in her mouth, obviously hesitant to enter the room. When one of the teachers spoke to her, she fell down on the floor and curled up in a ball. Her counselor believes that Susan has yet to resolve the trust-mistrust stage satisfactorily and that this impedes Susan's general social development.

Larry, who is eleven, has struggled with his reading disability ever since he entered school. The failure he has experienced has undermined his sense of value as a learner and compromised his resolution of the industry versus inferiority stage. He responds to teacher-assigned tasks with the simple response, "I can't." He has developed a strong distrust of his own capability as a learner, and this restricts his ability to recognize the skills he does have. Although he shows signs of beginning to deal with the identity stage (e.g., involvement with the peer group and disassociation from authority), his problems with the industry stage will likely compromise further development.

Erica is fifteen and receiving special education services for her learning disability. It appears that she is currently working on resolving the identity stage, as is appropriate for her age. Her teacher observes that Erica is trying to establish herself as an autonomous person with a name. She wants to be recognized by others and works very hard toward that end. Recently, she has become very concerned with her appearance. She wants to look her best. She wants her clothes to match, and she fusses with her appearance before school and after gym. She doesn't like wearing her glasses because she doesn't think they are as stylish as those worn by others. She is very conscious of her peer group and is struggling to balance fitting in with the group while still being herself.

time from the interaction of maturation with physical and social experience, proceeding only in interaction with other human beings. He noted that emotions are based on (1) a cognitive analysis of a situation, leading to (2) an alteration of affect (mood, feeling), which is followed by (3) an action or behavior.

The core emotions of joy, anger, guilt, sadness, pride, and fear serve as important indicators of who we are. Each human being is unique in terms of what we have strong feelings about and what we do with those feelings. These feelings and responses change over time, as do the explanations we give for our feelings. From two decades of observational research, Dupont (1989) identified a developmental sequence of stages of emotional development based on the explanations we give for our feelings, explanations that develop in a predictable sequence (see Table 13.2).

It should be noted that as emotional development proceeds, the lower stages do not disappear, but rather, coexist with and are integrated into the higher stages (e.g., individuals who have come to value being self-defined will nevertheless be happy at times simply because of pleasurable experiences). When individuals encounter conflicts between the values of various stages that have become integrated into their emotional selves, the higher stage will take precedence (e.g., functioning at the more advanced stage of valuing autonomy will lead the individual to resist problematic responses related to blind conformity in instances of peer pressure).

As we consider the social and emotional characteristics of learners with mild disabilities, an awareness of any delays in developing age-appropriate emotional cognitions may help us design more useful cognitive and behavioral interventions. Adolescent youngsters whose emotions still derive primarily from pleasure-seeking, freedom from pain, or responses of authority figures (i.e., explanations typical of younger children) will likely be

TABLE 13.2   Stages of Emotional Development

Explanations Given by the Individual for Their Feelings

1. Reasons given for emotions appear bizarre and irrational

2. Reasons for feelings relate to simple pleasure or displeasure, comfort or pain

3. Reasons for emotions relate to actions of authority figures and being allowed to get or have things that are desired

4. Reasons for feelings relate to being allowed to "go and do" or to being restricted from doing so by authority figures

5. Reasons for emotions relate to having friends and belonging; conformity is valued

6. Explanations for emotions relate to reciprocal relationships, and involve sensitivity to feelings of others; mutuality is valued

7. Reasons for emotions involve being self-defining and directed; autonomy is valued

8. Reasons for feelings reflect the need to be consistent with values and principles; integrity is valued

From "The Emotional Development of Exceptional Students," by H. Dupont, 1989, *Focus on Exceptional Children, 21*(1), p. 4. Copyright © 1989 by Love Publishing Company. Adapted and reprinted with permission.

impaired in the development of age-appropriate emotions and social behaviors. The emotional cognitions that underlie their behavior are similar to much younger children, and their behaviors are likely to be less age appropriate as well. Interventions must respect this level of development.

Consideration of the range of emotions expressed by a child or adolescent may also provide important diagnostic information. Children need to develop the ability to feel and express all of the core emotions in appropriate ways. As noted in Chapter 8, children who grow up in homes affected by alcohol or drug dependency or by child or spousal abuse frequently display a very restricted ability to feel anything, opting for feeling nothing (Black, 1981; Long & Morse, 1996). Attending to the range of expressed emotions and the explanations for them can be useful to therapists and others in assisting the emotional development of such youngsters (see In the Classroom 13.2).

Development of Social Perspective Taking

Social perspective taking is defined as the ability to relate to the viewpoints of others. It involves the coordination of multiple perspectives both within the self and socially between

---

IN THE CLASSROOM **13.2**

Emotional Development

Susan is seven years old and is in a class for children with emotional disorders. She seems to be delayed in emotional development, and all of her emotions are apparently related to her own pleasure or freedom from pain (a characteristic of younger children). She goes after the toys she wants, regardless of whose they are; she attends only those mainstream classes that she wants to attend. If she is sent to time-out for problems behaving during group time, she will sit there and cry, saying over and over, "I want to come back." She simply wants what she wants! The feelings or reactions of others have no bearing on the things she desires or seeks to avoid.

Mark is a sixth grader with mental retardation and a history of acting-out behaviors. His behavior and emotions depend to a large extent on the guidelines and restrictions placed on him by Mr. Chapman, his teacher. Mark exhibits a lot of resistance when his teacher does not grant a request or demand,

but he will usually end up complying. Occasionally he reacts violently and "trashes" the room, blaming Mr. Chapman for the occurrences. He clearly explains his feelings and emotions by what his teacher will allow him to do, or by reference to other authority figures in his life.

Jill, a seventh grade student with a learning disability, is served entirely in general education classes with consultant support. She interacts easily with others and her teacher feels that she has advanced to the stage of emotional development that values interactions with others. Her attitudes on any given day are dictated by how she is feeling about her relationship to her peer group. She seems to be very happy and gets right to work when things are going well between her and her friends. When she has had a disagreement with one of her friends, she becomes uncooperative and unwilling to carry out requests.

the self and others (Bradley & Meredith, 1991; Selman, 1980). For example, in intervening with a child who has just hurt another student, it is useful to consider whether the child has the ability to see the situation from the injured student's perspective, or to have empathy. Selman and others have hypothesized that social perspective taking is a developmental process similar to other social cognitions. Human beings make decisions based on their changing perceptions of others, and act on the basis of their ideas about the inherent social nature of behavior in a series of qualitatively different stages, as described in Table 13.3.

Selman's theory of social perspective taking has several implications for work with youngsters with various mild disabilities. Bradley and Meredith's (1991) study of social perspective taking among learners with mild mental retardation found that such youngsters exhibit developmental growth in perspective taking, but that the rate of growth is slower than typical peers, supporting the premise that their development is delayed, not defective. As

TABLE 13.3   Stages of Social Perspective Taking

Egocentric Perspective Taking (Ages 3–6)

The child relates to others as physical entities; recognizes that feelings and thoughts exist, but does not understand that others may not interpret a particular situation as they do; friends are simply those who are available to play at the time.

Subjective Perspective Taking (Ages 5–9)

The child understands that others have their own feelings and thoughts, although the interpretation of the feelings of others is based on the observer's experience; differentiates between intentional and unintentional acts; assumes that other's feelings and thoughts may be discerned from the physical indicators such as facial expressions; friends are those who do as one wishes.

Reciprocal Perspective Taking (Ages 7–12)

The young person becomes able to put himself/herself in the other's shoes; reflects on one's own actions from the perspective of the other; develops sense of reciprocity of thoughts and feelings, not merely actions; friends are those who like the same things, but friendships dissolve when that is no longer true.

Mutual Perspective Taking (Ages 10–15)

The young person is capable of stepping entirely outside the self and the situation; from this third-party perspective, the individual can simultaneously coordinate the perspectives of self and other; relationships are seen as ongoing systems whereby feelings and experiences are mutually shared.

Societal Perspective Taking (Ages 12–Adult)

Individual understands that all perspectives include multidimensional levels that may affect outcomes; capable of abstracting multiple and mutual perspectives to a societal or moral level shared by others; relationships are viewed as supportive but autonomous.

From "Interpersonal Development: A Study with Children Classified as Educable Mentally Retarded" by L. J. Bradley and R. C. Meredith, 1991, *Education and Training in Mental Retardation, 26*(2), pp. 134–135. Copyright © 1991 by Division on Mental Retardation and Developmental Disabilities of The Council for Exceptional Children. Adapted and reprinted with permission.

these youngsters grow older, the increasing gap may become problematic in social interactions and in their accomplishing the developmental tasks of adolescence. Social interventions with these students should take into account their level of social perspective taking.

The development of social perspective taking may be affected or delayed by other disabilities as well. In a review of studies of the social perspective taking ability of children with learning disabilities, Bryan (1991) found evidence that these students also exhibited deficits in perspective taking when compared to typical peers. One hypothesis for this finding is that the difficulty experienced by students with learning disabilities in understanding and using the communication tools needed to develop social cognitive skills may also impede their development of social perspective taking. Those with attention deficits may not be able to attend to environmental information efficiently enough to incorporate that information into their social schema. Those with emotional or behavioral disorders frequently display the negative effects of failing to develop age-appropriate levels of perspective taking. They frequently seem not to know, or even care, what others think or feel, and thus their ability or motivation to modify their behaviors and emotions based on this information is impeded. The degree to which children are successful in understanding the perspectives of others will be crucial to the development of their concept of what it means to be a person, a "self," and to the development of satisfying relationships with others (see examples in In the Classroom 13.3).

Social Competence and Cognitive Development

Social behaviors appear to depend on the development of essential social cognitive skills (Bryan, 1991; Kauffman, 2001). Social cognition involves the use of thinking skills (e.g., social perspective taking, social problem solving) to coordinate environmental events and social behaviors (Bryan, 1991). It appears that social cognition develops just as other cognitive skills do, and that a developmental perspective may be useful in understanding the social functioning of learners with mild disabilities (Siperstein, 1992). By helping young people develop their ability to cognitively process and act on social information, we give them the tools to manage their own responses to the environment and make it more reasonable to expect them to display increasing levels of self-responsibility.

Students with mild disabilities, as a group, tend to display deficits and delays in developing age-appropriate social cognitive skills and the behavioral repertoire needed to operate in a socially competent manner (Gumpel, 1994; Kavale & Forness, 1996; Vaughn, Zaragoza, Hogan, & Walker, 1993; Whalen & Henker, 1991). For example, the concept of the six-hour retarded child (President's Committee on Mental Retardation, 1970) discussed in Chapter 6 underscores the centrality of the inability to function competently in particular social environments as one of the indicators of disability. The AAMR (1992) proposed using an evaluation of an individual's social competence as a means of assessing adaptive behavior and confirming the presence or absence of mental retardation. While some have questioned that position (McGrew, Bruininks, & Johnson, 1996), it remains true that a variety of competencies are required for effective social functioning and that students with disabilities will be judged by the appropriateness of their social behaviors.

Central to the social cognitive approach is the concept of personal competence, a complex, multidimensional construct relating to an individual's ability to coordinate and

IN THE CLASSROOM **13.3**

Social Perspective Taking

David is a second grader with a learning disability. He seems to see the world solely from his own perspective, and subsequently has difficulty taking turns. Yesterday he took a ball out for recess and was throwing it up and down. His teacher asked if he wouldn't rather play with Philip, to which he answered, "Yes." However, when he threw the ball, he threw it so that Philip could not possibly catch it, then ran after it and threw it to himself again. He did not appear to be able to envision the game of catch from Philip's perspective. His teacher believes that he is still in the egocentric stage of perspective taking, and that this is hindering his social development.

Vinnie is an eighth grader in a program for students with emotional disabilities. In discussing a watch-stealing incident with Vinnie, Ms. Taylor realized that even though Vinnie appeared to understand that others looked at the theft as a bad thing, he seemed to excuse it because he "needed" the watch. Ms. Taylor also reflected on another incident: Vin-

nie had struck up a "friendship" with a new student for the mutual purpose of humiliating a third student. As long as they were in accord on this goal, the friendship remained intact; when that common goal ended, so did the friendship. From these incidents, Ms. Taylor feels that Vinnie displays a delay in development of social perspective taking, functioning primarily at the subjective stage, a stage more typical of elementary children.

Marie is an eleventh grader who has a language impairment. Most of the time, her teacher notes, she seems to understand that everyone has a perspective and that it might be different from hers. Last week, her class was discussing a piece of poetry. Marie listened intently and took into account each classmate's point of view. She was able to coordinate the different views expressed and to reference those ideas as she explained what she thought, indicating to her teacher that she is functioning within either the reciprocal or mutual perspective stage of social perspective taking.

effectively use a variety of skills to function in social contexts. A model of personal competence based on a variety of sources is presented in Figure 13.1. The model may be helpful in conceptualizing the complex interactions among the multiple abilities involved in personal competence, with each factor contributing uniquely to the ability to function in a socially and personally competent manner.

As Figure 13.1 indicates, a number of specific abilities contribute to an individual's personal competence, including:

- *Conceptual intelligence:* the intrinsic intellectual ability of the individual; the ability to process information, to solve abstract problems, and to understand and use symbolic processes such as language
- *Physical competence:* fine and gross motor skills; physical growth and development; general health status; deficits in hearing, vision, or mobility, as well as physical conditions such as seizures, that can compromise a learner's physical competence
- *Emotional competence:* the degree to which the individual is able to maintain an emotional "steady-state"; emotional competence is affected by the individual's personality,

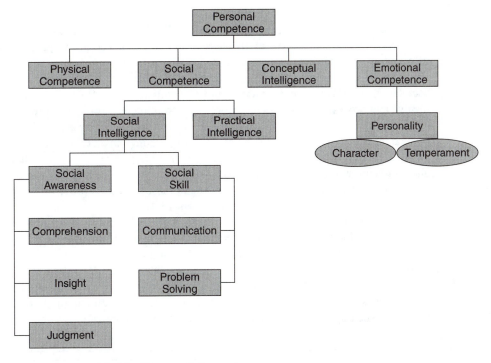

FIGURE 13.1   Model of Personal Competence

Based on AAMR, 1992; Greenspan & Granfield, 1992; Gumpel, 1992; Mathias, 1990; McGrew & Bruininks, 1990; McGrew, Bruininks, & Johnson, 1996.

including character and temperament, and is the dimension most often compromised when maladaptive behaviors are present

■ *Social competence:* the ability to respond appropriately in social situations and to carry out the functions associated with independent living; composed of two subcomponents:

Social intelligence, or the ability to understand social expectations and to interpret the behavior of others, to judge appropriately how to conduct oneself in social situations, and to select and use appropriate social strategies

Practical intelligence, or the ability to deal with the physical and mechanical aspects of life, including daily living and vocational skills, and to solve problems of everyday life.

Social Intelligence

Social intelligence is a critical component of social competence. It is the perception that an individual has deficits in social intelligence that most often leads to the identification of a disability (Gresham & Elliott, 1987; Sternberg, 1985). Low levels of social intelligence are frequently found to be related to functional failures in social settings such as school and work (Greenspan & Granfield, 1992). Teachers and others must not only consider the appropriateness of overt behaviors, they must also explore evidence of underlying social cognitive abilities, or social intelligence (Bryan, 1997; Gumpel, 1994; Leffert & Siperstein, 1996; Siperstein, 1992). The effectiveness of an individual's cognitive processing of social information provides evidence of the individual's social intelligence.

Social intelligence is composed of the two subcompetencies: social awareness and social skill. *Social awareness* refers to those cognitive abilities that allow the individual to receive and process relevant social information from the environment. It refers specifically to the comprehension of behavioral cues and to the accompanying insight about the meaning of such information, followed by the exercise of judgment in determining the relevance and value of that information. Adequate social awareness requires that students attend to actions and words around them, view that information from various perspectives, and interpret the cues using the mediator of language. Any one of these steps may prove difficult for students with cognitive disabilities (see In the Classroom 13.4).

In Chapter 10, it was noted that the concept of field dependence applies to social judgments as well. Field-dependent individuals are more likely to attend closely to and make use of social models and frames of reference in their immediate environment, or to be socially field dependent (Witkin et al., 1977), a concept related to social awareness. There is some evidence that such individuals may make more effective use of eye contact, facial cues, verbal messages, and other social components as a guide to social function. In unfamiliar environments, such behaviors are quite adaptive if they are accompanied by the social cognitive

---

IN THE CLASSROOM **13.4**

Social Intelligence: Social Awareness and Social Skill

Linda is a sixth grader with mild mental retardation who is served in a general education class for most of the day. Her deficits in social awareness, particularly in comprehension and judgment, affect her adjustment in that environment. One day another girl told her, in a very sarcastic tone and with facial expression to underscore the sarcasm, that her dress looked "real nice." The look on Linda's face made it clear that she wasn't sure what the other girl meant. She noted the discrepancy between voice, words, and actions, but she seemed at a loss as to the meaning of the communication, and she was therefore unable to respond effectively. Incidents such as this have caused her teacher to be very concerned about the effect of social awareness deficits on Linda's overall social adjustment.

Gary is twelve years old and is placed in a self-contained classroom as a result of his conduct disorder and associated ADHD. Because of his attentional deficits, his overall cognitive functioning is slowed, including his ability to appraise his emotions and to take the perspectives of others in social situations. He is quick to become frustrated, and his reactions to people and events are impulsive. His repertoire of responses is not well-developed, resulting in frequent exaggerated outbursts that are inappropriate to the stimulus. After an outburst, he experiences remorse. His teacher is heartened by his self-awareness in cases where he has overreacted, believing that it indicates that he is beginning to develop some initial competence in social awareness. His teacher hopes that this cognitive awareness will open up the opportunity for instruction in reading social cues more effectively before he reaches the frustration point, and in the use of more adaptive social skills.

skills necessary to process and give meaning to the information. A field-dependent social orientation can result in individuals' being more attuned to those with whom they interact and therefore more valued as friends. The negative aspect is the susceptibility of such individuals to follow the crowd indiscriminately, sometimes resulting in participation in behaviors that are not healthy, safe, or legal.

The second component of social intelligence is *social skill,* or the ability to select and use behaviors that lead to socially acceptable and personally satisfying outcomes (Goldstein & McGinnis, 1997; Gresham & Elliott, 1987; McGinnis & Goldstein, 1990, 1997). These behaviors comprise the person's response to the environment. Communication skills and problem-solving are central to an individual's level of social skill (see In the Classroom 13.4). Students with mild disabilities often have deficits in social skill, and therefore their responses to events are frequently unsatisfactory, ineffective, or unacceptable (Kavale & Forness, 1996; Short & Evans, 1990). Social skill includes learned behaviors (overt and covert) used in interpersonal interactions to achieve an environmental effect and response (Gumpel, 1994; Paul & Epanchin, 1991).

Emotional Competence

Emotional competence is related to a number of personality variables, including the nonintellectual attributes of temperament and character (AAMR, 1992; McGrew, Bruininks, & Johnson, 1996). Severe deficits in dimensions of personality (i.e., temperament and character), as well as in emotional competence in general, are held to be suggestive of a psychiatric condition or of emotional or behavioral disorders (Greenspan & Granfield, 1992). In fact, emotional competence is frequently defined by the absence of any maladaptive indicators such as externalizing, internalizing, or other asocial behaviors.

Character is defined as the collection of features and traits that form the individual nature of a person, including moral qualities, ethical standards, and principles. This aspect of personality is viewed as being malleable and susceptible to change when significant environmental pressures support change. Character deficits are frequently viewed as psychiatric conditions, including character disorders and other acting-out forms of psychopathology (Greenspan & Granfield, 1992).

Temperament is the behavioral style of an individual in interpersonal interactions. The term relates to the manner of the behavior, not the actions themselves. Temperament has been characterized as having a variety of aspects or components, most of which refer to the nature of the individual with regard to reactivity as well as other self-regulatory tendencies (see Table 13.4).

Temperament is generally presumed to be an inborn predisposition that is largely biological or genetic in origin and that is more stable than other personality factors (Keogh & Bess, 1991; Keogh & Pullis, 1980). Thomas and Chess (1977) studied the responses of infants and young children extensively and determined that the attributes listed in Table 13.4 tend to cluster into four styles: the easy child (40 percent); the difficult child (10 percent); the slow-to-warm-up child (15 percent); and uncertain (33 percent). Those children exhibiting the difficult child pattern may present more acting out behaviors at home and school. Those who are slow to warm up may present more passive or internalized clinical symptoms.

The individual's temperament, or behavioral style, interacts with the environment, affecting the responses from significant others (Thomas & Chess, 1977). The effect of the

TABLE 13.4   **Dimensions of Behavioral Style or Temperament**

Activity level
Rhythmicity (regularity, predictability)
Approach/withdrawal tendencies (response to new stimuli)
Adaptability
Threshold of responsiveness (or reactiveness to stimuli)
Intensity of reaction
Quality of mood
Distractibility
Attention span or persistence

Based on Thomas & Chess, 1977, pp. 21–22.

interaction of teacher–child or parent–child temperaments depends on the temperamental characteristics of both individuals. There is some evidence that children's temperament as well as their cognitive abilities and motivation can influence a teacher's opinion about their teachability (Cardell & Parmar, 1988; Keogh & Bess, 1991). When the child's temperament matches the teacher's expectation of teachability, the match and the interactions are likely to be positive and conducive to learning; when the child's style is inconsistent with the teacher's expectations, the teacher's evaluation of the child is more likely to be negative and the interactions less supportive.

Social Cognitive Delay

Social cognition follows a developmental pattern that is similar to that observed among other cognitive abilities. It is perhaps obvious that there will be individuals who, for a variety of reasons, are delayed in that developmental process. For example, as the research by Bradley and Meredith (1991) indicated, students with mental retardation commonly display social perspective taking skills that are characteristic of younger children. The term *social cognitive delay* may be used to refer to any such delays in developing age-appropriate, functional social cognitive skills and in applying those skills in social contexts (see In the Classroom 13.5).

One possible explanation of the inappropriate or immature behaviors exhibited by children and youth with disabilities may be that the individuals have one or more deficits or delays in general cognitive functioning. When these cognitive delays affect social development, the student may simply not have developed the necessary cognitive skills to cope effectively in the social arena. Difficulties in social problem solving may be related to deficits in general cognitive functioning, such as

- Attention: lack of attention to social cues
- Perception: misinterpretation of social cues, or attaching incorrect meaning to social cues
- Memory: poor memory of social cues as a situation unfolds
- Strategic control functions: lack of or poor selection of social skill strategies.

Failure to operate effectively in social contexts may be attributed to deficits in skill repertoire or deficits in performance (Gresham & Elliott, 1987; Kavale & Forness, 1996). First, the learner may never have developed the required social cognitive strategies. For a variety of reasons, the skills are simply not in the student's social skill repertoire. Such youngsters are said to have skill deficits. Alternatively, some students appear to possess the skills and can demonstrate them on cue in role-playing situations or sporadically in natural settings, but they may not be interpreting and using environmental cues reliably enough to determine when to appropriately use a skill (Kerr & Nelson, 1998). Such students are said to have performance deficits. Performance deficits can result when skills are taught in isolation in the classroom, resulting in the failure of the learner to generalize those skills to other appropriate settings (Gumpel, 1994). Learners with performance deficits are frequently punished for their inabilities because it is assumed that they could use the appropriate skill if they wanted to, and that their failure to do so is a matter of carelessness or choice, or simply a lack of motivation.

Another problem may be related to the degree to which a learner is able to demonstrate behavioral flexibility, or the ability to adjust behavior to respond to different situations, people, or settings (McGinnis & Goldstein, 1997). Students with mild disabilities may lack the behavioral flexibility needed to respond to changing situations, and therefore their responses may be seen as inappropriate or noncompliant (see In the Classroom 13.6). They may use fixed or stereotypic responses to situations rather than employing a full repertoire of adaptive social skills. Some learners with deficits in social cognitions may exhibit newness

---

IN THE CLASSROOM **13.5**

Social Cognitive Delay

Carmen is fourteen years old and is currently placed in a self-contained class for students with learning disabilities. He is the type of student who wants to be involved in everything that is going on in the room. His teacher describes him as a "neat kid" with a good sense of humor and a caring attitude toward others and who is a good conversationalist with adults. Unfortunately, Carmen does not see these positive qualities in himself, nor do his peers. He has a tendency to turn them off, and therefore they do not include him in social conversations and activities unless he initiates them. When he does interact with peers, he tends to engage in impulsive and inappropriate behaviors, similar to a younger child. It is common for Carmen to trip or poke other students, or to say inappropriate things to them regarding their personality, looks, family, or gender. He will barge into conversations when he was not invited, and then he will talk above the others to be included. Because this has been going on for so long, most of his peers won't have anything to do with him. Recently his tendency to act inappropriately in order to get attention has increased. When his teacher discussed a recent incident with him, he was unable to see why it was inappropriate. He is unable to differentiate between his actions and those of others. His teacher and counselor are beginning to work with him on social skills, including self-evaluation and self-regulation of his behavior.

IN THE CLASSROOM **13.6**

Lack of Behavioral Flexibility

Tom is fifteen years old and in a day program for youngsters with emotional disorders. He does not adjust his behavior well to fit different situations. For example, swearing is common within his friendship circle. However, he doesn't adjust his peer language for use at home or in class. He swears in class and does not even notice that he is using inappropriate language. When the teacher brings it to his attention, he seems surprised. His parents say that it is a problem at home as well, one they are working on particularly because there are younger children in the home.

Lee is ten years old and in a resource program for students with learning disabilities. Her teacher has noted that she uses a very limited number of social skills to deal with social situations: saying "I'm sorry" and hitting comprise the extent of her repertoire. Saying "I'm sorry" has seemed to work well for Lee in school, although hitting has not. She has been suspended several times for hitting other students. Nevertheless, she continues to respond to all situations with only those behaviors.

panic in change situations, responding to the new social demands with resistance or by withdrawing or acting out (Redl & Wineman, 1951).

When we note behaviors in a child that are suggestive of a less mature social cognitive stage, we must also address the following questions:

- Does a pattern of delay exist, or is this an isolated instance?
- Are the desired skills present in the training or classroom setting, and does the learner fail to generalize them to other environments?

With answers to these questions, we determine how the student's social cognitive development may have been affected. We can then address the problems by designing interventions that develop missing or faulty cognitive skills, enabling the youngster to address future social situations more adaptively. In dealing with social cognitive delay, teachers and parents need to evaluate the development of age-appropriate language and cognitive skills that contribute to the growth of social competence. When deficits are identified, coaching and feedback will be required to increase the student's ability to analyze social situations and to choose and implement effective responses (Gumpel, 1994). Punishment is rarely effective when the needed skills are not in the youngster's repertoire.

Behavior from an Ecological Perspective

Social-emotional characteristics and functioning can also be viewed from an ecological perspective. The ecological framework (Apter, 1982) holds that the source and explanation of behavioral or emotional disturbance lies in the interaction between the child and the environment. Behavioral ecologists assert that behavior is not simply the result of conflict within the individual, as psychodynamic theorists like Freud believed, or the outcome of inappropriate reinforcement, as behavioralists such as Skinner asserted. Rather, social ecologists believe that behavior results from the reciprocal interaction of personal variables, environment factors, and the quality of antecedent behaviors. Kauffman (2001) illustrated these interactions in his triadic reciprocal model (Figure 13.2). This model suggests that a given behavior (B′) is the result of the reciprocal interactions among and between the individual's personal traits (P), the environment (E), and prior or antecedent behaviors or events (B):

$$B' = (P, E, B)$$

Social ecologists believe that behaviors (B′) are interpretable only within the context of a consideration of the mutual effects of personal, environmental, and behavioral variables:

- Personal variables include the individual's thoughts, feelings, and perceptions as well as other personal traits, such as age, disability, ethnicity, language, religion, gender, sexual orientation, appearance, stature, and socioeconomic class.
- Environmental variables include both social and physical factors related to the setting in which the behavior occurs.
- Behavioral variables include the qualities of behaviors or events that are antecedent to the target behavior.

When considering behaviors from an ecological perspective, it is important to understand that most of the time all three influences are at work, although in some cases only one or two may be of significance. As we evaluate the problem behaviors of children, it is useful to consider whether any of the three variables is significantly more influential on a regular basis

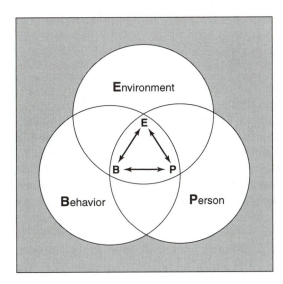

FIGURE 13.2   Triadic Reciprocal Model

This model illustrates the reciprocal influences of variables related to

E   environmental variables
B   antecedent behavior or event variables
P   person variables

The circles represent the environment, behavior, and person variables and their shared reciprocal effects.

Adapted from *Characteristics of Behavioral Disorders,* Sixth Edition (p. 124) by J. M. Kauffman. © 1997. Adapted by permission of Prentice-Hall Inc., Upper Saddle River, NJ.

IN THE CLASSROOM **13.7**

Ecological Interactions

Doug, age five, is a student in a preschool program for children with developmental delays. His teacher, Ms. Harper, has observed that environmental factors have a very strong influence on Doug's behavior. During the morning, there are nine other children in the classroom, several with severe acting-out behaviors. It appears to Ms. Harper that Doug's problem-solving is affected by these models of inappropriate behavior. Only four children remain after lunch, and Doug's behavior in this smaller, more socially skilled group improves significantly.

Debbie is a fifth grader with a learning disability. Her special education class joins a general education class for music. An incident last week illustrates the use of the triadic reciprocal model to analyze events. Some of the girls in the music class told Debbie that she was from the "stupid class."

Debbie didn't lash out at them or act inappropriately. She ignored them and then talked about it later to her teacher, who was able to help her articulate her feelings. Her teacher also provided her with reinforcement for using an effective response they had practiced in social skills lessons. In this case, Debbie's status as a student receiving special education services (a person variable) interacted with the taunting of the other girls (an event/behavior variable) in music class (an environmental variable) leading to Debbie's behavior, ignoring, which contained the problem. Her teacher is pleased that Debbie seems to be developing the social skills to deal with such events and to take care of things on her own, since her teachers cannot always be there to address problems for her.

---

and to consider the nature of the interactions that may be exacerbating the situation (see In the Classroom 13.7). A complete assessment of behavior requires attention to all three variables and their interactions, with such analysis leading to intervention suggestions, including enhancing positive forces and reducing or limiting negative aspects (Gable, 1996; Wehby & Symons, 1996).

Risk and Resilience

As noted throughout this chapter, most learners with mild disabilities present some social-emotional adjustment concerns in addition to concerns related to their primary area of disability. It is not unusual to find a child with mental retardation who also exhibits immature social behavior, or an adolescent with a learning disability who experiences periods of depression. The simple fact of having a disability appears to put the young person at risk for a variety of intrapersonal and interpersonal problems (Bender & Wall, 1994). IDEA 1997 confirmed this observation by requiring that behavioral planning be a part of the IEP for every child who exhibits problems in behavior and social interaction, regardless of the category of disability.

This concern invites us to consider potential outcomes for such students from an ecological perspective. Central to these outcomes is the concept of *risk,* defined by Keogh and Weisner (1993) as a "negative or potentially negative condition that impedes or threatens normal development" (p. 4). Risk factors identified in the literature (Morrison & Cosden, 1997) include

- Child factors, such as developmental delays, early antisocial behavior, disturbed peer relations, difficult temperament, and problematic biological or genetic factors
- Family and community factors, such as chronic poverty, problematic parenting skills, parental psychopathology, chronic family discord, family instability, and lack of social support to child and family
- School and peer group factors, such as school failure, dropping out of school, substance abuse, negative peer influence, lack of normative expectations for behavior, and alienation from school, family, or community.

Research into the phenomenon of risk has also identified a variety of protective factors that are associated with positive outcomes even in the presence of multiple risk factors. *Resiliency* is defined as the ability of the individual to resist the negative effects of stresses and to achieve a positive outcome. Protective factors associated with resiliency include

- Child factors, such as positive self-concept and social competence
- Family factors, such as consistent parenting, supportive family environment, and high but reasonable expectations
- School and community factors, including positive role models, positive school climate, appropriate curriculum, and availability of supportive adults.

An important research question, and one asked every day by parents and teachers, is "Why do some children succeed despite all odds, while others travel a destructive path to negative outcomes?" It is clear that there are no reliable linear links between a particular risk factor and an associated protective factor, and there is no magic answer that will assure a positive outcome for every child. Rather, outcomes are determined by complex interactions among the multiple risks and protective factors (Morrison & Cosden, 1997). The more risk factors present, the more likely the youngster will encounter difficulty. But even when the picture seems bleakest, some young people will survive and even thrive (see In the Classroom 13.8).

The Relationship Between Problems in Behavior and Problems in Learning

When discussing students who are served in special education for learning problems, it is assumed that their disabilities are related to academic learning. However, studies have repeatedly shown that when rated by teachers, students with disabilities of all kinds exhibit higher levels of problem behavior and have more social deficits than do typical youngsters (Forness & Kavale, 1991; Pearl, Donahue, & Bryan, 1986). It is generally observed that learners with mild disabilities frequently exhibit social deficits along with their academic learning deficiencies. To illustrate this fact, consider that three of the most recent definitions

Risk and Resiliency

Brad is a third grader whose learning disability makes learning to read, spell, and write difficult. He struggles with work that other classmates would find easy, but his classroom is rich in support from his classroom teacher, plus a consultant teacher for one period a day. His family is supportive at home. On a recent school day, Mrs. Shore, the consultant teacher, noted two events of interest. During the reading lesson, Brad listened intently and eagerly went back to his seat to complete an independent sequencing assignment. Halfway through the exercise, Brad realized that he didn't have enough room to paste the sentences. When he told his teacher, Mr. Jones explained Brad's error and told Brad to redo the exercise. At first Brad displayed frustration, but he persisted with the task, completing it in the allowed time. His face shone with pride!

Later in the morning, Brad was engaged in editing a paragraph with a classroom volunteer. After Brad read the paragraph aloud, the volunteer asked him to pick out his introductory and concluding sentences. He quickly realized that he didn't have a concluding sentence, and he wrote one more sentence. The volunteer helped him see that his new sentence was just another detail, and they worked for a while longer, resulting in his finally composing

an appropriate conclusion. Throughout the process, Brad persisted, with some frustration, but he persisted nevertheless.

As Mrs. Shore, the consultant teacher, reflected on these events, she was struck by Brad's resilience. Challenge after challenge, he kept on going. In spite of his learning difficulties, he persisted and achieved results. She wonders what keeps him going despite his misunderstandings and frequent errors.

One possibility is Brad's strong drive for competence. Completing a project gives him tangible evidence of his achievements, and he takes great pride in that. Another possibility is the assistance provided by both teachers. The school environment seems to work well for Brad, supporting his growth and achievement. Mrs. Shore then reflected on the supportive family Brad goes home to each day; expectations are high, but so is the love and encouragement to achieve those expectations. All in all, Brad's resilience appears to be the result of a number of protective factors working together to minimize the risk posed by his learning disability. Mrs. Shore's concern turns to those students whose risk factors overpower the available protective factors, and she wonders how she can help to improve the ratio.

---

of learning disabilities (NJCLD, ACLD, and ICLD) refer to socialization problems explicitly (Forness & Kavale, 1991; Hammill, 1990). The concept of social incompetence has also been central to the definition of mental retardation since Edgar Doll (1941) first defined mental retardation as social incompetence due to mental subnormality (Doll, 1941; Smith, J. D., 1997).

In order to understand why learners with mild disabilities often display inappropriate or ineffective social behavior, it is helpful to reconsider the critical features of their disabilities. Central to the functioning of most children with mild disabilities are their difficulties in understanding, processing, and using language, problems that are related to their cognitive processing of language (as discussed in Chapter 10). Since language facility appears essential to social learning and functioning, it is reasonable that disabilities in cognitive processing and language could hinder a child's development of socially skilled behavior. These deficits impair the student's learning of social rules and strategies generally acquired through observation of appropriate behavioral models.

To compound these problems, language mediates social learning, and social interaction is essential for language learning. This reciprocal process is disrupted by the inability of young people with disabilities to process and use language effectively and to demonstrate social competence through the use of language. Despite this, teachers of students with mild disabilities (like Nicki in Chapter 8) appear to believe that academic remediation is their primary responsibility. Development of social competence is rarely included as part of the child's IEP. If behavior is addressed at all, it is from the perspective of behavior management and control rather than remediation (Gresham, MacMillan, & Bocian, 1996; Nichols, 1992). The connection between these children's troubling behavioral problems and their disability-related difficulties in processing language is frequently ignored.

Such problems are sometimes compounded by the newcomer phenomenon. Students miss bits and pieces of classroom life while receiving services outside the general education classroom. They may also miss important input while in the classroom because of difficulties in attention or in processing oral language. This means that classroom conversation may not make much sense because they are missing specific pieces of background. Too often, this leads to avoidance strategies that result in these students' staying out of communicative interactions, appearing to be disinterested onlookers. Other students may avoid interacting with such students because their conversation often seems "weird." Since language learning requires interaction, the communicative differences grow. It is important to note that these problems are compounded for students who are learning English as a second language. Students with disabilities need a combination of social skill instruction along with the opportunity to practice skills in real contexts with feedback to help them develop their pragmatic language skills and to increase their levels of social competence.

Maladaptive Behavior

Thus far, the discussion has focused on the development of social-emotional characteristics and social competence, or adaptive behaviors. With some learners, however, the problem is not delayed or absent adaptive behavior but rather the presence of maladaptive behavioral responses to life events. McGrew and Bruininks (1990) concluded that while there is some overlap between the dimensions of adaptive and maladaptive behaviors, adaptive behavior seems more determined by conceptual, practical, and social intelligences as well as physical competence, while maladaptive behaviors appear to derive more directly from problems in the area of emotional competence.

In describing maladaptive behaviors, it is important to acknowledge that the difference between a child with serious maladaptive behavior problems and the typical child is not necessarily the presence or absence of a particular behavior such as hitting, being noncompliant, stealing, or crying, but rather the number of such occurrences and the time between instances. All children display some episodes of problem behaviors, as they grow and develop their social responses. However, most children exhibit significant reductions in aggressive behaviors as they mature and as they develop other ways of coping with frustrations. This is generally not true of children identified as having maladaptive behavior. Such children continue to demonstrate higher rates of problem behaviors and to a more serious degree than do other children (Kauffman, 2001; Rutherford & Nelson, 1995). Other relevant dimensions used to describe these behaviors are the degree to which they deviate from age-appropriate responses and their overt or covert nature.

Generally, youngsters with significant maladaptive behaviors will be identified for special education purposes as having a primary behavioral disorder. It is important to remember, however, that such students will also have problems in academic learning. Conversely, it is possible that a child whose primary disability is mental retardation, ADHD, or a learning disability may exhibit one or more serious maladaptive behaviors (Bryan, 1997; Reynolds & Miller, 1985; San Miguel, Forness, & Kavale, 1996). The degree to which the emotional needs of these students are met may depend on the extent to which programming is provided to develop their emotional competence, rather than focusing exclusively on academic activities.

Patterns of Maladaptive Behavior

Since problems with maladaptive behavior are common, it is important for teachers to have a basic understanding of various maladaptive behaviors and the ways in which problems in emotional competence may manifest themselves. Over the years, many different maladaptive behaviors in children and adolescents have been reported by parents, teachers, and other adults. Based on a statistical analysis of a large number of studies of maladaptive behaviors, Quay and Werry (1986) defined the following patterns or groupings:

- *Undersocialized aggressive conduct disorders* are antisocial externalizing behaviors that are aggressive, disruptive, and noncompliant and that significantly interfere with everyday functioning and the rights of others, leading others to conclude that the child is unmanageable. These behaviors violate major age-appropriate societal norms and rules.
- *Socialized aggressive conduct disorders* are antisocial externalizing behaviors that include involvement with peers in illegal acts or in behaviors that violate normative expectations. Behaviors in this category tend to be covert and are meant to be hard to detect and document. This dimension is predominantly a problem of older children and adolescents.
- *Anxiety-withdrawal-dysphoria disorders* consist of internalizing behaviors such as anxiety, fearfulness, panic, shyness, and depression.
- *Attention deficit disorders* are characterized by behaviors not in accordance with age-appropriate developmental expectations, including such characteristics as problems in concentration and attention, impulsivity, clumsiness, passivity, and lack of perseverance. (Attention deficit disorders were discussed in Chapter 9.)

Quay and Werry (1986) identified three additional groupings that were mentioned in a small number of studies and that represent more severe levels of disability: (1) schizoid-unresponsiveness (extreme introversion); (2) social ineptness (characterized by severely limited social skills); and (3) psychotic disorders, such as schizophrenia, observed only rarely in children.

Conduct Disorders.   Youngsters identified with conduct disorders display a large repertoire of age-inappropriate aggressive acts over a wide range of social situations. They exhibit frequent violations of socially appropriate standards of behavior. The actions of these children are contrary to adaptive patterns of behaviors such as cooperation, positive concern for others, and mutually beneficial social interactions (Rutherford & Nelson, 1995; Walker, Colvin, & Ramsey, 1995).

Although all children and youth engage in externalizing problem behaviors from time to time, youngsters with conduct disorders engage in such behaviors much more frequently and with greater intensity than their typical peers. These young people typically exhibit high rates of aggression at earlier ages, develop a larger repertoire of aggressive acts, exhibit aggression across a wider range of social situations, and persist in aggressive behavior for a longer period of time. Their behaviors lead them to be feared and rejected by peers, and they in turn perceive peers as hostile to them, setting up a vicious cycle of antisocial behavior.

A persistent pattern of antisocial behavior is exhibited by these students, impairing their everyday functioning at home and in school, and leading teachers and parents to identify them as incorrigible, unmanageable, or dangerous. The maladaptive behaviors are frequently accompanied by academic problems and may be related to social cognitive deficiencies (Walker et al., 1995; Wehby, 1994). Conduct disorders are more likely to result in the child's referral for evaluation than other types of emotional or behavioral disorders because they are so disruptive to classroom environments. In evaluating instances of aggressive behaviors associated with a conduct disorder, it is important to attempt to determine the needs that such behaviors might be meeting for the individual student (Rutherford & Nelson, 1995). For example, some students seem to seek attention for problem behavior rather than risk receiving no attention at all.

Behaviors associated with conduct disorders fall into two groups: overt (or undersocialized) and covert (or socialized). Undersocialized aggressive acts include teasing, threatening, fighting, bragging, sassing, swearing, arguing, disobeying, and being actively noncompliant. These behaviors quickly bring the attention of others, and the youngster is "in trouble," making it appear as if that outcome was the goal of the behavior in the first place. These behaviors are viewed as being undersocialized because the youngster appears to not have learned how to play the social game to get needs met and does not attempt to avoid getting caught. These behaviors are also labeled as undersocialized because the youngster does not appear to understand or appreciate the social undesirability of these actions and displays few, if any, guilt feelings when questioned about them (see In the Classroom 13.9).

Socialized aggressive acts include such behaviors as being passively negative or noncompliant, setting fires, lying, stealing, running away, engaging in substance abuse, and being truant. Youngsters engaging in these more secretive and less obvious behaviors are viewed as socialized, apparently having learned the social rule that you can behave inappropriately as long as you don't get caught. It is as if the youngster understands that it is important not to get caught doing something wrong and therefore acts out the aggressive feelings in more covert ways. Such behaviors are much more common among older children and adolescents and frequently involve their participation in an antisocial peer group (see In the Classroom 13.10).

IN THE CLASSROOM **13.9**

Conduct Disorders: Undersocialized Aggressive Type

Johnny is five years old and enrolled in kindergarten. His problem behaviors have just resulted in his referral for special education evaluation. Recently, Johnny became angry because his mother wouldn't take him to the park. In his rage, he took a butcher knife and ran toward her saying he would kill her. She locked herself and the baby in the bedroom until help arrived. Meanwhile, Johnny continued to pound on the bedroom door with the knife. His mother reported to the teacher that Johnny had been exhibiting violent and destructive behaviors since age two. At school, Johnny is verbally and physically aggressive toward the other children. He uses profanity, and when he has trouble expressing his feelings verbally, he lashes out physically. This causes the other children to become frightened, but Johnny is completely unaware of his effect on them. He reacts to crises in two very different ways. Sometimes he just gives up, throws his hands in the air, and says, "Forget it, I can't take it any more." His other reaction is to hit, pull hair, spit, and say, "I hate you" over and over. When he is angry with the teacher, he frequently tells her in great detail how he intends to kill her.

Delinquent, antisocial behavior in the context of an antisocial peer group may be viewed as socialized aggression or, alternatively, as social maladjustment. The behaviors (e.g., gang activity) are problematic to the school and community, but they do meet important relationship needs for the young person, and they are adaptive within the peer group. The combination of acting-out, externalizing behaviors with dependency on the deviant peer

IN THE CLASSROOM **13.10**

Conduct Disorders: Socialized Aggressive Type

Julia, age fourteen, has spent her entire school career in self-contained classes for students with behavioral disorders. At this time, her behaviors fall primarily within the category of conduct disorders, socialized aggressive type. Her teacher, Mr. Thomas, reports that Julia is a compulsive liar, sets fires, smokes marijuana, and engages in vandalism at school. These behaviors mystify Mr. Thomas. It is not clear whether Julia is angry at particular individuals or if she is just not able to control herself. Mr. Thomas thinks that Julia may believe that these actions will make her look "cool" to her friends. When Julia is confronted about her behaviors, she denies any connection to them, becoming enraged when she is not believed. Mr. Thomas reports that Julia hangs out with other girls who also display inappropriate behaviors to some degree, and it has become very difficult to control this group.

group presents particularly difficult intervention problems. Despite the problems presented by such young people, many school districts and states have begun to make the determination that these students are not eligible for special education services, basing this ruling on the exclusion of youngsters with social maladjustment from the IDEA classification. Such determinations tend to result in their exclusion from school and eventual incarceration.

Anxiety-Withdrawal-Dysphoria Disorders.   Individuals experiencing these disorders display extreme feelings of inferiority, embarrassment, self-consciousness, shyness, anxiety, or panic in normal situations, fearfulness that is not based on rational appraisal of the situation. They may exhibit feelings of depression, reluctance to try new things, withdrawal from social interaction, irritability, and a tendency to display "hurt feelings." They may be viewed as socially inept or as social isolates. Some youngsters exhibit fears and phobias relating to school environments that interfere with the ability to function. These behaviors are described as internalizing behaviors, since the child turns inward and withdraws into a shell (see In the Classroom 13.11). Such youngsters account for about 15 percent of all students identified as

---

IN THE CLASSROOM **13.11**

Anxiety-Withdrawal-Dysphoria Disorders

Billy, age thirteen, is a fifth grader with mild mental retardation and a history of parental neglect and abuse. He is currently placed in foster care. Billy shows no interest in things common to a thirteen-year-old. He is afraid to go to bed at night and sleeps with a teddy bear and a flashlight. Billy has learned not to trust others, and at times he does not even seem to trust himself. His nonverbal communication portrays a withdrawn, unhappy child who refrains from making eye-contact and walks in a slightly slouched manner. He appears to daydream for long periods of time; and he will isolate himself by drawing for hours, as if to withdraw from the present. His foster mother says she has noticed that he seems to have defined periods of depressed mood. He frequently sleeps all day and then stays up all night. He becomes anxious in new situations, and at these times his behavior can become disruptive, as he hits others and damages toys belonging to other children. On a recent behavioral evaluation, he achieved scores indicating clinical levels of deviance related to the withdrawal and anxious-depressed scales. Although Billy clearly qualifies as a student with mild mental retardation, the school district has just determined that the addition of services for depression is appropriate.

Maria is eighteen years old and in a transitional program for young adults with learning disabilities. Her teacher, Mr. Cutter, is concerned that without some sort of positive intervention, she will be lost as an adult. She appears to be extremely depressed, although this has never been formally diagnosed. She is wary of everything and seems socially withdrawn most of the time. When she first joined the class, her peers tried to include her in their activities. When she failed to respond, they began leaving her alone. She exhibits fearfulness that affects her ability to acquire the skills she will need for adult living because she is afraid to try. Mr. Cutter is afraid that Maria's wariness will deprive her of the opportunity to eventually participate fully in the normal activities most adults take for granted.

having emotional or behavioral disorders, although such problems are common among students with other types of disabilities as well (Falk, Dunlap, & Kern, 1996; Morrison & Cosden, 1997; Reynolds & Miller, 1985; San Miguel et al., 1996).

Some of these youngsters, including many with learning disabilities (Bryan, 1997) and mental retardation (Reynolds & Miller, 1985), are characterized primarily by social isolation, withdrawal, and lack of social skills. They engage in behaviors that drive others away, or they have deficiencies in the behaviors needed to establish social relationships. Their social behavior is generally viewed by themselves and others as inadequate. They either lack social skill (i.e., have skill deficits) or they fail to use the skills they have (i.e., have performance deficits).

Other learners display problem fears (i.e., anxiety disorders) that interfere with normal activities of childhood and adolescence. Some of these fears develop into full-scale phobias, fears that lead them to total avoidance of the feared situation. When school is the object of the phobia, it becomes very difficult to help the child through the educational system. These children exhibit definite signs of anxiety and even panic when required to attend school. Physical symptoms such as sweating, stomach aches, dizziness, and shortness of breath are very common. For these children, school becomes a threatening or aversive place, and the child seeks refuge at home (Kauffman, 2001). It is important to note that children who are truant are not considered school phobic, but rather as having a conduct disorder since their absence from school is generally an act of defiance to authority.

Obsessive-compulsive behaviors are also included in the group of anxiety disorders. Obsessions are persistent, repetitive, intrusive impulses or thoughts. They are images that the person cannot get out of his/her mind, such as constant worrying and repeating nonsense phrases. Compulsions are repetitive behaviors the individual performs over and over, that have no utility to the person, and that interfere with normal functioning, such as repeatedly washing hands or checking locked doors. These behaviors sometimes appear to perform an anxiety-reducing function for the individual.

Depression and related conditions are internalizing conditions characterized by depressed mood and a lack of interest in productive activity (Wright-Strawderman et al., 1996). There are three major types of depressive disorders: major depressive episodes or disorders (a combination of symptoms that seriously interfere with ordinary activity), dysthymia (less severe, but chronic symptoms that prevent an individual from functioning optimally), and bipolar depression (a condition characterized by extreme mood swings.)

Depression results from a complex interaction of a number of factors, with no single cause. It may be related to genetic or biochemical imbalances, or it may be a reaction to specific environmental events. School failure and depression may be reciprocal causal agents, given the importance placed on school performance. Factors that have been implicated include feelings of worthlessness, helplessness, hopelessness, isolation, experience of loss, disturbance in peer relationships, rejection, family disorganization, abuse, and fear of failure and humiliation (Guetzloe, 1988). Studies have found that students with disabilities such as learning disabilities, emotional or behavioral disorders, or mild mental retardation (Reynolds & Miller, 1985; Wenz-Gross & Siperstein, 1997; Wright-Strawderman et al., 1996) are more likely to experience depressed mood symptoms than their nondisabled counterparts, especially when placed in unsupportive classroom environments.

Since children's life experiences are qualitatively different from those of adults, adults and children may experience and exhibit depression differently as well. Childhood depression frequently results from or leads to academic problems and may also lead to unacceptable conduct including aggression, stealing, and social withdrawal. Common manifestations of depression in children include being sad and lonely. Learners experiencing depression may display an apathetic affect, low self-esteem, excessive guilt, school phobias, pessimism, avoidance of tasks or social experiences, physical complaints including lack of energy, and problems with eating or sleeping (Wright-Strawderman et al., 1996). Depression can be life-threatening: it is implicated in over 60 percent of suicides among young people. For this reason, and because depression is sometimes biochemical in origin, medical evaluation is generally indicated when depression is suspected. The DSM-IV indicators for the presence of depression include the following symptoms:

- Depressed or irritable mood
- Lack of interest in and inability to feel pleasure
- Disturbance of appetite (gain or loss); failure to gain weight appropriately
- Disturbance of sleep (insomnia or hypersomnia)
- Psychomotor agitation or immobility
- Lack of energy, fatigue
- Feelings of worthlessness, self-reproach, inappropriate guilt
- Inability to concentrate; indecisiveness
- Thoughts of suicide; suicide threats or attempts.

Reprinted with permission from the *Diagnostic and Statistical Manual of Mental Disorders, Fourth Edition Text Revision* (p. 356). Copyright © 2000 American Psychiatric Association.

At its most extreme, depression may result in suicidal thoughts or attempts (Guetzloe, 1988; Wright-Strawderman et al., 1996). It is suspected that some accidents are actually disguised or misreported suicides (Kauffman, 2001). Although rare, there are even documented cases of preschool youngsters attempting or completing suicide. Depression in students with learning disabilities has been associated with as many as 50 percent of completed youth suicides (San Miguel, Forness, & Kavale, 1996). Youngsters displaying a combination of the following risk factors should be considered at risk for potential suicide:

- Sudden changes in usual behaviors or affect (mood)
- School problems (academic, social, or disciplinary)
- Family or home problems (separation, divorce, abuse)
- Disturbed or disrupted peer relationships (including peer rejection or romantic breakups)
- Health problems (insomnia, loss of appetite)
- Substance abuse
- Giving away prized possessions
- Talking about suicide, making plans

- Situational events relating to the student or within the family, such as death of a family member or friend, pregnancy, abortion, arrest, loss of a job
- Sense of hopelessness.

The presence of maladaptive behaviors, both externalizing (e.g., conduct disorders) and internalizing (e.g., anxiety-withdrawal-dysphoric disorders), creates problems for the learner, the school, the family, and the community. Early identification of patterns of problem behavior allows for more effective interventions. Problem behaviors often coexist with other disabilities, and it is hypothesized that the effect of other disabilities on the effectiveness of the child's social cognitive functioning may exacerbate some of the emotional deficits (APA, 2000; San Miguel et al., 1996).

IDEA 1997 and Serious Discipline Problems

When youngsters present challenging behaviors in school environments, teachers and administrators need to be able to respond quickly and effectively to restore and preserve an environment that is safe and conducive to learning. These responses frequently involve a "change in placement" involving suspension or expulsion from school. It is widely (although incorrectly) believed that the ability of school personnel to respond quickly and decisively to problem behaviors is severely limited if the youngster happens to be a student who receives special education services. Teachers and administrators frequently believe that, if a student with a disability reacts aggressively, there is nothing they can do about it. They believe that suspensions are not allowed and that the child is exempt from the disciplinary measures that apply to other students. The responses of some students in problem situations seems to indicate that they also have been led to believe the same thing.

The Supreme Court, in *Honig* v. *Doe* (1988), ruled that, based on the IDEA principle of "zero reject," schools may not expel or suspend students when the problem behavior is directly related to their disability. The court also ruled that in such cases where it is determined that the behavior is a manifestation of the disability, schools may respond by reconvening the team and reviewing the student's program and placement to determine if modifications need to be made.

IDEA 1997 sought to clarify the requirements established in *Honig* v. *Doe* with regard to placement of students with challenging behaviors. It also sought to create new options for school administrators who need to be able to deal quickly and authoritatively with serious aggressive behaviors in situations where the safety of others in the school community is seriously threatened. These procedures are designed to protect the child's right to a free and appropriate education while giving school officials the means to preserve the right of others to a safe learning environment (Council for Exceptional Children, 1998a, 1998c; National Association of State Directors of Special Education, 1997; Yell & Shriner, 1997).

The fundamental IDEA requirement that every child receive a free and appropriate public education forms the basis of school responsibility for program planning and placement of children with challenging behaviors. Schools are required to respond in a timely manner to referrals by parents or others for the purpose of determining if a disability is present. In the presence of such behaviors, the student is considered to be covered under the provisions of the IDEA with respect to responses to challenging behavior if it can be shown that the school had reason to know that a disability might be present. If the school had no knowledge of the possible disability, then implementation of the general code of conduct, including suspensions, is allowed.

Once the child is identified as having a disability, the IEP team must consider and include in the IEP any interventions, strategies, and supports (including behavior management plans) required for a child whose behavior impedes learning, regardless of disability classification. Congress intends for a functional behavioral assessment to be performed for every student with problem behavior, regardless of the disability, and for an individualized, proactive intervention plan to be developed for all such students.

When a child with a disability engages in behaviors that would have resulted in disciplinary action if the child did not have a disability, school officials are allowed to impose such sanctions as are provided for in the general code of conduct as long as the discipline does not result in removal from the established school placement. Removal from school, including suspension, expulsion, and placement in an alternative setting, is regarded as a change in placement for the child. For this reason, all changes in placement must be reviewed by the IEP team before they are implemented. In addition, IDEA 1997 requires that children with disabilities shall not be deprived of educational services even if they have been suspended or expelled from school.

The exception to this general provision is that school officials may order the removal of a child to an alternative educational placement or suspension for up to ten days if continuation of the current placement involves danger to the child or others. Students with disabilities who bring firearms to school or who possess, use, or sell illegal drugs may be placed in an alternative education setting for up to forty-five days. IDEA 1997 allows school officials to report illegal activity to appropriate law enforcement agencies and to forward special education and disciplinary records as well.

IDEA 1997 specifies procedural guidelines for evaluating the placements of children who have been removed from school under the above provisions. Before the tenth day, the IEP team is required to conduct a functional behavioral assessment, to develop an appropriate behavioral plan if one is not in place, and to review and revise any plan or placement already in place. Should the school or parents disagree with the evaluation of the team, the law provides for procedural due process. The IDEA further provides that the child should remain in the alternative educational setting pending the outcome of any due process proceedings.

A hearing officer may order placement in an alternative interim educational setting for up to forty-five days if the school can show that continuation of the current school placement is likely to result in injury to the child or others. In addition, the hearing officer must review the student's current intervention program and placement, determining if the school has made reasonable efforts to implement the current placement plan. Any alternative interim educational placement must meet the following requirements:

- The child will continue to receive appropriate educational services.
- The alternative educational placement will include services and modifications designed to address the behavior of concern.

Central to all of these reviews is the process of *manifestation determination*. If a change of placement is to exceed ten days, the IEP team must review the facts of the case and determine the relationship, if any, between the behavior and the disability. The team may determine that the behavior is not a manifestation of the disability and the child may be disciplined in accordance with the general code of conduct of the school if the following criteria are met:

■ The child's program and placement are found to be appropriate, designed to meet the child's needs, and implemented appropriately
■ The disability does not impair the child's ability to understand the consequences of the behavior
■ The disability does not impair the child's ability to control his/her own behavior.

An appropriate behavioral intervention plan and placement are the best protection for school officials. Individualized behavioral intervention plans should be a part of the IEP for any youngsters who present a pattern of maladaptive behaviors, regardless of disability category. Such plans, now required by IDEA 1997 as part of the IEP, will identify the behavioral expectations, the inappropriate behaviors of concern, and the positive and negative consequences that are associated with both the expectations and the inappropriate behavior. The team should proactively consider interventions to ameliorate the problem behavior as well as the disciplinary process that will be followed if misbehavior occurs. A crisis response plan should also be specified in advance. This kind of effective preparation will assist students in managing their own behaviors and will ensure that, in an emergency, an alternative plan is ready to be implemented.

Focus on Culture and Diversity

Of all the diversities students bring with them to the classroom, the family is the most central. The family represents the unique combination of cultural forces affecting the learner's life. It is the family from which the student comes and the family to which the student returns. When educators consider how to most effectively support a learner with deficits in social-emotional functioning, the family must be part of the discussion (Obiakor, Utley, Smith, & Harris-Obiakor, 2002; Raymond, 1997). Rather than blaming the family for the student's problems, educators must work proactively to build connections with the family. With the school and family working as a team, cultural differences become part of what enriches the quality of classroom life, and the interventions developed are more likely to succeed.

Students with emotional and behavioral disorders generally benefit from comprehensive integrated services, and this requires collaboration with families. When families are from diverse backgrounds (e.g., race, language, religion, sexual orientation, socio-economic status, family structure), such collaborations require significant sensitivity. Involving families in designing positive supports for the student with problem behaviors (Fox, Vaughn, Wyatte, & Dunlap, 2002) allows educators to acquire a greater understanding of the needs that lead the child to engage in those behaviors. Collaboration with families helps educators see the problem from the parents' perspectives, and interventions can be evaluated with an eye to their cultural acceptability and perceived validity. School and family become supportive of one another, and the likelihood of positive outcomes increases.

Resources on the Web

IDEAS That Work

www.ideapractices.org

> Provides comprehensive information and updates on IDEA regulations relating to responses to problem behaviors, links to federal publications concerning special education, and a variety of other resources for teachers and parents.

National Information Center for Children and Youth with Disabilities

www.nichcy.org

> Provides information on a variety of topics related to students with disabilities, including the new requirements for functional behavioral assessment and positive behavioral supports.

Center for Effective Collaboration and Practice

www.cecp.air.org

> Provides resources related to assessment and services for students with problem behaviors, including functional behavioral assessments and design of positive behavior support plans.

Summary

Social-emotional characteristics can be studied from a number of perspectives, including the developmental and the ecological perspectives. Erikson's theory of psychosocial development proposes that human behavior develops from the result of social challenges that must be addressed and resolved for healthy adaptation to occur. In the span of a human life, each person is faced with the need to resolve challenges associated with trust, autonomy, initiative, industry, identity, intimacy, generativity, and ego integrity. Failure to resolve these crises in a positive balance may lead to adjustment problems in later development.

Emotions are the window on the inner psychological development of human beings. The core emotions of joy, pride, sadness, guilt, fear, and anger communicate much about what we value. The explanations given for a particular feeling develop over time and provide clues about the individual's development as a social being.

Selman studied the social cognitive skills involved in social perspective taking as a developmental process. He discovered that the skill of being able to take the perspective of another or of society develops just as emotions do.

Skills in social cognition are essential to the development of socially skilled behavior. The level of personal competence derives from the interaction of physical competence, conceptual intelligence, emotional competence, and social competence (which is composed of social intelligence and practical intelligence). Social intelligence includes skills associated with social awareness and social skill.

Emotional competence is related to the development of a variety of personality characteristics including character and temperament. Character relates to the values and principles that guide an individual's behavioral choices. Temperament is believed to be an inborn characteristic related to behavioral style; it refers to the way individuals react to stimuli and regulate themselves.

The ecological perspective holds that behaviors or behavioral patterns can only be understood by analyzing the interactions among the person, the environment, and any antecedent behavioral variables. Another example of research with an ecological focus is the work on the relationship of risk factors and protective factors resulting in the resilience displayed by some learners.

Maladaptive behaviors are present in some learners with mild disabilities, including, but not restricted to, those with emotional or behavioral disorders. Conduct disorders include those externalizing aggressive behaviors that cause disruption in classrooms, homes, and communities. Anxiety-withdrawal-dysphoria disorders are represented by internalizing behaviors such as anxiety and panic disorders, obsessions, compulsions, phobias, and depression.

IDEA 1997 addressed the special concerns related to youngsters with challenging behaviors. The law now requires that all children with any disability who present problems in behavior must have that behavior assessed using a functional behavioral assessment. The behavior must then be addressed as part of the IEP planning and placement process.

SAMMY: A Case Study

Sammy is a sixteen-year-old male of African-American heritage. He lives in a small southern town with his mother, father, and younger brother. Sammy's mother and father are both employed at low-wage service jobs. Over the years, they have tried to arrange their work schedules so that one of them has been available when the children were not in school. Sammy's mother has been very involved with the children's education, coming for conferences, seeking solutions to problems. She has voiced some frustration with the system, however, and has recently sought the assistance of the state protection and advocacy office.

Sammy began his elementary schooling at Tate Elementary. Tate was not his home school, but under the district's majority-minority transfer de-

segregation plan, his mother arranged for him to enter Tate, which had a majority white enrollment. She believed that an integrated school would provide her children with a better education than was available in their segregated neighborhood school. During first grade, Sammy experienced difficulty with the beginning reading process and with staying on task. He was referred for special education evaluation, which indicated that he was eligible for services as a child with a learning disability. He was served in Tate's resource program for the next two years, with minimal progress.

The following year, the school district opened a new self-contained program for students like Sammy. His underachievement was severe enough to qualify for that class, so he was transferred to

South Elementary School. Ms. Cole, his teacher reported that during the next two years, Sammy began to make some progress in reading, but mathematics was still difficult. He had difficulty completing his math assignments and was frequently off-task, unable to sustain attention. He also experienced continuing problems with impulse control and displays of anger. Sammy impressed Ms. Cole as having significant intellectual ability despite his reading and behavior problems. She helped him gain a position on the school's "Odyssey of the Mind" team, and she was pleased to see him experience success with that group.

During his second year at South Elementary, Sammy was mainstreamed for science in a fourth grade class. Academically he was passing, but his behavior was erratic. He had particular problems dealing with teasing. A behavior contract was initiated whereby he earned a star for each class period his behavior met the stated guidelines, and this seemed to have a positive effect.

At the end of that year, it was decided that Sammy had made sufficient progress, and that he should return to Tate School in a regular fourth grade class with resource help. It was suggested that he be put on an organizational behavior contract and receive instruction in anger management. Unfortunately, the fourth grade teacher was not willing to provide extra support and was, in fact, overtly negative and sarcastic toward Sammy's behavior. In addition, the resource position was vacant for the first two months of the year, so there was no transition support. Sammy's behavior deteriorated, and his academic progress evaporated. In January, he was

sent back to the self-contained class at South, where he stayed for the remainder of elementary school. It seemed as if Sammy had decided that life was easier in the self-contained classroom, so that was where he wanted to be.

He moved to the self-contained class at the junior high school in seventh grade, and his behavior became more violent. He was frequently involved in fights and was suspended a number of times. When he was fifteen, Sammy was socially promoted to ninth grade at the high school, although he had not met the state-mandated criteria for exiting eighth grade. In ninth grade, he was involved in a fight and suspended. His mother asked that he be placed in the alternative program for out-of-school youth. She did not understand that by doing so she was removing him from coverage under the IDEA. The school district said that since she had removed him from school, they no longer had an obligation to serve him. He was soon expelled from the alternative program for fighting, and he was placed under the jurisdiction of the Department of Youth Services.

His mother is literally at her wits' end. She can no longer handle his emotional outbursts at home, and she feels that the school and other agencies just want to get rid of Sammy. She knows that Sammy needs help emotionally and academically. Sammy's mother and the advocate have requested that the school revisit Sammy's case and evaluate the possibilities for reinstituting services. At the request of Sammy's mother, the following historical information was provided to the multidisciplinary team by Ms. Cole, Sammy's special education teacher in third and fourth grade.

To Whom It May Concern:

I have been asked by Sammy's mother to provide some historical information that may be useful in Sammy's future educational placement and planning. I served as Sammy's teacher in the self-contained class for students with learning disabilities when he was nine to eleven years old. Although I have not worked directly with Sammy since that time, I have kept in touch with the family and followed Sammy's journey through the school system.

When Sammy was a student in my class, he was classified as a third grader. He was reading at an average second-grade level and had difficulty completing math assignments. His primary problems at the time were work-habit related, including attention to task, task completion, and goal setting and attainment. He also exhibited periodic problems with impulse control in unstructured settings. This manifested itself by his engaging in fighting on the playground when teased. The

(continued)

failure to control his impulses appeared to increase when he was under stress, such as during statewide testing periods. It is unclear to me now whether his learning disabilities led to the behavioral problems or whether the behavioral problems resulted in his difficulty profiting from instruction. In any case, both areas impeded his academic and social progress.

Under certain circumstances, Sammy demonstrated average to excellent cognitive abilities. When he was ten, Sammy was invited to fill a slot on an Odyssey of the Mind team. He was the only member of the team who was not identified by the school system as gifted and talented, but observation of his interactions in the group would not have called attention to this fact. Because the competition relied on nonverbal exhibition of creative thinking, he was not disadvantaged by his poor reading skills. On the contrary, his capability in logical problem-solving proved to be an asset to the team, resulting in their winning second place at the regional competition and moving on to compete at the state level. In addition, although he was the only African American student on the team, he interacted well with the other members; ethnic diversity was never an issue. This experience indicated to me that when given a challenging environment that did not present assaults on his self-esteem, Sammy had the cognitive ability to function well. It also demonstrated that he was able to control his behavior as well as any other child, given clear goals, supportive leadership, and interesting tasks. I saw him grow during that semester, and this growth was evidenced in his work at school as well.

By the time he was eleven, Sammy had made sufficient academic and behavioral progress that mainstreaming for fourth-grade science was initiated. He had some difficulty with the work expectations at first, but with assistance and oral testing he was able to attain passing grades. He then began to eat lunch and have recess with that class. Behavior became a recurrent problem, primarily when he would "lose it" on the playground. We initiated a behavioral contract to help him monitor his behavior and work habits, and there was improvement. By the end of the year it was decided that he was ready for a less restrictive placement. His reading was at a lower third-grade level, and so he was recommended for placement in a regular fourth grade at his home elementary school. It was expected that his resource teacher and general education teacher would work closely with him during the transition to mainstream programming. Unfortunately, for a variety of reasons primarily related to staffing problems during that period, the needed close support and monitoring apparently did not occur. The reported negative behaviors increased, and Sammy was returned to the self-contained class in the spring of that year.

In summary, Sammy has manifested a number of problems in the past that have interfered with his progress in school. His problems have primarily involved his inability to set and work toward self-defined goals, to accept the restrictions placed on him by societal expectations, and to control his impulses. While he appears to have some perceptual and cognitive disabilities as well, it appears to me that the behavioral aspects were primarily responsible for restricting his performance. He needed then, and likely still does need, assistance, coaching, and support for developing cognitive processes to accomplish what he needs to do and to refrain from actions that are detrimental to himself and others. Such programs exist, and I sincerely hope that the planning team can design a program that will help him meet these needs so that his considerable talents can be unleashed. The frustration he must feel at this point, after all these years of being shuffled from program to program without developing the skills he needs, must be seriously undermining his self-esteem.

Sincerely,

Susan Cole

The following psychoeducational report was prepared by the school psychologist for the multi-disciplinary team meeting requested by Sammy's mother:

Downing County School District
Psychoeducational Report

Name: Sammy
Age: 16 years, 2 months
School: Senior High (not currently enrolled)
Grade: 9

Reason for Referral   Sammy was referred for evaluation by the State Advocacy Office in order to aid in educational placement and planning.

Background Information   Sammy is a sixteen-year-old male who was attending the senior high school until three months ago when his mother withdrew him from school while he was under suspension for fighting. Sammy is currently on probation with the Department of Youth Services for fighting at school. Even though he was never expelled from school by the district, he entered an alternative program for dropouts operated by the school district. Sammy was dropped from that program two weeks later, again for fighting. Up until his enrollment in the alternative school, Sammy had been suspended for twenty-one days this year. Triennial evaluations over the last eight years all found Sammy to be functioning in the low-average range intellectually. Sammy is currently receiving counseling through the community mental health clinic.

Behavioral Observations   Sammy was alert and outgoing during the testing. Eye contact was satisfactory. Sammy's general behavior during the testing session can be described as at ease, courteous, cooperative, cheerful, interested, and involved. Sammy attended well to initial instructions and moved rapidly into the test items. He responded well to the highly structured setting of the testing situation and related warmly and appropriately to the examiner. Sammy seemed to understand most instructions, although it had been previously noted that his listening skills were poor. His vocabulary was extensive, and he was very talkative in the testing session.

Test Results and Interpretation

Wechsler Intelligence Scale for Children-III (WISC-III)
Sammy's level of intellectual functioning on the WISC-III was within the low-average range.

Full Scale IQ	84	Verbal IQ	82
		Performance IQ	87

Subtest Scaled Scores (10 represents average performance)

Verbal Subtests		*Performance Subtests*	
Information	7	Picture Completion	10
Similarities	6	Picture Arrangement	12
Arithmetic	6	Block Design	7
Vocabulary	9	Object Assembly	8
Comprehension	8	Coding	4

Peabody Picture Vocabulary Test-Revised (PPVT)
Standard Score	84
Percentile	14
Age Equivalent	12 years, 7 months

(continued)

Peabody Individual Achievement Test (PIAT)

The PIAT indicates that Sammy's reading recognition is significantly below ability level, although his reading comprehension is comparable to ability level.

Subtest	Standard Score	Grade Equivalent
Reading Recognition	64	4.8
Reading Comprehension	84	6.4
Total Reading	74	5.1

Wide Range Achievement Test-Revised (WRAT)

The WRAT indicates severe academic deficiencies in all three academic areas.

Subtest	Standard Score	Percentile	Grade Equivalent
Decoding	65	1 %tile	3 end
Spelling	59	7 %tile	3 grade
Arithmetic	62	1 %tile	4 end

Conclusions   This evaluation indicates that Sammy is functioning intellectually in the low-average range. His receptive language is comparable to his estimated mental age. His academic achievement in reading recognition, spelling, and arithmetic is severely deficient. Sammy appears to have poor listening skills, with better developed visual processing skills. Sammy attempted to make manipulatives to use during the arithmetic subtest of the WISC-III. Some adjustment problems are apparent in the school setting; however, Sammy's behavior throughout the evaluation was exemplary, indicating that he can control his emotions. Lack of academic achievement no doubt contributes to his frustration, leading to his inappropriate behaviors. The assessment indicates that Sammy should probably continue to be classified as a student with a learning disability.

DISCUSSION

Review the historical and current evaluation information you have been provided about Sammy. Make a list of the strengths and needs indicated by this case material.

Given this information, do you concur with the school psychologist's conclusions about classification? What are the implications of that classification? What are the implications for programming in this information? What implications do you see in this case about the interaction between learning disabilities and behavioral disorders?

POLICY STATEMENTS

Council for Exceptional Children:
Labeling and Categorizing of Children
Inclusive Schools and Community Settings

National Association of School Psychologists:
Rights Without Labels

Council for Learning Disabilities:
Measurement and Training of Perceptual and Perceptual-Motor Functions

Labeling and Categorizing of Children—Council for Exceptional Children*

The field of special education is concerned with children who have unique needs and with school programs that employ specialized techniques. As a result of early attitudes and programs that stressed assistance for severely handicapped children, the field developed a vocabulary and practices based on the labeling and categorizing of children. In recent decades, labeling and categorizing was extended to children with milder degrees of exceptionality. Unfortunately, the continued use of labels tends to rigidify the thinking of all educators concerning the significance and purposes of special education and thus to be dysfunctional and even harmful for children.

Words such as "defective," "disabled," "retarded," "impaired," "disturbed," and "disordered," when attached to children with special needs, are stigmatic labels that produce unfortunate results in both the children and in the community's attitudes toward the children. These problems are magnified when the field organizes and regulates its programs on the basis of classification systems that define categories of children according to such terms. Many of these classifications are oriented to etiology, prognosis, or necessary medical treatment rather than to educational classifications. They are thus of little value to the schools. Simple psychometric thresholds, which have sometimes been allowed to become pivotal considerations in educational decision making, present another set of labeling problems.

Special education's most valuable contribution to education is its specialized knowledge, competencies, values, and procedures for individualizing educational programs for individual children, whatever their special needs. Indeed, special educators at their most creative are the advocates for children who are not well served by

(continued)

schools except through special arrangements. To further the understanding and servicing of such children, special educators as well as other educational personnel should eliminate the use of simplistic categorizing.

No one can deny the importance of some of the variables of traditional significance in special education such as intelligence, hearing, and vision. However, these variables in all their complex forms and degrees must be assessed in terms of educational relevance for a particular child. Turning them into typologies that may contribute to excesses in labeling and categorizing children is indefensible and should be eliminated.

In the past, many legislative and regulatory systems have specified criteria for including children in an approved category as the starting point for specialized programming and funding. This practice places high incentives on the labeling of children and undoubtedly results in the erroneous placement of many children.

It is desirable that financial aids be tied to educational programs rather than to children and that systems for allocating children to specialized programs be much more open than in the past.

Special educators should enhance the accommodative capacity of schools and other educational agencies to serve children with special needs more effectively. In identifying such children, special educators should be concerned with the identification of their educational needs, not with generalized labeling or categorizing of children.

Decisions about the education of children should be made in terms of carefully individualized procedures that are explicitly oriented to children's developmental needs.

To further discourage the labeling and categorizing of children, programs should be created on the basis of educational functions served rather than on the basis of categories of children served.

Regulatory systems that enforce the rigid categorization of pupils as a way of allocating them to specialized programs are indefensible. Financial aid for special education should be tied to specialized programs rather than to finding and placing children in those categories and programs.

*From "Labeling and categorizing of children" in *CEC Policies for Delivery of Services to Exceptional Children*, Council for Exceptional Children. Reprinted with permission.

Inclusive Schools and Community Settings—Council for Exceptional Children*

The Council for Exceptional Children (CEC) believes all children, youth, and young adults with disabilities are entitled to a free and appropriate education and/or services that lead to an adult life characterized by satisfying relations with others, independent living, productive engagement in the community, and participation in society at large. To achieve such outcomes, there must exist for all children, youth, and young adults a rich variety of early intervention, educational, and vocational program options and experiences. Access to these programs and experiences should be based on individual educational need and desired outcomes. Furthermore, students and their families or guardians, as members of the planning team, may recommend the placement, curriculum option, and the exit document to be pursued.

CEC believes that a continuum of services must be available for all children, youth, and young adults. CEC also believes that the concept of inclusion is a meaningful goal to be pursued in our schools and communities. In addition, CEC believes children, youth, and young adults with disabilities should be served whenever possible in general education classrooms in inclusive neighborhood schools and community settings. Such settings should be strengthened and supported by an infusion of specially trained personnel and other appropriate supportive practices according to the individual needs of the child.

Policy Implications

Schools. In inclusive schools, the building administrator and staff with assistance from the special education administration should be primarily responsible for the education of children, youth, and young adults with disabilities. The administrator(s) and other school personnel must have available to them appropriate support and technical assistance to enable them to fulfill their responsibilities. Leaders in state/provincial and local governments must redefine rules and regulations as necessary, and grant school personnel greater authority to make decisions regarding curriculum, materials, instructional practice, and staffing patterns. In return for greater autonomy, the school administrator and staff should establish high standards for each child and youth and should be held accountable for his or her progress toward outcomes.

Communities. Inclusive schools must be located in inclusive communities; therefore, CEC invites all educators, other professionals, and family members to work together to create early intervention, educational, and vocational programs and experiences that are collegial, inclusive, and responsive to the diversity of children, youth, and young adults. Policy makers at the highest levels of state/provincial and local government, as well as school administration, also must support inclusion in the educational reforms they espouse. Further, the policy makers should fund programs in nutrition, early intervention, health care, parent education, and other social support programs that prepare all children, youth, and young adults to do well in school. There can be no meaningful school reform, nor inclusive schools, without funding of these key prerequisites. As important, there must be interagency agreements and collaboration with local governments and business to help prepare students to assume a constructive role in an inclusive community.

Professional Development. And finally, state/provincial departments of education, local educational districts, and colleges and universities must provide high-quality preservice and continuing professional development experiences that prepare all general educators to work effectively with children, youth, and young adults representing a wide range of abilities and disabilities, experiences, cultural and linguistic backgrounds, attitudes, and expectations. Moreover, special educators should be trained with an emphasis on their roles in inclusive schools and community settings. They also must learn the importance of establishing ambitious goals for their students and of using appropriate means of monitoring the progress of children, youth, and young adults.

*From "Inclusive Schools and Community Settings" in *CEC Policies for Delivery of Services to Exceptional Children,* (p. 5–6). Copyright © 1994 by The Council for Exceptional Children. Reprinted with permission.

Rights Without Labels
National Coalition of Advocates for Students
National Association of School Psychologists*
National Association of Social Workers

The Rights Without Labels concept has been developed to address problems associated with the classification and labeling of children as "handicapped" for educational purposes. This classification establishes certain legal rights for children and parents, often including funds for schools offering specialized services.

Problems permeate this system: unreliability of classification; lack of instructional relevance for some classifications; exclusion of children from regular education; and the stigmatization of classified children. Moreover, removing these classifications and labels to return a student to regular education has proved very difficult.

(continued)

The Rights Without Labels guidelines presented here have special significance for children with academic and/or behavioral difficulties who are frequently classified as learning disabled, educable mentally retarded, or behavior disordered/emotionally disturbed. Our intention, however, is to apply these guidelines to as broad a range of exceptionalities as is feasible and in no way to diminish opportunities for even the severely/profoundly handicapped student to be served in settings with their non-handicapped peers.

The Rights Without Labels guidelines are based on the assumption that it would be desirable at this time to conduct programs wherein efforts are made to serve children who have special needs without labeling them or removing them from regular education programs. Research indicates that several factors are critical to the success of such experimental programs.

Pre-referral Screening/Intervention

Attempts must be made at the very outset to ameliorate educational difficulties through the use of pre-referral screening/intervention methods conducted by regular school personnel with the support of resources typically limited to special education (i.e., school psychologists, teachers, social workers, speech therapists, etc.). This benefits all children, especially those experiencing educational problems, while helping to identify students with characteristics consonant with legal definitions of handicapped conditions. Such practices will engender an abiding respect for students' rights under the law not to be evaluated in the absence of genuine suspicion of a handicap.

Curriculum Based Assessment

Secondly, identification and evaluation methods must include curriculum based assessment procedures. Research demonstrates these procedures provide reliable measures of student performance and produce relevant information for instructional planning. Most importantly, they fulfill the evaluation protection criteria set out in P.L. 94-142. The primary purpose of these procedures is not to classify or label children, but rather to identify specific curriculum and instructional deficits and strengths in order to provide a framework to develop appropriate educational programs. Individualized Education Programs (IEP) continue to be required, as well as

related services provided in accordance with current legal guidelines.

Special Resources in Regular Settings

The traditional array of special education supplementary aids, services, and resources (including teachers/aides) are available to children only outside the regular classroom. Our goal is to broaden the classroom situation within which special education resources can be used and to reverse the practice of moving handicapped students to special education situations outside regular classes and schools. Instead, special education resources can be transferred into the non-categorically identified students' regular classroom setting.

Rights Without Labels Guidelines

These guidelines are stated positively as principles for programs which professionals, advocates, and parents may wish to examine. The checklist format is provided for use in developing experimental programs in local or state systems.

Guidelines for Assuring Rights Without Labels in Regular/Special Education Programs

I. ASSURANCES: Any proposed alternative non-categorical program or system shall:
 A. Ensure that the fundamental rights afforded handicapped students and their parents under P.L. 94-142 are maintained and safeguarded. These include, but are not limited to:
  (1) Standards for fair and unbiased identification and evaluation of children who would qualify as "handicapped" in a categorical system.
  (2) Individualized Education Programs (IEPs) for all students who would otherwise qualify under a categorical system.
  (3) Specialized instruction and related services for students who would otherwise qualify under a categorical system.
  (4) Least Restrictive Environment (LRE) standards in determining educational placements.
  (5) Appointment of surrogate parents when appropriate.

(6) Non-discriminatory discipline procedures.

(7) All timeline standards governing the above practices and procedures.

(8) Parental rights in the identification, evaluation, IEP's, and placement of students who would otherwise qualify under a categorical system.

(9) Due Process rights for parents and students who wish to pursue concerns/complaints regarding educational evaluations, programs, and placements.

(10) Local advisory boards to assist local educational agencies (LEAs) in planning for the provision of appropriate educational services.

B. Provide parents of handicapped students with an alternative to selecting a traditional categorical approach to classification.

C. Provide full disclosure of the non-categorical system to parents including an explanation of resources, services, and rights that will be afforded students in this system.

II. GENERAL QUALITY FOR ALTERNATIVE PROGRAM: Any proposed non-categorical program or system shall:

A. Employ pre-referral screening/intervention measures and utilize evaluation procedures that include curriculum based assessment.

B. Employ methodology known to be associated with effective teaching/learning (for example, provide students with orderly and productive environments, ample learning/teaching time, systematic and objective feedback on performance, well-sequenced curricula, etc.).

C. Focus attention on basic skills as priority areas for instruction (for example, language, self-dependence, reasonable social behavior, mathematics, health and safety, etc.).

D. Provide procedures to identify and respond to the individual needs of all students, and in particular, those who may need modifications in their school programs.

E. Provide for special education aids, services, and resources to be delivered in regular education settings.

III. ASSESSMENT OF OUTCOMES: Any proposed non-categorical program shall:

A. Have an objective methodology for assessing the educational progress of students in major curriculum domains (including academic, social, motivational, and attitudinal variables) and for comparing such progress with results in traditional programs.

B. Contain and utilize a cost-benefit analysis to compare costs with traditional programs.

IV. TEACHING STAFF AND FACILITIES: Any proposed non-categorical program shall:

A. Include instruction and services by teachers and staff who are qualified in accordance with current state certification standards.

B. Include a delivery system that provides continuing staff development responsive to the training needs of the teaching staff and administrative personnel who will be implementing the requirements of the non-categorical program.

C. Include appropriate instructional materials and other resources.

D. Include assurances that funding levels and personnel allocations will not be decreased during the experimental period or as a result of successful alternative service delivery.

NOTE: To provide these assurances, it is assumed that as part of the experimental procedures, it would be common to conduct a dual classification system, whereby, for example, a student who might be classified as "learning disabled" in a traditional system would actually be so identified. Although the student's record would reflect the traditional classification, the student would be considered in need of "supplemental services" (i.e., regular and special education services) for purposes of his/her participation in the non-categorical program. Only by such a dual system could assurances concerning "rights" be offered and safeguarded. Over the long term, the traditional classification system might be modified if all stake-holders are satisfied about the new procedure.

*Position statement of the National Association of School Psychologists. Reprinted with permission.

Measurement and Training of Perceptual and Perceptual-Motor Functions—Council for Learning Disabilities*

The Board of Trustees of the Council for Learning Disabilities opposes the measurement and training of perceptual and perceptual-motor functions as part of learning disability services. The Board of Trustees of the Council for Learning Disabilities takes this position because:

1. An extensive body of research has failed to establish the value of assessing perceptual and perceptual-motor functions when identifying individuals with learning disabilities. Moreover, there is strong consensus that the instrumentation in this area lacks the necessary technical adequacy for diagnosing learning disabilities and for determining eligibility for learning disability programs;
2. There is little or no empirical support for claims that the training of perceptual and perceptual motor functions improves either the academic performance or the perceptual or perceptual-motor functions of learning disabled individuals. Therefore, such training must be characterized at best as experimental and nonvalidated;
3. Since little scientific evidence exists to show that assessment and training of perceptual and

perceptual-motor functions are beneficial to learning disabled individuals, schools must view the time, money, and other resources devoted to such activities as wasteful, as an obstruction to the provision of appropriate services, and as unwarranted for any purposes other than those of pure research.

The Board of Trustees of the Council for Learning Disabilities makes the following recommendations:

1. A moratorium on assessment and training of perceptual and perceptual-motor functions in education should be instituted;
2. Assessment and remediation of learning disabilities should focus on primary disorders (i.e., listening, speaking, reading, writing, reasoning, and mathematics) as specified in the definition of learning disabilities adopted by the National Joint Committee on Learning Disabilities and in federal rules and regulations;
3. That aspect of the learning disabilities definition in P.L. 94-142 which refers to *basic psychological processes* should not be interpreted to require measurement and training of perceptual and perceptual-motor functions.

*Reprinted by permission, Council for Learning Disabilities.

LEGISLATION AND LITIGATION

Major Legislation Affecting Students with Disabilities

P.L. 89-10	*Elementary and Secondary Education Act of 1965*
P.L. 93-112	*Section 504 of the Amendments to the Vocational Rehabilitation Act of 1973*
P.L. 94-103	*Developmental Disabilities Assistance and Bill of Rights Act of 1974* (reauthorized in 1996)
P.L. 94-142	*Education for all Handicapped Children Act of 1975*
P.L. 99-457	*Education for all Handicapped Children Act Amendments of 1986*
P.L. 101-336	*Americans with Disabilities Act (ADA) of 1990*
P.L. 101-476	*Individuals with Disabilities Education Act Amendments of 1990*
P.L. 105-17	*Individuals with Disabilities Education Act Amendments of 1997*

Court Cases

Board of Education v. *Rowley,* 458 U.S. 176 (1982)

Brown v. *Board of Education,* 347 U.S. 483 (1954)

Buck v. *Bell,* 274 U.S. 200 (1927)

Cedar Rapids Community School v. *Garrett F.,* 119 S.Ct. 992 (1999)

Daniel R.R. v. *State Board of Education,* 874 F2d 1036 (5th Cir. 1989)

Diana v. *State Board of Education,* C.A. No. C-70-37 (N.D. CAl., July 1970)

Hobson v. *Hanson,* 269 F.Supp. 401 (D.D.C. 1967)

Honig v. *Doe,* 484 U.S. 305 (1988)

Jose P. v. *Ambach,* 551EHLR245 & 412 (E.D.N.Y. 1979)

Larry P. v. *Riles,* 793 F2d. 969 (9th Cir. 1984) (previous rulings in 1972, 1979)

Mills v. *District of Columbia Board of Education,* 348 F.Supp. 866 (D.D.C. 1972)

Oberti v. *Board of Education,* 995 F.2nd 1204 (3rd Cir. 1993)

New Mexico Association for Retarded Citizens v. *New Mexico,* 495 F.Supp. 391 (D.N.M. 1980)

PASE v. *Hannon,* 506 F.Supp. 831 (N.D. Ill. 1980)

Pennsylvania Association for Retarded Citizens (PARC) v. *Pennsylvania,* 334 F. Supp. 1257 (E.D. Pa. 1971); 343 F.Supp. 279 (E.D. Pa. 1971, 1972)

Timothy W. v. *Rochester (NH) School District,* 875 F.2nd 954 (1st Cir. cert denied, 493 US 983 (1989)

Wyatt v. *Stickney,* 344 F.Supp. 373 (M.D.Ala. 1972)

academic learning disabilities   specific learning disabilities that are manifested by difficulty in school learning in such areas as reading, written expression, spelling, handwriting, mathematics, and content learning

academic learning time   the amount of time students actually spend actively engaged in learning activities with a high rate of success

academic responding time   amount of time students actually spend in responding to academic tasks/challenges as opposed to waiting or engaging in task management activities

accommodation   the process of handling new information by altering existing schema to incorporate new and contradictory information and experiences

acquisition   the first stage in learning, which takes the learner from little or no knowledge to basic mastery of the concept or skill

adaptation   the process by which existing schema are modified, using either assimilation or accommodation to make changes to the individual's cognitive organizational structures

adaptive behavior   skills and behaviors involving everyday functions used by individuals for meeting environmental demands and for functioning in a competent manner

ADHD   acronym for attention-deficit/hyperactivity disorder

affect   the collected feelings, moods, or emotions displayed by an individual

affiliation   one of the sources of intrinsic human motivation, which involves the desire to join with others in a common interest or purpose

alertness   the stage in the attention process in which the individual determines that attention is required; characterized by a readiness to attend to sensory input or to a cognitive task

alternative educational setting (AES)   temporary placement allowed by the 1997 IDEA amendments for use when a student's behavior is a threat in the classroom

Americans with Disabilities Act   legislation that prohibits discrimination based on disability in employment, public accommodations, governmental services, transportation, and telecommunication services

anencephaly   a congenital condition involving the absence of part or all of the brain

anxiety   a psychiatric condition characterized by fear and excessive worries, which results in demonstrated distress, tension, or uneasiness

aphasia   the loss or absence of the ability to use spoken and written language; *developmental aphasia* refers to children who fail to develop oral language skills as expected, with the presumption that central nervous system dysfunction is the cause

apprehension   catching or registering a stimulus in the sensory register for use in subsequent cognitive processing

appropriating   the process by which a learner assumes the skills demonstrated by a teacher or guide

assimilation   the addition of new and complementary information into an individual's existing cognitive schema

atrophy   the wasting away of a body part or skill due to lack of use or to degenerative processes

attention   the strategic control function that allows the learner to focus on the relevant aspects of a task or concept long enough to process the information

attention-deficit/hyperactivity disorder   a condition characterized by inattention and/or hyperactivity and impulsivity that compromises the individual's ability to process cognitive information and to learn

attributions for success or failure   the reasons given by individuals for their success or failure

auditory association   the ability to relate ideas, find relationships, make associations, and categorize information obtained by listening

auditory blending   the ability to make a complete word by blending the individual phonological elements, and to perceive the whole as a combination of the parts

auditory closure   the ability to identify words and other auditory elements that have been presented in incomplete form or that have unclear elements

auditory discrimination   the ability to recognize differences between sounds and to make perceptual judgments between auditory stimuli with very similar sounds

auditory figure-ground discrimination   the ability to distinguish a sound from its background

auditory memory   the ability to recognize and recall previously presented auditory stimuli or a sequence of items presented auditorially

auditory perception   the ability to interpret auditory stimuli and to attach meaning to what is heard

automaticity   the stage of learning following acquisition in which the learner's goal is to maintain accuracy while increasing the rate of accurate production and to perform tasks with little conscious cognitive effort

autonomy   independence or freedom; the capability of acting in accordance with one's own will and effort

behavioral flexibility   the ability to adjust one's behavior to different situations, people, or settings

biological constructivism   Piaget's theory that an individual learner is inherently predisposed to process stimuli and information in predictable patterns

borderline mental retardation   a term used in the past to describe individuals with measured IQs of 75–80 who display some indications of mental retardation but whose performance approximates that of typical individuals

bound morphemes   a unit of language (such as a prefix, suffix, or an inflected ending) that has meaning only when combined with a free-standing morpheme or word

cerebral hemispheric dominance   the theory that each side, or hemisphere, of the brain controls particular functions and that one hemisphere is stronger than the other in most individuals, affecting individual performance

character   the combined traits that shape a person's nature and contribute to the establishment of the individual's personality

chronicity   the characteristic of being of long or indeterminate duration or of recurring frequently

chunk   a collection of stimuli or symbols that is treated as a unit for ease in cognitive processing

chunking   the process of subdividing content into subunits for easier cognitive processing

classification   the process of assigning individuals into groups or categories by the use of agreed-upon criteria; also a Piagetian developmental task in which the learner becomes able to group items in categories

classification system   the formal taxonomy of categories and levels of disability, combined with the criteria by which classification decisions are made

clustering   the process of grouping elements to assist in cognitive processing

cognitive stages   periods of development that are characterized by a specific level of cognitive sophistication

cognitive style   the way in which learners typically approach and structure stimuli and derive meaning from their experiences

comorbidity   the coexistence of two or more conditions in the same individual

comparison   the cognitive process of determining if two stimuli are the same or if they are members of the same class of objects

competence   possessing the skills needed for skillful performance of expected functions

comprehension   the process of interpreting and deriving meaning from oral or written communication

compulsions   a condition characterized by the intrinsic need to perform repetitive actions that appear to others to be irrational or against one's will

conceptual intelligence   the intrinsic intellectual ability of an individual, as well as the ability to process information, solve abstract problems, and understand and use symbolic processes such as language

concrete operations   Piaget's third stage of cognitive development, characterized by the growing ability of children to think logically about concepts in their own experience, but still remain unable to deal with abstractions

conditional knowledge   a component of long-term memory consisting of the knowledge that an individual uses to determine when or whether to utilize a particular cognitive process or knowledge base

conduct disorders   a pattern of behavior characterized by frequent occurrences of serious levels of aggression, destruction of property, and violations of family and community norms and standards

connotative   relating to the meanings associated with words; used to refer to those enhanced meanings beyond the basic definition

content   the aspect of language that includes elements related to meaning, including morphology and semantics

context   the combined variables that characterize the environment in which a pragmatic language or social event occurs

criterion-referenced assessment   the process of gathering information about which skills a learner has mastered

cross-categorical programs   a model of service delivery in which services are provided to children with different conditions in the same setting; with interventions designed to meet student abilities and needs rather than being based on disability categories

culturally fair   the term used to describe instruments and assessment processes designed to accurately assess the performance of individuals from culturally and linguistically diverse backgrounds

culturally normative   the concept that behaviors must be evaluated in the context of the culture in which they occur; behaviors that are adaptive for an individual in a particular setting may be viewed as normative for that setting

culture   the attitudes, beliefs, values, traditions, and customs shared by a group of people and which are derived from their shared heritage

curriculum-based assessment   the process of creating assessment instruments related to the curriculum that has been taught in a particular school or classroom

declarative knowledge   knowledge that deals with factual information and the acquisition of related concepts

declarative memory   the long-term storage facility used for factual and conceptual information

definition   the criteria used to establish the identity of a condition; the criteria may be conceptual, referring to the nature of the condition, or they may be operational and outline procedures used to place individuals into diagnostic categories

denotative   referring to the explicit, primary meaning of a word, indicating the meaning generally held by most people in that culture

depression   a condition characterized by prolonged depressed mood and lack of interest in ordinary activities, including those generally viewed as pleasurable

developmental delay   a noncategorical classification term defined in IDEA 1997 for use with children ages 3–9, and identified by documentation of a delay in development of physical, cognitive, communication, social-emotional, and/or adaptive skills

developmental disability   a chronic condition characterized by significant impairment in functioning that results from mental and/or physical impairments, is manifested before age 22, and results in substantial functional limitations in three or more major life activities

developmental learning disabilities   specific learning disabilities that affect functions such as attention, perception, memory, and language

developmental period   that period of life during which rapid physical, intellectual, social, and emotional development is occurring, culminating in transition to adult status at about age 18

deviance   a condition characterized by behavior that significantly departs from the accepted and expected normative behavior

diagnosis   the result of a diagnostic process that describes an individual's condition, including etiology, current manifestation of the condition, treatment requirements, and prognosis

dichotomous   belonging to one of only two possible and mutually exclusive categories

differentiation   Piaget's theory that learning begins when individuals distinguish between and among various environmental stimuli and recognize specific stimuli as new information

disability   a describable, measurable condition in which an expected, specific human ability is curtailed or absent

discrepancy   a difference from expectations or an inconsistency

disequilibrium   an unsteady cognitive state resulting from new information or experiences that need to be incorporated into existing cognitive schema

displacement   the phenomenon of losing specific cognitive information due to limited storage capacity during processing

distractibility   a condition described by the individual's tendency to attend to multiple and irrelevant stimuli rather than to focus on the most relevant stimulus

Down syndrome   a condition characterized by multiple physical abnormalities as well as by some impairment of intellectual functioning; results from a chromosomal defect affecting the 23rd chromosomal pair

due process procedures   set of procedures designed to protect the right to receive notice of and to challenge governmental actions

dyscalculia   severe disabilities in mathematical processing

dysgraphia   severe disabilities in written expression and in performing the motoric functions associated with handwriting

dyslexia   severe disabilities in reading, including failure to learn to read or to read fluently and effectively

ecological assessment   process that considers behaviors in the context of the individual's environment and assesses the effect of the interactions between and among environmental factors and the individual's behaviors for the purpose of designing effective interventions

educable   an obsolete term used to describe students with mild retardation who were believed to be capable of becoming functionally literate and to lead independent or semi-independent lives

Education for All Handicapped Children Act   legislation passed in 1975 as P.L. 94–142 that guaranteed a free, appropriate, public education to all children in the United States

elaboration   cognitive mnemonic strategies by which storage of information in long-term memory is supported by strengthening the meaning of the stimulus through use of semantic or visual enhancements

emotional competence   the degree to which the individual is able to maintain an emotional "steady-state"

emotional disturbance   the term used in IDEA 1997 for learners with emotional or behavioral disorders

emotional or behavioral disorders   disability that is characterized by the presence of severe problem behavior(s) that are markedly different from typical peers, have existed for a prolonged period of time, and are affecting the student's educational performance

encephalitis   inflammation of the brain related to an infection

encoding   the component of the process of perception that involves the formation of a mental representation of the stimulus, including its interpretation in terms of attributes, associations, or meaning

endogenous retardation   term proposed by Strauss to refer to individuals with mental retardation whose condition is associated with congenital causal factors

equilibration   the process by which a learner resolves the unsteady cognitive state created by new information, using the cognitive functions of organization and adaptation, resulting in a new level of equilibrium and cognitive competence

etiology   study of the factors that appear to cause or contribute to a disability, including biomedical, social, and behavioral factors

eugenics   philosophy that holds that it is possible to improve the characteristics of a population by discouraging reproduction by those believed to have inferior characteristics and encouraging procreation by those with desirable traits

executive control functions   cognitive functions involved in monitoring and evaluating the effectiveness of cognitive processing, directing the flow of information, and making resource allocations among the structural storage components of memory

exogenous retardation   term proposed by Strauss to refer to those individuals with mental retardation whose condition is associated with brain injury

expressive language   communication process that involves speaking and writing for the purpose of transferring information from the communicator to the reader or listener

externalizing behaviors   problem behaviors that are characterized by acting out, aggressive actions, where the target of the behaviors and the effect is outside of the individual

external locus of control   belief of learners that their success or failure is due to factors outside themselves, such as chance, fate, or the actions of others

extrinsic motivation   motivation related to the desire to earn a reward or avoid punishment

FAPE   acronym for *free and appropriate public education*

field dependence   the degree to which an individual's perceptual and cognitive judgments are dependent on the surrounding environment

field independence   the degree to which an individual is able to interpret perceptual information independently by attending to and considering relevant information from the environment and comparing it to internal standards

field sensitive   an alternative term for field dependence, which recognizes the positive aspects of interpreting some perceptual information with reference to the surrounding environment and which is characteristic of individuals in some cultures

fetal alcohol effects (FAE)   condition related to fetal alcohol syndrome in which the effects of a mother's drinking on the developing fetus are present but less severe

fetal alcohol syndrome (FAS)   a condition resulting from ingestion of alcohol by the mother during the prenatal period, which results in the child's displaying mental retardation, drooping eyelids and other facial abnormalities, heart defects, reduced physical size throughout life, and other evidence of central nervous system dysfunction

figure-ground discrimination   the ability to distinguish an object or sound from its background

form   components of language associated with the structure of language, including phonology, morphology, and syntax

formal operations   Piaget's final stage in cognitive development, characterized by the ability to think abstractly and to use reasoning for learning

formative evaluation   evaluation conducted in the context of ongoing activity for the purposes of making changes

fragile X syndrome   a common inherited cause of mental retardation associated with a fragile site on the X chromosome; defects include mental retardation as well as other learning and behavioral problems and physical differences

free and appropriate education (FAPE)   the core right in the IDEA, which guarantees to every child an education designed to meet his/her needs provided at no cost to the parents

free morphemes   the smallest units of language that can exist by themselves and convey meaning

functional behavioral assessment   the gathering of information to accurately describe a problem behavior, the contexts in which it occurs, and the function or need it fulfills for the student

general education curriculum the curriculum established by a school, district, or state for use by all children, which specifies the goals and objectives viewed as essential for later functioning; pertains to the content of instruction, not the way it is taught nor the setting in which it occurs

general education initiative (GEI) the philosophy that students with disabilities can and should be educated within the general education classroom setting, with supports and modifications to teaching strategies as needed; formerly called the regular education initiative

generalization the use of learned skills in settings or situations other than those under which the skill was trained

grapheme the written symbols used alone or in combinations to represent sounds in a language; a *phonogram*

habilitation the process of providing training in necessary life skills to individuals who have not acquired those skills previously

handicap restriction on the performance of a desired function due to environmental barriers; results from interaction of a disability with an environment that cannot or will not modify to accommodate the disability and permit the function

handicapism attitude that any individual with a disability must also be handicapped or unable to perform necessary life functions

haptic perception the ability to ascribe meaning to tactile (touch) and kinesthetic (movement) stimuli

heritability characteristic of traits believed to be inherited or controlled by genetic components

high-prevalence disabilities conditions that occur relatively frequently in society

hydrocephalus condition characterized by relatively large head, related to an increase in the amount of cerebrospinal fluid leading to increased pressure on brain structures

hyperactivity condition characterized by an unusually high level of activity and restlessness

hypoactivity condition characterized by an unusually low level of activity

hypoxia a condition characterized by inadequate oxygenation of the blood

IDEA acronym for the Individuals with Disabilities Education Act

imagery memory strategy that involves pairing a concept with a visual image to enhance the strength of the concept in long-term memory

immediate memory structural component that includes the working and short-term memories and that is devoted to active processing of information prior to storage or output

impulsivity cognitive style that is characterized by failure to think about an action before taking it

incidence the percentage of individuals who will at some point in their lives develop a particular condition

inclusion educational practice of providing within the general education setting all the educational services students with disabilities require

individualized education program (IEP) written plan for individualized instructional services developed annually for each child with a disability

individualized family service program (IFSP) written plan for individualized educational services developed annually for each preschool child with a disability

individualized transition program (ITP)   written plan developed annually for every student with a disability at least by age 14, identifying the student's needs with respect to ultimate transition to adult living

Individuals with Disabilities Education Act   special education legislation that guarantees a free, appropriate, public education to all children in the United States

inner language   the use of language and linguistic concepts in internal cognitive processing of information

insight   the skills involved in determining the meaning of social information and its relevance to the individual

intelligence quotient (IQ)   standard score from a norm-referenced intelligence test such as the WISC-III or the Stanford Binet; a score of 100 indicates average intellectual functioning

interference   cognitive condition resulting from the identification of a discrepancy between new information and previously stored material, leading to the modification or loss of information deemed inaccurate

internalizing behaviors   problem behaviors characterized by social withdrawal, including anxiety, depression, fears, and phobias

internal locus of control   belief of learners that their success or failure is due to the personal effort they have exerted

intrinsic motivation   motivation related to needs within an individual for competence, belonging, and self-determination

involuntary attention   the attribute of tasks that forces or commands attention by an individual

I-plans   individualized education program (IEP), individualized family service program (IFSP), and individualized transition program (ITP)

IQ   acronym for *intelligence quotient*

judgment   skills used to determine the relevance and value of social information prior to framing behavioral responses

kinesthetic   of or related to the sensation of bodily movement

labeling   the process of attaching a name to the disability category to which a child has been assigned

language   any method or code employing signs, symbols, or gestures used for communicating ideas meaningfully

language disabilities   condition characterized by impaired ability to develop, understand, and use language

learned helplessness   belief that one's own efforts will not be sufficient to positively affect outcomes

learning   process by which experience and practice result in a stable change in an individual's behavior that is not explained simply by maturation, growth, or aging; the process of moving from a state of "not knowing" to "knowing"

learning disability   condition attributed to deficits in psychological process involved in the understanding and use of language and identified by the presence of a severe discrepancy between ability and achievement and the absence of other disabilities that may be causing the learning problems

learning styles theory   theory that each person possesses certain characteristics that interact with specific learning experiences and environments, resulting in enhancement of learning or in making learning more difficult

least restrictive environment   term used in IDEA to refer to the principle that children with disabilities should be educated with their typical peers as often as possible, and that removal to more specialized or restrictive settings should occur only when it is not possible, even with the provision of supplementary aids and supports, to serve a student with a disability in the general education setting

lexicon   the vocabulary (collection of morphemes) used by an individual; the vocabulary of a language

locus of control   the degree to which individuals perceive that there is a connection between their actions and the outcomes achieved

long-term memory   main cognitive storage component, with virtually unlimited storage capacity; information stored in long-term memory is considered to be permanent and, if stored effectively, remains accessible throughout life

mainstreaming   temporal, physical, instructional, and/or social integration of children with disabilities with their typical peers in settings or activities where their disability is not a problem and where the need for accommodations is minimal

maintenance   stage of learning that follows mastery and proficiency, the goal of which is to maintain a high level of performance over time

maladaptive behavior   behavior that interferes with normal interpersonal interactions and that is personally unsatisfying or socially unacceptable

manifestation determination   the procedural requirement of the IDEA that the IEP team must review the facts of disciplinary cases involving students with disabilities and determine the relationship, if any, between the behavior and the disability before proceeding with disciplinary actions or interventions

Mendelian trait   characteristic related to genetic factors and governed by the laws of heredity

mental retardation   disability characterized by significantly subaverage intellectual functioning, accompanied by impairments in the skills needed for everyday functioning

metacognition   awareness of one's own thinking processes and the accompanying ability to direct and monitor one's own cognitive processing

metacognitive regulation   cognitive abilities involved in self-instruction, self-monitoring, and self-evaluation of the efficiency and accuracy of thinking behaviors

metacomprehension   awareness of one's effectiveness in understanding oral or written language

microcephalus   congenital condition characterized by an abnormally small skull and resultant brain damage and mental retardation

mild disabilities   disabilities that impair some functions needed for learning and everyday activities, but that nevertheless allow many functions to be performed normally

mild mental retardation   level of retardation characterized by IQ in the 55–70 range

minimal brain dysfunction   term proposed by Task Force I for the condition now referred to as *learning disabilities*

mnemonic   of or pertaining to memory

mnemonics   specific techniques involving the use of memory cues that are used for assisting storage in memory

mnemonic strategies   cognitive procedures used to achieve the storage of information in long-term memory

moderate disabilities   disabilities that more severely affect the individual's ability to function and that may require more intensive and continuing supports

modified curriculum   curriculum in which modifications or substitutions are made in particular goals and objectives related to the content of instruction

morpheme   smallest meaningful unit in a language; a word

morphology   study of morphemes

motivation   force or drive from either intrinsic or extrinsic sources that leads an individual to act a certain way

multiple-gated screening   multistep screening process for assessing children for possible disabilities

multiple intelligences   theory that each individual possesses a number of separate talents or intelligences and that learners may have a variety of ways to approach a learning task most meaningfully

nature versus nurture   debate concerning the relative importance of inborn traits ("nature") and environmental events ("nurture") in determining the eventual functioning level of an individual

newcomer phenomenon   condition resulting from the return of an individual to an environment after an absence in which the individual is unable to quickly resume activity due to missing information

newness panic   condition of anxiety in which a person responds inappropriately in a situation perceived as new

noncategorical programs   service delivery models that base programming on identified strengths and needs of students instead of categorical labels

nondiscriminatory evaluation   evaluation procedures using tests that do not discriminate against students with respect to racial, linguistic, or cultural background

normalization   philosophy that supports making services available to individuals with disabilities in ways that are as close as possible to the norms and patterns of mainstream society

norm-referenced tests   tests that provide scores that allow comparison of the performance of a specific child to typical children of that age or grade

object recognition   ability to recognize the essential nature of an object

obsessions   repetitive and intrusive thoughts, impulses, or worries, unrelated to real-life demands that interfere with the ability of the individual to handle everyday tasks

oppositional defiant disorder   pattern of behavior characterized by active noncompliance and other forms of hostile responses to requests by teachers and parents

ordering   arrangement of items in some logical sequence as a means of facilitating storage and retrieval from long-term memory

organization   process by which individual learners are prompted by internal self-regulatory processes to fit new information into existing cognitive organizational structures and to relate new concepts to previous learning

paired associates   connection of a new concept with a concept already in the learner's repertoire

perception   recognition and labeling of sensory stimuli; attaching meaning to auditory, visual, and haptic stimuli

perceptual integration   process used to match an encoded stimulus with a previously stored mental representation

perceptual overload   tendency for information from one sensory input system to interfere with the processing of information coming in from another

perceptual speed efficiency with which an individual is able to attach meaning to relevant sensory stimuli

performance deficits social skill deficits relating to problems in the decision making required to activate appropriate social skills; the required skill is in the person's repertoire, but the individual does not recognize environmental cues that prompt the use of the skill

perinatal the period from the 20th week of pregnancy to the 28th day of the life of a newborn

perseveration condition characterized by repetition of a behavior past the point of usefulness

personal competence an individual's ability to coordinate and effectively use a variety of skills to function in social contexts and to respond to environmental demands

personality pattern of an individual's behavioral characteristics, including attributes of character and temperament

pervasive disorder disorder that affects most aspects of development and functioning

phenylketonuria (PKU) genetic condition that prevents the metabolism of the amino acid phenylalanine

phobia irrational fear that prevents an individual from performing necessary functions

phoneme smallest unit of sound in a language

phonogram written symbols used alone or in combinations to represent sounds in a language; a grapheme

phonological awareness the recognition of sounds and the understanding that words can be segmented into individual phonemes and syllables

phonology study of the linguistic system of a language involving individual sounds and letters and the way they are combined

physical competence adequacy of performance related to abilities in fine and gross motor skills, as well as physical development and health status

PKU acronym for *phenylketonuria*

P.L. 94–142 the Education for All Handicapped Children Act of 1975

placental insufficiency condition involving the inefficient transfer of nutrients by the placenta to the fetus in the last trimester of pregnancy

poor delay of response deficiency in the ability to reflect before acting and to refrain from carrying out actions that on reflection would be seen to be undesirable or ineffective; a lack of tolerance for delay within tasks and a reduced ability to delay responses

positive behavioral supports a proactive approach to addressing problem behaviors by assuring that it is possible for learners to meet important needs while engaging in socially acceptable behavior

postnatal the period after childbirth

practical intelligence the ability to deal with the physical and mechanical aspects of life, including daily living and vocational skills

pragmatics the study of language within a social context; the functional use of language

prenatal the period beginning with conception and ending at birth

preoperational the second stage of Piaget's theory of cognitive development, in which the child begins to use symbols for thinking but does not use logic to process cognitive information

prereferral problem-solving process prior to formal referral involving gathering information about a child's difficulty in performing necessary tasks and designing interventions to address those problems

prevalence   the total number of individuals with a particular condition in the population at a given time

primary prevention   to change the conditions associated with a condition so that it does not occur in the first place

proactive behaviors   behaviors designed to cause something to happen; purposeful behaviors designed to achieve a desired end

procedural knowledge   information related to the performance of specific tasks; a system of *condition-action* rules

procedural memory   the long-term storage facility used for processes and skills

production   the expressive channel of language, composed of speaking and writing

production channel   communication processes used to transmit messages from one person to another by means of speaking or writing

productions   condition-action rules stored in long-term memory as a string of connected steps in a process and used to facilitate access to procedural knowledge

proficiency   stage of learning following demonstration of mastery, the goal of which is to achieve automatic and fluent skill performance

profound disability   pervasive and severe level of impairment, resulting in significant restrictions of the abilities required to carry out typical functions

psychoactive drug   substance that affects mental activity or behavior

psycholinguistics   study of the psychological processes involved in the understanding and use of language

psychometric thresholds   cutoff scores on norm-referenced instruments used to make classification decisions

psychotic disorder   emotional or behavioral disorder characterized by extreme departures from typical behavior that present serious barriers to ordinary activities

reaction range   potential range of expression of a genetically directed trait; extent to which environment hinders or enhances the development of an innate capability

reactive behaviors   behaviors that occur in response to a particular condition or stimulus

receptive language   communication functions used to receive information from the environment, including the skills of listening and reading

reflectivity   cognitive style characterized by the presence of an effective deliberative process in which the individual thinks about the action before acting

regular education initiative (REI)   older term for the *general education initiative*

rehabilitation   process of restoring an individual to a prior level of skill and functioning; activities needed to regain a function that was lost due to injury or disease

rehearsal   cognitive strategy involving simple repetition, used to store less complex concepts in long-term memory

relatedness   source of motivation related to the human need for belonging and nurturing, including the need or desire to develop affiliations, a sense of belonging, or friendships

reliability   extent to which other evaluators would be expected to arrive at the same conclusion about a classification

resiliency   ability of an individual to resist or overcome the negative effects of environmental stress and to achieve a positive outcome

reversion   period of early learning in which students experience some measure of success but still make significant numbers of errors

risk   negative or potentially negative situation that impedes or threatens the achievement of desired goals

scaffolding instruction   Vygotsky's term for the role of teachers and others in supporting the learners' development

schema   a concept or intellectual structure that organizes perceptions of the world in a systematic manner

schizophrenia   pervasive and severe psychotic condition characterized by distortions in thinking and bizarre behaviors

secondary prevention   to identify a condition as early as possible and change the environment so that the person is affected as little as possible and the duration of the disorder is shortened

Section 504 of the Vocational Rehabilitation Act   legislation that guarantees equal access for persons with disabilities to all programs and services supported by federal funds

seizure disorder   disorder characterized by temporary abnormalities in neurological activity and periods of unregulated electrical discharges in the brain

selective attention   the ability to focus on relevant stimuli without being distracted by irrelevant environmental factors

self-concept   an individual's sense of personal identity

self-determination   being able to act as the primary causal agent in one's life and to make choices and decisions

semantic elaboration   a memory strategy utilizing verbal enhancement of the concept(s) to be stored in long-term memory

semantic memory   the unit in long-term memory storage that deals with factual information and the acquisition of related concepts; alternative term for *declarative memory*

semantics   the component of spoken and written language that focuses on the meaning of phrases, sentences, and more complex and longer expressions

sensorimotor   the first of Piaget's cognitive stages, in which the individual acquires knowledge through sensory input and motoric activity

sensory encoding   process of translating sensory input into a representational form that can be manipulated in a person's working memory and stored in long-term memory

sensory register   the structural component that receives and stores sensory stimuli briefly, prior to cognitive processing by the strategic control functions of attention and perception; also called the *sensory store*

seriation   process of arranging or ability to arrange items in a series along a specific dimension

serious emotional disturbance   the term used in P.L. 94–142 for students with emotional or behavioral disorders; IDEA 1997 removed the word *serious*

severe disabilities   conditions that affect major life functions to the point that the individual is dependent on external and intensive supports to perform activities

short-term memory   temporary storage device for information being processed for a specific cognitive purpose; storage buffer for auditory, visual, and/or other sensory stimuli; mediator between input, processing, and output

significantly subaverage   scores on a norm-referenced test that are more than two standard deviations below the mean and that indicate significant levels of difference

six-hour retarded child   concept developed in the 1970s to describe children who appear to have mental retardation only in school contexts and who are able to function in ways consistent with norms outside the classroom

skill deficits   absence of needed social skills in the individual's repertoire

social awareness   abilities that allow an individual to receive and process relevant social information from the environment

social cognitive delay   delay in developing age-appropriate functional social cognitive skills and in applying those skills in social contexts

social competence   ability to respond appropriately in social situations and to carry out the functions associated with independent living

social constructivism   Vygotsky's theory that learning occurs through participation in social or culturally embedded experiences

Social Darwinism   theory that the social order is a result of the natural selection of those individuals with social skills most conducive to effective social adaptation

social field dependence   trait possessed by individuals who attend closely to and make use of social models and frames of reference in their immediate environment as they make decisions about how to act in a given situation

social intelligence   abilities associated with *social awareness* and *social skill*

socialized aggressive behaviors   antisocial behaviors that are characterized by covertness and that frequently occur in the context of a negative peer culture

social learning theory   theory proposed by Bandura that learning occurs as the individual observes and imitates social models in the immediate environment

social skill   ability to select and use behaviors that lead to socially acceptable and personally satisfying outcomes

spatial relations   ability to perceive the position of physical objects in space in relation to oneself and other objects

spina bifida   congenital malformation of the spinal column in which the structures that protect the spinal cord do not fully develop, frequently involving some degree of paralysis

standard deviation   measure of the variability of scores

standard English   version of English that is used most widely in public oral and written discourse in the United States

stigma   a condition that is viewed negatively and that causes the individual to be viewed negatively as well

strategic control components   cognitive functions involved in using appropriate strategies for specific task completion, including attention, perception, and storage and retrieval strategies

Strauss syndrome   term proposed in the 1950s for a condition characterized by distractibility, hyperactivity, and perceptual motor problems; individuals with this condition today are referred to as having *learning disabilities*

structural components   storage elements of the cognitive model, including the sensory register, the immediate memory, and the long term memory

summative evaluation   evaluation performed at the conclusion of an activity or program for the purpose of making judgments about the outcome

surrogate parent   person appointed to serve in place of the biological parents for the purpose of advocating for and protecting a child's rights in due process and legal proceedings

sustained attention   ability to maintain focus on incoming information over a sufficient period of time for effective cognitive processing to occur and to evaluate and withhold responses to other incidental or nonrelevant stimuli

syntax   component of language that involves knowledge and application of the rules governing the use of classes of words; the grammar of a language

tabula rasa   concept proposed by John Locke that all of our ideas are derived from our experiences, that we enter the world as a "blank slate" upon which experience records information

tactile   of or pertaining to the sense of touch

tactile defensiveness   condition characterized by extreme sensitivity and discomfort in response to the slightest tactile stimulation or touch

task analysis   the process of identifying the prerequisite and component skills that must be mastered to achieve a specific terminal objective

temperament   behavioral style relating to how an individual interacts with others

tertiary prevention   actions taken to provide support in educational and social environments over the life span to maximize level of functioning and prevent a condition from deteriorating any more rapidly than necessary

Tourette syndrome   chronic, hereditary tic disorder characterized by multiple motor and vocal tics

trainable   obsolete term to describe students with moderate levels of retardation who were believed to be capable of learning basic self-care skills and of working in unskilled jobs with supervision

triadic reciprocal model   conceptual framework that holds that a given behavior is a result of interactions among personal, environmental, and behavioral variables and that behaviors can only be understood in an ecological context

triangulate   to use several sources to confirm the value and meaning of information

undersocialized aggressive behaviors   antisocial behaviors characterized by acting-out behaviors

Universal Design for Learning (UDL)   the principles that hold that curricular materials, instructional methods, and learning environments should be designed so as to flexibly support and challenge as many of the students as possible

use   aspect of language that deals with the functional application of oral and written language skills

VAKT   an acronym for one of the multisensory teaching procedures that make use of input from visual, auditory, kinesthetic, and tactile sources to enhance the stimulus for learning

vigilance   continuous monitoring of stimuli combined with evaluative capacity to reject those that are not relevant to the task at hand

visual acuity   the degree to which visual capability allows discernment of objects at specific distances

visual closure   ability to identify figures that are presented in incomplete form

visual discrimination   ability to identify dominant features of objects and to use that ability to discriminate among a variety of objects

visual figure-ground discrimination   ability to distinguish an object from its background, to lift the relevant visual stimulus from its visual background

visual memory   ability to recall dominant features of a stimulus no longer physically present, or to recall the sequence of items presented visually

visual-motor integration   incorporation of the perception of visual stimuli with a particular motor activity, as in copying, drawing, and writing

visual perception   ability to attach meaning to visual stimuli

voluntary attention   tasks which require effort to act consciously and to actively focus on and control the cognitive processing of stimuli

working memory   component of the immediate memory used for temporary storage and manipulation of information from incoming stimuli and information retrieved from long-term memory

written expression   use of handwriting, spelling, and composition to communicate with others

zero reject   the principle that all children must receive a free appropriate public education (FAPE) regardless of the severity of their disabilities

zone of proximal development   range of learnings that students can achieve when they are engaged in meaningful activities with competent others

REFERENCES

Aaron, P. G. (1997). The impeding demise of the discrepancy formula. *Review of Educational Research, 67*(4), 461–502.

Aber, M. E., Bachman, B., Campbell, P., & O'Malley, G. (1994). Improving instruction in elementary schools. *Teaching Exceptional Children, 26*(3), 42–50.

Achenbach, T. M. (1991). *Child behavior checklist.* Burlington, VT: University of Vermont.

Adelman, H. S., & Taylor, L. (1990). Intrinsic motivation and school misbehavior: Some intervention implications. *Journal of Learning Disabilities, 23*(9), 541–550.

Algozzine, B., Morsink, C. V., & Algozzine, K. M. (1988). What's happening in self-contained special education classrooms? *Exceptional Children, 55*(3), 259–265.

Algozzine, B., & Ysseldyke, J. E. (1988). Questioning discrepancies: Retaking the first step 20 years later. *Learning Disability Quarterly, 11,* 307–318.

Algozzine, B., Ysseldyke, J. E., & Campbell, P. (1994). Strategies and tactics for effective instruction. *Teaching Exceptional Children, 26*(3), 34–36.

Allen, V. L., & Greenberger, D. B. (1980). Destruction and perceived control. In A. Baum & J. E. Singer (Eds.), *Advances in environmental psychology: Vol. 2, Applications of personal control* (pp. 85–109). Hillsdale, NJ: Erlbaum.

Alley, G., & Deshler, D. D. (1979). *Teaching the learning disabled adolescent: Strategies and methods.* Denver: Love.

Allinder, R. M. (1996). When some is not better than none: Effects of differential implementation of curriculum-based measurement. *Exceptional Children, 62*(6), 525–535.

American Association on Mental Retardation (AAMR). (1992). *Mental retardation: Definition, classification, and systems of support.* Washington, DC: Author.

American Association on Mental Retardation (AAMR). (2002). *Mental retardation: Definition, classification, and systems of support* (10th ed.). Washington, DC: Author.

American Psychiatric Association (APA). (1968). *Diagnostic and statistical manual of mental disorders* (2nd ed.). Washington, DC: Author.

American Psychiatric Association (APA). (1980). *Diagnostic and statistical manual of mental disorders* (3rd ed.). Washington, DC: Author.

American Psychiatric Association (APA). (1987). *Diagnostic and statistical manual of mental disorders* (3rd. ed. rev.). Washington, DC: Author.

American Psychiatric Association (APA). (1994). *Diagnostic and statistical manual of mental disorders* (4th ed.). Washington, DC: Author.

American Psychiatric Association (APA). (2000). *Diagnostic and statistical manual of mental disorders, 4th ed., text revision.* Washington, DC: Author.

American Psychological Association (APA). (1985). *Standards for educational and psychological testing.* Washington, DC: Author.

American Psychological Association (APA). (2001). *Publication manual of the American Psychological Association* (5th ed.). Washington, DC: Author.

Anderson, J. R. (1983). *The architecture of cognition.* Cambridge, MA: Harvard University Press.

Angoff, W. H. (1988). The nature-nurture debate, attitudes, and group differences. *American Psychologist, 43*(9), 713–720.

Apter, S. J. (1982). *Troubled children/troubled systems.* New York: Pergamon.

Apter, S. J., & Conoley, J. C. (1984). *Childhood behavioral disorders and emotional disturbance: An introduction to teaching troubled children.* Englewood Cliffs, NJ: Prentice-Hall.

Arent, R. P. (1992). *Trust building with children who hurt.* West Nyack, NY: Center for Applied Research in Education.

Ariel, A. (1992). *Education of children and adolescents with learning disabilities.* New York: Merrill.

Armstrong, T. (1994). *Multiple intelligences in the classroom.* Alexandria, VA: Association for Supervision and Curriculum Development.

Armstrong, T. (1995, October 18). ADD as a social invention. *Education Week, 44,* 33.

Ashbaker, M. H., & Swanson, H. L. (1996). Short-term memory and working memory operations and their contributions to reading in adolescents with and without learning disabilities. *Learning Disabilities Research and Practice, 11*(4), 206–213.

Association of Children with Learning Disabilities (ACLD). (1986). ACLD description: Specific learning disabilities. *ACLD Newsbriefs, 166,* 15–16.

Baker, J. M., & Zigmond, N. (1990). Are regular education classes equipped to accommodate students with learning disabilities? *Exceptional Children, 56*(6), 515–526.

Balk, D. (1983). Learned helplessness: A model to understand and overcome a child's extreme reaction to failure. *Journal of School Health, 53*(6), 365–369.

Bandura, A. (1986). *Social foundations of thought and action: A social cognitive theory.* Englewood Cliffs, NJ: Prentice Hall.

Barkley, R. A. (1993). A new theory of ADHD. *ADHD Report, 1*(5), 1–4.

Barnhill, G. P. (2001). What is Asperger Syndrome? *Intervention in School and Clinic, 36*(5), 259–265.

Bashir, A. S., & Scavuzzo, A. (1992). Children with language disorders: Natural history and academic success. *Journal of Learning Disabilities, 25*(1), 53–65.

Bateman, B. (1965). An educational view of a diagnostic approach to learning disorders. In J. Hellmuth (Ed.), *Learning Disorders: Vol. 1* (pp. 219–239). Seattle: Special Child Publications.

Bender W. N., & Wall, M. E. (1994). Social-emotional development of students with learning disabilities. *Learning Disabilities, 17*(4), 323–341.

Bickel, W. E., & Bickel, D. D. (1986). Effective schools, classrooms, and instruction: Implications for special education. *Exceptional Children, 52*(6), 489–500.

Biklen, D. (1985). *Achieving the complete school.* New York: Columbia University Press.

Billingsley, B. S., & Wildman, T. M. (1990). Facilitating reading comprehension in learning disabled students: Metacognitive goals and instructional strategies. *Remedial and Special Education, 11*(2), 18–31.

Black, C. (1981). *It will never happen to me!* New York: Ballantine.

Blackman, H. P. (1989). Special education placement: Is it what you know or where you live? *Exceptional Children, 55,* 459–462.

Blackman, S., & Goldstein, K. M. (1982). Cognitive styles and learning disabilities. *Journal of Learning Disabilities, 15*(2), 106–114.

Blanton, R. L. (1975). Historical perspectives on the classification of mental retardation. In N. Hobbs (Ed.), *Issues in the classification of children: Vol. 1* (pp. 164–193). San Francisco: Jossey-Bass.

Bloom, L. (1988). What is language? In M. Lahey (Ed.), *Language disorders and language development* (pp. 1–19). New York: Macmillan.

Bloom, L., & Lahey, M. (1978). *Language development and language disorders.* New York: John Wiley and Sons.

Bogdan, R., & Taylor, S. J. (1976). The judged, not the judges. *American Psychologist, 31*(1), 47–52.

Bogdan, R., & Taylor, S. J. (1994). *The social meaning of mental retardation: Two life stories.* New York: Teachers College Press.

Borkowski, J. G., & Kurtz, B. E. (1987). Metacognition and executive control. In J. G. Borkowski & J. D. Day (Eds.), *Cognition in special children: Comparative approaches to retardation, learning disabilities, and giftedness* (pp. 123–152). Norwood, NJ: Ablex.

Borkowski, J. G., Weyhing, R. S., & Turner, L. A. (1986). Attributional retraining and the teaching of strategies. *Exceptional Children, 53*(2), 130–137.

Bower, E. M. (1960). *Early identification of emotionally handicapped children in school.* Springfield, IL: Charles C. Thomas.

Bower, E. M. (1982). Defining emotional disturbance: Public policy and research. *Psychology in the Schools, 19*(1), 55–66.

Bradley, L. J., & Meredith, R. C. (1991). Interpersonal development: A study with children classified as educable mentally retarded. *Education and Training in Mental Retardation, 26*(2), 130–141.

Brehm, S. S., & Brehm, J. W. (1981). *Psychological reactance: A theory of freedom and control.* New York: Academic Press.

Brigance, A. H. (1981). *Inventory of essential skills.* North Billerica, MA: Curriculum Associates.

Brigance, A. H. (1991). *Inventory of early development* (rev. ed.). North Billerica, MA: Curriculum Associates.

Brigance, A. H. (1999). *Comprehensive inventory of basic skills* (rev. ed.). North Billerica, MA: Curriculum Associates.

Brophy, J., & Good, T. L. (1986). Teacher behavior and student achievement. In M. C. Wittrock (Ed.), *Handbook of research on teaching* (3rd ed.) (pp. 328–375). New York: MacMillan.

Brown, L., & Hammill, D. (1990). *Behavior rating profile–2.* Austin, TX: Pro-Ed.

Bruner, J. (1990). *Acts of meaning.* Cambridge, MA: Harvard University Press.

Bryan, T. (1991). Assessment of social cognition: Review of the research in learning disabilities. In H. L. Swanson (Ed.), *Handbook of the assessment of learning disabilities: Theory, research, and practice* (pp. 285–311). Austin, TX: Pro-Ed.

Bryan, T. (1997). Assessing the personal and social status of students with learning disabilities. *Learning Disabilities Research and Practice, 12*(1), 63–76.

Burleigh, M. (1994). *Death and deliverance: "Euthanasia" in Germany c. 1900–1945.* Cambridge, England: Cambridge University Press.

Bursuck, W., Polloway, E. A., Plante, L., Epstein, M. H., Jayanthi, M., & McConeghy, J. (1996). Report card grading and adaptations: A national survey of classroom practices. *Exceptional Children, 62*(4), 301–318.

Bussing, R., Zima, B. T., Belin, T. R., & Forness, S. R. (1998). Children who qualify for LD and SED programs: Do they differ in level of ADHD symptoms and comorbid psychiatric conditions? *Behaviorial Disorders, 23*(2), 85–97.

Buzzell, J. B., & Piazza R. (1994). *Case studies for teaching special needs and at-risk students.* Albany, NY: Delmar.

Calculator, S. N. (1985). Describing and treating discourse problems in mentally retarded children: The myth of mental retardese. In D. N. Ripich & F. M. Spinelli (Eds.), *School discourse problems* (pp. 135–147). San Diego, CA: College Hill Press.

Candler, A. C., & Hildreth, B. L. (1990). Characteristics of language disorders in learning disabled students. *Academic Therapy, 25*(3), 333–343.

Cannon, G. S., Idol, L., & West, J. F. (1992). Educating students with mild handicaps in general classrooms: Essential teaching practices for general and special educators. *Journal of Learning Disabilities, 25*(5), 300–317.

Carbo, M. (1987). Matching reading styles: Correcting ineffective instruction. *Educational Leadership, 45*(2), 55–62.

Carbo, M., & Hodges, H. (1988). Learning styles strategies can help students at risk. *Teaching Exceptional Children, 20*(4), 55–58.

Cardell, C. D., & Parmar, R. S. (1988). Teacher perceptions of temperament characteristics of children classified as learning disabled. *Journal of Learning Disabilities, 21*(8), 497–502.

Carpenter, D. (1985). Grading handicapped pupils: Review and position statement. *Remedial and Special Education, 6*(4), 54–59.

Carroll, J. B. (1963). A model of school learning. *Teachers College Record, 64*(8), 723–733.

Carroll, J. B. (1976). Psychometric tests as cognitive tasks: A new "structure of intellect." In L. B. Resnick (Ed.), *The nature of intelligence* (pp. 27–56). Hillsdale, NJ: Erlbaum.

Carroll, J. B. (1981). Ability and task difficulty in cognitive psychology. *Educational Researcher, 10*(1), 11–21.

Cartledge, G. (1999). African-American males and serious emotional disturbance: Some personal perspectives. *Behavioral Disorders, 25*(1), 76–79.

Center, D. B. (1989). Social maladjustment: Definition, identification, and programming. *Focus on Exceptional Children, 22*(1), 1–12.

Checkly, K. (1997). The first seven . . . and the eighth: A conversation with Howard Gardner. *Educational Leadership, 55*(1), 8–13.

Cheney, C. O., & Sampson, K. (1990). Issues in identification and service delivery for students with conduct disorders: The "Nevada" solution. *Behavioral Disorders, 15,* 174–179.

Cheney, D., & Muscott, H. S. (1996). Preventing school failure for students with emotional and behavioral disabilities through responsible inclusion. *Preventing School Failure, 40*(3), 109–116.

Chomsky, N. A. (1957). *Syntactic structures.* The Hague: Moulton.

Chomsky, N. A. (1965). *Aspects of the theory of syntax.* Cambridge, MA: MIT Press.

Christenson, S. L., Ysseldyke, J. E., & Thurlow, M. L. (1989). Critical instructional factors for students with mild handicaps: An integrative review. *Remedial and Special Education, 10*(5), 21–31.

Clarizio, H. F. (1992). Social maladjustment and emotional disturbance: Problems and positions II. *Psychology in the Schools, 29,* 331–341.

Clarizio, H. F., & Klein, A. P. (1995). Assessing the severity of behavior disorders: Rankings based on clinical and empirical criteria. *Psychology in the Schools, 32,* 77–85.

Claxton, C. S., & Murrell, P. H. (1987). *Learning styles: Implications for improving educational practices.* (ASHE-ERIC Higher Education Report No. 4.). Washington, DC: Association for the Study of Higher Education.

Clements, S. D. (1966). Minimal brain dysfunction in children: Terminology and identification (*NINDB Monograph No. 3,* Public Health Service Publication No. 1415). Washington, DC: U.S. Department of Health, Education and Welfare.

Cline, D. H. (1990). A legal analysis of initiatives to exclude handicapped/disruptive students from special education. *Behavioral Disorders, 15*(3), 159–173.

Coleman, J. M., Pullis, M. E., & Minnett, A. M. (1987). Studying mildly handicapped children's adjustment to mainstreaming: A systemic approach. *Remedial and Special Education, 8*(6), 19–30.

Conte, R. (1991). Attention disorders. In B. Y. L. Wong (Ed.), *Learning about learning disabilities* (pp. 59–101). San Diego, CA: Academic Press.

Cook, S. B., Scruggs, T. E., Mastropieri, M. A., & Casto, G. C. (1985–86). Handicapped students as tutors. *Journal of Special Education, 19*(4), 486–492.

Cotugno, A. J. (1987). Cognitive control functioning in hyperactive and nonhyperactive learning disabled children. *Journal of Learning Disabilities, 20*(9), 563–567.

Council for Children with Behavioral Disorders. (1990). Position paper on the provision of service to children with conduct disorders. *Behavioral Disorders, 15*(3), 180–189.

Council for Children with Behavioral Disorders. (In preparation). Best assessment and instructional practices for culturally and linguistically diverse children and youth. *Behavioral Disorders.*

Council for Exceptional Children. (1994a). Inclusive schools and community settings. In *CEC policies for delivery of services to exceptional children* (pp. 5–6). Reston, VA: Author.

Council for Exceptional Children. (1994b). Labeling and categorizing of children. In *CEC policies for delivery of services to exceptional children* (p. 7). Reston, VA: Author.

Council for Exceptional Children. (1998a). *IDEA 1997: Let's make it work.* Reston, VA: Author.

Council for Exceptional Children. (1998b). IDEA 1997: IDEA reauthorization: Focus on the IEP and performance assessment. (Teleconference, January 21, 1998).

Council for Exceptional Children. (1998c). IDEA 1997: IDEA reauthorization: Focus on classroom management and discipline. (Teleconference, May 12, 1998).

Council for Learning Disabilities. (1987a). CLD position statements: Use of discrepancy formulas in the identification of learning disabled individuals. *Learning Disability Quarterly, 9,* 245.

Council for Learning Disabilities. (1987b). Measurement and training of perceptual and perceptual-motor functions. *Journal of Learning Disabilities, 20*(6), 350.

Coutinho, M., & Malouf, D. (1993). Performance assessment and children with disabilities: Issues and possibilities. *Teaching Exceptional Children, 25*(4), 63–67.

Coutinho, M. J., Oswald, D. P., & Best, A. M. (2002) The influence of sociodemographics and gender on the disproportionate identification of minority students as having learning disabilities. *Remedial and Special Education, 23*(1), 49–59.

Coutinho, M. J., Oswald, D. P., & Forness, S. R. (2002). Gender and sociodemographic factors and the disproportionate identification of culturally and linguistically diverse students with emotional disturbance. *Behavioral Disorders, 27*(2), 109–125.

Cranston-Gingras, A., & Mauser, A. J. (1992). Categorical and noncategorical teacher certification in special education: How wide is the gap? *Remedial and Special Education, 13*(4), 6–9.

Cruickshank, W., Bentzen, F., Ratzeburgh, F., & Tannhauser, M. (1961). *Teaching methods for brain-injured and hyperactive children.* Syracuse, NY: Syracuse University Press.

Cullinan, D., Epstein, M. H., & McLinden, D. (1986). Status and change in state administrative definitions of behavior disorder. *School Psychology Review, 15*(3), 383–392.

Darwin, C. (1859). *The origin of species by means of natural selection or the preservation of favored races in the struggle for life.* New York: D. Appleton.

Davila, R. R., Williams, M. L., & MacDonald, J. T. (1991). *Clarification of policy to address the needs of children with attention deficit disorders within general and/or special education.* Washington, DC: U.S. Department of Education, Office of Special Education and Rehabilitative Services.

Dean, A. V., Salend, S. J., & Taylor, L. (1993). Multicultural education: A challenge for special educators. *Teaching Exceptional Children, 26*(1), 40–43.

Deci, E. L., & Chandler, C. L. (1986). The importance of motivation for the future of the LD field. *Journal of Learning Disabilities, 19*(10), 587–594.

Deci, E. L., & Ryan, R. M. (1985). *Intrinsic motivation and self-determination in human behavior.* New York: Plenum.

Dellarosa, D. (1988). A history of thinking. In R. J. Sternberg & E. E. Smith (Eds.), *The psychology of human thought* (pp. 1–18). Cambridge, England: Cambridge University Press.

Denham, C., & Lieberman A. (1980). *Time to learn.* Washington, DC: National Institute of Education.

Denning, C. B., Chamberlain, J. A., & Polloway, E. A. (2000). An evaluation of state guidelines for mental retardation: Focus on definition and classification practices. *Education and Training in Mental Retardation and Developmental Disabilities, 35*(2), 226–232.

Deno, E. (1970). Special education as developmental capital. *Exceptional Children, 37,* 229–240.

Deno, S., Maruyama, G., Espin, C., & Cohen, C. (1990). Educating students with mild disabilities in general education classrooms: Minnesota alternatives. *Exceptional Children, 57*(2), 150–161.

Derry, S. J. (1990). Remediating academic difficulties through strategy training: The acquisition of useful knowledge. *Remedial and Special Education, 11*(6), 19–31.

Deshler, D. D., Ellis, E. S., & Lenz, B. K. (1996). *Teaching adolescents with learning disabilities* (2nd ed.). Denver: Love.

Dever, R. B. (1990). Defining mental retardation from an instructional perspective. *Mental Retardation, 28*(3), 147–153.

Dever, R. B., & Knapczyk, D. R. (1997). *Teaching persons with mental retardation: A model for curriculum development and teaching.* Madison, WI: Brown and Benchmark.

Dingman, H., & Targan, G. (1960). Mental retardation and the normal curve. *American Journal of Mental Deficiency, 64,* 991–994.

Division for Learning Disabilities. (1991, November). DLD statement on appropriate educational interventions for students identified as having attention deficit disorders. Paper presented at the hearing of CEC Task Force, New Orleans, LA.

Doll, E. A. (1941). The essentials of an inclusive concept of mental deficiency. *American Journal of Mental Deficiency, 46,* 214–229.

Drew, C. J., Logan, D. R., & Hardman, M. L. (1988). *Mental retardation: A life cycle approach,* (4th ed.). Columbus, OH: Merrill.

Dunn, L. M. (1968). Special education for the mentally retarded: Is much of it justified? *Exceptional Children, 35*(1), 5–22.

Dunn, R. (1995). *Strategies for educating diverse learners.* Bloomington IN: Phi Delta Kappa.

Dupont, H. (1989). The emotional development of exceptional students. *Focus on Exceptional Children, 21*(9), 1–9.

Edgerton, R. B. (1967). *The cloak of competence: Stigma in the lives of the mentally retarded.* Berkeley, CA: University of California Press.

Egnor, D. E. (1996). Individuals with Disabilities Education Act—Amendments. *Focus on Autism and Other Developmental Disabilities, 11*(4), 1–4.

Elkind, D. (1981). *The hurried child: Growing up too fast too soon.* Reading, MA: Addison Wesley.

Ellis, E. S. (1993). Integrative strategy instruction: A potential model for teaching content area subjects to adolescents with learning disabilities. *Journal of Learning Disabilities, 26*(6), 358–383.

Ellis, E. S., Lenz, B. K., & Sabornie, E. J. (1987). Generalization and adaptation of learning strategies to natural environments: Part 1: Causal agents. *Remedial and Special Education, 8*(1), 6–20.

Englert, C. S. (1984). Effective direct instruction practices in special education settings. *Remedial and Special Education, 5*(2), 38–47.

Epstein, M. A., Shaywitz, S. E., Shaywitz, B. A., & Woolston, J. L. (1991). The boundaries of attention deficit disorder. *Journal of Learning Disabilities, 24*(2), 78–86.

Epstein, M. H., & Cullinan, D. (1983). Academic performance of behaviorally disordered and learning disabled pupils. *Journal of Special Education, 17*(3), 303–307.

Epstein, M. H., Cullinan, D., & Sabatino, D. A. (1977). State definitions of behavior disorders. *Journal of Special Education, 11*(4), 417–425.

Erikson, E. (1963). *Childhood and society* (2nd ed.). New York: Norton.

Falk, G. D., Dunlap, G., & Kern, L. (1996). An analysis of self-evaluation and videotape feedback for improving the peer interactions of students with externalizing and internalizing behavioral problems. *Behavioral Disorders, 21*(4), 261–276.

Faust, M. S., & Faust, W. L. (1980). Cognitive constructing: Levels of processing and developmental change. In B. K. Keogh (Ed.), *Advances in special education: A research annual: Basic constructs and theoretical orientations: Vol. 1* (pp. 1–54). Greenwich, CT: JAI Press.

Ferguson, D. L. (1994). Is communication really the point? Some thoughts on interventions and membership. *Mental Retardation, 32*(1), 7–18.

Field, S., Hoffman, A., & Posch, M. (1997). Self-determination during adolescence: A developmental perspective. *Remedial and Special Education, 18*(5), 285–293.

Fisher, J. B., Schumaker, J. B., & Deshler, D. D. (1995). Searching for validated inclusive practices: A review of the literature. *Focus on Exceptional Children, 28*(4), 1–20.

Foley, R. M., & Epstein, M. H. (1992). Correlates of the academic achievement of adolescents with behavioral disorders. *Behavioral Disorders, 18*(1), 9–17.

Forness, S. R., & Kavale, K. A. (1988). Pharmocological treatment: A note on classroom effects. *Journal of Learning Disabilities, 21*(3), 144–147.

Forness, S. R., & Kavale, K. A. (1991). Social skills deficits as primary learning disabilities. *Learning Disabilities: Research and Practice, 6*(1), 44–49.

Forness, S. R., & Knitzer, J. (1992). A new proposed definition and terminology to replace "serious emotional disturbance" in Individuals with Disabilities Education Act. *School Psychology Review, 21*(1), 12–20.

Forns-Santacana, M., Amador-Campos, J. A., & Roig-Lopez, F. (1993). Differences in field dependence-independence cognitive style as a function of socioeconomic status, sex, and cognitive competence. *Psychology in the Schools, 30*(2), 176–186.

Fox, L., Vaughn, B. J., Wyatte, M. L., & Dunlap, G. (2002). "We can't expect other people to understand": Family perspectives on problem behavior. *Exceptional Children, 68*(4), 437–450.

Frankenberger, W., & Fronzaglio, K. (1991). A review of states' criteria and procedures for identifying children with learning disabilities. *Journal of Learning Disabilities, 24*(8), 495–500.

Frick, P., & Lahey, E. (1991). Nature and characteristics of attention deficit hyperactivity disorder. *School Psychology Review, 20*(2), 163–173.

Frostig, M., Lefever, D. W., & Whittlesey, J. B. (1964). *The Marianne Frostig developmental test of visual perception.* Palo Alto, CA: Consulting Psychology Press.

Fuchs, L. S., & Fuchs, D. (1986). Effects of systematic formative evaluation: A meta-analysis. *Exceptional Children, 53*(3), 199–208.

Gable, R. A. (1996). A critical analysis of functional assessment: Issues for researchers and practitioners. *Behavioral Disorders, 22*(1), 36–40.

Gallagher, J. J., Beckman, P., & Cross, A. H. (1983). Families of handicapped children: Sources of stress and its amelioration. *Exceptional Children, 50*(1), 10–18.

Galton, F. (1869, 1978). *Hereditary genius: An inquiry into its laws and consequences.* London: J. Friedman.

Garcia, E. (1994). *Understanding and meeting the challenge of student cultural diversity.* Boston: Houghton Mifflin.

Gardner, H. (1983). *Frames of mind.* New York: Basic Books.

Gardner, H. (1991). *The unschooled mind: How children think and how schools should teach.* New York: Basic Books.

Gardner, H. (1993). *Multiple intelligences: The theory in practice.* New York: Basic Books.

Gardner, H. (1995). Reflections on multiple intelligences: Myths and messages. *Phi Delta Kappan, 77*(3), 206–209.

Gardner, H. (1996). Probing more deeply into the theory of multiple intelligences. *NASSP Bulletin, 80*(583), 1–7.

Gargiulo, R. M. (2003). *Special education in contemporary society: An introduction to exceptionality.* Belmont, CA: Wadsworth.

Gartner, A., & Lipsky, D. K. (1987). Beyond special education: Toward a quality system for all students. *Harvard Educational Review, 57*(4), 123–157.

Gazaway, R. (1969). *The longest mile.* New York: Doubleday.

Geisthardt, C., & Munsch, J. (1996). Coping with school stress: A comparison of adolescents with and without learning disabilities. *Journal of Learning Disabilities, 29*(3), 287–296.

Gersten, R., Brengelman, S. & Jiménez, R. (1994). Effective instruction for culturally and linguistically diverse students: A reconceptualization. *Focus on Exceptional Children, 27*(1), 1–16.

Giangreco, M. F., Edelman, S. W., Luiselli, T. E., & MacFarland, S. Z. C. (1997). Helping or hovering: Effects of instructional assistant proximity on students with disabilities. *Exceptional Children, 64*(1), 7–18.

Gibbs, D. P., & Cooper, E. B. (1989). Prevalence of communication disorders in students with learning disabilities. *Journal of Learning Disabilities, 22*(1), 60–63.

Giordano, G. (1984). Analyzing and remediating writing disabilities. *Journal of Learning Disabilities, 17*(2), 78–83.

Glasser, W. (1986). *Control theory in the classroom.* New York: Harper Row.

Glasser, W. (1990). *The quality school: Managing students without coercion.* New York: Harper.

Goddard, H. H. (1912). *The Kallikak family: A study in the heredity of feeble-mindedness.* New York: MacMillan.

Goldstein, A. P., & McGinnis, E. (1997). *Skillstreaming the adolescent: New strategies and perspectives for teaching prosocial skills* (rev. ed.). Champaign, IL: Research Press.

Goodman, G., & Poillion, M. J. (1992). ADD: Acronym for any dysfunction or difficulty. *Journal of Special Education, 26*(1), 37–56.

Graham, S. (1985). Teaching basic academic skills to learning disabled students: A model of the teaching-learning process. *Journal of Learning Disabilities, 18*(9), 528–534.

Greenspan, S., & Granfield, J. M. (1992). Reconsidering the construct of mental retardation: Implications of a model of social competence. *American Journal on Mental Retardation, 96*(4), 442–453.

Gresham, F. M. (1991). Conceptualizing behavior disorders in terms of resistance to intervention. *School Psychology Review, 20*(1), 23–36.

Gresham, F. M., & Elliott, S. N. (1987). The relationship between adaptive behavior and social skills: Issues in definition and assessment. *Journal of Special Education, 21*(1), 167–181.

Gresham, F. M., MacMillan, D. L., & Bocian, K. (1996). "Behavioral earthquakes": Low frequency, salient behavioral events that differentiate students at-risk for behavioral disorders. *Behavioral Disorders, 21*(4), 277–292.

Grice, H. P. (1989). *Studies in the ways of words.* Cambridge, MA: Harvard University Press.

Grolnick, W. S., & Ryan, R. M. (1990). Self-perceptions, motivation, and adjustment in children with learning disabilities: A multiple group comparison study. *Journal of Learning Disabilities, 23*(3), 177–184.

Grossman, H. J. (Ed.). (1973). *Manual on terminology and classification in mental retardation.* Washington, DC: American Association on Mental Deficiency.

Grossman, H. J. (Ed.). (1983). *Classification in mental retardation: 1983 revision.* Washington, DC: American Association on Mental Deficiency.

Guetzloe, E. (1988). Suicide and depression: Special education's responsibility. *Teaching Exceptional Children, 20*(4), 25–28.

Guetzloe, E. (1998). Proposed definition of emotional disturbance. *CCBD Newsletter, 11*(4), 1.

Gumpel, T. (1994). Social competence and social skills training for persons with mental retardation: An expansion of a behavioral paradigm. *Education and Training in Mental Retardation and Developmental Disabilities, 29*(3), 194–201.

Guterman, B. R. (1995). The validity of categorical learning disabilities services: The consumer's view. *Exceptional Children, 62*(2), 111–124.

Hallahan D. P., & Kauffman, J. M. (1977). Labels, categories, behaviors: ED, LD, and EMR reconsidered. *Journal of Special Education, 11*(2), 139–149.

Hallahan, D. P., Kauffman, J. M., & Lloyd, J. W. (1985). *Introduction to learning disabilities* (2nd ed.). Englewood Cliffs, NJ: Prentice Hall.

Hallahan, D. P., Kauffman, J. M., & Lloyd, J. W. (1999). *Introduction to learning disabilities* (2nd ed.). Boston, MA: Allyn and Bacon.

Hallahan, D. P., & Reeve, R. R. (1980). Selective attention and distractibility. In B. K. Keogh (Ed.), *Advances in special education: A research annual: Basic constructs and theoretical orientations: Vol. 1* (pp. 141–182). Greenwich, CT: JAI Press.

Hallenbeck, M. J. (1996). The cognitive strategy in writing: Welcome relief for adolescents with learning disabilities. *Learning Disabilities Research and Practice, 11*(2), 107–119.

Hammill, D. (1990). On defining learning disabilities: An emerging consensus. *Journal of Learning Disabilities, 23*(2), 74–84.

Haring, N. G., & Phillips, E. L. (1962). *Educating emotionally disturbed children.* New York: McGraw Hill.

Hasselbring, T. S., Goin, L. J., & Bansford, J. D. (1988). Developing math automaticity in learning handicapped children: The role of computerized drill and practice. *Focus on Exceptional Children, 20*(6), 1–7.

Hayes, B. K., & Taplin, J. E. (1993). Development of conceptual knowledge in children with mental retardation. *American Journal on Mental Retardation, 98*(2), 293–303.

Hayes, J. R. (1989). *The complete problem solver* (2nd ed.). Hillsdale, NJ: Erlbaum.

Haynes, M. C., & Jenkins, J. R. (1986). Reading in special education resource rooms. *American Educational Research Journal, 23*(2), 161–190.

Hearne, D., & Stone, S. (1995). Multiple intelligences and underachievement: Lessons from individuals with learning disabilities. *Journal of Learning Disabilities, 28*(7), 439–448.

Heber, R. (1959). A manual on terminology and classification in mental retardation. *American Journal on Mental Deficiency, 62* (Monograph Supplement).

Heumann, J. E., & Warlick, K. R. (2000). Questions and answers about provisions in the Individuals with Disabilities Education Act Amendments of 1997 related to students with disabilities and state and district-wide assessments (OSEP Memo 00-24). Retrieved October 12, 2002, from http://www.dssc.org/frc/AssessmentQ&A.html.

Hewett, F. M. (1968). *The emotionally disturbed child in the classroom.* Boston: Allyn and Bacon.

Hinshelwood, J. (1917). *Congenital word blindness.* London: H. K. Lewis.

Hobbs, N. (1975a). *The futures of children: Categories, labels and their consequences.* San Francisco: Jossey-Bass.

Hobbs, N. (1975b). *Issues in the classification of children: Vol. 1.* San Francisco: Jossey-Bass.

Hobbs, N. (1975c). *Issues in the classification of children: Vol. 2.* San Francisco: Jossey-Bass.

Hoerr, T. R. (1996). *Implementing multiple intelligences: The New City School experience.* Bloomington, IN: Phi Delta Kappa Educational Foundation.

Hoge, G., & Datillo, J. (1995). Recreation participation patterns of adults with and without mental retardation. *Education and Training in Mental Retardation and Developmental Disabilities, 30*(4), 283–298.

Hoover, J. J. (1987). Preparing special educators for mainstreaming: An emphasis upon curriculum. *Teacher Education and Special Education, 10*(2), 58–64.

Hresko, W. P. (1996). Oral language. In D. K. Reid, W. P. Hresko, & H. L. Swanson, (Eds.), *Cognitive approaches to learning disabilities* (3rd ed.) (pp. 433–496). Austin, TX: Pro-Ed.

Illinois Department of Rehabilitation Services. (1994). Handicapping language: A guide for journalists and the public. *Remedial and Special Education, 15*(1), 60–62.

Interagency Committee on Learning Disabilities. (1987). *Learning disabilities: A report to the U.S. Congress.* Bethesda, MD: National Institutes of Health.

Itard, J. M. G. (1801, 1962). *The wild boy of Aveyron.* (G. Humphrey & M. Humphrey, Trans.). Englewood Cliffs, NJ: Prentice-Hall.

Javorsky, J. (1996). An examination of youth with attention deficit/hyperactivity disorder and language learning disabilities: A clinical study. *Journal of Learning Disabilities, 29*(3), 247–258.

Jenkins, J. R., Pious, C. G., & Peterson, D. L. (1988). Categorical programs for remedial and handicapped students: Issues of validity. *Exceptional Children, 55*(2), 147–158.

Jensen, A. R. (1969). How much can we boost IQ and scholastic achievement? *Harvard Educational Review, 39,* 1–123.

Jerger, M. A. (1996). Phoneme awareness and the role of the educator. *Intervention in School and Clinic, 32*(1), 5–13.

Johnson, D. J., & Croasmun, P. A. (1991). Language assessment. In H. L. Swanson (Ed.), *Handbook on the assessment of learning disabilities: Theory, research, and practice* (pp. 229–248). Austin, TX: Pro-Ed.

Johnson, D. W., & Johnson, R. T. (1996). Peacemakers: Teaching students to resolve their own and schoolmates' conflicts. *Focus on Exceptional Children, 28*(6), 1–11.

Johnson, D. W., Johnson, R. T., Holubec, E. J., & Roy, P. (1984). *Circles of learning: Cooperation in the classroom.* Reston, VA: ASCD.

Johnston, C. L. (1984). The learning disabled adolescent and young adult: An overview and critique of current practices. *Journal of Learning Disabilities, 17*(7), 386–390.

Joint Committee on Testing Practices. (1988). *Code of fair testing practices in education.* Washington, DC: Author.

Kameenui, E. J., & Simmons, D. (1990). *Instructional strategies: The prevention of academic learning problems.* Columbus, OH: Merrill.

Kauffman, J. M. (1977). *Characteristics of children's behavior disorders.* Columbus, OH: Merrill.

Kauffman, J. M. (1997). *Characteristics of behavior disorders of children and youth* (6th ed.). Columbus, OH: Merrill.

Kauffman, J. M. (2001). *Characteristics of behavior disorders of children and youth* (7th ed.). Columbus, OH: Merrill.

Kavale, K. A., & Forness, S. R. (1983). Hyperactivity and diet treatment: A meta-analysis of the Feingold hypothesis. *Journal of Learning Disabilities, 16*(6), 324–330.

Kavale, K. A., & Forness, S. R. (1985). Learning disability and the history of science: Paradigm or paradox? *Remedial and Special Education, 6*(4), 12–23.

Kavale, K. A., & Forness, S. R. (1996). Social skill deficits and learning disabilities: A meta analysis. *Journal of Learning Disabilities, 29*(3), 226–237.

Kavale, K. A., Hirshoren, A., & Forness, S. R. (1998). Meta-analytic validation of the Dunn and Dunn model of learning-style preferences: A critique of what was Dunn. *Learning Disabilities Research and Practice, 13*(2), 75–80.

Kavale, K., & Mattson, P. D. (1983). "One jumped off the balance beam": Meta-analysis of perceptual-motor training. *Journal of Learning Disabilities, 16*(3), 165–173.

Keogh, B. K., & Bess, C. R. (1991). Assessing temperament. In H. L. Swanson (Ed.), *Handbook of the assessment of learning disabilities: Theory, research, and practice* (pp. 313–330). Austin, TX: Pro-Ed.

Keogh, B. K., & Donlon, G. M. (1972). Field dependence, impulsivity, and learning disabilities. *Journal of Learning Disabilities, 5*(6), 331–336.

Keogh, B. K., & Margolis, J. (1976). Learn to labor and wait: Attentional problems of children with learning disorders. *Journal of Learning Disabilities, 9*(5), 276–286.

Keogh, B. K., & Pullis, M. E. (1980). Temperament influences on the development of exceptional children. In B. K. Keogh (Ed.), *Advances in special education: A research annual: Basic constructs and theoretical orientations: Vol. 1* (pp. 239–276). Greenwich, CT: JAI Press.

Keogh, B. K., & Weisner, T. (1993). An ecocultural perspective on risk and protective factors in children's development: Implications for learning disabilities. *Learning Disabilities Research & Practice, 8*(1), 3–10.

Kephart, N. C. (1960). *The slow learner in the classroom.* Columbus, OH: Merrill.

Kerr, M. M., & Nelson, C. M. (1998). *Strategies for managing behavior problems in the classroom* (3rd ed.). Upper Saddle River, NJ: Merrill.

Kerr, M. M., Nelson, C. M., & Lambert, D. L. (1987). *Helping adolescents with learning and behavior problems.* Columbus, OH: Merrill.

Kidder, T. (1989). *Among schoolchildren.* Boston: Houghton Mifflin.

Kirk, S. A. (1963). Behavioral diagnosis and remediation of learning disabilities. In *Proceedings of the Conference on the Exploration into the Problems of the Perceptually Handicapped Child.* Chicago: Reprinted in Kirk, S. A., & McCarthy, J. (Eds.). (1975). *Learning disabilities: Selected ACLD Papers.* Boston: Houghton Mifflin.

Kirk, S. A. (1987). The learning disabled preschool child. *Teaching Exceptional Children, 19*(2), 78–80.

Kirk, S. A., & Chalfant, J. C. (1984). *Academic and developmental learning disabilities.* Denver, CO: Love.

Kirk, S. A., Gallagher, J. J., & Anastasiow. (2003). *Educating exceptional children* (10th ed.). Boston: Houghton Mifflin.

Kirk, S. A., & Kirk, W. D. (1971). *Psycholinquistic learning disabilities: Diagnosis and remediation.* Urbana, IL: University of Illinois Press.

Kirk, S. A., & McCarthy, J. (Eds.). (1975). *Learning disabilities: Selected ACLD papers.* Boston: Houghton Mifflin.

Kirk, S. A., McCarthy, J., & Kirk, W. D. (1968). *Illinois Test of Psycholinguistic Abilities* (rev. ed.). Urbana IL: University of Illinois Press.

Klorman, R. (1991). Cognitive event-related potentials in attention deficit disorder. *Journal of Learning Disabilities, 24*(3), 130–140.

Knoblock, P. (1983). *Teaching emotionally disturbed children.* Boston: Houghton Mifflin.

Kohn, A. (1993). *Punished by rewards: The trouble with gold stars, incentive plans, A's, praise, and other bribes.* New York: Houghton Mifflin.

Kortering, L. J., & Blackorby, J. (1992). High school dropout and students identified with behavioral disorders. *Behavioral Disorders, 18*(1), 24–32.

Krauss, M. W. (1990). In defense of common sense. *American Journal on Mental Retardation, 95*(1), 19–21.

Krupski, A. (1980). Attention processes: Research, theory, and implications for special education. In B. K. Keogh (Ed.), *Advances in special education: A research annual: Basic constructs and theoretical orientations: Vol. 1* (pp. 101–140). Greenwich, CT: JAI Press.

Krupski, A. (1981). An interactional approach to the study of attention problems in children with handicaps. *Exceptional Education Quarterly, 2*(3), 1–10.

Krupski, A. (1986). Attention problems in youngsters with learning handicaps. In J. K. Torgesen & B. Y. L. Wong (Eds.), *Psychological and educational perspectives on learning disabilities* (pp. 161–192). Orlando, FL: Academic Press.

Krupski, A. (1987). Attention: The verbal phantom strikes again—A response to Samuels. *Exceptional Children, 54*(1), 62–65.

Lahey, B. B., Applegate, B., McBurnett, K., Biederman, J., Greenhill, L., Hynd, G. W., Barkley, R. A., Newcorn, J., Jensen, P., Richters, J., Garfinkel, B., Kerdyk, L., Frick, P. J., Ollendick, T., Perez, D., Hart, E. L. Waldman, I., & Shaffer, D. (1994). DSM-IV field trials for attention deficit hyperactivity disorder in children and adolescents. *American Journal of Psychiatry, 151*(11), 1673–1685.

Lahey, B. B., & Carlson, C. L. (1991). Validity of the diagnostic category of attention deficit disorder without hyperactivity. *Journal of Learning Disabilities, 24*(2), 110–120.

Lahey, M. (1988). *Language disorders and language development.* New York: Macmillan.

Lane, H. (1976). *The wild boy of Aveyron.* Cambridge, MA: Harvard University Press.

Lapadat, J. C. (1991). Pragmatic language skills of students with language or learning disabilities: A quantitative synthesis. *Journal of Learning Disabilities, 24*(3), 147–158.

Larrivee, B. (1986). Effective teaching for mainstreamed students is effective teaching for all students. *Teacher Education and Special Education, 9*(4), 173–179.

Lavoie, R. D. (1989). *Understanding learning disabilities: How difficult can this be? The F. A. T. city workshop.* Alexandria, VA: PBS Video.

Leal, L., & Raforth, M. A. (1991). Memory development: What teachers do does make a difference. *Intervention in School and Clinic, 26*(4), 234–237.

Leffert, J. S., & Siperstein, G. N. (1996). Assessment of social-cognitive processes in children with mental retardation. *American Journal on Mental Retardation, 100*(5), 441–455.

Lenz, B. K., Bulgren, J., & Hudson, P. J. (1990). Content enhancement: A model for promoting the acquisition of content by individuals with learning disabilities. In T. Scruggs & B. Y. L. Wong (Eds.), *Intervention research in learning disabilities* (pp. 122–165). New York: Springer-Verlag.

Lerner, J. W. (1993). *Learning disabilities: Theories, diagnosis, and teaching strategies* (6th ed.). Boston: Houghton Mifflin.

Lerner, J. W., & Lerner, S. R. (1991). Attention deficit disorder: Issues and questions. *Focus on Exceptional Children, 24*(3), 1–17.

Lerner, J. W., Lowenthal, B., & Lerner, S. (1995). *Attention deficit disorders: Assessment and teaching.* Pacific Grove, CA: Brooks/Cole.

Levin, T., & Long, R. (1981). *Effective instruction.* Alexandria, VA: ASCD.

Licht, B. G., & Kistner, J. A. (1986). Motivational problems of learning disabled children: Individual differences and their implications for treatment. In J. K. Torgesen & B. Y. L. Wong (Eds.), *Psychological and educational perspectives on learning disabilities* (pp. 225–255). Orlando, FL: Academic Press.

Lipsky, D. K., & Gartner, A. (1987). Capable of achievement and worthy of respect: Education for all handicapped children as if they were full-fledged human beings. *Exceptional Children, 54*(1), 69–74.

Lloyd, J. W. (1984). How should we individualize instruction—or should we? *Remedial and Special Education, 5*(1), 7–15.

Locke, J. (1690, 1894). *An essay concerning human understanding: Vol. 1* (A. C. Fraser, Ed.). Oxford, England: Oxford University Press.

Long, N. J. (1990). Life space interviewing. *Beyond Behavior, 2*(1), 10–15.

Long, N. J., & Morse, W. C. (1996). *Conflict in the classroom: The education of at-risk and troubled students* (5th ed.). Austin, TX: Pro-Ed.

Long, N. J., Morse, W. C., & Newman, R. G. (Eds.).(1965). *Conflict in the classroom.* Belmont, CA: Wadsworth.

MacMillan, D. L. (1982). *Mental retardation in school and society.* Boston: Little, Brown.

MacMillan, D. L., & Forness, S. R. (1998). The role of IQ in special education placement decisions: Primary and determinative or peripheral and inconsequential? *Remedial and Special Education, 19*(4), 239–253.

MacMillan, D. L., Gresham, F. M., & Siperstein, G. M. (1993). Conceptual and psychometric concerns about the 1992 AAMR definition of mental retardation. *American Journal on Mental Retardation, 98*(3), 325–335.

MacMillan, D. L., Gresham, F. M., & Siperstein, G. M. (1995). Heightened concerns over the 1992 AAMR definition: Advocacy versus precision. *American Journal on Mental Retardation, 100*(1), 87–97.

MacMillan, D. L., Keogh, B. K., & Jones, R. L. (1986). Special education research on mildly handicapped learners. In M. C. Wittrock (Ed.), *Handbook of research on teaching* (3rd ed.) (pp. 686–724). New York: Macmillan.

MacMillan, D. L., Siperstein, G. N., & Gresham, F. M. (1996). A challenge to the viability of mild mental retardation as a diagnostic category. *Exceptional Children, 62*(4), 356–371.

Marston, D., Deno, S. L., Kim, D., Diment, K., & Rogers, D. (1995). Comparison of reading approaches for students with mild disabilities. *Exceptional Children, 61*(1), 20–37.

Martin, R. P. (1992). Child temperment: Effects on special education and outcomes. *Exceptionality, 3*(2), 99–115.

Masland, R., Sarason, S., & Gladwin, T. (1958). *Mental subnormality.* New York: Basic Books.

Maslow, A. (1954). *Motivation and personality.* New York: Harper and Row.

Mastropieri, M. A., & Scruggs, T. E. (1991). *Teaching students ways to remember: Strategies for learning mnemonically.* Cambridge, MA: Brookline Books.

Mastropieri, M. A., Scruggs, T. E., & Butcher, K. (1997). How effective is inquiry learning for students with mild disabilities? *Journal of Special Education, 31*(2), 199–211.

Mathias, J. L. (1990). Social intelligence, social competence, and interpersonal competence. In N. W. Bray (Ed.), *International Review of Research in Mental Retardation: Vol. 16* (pp. 125–160). San Diego, CA: Academic Press.

McConnell, M. E., Hilvitz, P. B., & Cox, C. J. (1998). Functional assessment: A systematic process for assessment and intervention in general and special education classrooms. *Intervention in School and Clinic, 34*(1), 10–20.

McCormick, P. K., Campbell, J. W., Pasnak, R., & Perry, P. (1990). Instruction on Piagetian concepts for children with mental retardation. *Mental Retardation, 28*(6), 359–366.

McFarland, C. F. Jr., & Weibe, D. (1987). Structure and utilizatiuon of knowledge among special children. In J. G. Borkowski & J. D. Day (Eds.), *Cognition in special children: Comparative approaches to retardation, learning disabilities, and giftedness* (pp. 87–121). Norwood, NJ: Ablex.

McGinnis, E., & Goldstein, A. P. (1990). *Skillstreaming in early childhood: Teaching prosocial skills to the preschool and kindergarten child.* Champaign, IL: Research Press.

McGinnis, E., & Goldstein, A. P. (1997). *Skillstreaming the elementary child: New strategies and perspectives for teaching prosocial skills (rev. ed.).* Champaign, IL: Research Press.

McGrew, K. S., & Bruininks, R. H. (1990). Defining adaptive and maladaptive behavior within a model of personal competence. *School Psychology Review, 19*(1), 53–73.

McGrew, K. S., Bruininks, R. H., & Johnson, D. R. (1996). Confirmatory factor analytic investigation of Greenspan's model of personal competence. *American Journal on Mental Retardation, 100*(5), 533–545.

McIntyre, T. (1993). Reflections on the new definition: Who still falls through the cracks and why. *Behavioral Disorders, 18*(2), 148–160.

McIntyre, T. (1996). Guidelines for providing appropriate services to culturally diverse students with emotional and/or behavioral disorders. *Behavioral Disorders, 21*(2), 137–144.

McLeskey, J. (1992). Students with learning disabilities at the primary, intermediate and secondary grade levels: Identification and characteristics. *Learning Disability Quarterly, 15*(1), 13–19.

McLeskey, J., & Waldron, N. L. (1991), Identifying students with learning disabilities: The effect of implementing statewide guidelines. *Journal of Learning Disabilities, 24*(8), 501–506.

McLeskey, J., Waldron, N. L., & Wornhoff, S. A. (1990). Factors influencing the identification of black and white students with learning disabilities. *Journal of Learning Disabilities, 23*(6), 362–366.

McLoughlin, J. A., & Lewis, R. B. (1994). *Assessing special students* (4th ed.). New York: Merrill.

Mehring, T. A., & Colson, S. E. (1990). Motivation and mildly handicapped learners. *Focus on Exceptional Children, 22*(5), 1–14.

Meichenbaum, D. (1977). *Cognitive behavior modification.* New York: Plenum.

Melamed, L. E., & Melamed, E. C. (1982). Refining our approach to perceptual disorders. *Academic Therapy, 17*(3), 351–357.

Melton, L., & Pickett, W. (1997). *Using multiple intelligences in middle school reading.* Bloomington, IN: Phi Delta Kappa Educational Foundation.

Mental Health and Special Education Coalition. (1991). *Fact sheets: Definition of "seriously emotionally disturbed" under Individuals with Disabilities Education Act; Overview of proposed alternative to definition of "seriously emotionally disturbed" under Individuals with Disabilities Education Act; Clarification of changes proposed to terminology and definition.* Alexandria, VA: National Mental Health Association.

Mercer, C. D. (1987). *Students with learning disabilities* (3rd ed.). Columbus, OH: Merrill.

Mercer, C. D., Jordan, L., Allsopp, D. H., & Mercer, A. R. (1996). Learning disabilities definitions and criteria used by state education departments. *Learning Disabilities Quarterly, 19*(4), 217–232.

Mercer, C. D., King-Sears, P., & Mercer, A. R. (1990). Learning disabilities definitions and criteria used by state education departments. *Learning Disability Quarterly, 13*(3), 141–152.

Mercer, J. (1973). *Labeling the mentally retarded: Clinical and social perspective on mental retardation.* Berkley, CA: University of California.

Merrill, E. C. (1990). Attentional resource allocation and mental retardation. In N. W. Bray (Ed.), *International review of research in mental retardation: Vol. 16* (pp. 51–88). San Diego, CA: Academic Press.

Mills, R. P. (1996). Statewide portfolio assessment: The Vermont experience. In J. B. Baron & D. P. Wolf (Eds.), *Performance-based student assessment: Challenges and possibilities: Ninety-fifth Yearbook of the National Society for the Study of Education: Part 1* (pp. 192–214). Chicago: University of Chicago.

Mira, M. P., & Tyler, J. S. (1991). Students with traumatic brain injury: Making the transition from hospital to school. *Focus on Exceptional Children, 23*(5), 1–12.

Montessori, M. (1912, 1964). *The Montessori method.* New York: Schocken.

Morrison, G. M., & Cosden, M. A. (1997). Risk, resilience and adjustment of individuals with learning disabilities. *Learning Disability Quarterly, 20*(1), 43–60.

Morsink, C. V., Soar, R. S., Soar, R. M., & Thomas, R. (1986). Research on teaching: Opening the door to special education classrooms. *Exceptional Children, 53,* 320–340.

Munk, D. D., & Bursuck, W. D. (2001). Preliminary findings on personalized grading plans for middle school students with learning disabilities. *Exceptional Children, 67*(2), 211–234.

Murphy, V., & Hicks-Stewart, V. (1991). Learning disabilities and attention-deficit-hyperactivity disorder: An interactional perspective. *Journal of Learning Disabilities, 24*(7), 386–388.

Myles, B. B., & Simpson, R. L. (2001). Understanding the hidden curriculum: An essential social skill for children and youth with Asperger Syndrome. *Intervention in School and Clinic, 36*(5), 279–286.

National Advisory Committee on Handicapped Children (NACHC). (1968). *Special education for handicapped children: First annual report.* Washington, DC: HEW.

National Association of School Psychologists, National Coalition of Advocates for Students, & National Association of Social Workers. (1987, May 5). Forum: Rights without labels. *Education Week,* p. 22.

National Association of State Directors of Special Education (NASDSE). (1997). *Comparison of key issues: Current law and 1997 IDEA amendments.* Washington, DC: Author.

Nevin, J. A. (1988). Behavioral momentum and the partial reinforcement effect. *Psychological Bulletin, 103*(1), 44–56.

Nichols, J. G., McKenzie, M., & Shufro, J. (1994). Schoolwork, homework, life's work: The experience of students with and without learning disabilities. *Journal of Learning Disabilities, 27*(9), 562–569.

Nichols, P. (1992). The curriculum of control: Twelve reasons for it, some arguments against it. *Beyond Behavior, 3*(2), 5–11.

Nirje, B. (1969). The normalization principle and its human management implications. In R. B. Kugel & W. Wolfensberger (Eds.), *Changing patterns in residential services for the mentally retarded* (pp. 179–195). Washington, DC: President's Committee on Mental Retardation.

Obiakor, F. E., Utley, C. A., Smith, R., & Harris-Obiakor, P. (2002). The Comprehensive Support Model for culturally diverse exceptional learners: Intervention in an age of change. *Intervention in School and Clinic, 38*(1), 14–27.

O'Reilly, M. F., & Glynn, D. (1995). Using a process social skills training approach with adolescents with mild intellectual disabilities in a high school setting. *Education and Training in Mental Retardation and Developmental Disabilities, 30*(3), 187–198.

Ortiz, A. A. (1997). Learning disabilities occurring concomitantly with linguistic differences. *Journal of Learning Disabilities, 30*(3), 321–332.

Orton, S. T. (1937). *Reading, writing and speech problems in children.* New York: Norton.

Otto-Flynn, K. (undated). *When mainstreaming fails.* Unpublished manuscript.

Overton, T. (1996). *Assessment in special education: An applied approach* (2nd ed.). Upper Saddle River, NJ: Merrill.

Owens, R. E. Jr. (1999). *Language disorders: A functional approach to assessment and intervention* (3rd ed.). Boston: Allyn & Bacon.

Papilia, D. E., & Olds, S. W. (1990). *A child's world: Infancy through adolescence.* New York: McGraw-Hill.

Paris, S. G., & Winograd, P. (1990). Promoting metacognition and motivation of exceptional children. *Remedial and Special Education, 11*(6), 7–15.

Pasnak, R., Whitten, J. C., Perry, P., Waiss, S., Madden, S. E., & Watson-White, S. A. (1995). Achievement gains after instruction on classification and seriation. *Education and Training in Mental Retardation and Developmental Disabilities, 30*(2), 109–117.

Patton, J. M. (1998). The disproportionate representation of African Americans in special education: Looking behind the curtain for understanding and solutions. *Journal of Special Education, 32,* 25–31.

Paul, J. L., & Epanchin, B. C. (1991). *Educating emotionally disturbed children and youth: Theories and practices for teachers* (2nd ed.). New York: Merrill.

Payne, J. S., & Patton, J. R. (1981). *Mental retardation.* Columbus, OH: Merrill.

Peacock Hill Working Group. (1991). Problems and promises in special education and related services for children and youth with emotional or behavioral disorders. *Behavioral Disorders, 16*(4), 299–313.

Pearl, R., Donahue, M., & Bryan, T. (1986). Social relationships of learning-disabled children. In J. K. Torgeson & B. Y. L. Wong (Eds.), *Psychological and educational perspectives on learning disabilities* (pp. 193–224). Orlando, FL: Academic Press.

Perry, P., Pasnak, R., & Holt, R. W. (1992). Instruction on concrete operations for children who are mildly mentally retarded. *Education and Training in Mental Retardation, 27*(3) 273–281.

Piaget, J. (1960). *The psychology of intelligence* (M. Piercy & D. E. Berlyne, Trans.). London: Routledge & Kegan Paul.

Plomin, R. (1995). Genetics and children's experiences in the family. *Journal of Child Psychology and Psychiatry, 36,* 33–68.

Podell, D. M., Tournaki-Rein, N., & Lin, A. (1992). Automatization of mathematics skills via computer assisted instruction among students with mild retardation. *Education and Training in Mental Retardation, 27*(3), 200–206.

Polloway, E. A., & Patton, J. R. (1988). Conceptualizing the identification of learning disabilities: A decision-making model. *Education and Treatment of Children, 11*(2), 179–194.

Polloway, E. A., Patton, J. R., Smith, J. D., & Roderique, T. W. (1991). Issues in program design for elementary students with mild retardation: Emphasis on curriculum development. *Education and Training in Mental Retardation, 26*(2), 142–150.

Pomplun, M. (1997). When students with disabilities participate in cooperative groups. *Exceptional Children, 64*(1), 49–58.

Poplin, M., & Phillips, L. (1993). Sociocultural aspects of language and literacy: Issues facing educators of students with learning disabilities. *Learning Disability Quarterly, 16*(4), 245–255.

Posner, M. I., & Boies, S. J. (1971). Components of attention. *Psychological Review, 78*(5), 391–408.

President's Committee on Mental Retardation (PCMR). (1970). *The six-hour retarded child.* Washington, DC: U.S. Government Printing Office.

Pruess, J. B., Vadasy, P. F., & Fewell, R. R. (1987). Langauge development in children with Down syndrome: An overview of recent research. *Education and Training in Mental Retardation, 22*(1), 44–55.

Prutting, C. A. (1982). Pragmatics as social competence. *Journal of Speech and Hearing Disorders, 47*(2), 123–134.

Prutting, C. A., & Kirchner, D. M. (1987). A clinical appraisal of the pragmatic aspects of language. *Journal of Speech and Hearing Disorders, 52*(2), 105–119.

Quay, H. C., & Peterson, D. (1987). *Revised behavior problem checklist.* Miami: Author.

Quay, H. C., & Werry, J. S. (Eds.). (1986). *Psychopathological disorders of childhood* (3rd ed.). New York: John Wiley.

Raymond, E. B. (1997). It's all in the family: Working with gays and lesbians in family contexts. *Reaching Today's Youth, 1*(3), 32–36.

Redl, F., & Wineman, D. (1951). *Children who hate.* New York: Free Press.

Reid, D. K., & Button, L. J. (1995). Anna's story: Narratives of personal experience about being learning disabled. *Journal of Learning Disabilities, 28*(10), 602–614.

Reid, D. K., Hresko, W. P., & Swanson, H. L. (Eds.). (1996). *Cognitive approaches to learning disabilities* (3rd ed.). Austin, TX: Pro-Ed.

Reid, D. K., & Stone, C. A. (1991). Why is cognitive instruction effective? Underlying learning mechanisms. *Remedial and Special Education, 12*(3), 8–19.

Reilly, T. F. (1991). Cultural bias: The albatross of assessing behavior-disordered children and youth. *Preventing School Failure, 36*(1), 50–53.

Reschley, D. J. (1988). Minority mild mental retardation: Legal issues, research findings and reform trends. In M. C. Wang, M. C. Reynolds & H. C. Walberg (Eds.), *Handbook of special education. Vol. 2* (pp. 23–41). Oxford, England: Pergamon Press.

Reynolds, M. C. (1989). An historical perspective: The delivery of special education to mildly disabled and at-risk students. *Remedial and Special Education, 10*(6), 7–11.

Reynolds, M. C., & Heistad, D. (1997). 20/20 analysis: Estimating school effectiveness in serving students at the margins. *Exceptional Children, 63*(4), 439–449.

Reynolds, W. M., & Miller, K. L. (1985). Depression and learned helplessness in mentally retarded and nonmentally retarded adolescents: An initial investigation. *Applied Research in Mental Retardation, 6,* 295–306.

Richards, G. P., Samuels, S. J., Turnure, J. E., & Yselldyke, J. E. (1990). Sustained and selective attention in children with learning disabilities. *Journal of Learning Disabilities, 23*(2), 129–136.

Richardson, V., & Anders, P. L. (1998). A view from across the Grand Canyon. *Learning Disabilities Quarterly, 21*(1), 85–97.

Ripich, D. N., & Spinelli, F. M. (1985). *School discourse problems.* San Diego, CA: College Hill Press.

Robinson, G. A., Patton, J. R., Polloway, E. S., & Sargent, L. R. (Eds.). (1989). *Best practices in mild mental retardation.* Reston VA: Council for Exceptional Children.

Roccio, C. S., Hynd, G. W., Cohen, M. J., & Gonzalez, J. J. (1993). Neurological basis of attention deficit hyperactivity disorder. *Exceptional Children, 60*(2), 118–124.

Rosenshine, B. V. (1986). Synthesis of research on explicit teaching. *Educational Leadership, 43*(7), 60–69.

Rosenshine, B. V., & Stevens, R. (1986). Teaching functions. In M. C. Wittrock (Ed.), *Handbook of research on teaching* (3rd ed.) (pp. 376–391). New York: Macmillan.

Ross, R. P. (1995). Impact on psychologists of state guidelines for evaluating underachievement. *Learning Disability Quarterly, 18*(1), 43–56.

Rotter, J. B. (1966). Generalized expectancies for internal versus external control of reinforcement. *Psychological Monographs, 80*(609).

Rowitz, L. (1986). Multiprofessional perspectives on prevention. *Mental Retardation, 24*(1), 1–3.

Rubin R. A., & Balow, B. (1978). Prevalence of teacher identified behavior problems: A longitudinal study. *Exceptional Children, 45,* 102–111.

Ruhl, K. L., Hughes, C. A., & Camarata, S. M. (1992). Analysis of the expressive and receptive language characteristics of emotionally handicapped students served in public school settings. *Journal of Childhood Disorders, 14*(2), 165–176.

Rutherford, R. B., & Nelson, C. M. (1995). Management of aggressive and violent behavior in schools. *Focus on Exceptional Children, 27*(6), 1–15.

Ryan, E. B., Short, E. J., & Weed, K. A. (1986). The role of cognitive strategy training in the improving of academic performance of learning disabled children. *Journal of Learning Disabilities, 19*(9), 521–529.

Safford, P. L., & Safford, E. J. (1996). *A history of childhood and disability.* New York: Teachers College Press.

Safford, P. L., & Safford, E. J. (1998). Visions of the special class. *Remedial and Special Education, 19*(4), 229–238.

Safran, S. P. (2001). Asperger Syndrome: The emerging challenge to special education. *Exceptional Children, 67*(2), 151–160.

Salend, S. J. (1998). Using portfolios to assess student performance. *Teaching Exceptional Children, 31*(2), 36–43.

Salend, S. J. (2001). *Creating inclusive classrooms: Effective and reflective practices.* (4th ed.). Upper Saddle River, NJ: Merrill.

Salend, S. J., & Garrick Duhaney, L. M. (2002). Grading students in inclusive settings. *Teaching Exceptional Children, 34*(3), 8–15.

Salend, S. J., Garrick Duhaney, L. M., & Montgomery, W. (2002). A comprehensive approach to identifying and addressing issues of disproportionate representation. *Remedial and Special Education, 23*(5), 289–299.

Samuels, S. J. (1987). Information processing abilities and reading. *Journal of Learning Disabilities, 20*(1), 18–22.

Sands, D. J., Adams, L., & Stout, D. M. (1995). A state-wide exploration of the nature and use of curriculum in special education. *Exceptional Children, 62*(1), 68–83.

Sands, D. J., & Doll, B. (1996). Fostering self-determination: A developmental task. *Journal of Special Education, 30*(1), 58–76.

San Miguel, S. K., Forness, S. R., & Kavale, K. A. (1996). Social skills deficits in learning disabilities: The psychiatric comorbidity hypothesis. *Learning Disability Quarterly, 19*(4), 252–261.

Santos, K. E. (1992). Fragile X syndrome: An educator's role in identification, prevention, and intervention. *Remedial and Special Education, 13*(2), 32–39.

Schnitzer, S. (1993). Designing an authentic assessment. *Educational Leadership, 50*(7), 32–35.

Schoenbrodt, L., Kumin, L., & Sloan, J. M. (1997). Learning disabilities existing concomitantly with communication disorder. *Journal of Learning Disabilities, 30*(3), 264–281.

Schrunk, D. H. (1992). Theory and research on student perceptions in the classroom. In D. H. Schrunk & J. L. Meece (Eds.), *Student perceptions in the classroom* (pp. 3–23). Hillsdale, NJ: Erlbaum.

Schulte, A. C., Osborne, S. S., & McKinney, J. D. (1990). Academic outcomes for students with learning disabilities in consultation and resource programs. *Exceptional Children, 57*(2), 162–172.

Schultz, G. P., & Switzky, H. N. (1994). The development of intrinsic motivation in students with learning problems: Suggestions for more effective instructional practice. *Preventing School Failure, 34*(2), 14–19.

Schumm, J. S., Vaughn, S., & Leavell, A. G. (1994). Planning pyramid: A framework for planning for diverse student needs during content area instruction. *Reading Teacher, 47*(8), 608–615.

Scott, K., & Carren, D. (1987). The epidemiology and prevention of mental retardation. *American Psychologist, 42*(8), 801–804.

Seligman, M. E. P. (1975). *Helplessness: On depression, development and death.* San Francisco: W. H. Freeman.

Selman, R. L. (1980). *The growth of interpersonal understanding: Developmental and clinical analyses.* New York: Academic Press.

Shaywitz, B. A., Shaywitz, S. E., Fletcher, J. M., Pugh, K. R., Gore, J. C., Constable, R. T., Fulbright, R. K., Skudlarski, P., Liberman, A. M., Shankweiler, D. P., Katz, L., Bronen, R. A., Marchione, K. E., Holahan, J. M., Francis, D. J., Klorman, R., Aram, D. M., Blachman, B. A., Stuebing, K. K., & Lacadie, C. (1997). The Yale Center for the Study of Learning and Attention: Longitudinal and neurobiological studies. *Learning Disabilities, 8*(1), 21–29.

Shaywitz, S. E., & Shaywitz, B. A. (1988). Attention deficit disorder: Current perspectives. In J. Kavanagh & T. J. Truss (Eds.), *Learning disabilities: Proceedings of the national conference* (pp. 369–567). Parkton, MD: York Press.

Shaywitz, S. E., & Shaywitz, B. A. (1991). Introduction to the special series on attention deficit disorder. *Journal of Learning Disabilities, 24*(2), 68–71.

Shinn, M. R., Powell-Smith, K. A., Good, R. H. III, & Baker, S. (1997). The effects of reintegration into general education reading instruction for students with mild disabilities. *Exceptional Children, 64*(1), 59–79.

Shinn, M. R., Ysseldyke, J. E., Deno, S. L., & Tindal, G. A. (1986). A comparison of differences between students labeled learning disabled and low achieving on measures of classroom performance. *Journal of Learning Disabilities, 19*(9), 545–552

Shore, S. (2001). Understanding the Autism Spectrum: What teachers need to know. *Intervention in School and Clinic, 36*(5), 293–299, 305.

Short, E. J., & Evans, S. W. (1990). Individual difference in cognitive and social problem-solving skills as a function of intelligence. In N. W. Bray (Ed.), *International review of research in mental retardation: Vol. 16* (pp. 89–123). San Diego, CA: Academic Press.

Silver, L. B. (1990). Attention-deficit/hyperactivity disorder: Is it a learning disability or a related disorder? *Journal of Learning Disabilities, 23*(7), 394–397.

Simmons, D. C., & Kameenui, E. J. (1996). A focus on curriculum design: When children fail. *Focus on Exceptional Children, 28*(7), 1–16.

Simmons, D. C., Kameenui, E. J., & Chard, D. J. (1998). General education teachers' assumptions about learning and students with learning disabilities: Design-of-instruction analysis. *Learning Disability Quarterly, 21*(1), 6–21.

Siperstein, G. N. (1992). Social competence: An important construct in mental retardation. *American Journal on Mental Retardation, 96*(4), iii–vi.

Siperstein, G. N., & Leffert, J. S. (1997). Comparison of socially accepted and rejected children with mental retardation. *American Journal on Mental Retardation, 101*(4), 339–351.

Skeels, H. M., & Dye, H. B. (1939). A study of the effects of differential stimulation on mentally retarded children. *Program of the American Association of Mental Deficiency, 44,* 114–136.

Skinner, B. F. (1953). *Science and human behavior.* New York: Macmillan.

Skinner, B. F. (1974). *About behaviorism.* New York: Knopf.

Sleeter, C. E. (1986). Learning disabilities: The social construction of a special education category. *Exceptional Children, 53*(1), 46–54.

Smith, C. R. (1991). *Learning disabilities: The interaction of the learner, task and setting.* Boston: Allyn and Bacon.

Smith, C. R. (1998). From gibberish to phonemic awareness. *Teaching Exceptional Children, 30*(6), 20–25.

Smith, J. D. (1985). *Minds made feeble: The myth and legacy of the Kallikaks.* Rockville, MD: Aspen.

Smith, J. D. (1994). The revised AAMR definition of mental retardation: The MRDD position. *Education and Training in Mental Retardation and Developmental Disabilities, 29*(3), 179–183.

Smith, J. D. (1997). Mental retardation as an educational construct: Time for a new shared view? *Education and Training in Mental Retardation and Developmental Disabilities, 32*(3), 167–173.

Smith, J. D. (1998). The history of special education: Essays honoring the bicentennial of the work of Jean Itard (Special issue). *Remedial and Special Education, 19*(4).

Smith, T. E. C. (1998). Introduction to the special series. *Remedial and Special Education, 19*(4), 194–195.

Smith, T. E. C., & Puccini, I. K. (1995). Position statement: Secondary curricula and policy issues for students with mental retardation. *Education and Training in Mental Retardation and Developmental Disabilities, 30*(4), 275–282.

Snider, V. E. (1992). Learning styles and learning to read: A critique. *Remedial and Special Education, 13*(1), 6–18.

Speece, D. L., & Harry, B. (1997). Classification for children. In J. W. Lloyd, E. J. Kameenui, & D. Chard (Eds.), *Issues in educating students with disabilities* (pp. 63–73). Mahwah, NJ: Lawrence Erlbaum.

Spradley, J. P. (1979). *The ethnographic interview.* New York: Holt.

Spradley, J. P. (1980). *Participant observation.* New York: Holt.

Stainback, S., & Stainback, W. (1987). Integration vs. cooperation: A commentary on "Educating children with learning problems: A shared responsibility." *Exceptional Children, 54*(1), 66–68.

Stainback, S., & Stainback, W. (1988). Letter to the editor. *Journal of Learning Disabilities, 21*(8), 452–453.

Stainback, W., & Stainback, S. (1984). A rationale for the merger of special and regular education. *Exceptional Children, 51*(2), 102–111.

Stainback, W., & Stainback, S. (1996). *Controversial issues confronting special education: Divergent perspectives* (2nd ed.). Boston: Allyn and Bacon.

Steinberg, Z., & Knitzer, J. (1992). Classrooms for emotionally and behaviorally disturbed students: Facing the challenge. *Behavioral Disorders, 17*(2), 145–156.

Sternberg, R. J. (1984). Mechanisms of cognitive development: A componential approach. In R. J. Sternberg (Ed.), *Mechanisms of cognitive development* (pp. 163–186). New York: Freeman.

Sternberg, R. J. (1985). *Beyond IQ: A triarchic theory of human intelligence.* Cambridge, England: Cambridge University Press.

Sternberg, R. J. (1986). Cognition and instruction: Why the marriage sometimes ends in divorce. In R. F. Dillon & R. J. Sternberg, *Cognition and instruction* (pp. 375–382). Orlando, FL: Academic Press.

Sternberg, R. J. (1988). Intelligence. In R. J. Sternberg & E. E. Smith (Eds.), *The psychology of human thought* (pp. 267–308). Cambridge, England: Cambridge University Press.

Stevens, G. D., & Birch, J. W. (1957). A proposal for clarification of the terminology used to describe brain injured children. *Exceptional Children, 23,* 346–349.

Stipek, D. J. (1993). *Motivation to learn: From theory to practice* (2nd ed.). Boston: Allyn and Bacon.

Stolzenberg, J., & Cherkes-Julkowski, M. (1991). ADHD and LD connections. *Journal for Learning Disabilities, 24*(4), 194–195.

Stone, C. A., & Reid, D. K. (1994). Social and individual forces in learning: Implications for instruction of children with learning difficulties. *Learning Disability Quarterly, 17*(1), 72–86.

Strauss, A. A., & Kephart, N. C. (1955). *Psychopathology and education in the brain-injured child: Volume 2: Progress in theory and in clinic.* New York: Grune & Stratton.

Strauss, A. A., & Lehtinen, L. E. (1947). *Psychopathology and education in the brain-injured child.* New York: Grune & Stratton.

Sugai, G. A., & Horner, R. H. (2002). Introduction to the special series on positive behavior support in schools. *Journal of Emotional and Behavioral Disorders, 10*(3), 130–135.

Sugai, G. A., Horner, R. H., & Sprague, J. R. (1999). Functional-assessment-based behavior support planning: Research to practice to research. *Behavioral Disorders, 24*(3), 253–257.

Swanson, H. L. (1987). Information processing theory and learning disabilities: An overview. *Journal of Learning Disabilities, 20*(1), 3–7.

Swanson, H. L. (1991). Cognitive assessment approach I. In D. K. Reid, W. P. Hresko, & H. L. Swanson (Eds.), *A cognitive approach to learning disabilities* (2nd ed.) (pp. 251–273). Austin, TX: Pro-Ed.

Swanson, H. L. (1994). Short-term memory and working memory: Do both contribute to our understanding of academic achievement in children and adults with learning disabilities? *Journal of Learning Disabilities, 27*(1), 34–50.

Swanson, H. L., Cochran, K. F., & Ewers, C. A. (1990). Can learning disabilities be determined from working memory performance? *Journal of Learning Disabilities, 23*(1), 59–67.

Swanson, H. L., & Cooney, J. B. (1991). Learning disabilities and memory. In B. Y. L. Wong (Ed.), *Learning about learning disabilities* (pp. 103–127). San Diego, CA: Academic Press.

Switzky, H. N., & Schultz, G. F. (1988). Intrinsic motivation and learning performance: Implications for individual educational programming for learners with mild handicaps. *Remedial and Special Education, 9*(4) 7–14.

Tallmadge, G. K., Gamel, N. N., Munson, R. G., & Hanley, T. V. (1985). *Special study of terminology: Comprehensive review and evaluation report.* Mountain View, CA: SRA Technologies.

Taylor, R. L. (1997). *Assessment of exceptional students: Educational and psychological procedures* (4th ed.). Boston: Allyn and Bacon.

Teeter, P. A. (1991). Attention deficit hyperactivity disorder: A psychoeducational paradigm. *School Psychology Review, 20*(2), 266–280.

Thomas, A., & Chess, S. (1977). *Temperament and development.* New York: Brunner/Mazel.

Thomas, A., & Chess, S. (1984). Genesis and evolution of behavioral disorders: From infancy to early adult life. *American Journal of Psychiatry, 141*(1), 1–9.

Torgeson, J. K. (1991). Learning disabilities: Historical and conceptual issues. In B. Y. L. Wong (Ed.), *Learning about learning disabilities* (pp. 3–37). San Diego, CA: Academic Press.

Torgeson, J., & Kail, R. V. Jr. (1980). Memory processes in exceptional children. In B. K. Keogh (Ed.), *Advances in special education: A research annual: Basic constructs and theoretical orientations: Vol. 1* (pp. 55–99). Greenwich, CT: JAI Press.

Torgeson, J. K., Kistner, J. A., & Morgan, S. (1987). Component processes in working memory. In J. G. Borkowski & J. D. Day (Eds.), *Cognition in special children: Comparative approaches to retardation, learning disabilities, and giftedness* (pp. 49–86). Norwood, NJ: Ablex.

Torgeson, J. K., Morgan, S. T., & Rashotte, C. A. (1994). Longitudinal studies of phonological processing and reading. *Journal of Learning Disabilities, 27*(3), 276–286.

Treiber, F. A., & Lahey, B. B. (1983). Toward a behavioral model of academic remediation with learning disabled children. *Journal of Learning Disabilities, 16*(2), 111–116.

Trent, J. W. (1998). Defectives at the World's Fair: Constructing disability in 1904. *Remedial and Special Education, 19*(4), 201–211.

Trent, S. C., Artiles, A. J., & Englert, C. S. (1998). From deficit thinking to social constructivism: A review of special education theory, research, and practice from a historical perspective. In P. D. Pearson & A. Iran-Nejad, *Review of Research in Education: Vol. 23* (pp. 227–307). Washington, DC: American Educational Research Association.

Turnbull, H. R., & Turnbull, A. P. (1998). *Free appropriate public education: The law and children with disabilities* (5th ed.). Denver: Love.

U.S. Department of Education (1991). *To assure the free, appropriate public education of all handicapped children (1978–1990.); Thirteenth annual report to Congress on the implementation of the Individuals with Disabilities Education Act: Data analysis systems (DANS).* Washington, DC: Government Printing Office.

U.S. Department of Education. (1994). *Sixteenth annual report to Congress on the implementation of the Individuals with Disabilities Education Act: Data analysis systems (DANS).* Washington, DC: Government Printing Office.

U.S. Department of Education. (1995). *Seventeenth annual report to Congress on the implementation of the Individuals with Disabilities Education Act: Data analysis systems (DANS)*. Washington, DC: Government Printing Office.

U.S. Department of Education. (1997a). Assistance to states for the education of children with disabilities: Proposed Rule. *Federal Register, 62*(204), 55026–55135.

U.S. Department of Education. (1997b). *Nineteenth annual report to Congress on the implementation of the Individuals with Disabilities Education Act: Data analysis systems (DANS)*. Washington, DC: Government Printing Office.

U.S. Department of Education. (1998). *Twentieth annual report to Congress on the implementation of the Individuals with Disabilities Education Act: Data analysis systems (DANS)*. Washington, DC: Government Printing Office.

U.S. Department of Education. (1999). Individuals with Disabilities Education Act: Part 300. Assistance to states for the education of children with disabilities. *Federal Register, 64*(8), 12418–12480.

U.S. Department of Education. (2001). *Twenty-third annual report to Congress on the implementation of the Individuals with Disabilities Education Act: Data analysis systems (DANS)*. Washington, DC: Government Printing Office.

U.S. Office of Education. (1976). Education of handicapped children. *Federal Register, 41*, 52405.

U.S. Office of Education. (1977a). Assistance to the states for the education of handicapped children: Procedures for evaluating learning disabilities. *Federal Register, 42*, 65082–65085.

U.S. Office of Education. (1977b). Implementation of Part B of the Education of the Handicapped Act. *Federal Register, 42*(163), 42474–42518.

U.S. Office of Special Education and Rehabilitative Services. (1993, February 10). Invitation to comment on the regulatory definition of "serious emotional disturbance" and the use of this term in the Individuals with Disabilities Education Act. *Federal Register, 58*(26), 7938.

U.S. Office of Special Education Programs. (1999). Universal design: Ensuring access to the general education curriculum. *Research Connections in Special Education, 5*, 1–5.

Utley, C. A., Lowitzer, A. C., & Baumeister, A. A. (1987). A comparison of the AAMD's definition, eligibility criteria, and classification schemes with state departments of education guidelines. *Education and Training in Mental Retardation, 22*(1), 35–43.

Vandervelden, M. C., & Siegel, L. S. (1997). Teaching phonological processing skills in early literacy: A developmental approach. *Learning Disability Quarterly, 20*(2), 63–81.

Vaughn, S., Moody, S. W., & Schumm, J. S. (1998). Broken promises: Reading instruction in the resource room. *Exceptional Children, 64*(2), 211–225.

Vaughn, S., & Schumm, J. S. (1995). Responsible inclusion for students with learning disabilities. *Journal of Learning Disabilities, 28*(5), 264–270, 290.

Vaughn, S., Zaragoza, N., Hogan, A., & Walker, J. (1993). A four-year longitudinal investigation of the social skills and behavior problems of students with learning disabilities. *Journal of Learning Disabilities, 26*(6), 404–412.

Venn, J. (1994). *Assessment of students with special needs*. New York: Merrill.

Villa, R. A., & Thousand, J. S. (1988). Enhancing success in heterogeneous classrooms and schools: The powers of partnership. *Teacher Education and Special Education, 11*(4), 144–154.

Vygotsky, L. S. (1962). *Thought and language*. Cambridge, MA: MIT Press.

Vygotsky, L. S. (1978). *Mind in society*. Cambridge, MA: Harvard University Press.

Vygotsky, L. S. (1987). Thinking and speech. In R. Rieber & A. S. Carton (Eds.), *Collected works of L. S. Vygotsky: Vol. 1: Problems of general psychology* (pp. 39–285). New York: Plenum.

Walker, H. M. (1983). *The Walker problem behavior identification checklist.* Los Angeles: Western Psychological Services.

Walker, H. M., Colvin, G., & Ramsey, E. (1995). *Antisocial behavior in school: Strategies and best practices.* Pacific Grove, CA: Brooks/Cole.

Walker, H. M., & Severson, H. H. (1992). *Systematic screening for behavior disorders (SSBD): User's guide and administration manual* (2nd ed.). Longmont, CO: Sopris West.

Walker, H. M., Severson, H., Stiller, B., Williams, G., Haring, N., Shinn, M., & Todis, B. (1988). Systematic screening of pupils in the elementary age range at risk for behavior disorders: Development and trial testing of a multiple gating model. *Remedial and Special Education, 9,* 8–14.

Wallace, G., Cohen, S. B., & Polloway, E. A. (1987). *Language arts: Teaching exceptional students.* Austin, TX: Pro-Ed.

Wang, M. C., Reynolds, M. C., & Walberg, H. J. (1986). Rethinking special education. *Educational Leadership, 44*(1), 26–31.

Wegsheider, S. (1981). *Another chance: Hope and health for the alcoholic family.* Palo Alto, CA: Science and Behavior Books.

Wehby, J. H. (1994). Issues in the assessment of aggressive behavior. *Preventing School Failure, 38*(3), 24–28.

Wehby, J. H., & Symons, F. J. (1996). Revisiting conceptual issues in the measurement of aggressive behavior. *Behavioral Disorders, 22*(1), 29–35.

Wehmeyer, M. L. (1992). Self determination and the education of students with mental retardation. *Education and Training in Mental Retardation, 27*(4), 302–314.

Wehmeyer, M. L. (1994). Perceptions of self-determination and psychological empowerment of adolescents with mental retardation. *Education and Training in Mental Retardation, 29*(1), 9–21.

Wehmeyer, M. L., Agran, M., & Hughes, C. (1998). *Teaching self-determination to students with disabilities: Basic skills for successful transition.* Baltimore: Paul Brookes.

Wehmeyer, M. L., Kelchner, K., & Richards, S. (1996). Essential characteristics of self-determined behavior of individuals with mental retardation. *American Journal on Mental Retardation, 100*(6), 632–642.

Wehmeyer, M. L., & Schwartz, M. (1997). Self-determination and positive adult outcomes: A follow-up study of youth with mental retardation or learning disabilities. *Exceptional Children, 63*(2), 245–255.

Welch, M. (1997). The MATS form: A collaborative decision-making tool for instructional adaptations. *Intervention in School and Clinic, 32*(3), 142–147.

Wenz-Gross, M., & Siperstein, G. N. (1997). Importance of social support in the adjustment of children with learning problems. *Exceptional Children, 63*(2), 183–193.

Westling, D. L. (1986). *Introduction to mental retardation.* Englewood Cliffs, NJ: Prentice-Hall.

Whalen, C. K., & Henker, B. (1991). Social impact of stimulant treatment for hyperactive children. *Journal of Learning Disabilities, 24*(4), 231–241.

Will, M. C. (1986). Educating children with learning problems: A shared responsibility. *Exceptional Children, 52*(5), 411–415.

Williams, K. (2001). Understanding the student with Asperger Syndrome: Guidelines for teachers. *Intervention in School and Clinic, 36*(5), 287–292.

Willows, D. M. (1991). Visual processes in learning disabilities. In B. Y. L. Wong (Ed.), *Learning about learning disabilities* (pp. 163–193). San Diego, CA: Academic Press.

Wing, L. (1981). Asperger's Syndrome: A clinical account. *Psychological Medicine, 11*(1), 115–129.

Winzer, M. A. (1993). *The history of special education: From isolation to integration.* Washington, DC: Gallaudet University Press.

Winzer, M. A. (1998). A tale often told: The early progression of special education. *Remedial and Special Education, 19*(4), 212–218.

Witkin, H. A., Moore, C. A., Goodenough, D. R., & Cox, P. W. (1977). Field-dependent and field independent cognitive styles and their educational implications. *Review of Educational Research, 47*(1), 1–64.

Wodrich, D. J., & Barry, C. T. (1991). A survey of school psychologists' practices for identifying mentally retarded students. *Psychology in the Schools, 28*(2), 165–171.

Wodrich, D. J., & Joy, J. E. (1986). *Multidisciplinary assessment of children with learning disabilities and mental retardation.* Baltimore: Paul H. Brookes.

Wolfensberger, W. (1972). *The principle of normalization in human services.* Toronto, Canada: National Institute on Mental Retardation.

Wong, B. Y. L. (1991). Relevance of metacognition to learning disabilities. In B. Y. L. Wong (Ed.), *Learning about learning disabilities* (pp. 231–258). San Diego, CA: Academic Press.

Wood, F. (1982). Defining disturbing, disordered, and disturbed behavior. In F. Wood & K. Laken (Eds.), *Disturbing, disoriented, or disturbed?* (pp. 3–16). Reston, VA: CEC.

Wood, M. M. (1975). *Developmental therapy.* Baltimore: University Park Press.

Wood, M. M., & Long, N. J. (1991). *Life space intervention: Talking with children and youth in crisis.* Austin, TX: Pro-Ed.

Wright, D., Pillard, E. D., & Cleven, C. A. (1990). The influence of state definitions of behavior disorders on the number of children served under P.L. 94–142. *Remedial and Special Education, 11*(5), 17–22, 38.

Wright-Strawderman, C., Lindsey, P., Navarette, L., & Flippo, J. R. (1996). Depression in students with disabilities: Recognition and intervention strategies. *Intervention in School and Clinic, 31*(5), 261–275.

Wyer, R. S., & Srull, T. K. (1989). *Memory and cognition in its social context.* Hillsdale, NJ: Erlbaum.

Yell, M. L., Rogers, D., & Rogers, E. L. (1998). The legal history of special education: What a long, strange trip it's been! *Remedial and Special Education, 19*(4), 219–228.

Yell, M. L., & Shriner, J. G. (1997). The IDEA Amendments of 1997: Implications for special and general education teachers, administrators, and teacher trainers. *Focus on Exceptional Children, 30*(1), 1–19.

Ysseldyke, J. E. (1983). Current practices in making psychoeducational decisions about learning disabled students. *Journal of Learning Disabilities, 16*(4), 226–233.

Ysseldyke, J. E., & Algozzine, R. (1983). LD or not LD: That's not the question! *Journal of Learning Disabilities, 16*(1), 29–31.

Ysseldyke, J. E., Algozzine, R., & Epps, S. (1983). A logical and empirical analysis of current practice in classifying students as handicapped. *Exceptional Children, 50,* 160–165.

Ysseldyke, J. E., Algozzine, R., & Thurlow, M. L. (2000). *Critical issues in special education* (3rd ed.). Boston: Houghton Mifflin.

Ysseldyke, J. E., Thurlow, M. L., Wotruba, J. W., & Nania, P. A. (1990). Instructional arrangements: Perceptions from general education. *Teaching Exceptional Children, 22*(4), 4–8.

Zigler, E., & Hodapp, R. M. (1986). *Understanding mental retardation.* Cambridge, England: Cambridge University Press.

Zigler, E., Hodapp, R. M., & Edison, M. R. (1990). From theory to practice in the care and education of mentally retarded individuals. *American Journal on Mental Retardation, 95*(1), 1–12.

Zirpoli, T. J., & Melloy, K. J. (1993). *Behavior management: Applications for teachers and parents.* New York: Merrill.

INDEX